ENCYCLOPEDIA OF AFRICAN AMERICAN WOMEN WRITERS

ENCYCLOPEDIA OF AFRICAN AMERICAN WOMEN WRITERS

Volume 2

Edited by Yolanda Williams Page

GREENWOOD PRESS
Westport, Connecticut • London

Library of Congress Cataloging-in-Publication Data

Encyclopedia of African American women writers / edited by Yolanda Williams Page.

p. cm.

Includes bibliographical references and index.

ISBN 0-313-33429-3 (set : alk. paper)—ISBN 0-313-34123-0 (vol 1 : alk. paper)—
ISBN 0-313-34124-9 (vol 2 : alk. paper) 1. American literature—African American authors—
Encyclopedias. 2. American literature—Women authors—Encyclopedias. 3. American
literature—20th century—Encyclopedias. 4. African American women authors—Biography—
Encyclopedias. 5. African American women—Encyclopedias. I. Page, Yolanda Williams.

PS153.N5E49 2007

810.9'896073—dc22   2006031193

British Library Cataloguing in Publication Data is available.

Library of Congress Catalog Card Number: 2006031193

ISBN-10: 0-313-33429-3 (set)   ISBN-13: 978-0-313-33429-0
        0-313-34123-0 (vol. 1)   978-0-313-34123-6
        0-313-34124-9 (vol. 2)   978-0-313-34124-3

First published in 2007

Greenwood Press, 88 Post Road West, Westport, CT 06881
An imprint of Greenwood Publishing Group, Inc.
www.greenwood.com

Printed in the United States of America

The paper used in this book complies with the
Permanent Paper Standard issued by the National
Information Standards Organization (Z39.48-1984).

10 9 8 7 6 5 4 3 2 1

To my two favorite beaus, David and William

CONTENTS

Preface   xiii

List of Authors by Genre   xv

Chronological List of Authors   xix

Volume 1

Elizabeth Laura Adams
(1909–1982)
   Hermine Pinson   1

Octavia Victoria Rogers Albert
(1853–1889)
   Iva Balic   7

Clarissa Minnie Thompson
Allen (?–?)
   Elizabeth Marsden   9

Mignon Holland Anderson
(1945–)
   Teresa Clark Caruso   11

Maya Angelou (1928–)
   Joi Carr   13

Tina McElroy Ansa (1949–)
   Tarshia L. Stanley   19

Doris Jean Austin (1949–1994)
   Imani Lillie B. Fryar   23

Nikki Baker (1962–)
   Kimberly Downing Braddock   26

Toni Cade Bambara (1939–1995)
   Rochelle Spencer   28

Gwendolyn Bennett (1902–1981)
   Sue E. Barker   35

Marita Bonner (1898–1971)
   Sophie Blanch   39

Candy Dawson Boyd (1946–)
   Bennie P. Robinson   43

Joanne Braxton (1950–)
   Tanya N. Clark   46

Gwendolyn Brooks (1917–2000)
   Bridget Harris Tsemo   49

Linda Beatrice Brown (1939–)
   Teresa Clark Caruso   56

Annie Louise Burton
(1858–1910)
   Gabriel A. Briggs   59

Olivia Ward Bush-Banks (1869–1944)
   Susan M. Stone   61

Octavia Butler (1947–2006)
   Keren Omry   64

Jeannette Franklin Caines
(1938–2004)
   Eric Sterling   71

Bebe Moore Campbell (1950–)
   Tenille Brown   74

Barbara Chase-Riboud (1939–)
   Ginette Curry   76

Alice Childress (1916–1994)
   Carol Bunch Davis   79

Barbara T. Christian
(1943–2000)
   Sharon L. Barnes   85

Pearl T. Cleage (1948–)
   Adrienne Cassel   88

Michelle Cliff (1946–)
   Lopamudra Basu   92

Lucille Clifton (1936–)
   Patricia Kennedy Bostian   94

Wanda Coleman (1946–)
   Terri Jackson Wallace   101

Eugenia W. Collier (1928–)
T. Jasmine Dawson   103

Kathleen Conwell Collins
(1942–1988)
Chandra Tyler Mountain   106

Anna Julia Hayward Cooper
(1858–1964)
Gloria A. Shearin   112

J. California Cooper (?–)
Adrienne Carthon   116

Jayne Cortez (1936–)
Ruth Blandón   121

Margaret Esse Danner
(1910–1984)
Claire Taft   127

Edwidge Danticat (1969–)
Jana Evans Braziel   132

Doris Davenport (1949–)
Denise R. Shaw   141

Angela Y. Davis (1944–)
Deirdre Osborne   145

Lucy Delaney (1830–1890)
Dave Yost   149

Toi(Nette) Marie Derricotte
(1941–)
Karen S. Sloan   151

Alexis De Veaux (1948–)
Bennie P. Robinson   155

Edwina Streeter Dixon
(1907–2002)
*Kevin L. Cole and
Katherine Madison*   161

Rita Dove (1952–)
Laura Madeline Wiseman   163

Kate Drumgoold
(1858?–1898)
Karen S. Sloan   169

Shirley Graham DuBois
(1896–1977)
Rebecca Walsh   171

Alice Dunbar-Nelson (1875–1935)
Denisa E. Chatman-Riley   174

Grace Edwards-Yearwood
(1934?–)
Jasmin J. Vann   180

Zilpha Elaw (1790?–1846?)
Nancy Kang   182

Mari Evans (1923–)
Jessica Allen   186

Sarah Webster Fabio
(1928–1979)
Richard A. Iadonisi   191

Jessie Redmon Fauset (1882–1961)
Joy R. Myree-Mainor   193

Carolyn Ferrell (1962–)
Alex Feerst   200

Julia Fields (1938–)
Jacqueline Imani Bryant   202

Julia A. J. Foote (1823–1900)
Ann Beebe   204

Patrice Gaines (1949–)
Amanda J. Davis   207

Patricia Joann Gibson (1951–)
Sarah Estes Graham   209

Mercedes Gilbert (1889–1952)
Marlo David Azikwe   211

Nikki Giovanni (1943–)
Jane M. Barstow   213

Marita Golden (1950–)
DaMaris Hill   218

Jewelle Gomez (1948–)
Josie A. Brown-Rose   223

Eloise Greenfield (1929–)
Elissa Gershowitz   227

Angelina Weld Grimké
(1880–1958)
Gloria A. Shearin   229

Rosa Guy (1925–)
Julie Ellam   235

Beverly Guy-Sheftall (1946–)
Lynnell Thomas   237

Madame Emma Azalia Smith
Hackley (1867–1922)
Lisa Pertillar Brevard   241

Virginia Hamilton (1936–2002)
Myisha Priest   244

Lorraine Hansberry (1930–1965)
Kelly O. Secovnie   251

Joyce Hansen (1942–)
Dorsia Smith   259

Frances Ellen Watkins Harper
(1825–1911)
Valerie Palmer-Mehta   261

Juanita Harrison (1887–19??)
Sarah Boslaugh   264

Safiya Henderson-Holmes
(1950–2001)
Shamika Ann Mitchell   266

Carolivia Herron (1947–)
Rachelle D. Washington   268

Frenchy Jolene Hodges
(1940–)
Katarzyna Iwona Jakubiak   271

bell hooks (1952–)
Peggy J. Huey   273

Pauline Elizabeth Hopkins
(Sara A. Allen) (1859–1930)
Jeehyun Lim   278

Zora Neale Hurston
(1891–1960)
Warren J. Carson   283

Angela Jackson (1951–)
Judy Massey Dozier   292

Elaine Jackson (1943–)
Raymond Janifer   296

Mae Jackson (1946–)
Heather Hoffman Jordan   299

Mattie Jane Jackson (1843–?)
Tabitha Adams Morgan   301

Rebecca Cox Jackson
(1795–1871)
Joshunda Sanders   303

Harriet Ann Jacobs (1813–1897)
Mary McCartin Wearn   305

Amelia E. Johnson (1858–1922)
Sathyaraj Venkatesan   309

Georgia Douglas Johnson
(1877–1966)
Maria J. Rice   312

Helen Johnson (1906–1995)
Wendy Wagner   317

Gayl Jones (1949–)
Helen Doss   321

June Jordan (1936–2002)
Roy Pérez   326

Elizabeth Hobbs Keckley
(1818–1907)
Regina V. Jones   331

Adrienne Kennedy (1931–)
Nita N. Kumar   334

Jamaica Kincaid (1949–)
Maria Mikolchak   341

Volume 2

Pinkie Gordon Lane (1923–)
Julia Marek Ponce   347

Nella Larsen (1891–1964)
Frank A. Salamone   350

Kristin Hunter Lattany (1931–)
David M. Jones   355

Andrea Lee (1953–)
Barbara Boswell   360

Helene Elaine Lee (1959–)
Lena Marie Ampadu   364

Jarena Lee (1783–?)
Christopher J. Anderson   366

Audre Geraldine Lorde
(1934–1992)
Heejung Cha   369

Naomi Long Madgett (1923–)
Shayla Hawkins   378

Paule Marshall (1929–)
Kalenda C. Eaton   382

Sharon Bell Mathis (1937–)
Loretta G. Woodard   388

Victoria Earle Matthews
(1861–1898)
Heidi Stauffer   391

Colleen J. McElroy (1935–)
Roxane Gay   393

Patricia McKissack (1944–)
Rebecca Feind   397

Terry McMillan (1951–)
Yolanda Williams Page   399

Louise Meriwether (1923–)
Bridgitte Arnold   402

May Miller (1899–1995)
Miranda A. Green-Barteet   406

Arthenia J. Bates Millican
(1920–)
Rebecca Feind   411

Mary Monroe (1949–)
Freda Fuller Coursey   413

Anne Moody (1940–)
Meta Michond Cooper   416

Opal J. Moore (1953–)
Kellie D. Weiss   420

Toni Morrison (1931–)
Deborah M. Wolf   423

Gertrude Bustill Mossell
(1855–1948)
Amanda Wray   434

Harryette Mullen (1953–)
Ordner W. Taylor, III   436

Beatrice Murphy (1908–1992)
Judy L. Isaksen   439

Pauli Murray (1910–1985)
Christina G. Bucher   441

Gloria Naylor (1950–)
Pratibha Kelapure   444

Barbara Neely (1941–)
A. Mary Murphy   449

Diane Oliver (1943–1966)
Joseph A. Alvarez   451

Brenda Marie Osbey (1957–)
Trimiko C. Melancon   453

Pat Parker (1944–1989)
Linda Garber   457

Suzan-Lori Parks (1964–)
Marla Dean   459

Ann Petry (1908–1997)
Yolanda Williams Page   465

Ann Plato (1820?–1860)
Tinola N. Mayfield   468

Connie Porter (1959–)
Tamra E. DiBenedetto   470

Eliza Potter (1820–?)
Karen C. Summers   472

Mary Prince (1788–?)
Babacar M'Baye   474

Nancy Prince (1799–?)
Dave Yost   477

Aishah Rahman (1939–)
Joan McCarty   480

Alice Randall (1959–)
Louis M. Palmer, III   483

Henrietta Cordelia Ray
(1849–1916)
Megan K. Ahern   486

Jewell Parker Rhodes (?–)
Tatia Jacobson Jordan   488

Carolyn Marie Rodgers (1943–)
Adenike Marie Davidson   493

Mona Lisa Saloy (1950–)
  Delicia Dena Daniels   495

Sonia Sanchez (1934–)
  Ben Fisler   497

Dori Sanders (1934–)
  Chandra Wells   503

Mary Seacole (1805–1881)
  Nanette Morton   508

Fatima Shaik (1952–)
  Sharon T. Silverman   511

Ntozake Shange (1948–)
  Cammie M. Sublette   514

Ann Allen Shockley (1927–)
  Adriane Bezusko   522

Amanda Berry Smith
(1837–1915)
  Mary G. De Jong   527

Anna Deavere Smith (1950–)
  Yolanda Williams Page   529

Ellease Southerland (1943–)
  Kate Falvey   532

Maria W. Stewart (1803–1879)
  Rhondda Robinson Thomas   536

Barbara Summers (1944–)
  Firouzeh Dianat   540

Ellen Tarry (1906–)
  Kevin Hogg   542

Claudia Tate (1946–2002)
  Angela Shaw-Thornburg   544

Mildred D. Taylor (1943–)
  Shawntaye M. Scott   547

Susie King Taylor (1848–1912)
  Laura Gimeno Pahissa   550

Lisa Teasley (1962–)
  Jeremy Griggs   552

Lucy Terry (1730–1812)
  Debbie Clare Olson   554

Joyce Carol Thomas (1938–)
  Elizabeth Malia   556

Era Bell Thompson (1905–1986)
  Kevin L. Cole   561

Katherine Davis Chapman
Tillman (1870–?)
  Gerri Reaves   563

Ruth D. Todd (1878?–?)
  Amy L. Blair   567

Mary Elizabeth Vroman
(1925–1967)
  Jean Forst   569

Gloria Wade-Gayles (1938–)
  Cameron Christine Clark   572

Alice Walker (1944–)
  Su-lin Yu   578

Margaret Walker (1915–1998)
  Aimable Twagilimana   589

Mildred Pitts Walter (1922–)
  Gerardo Del Guercio   595

Marilyn Nelson Waniek (1946–)
  Jacob Nelson Wilkenfeld   598

Ida B. Wells-Barnett (1862–1931)
  Joy. M. Leighton   601

Dorothy West (1907–1988)
  Pearlie Mae Peters   606

Phillis Wheatley (1753–1784)
  Pratibha Kelapure   610

Paulette Childress White (1948–)
  Jessica Margaret Brophy   614

Brenda Wilkinson (1946–)
  Tamara Zaneta Hollins   616

Fannie Barrier Williams
(1855–1944)
  Ted Morrissey   620

Sherley Anne Williams
(1944–1999)
  Gretchen Michlitsch   624

Harriet E. Wilson (1828?–1863?)
  Katie Rose Guest   629

Sarah Elizabeth Wright (1928–?)
  Althea Rhodes   633

Shay Youngblood (1959–)
  Samira C. Franklin   636

*Appendix: List of Awards
and Authors*   641

Bibliography of Works   647

Index   653

*About the Editor and
the Contributors*   665

PREFACE

Since its inception, the African American literary tradition has been very vital to African American culture. Historically not only has the literature provided insight into various aspects of the African American experience, but it has also served as a source of activism. For example, during the colonial period it was used to prove that blacks, like writers of nonAfrican descent, could successfully produce a variety of belletristic and practical genres of writing; thus giving lie to the justification for the enslavement of black people. Later, during the reconstruction era the literature was used to emphasize African Americans' similarities to other educated Americans and to protest their exclusion from the American mainstream. Today, it continues to serve as a political and social conduit, the majority of it being used to promote ideas, philosophies and causes, while the rest is simply written with the purpose to entertain or as a platform for the author to express himself.

Although the preponderance of African American literature that exists is written by African American males, African American women writers have also produced an impressive body of the literature. In fact, the tradition began with a black woman, Lucy Terry whose ballad poem "Bars Fight" was recited for a century before it was published in 1855. Although some works by African American women were published near or at the turn of the twentieth century, when they enjoyed modest popularity, the vast majority of it was published during the Harlem Renaissance and in the years after the 1970s, as women writers, in general, gained increased access to the marketplace.

The *Encyclopedia of African American Women Writers* provides a comprehensive reference to literature by African American women. One hundred sixty-eight writers are included in this sourcebook. While this work is by no means exhaustive, it does provide coverage of many African American women writers. Many of them are established and canonized, others are emerging, while some are obscure, forgotten writers that this author seeks to bring to the critical attention of contemporary students and scholars. This work is an extensive study of the well-known, not so known and unknown African American women writers from 1746 to present; it provides a thorough examination of their lives, major works and the critical reception of that work.

While this sourcebook's focus is writers of African American descent, Caribbean authors such as Michelle Cliff, Edwidge Danticat, and Jamaica Kincaid have been included because they are closely identified with the African American literary tradition; the themes of their writing resonate aspects of African American life and experience. In addition, their inclusion iterates that the experience of the African Diaspora is not exclusive.

The *Encyclopedia of African American Women Writers* is not the first work of its kind, but it fills an important information gap in that it is genre inclusive. That is, the entries include women who write in a variety of belletristic forms: autobiography, drama, essay, fiction and poetry. Also included are cultural/literary theorists and children/young adult writers.

The *Encyclopedia of African American Women Writers* has been written so that the user will find it helpful no matter his stage of research. Advanced high school students, undergraduates and users of community college and public libraries will all find the information accessible. The book includes an alphabetical list of authors as well as a chronological list of authors, a list of authors by genre, and a list of authors and awards. Too, graduate students and seasoned scholars in the initial stage of research will find this text useful, for each entry includes primary and secondary sources. Entries are written in chapter format and consist of five parts: (1) heading-which includes the writer's name, year of birth and year of death (if applicable); (2) biographical narrative-which consists of a concise writer biographical profile; (3) majors works-which consists of a discussion of the writer's works. Motifs and themes are also highlighted; (4) critical reception-which consists of critical response to the author's work; and (5) bibliography which-consists of a list of the author's work and a list of studies of the author's work. Entries vary in length from 750 words to 5000 words.

ACKNOWLEDGMENTS

There are many to whom I am indebted for the completion of this book. I thank George Butler at Greenwood Press for considering this a worthy project. Thanks to my Dillard University family for providing me a research award that allowed me to complete the preliminary work on this project. Thanks also to my undergraduate assistant, La-Chandra Pye, for helping with the administrative aspects of this project. I especially express gratitude to the contributors of this book. Without you this project would not have come to fruition. Lastly, I thank my friends and family, especially my mother and my sister, for their words of encouragement and support.

LIST OF AUTHORS BY GENRE

Autobiography
Maya Angelou
Annie Louise Burton
Lucille Clifton
Angela Y. Davis
Lucy Delaney
Kate Drumgoold
Zilpha Elaw
Julia A. J. Foote
Juanita Harrison
bell hooks
Mattie Jane Jackson
Rebecca Cox Jackson
Harriet Jacobs
Elizabeth Hobbs Keckley
Adrienne Kennedy
Jarena Lee
Audre Geraldine Lorde
Anne Moody
Pauli Murray
Eliza Potter
Mary Seacole
Notzake Shange
Amanda Berry Smith
Susie King Taylor
Era Bell Thompson

Biography
Elizabeth Laura Adams
Octavia Victoria Rogers Albert
Anna Julia Hayward Cooper
Shirley Graham DuBois
Pauli Murray
Ann Plato
Henrietta Cordelia Ray

Children's Literature
Candy Boyd (Marguerite Dawson)
Gwendolyn Brooks
Jeannette Franklin Caines
Lucille Clifton
Alexis DeVeaux

Eloise Greenfield
Virginia Hamilton
Carolivia Herron
bell hooks
Amelia E. Johnson
Sharon Bell Mathis
Patricia McKissack
Louise Meriwether
Opal J. Moore
Connie Porter
Fatima Shaik
Ellen Tarry
Mildred D. Taylor
Mildred Pitts Walter
Brenda Wilkinson

Criticism
Joanne Braxton
Barbara T. Christian
Sarah Webster Fabio
Beverly Guy-Sheftall
bell hooks
Toni Morrison
Claudia Tate
Gloria Wade-Gayles

Drama
Maya Angelou
Marita Bonner
Olivia Ward Bush-Banks
Alice Childress
Pearl T. Cleage
Kathleen Conwell Collins
J. California Cooper
Alexis DeVeaux
Rita Dove
Shirley Graham DuBois
Mari Evans
Julia Fields
Patricia Joann Gibson
Mercedes Gilbert
Angelina Weld Grimké

Rosa Guy
Lorraine Hansberry
Zora Neale Hurston
Angela Jackson
Elaine Jackson
Mae Jackson
Gayl Jones
June Jordan
Adrienne Kennedy
May Miller
Suzan-Lori Parks
Aishah Rahman
Sonia Sanchez
Ntozake Shange
Anna Deavere Smith
Katherine Davis Chapman Tillman
Shay Youngblood

Essay
Clarissa Minnie Thompson Allen
Tina McElroy Ansa
Doris Jean Austin
Toni Cade Bambara
Marita Bonner
Olivia Ward Bush-Banks
Octavia Butler
Barbara Chase-Riboud
Alice Childress
Barbara T. Christian
Pearl T. Cleage
Eugenia W. Collier
Anna Julia Hayward Cooper
Edwidge Danticat
Angela Y. Davis
Rita Dove
Mari Evans
Nikki Giovanni
Jewelle Gomez
Angelina Weld Grimké
Virginia Hamilton
Frances Ellen Watkins Harper
Pauline Elizabeth Hopkins (Sara A. Allen)
Gayl Jones
June Jordan
Jamaica Kincaid
Audre Geraldine Lorde
Paule Marshall
Louise Meriwether

Opal J. Moore
Gertrude Bustill Mossell
Gloria Naylor
Ann Petry
Ann Plato
Ann Allen Shockley
Ellease Southerland
Maria W. Stewart
Lisa Teasley
Era Bell Thompson
Katherine Davis Chapman Tillman
Alice Walker
Margaret Walker
Ida B. Wells-Barnett
Fannie Barrier Williams

Etiquette Book
Madame Emma Azalia Smith Hackley

Memoir
Toi(nette) Marie Derricotte
bell hooks
Dori Sanders
Era Bell Thompson

Mystery
Barbara Neely

Novel
Clarissa Minnie Thompson Allen
Tina McElroy Ansa
Doris Jean Austin
Nikki Baker
Toni Cade Bambara
Candy Dawson Boyd
Gwendolyn Brooks
Linda Beatrice Brown
Bebe Moore Campbell
Barbara Chase-Riboud
Alice Childress
Pearl T. Cleage
Michelle Cliff
Kathleen Conwell Collins
J. California Cooper
Edwidge Danticat
Rita Dove
Grace Edwards-Yearwood
Jessie Redmon Fauset
Patrice Gaines
Marita Golden

Jewelle Gomez
Joyce Hansen
Frances Ellen Watkins Harper
Pauline Elizabeth Hopkins (Sara A. Allen)
Zora Neale Hurston
Angela Jackson
Amelia E. Johnson
Gayl Jones
June Jordan
Jamaica Kincaid
Pinkie Gordon Lane
Nella Larsen
Kristin Hunter Lattany
Andrea Lee
Helen Elaine Lee
Paule Marshall
Terry McMillan
Louise Meriwether
Mary Monroe
Toni Morrison
Gloria Naylor
Suzan-Lori Parks
Ann Petry
Connie Porter
Alice Randall
Jewell Parker Rhodes
Dori Sanders
Fatima Shaik
Ann Allen Shockley
Ellease Southerland
Barbara Summers
Lisa Teasley
Katherine Davis Chapman Tillman
Mary Elizabeth Vroman
Alice Walker
Margaret Walker
Dorothy West
Sherley Anne Williams
Harriet E. Wilson
Sarah Elizabeth Wright
Shay Youngblood

Novella
Ruth D. Todd

Poetry
Maya Angelou
Gwendolyn Bennett
Joanne Braxton

Gwendolyn Brooks
Linda Beatrice Brown
Olivia Ward Bush-Banks
Barbara Chase-Riboud
Pearl T. Cleage
Michelle Cliff
Lucille Clifton
Wanda Coleman
Eugenia W. Collier
Jayne Cortez
Margaret Esse Danner
Doris Davenport
Toi(nette) Marie Derricotte
Alexis DeVeaux
Rita Dove
Alice Dunbar-Nelson
Mari Evans
Sara Webster Fabio
Julia Fields
Patrice Gaines
Mercedes Gilbert
Nikki Giovanni
Marita Golden
Jewelle Gomez
Rosa Guy
Frances Ellen Watkins Harper
Frenchy Jolene Hodges
Safiya Henderson-Holmes
bell hooks
Pauline Elizabeth Hopkins (Sara A. Allen)
Angela Jackson
Mae Jackson
Amelia E. Johnson
Georgia Douglas Johnson
Helen(e) Johnson
Gayl Jones
June Jordan
Audre Geraldine Lorde
Naomi Long Madgett
May Miller
Arthenia J. Bates Millican
Opal J. Moore
Gertrude Bustill Mossell
Harryette Mullen
Beatrice Murphy
Pauli Murray
Brenda Marie Osbey
Pat Parker

Ann Petry
Ann Plato
Henrietta Cordelia Ray
Carolyn Marie Rodgers
Mona Lisa Saloy
Sonia Sanchez
Ntozake Shange
Ellease Southerland
Lucy Terry
Joyce Carol Thomas
Katherine Davis Chapman Tillman
Gloria Wade-Gayles
Alice Walker
Margaret Walker
Marilyn Nelson Waniek
Phillis Wheatley
Sherley Anne Williams
Sarah Elizabeth Wright

Science Fiction
Octavia Butler

Short Fiction
Mignon Holland Anderson
Tina McElroy Ansa
Toni Cade Bambara
Gwendolyn Bennett
Marita Bonner
Olivia Ward Bush-Banks
Octavia Butler
Michelle Cliff
Wanda Coleman
Eugenia W. Collier
Kathleen Conwell Collins
J. California Cooper
Edwidge Danticat
Edwina Streeter Dixon
Rita Dove
Alice Dunbar-Nelson
Mari Evans
Carolyn Ferrell
Julia Fields
Jewelle Gomez
Angelina Weld Grimké
Frances Ellen Watkins Harper
Carolivia Herron
Frenchy Jolene Hodges
Zora Neale Hurston
Amelia E. Johnson

Adrienne Kennedy
Jamaica Kincaid
Nella Larsen
Kristin Hunter Lattany
Andrea Lee
Paule Marshall
Victoria Earle Matthews
Colleen J. McElroy
Patricia McKissack
Louise Meriwether
Arthenia J. Bates Millican
Mary Monroe
Opal J. Moore
Toni Morrison
Barbara Neely
Diane Oliver
Ann Petry
Carolyn Rodgers
Ann Allen Shockley
Ellease Southerland
Barbara Summers
Lisa Teasley
Ruth D. Todd
Mary Elizabeth Vroman
Dorothy West
Paulette Childress White
Shay Youngblood

Slave Narrative
Harriet Ann Jacobs
Lucy Delaney
Mattie Jane Jackson
Elizabeth Hobbs Keckley
Mary Prince

Travel Literature
Juanita Harrison
Andrea Lee
Colleen McElroy
Nancy Prince
Mary Seacole

Young Adult Literature
Rosa Guy
Joyce Hansen
Sharon Bell Mathis
Joyce Carol Thomas
Mildred Pitts Walter
Brenda Wilkinson

CHRONOLOGICAL LIST OF AUTHORS

The dates to the right of the author's name indicate the date of the author's initial publication.

Lucy Terry (1746)
Phillis Wheatley (1767)
Mary Prince (1831)
Maria W. Stewart (1831)
Jarena Lee (1836)
Zilpha Elaw (1840)
Ann Plato (1841)
Nancy Prince (1850)
Rebecca Cox Jackson (1857)
Mary Scacole (1857)
Frances Ellen Watkins Harper (1859)
Eliza Potter (1859)
Harriet E. Wilson (1859)
Harriet Ann Jacobs (1861)
Mattie Jane Jackson (1866)
Elizabeth Hobbs Keckley (1868)
Julia A. J. Foote (1879)
Clarissa Minnie Thompson Allen (1885)
Octavia Victoria Rogers Albert (1890)
Amelia E. Johnson (1890)
Lucy Delaney (1891)
Ida B. Wells-Barnett (1892)
Anna Julia Hayward Cooper (1892)
Victoria Earle Matthews (1893)
Henrietta Cordelia Ray (1893)
Amanda Berry Smith (1893)
Katherine Davis Chapman
    Tillman (1893)
Gertrude Bustill Mossell (1894)
Kate Drumgoold (1898)
Olivia Ward Bush-Banks (1899)
Alice Dunbar-Nelson (1899)
Pauline Elizabeth Hopkins
    (Sara A. Allen) (1900)
Angelina Weld Grimké (1900)
Susie King Taylor (1902)
Ruth D. Todd (1902)
Fannie Barrier Williams (1902)

Annie Louise Burton (1909)
Madame Emma Azalia Smith
    Hackley (1916)
Georgia Douglas Johnson (1918)
May Miller (1920)
Gwendolyn Bennett (1923)
Jessie Redmon Fauset (1924)
Helen(e) Johnson (1926)
Dorothy West (1926)
Marita Bonner (1927)
Nella Larsen (1928)
Mercedes Gilbert (1931)
Shirley Graham DuBois (1932)
Zora Neale Hurston (1934)
Juanita Harrison (1937)
Ann Petry (1939)
Ellen Tarry (1940)
Elizabeth Laura Adams (1941)
Naomi Long Madgett (1941)
Margaret Walker (1942)
Gwendolyn Brooks (1945)
Beatrice Murphy (1945)
Alice Childress (1949)
Rosa Guy (1954)
Sara Elizabeth Wright (1955)
J. California Cooper (1956)
Pauli Murray (1956)
Lorraine Hansberry (1958)
Paule Marshall (1959)
Margaret Esse Danner (1962)
Julia Fields (1962)
Adrienne Kennedy (1963)
Pat Parker (1963)
Mary Elizabeth Vroman (1963)
Kristin Hunter Lattany (1964)
Ellease Southerland (1964)
Diane Oliver (1965)
Louise Meriwether (1967)

Alice Walker (1967)
Mari Evans (1968)
Sarah Webster Fabio (1968)
Audre Geraldine Lorde (1968)
Anne Moody (1968)
Carolyn Marie Rodgers (1968)
Lucille Clifton (1969)
Jayne Cortez (1969)
Mae Jackson (1969)
June Jordan (1969)
Sharon Bell Mathis (1969)
Arthenia J. Bates Millican (1969)
Sonia Sanchez (1969)
Mildred Pitts Walter (1969)
Maya Angelou (1970)
Nikki Giovanni (1970)
Toni Morrison (1970)
Ann Allen Shockley (1970)
Pearl T. Cleage (1971)
Angela Y. Davis (1971)
Patricia Joann Gibson (1971)
Frenchy Jolene Hodges (1971)
Elaine Jackson (1971)
Toni Cade Bambara (1972)
Eugenia W. Collier (1972)
Pinkie Gordon Lane (1972)
Aishah Rahman (1972)
Paulette Childress White (1972)
Sherley Anne Williams (1972)
Jeannette Franklin Caines (1973)
Alexis De Veaux (1973)
Virginia Hamilton (1973)
Mildred D. Taylor (1973)
Joyce Carol Thomas (1973)
Angela Jackson (1974)
Barbara Chase-Riboud (1974)
Ntozake Shange (1974)
Gayl Jones (1975)
Brenda Wilkinson (1975)
Mignon Holland Anderson (1976)
Octavia Butler (1976)
Joanne Braxton (1977)
Wanda Coleman (1977)
Edwina Streeter Dixon (1977)
Toi(nette) Marie Derricotte (1978)
Eloise Greenfield (1978)
Beverly Guy-Sheftall (1979)

Gloria Wade-Gayles (1979)
Barbara T. Christian (1980)
Michelle Cliff (1980)
Kathleen Conwell Collins (1980)
Doris Davenport (1980)
Rita Dove (1980)
Jewelle Gomez (1980)
Joyce Hansen (1980)
Marilyn Nelson Waniek (1980)
bell hooks (1981)
Andrea Lee (1981)
Harryette Mullen (1981)
Barbara Neely (1981)
Gloria Naylor (1982)
Marita Golden (1983)
Jamaica Kincaid (1983)
Brenda Marie Osbey (1983)
Claudia Tate (1983)
Linda Beatrice Brown (1984)
Colleen J. McElroy (1984)
Mary Monroe (1985)
Bebe Moore Campbell (1986)
Doris Jean Austin (1987)
Candy Dawson Boyd (1987)
Terry McMillan (1987)
Fatima Shaik
Grace Edwards-Yearwood (1988)
Patricia McKissack (1988)
Tina McElroy Ansa (1989)
Opal J. Moore (1989)
Suzan-Lori Parks (1989)
Barbara Summers (1989)
Shay Youngblood (1989)
Safiya Henderson-Holmes (1990)
Mona Lisa Saloy (1990)
Dori Sanders (1990)
Nikki Baker (1991)
Carolivia Herron (1991)
Connie Porter (1991)
Anna Deavere Smith (1992)
Jewell Parker Rhodes (1993)
Edwidge Danticat (1994)
Carolyn Ferrell (1994)
Patrice Gaines (1994)
Helen Elaine Lee (1994)
Lisa Teasley (1997)
Alice Randall (2001)

PINKIE GORDON LANE (1923–)

BIOGRAPHICAL NARRATIVE

Pinkie Gordon Lane, the first African American poet laureate of Louisiana, was born Pinkie Rose Gordon in Philadelphia, Pennsylvania, on January 13, 1923, to William and Inez Gordon. Both her parents died before she reached the age of twenty-five, and she was forced to sell the family house in order to enroll in college. In 1945, she entered Spelman College in Atlanta, Georgia, on a four-year academic scholarship. In 1948, while attending Spelman College, she married Ulysses Simpson Lane. She graduated magna cum laude in 1949, with a bachelor's degree in English and art. She taught English in the public schools of Florida and Georgia for six years; then she and her husband moved back to Atlanta in 1955.

In 1956, Lane graduated from Atlanta University with a master's degree in English, and she moved with her husband to Baton Rouge, Louisiana, where she still resides. She began teaching at Leland College in Baker, Louisiana, in 1957. In 1959, she became an instructor of English at Southern University in Baton Rouge, where she later became a full professor, and then director of the English department. Gordon Edward Lane, her only child, was born in 1963. Her husband died seven years later, in 1970.

While working as an instructor at Southern University in 1960, a colleague gave Lane a copy of *A Street in Bronzeville* by Gwendolyn Brooks. This was the first time Lane had read a book of poems by an African American woman author, and Lane began writing poems herself. She had previously written works of fiction, mainly short stories. Her first poem was published in *Phylon* in 1961. She published a number of other poems in journals and magazines, including the *Journal of Black Poetry*, *Pembroke Magazine*, *Southern Review*, and *Callaloo*. Her first book of poems, *Wind Thoughts*, was published in 1972. Since that time she has published four other volumes of poetry: *The Mystic Female* (1978), which was nominated for the Pulitzer Prize in 1979; *I Never Scream: New and Selected Poems* (1985); *Girl at the Window* (1991); and *Elegy for Etheridge* (2000).

Lane became the first African American woman to receive a doctoral degree from Louisiana State University, in Baton Rouge, when she graduated in 1967. She became the first African American poet laureate of Louisiana in 1989, a position which she held until 1992. She has received numerous awards throughout her career, including the National Award for Achievement in Poetry from the College Language Association in 1988 and the Image Award from the NAACP in 1990, and she was inducted into the Louisiana Black History Hall of Fame in 1991.

MAJOR WORKS

Even though Lane began writing poetry in the 1960s, her work is in many ways different from other writers of the Black Arts Movement. When she first began writing in 1961, Lane used both the Italian and Elizabethan sonnet forms as models for her poetry.

Later she began to experiment with other forms, and eventually shifted to writing free verse. Her first volume of poems, *Wind Thoughts*, contains examples of each of these forms. Perhaps the most striking poems of this volume are the "Poems to My Father," which have also been reprinted in a number of Lane's later books. Throughout her work it is clear that Lane's father had a profound influence on her life. In "Poems to My Father" Lane deals with the pain caused by her father's drunkenness and neglect, but at the same time she expresses her love for him. Her poetry describes the inward wrestlings of her mind and soul with such themes as love, suffering, and death. While Lane deals with these themes from a very personal point of view, they also have broader significance.

In *The Mystic Female*, Lane's second volume of poetry, she focuses on the everyday experiences of life, but often through a mystical or even metaphysical lens. She often uses her poetry as a means of reaction to situations that are taking place in the world around her. The poem "Sexual Privacy of Women on Welfare" reacts to the questions on a welfare application, poignantly revealing the pain and loneliness which many women on welfare face. The imagery in this volume is often very vivid. Having minored in art at Spelman College, Lane learned how to use her poems to "paint" a detailed picture of the people, and especially the places, in her poems. In the Baton Rouge poems, Lane describes the town of Baton Rouge as it grows and expands into a large city. Many of Lane's poems describe scenes in nature, and her poems engage the senses as they describe the sights, smells, and sounds of the Louisiana landscape.

Lane's poems are divided into three sections in *I Never Scream*—"Metaphors," "People," and "Love." Lane was greatly influenced by Anne Sexton's use of metaphor, and this is reflected in the poems in the first section. The second section is written for or about significant people in Lane's life. In "Four Poems for Gordon," Lane describes her experiences as a mother, and the struggle she faces as her son grows older. Like the many other elegies and eulogies in Lane's work, the poem "Dying" was written for Lane's late husband, and deals with the desire for life amidst the crushing reality of death. A number of poems in this volume and her later volumes are dedicated to other authors such as Gwendolyn Brooks, Sonia Sanchez, and Etheridge Knight. The final section of this book deals with issues of love, particularly the madness and pain—as well as the hope and ecstasy—that it brings. *Girl at the Window* and *Elegy for Etheridge*, Lane's most recent works, pick up many of the same themes from her previous volumes. A central focus of all of Lane's poetry is her subjective experience of everyday life. Many of her poems are autobiographical in nature, and concern Lane's experiences as a teacher, writer, and editor. In "While Working towards the Ph.D. Degree," Lane recounts the difficulties of trying to balance a career and a family.

CRITICAL RECEPTION

Although Lane's work has not generated the same amount of criticism as other contemporary poets, her poems have elicited a number of different critical responses. One area that many critics have noted is Lane's concern with place, culture, and family. The distance between Lane's childhood home of Philadelphia and her current home in Louisiana is of particular interest because they are "points metaphors of mental occurences [*sic*] within the poet/speaker" ("Evocations," Bryan 57). These descriptions of place, culture, and family have been examined primarily for their significance to Louisiana literature, mainly as a record of Southern place. However, critics have also discussed how her depictions provide an important history of African American life and experience.

Along with depictions of place, critics have noted a number of other significant aspects in Lane's work. Some critics have responded to the lyric quality of Lane's language, and the vivid images in her poems. Other critics have mentioned Lane's use of emotion and mysticism, particularly in *The Mystic Female*. Furthermore, her poems are sometimes called "quiet poems," taken from her poem by the same name, because they deal with broad issues in a personal, "quiet" way.

There is much work left to be done in the study of Lane's poetry. It would be interesting to explore Lane's work from a feminist perspective. Also, the process of intertextuality in the poems has not been explored fully. These and other future analyses of the poems could prove profitable in helping the reader better understand and appreciate Lane's work.

BIBLIOGRAPHY

Works by Pinkie Gordon Lane

Elegy for Etheridge. Baton Rouge: Louisiana State University Press, 2000.
Girl at the Window. Baton Rouge: Louisiana State University Press, 1991.
I Never Scream: New and Selected Poems. Detroit: Lotus Press, 1985.
The Mystic Female. Fort Smith, AR: South & West, 1978.
Wind Thoughts. Fort Smith, AR: South & West, 1972.

Studies of Pinkie Gordon Lane's Works

Bryan, Violet Harrington. "Evocations of Place and Culture in the Works of Four Contemporary Black Louisiana Writers: Brenda Osbey, Sybil Kein, Elizabeth Brown-Guillory, and Pinkie Gordon Lane." *Louisiana Literature* 4.2 (1987): 49–60.
———. "Interview with Pinkie Gordon Lane." *Xavier Review* 17.2 (1997): 16–24.
Cockram, Pati. "Graceful, Musical Language: *The Island Itself* by Roger Fanning and *Girl at the Window* by Pinkie Gordon Lane." *American Book Review* 15.1 (1993): 30.
Craig, Marilyn B. "Pinkie Gordon Lane." In *Afro-American Poets Since 1955*, edited by Trudier Harris-Lopez and Thadious M. Davis, 212–16. *Dictionary of Literary Biography*, vol. 41. Detroit: Gale Research Co., 1985.
Henderson, Stephen. *Understanding the New Black Poetry, Black Speech, and Black Music as Poetic References*. New York: William Morrow & Co., 1973.
Moore, Lenard D. "Review: Witnesses: African American Poetry of History, Family, and Place." *African American Review* 28.2 (1994): 311–15.
Newman, Dorothy. "Review: Lane's Mystic Female." *Callaloo* (1979): 153–55.
Roland, Lillian D. "Review." *Black American Literature Forum* 20.3 (1986): 294–98.

Julia Marek Ponce

NELLA LARSEN (1891–1964)

BIOGRAPHICAL NARRATIVE

Nella Larsen, a folklorist, novelist and short fiction writer, was born in 1891 in Chicago, Illinois. Her father, Peter Walker, was a West Indian. Her mother, Mary Hanson, was Danish. Her parents may or may not have separated after her birth. Her mother may or may not have married a white man named Peter Larsen. Because Nella Larsen was secretive about her family history, it is difficult to know the truth. There are those who say that Walker and Larsen were the same man. Larsen, according to the stories, was Walker passing as white to get a job on the Chicago railroad. Nella Larsen, thus, may have learned early the basic lesson of her classic novels.

Larsen spent her childhood in Chicago. While there, she went to public schools. In 1907 she went to Fisk University's Normal School, staying until 1910. This experience served to separate her from her family of birth through bringing her closer to Afrcian American culture and away from her parents' rejection. Her parents sent her to Fisk in an effort to further hide her. Larsen had found herself excluded time after time from the family. For example, Larsen's mother failed to report her to census takers. After finishing Fisk on her own without her parents' help, she then attended the University of Copenhagen in Denmark, from 1910 to 1912, demonstrating her pull toward her bicultural culture. Upon returning to the United States in 1912, she successfully embarked upon a three-year nursing program.

Between 1912 and 1915, she studied nursing in New York. When she graduated, she went to the south to work at Tuskegee Institute in Alabama. There she became the head nurse at John Andrew Memorial Hospital and Nurse Training School. Larsen, however, was never comfortable in the south although she was most comfortable in African American settings. Therefore, she left Alabama and returned to a nursing position in New York.

There she met and married Elmer Imes in 1919. Larson's marriage to the physicist made social prominence easily available. This prominence enabled her to meet people who were significant in the Harlem Renaissance. At the same time, she began working in the Harlem branch of the New York Public Library while she attended Columbia University, majoring in library science.

At this time she began to publish her writings, starting with two articles for children. These were articles describing Danish games, which Larsen published in the children's magazine *Brownies' Book*. Larsen wrote a few pieces of fiction under the pen name Allen Semi (Semi is a reversal of Imes).

She published two captivating novels, *Quicksand* (1928) and *Passing* (1929), and three fine short stories, "Freedom" (1926), "The Wrong Man" (1926), and "Sanctuary" (1930). In 1930, Larsen won a Guggenheim Fellowship, the first African American woman to receive it.

A reader of *Forum* magazine accused Larsen of plagiarizing her short story "Sanctuary" from Sheila Kaye-Smith's "Mrs. Adis." Even though Larsen proved that she had written her story prior to Kaye-Smith's work, she felt rejected—a constant theme in her life to that point. Coupled with her marital problems, this charge helped end her writing career.

The trauma of an ugly divorce in 1933 interrupted her career forever. Her mother-in-law, a light-skinned woman, foreshadowed the breakup through her antipathy toward Larsen. Her husband's affair, significantly, was with Ethel Gilbert, a white staffer at Fisk University, where he taught. The popular press blamed Larsen's writing career for the breakup, claiming that her preoccupation with success had prevented her from living up to her marital responsibilities. Supposedly, Larsen attempted suicide in her despair. Whether she did or not, Larsen stopped writing, moved to the Lower East Side, and cut herself off from former contacts.

Unfortunately, she never published another novel again. Instead of leading to further triumphs, the Guggenheim marked the end of her public career. She retreated to private life and worked as a nurse in New York until she died in 1964. Larsen was found dead in her apartment.

MAJOR WORKS

Nella Larsen was a woman ahead of her time. Her writings express her desire to identify with both her "racial" backgrounds and heritages. Additionally, she was aware of what today is called the woman's issue as well as of social class. Freedom, for her, was indeed indivisible. She brought this passion for justice to her all-too-few fictional writings, demonstrating, as Barbara Smith notes, "that the politics of sex as well as the politics of race and class are crucially interlocking factors in the works of Black women writers" (170). This works in Larsen's fiction toward a fuller picture of identity, its establishment, maintenance, and meaning.

Larsen's work probes the way in which people's identity can be lost behind labels, or in the jargon "signifiers." There is a danger of people being lost behind these labels and being confused with them. The person is lost behind that which signifies her or him. Thus, the idea of "passing," for example, is one that should not exist. It is in itself demeaning. It is the result of setting one "racial" identity above another, forcing people to deny their full heritage.

Larsen interestingly enough uses the term "passing" in a double meaning of both "passing" as white, crossing the color line, and of dying, passing to another world. In both cases, essential identity is submerged; one, by social exigencies, the other, through natural ones. Irene Westover Redfield and Clare Kendry Bellew, the major protagonists of *Passing*, have to deal with the label "nigger," which threatens to swallow up their identity and submerge them so that they "pass" from sight. The label, in sum, hides or obliterates the identity.

Both Clare and Irene seek recognition and both "pass" to attain it. White racism overdetermines their efforts to achieve recognition. Clare passes by crossing the color barriers and "passing" as white. Irene, however, passes through assimilating and embracing white values, including those concerning feminine beauty. Irene is a member of the black bourgeoisie. Clare, however, comes from an impoverished background. Her father was an alcoholic janitor. Moving in with her white great-aunts does not make matters better for these two women.

Larsen further plays on the dark-white theme through having Clare (her name means "light") renamed "Nig," short for the despised word "nigger," by her husband. Her husband is ignorant of Clare's background and those of her friends, who also disguise their African American heritage. Thus he is free to proclaim his racism openly, claiming that Clare is getting darker daily and soon will be a "nigger." He continues his speech stating what he means by that term and makes clear his hatred for African Americans, inadvertently denying his wife's true identity and individual humanity.

Larsen neatly displays the imbalance not only in black-white relationships but also in male-female ones. Irene who seeks to maintain her African American identity while assimilating white bourgeois values is in danger of accepting the white "truth" of African American inferiority. Not only is she in danger of losing her identity, but she is also cooperating through her silence in the furtherance of her own oppression.

Irene finds the situation intolerable but is helpless to change it. The dilemma it sets up in her mind leads to her increasing mental deterioration and descent into mental illness. She has no control of the situation. The issue of power is central to Larsen's fiction. The ability of people to humiliate others through casual words is part of that power. Clare is thrown into deep despair when her husband Bellew greets her with a casual "Hello, Nig."

Irene herself, however, applies racist terms unthinkingly to less advantaged and darker-skinned African Americans, showing her assimilation of racist values. She dehumanizes others through her use of language, losing the individual behind the symbol. She terms other African Americans who are somehow beneath her as "nigger," "Nig," "boy," and so on. She uses the term "creature" as an unreflective derogatory term.

Certainly, this internalization of white "values" and their projection on others is a classic example of seeking to separate oneself from a "spoiled" category, a kind of Freudian process in which we "pass" on the blame of our stigma to others. Irene's major fault is beyond her control. White society "labels" her black. In spite of what she does personally, she will be blamed for the reputed deficiencies of African Americans. To defend herself, she projects her fears onto others and "blames" less-fortunate victims for the situation.

Larsen poignantly depicts this situation early in the novel. After Irene faints on the street, a cab driver who takes Irene for white brings her to an exclusive hotel, the Drayton. While there Irene worries that she may be found out as not white and expelled, reminding her of past humiliations. The segregation she faces is as oppressive as the August sun that caused her to faint. Larsen states that Irene became aware of a woman staring at her. At once she feels that she has been found out. Her first thought is that she will be humiliated again.

In *Passing*, Larsen constructs a self-aware novel of passing, one that realizes it is part of a genre that stretches back through black and white literature and would go forward into the future. It includes such writers as Eugene Chesnutt, Fannie Hurst, Mark Twain, and others. Larsen repeats the theme of racial pride but with a deep strain of inevitable tragedy. Those who pass in her novel do not find peace or happiness in doing so, whether that passing is physical or psychological.

Although Larsen follows the general model of the passing genre of fiction, she adds a major new element. Thus, Larsen's novel has the following generic characteristics: (1) a chiaroscuro style, (2) a theme of racial justice, (3) a return home, (4) secrecy and exposure, and (5) the heroine's death. However, Larsen's contribution and genius is in putting in a concern over the language and message of the tale.

Quicksand, the first of her two novels, depicts a different aspect of loss of identity. It, too, draws on autobiographical details, detailing the quest for racial and sexual identity as part of the construction of an overall identity. Helga Crane, the main character, finds herself trapped in the restrictions and necessities of motherhood. Moreover, Helga is illegitimate and has a white and an African American parent. There is no place for her in post–Civil War American society.

Larsen adds to the problem of sex, race, women's place in society, and the issue of social class. The final paragraph of the book brings many of Larsen's themes together, especially sex, race, and class:

It was so easy and so pleasant to think about freedom and cities, about clothes and books, about the sweet mingled smell of Houbigant and cigarettes in softly lighted rooms filled with inconsequential chatter and laughter and sophisticated tuneless music. It was so hard to think out a feasible way of retrieving all these agreeable, desired things. Just then. Later. When she got up. By and by. She must rest. Get strong. Sleep. Then, afterward, she could work out some arrangement. So she dozed and dreamed in snatches of sleeping and waking, letting time run on. Away. *AND HARDLY* had she left her bed and become able to walk again without pain, hardly had the children returned from the homes of the neighbors, when she began to have her fifth child.

Larsen recounts the psychological world of a middle-class black woman. She avoids a materialistic economic explanation for Helga's problems. Helga is not simply a symbol of a racist victim. She is a well-rounded individual who has some responsibility for her problems. She is a seductress. She is aggressive in pursuing her own goals. The novel is not simply one of victimization and oppression. These certainly are elements of the story, of Helga's reality. However, Larsen universalizes Helga's plight through her careful creation of an individual who is deeper than stereotypes can make her. These aspects of Helga's personality, her seductiveness and aggressiveness, implicate her in her own fate and place this masterpiece in the realm of tragedy and not melodrama.

CRITICAL RECEPTION

Nella Larsen is considered one of the more sophisticated authors of the Harlem Renaissance. Her novels *Quicksand* and *Passing* have become part of the literary canon in many universities. There have been numerous discussions of her novels and to a lesser extent short stories over the years. As the feminist movement and sensibility emerged, the depth of Larsen's perception as well as her influence became better appreciated.

Even in her lifetime, however, Larsen earned great praise. She received a Guggenheim Fellowship, earned critical praise, and was influential in the Harlem Renaissance movement. Larsen's *Quicksand* received better reviews than Claude McKay's *Home to Harlem*. Larsen also won a Harmon Award in 1928. Unfortunately, Nella Larsen's treatment of sexuality was rejected at the time by not only white editors but also the NAACP and black women social leaders. These black leaders felt that her openness jeopardized the cause of racial advance and played to stereotypes concerning black sexual license.

Larsen's last three novels were never published. The publisher's readers found merit in *Mirage*. However, Larsen chose not to rewrite them and never published another thing. So far no manuscripts of these works have come to light so that modern readers may judge for themselves.

More recent commentators have noted how far in advance her combination of gender, class, and race actually was. She advocated an understanding of the intertwining of these issues and an understanding of the importance of the individual. Her work was subtle and sophisticated. Her characters were well-rounded, in-depth individuals, not representatives of personal stands. Neither were they stereotypes. Their complexities gave them humanity. Larsen's oeuvre was small, but it was significant and influential.

BIBLIOGRAPHY

Works by Nella Larsen

The Complete Fiction of Nella Larsen: Passing, Quicksand and the Short Stories, edited by Marita Golden. New York: Anchor Books, 2003.
"Freedom" (1926). In *The Complete Fiction of Nella Larsen: Passsing, Quicksand and the Stories*. Ed. Charles Larson. New York: Anchor, 2001.
Passing. New York: Penguin Classics, 1929.
Quicksand and Passing (reprint). New Brunswick, NJ: Rutgers University Press, 1986.
"Sanctuary" (1930). In *The Complete Fiction of Nella Larsen: Passsing, Quicksand and the Stories*. Ed. Charles Larson. New York: Anchor, 2001.
"The Wrong Man" (1926). In *The Complete Fiction of Nella Larsen: Passsing, Quicksand and the Stories*. Ed. Charles Larson. New York: Anchor, 2001.

Studies of Nella Larsen's Works

Bennett, Juda. *The Passing Figure: Racial Confusion in Modern American Literature*. New York: Peter Lang, 1996.
Davis, Thadious. *Nella Larsen: Novelist of the Harlem Renaissance*. Baton Rouge: Louisiana State University Press, 1994.
Larson, Charles. *An Intimation of Things Distant: The Collected Fiction of Nella Larsen*. New York: Anchor, 1992.
McLendon, Jacquelyn Y. *The Politics of Color in the Fiction of Jessie Fauset and Nella Larsen*. Charlottesville: University Press of Virginia, 1995.
Mille, Erica M., and Erick Miller. *The Other Reconstruction: Where Violence and Womanhood Meet in the Writings of Ida B. Wells-Barnett, Angelina Weld Grimke, and Nella Larsen*. New York: Garland, 1999.
Tate, Claudia. *Psychoanalysis and Black Novels: Desire and the Protocols of Race*. New York: Oxford University Press, 1998.

Other Works

Smith, Barbara. *Toward a Black Feminist Criticism*. New York: Out and Out Books, 1981.

Frank A. Salamone

KRISTIN HUNTER LATTANY (1931–)

BIOGRAPHICAL NARRATIVE

Kristin Hunter Lattany, a distinctive voice in American literature, was born on September 12, 1931, in Philadelphia, Pennsylvania. Her parents, George and Mabel Eggleston, were professionally employed at a time when legal discrimination was common in the United States. Despite these challenges, both parents managed dual careers, George as a school principal and army colonel, and Mary as a pharmacist and schoolteacher. The influences of Lattany's family and hometown are evident in her fiction, particularly in her depiction of educated African American characters and her use of the regions around Philadelphia and western New Jersey as settings.

Lattany began her writing career as a columnist for the *Pittsburgh Courier* at age fourteen. A few years later, she enrolled at the University of Pennsylvania, graduating with a degree in education. She married Joseph Hunter in 1952 and worked as an elementary schoolteacher and an advertising writer. In the early 1960s, Lattany gained a foothold in the academic and literary worlds that she would sustain for four decades. She earned a research assistantship at the University of Pennsylvania in 1961, where she would later serve for twenty-three years as an English professor. Her early work was published under the name Kristin Hunter, including her first novel, *God Bless the Child*. Two more published novels would follow before the end of the 1960s. She married John Lattany in 1968, and completed eleven full-length works of adult and adolescent fiction by 2003.

MAJOR WORKS

In her career as a novelist, Kristin Hunter Lattany has developed a distinctive voice in late twentieth and early twenty-first century American literature. Her work is topical, addressing political and cultural issues that have arisen in the United States since the civil rights movement, especially inequalities and miscommunication in American race relations. Through effective characterization, Lattany explores the promising and problematic traits characters inherit from family, contradiction and compromise in work life, and the ways that communities form among small circles of people for personal growth or political activism. Stylistically, Lattany's use of realism makes her work accessible to diverse audiences—academic, popular, adolescent, and adult.

Lattany's first novel, *God Bless the Child* (1964), was a critical and popular success. The novel provides a hard look at issues in the inner cities of the 1960s, including a lack of jobs and adequate housing, family instability, and ethnic tensions between white business owners and African American employees and customers. The novel's mood is shaped by the specter of "The Man," a symbolic representation of a white power structure that benefited from rackets such as the heroin trade and "the numbers." The institutional power of "the man" is projected in the novel by powerful underlings such as

Benny, an Italian-American restaurant owner who exerts direct control over numbers runners, pimps, and other crime figures.

The protagonist of *God Bless the Child* is Rosie Fleming, a young African American woman whose efforts to become wealthy at any cost lead to unforeseen consequences. In her formative years, Rosie witnesses contrasting strategies for survival among the most important women in her life, her mother and her grandmother. Her mother, Queenie, earns enough in her work as a hairdresser to keep the rent paid on a roach-infested apartment and to insure the family's basic survival, but she also gives away money to a womanizing boyfriend and is an alcoholic. Ironically, Queenie's boyfriend is known to Rosie at first as "Uncle Roscoe," though there are no illusions that he or previous boyfriends were ever Rosie's real uncle.

The second powerful parental figure in the novel is Rosie's grandmother, Lourinda Baxter Huggs. Lourinda works for years in a white family household. She is convinced that her employers embody the strength of character and good taste that would make appropriate models for African Americans to follow. Readers, however, are invited to consider the futility of pursuing an image of success based strictly on material possessions and requiring the repudiation of one's familiar notions of home.

Two years later Lattany published her second novel, *The Landlord*. In this novel a young Jewish man of inherited means, Elgar Enders, purchases an inner city apartment building but is unable initially to collect rent from his tenants. Later, he moves into one of the apartments and becomes friendly, even intimate, with some of the tenants, with comic results. Audience response to the novel was positive and sustained enough to support production of a film version in 1970 starring Pearl Bailey, Beau Bridges, and Lee Grant. The novel illustrates Lattany's ability to write sympathetically about characters of various ethnicities.

Lattany's third novel of the 1960s, *The Soul Brothers and Sister Lou* (1968), was the first of several texts she wrote for adolescent readers in the vein of other socially conscious young adult fiction such as Louise Meriwether's *Daddy Was a Numbers Runner* (1970), Toni Cade Bambara's *Gorilla, My Love* (1972), and Alice Childress's *A Hero Ain't Nothin' but a Sandwich* (1973). *The Soul Brothers and Sister Lou* depicts the adolescence of Louretta Hawkins, who is living in the inner city with a large, multigenerational, single-parent family. The story revolves around Louretta, her family, and several young men from her neighborhood who are disillusioned by the atmosphere of violence and economic stagnation in the inner city. However, prospects change for everyone when Louretta convinces her ambitious brother William to rent an abandoned church. The space allows her brother to pursue his dream of a printing business, while the teenagers gain a place to rehearse their singing with hopes of a music career.

The Soul Brothers and Sister Lou seems to embody the author's disillusionment and optimism about the role of identity movements in improving the lives of African Americans, a topic she returns to repeatedly in her later work. In an interview published in *Black Women Writers at Work* (1983), Lattany states that "as Americans, we believe that all problems can be solved, that all questions have answers" (Tate 84), and these assumptions are implicit in social movements based on race and gender identity. Lattany then weighs the gains and losses of the civil rights and feminist movements. She suggests that "the women's movement has eclipsed many black concerns and diluted black gains" (Tate 80), and does not identify strongly with an African American female standpoint as a particular way of writing. Instead, she marvels at "the enormous and varied adaptations of black people to the distorting, terrifying restrictions of society" (84).

After the 1960s, Lattany continued to publish adult fiction and adolescent literature. Two collections of adolescent short fiction appeared in the early 1970s, *Boss Cat* (1971) and *Guest in the Promised Land* (1973), followed by *The Survivors* (1975), a novel with an adult-child friendship plot that may also appeal to young readers. Her next major work was *The Lakestown Rebellion* (1978), a treatment of African American community life and collective action to save an all–African American town from a misdirected urban renewal project. Related themes were raised earlier in *The Landlord*, but Lattany gives these themes a more earnest treatment in this novel, with Lakestown modeled after the real-life town of Lawnside, New Jersey. The reputation of the novel was strong enough that it was republished in 2003 by Coffee House Press, in a limited reissue series of key texts from the Black Arts Movement.

Since the 1970s, Lattany has published four novels, *Lou in the Limelight* (1981), a sequel to *The Soul Brothers and Sister Lou*, *Kinfolks* (1996), *Do Unto Others* (2000), and *Breaking Away* (2003). Among these, *Lou in the Limelight* responded to popular demand for a continuation of the story of Louretta and her compatriots. Lattany returns to adult themes in her last three texts with reflective views of the social changes that were set in motion during her early adulthood. *Kinfolks* tells the story of Patrice Barber and Cherry Hopkins, both parents and close friends who must come to terms with their histories of growing up in the 1960s in order to advise their children on their emerging sexualities and other matters of identity and behavior. *Do Unto Others* raises the subject of African American relationships with Africa, in terms of both ancestry and the present. The protagonist, Zena Lawson, becomes the latest in a list of memorable African American female characters in Lattany's fiction, and the novel takes a critical look at the Afrocentricity movement of the 1980s and 1990s.

Breaking Away, Lattany's most recent novel, blends the methods of realism and historical fiction to examine cultural debates in higher education. The protagonist is Bethesda Barnes, an African American professor in an English department at a New Jersey university. She is an untenured professor who does not participate actively in department politics, but she is confident in her teaching skills. The novel's primary conflict surrounds Dr. Barnes's response when several black female students report to her that they have been verbally harassed by a group of white students. The harassment occurred around midnight, when the students were practicing for a step show. Dr. Barnes puts aside her own skepticism about African American sororities and the artistic legitimacy of step shows in order to support and advise the students. However, internal conflicts prove difficult to resolve, especially her personal struggles after the death of her father, instability in her romantic life, and her department's opposition to her support for the students. Once again, the novel suggests that the mass activism of the 1960s did not resolve the dilemmas that most African Americans face in everyday life, even if they are privileged enough to attend or even teach at an elite university.

CRITICAL RECEPTION

Only a small number of critical studies of Lattany's fiction have been published to date. The dearth of criticism may be attributable to Lattany's realist aesthetics. While Lattany has been effective as a satirist, she does not engage in formal experiments as have Ishmael Reed or Percival Everett, and her historical writing bears little resemblance stylistically to the celebrated recent authors of that genre—Toni Morrison, Charles Johnson, and Sherley Anne Williams, for instance. Thus, while African American realist writers of significant force and power remain a part of the literary landscape (Terry McMillan and Bebe Moore Campbell are examples), Lattany's recent texts have not benefited from widespread national review or careful critical analysis by established scholars.

Of the published commentary that is currently available, Gerald Early's "Working Girl Blues: Mothers, Daughters, and the Image of Billy Holiday in Kristin Hunter's *God Bless the Child*" is most effective at placing Hunter's work within a larger context of African American aesthetics, although the article examines only Lattany's first novel. In his analysis, Early argues that the thematic content of Billie Holiday's song provides a better starting point for understanding Lattany's text than do the naturalist novels of the early twentieth century by Theodore Drieser, an author who is often mentioned as a source point for Lattany's early work. Early compares the characterization of Rosie Fleming in the text to the tragic life of Billie Holiday, whose rise from poverty to wealth and celebrity also provided no escape from oppression. In Early's words, Rosie "can only be driven mad by the horror of it all, much as Billie Holiday was driven to drugs, to drink, and finally to inertia as she became overwhelmed by the horror of American culture's utopian vision of bourgeois success" (438).

Reviews from her first decade of writing also help to explain Lattany's unique vision and qualities and may also help explain why critics have been slow to take up her work. From that period, noted editor Abraham Chapman provides perhaps the most balanced and thoughtful assessment of her work. In his review of *The Landlord*, Chapman criticizes the "artistic and structural flaws" of the novel, especially Elgar's psychologist Borden, whose conversations with Elgar are a too-convenient device for character development, and Chapman also finds elements of the novel's resolution unrealistic. However, Chapman recognizes Lattany's skill in moving away from ideological dogma while effectively using a familiar set of realist tools: chronological time, sympathetic characters, and clear displays of causes and effects within the plot. As a capstone assessment, Chapman writes that "Kristin Hunter, whose first novel was *God Bless the Child*, here negates any idea that all American Negro writing is didactic and dead earnest and bitter and full of the mystique of race; she explodes the stereotype of the so-called 'Negro Novel'" (45).

Reviewing *The Soul Brothers and Sister Lou*, Zena Sutherland writes in memorable terms that might apply to the fiction of Lattany's later years as well. Sutherland complements the novel's depiction of "the maturing of a young girl who learns to appreciate her racial heritage during those difficult years when self-acceptance and self-identity are problems for all adolescents. This is indeed a book for our times" (37). In her larger body of fiction, Lattany implies that the process of maturing and appreciating one's racial heritage extends into middle age, and is not confined to the struggles faced by Louretta Hawkins, Rosie Fleming, or the young people of the inner city. Instead, Lattany suggests imaginative ways that Americans of all races might examine their relationships to the legacy of racial division that continues into the twenty-first century, even if solutions to these dilemmas remain elusive.

BIBLIOGRAPHY

Works by Kristin Hunter Lattany

Boss Cat. New York: Avon Books, 1971.
Breaking Away. New York: Ballantine/One World, 2003.
Do Unto Others. New York: One World/Ballantine, 2000.

God Bless the Child. New York: Bantam, 1964.

Guest in the Promised Land. New York: Scribner, 1973.

Kinfolks. New York: Ballantine, 1996.

The Lakestown Rebellion. New York: Scribner, 1978. Reprint, Minneapolis: Coffee House Press, 2003.

The Landlord. New York: Scribner, 1966.

Lou in the Limelight. New York: Scribner, 1981.

The Soul Brothers and Sister Lou. New York: Scribner, 1968.

The Survivors. New York: Scribner, 1975.

Studies of Kristin Hunter Lattany's Works

Ballantine Reader's Circle and Random House, Inc. *Kinfolks*. Reading Group Guide and Interview with Kristin Lattany. http://www.readinggroupguides.com/guides/kinfolks-author.asp (accessed May 1, 2005).

Bogart, Gary. "Kristin Hunter Lattany." *Wilson Library Bulletin* 50.2 (October 1975): 115ff.

Brooks, Gwendolyn. "Tenant Problem: A Review of *The Landlord* by Kristin Hunter Lattany." *Washington Post*, May 8, 1966, 14.

Buckmaster, Henrietta. Rev. of *God Bless the Child*. *Christian Science Monitor*, September 10, 1964, 7.

Chapman, Abraham. "White Invisible Man." Rev. of *The Landlord*. *Saturday Review* 49.20 (May 14, 1966): 45.

Davis, Thadious, and Trudier Harris. *Dictionary of Literary Biography (African-American Fiction Writers after 1945)*, vol. 33. Detroit: Gale Research Group, 1984.

Early, Gerald. "Working Girl Blues: Mothers, Daughters and the Image of Billie Holiday in Kristin Hunter's *God Bless the Child*." *Black American Literature Forum* 20.4 (Winter 1986): 423–42.

Heins, Paul. *Horn Book Magazine* 49 (August 1973): 386.

Johnson, Becky. *Voices of Youth Advocates* 4.6 (February 1982): 33.

Kaye, Marilyn. *New York Times Book Review*, February 21, 1982, 35.

Kirkus Review 46.6 (March 15, 1987): 325.

Nelson, Emmanual, ed. *Contemporary African-American Novelists: A Bio-Biographical Critical Sourcebook*. Westport, CT: Greenwood Press, 1999.

Saal, Rollen. "What Made Rosie Run?" Rev. of *God Bless the Child* by Kristin Hunter Lattany. *New York Times Book Review*, September 20, 1964, 36.

Schraufnagel, Noel. "Kristin Hunter." Salem Press. *MagillOnLiterature Plus*. Ebscohost Research Databases/Academic Search Elite (accessed April 18, 2005).

Stanton, Junious. "Saving a Black Haven." Rev. of *Lakestown Rebellion*, reprint edition. *Black Issues Book Review* 5.4 (July/August 2003): 50–51.

Sutherland, Zena. *Saturday Review* 51 (October 19, 1968): 37.

Tate, Claudia. *Black Women Writers at Work*. New York: Continuum, 1983.

Zaleski, Jeff. "Breaking Away" (review). *Publishers Weekly* 250.9 (March 3, 2003): 51.

David M. Jones

ANDREA LEE (1953–)

BIOGRAPHICAL NARRATIVE

Born in Philadelphia in 1953, fiction and travel writer, Andrea Lee spent most of her childhood in a middle-class suburb of the city. Reflecting on her childhood, Lee has written that she was part of "an affluent, extremely bookish, extremely middle-class Afro-American family, in which the adults, at least, would have been horrified to hear themselves called Afro-Americans" ("Double Lives" 60). Though her parents were actively involved in the civil rights movement, Lee describes them as consummate outsiders, who felt apart "from the poorer, blacker masses with whom they were declaring solidarity" (60–61) while distrusting white, mainstream America. Consequently, Lee and her two brothers "grew adept at assimilation without absorption, at double lives . . . we went everywhere and belonged nowhere" (61).

Lee obtained a bachelor's and master's degree in English from Harvard University. While pursuing her master's degree, she accompanied her husband, a doctoral student in Russian history, to the Soviet Union in 1978. *Russian Journal*, published in 1981, was the result of Lee's ten-month Russian sojourn. It was nominated for the American Book Award for General Nonfiction in 1981, and garnered the Jean Stein Award from the National Academy of Arts and Letters in 1984.

Lee published the bildungsroman *Sarah Phillips* in 1984, followed by a short-story anthology, *Interesting Women*, in 2002. Throughout her writing career Lee has worked as a staff writer for the *New Yorker*, later becoming an occasional contributor. Lee now lives in Turin, Italy, with her Italian spouse and son.

MAJOR WORKS

Lee published *Russian Journal* in 1981, after living in Russia for ten months. Predating the glasnost and perestroika era, *Russian Journal* provides an intriguing glimpse into the mechanisms of Soviet Russia. The work comprises a series of vignettes centered around a cast of exotic young students and artists the author encounters or befriends. This collection succeeds in capturing a particular moment in USSR history when, underneath the surface of seeming compliance with an authoritarian regime, the society's foundations are crumbling.

With rich description, Lee evokes a sense of place—be it in her descriptions of a Leningrad sunset or the Moscow metro, "heavy with the odors of sharp tobacco, sausage, and perspiring human flesh" (*Russian Journal* 7), or the ancient babushki sweeping streets in their black dresses and shawls. Through her writing, the imagined Russia of her childhood—that "mysterious counterweight to the known world of America" (*Russian Journal* 4)—takes on a new and animated form as Lee discovers some of what lies beneath the surface of "official" metanarratives of Russian life.

In 1984 Lee published *Sarah Phillips*, a collection of interlinked short stories that charts an African American girl's coming-of-age between 1963 and 1974. Though initially written separately, the stories form a seamless narrative arch, which excavates the intersections of race, gender, and class in the United States and Paris, France. Through Sarah Phillip's first-person narrative, Lee sketches a complex picture of African American racial identity, as it is mediated by class, gender, and location. Firmly ensconced in a middle-class milieu, which includes private boarding schools and summer vacations in Europe, Sarah emerges from adolescence "tall and lanky and light-skinned, quite pretty in a nervous sort of way; . . . with an unfocused snobbery, vague literary aspirations, and a lively appetite for white boys" (*Sarah Phillips* 4). Lee explores the tensions generated when this young, African American female subject enters the ostensibly racially integrated world that her parents' generation had fought for during the civil rights movement; and the alienation Sarah feels from members of her own race. Sarah Phillips's class privilege initially buffers her against racism in the United States; yet this protection leaves her vulnerable when she encounters racism and sexism as a young adult. When her French lover taunts her for being the product of the rape of an Irishwoman by "a jazz musician as big and black as King Kong, with sexual equipment to match" (*Sarah Phillips* 11), Sarah does not know how to respond, and misreads his comment as "part of our special brand of humor" (*Sarah Phillips* 12). Sarah's ambivalence toward racism and sexism, and her lack of awareness of her own subjugation as an African American woman becomes a motif throughout the novel.

In *Interesting Women* (2002), Lee continues the theme of exploring African American female subjectivity, this time using a wide array of characters and international settings for her short stories. If Lee has any agenda beyond the aesthetic, it is disrupting stereotypical notions of what it means to be black, American, and a woman. In *Interesting Women* the protagonists' racial identities are not always made explicit. Those who are African American exist in such diverse contexts and locations that there is very little—except perhaps their upper-middle class position—that marks them as coming from the same community. As in *Sarah Phillips*, most of Lee's African American protagonists seemingly fail to recognize or interrogate their privilege within a world of white domination. Often, these women exist in troubled relation to indigenous African American women in the locales they visit as holidaymakers. Lee shows how the privileged African American woman's identity is shored up through her othering of non-U.S., working-class black women living in places like Madagascar and the Honduras. Ultimately, Lee's project is one of deconstructing the idea of a unitary, African American female subject, and, by extension, the idea that an African American woman writer's primary literary preoccupation should be issues of race.

CRITICAL RECEPTION

Most criticism of Lee's work centers around *Sarah Phillips*. Valerie Smith and Donald Gibson note that the text often produces discomfiture in their students. Smith cites Lee's transgression of the conventional bounds of what is considered "black women's writing" as one source of this discomfit.

Mary Helen Washington's 1985 review of *Sarah Phillips* positions the novel within a tradition of African American novelists such as Nella Larsen and James Weldon Johnson, who created privileged black narrators struggling with identity while moving between white and African American worlds. However, Sarah differs from these authors' protagonists in that she fails to become the "perceptive narrator" who understands the tensions generated between these two worlds, and who interrogates the ways in which her social status mitigates the impact of racism. Sarah Phillips, argues Washington, initially grapples with issues of racial identity and privilege, but by the middle of the novel her voice shifts from a "privileged kid" to that of "the privileged narrator, no longer willing to struggle over issues of race and class, unable to bear the 'alarming knowledge' that these issues must reveal" (Washington 3).

Other critics have praised *Sarah Phillips* for illuminating the complexity and multiplicity of African American identity and experience. Gibson argues that there is a need to engage with this text "because of what it reveals about the intersection of class values with those of color and race" (Gibson 164). Smith concurs, asserting that Sarah's silence in the face of racism, and her seeming complicity with those who taunt her, signifies Lee's problematizing of what it means to be a resisting, African American subject in postintegration America. Since racism has shifted to manifest itself more subtly after the civil rights movement, argues Smith, the nature of resistance has changed too, so that black subjects have a wider range of responses from which to choose. Sometimes, responses to racism can include not responding at all.

Don Enomoto describes *Sarah Phillips* as a text that defies theoretical classification, thus inhabiting the liminal space between theory and tradition. For Enomoto, Lee's transgressive and boundary-crossing writing "delineates the limitations of modernism, postmodernism, and traditional black criticism, and suggests that our hope lies in the ability to combine the best aspect of each perspective" (Enomoto 215). However, as Adrienne McCormick points out, Enomoto's position does not allow for Lee's work to be situated as postmodernism *within* an African American literary tradition (emphasis hers). Locating Lee's work at this intersection may be the closest we can come to situating an *oeuvre* that has thus far defied all literary categorization.

BIBLIOGRAPHY

Works by Andrea Lee

"Double Lives." In *They Went: The Art and Craft of Travel Writing*, edited by William Zinsser, 57–74. Boston: Houghton Mifflin Company, 1991.
Interesting Women: Stories. New York: Random House, 2002.
Russian Journal. New York: Random House, 1981.
Sarah Phillips (reprint). Boston: Northeastern University Press, 1993.

Studies of Andrea Lee's Works

Enomoto, Don. "Irreconcilable Differences: 'Creative Destruction' and the Fashioning of a Self in *Sarah Phillips*." *MELUS* 24.1 (Spring 1999): 209–34.
Gibson, Donald B. "Review: Andrea Lee. *Sarah Phillips*." *African American Review* 29.1 (1995): 164–66.
Hogue, W. Lawrence. "The Limits of Modernity: Andrea Lee's *Sarah Phillips*." *MELUS* 19.4 (Winter 1994): 75–90.
King, Nicole. "'You Think Like You White': Questioning Race and Racial Community through the Lens of Middle-Class Desire(s)." *Novel: A Forum on Fiction* 35.2/3 (Spring/Summer 2002): 211–31.

McCormick, Adrienne. "Is This Resistance? African-American Postmodernism in *Sarah Phillips*." *Callaloo* 27.3 (2004): 808–28.

Smith, Valerie. "Foreword." In *Sarah Phillips*, edited by Andrea Lee, ix–xxi. Boston: Northeastern University Press, 1993.

Washington, Mary Helen. "Young, Gifted and Black." *Women's Review of Books* II.6 (March 1985): 3–4.

Barbara Boswell

HELEN ELAINE LEE (1959–)

BIOGRAPHICAL NARRATIVE

Born in Detroit, Michigan, novelist Helen Elaine Lee was reared by a mother who was a college professor of comparative literature, Dorothy Lee, and an attorney, George Lee. Their presence instilled in her a love of, respect for, and fascination with, books and a facility with language. Thus, her becoming a writer seemed a natural outgrowth of the values passed to her during her early years. Following in the footsteps of her father, she became a Harvard-trained lawyer, and earned the J.D. degree in 1985. She supported herself through practicing law full time in Washington, D.C., until she could sustain herself financially as a writer. Her first book, *The Serpent's Gift*, was warmly received by her audience. After her success as a writer, Lee secured a professorship in the Program in Writing and Humanistic Studies at the Massachusetts Institute of Technology.

MAJOR WORKS

Lee's first successful novel, *The Serpent's Gift* (1994), is set in a small Midwestern town, Black Oak, in 1910. Inspired by her own close-knit family, it explores love and the survival techniques that African American families used to keep families intact during significant historical eras, including the Depression, the Great Migration, Jim Crow, World War II, and the civil rights movement. Early in the story, Eula Smalls, a victim of domestic violence, finds refuge in the home of the Staples family. She moves in with her children, LaRue and Vesta, after her husband dies accidentally. Lee deftly captures the African American folk and storytelling tradition through make-believe characters that LaRue invents to escape the pain of his family's past. Confronted with color prejudice and haunted by the stigma of her father's death, Vesta finds comfort in the sisterly relationship with Ouida Staples and later in rearing the child left behind by Ruby Staples's premature death. After a brief failed marriage and several love affairs, Ouida finds true love with a woman, reflecting Lee's own lesbianism. The book attunes the reader to the possibility of humanity's advancing to new beginnings linked to the symbolism of the snake's rebirth.

Lee's second novel, *Water Marked* (1999), continues the emphasis on family history. The story focuses on estranged sisters, Sunday and Delta Owens, who try to reconcile their past and gain a better understanding of themselves by becoming better acquainted with their father, Mercury, whom they believed was deceased. For most of their lives, the sisters were raised by their mother and grandmother. Although the two matrons were good providers, they failed to give the sisters a sense of their family's heritage. It is through Mercury, who had faked his own suicide and disappeared when their mother was pregnant with Sunday, that they are able to acquire knowledge of their familial legacy. As a writer, Lee has Sunday and Delta reconstruct their past through swapping stories, remembering childhood incidents, and collecting oral histories from community members.

CRITICAL RECEPTION

Though Lee has been recognized as a talented writer, her works have not amassed volumes of critical studies. As a testament to her literary skill, her first novel won a Black Caucus of the American Library Association First Novel Award (1995). The criticism, mostly editorial reviews, published on *The Serpent's Gift* is largely favorable. No full-length books or lengthy critical treatises exist. One reviewer regards her strength as being lyrical and richly textured and comments that her hurried pace in telling the story shortchanges plot and character along the way (Kirkus Reviews, 166). Other critics agree that the character LaRue's storytelling emerges as a vibrant facet of the story, fashioned after the African and African American oral traditions of Anansi the spider and Br'er Rabbit. Others, however, think his stories become less charming as they progress. One admiring critic praises her ability to seduce her readers with her use of the color blue and to weave together family stories with exquisite lyricism (Davis).

BIBLIOGRAPHY

Works by Helen Elaine Lee

The Serpent's Gift. New York: Scribner, 1994.
Water Marked. New York: Scribner, 1999.

Studies of Helen Elaine Lee's Works

Davis, Sandra D. "The Storyteller's Gift." *Detroit Free Press* (1994): E1, E3.
Review of *Serpent's Gift. Kirkus Reviews.* February 15, 1994: 166.
Rowell, Charles. "An Interview with Helen Elaine Lee." *Callaloo* 23.1 (2000): 139–50.
Woods, Paula L. "Tell Your Friends." *Los Angeles Times Book Review* (1994): 3, 13.

Lena Marie Ampadu

JARENA LEE (1783—?)

BIOGRAPHICAL NARRATIVE

Jarena Lee, itinerant minister and author, was born in 1783 to a free African American family at Cape May, New Jersey. In 1804, at age twenty-one, Lee attended a religious meeting of an itinerant Presbyterian missionary whose sermon, Lee claimed, challenged her to change from her sinful ways and seek a relationship with God. Shortly after her conversion to Christianity, Lee began attending the religious services of a Methodist Episcopal church in Philadelphia. In her quest to be used by God, Lee sought to attain sanctification, which she believed would help her end a lifelong struggle with selfish ambitions and set her apart as a Christian worker. Shortly thereafter, following an intense session in prayer, Lee recorded, "That very instant, as if lightning had darted through me, I sprang to my feet, and cried, 'The Lord has sanctified my soul!'" (Religious Experience, 13).

In 1809, Lee heard a divine voice telling her to "Go preach the Gospel," which confirmed her "call" to ministry. Lee met with Richard Allen, a bishop in the African Methodist Episcopal (AME) Church, to discuss her desire to preach and serve as a licensed minister. Allen's response was less than enthusiastic declaring the Church *Discipline* "knew nothing at all about it—that it did not call for women preachers." Lee would not let the response of Bishop Allen deter her future work. In 1811, Lee married the minister of a small AME Church outside Philadelphia. Six years later, Lee returned to Philadelphia following the deaths of her husband and four of her six children. In 1818 or 1819, while in the presence of Bishop Allen at an AME service, Lee rose to her feet to offer an exhortation on the sermon. Upon hearing her words, Allen rescinded his earlier concerns, giving Lee permission to hold meetings in her home, to comment on public sermons, and to travel as an itinerant speaker.

Lee traveled thousands of miles throughout the United States and spoke in venues from Upstate New York to Maryland to Ohio. Lee's itinerancy took her into the camp meetings, homes, and churches of Quaker, Presbyterian, and Baptist adherents. During her preaching tours Lee spoke at a number of multiracial church gatherings, including religious meetings in Maryland with slaveholders in attendance. In 1836 Lee published her spiritual autobiography, *The Life and Religious Experience of Jarena Lee*. In 1849, Lee edited and published a second version of her autobiography, *Religious Experience and Journal of Mrs. Jarena Lee*, which included comments on the social and religious concerns of her day. No official documentation exists indicating the year or location of her death.

MAJOR WORKS

Jarena Lee sold copies of both versions of her spiritual autobiography at camp meetings, churches, and revivals. For Lee, the publications provided literary evidence of her "calling" by God and documented her religious experiences including her conversion to Christianity and subsequent spiritual empowerment through sanctification. An example of her work reveals a sense of relief following her conversion to Christianity: "Great was the ecstacy [*sic*] of my mind, for I felt that not only the sin of malice was pardoned, but all other sins were swept away together. That day was the first when my heart had believed, and my tongue had made confession unto salvation" (Religious Experience, 4).

Lee's text provides a spiritual narrative of the life and journey of an African American woman in antebellum America. Lee's work shows how racism and sexism pervaded American religious culture as she dealt with inequity not only as an African American but also as a woman who desired authorization to speak for the African Methodist Episcopal Church. Lee worked on the periphery of an American environment that discriminated her not only because she was an African American in a slave-holding country but also because she was a woman in a male-dominated ecclesiastical system.

Lee's autobiography suggests the itinerant did not allow these conditions to keep her out of the public sphere of influence. Lee believed God gave her authority to speak, to leave her children in the hands of others during her travels, and to write about her life and freedom found as a Christian African American woman. These indications of divine guidance provoked her to travel thousands of miles throughout the United States and to write her experiences in autobiographical form for the benefit of future generations.

CRITICAL RECEPTION

Scholars of Jarena Lee note that her writings constitute early examples of African American spiritual autobiography. The narrative style of Lee emphasizes religious themes of Christian conversion, sanctification, and the self-described journeys of a black itinerant exhorter. In her autobiography, Lee intended to evoke a response from readers that would "change the hearts of the men and women" toward an "escape from sinfulness" resulting in "the achievement of salvation" (McKay 140–41).

The works of Jarena Lee convey concern and victory over sexism and racism in antebellum America. Scholars note the difficulties experienced by Lee as a woman who desired permission to speak publicly within her own African Methodist Episcopal Church. Discriminated against because of her gender, Lee found solace that God, and not the all-male leadership of the AME Church, chose to exhort her to write her own story. Lee cherished the African American community within the AME tradition yet branched out and held revivals for gatherings of men and women, both black and white. Her willingness to travel into Maryland, a slave state, demonstrated her social and religious convictions to preach to slave owners even at the possible expense of her own personal safety.

Through her writings Jarena Lee established her identity as a confident African American woman and informed readers of her personal feelings of accomplishment and self-respect. In her autobiography Lee expressed notions of liberty and Christian freedom that, for today's reader, as Frances Smith Foster suggests, "can enrich our concepts of history and literature and thus of our notions of selfhood" (*Niether Auction Block Nor Pedestal*, 129).

BIBLIOGRAPHY

Works by Jarena Lee

The Life and Religious Experience of Jarena Lee, a Coloured Lady, Giving an Account of Her Call to Preach the Gospel. Philadelphia: Printed and Published for the Author, 1836. Reprint, Nashville: African Methodist Episcopal Church Sunday School Union/Legacy Publishing, 1991.

Religious Experience and Journal of Mrs. Jarena Lee, Giving an Account of Her Call to Preach the Gospel, Revised and Corrected from the Original Manuscript Written by Herself. Philadelphia: Published for the Author, 1849.

Studies of Jarena Lee's Works

Andrews, William, ed. *Sisters of the Spirit: Three Black Women's Autobiographies of the Nineteenth Century*. Bloomington: Indiana University Press, 1986.

Dodson, Jualynne. "Nineteenth-Century A.M.E. Preaching Women." In *Women in New Worlds*, edited by Hilah F. Thomas and Rosemary Skinner Keller, 276–89. Nashville: Abingdon Press, 1981.

Foster, Frances Smith. "Adding Color and Contour to Early American Self-Portraitures: Autobiographical Writings of Afro-American Women." In *Conjuring: Black Women, Fiction, and Literary Tradition*, edited by Marjorie Pryse and Hortense J. Spillers, 25–38. Bloomington: Indiana University Press, 1985.

———. "Neither Auction Block Nor Pedestal: 'The Life and Religious Experience of Jarena Lee, A Coloured Lady.'" In *The Female Autograph: Theory and Practice of Autobiography from the Tenth to the Twentieth Century*, edited by Domna C. Stanton, 126–30. Chicago: University of Chicago Press, 1984.

Gates, Henry Louis, Jr., ed. *Spiritual Narratives*. With an introduction by Sue E. Houchins. New York: Oxford University Press, 1988.

McKay, Nellie Y. "Nineteenth-Century Black Women's Spiritual Autobiographies: Religious Faith and Self-Empowerment." In *Interpreting Women's Lives: Feminist Theory and Personal Narratives*, edited by The Personal Narratives Group, 139–54. Bloomington: Indiana University Press, 1989.

Peterson, Carla L. *"Doers of the Word": African-American Women Speakers and Writers in the North*. New York: Oxford University Press, 1995.

Christopher J. Anderson

AUDRE GERALDINE LORDE (1934–1992)

BIOGRAPHICAL NARRATIVE

Audre Geraldine Lorde, a prolific writer, poet, teacher, and activist, was born on February 18, 1934, in New York City as the youngest daughter of Frederic Byron and Linda Belmar Lorde, who immigrated from Grenade in the West Indies and settled in Harlem during the Depression. In her autobiographical work *Zami: A New Spelling of My Name* (1982), Lorde reveals her precocious awareness of self-renaming at the age of four: "I did not like the tail of the Y hanging down below the line in Audrey . . . I used to love the evenness of AUDRELORDE . . ." (24). Later on, she took the African name Gambda Adisa, meaning "warrior: she who makes her meaning clear," and also used the pseudonym Rey Domini. In 1990, Lorde self-assuredly stated that "I am a Black lesbian feminist warrior poet mother and I am still making trouble." With a powerful, angry voice, she critically redefined and embraced human differences as sources of power (*Sister Outsider* 115). Indeed, her work and life expands, deepens, and enriches our understanding of relationships between self and others in terms of racial, gender, sexual, class, and cultural differences.

Lorde was tongue-tied and nearsighted to the degree that doctors declared her legally blind. At the age of four, her mother, Linda, taught her to talk, read, and write. In *Zami*, Lorde recounts that as a little girl she was often spat upon on the street, and her mother, whom she remembered as a very powerful woman, remained silent about such humiliation and racial hatred. She went to Catholic grammar schools such as St. Mark's School where she faced a patronizing racism and St. Catherine's School where, as the first black student, she experienced hostile racist treatments. In addition, while her mother was light enough to pass for white, Lorde was darker skinned than her sisters, Phyllis and Helen. Lorde painfully sensed her light-skinned mother's internalized racism toward the darker skinned. At the age of twelve or thirteen, she began to write poems to express her feelings. "I would recite a poem, and somewhere in that poem would be the feeling, the vital piece of information" (*Sister Outsider* 82). She attended Hunt High School, where she befriended others who were outcast poets called "the sisterhood of rebels." When she was fifteen, her first poem appeared in *Seventeen* magazine.

The teenaged Lorde came to rebel at her strict parents. Two weeks after graduating from high school, she moved out of her parents' home. In order to support herself, she worked at various jobs, including a nurses' aide, medical clerk, factory worker, and social worker, and went through painful experiences of abortion, loneliness, isolation, and hunger. Lorde attended Hunter College in New York from 1951 to 1959 and obtained a bachelor's degree. In 1954 she studied at the National University of Mexico for one year, where she confirmed her identity as a lesbian and a poet. Upon her return to New York, she became actively engaged in the predominantly white gay culture in Greenwich Village and went to pursue her master's degree in library science at Columbia University. On graduation in 1961, Lorde worked as librarian at Mount Vernon Public Library until 1963. On March 31, 1962, she married white attorney Edwin Ashley

Rollins and gave birth to a daughter, Elizabeth, and a son, Jonathan. Her interracial marriage was little known and ended in divorce in 1970. During the 1960s, Lorde was actively engaged in political movements such as the civil rights movement, antiwar movement, and feminist movement.

From 1966 to 1968, Lorde worked as head librarian at Town School Library in New York City. In 1968, her first collection of poetry, *The First Cities*, was released, and she received a National Endowment for the Arts grant. In the same year, she accepted a teaching position and became the poet in residence at Tougaloo College, a small black college in Jackson, Mississippi, where racial violence, even after the civil rights movement (1955–1965), seriously remained. This teaching experience greatly affected her social and political consciousness as an artist and activist in a racist, capitalist, patriarchal, and homophobic society. Lorde since held various academic positions including lecturerships in creative writing at City College and in the Education Department at Herbert H. Lehman College, and an associate professor in English at John Jay College of Criminal Justice and Hunter College.

In 1978, Lorde was diagnosed with breast cancer, resulting in a mastectomy but she became more focused on writing and social activism. In 1979, she was a featured speaker at the first national march for lesbian and gay liberation in Washington, D.C. In the early 1980s, furthermore, closely working with women of color in other countries, Lorde actively helped to found groundbreaking female organizations such as Kitchen Table: Women of Color Press and the Sisterhood in Support of Sisters in South Africa. As a poet, teacher, and activist, Lorde raised an awareness of interlocking oppression in terms of power relations and taught the powerless to break silence and express their feelings for freedom from all oppression. At the forefront of the feminist movement, she emphasized difference as a creative force, not as a fearful element, to transform unnecessary divisions among women suffering in various forms and degrees of patriarchal oppression. Lorde became a powerful voice for people of color, women, and the lesbian and gay community.

From 1968 to 1993, Lorde published about a dozen collections of poetry and six books of prose and gave numerous lectures throughout the United States and Europe. Her best-known prose works are *The Cancer Journals* (1980), which narrates her survival and struggle with her own fear and despair as well as cancer, and *Zami: A New Spelling of My Name* (1982), which innovatively describes the process of her becoming a poet. Her collections of essays and speeches, *Sister Outsider* and *A Burst of Light*, were released in 1984 and 1988 respectively. Her poetry publications include *Coal* (1976), *The Black Unicorn* (1978), and *Undersong: Chosen Poems Old and New* (1993), and more. Moreover, in recognition of her art and activism, Lorde received numerous awards and honorary doctorates. In 1972, Lorde was given a Creative Artists Public Service grant. In 1974, her third poetry volume, *From a Land Where Other People Live* (1973), was nominated for a National Book Award. And *The Cancer Journals* won the American Library Association Gay Caucus Book for the Year Award in 1981. Lorde also received the American Book Award for her prose collection, *A Burst of Light*. In 1991, she became the recipient of the Walt Whitman Citation of Merit and was named the poet laureate of New York from 1991 to 1993.

Two weeks before her fiftieth birthday in 1984, Lorde was diagnosed with liver cancer. Struggling with cancer, she continued with a scheduled teaching trip to Europe. Lorde died on November 17, 1992, in St. Croix, Virgin Islands. However, her courageous spirit, outspoken voice, and rich literary legacy are much alive to give hope and strength in surviving to the next generation. As her work continuously touches and amplifies our lives with creativity and vitality, Lorde has been and will be remembered as a talented poet, inspirational teacher, passionate mother, strong-willed woman, and energetic fighter for civil justice and racial/sexual equality.

MAJOR WORKS

Lorde is a prolific writer. Thematically, throughout various genres including poetry, fictionalized autobiography, political essays, and personal journals, Lorde emphasizes the need of a speaking voice for women. Keenly aware of the oppression she faced as a black lesbian, she openly expresses her struggle and anger. With force and clarity, she opposes racial injustice, gender inequality, sexual oppression, urban blight, and global exploitation through her writing and speech. Lorde refuses to be defined in the discourses of race prejudice, gender bias, and sexual oppression and continuously reclaims self-representation as a black lesbian working-class woman and mother of two interracial children. Furthermore, in order to create female solidarity and to realize equality among women, Lorde challenges dominant movements in feminism exclusively mobilized in the interests of relatively privileged women, that is, white, Eurocentric, bourgeois, and educated women. In much of her work, with an eloquent and powerful voice, she redefines difference on multiple fronts of the feminist movement, deals with the politics of location and identity, and envisions useful strengths and hope for positive change and spiritual renewal.

During the 1960s, when the Black Arts Movement was radically initiated, Lorde's poems regularly appeared in several anthologies and literary magazines. In 1968, her first collection of poems, *The First Cities*, was released by the Poets Press. Critics reviewed it as an innovative, refreshing, and introspective book. Focusing on feelings and relationships, Lorde describes the self-celebration of being a black woman: "I am black because I come from the earth's inside" (*Coal*). In addition, she expresses her personal suffering. For instance, in "Father, Son and Holy Ghost," Lorde grieves over her father's death and infidelity in a straightforward manner: "I have not ever seen my father's grave/ . . . / Each week/ A different woman has my mother's face." It was followed by *Cables to Rage*, which was published in London in 1970. While teaching poetry at Tougaloo College, Lorde wrote most of the poems contained in this volume, which deal with themes such as human love, betrayal, hunger, and child bearing/rearing/ and nurturing. And, for the first time, she overtly expresses her lesbianism: "No Martha I do not know if we shall ever/ sleep in each other's arms again" ("Martha").

Later on, the poems in these two books reappeared in her fifth volume of poetry, titled *Coal*. It was released by a major publisher, W. W. Norton and Company, in 1976. In *Coal*, Lorde describes unfair and brutal treatments of women in social, political, and cultural contexts. She was acclaimed for her poetic language and creative metaphor and began to receive public attention and wider readership.

Lorde's third volume of poetry, *From a Land Where Other People Live*, was nominated for the National Book Award for Poetry in 1973. This book reflects her personal experiences as a woman, mother, daughter, lover, and teacher in complex contexts of racial oppression, social injustice, and gender struggle. She further develops her angry voice with a focus on a mother-daughter relationship: "I learned from you/ to define myself/ through your denials" ("Black Mother Woman") and a maternal concern for children: "My children have gone to the wood/ . . . / Let their journey be free from ghosts" ("Signs"). In the following collection of poems, *New York Head Shop and Museum* (1974), which is dedicated to "The Chocolate People of America," Lorde continues to express her radical socialist politics and calls for immediate actions for change: "I am/ are you/ Ready" ("Now"). She goes on to narrate harshness in life as a black woman and a mother of black children with decaying images of New York City: "Past questioning the necessities of blood/ or why it must be mine or my children's time" ("New York City 1970").

In 1978, Lorde's seventh collection of sixty-seven poems, *The Black Unicorn*, was released, and it was well received as her most successful and rich volume. By exploring African matriarchal myths, which are reflected in poems such as "From the House of Yemanja," "Coniagui Women," "Dahomey," and "12th Street and Abomey," Lorde cultivates her poetic vision of a black transatlantic culture and tradition. In the opening poem, "The Black Unicorn," she critically and metaphorically points out the misrepresentations of Africa and its people: "The black unicorn was mistaken/ for a shadow/ or symbol/. . ./ the black unicorn is not free." Furthermore, in adamantly questing for freedom, Lorde defines not only her womanhood and blackness, "I am woman and not white" ("A Woman Speaks"), but also evinces her lesbianism: "I dream of a place between your breasts/ to build my house like a haven" ("Woman"). In many of her poems, Lorde characteristically expresses a deep maternal love for children. The poem "Power" demonstrates that Lorde is greatly enraged by a real-life incident where a white policeman killed a ten-year-old black boy but was acquitted: "A dead child dragging his shattered black/ face off the edge of my sleep." This volume of poetry monumentally reconfirms her ability and creativity as a poet.

Lorde's final collection of thirty-nine poems, *The Marvelous Arithmetics of Distance: Poems 1987–1992*, was published in August 1993. Facing her own mortality in the advanced stage of cancer, she reflects on her past in terms of Caribbean heritage, family, and parenting in poems including "Legacy-Hers," "Inheritance-His," "Prism," "For Craig," and more. As always, Lorde shows her anger toward social and political injustice as well as racial and sexual oppression in a global context in poems such as "Peace on Earth: Christmas, 1989," "East Berlin," "jessehelms," and others. One of the most remarkable poems in this commanding and poignant volume is "Today Is Not the Day," in which Lorde relentlessly claims her ownership over her art and her life: "I am dying/ but I do not want to do it/ looking the other way." Indeed, she insightfully looks at life even in front of death.

In her numerous essays and speeches arising from her radical social and political consciousness, Lorde emphasizes the significance of writing, language, and voice to women, and the roles of women writers and artists in a male-dominated society where women's voices are intentionally silenced, and their feelings are distorted. In one of her best-known essays, "Poetry Is Not a Luxury," Lorde redefines the meaning of poetry as "a revelatory distillation of experience, not the sterile word play" (37). This essay first appeared in *Chrysalis: A Magazine of Female Culture* in 1977. Lorde argues that for women, writing poetry is a necessity of existence, not a luxury: "The white fathers told us: I think, therefore I am. The black mother within each of us—the poet—whispers in our dreams: I feel, therefore I can be free" (38). She compares the process of writing poetry with a process of creating a new life embedded in possibilities and strengths. Therefore, poetry becomes the revolutionary foundation for not only women's freedom and empowerment but also their survival and change. Indeed, through her poems, which illuminate her fears, pain, love, and concerns, Lorde names her dreams to be realized and encourages women to see, feel, speak, and dare for their dreams, hopes, and survival.

In another well-known essay, titled "Uses of the Erotic: The Erotic as Power," delivered at the Fourth Berkshire Conference on the History of Women, Mount Holyoke College (1978), Lorde further analyzes women's feelings in terms of power. She critically points out that just as blackness is considered inferior, the erotic is contemptibly seen as a sign of female inferiority: "We have been taught to suspect this resource, vilified, abused, and devalued within western society" (53). Instead, by distinguishing eroticism from pornography, which results in the abuse of feeling, she vigorously speaks in defense of the erotic as an enlightening force within women's lives: "The erotic is a resource within each of us that lies in a deeply female and spiritual plane, firmly rooted in the power of our unexpressed or unrecognized feeling" (53). In doing so, Lorde challenges an exclusively European-American male tradition producing, and produced by, a patriarchal antierotic society.

What is more, Lorde vigorously criticizes homogenous generalization and representation in academic feminist discourse based on an umbrella usage of the term "woman," which became a shield for one woman's privileges linked to another woman's exploitation. In essays such as "Age, Race, Class, and Sex: Women Redefining difference," she indicates institutionalized rejection of difference and emphasizes the creative function of difference and interdependency among women. As her famous dictum "The Master's Tools Will Never Dismantle the Master's House" implies, Lorde argues that "survival is not an academic skill," and without a proper understanding of difference—race, sexuality, class, and age—within the lives of women, women hardly attain a full freedom that "allows the *I* to *be*, not in order to be used, but in order to be creative" ("The Master's Tools," 111–12). While criticizing the misnaming of human differences, Lorde goes on to assert that black sexism perpetuates white racist patriarchal social order. Thus, difference should be recognized as a crucial strength and force for change and true liberation, not as a cause for separation and suspicion.

At the crossroads of her existence, Lorde fought cancer and won. *The Cancer Journals*, a chronicle of her experiences of painful struggles with breast cancer and mastectomy, was published in 1980. This book raises public awareness of women's health issues and contributes to the redefinition of a stereotyped feminine beauty. It won the American Library Association Gay Caucus Book for the Year Award in 1981. As in other essays, Lorde begins the book with the self-definition: "I am a post-mastectomy woman who believes our feelings need voice in order to be recognized, respected, and used" (9). In spite of her confrontation with mortality, Lorde refused to be silenced by her pain and fear about cancer and further keenly realized the function of cancer in a profit economy.

Alice Walker states that *The Cancer Journals* "has taken away some of my fear of cancer, my fear of incompleteness, my fear of difference. This book teaches me that with one breast or none, I am still me." To be sure, by making visible her fears, Lorde was empowered to survive: "I was fighting the devil of despair within myself for my own soul" (77). In addition, while recovering from a radical mastectomy, she learned to love and embrace a new difference in her body. By documenting her experience with cancer and pain and affirming her survival, Lorde distinctively conveys that speaking, not silence, underlines the possibilities of self-healing and the richness of self-conscious living. It cannot be denied that her painful experience and strength serve as encouragement for other women to speak and act out of their experiences with threats of death.

In 1982, Lorde's autobiographical *Zami: A New Spelling of My Name* was released. Lorde calls it "a biomythography" mingling of Caribbean and African cultural heritages with everyday life in New York. Indeed, by blending various genres, including autobiography, fiction, history, and mythology, *Zami* reflects her life from her childhood in Harlem to her midtwenties in New York City in chronological order. Lorde is acclaimed for her rich craft of vivid description and charming characterization with poetic language and erotic images. In *Zami*, as a necessary part of the (re)constructing process of the multiple selves, Lorde narrates her Caribbean-American experience, lesbianism, and anger at racism and heterosexism. In other words, *Zami* describes her quest for identity as a black girl, black woman, and black lesbian, during conflicting periods from the poverty ridden 1930s, to the war-devastated 1940s, and to the anticommunist hysteria inflicted 1950s: "To the journeywoman pieces of myself. Becoming. Afrekete" (5). In fact, as the title implies, *Zami* shows Lorde's transformation from the passive *be* to the active *being*; it is a fictionalized record of how she became a poet.

In the first part of *Zami,* Lorde vividly depicts her childhood episodes scarred by cruelties of racism and poverty. The young Lorde was insatiably curious and fascinated by her discovery of a visual world with language. Growing up, Lorde was greatly influenced and angered by her mother who dreamed of returning home to Grenville, Grenada, and told stories about the West Indies. By narrating her difficult relationship with her mother, Lorde came to realize that her mother's strength and courage enriched her inner development of voice as a poet: "I am a reflection of my mother's secret poetry as well as her hidden anger" (32). In the epilogue, Lorde explains that *Zami* is "[a] Carriacou name for women who work together as friends and lovers" (255). To realize the integration of her life, her being, and her creative work, Lorde explores physical and psychological experiences with other women, including Gennie, Ginger, Muriel, and Afrekete, and social rejection.

Indeed, Lorde's relationships with other women as well as her mother are central in *Zami*. And these relationships, in terms of sexual intimacy and emotional interdependence, expose her vulnerability and sensibility as a young black woman battling racism and heterosexism. For instance, at Hunt High School in New York, Lorde befriended a girl named Gennie, who became the first true friend that she was ever conscious of loving, but their relationship ended with Gennie's suicide. Nevertheless, Gennie left her significant print upon Lorde's life. Much later on, through the memories of Gennie, Lorde came to realize the importance of her voice: "I lost my sister, Gennie, to my silence and her pain and despair, to both our angers and to a world's cruelty" (251). Ultimately, *Zami* carries not only Lorde's reflections on her struggle to rename and embrace her myriad selves mingled with words of young, girl, black, lesbian, woman, and poet, but it also celebrates women's power and ancestral black mothers.

Lorde's last collection of essays, *A Burst of Light*, was published in 1988. It won the American Book Award for 1989. It includes an interview with Susan Leigh Star, in which Lorde discusses sadomasochism as "an institutionalized celebration of dominate/subordinate relationships" in the lesbian-feminist community (14). Also, her selected daily journals from January 1984 to August 1987, titled "A Burst of Light: Living with Cancer," narrates her continuous battles with liver cancer spread from the breast cancer she had six years before. Like *Zami*, which is poetically presented, these essays have the poetic quality combined with her great sensibility and powerful insight to living with cancer and its meanings. Lorde courageously takes the struggle with cancer as "another face of that continuing battle for self-determination and survival that Black women fight daily, often in triumph" (49); in a way, it is "an act of political warfare" (131). Also, she states that it would be certainly worth telling of her personal struggle if one black woman gains hope and strength from her story. In turn, the journals illustrate her strongly determined will, despite a reality of cancer, to live fully, love deeply, write passionately, resist fiercely, and speak out vigorously: "I work, I love, I rest, I see and learn. And I report" (134).

CRITICAL RECEPTION

Audre Lorde is one of the most influential activists and respected writers in the feminist movement from the midtwentieth century to today. Lorde's work has been reviewed in many national publications and is internationally recognized. Also, her writing is widely taught in women's studies, gay and lesbian studies, American cultural studies, and literature courses and translated into several languages. There are numerous critical articles and books about her life, philosophy, social and political activism, and writing.

Adrienne Rich calls Lorde "the Amazon warrior" and states that her work offers women a new and deeply feminist challenge. By inscribing her own experiences as a black lesbian, Lorde strengthened the connection between women's rights, civil rights, and gay rights movements. In essence, dealing with internalized racism, sexism, and homophobia in women's lives in terms of power and knowledge, Lorde's work draws special attention to the dynamics of solidity among women across differences of ethnicity, sexuality, culture, age, class, and others.

Barbara Christian, in "The Dynamics of Difference: Book Review of Audre Lorde's *Sister Outsider*," acclaims Lorde's powerful, eloquent voice as a black, lesbian, feminist, poet, and mother, which stresses the importance of the concept of difference in self-formation and in relation to others and demonstrates the connections between sexism, racism, ageism, homophobia, classism, and between people as well. She defines Lorde's collection of essays as "another indication of the depth of analysis that black women writers are contributing to feminist thought" (210).

In *Women Reading Women Writing*, AnnaLouise Keating analyses Lorde's dynamic formation of gendered and ethnic identities in terms of an ongoing process of "interactional self-naming," in Lorde's semiautobiographical fiction, poetry, and prose. She points out that "silence—the absence of language and the refusal to name—plays a significant role in Lorde's interactional self-naming" (147). Keating goes on to argue that Lorde reinvents her own gender/ethnic identity and her readers' as well through formative, disruptive, and transformational language.

In "Audre Lorde's Life Writing: The Politics of Location," Lori L. Walk discusses that with the concept of positionality constantly reproduced by and within the social matrix, Lorde's life-writing brings the often tangible theories into realizable political action, self-determination, and means of survival and uses the erotic, the lyrical, and the mythological to build home for her myriad selves. In the article, by comparing Lorde's concept of positionality with those of postmodern theorists such as Merleau-Ponty, Butler, Bakhtin, and others, Walk explores Lorde's poetic language, the symbol of the mother, the erotic desire, the black woman's body, as well as her life-struggle inscribed in her work. Walk concludes that "[a]ll writing is life-writing for Audre Lorde," whose language is "action, and with it she makes her power a permanent location for all fluid identities to use as refuse, a home-place" (833).

In *Warrior Poet: A Biography of Audre Lorde*, by capturing Lorde's charismatic and complex personality, biographer Alexis De Veaux mentions that "the three themes of escape, freedom, and self-actualization were crucial determinants" of Lorde's life from a difficult childhood to a celebrated literary career (xi). Also, while tracing her public and private life, she describes that Lorde's erotic lesbianism and Caribbean cultural heritage are central to her development of the multiple selves and searching for a home. Ultimately, the narrative of Lorde's life deepens our understanding of and appreciation for her literary legacy.

Having worked for eight years in collaboration with Lorde to make a film titled *A Litany for Survival: The Life and Work of Audre Lorde,* Ada Gay Griffith comments that "Audre Lorde has been a pioneer in making available her voice as a teacher, a survivor, an activist, and a crusader against bigotry." The documentary film profiles this fascinating woman's extraordinary life through a series of interviews with her family, lovers, colleague poets and activists, who acknowledge Lorde's political and artistic accomplishments and pay tributes to her wisdom, strength, endurance, and inspirational force.

Many critics and readers appreciate that Lorde articulates her critical ideas on race, sexuality, gender, and human difference in groundbreaking ways. Through her work and life, Lorde relentlessly attempts to transform a society marked by injustice and inequality and make women's voices heard. As many critical articles demonstrate, by cultivating the concept of the interconnectedness among women across difference, Lorde painstakingly argues that while women's silence, even if strategic silence, serves as denial of societal oppressions, women's speaking makes their fears and pains visible, and in doing so realizes their survival and freedom. In addition, critics indicate that in various forms and manners, love and anger almost always underlie her writing and activism to make a better world. As in the last poem of her ninth volume, *Our Dead Behind Us* (1986), Lorde firmly states that "I believe in the holy ghost mother" whose name has been lost in time; likewise, her readers will genuinely remember her as "Mother loosen my [their] tongue and adorn me [them] with a lighter burden" ("Call").

BIBLIOGRAPHY

Works by Audre Geraldine Lorde

Between Our Selves. Point Reyes, CA: Eidolon, 1976.
The Black Unicorn. New York: Norton, 1978.
A Burst of Light. Ithaca, NY: Firebrand, 1988.
Cables to Rage. London: Breman, 1970.
The Cancer Journals. Argyle, NY: Spinsters Ink, 1980.
Chosen Poems Old and New. New York: Norton, 1982.
Coal. New York: Norton, 1976.
The First Cities. New York: Poets, 1968.
From a Land Where Other People Live. Detroit: Broadside, 1973.
I Am Your Sister: Black Women Organizing Across Sexualities. New York: Women of Color, 1985.
The Marvelous Arithmetics of Distance: Poems 1987–1992. New York: Norton, 1993.
Need: A Chorale for Black Women Voices. New York: Women of Color, 1990.
New York Head Shop and Museum. Detroit: Broadside, 1974.
Our Dead Behind Us. New York: Norton, 1986.

Sister Outsider: Essays and Speeches. Trumansburg, NY: Crossing, 1984.
Uses of the Erotic: The Erotic as Power. New York: Out & Out, 1978.
Zami: A New Spelling of My Name. Trumansburg, NY: Crossing, 1982.

Studies of Audre Geraldine Lorde's Works

Abod, Jennifer. *The Edge of Each Other's Battles: The Vision of Audre Lorde.* Long Beach, CA: Profile Productions, 1990.

"Audre Lorde: A Special Section." *Callaloo* 14.1 (1991): 39–95.

Brooks, Jerome. "In the Name of the Father: The Poetry of Audre Lorde." In *Black Women Writers (1950–1980): A Critical Evaluation*, edited by Mari Evans, 269–76. Garden City, NY: Anchor/Doubleday, 1984.

Christian, Barbara. "The Dynamics of Difference: Book Review of Audre Lorde's *Sister Outsider.*" *Black Feminist Criticism: Perspectives on Black Women Writers.* New York: Pergamaon, 1985.

De Veaux, Alexis. *Warrior Poet: A Biography of Audre Lorde.* New York: Norton, 2004.

Griffith, Ada Gay, and Michelle Parkerson. *A Litany for Survival: The Life and Work of Audre Lorde.* New York: Third World Newsreel, 1994.

Hall, Joan Wylie. *Conversations with Audre Lorde.* Jackson: University Press of Mississippi, 2004.

Heacock, Maureen C. "The 'Sharpened Edge' of Audre Lorde: Visions and Re-visions of Community, Power, and Language." In *Sharpened Edge: Women of Color, Resistance, and Writing*, edited by Stephanie Athey, 165–85. Westport, CT: Praeger, 2003.

Kader, Cheryl. "'The Very House of Difference': *Zami*, Audre Lorde's Lesbian-Centered Text." In *Critical Essays: Gay and Lesbian Writers of Color*, edited by Emmanuel S. Nelson, 181–94. New York: Haworth, 1993.

Keating, AnnaLouise. *Women Reading Women Writing: Self-Invention in Paula Gunn Allen, Gloria Anzaldua and Audre Lorde.* Philadelphia: Temple University Press, 1996.

Major, William. "Audre Lorde's *The Cancer Journals*: Autopathography as Resistance." *Mosaic* 35.2 (2002): 39–56.

Tate, Claudia. *Black Women Writers at Work.* New York: Continuum, 1984.

Walk, Lori L. "Audre Lorde's Life Writing: The Politics of Location." *Women's Studies* 32.7 (2003): 815–34.

Wood, Deborah. "Interview with Audre Lorde." In *The Memory and Spirit of Frances, Zora, and Lorraine: Essays and Interviews on Black Women and Writing*, ed. Juliette Bowles, 11–22. Washington, DC: Howard University Press, 1979.

Heejung Cha

NAOMI LONG MADGETT (1923–)

BIOGRAPHICAL NARRATIVE

Though she would earn lasting acclaim as a poet and publisher in Detroit, Michigan, Naomi Long Madgett's life and literary journey began in the southern United States. Born Naomi Cornelia Long in Norfolk, Virginia, on July 5, 1923, Madgett was the youngest of three children and the only daughter of the Rev. Clarence Marcellus Long and Maude Selena Long (née Hilton), a homemaker and former teacher. Before Madgett's second birthday, she and her family moved to East Orange, New Jersey, after her father was appointed pastor of Calvary Baptist Church.

It was in New Jersey that Madgett, who was quiet and introverted, first encountered poetry. Reverend Long encouraged his daughter to read, and in his personal library Madgett read mythological stories, fables, and poems by Henry Wadsworth Longfellow and Alfred Tennyson. Reverend Long also aided his daughter's future writing and publishing career by providing her with books that showcased the talents of African American poets. Two such volumes were the Robert Kerlin anthology *Negro Poets and Their Poems* and an adult education textbook titled *An Anthology of Negro Poetry.* In them Madgett discovered poems by notable African American poets including Langston Hughes, Paul Laurence Dunbar, Georgia Douglas Johnson, and Anne Spencer. Madgett's exposure to African American verse filled the educational void left by her school curriculum (which did not recognize or permit discussion of African American achievements) and also inspired Madgett to write her own poetry. Many of Madgett's childhood poems were published in her grammar school newspaper, and by the time she was twelve, Madgett had written over 100 poems. One of them, "My Choice," was published on the youth page of the *Orange Daily Courier* (Madgett's hometown newspaper) in 1935. In 1937, after Reverend Long received a pastoral appointment to another church, Madgett and her family moved to St. Louis, Missouri. At that time, schools in Missouri were racially segregated. So Madgett entered the all–African American Charles Sumner High School in January 1938. But the school held high standards for its students, and Madgett's academic studies and creativity flourished. As a teenager, Madgett met Langston Hughes for the first time, who encouraged her writing and, later, upon their second meeting, interrupted his own poetry presentation to read some of Madgett's poems. In 1939, Madgett's father secured a contract with a small New York press to publish a book of his daughter's poetry. In 1941, when Madgett was seventeen, her first book, *Songs to a Phantom Nightingale,* was released a few days after her high school graduation. And, about one year before his death, Harlem Renaissance poet Countee Cullen invited Madgett to his home, read some of her poetry, and praised her efforts.

In 1945, Madgett received a Bachelor of Arts degree in English from Virginia State University in Petersburg. Soon after, she married Julian Fields Witherspoon. In April 1946, the couple moved to Detroit, where Witherspoon lived before enlisting in the armed services. For several months, Madgett worked part time as a copyreader and writer at the *Michigan Chronicle*. But she left that job before giving birth to her only child, Jill Witherspoon Boyer, in April 1947. Madgett's marriage soon dissolved. Subsequently, she worked as a service representative at the Michigan Bell Telephone Company. Madgett continued writing poetry, however, and within three years, some of her work appeared in two important anthologies: *The Poetry of the Negro, 1746–1949*, edited by Langston Hughes and Arna Bontemps, and *American Literature by Negro Authors* (1950), edited by Herman Dreer.

In 1954, Madgett returned to college and earned a master's degree from Wayne State University. The following September, she started a twelve-year career as a high school teacher in the Detroit public schools. In 1968, Madgett became a professor of English at Eastern Michigan University and taught there until her retirement in 1984.

MAJOR WORKS

Madgett's second poetry collection, *One and the Many*, was published in 1956 followed by her third book, *Star by Star*, in 1965. But it was not until the 1970s, after Madgett tried and failed to find a publisher for her fourth poetry manuscript, that she would establish one of the most acclaimed and enduring publishing companies in the history of African American literature.

Madgett's nine poetry collections are lyrical distillations of her quietness, her respect for humanity, and her pride in the perseverance, ingenuity, and accomplishments of African Americans. Critics characterize Madgett's poems as elegant, introspective analyses of universal emotions and life experiences. Madgett's contemplative verse was a stark contrast to the inflamed and confrontational political poetry of the Black Arts Movement. During the late 1960s and 1970s, the American publishing industry was flooded with poems by African American authors that glamorized crime, broken families, ghetto life, and were openly hostile and racist toward white people. Such poems came to define the Black Arts Movement and were, ironically, lucrative for white publishing companies. Madgett's poetry, however, tended to explore and transcend race rather than exploit it, and was rejected by white and African American editors.

In 1972, with the help of three friends and her third husband, Leonard Patton Andrews, Madgett established Lotus Press to publish *Pink Ladies in the Afternoon*, her fourth book. In 1974, Madgett and her husband gained sole ownership of Lotus Press. For years afterward, Madgett, with the rare help of an intern or volunteer, executed every publishing duty of Lotus Press, from typing and layout to bookkeeping and promotion, entirely by herself.

Madgett's unfailing commitment to poetry and Lotus Press has paid off. In its more than thirty years of existence, the press has helped establish or promote the careers of prominent African American authors such as Gayl Jones, Toi Derricotte, E. Ethelbert Miller, Haki Madhubuti, Claude Wilkinson, and Dudley Randall. The annual Naomi Long Madgett Poetry Award, established in 1993, grants the winning poet 500 dollars and publication of his or her manuscript, and is one of the most revered prizes in African American poetry. Also in 1993, Madgett (in what would end up in a short-lived arrangement) turned distribution of Lotus Press books over to Michigan State University, which established the Lotus Press Series and named Madgett its senior editor. Lotus Press now handles its own distribution.

In the past twenty years, Madgett has been able to devote more time to her own writing projects. In 1988, Third World Press published Madgett's book *Octavia and*

Other Poems, her most challenging and personal favorite of all her poetry collections. The book is a tribute to Octavia Long, Madgett's paternal aunt who died of tuberculosis before Madgett was born, and to whom Madgett bore a striking resemblance. Madgett has also completed a memoir titled *Pilgrim Journey*, and in 2004, Lotus Press released *Connected Islands: New and Selected Poems*, Madgett's ninth and most recent poetry collection.

CRITICAL RECEPTION

In April 2001, Madgett was appointed Poet Laureate of Detroit, and a bronze bust of Madgett sculpted by Artis Lane was unveiled in the summer of 2005 at the Charles H. Wright Museum of African American History.

Most of the information regarding Madgett's work appears in reference works such as *Black Women In America* and *Contemporary Authors Autobiography Series*, among others. Most of these works describe Madgett's poetry as personal, dealing with themes such as faith, integrity and sense of responsibility (Wedge 469).

Madgett's unpublished poetry and other documents related to her writing and Lotus Press are archived in the Special Collections Library at the University of Michigan in Ann Arbor.

BIBLIOGRAPHY

Works by Naomi Long Madgett

Adam of Ifé: Black Women in Praise of Black Men. Detroit: Lotus Press, 1992.
Connected Islands: New and Selected Poems. Detroit: Lotus Press, 2005.
Deep Rivers, A Portfolio: Twenty Contemporary Black American Poets. Detroit: Lotus Press, 1978.
Exits and Entrances. Detroit: Lotus Press, 1978.
Hymns Are My Prayers. (Poster-poems.) Detroit: Lotus Press, 1994.
A Milestone Sampler: 15th Anniversary Anthology. Detroit: Lotus Press, 1988.
Octavia and Other Poems. Chicago: Third World Press, 1988.
Octavia: Guthrie and Beyond. Detroit: Lotus Press, 2002.
One and the Many. Exposition, 1956.
Phantom Nightingale: Juvenilia. Detroit: Lotus Press, 1981.
Pink Ladies in the Afternoon. Detroit: Lotus Press, 1972. Reprint, 1990.
Remembrances of Spring: Collected Early Poems. East Lansing: Michigan State University Press, 1993.
Songs to a Phantom Nightingale. New York: Fortuny's, 1941.
Star by Star. Detroit: Harlo, 1965. Reprint, Detroit: Evenhill, 1970.

Studies of Naomi Long Madgett's Work

Deck, Alice A. "Madgett, Naomi Long." In *Black Women in America, Volume 2*, edited by Darlene Clark Hine, 741–43. Bloomington: Indiana University Press, 1994.
Madgett, Naomi Long. "Naomi Long Madgett." In *Contemporary Authors Autobiography Series*, edited by Shelly Andrews, 193–213. Detroit: Gale Research, 1996.
Sedlack, Robert P. "Madgett, Naomi Long." In *The Oxford Companion to Women's Writing in the United States*, edited by Cathy N. Davidson and Linda Wagner-Martin, 535–36. New York: Oxford University Press. 1995.

————. "Naomi Long Madgett." In *Dictionary of Literary Biography, Volume 76: Afro-American Writers*, edited by Trudier Harris, 104–12. Detroit: Gale Research, 1988.

Warren, Nagueyalti. "Naomi Long Madgett." In *Notable Black American Women, Book I*, edited by Jessie Carney Smith, 716–19. Detroit: Gale Research, 1992.

Wedge, George F. "Madgett, Naomi Long." In *The Oxford Companion to African American Literature*, edited by William L. Andrews, Frances Smith Foster, and Trudier Harris, 468–69. New York: Oxford University Press, 1997.

Shayla Hawkins

PAULE MARSHALL (1929–)

BIOGRAPHICAL NARRATIVE

Paule Marshall is a novelist, short-fiction writer, essayist, and educator. She was born Valenza Pauline Burke in Brooklyn, New York, to parents who immigrated to America from the Caribbean island of Barbados. Marshall's childhood experiences of growing up in an immigrant West Indian community inform her writing style and thematic approach. Marshall often attributes her cultural knowledge and passion for narratives to the ritualistic storytelling and diverse conversations she witnessed in her mother's kitchen, a place where her mother and other female members of the community would gather to discuss culture, and national and international politics.

Marshall began her writing career at a young age, first trying poetry, but quickly realizing that "poetry was not for (her)." Upon graduating from high school, she attended Brooklyn College, where she received a bachelor's degree in English literature (1953). After graduating from college, Marshall pursued a master's degree at Hunter College, before deciding to become a librarian. After leaving her work at the library, Marshall became the "only woman on staff" at *Our World,* a 1950s-era African American magazine (quoted in *Voices from the Gaps*). During this time in her life, she married (1950), had a child (1959), and finished her first novel, titled *Browngirl, Brownstones* (1959). The novel tells the story of Selina Boyce, a young girl growing up in a Barbadian community located in Brooklyn, New York.

Marshall followed the success of *Browngirl, Brownstones* with a collection of four novellas, titled *Soul Clap Hands and Sing* (1961). In this work, Marshall delves deeper into the intricacies of the Pan-African experience by exploring four different locales (Brazil, Barbados, Brooklyn, and British Guyana) that speak to a shared African heritage. Her seminal novel *The Chosen Place, The Timeless People* (1969), which retraces themes of place, Afro-Caribbean identity, home, and responsibility, placed Marshall at the forefront of African American literature and secured her place within the literary canon. Marshall followed *The Chosen Place* with *Praisesong for the Widow* (1983), a novel that charts the protagonist's (Avey Johnson) path to healing and self-discovery. Also published in 1983 was a collection of short stories titled *Reena, and Other Stories* (1983). Included is the essay "From the Poets in the Kitchen," which highlights the creative power of her mother and other women in the community in which she was reared. By the end of the twentieth century, Marshall produced two more novels, *Daughters* (1991) and *The Fisher King* (2000). These further explore female responsibility and the contentious relationships between African American and Caribbean families, respectively.

Throughout her career, Paule Marshall's writing and creativity have received high acclaim, including a Guggenheim Fellowship (1960), a National Institute of Arts Award (for *Soul Clap Hands and Sing*), the John Dos Passos Award for Literature, the Columbus Foundation American Book Award (for *Praisesong for the Widow*), and a MacArthur "Genius" Award (1992). She has also received the PEN/Faulkner Award for her excellence in the field of literature. In addition, Marshall's works have been included in countless anthologies of African American and American literature, and are widely taught in universities.

Paule Marshall currently holds the Helen Gould Sheppard Chair of Literature and Culture in the Creative Writing Department at New York University.

MAJOR WORKS

In her novels, Paule Marshall places family, community, identity, class, gender, and nationality at the forefront. When writing women's experiences, she masters the ability to "use words as a weapon" through her rich portrayals of African American and Caribbean American life cultural experience including the inevitable connections between the two diverse worlds.

Browngirl, Brownstones is a coming-of-age novel set against the backdrop of a close-knit Caribbean community in Brooklyn, New York. The protagonist, Selina Boyce, is the daughter of Barbadian immigrant parents who must face the challenges of residing in a foreign land. The story follows Selina's attempt to understand her life, family community, and the larger world as a young woman caught between West Indian culture and the myth of the "American Dream." The novel moves within the Caribbean American experience from the inside out, making it possible to see the members of the community through Selina's eyes.

Selina's parents are integral to her growth as both represent different views of the immigrant Caribbean community in New York, post–World War II. Her father, Deighton, is a mild-mannered, dreamy, and passionate man who remains optimistic in his constant quest for purpose. Selina's mother, Silla, on the other hand, is presented as stern and rough, a woman who believes that hard work and ambition are the ultimate keys to success in America. She often berates Deighton for being irresponsible with money. In reference to his actions, she remarks, "But what kind of man he is, nuh? Here every Bajan is saving if it's only a dollar a week and buying house and he wun save a penny. He ain got nothing and ain looking to get nothing" (24).

As the novel progresses, Selina makes mature choices and many mistakes. Marshall allows the character to build and grow as a young woman who is not yet "grown" but definitely growing. In addition, Selina is forced to make choices between her loyalty to a mythic Caribbean homeland that she envisions through her father's stories and dreams and accepting her reality as an American. Ultimately, Selina chooses to forge her own identity as a Caribbean American woman.

Marshall's next major work, *The Chosen Place, The Timeless People* provides an examination of life on fictional Bourne Island, where African-descended islanders separate themselves according to color, caste, and British education. Those who live in "Bournehills," the underdeveloped portion of the island, retain a rich cultural heritage that their middle and upper class black counterparts cannot understand. The novel opens with white American representatives of CASR (Center for Applied Social Research) converging on the island in an attempt to help the poor of Bournehills progress socially and economically. Saul Amron, a Jewish sociologist who is conflicted within, leads the crew. He desires to be more than a cultural outsider, but wrestles with his responsibility to the "folk" and to his conservative white spouse.

The lives and stories of the island's inhabitants are told through Merle Kinbona, a woman who, despite being deemed the "perfect cultural broker," is the voice of the people. As her surname suggests, she represents the "family goods" (kin means "family," bon means "good") of a community that is unable and often unwilling to speak for themselves. Through her attempts at self-forgiveness for past wrongs and a desire to remake herself whole, Merle becomes a savior for those who remain grounded in a glorious history of black resistance and strength.

Several motifs and themes exist in the novel, including the debilitating yoke of slavery and colonization, the postcolonial subject, place consciousness, the African diaspora, the ocean as burial ground, creolization, class, social progress, and revolution.

In another of Marshall's major works, *Praisesong for the Widow*, Avatara "Avey" Johnson embarks on a cultural quest of epic proportions. When the novel opens, Avey, a middle-aged successful African American woman, is indifferent and emotionally detached from the rest of the world. Her hardworking husband is deceased and her relationship with her daughter is waning. In addition, class and upward mobility have made it possible for Avey to disregard her cultural memories and exist as a member of an amnesiac African American middle class.

When Avey is snatched from her destructive reality on an annual cruise and forced to recall the early years of struggle with her husband, she realizes that she does not know the person she has become. On the same cruise, Avey encounters the spirit of another reminder, her Great Aunt Cuney, a woman who introduced a much younger Avey to the power of storytelling and African heritage. Through dreams and nightmares, Avey is made to revisit her early life in New York as a young wife and mother, as well as the summers she spent in the lowlands of South Carolina with her aunt. Remembering these experiences prepares Avey for a series of events that take her to the small Caribbean island of Carriacou, a place where she learns to love herself, forgive past wrongs, and rediscover her cultural "roots."

In several of Marshall's major works, the protagonist embarks on a reverse Middle Passage in order to fully heal and accept his or her self. *Praisesong for the Widow* is another example of this quest. Through various methods, the novel takes Avey physically and psychically from New York to South Carolina, to Grenada, and then Carriacou. As she moves further south, she encounters "Africanisms" in the form of Creole language, dance, music, tradition, food, and community. Avey unwittingly travels back through the African slave route, and this becomes the only way that she can become liberated from the strictures of her present life. Her "praisesong" draws her into a place where she can fully understand the true meaning of her name (Avatara) as it relates to mental and physical survival in the New World.

Women's lives are central to Paule Marshall's examination of African American and Caribbean American experiences. She continues the pattern of the female protagonist in her next novel, *Daughters* (1991). *Daughters* invokes a young woman, Ursa Mackenzie, who matures through an increasing responsibility to those around her. Like *Browngirl, Brownstones*, Ursa's parents inform her decisions, and their influence adjusts the way she understands the world. Set in New York and the fictional island of Triunion, the novel explores the choices one must make between motherhood and abortion, and the importance of legacies. Ursa is caught between her role as a researcher and her role as the daughter of a prominent Triunion official (the PM) and an American mother, Estelle.

As in other works by Marshall, Ursa's travels are integral to her character. She is born in Triunion, and lives in New York, a place she calls home. In the novel, Ursa's mother beckons her "home" because she feels that Ursa is the only one who can prevent the PM from making a grand political mistake. The movement to and from the Caribbean and the United States mirrors Ursa's own internal angst. Like other Marshall heroines, she is born into two worlds, both competing for her loyalty while Ursa is forced to decide which experience is greater, if any.

Proving the power of her craft and the universality of her writing, Marshall ushered in the new century with her latest novel, *The Fisher King* (2000). While the themes in this work are similar to Marshall's other writings, there exists a further level of complexity regarding place, acculturation, family, and flight. The novel tells the story of a deceased expatriate jazz musician Sonny-Rett Payne and his family's inability to love unconditionally, across cultural lines.

Similar to other novels with musical themes, *The Fisher King* embodies the jazz essence and moves in cadenced tempos. As a slight departure from the female protagonist present in her previous works, Marshall introduces the characters through Sonny Carmichael Payne's eyes. Throughout the novel, Sonny (Sonny-Rett's Parisian-born grandson) exists as a foreign-born child attempting to understand his distant and troubled American and West Indian family members in the United States. Viewing the actions through his eyes permits a multilayered representation of cultural conflict, interpreted from the outside.

While it appears that Marshall has departed from the female-centered novel, by making the principal character a young boy, Sonny's experience in Brooklyn is informed by the women who power the novel and the family. Hattie, another primary character, serves as young Sonny's nurturer and protector in France and in the United States. Their relationship at home and abroad is maintained by the connection to Sonny-Rhett's legacy. Therefore, Marshall positions both characters, young and old, "American" and French, as the physical embodiments of the expatriate identity. Young Sonny's great-grandmothers represent two opposite worlds, one a West Indian immigrant, and the other a middle-class African American. Their separation is further depicted by each living on the opposite side, of the street from the other. The women desire young Sonny and "hold on for [him]" because he is the evidence of their love—the grandchild of their children who fled to France escaping America's racial history and their families' bitter divide. In *The Fisher King,* Marshall is able to explore the consequences of separation and insularity throughout generations.

Marshall is unapologetically invested in creating works that address the specific experiences of the Afro-Caribbean subject. Her own experiences inform her writing and add depth to the larger meaning. Simultaneously, Marshall's novels place West Indian immigrant experience in contrast with African American experience in order to show the commonalities between the two cultures. The stories she tells require that the reader complicate his or her own notions of identity, location, class, gender, language, and kinship, and attempt to deconstruct how social and cultural divisions affect the progress of the global black community.

CRITICAL RECEPTION

Paule Marshall has indelibly forged a place within the history and tradition of African American literature. Her vivid descriptions of the immigrant experience serve as the foundation for much of the writings by contemporary Afro-Caribbean and African American writers. Her first novel, *Browngirl, Brownstones*, has been frequently read and analyzed for more than forty-five years after its first publication. Likewise, any anthology of African American literature would be incomplete without either one of her short stories or an excerpt from one of her full-length novels. Her work remains a favorite among scholars because of the groundbreaking discussions of hybridity and dual-consciousness within the black experience, the general thematic consistency, and craft of storytelling evident in each of Marshall's works. There is little doubt that Paule Marshall has become a legend within the literary canon.

Since Marshall's work has been widely received for a number of years, there has been much critical response to it. For example, Martin Japtok is compelled by the recreation of the natural Caribbean setting in Marshall's works, specifically "To Da-Duh, in Memoriam." In discussing her short story, he connects the Caribbean "flora and fauna" to the colonial history of the West Indies. He states, "Paule Marshall shows the inescapability of this history by inscribing it into the very landscape" (476).

Carole Boyce Davies has referenced Paule Marshall's works in several of her writings, noting the "heritage/ancestry relationship." She further observes, "There is a definite Pan-Africanist focus in the relationship to heritage in *Praisesong [for the Widow]* and in several other Marshall works" (61). Davies also states that Avey (*Praisesong for the Widow*) must undergo a maturation process in order to return to the United States—an important statement given the fact that Avey is "middle-aged" when she embarks on her journey toward identity transformation.

Lori Leibovich, in the *New York Times* review of *The Fisher King*, is disappointed by the novel's "abrupt ending," but writes, "Marshall's prose is full of expert dialogue, mellifluous rhythms and sharply drawn portraits of Sonny-Rett's loved ones."

In addition to scholarly essays and reviews, there have been several full-length critical studies of Paule Marshall's work, including but not limited to Eugenia Delamotte's *Places of Silence, Journeys of Freedom: The Fiction of Paule Marshall* (1998), Dorothy Denniston's *The Fiction of Paule Marshall: Reconstructions of History, Culture, and Gender* (1995), and Joyce Owen Pettis's *Toward Wholeness in Paule Marshall's Fiction* (1995).

BIBLIOGRAPHY

Works by Paule Marshall

Browngirl, Brownstones (reprint). New York: Feminist Press at CUNY.
The Chosen Place, The Timeless People. New York: Vintage, 1969.
Daughters. London: Serpent's Tail, 1991.
The Fisher King. New York: Simon & Schuster, 2000.
Praisesong for the Widow. New York: Penguin, 1983.
Reena, and Other Stories. New York: The Feminist Press at CUNY, 1983.
Soul Clap Hands and Sing. New York, Atheneum, (1961).

Studies of Paule Marshall's Works

Alexander, Simone James. *Mother Imagery in the Novels of Afro-Caribbean Women.* Columbia: University of Missouri Press, 2001.
Brownley, Martine Watson. *Deferrals of Domain: Contemporary Women Novelists and the State.* New York: St. Martin's Press, 2000.
Coser, Stelamaris. *Bridging the Americas: The Literature of Paule Marshall, Toni Morrison, and Gayl Jones.* Philadelphia: Temple University Press, 1995.

Davies, Carole Boyce, and Elaine Savory Fido. *Out of the Kumbla: Caribbean Women and Literature*, 2nd ed. Trenton: African World Press, 1994.

Delamotte, Eugenia C. *Places of Silence, Journeys of Freedom: The Fiction of Paule Marshall.* Philadelphia: University of Pennsylvania Press, 1998.

Denniston, Dorothy Hamer. *The Fiction of Paule Marshall: Reconstructions of History, Culture, and Gender.* Knoxville: University of Tennessee Press, 1995.

Hathaway, Heather. *Caribbean Waves: Relocating Claude McKay and Paule Marshall.* Bloomington: Indiana University Press, 1999.

Japtok, Martin. "Sugarcane as History in Paule Marshall's 'To Da-Duh, in Memoriam.'" *African American Review* 34 (2000): 475–82.

Leibovich, Lori. "Sounds Good, Feels Bad." *New York Times* (November 26, 2000).

Liddell, Janice Lee. "Voyages beyond Lust and Location: The Climacteric as Seen in Novels by Sylvia Winter Beryl Gilroy, and Paule Marshall." In *Arms Akimbo: Africana Women in Contemporary Literature*, edited by Janice Lee Liddell and Yakini B. Kemp. Gainesville: University Press of Florida, 1999.

Pettis, Joyce Owen. *Toward Wholeness in Paule Marshall's Fiction.* Charlottesville: University Press of Virginia, 1995.

Kalenda C. Eaton

SHARON BELL MATHIS (1937–)

BIOGRAPHICAL NARRATIVE

Sharon Bell Mathis, a columnist, librarian, interviewer, and educator, emerged in the 1970s as one of the most gifted, prolific writers of literature for children and young adults. Although Mathis had published most of her award-winning works by the mid-1970s, she has devoted much of her life to writing for and about black children. Mathis states, "I write to salute the strength in Black children and to say to them, 'Stay strong, stay Black and stay alive'" (Commire 162). In 1984, Mathis received the Wallace Johnson Memorial Award for Outstanding Contributions to the Literary Arts, and the Arts and Letters Award from the Boys and Girls Club of Greater Washington. Two years later, she was honored with the Outstanding Writer Award from the Writing-to-Read Program, D.C. Public Schools.

Born in Atlantic City, New Jersey, to John Willie and Alice Mary (Frazier) Bell, Mathis was raised in Brooklyn, New York, where she attended parochial schools. Exposed early to a wide range of literary works, various theatrical productions, and to her mother's extensive collection of books, Mathis was encouraged by her parents and her high school teachers to write short fiction and poetry. After graduating from Morgan State College (now Morgan State University) with a B.A. in sociology and after beginning her lifelong professional career as a teacher, Mathis became a writer.

In 1969, Mathis launched her literary career with her first story for children, "The Fire Escape," which appeared in *News Explorer*. While teaching junior high school, she published her first book, *Brooklyn Story* (1970), as part of the Challenger Book series, and her two poems, "Ladies Magazine" and "R.S.V.P.," were included in Nikki Giovanni's anthology, *Night Comes Softly: An Anthology of Black Female Voices*. Mathis's second book, *Sidewalk Story* (1971), received an award from the Council on Interracial Books for Children in 1970. Her third book, *Teacup Full of Roses* (1972), won the Child Study Association of America's Children's Books of the Year Award, the American Library Association's Notable Book Award, and was a runner-up for the Coretta Scott King Award. In 1973, she published her juvenile biography, *Ray Charles*, winner of the Coretta Scott King Award in 1974. *Listen for the Fig Tree* (1973) was followed by *The Hundred Penny Box* (1975), a Boston Globe-Horn Book Honor Book, and *Cartwheels* (1977). After a long hiatus, Mathis published her two volumes of poetry, *Red Dog, Blue Fly: Football Poems* (1991) and *Running Girl: The Diary of Ebonee Rose* (1997). In 1995, Mathis retired from the school system. Currently, she is working on the young adult novels *Sammy's Baby* and *Carrotsticks and Marshmallows*.

MAJOR WORKS

In Mathis's most popular award-winning novel, *Teacup Full of Roses*, she focuses on a family torn apart by one son's drug addiction and on another son's unsuccessful attempt to keep the family together. Set in the ghetto of Washington, D.C., within a one-week span, the book is filled with suspense and tension as Mathis introduces and develops her main characters through their actions. The protagonist is Joe Brooks, a seventeen-year-old storyteller, who uses the title phrase to describe a kind of utopia "where trouble never comes." As Joe takes on the role of "savior" throughout the novel, he learns, despite his love for his family and his girlfriend, Ellie, that he can save only himself in a world where his own dream is threatened by the realities of ghetto life. He loses his brother Paul, an artistic twenty-four-year-old heroin addict, to drugs. He loses Davey, his idealistic fifteen-year-old younger brother, who is an athlete and honor student, to street violence. Mattie Brooks, the uptight, hardworking mother, is completely consumed by Paul's drug problem. Isaac Brooks, the sick and unemployed father, tries to please his wife Mattie, but reads the newspaper and watches television to escape her constant nagging. The last of the family members, Joe's Aunt Lou, and Isaac's oldest sister, is an eccentric, elderly woman lost in a world of spirits. Not surprisingly, it is the aunt who warns Joe of trouble and encourages him to be strong. By the end of the novel, the focal point is indeed survival, physically, mentally, emotionally, and spiritually.

In Mathis's heartbreaking, fast-paced narrative, her sensitivity and clever use of foreshadowing, poetic language, dialogue, strong black images, and a loving tone add tremendous depth to the realistic portrayal of her characters' lives. Moreover, her genuine perception of the human condition allows readers to discover that her characters are caring, everyday people who, even with their weaknesses and limitations, have "pride in appearances, faith in education, hard work and the hope for a better life through sacrifice" (Harris 8).

CRITICAL RECEPTION

All of Mathis's critics agree that she writes honestly and respectfully about black people and their relationships with families, neighbors, and friends, and their coming to terms with themselves and with those whom they love. Writing for *Black World*, Eloise Greenfield agrees that Mathis writes of "real people" and identifies her talent as being rooted in "a profound knowledge of people and an infinite love and respect for Black children" (86). Janet Harris observes that Mathis "weaves her plots with sure authority and creates her characters with economy and veracity" (8). Judy Richardson states that the book has "... an ending which is realistically hopeful, giving the young reader a sense of his [or her] own inner strength" (381). Karen Hanley also praises the book and concludes that what makes it memorable is its "[p]owerfully motivated characters, skillful foreshadowing, and taut storyline" (647).

BIBLIOGRAPHY

Works by Sharon Bell Mathis

Brooklyn Story. New York: Hill & Wang, 1970.
Cartwheels. New York: Scholastic, 1977.
The Hundred Penny Box. New York: Viking, 1975.
Listen for the Fig Tree. New York: Viking, 1973.
Ray Charles. New York: Crowell, 1973.
Red Dog, Blue Fly: Football Poems. New York: Viking, 1991.
Running Girl: The Diary of Ebonee Rose. New York: Harcourt Brace, 1997.

Sidewalk Story. New York: Viking, 1971. Reprint, New York: Penguin, 1986.
Teacup Full of Roses. New York: Viking, 1972. Reprint, New York: Penguin, 1987.

Studies of Sharon Bell Mathis's Works

Commire, Anne, ed. "Mathis, Sharon Bell." In *Something about the Author*, vol. 7, p. 162. Detroit: Gale, 1975.

Foster, Frances Smith. "Sharon Bell Mathis." In *Dictionary of Literary Biography: Afro-American Fiction Writers after 1955*, vol. 33, edited by Thadious M. Davis and Trudier Harris, 170–73. Detroit: Gale, 1984.

Gottlieb, Annie. Rev. of *The Hundred Penny Box* by Sharon Bell Mathis. *New York Times*, May 4, 1975, 20.

Greenfield, Eloise. Rev. of *Teacup Full of Roses* by Sharon Bell Mathis. *Black World* (August 1973): 86–87.

Hanley, Karen Stang. "Mathis, Sharon Bell." *Twentieth Century Children's Writers.* New York: St. Martin's, 1978.

Harris, Janet. Rev. of *Teacup Full of Roses* by Sharon Bell Mathis. *New York Times*, September 10, 1972, 8.

Kutenplon, Deborah, and Ellen Olmstead, eds. "Mathis, Sharon Bell." In *Young Adult Fiction by African American Writers. 1968–1994: A Critical and Annotated Guide*. New York: Garland, 1996.

Liggins, Saundra. "Mathis, Sharon Bell." In *The Oxford Companion to African American Literature*, edited by William L. Andrews, Francis Smith Foster, and Trudier Harris, 483–84. New York: Oxford University Press, 1997.

Metzger, Linda, ed. "Mathis, Sharon Bell." In *Black Writers: A Selection of Sketches from Contemporary Authors*. Detroit: Gale, 1989.

Richardson, Judy. "Black Children's Books: An Overview." *Journal of Negro Education* (Summer 1974): 380–400.

Loretta G. Woodard

VICTORIA EARLE MATTHEWS (1861–1898)

BIOGRAPHICAL NARRATIVE

Victoria Earle Matthews was born into slavery in Fort Valley, Georgia, where she remained for eight years until her mother returned to claim her around 1869. She published three short stories: "Aunt Lindy: A Story Founded on Real Life" (1889), "Eugenia's Mistake: A Story" (1892), and "Zelika: A Story" (1892). Matthews was also known for her philanthropy, journalistic efforts, and speeches meant to improve the plight of African American woman. She hailed racial uplift and Christian values, which were apparent in her efforts to investigate the problems that southern African American women were facing in areas of unfair employment. She rallied support through her speeches and short stories, became president of the Woman's Loyal Union, and was later named chairman of the National Federation of Afro-American Women, which she helped establish.

MAJOR WORKS

The major themes in Matthews's literature relate to racial uplift, Christian values, and African American womanhood. These are apparent in one of Matthews's most well-known stories, "Aunt Lindy: A Story Founded on Real Life," and speak toward Matthews's dedication to the improvement of conditions for African Americans during the Reconstruction era. "Aunt Lindy" depicts a small town's struggle to fight and recover from a devastating fire. Many perish in the flames of this disaster, and Aunt Lindy is asked to care for one dying man, who she later discovers is her former slave master. In the end, it even seems as if Aunt Lindy's benevolence toward her cruel master is divinely rewarded.

Matthews uses the short story to perpetuate a new ideology of forgiveness and Christian ethics, despite the suffering endured by the former slave. One of the messages inherent in the story is the reconstruction of the traditional African American female role through Aunt Lindy. Lindy defies the typically submissive traits usually attributed to older African American characters and embraces intelligence and fortitude instead. Whether this is a result of the fact that Matthews is a former slave herself, or an effort to reconfigure the preconceived notion of the mentality of the slave, her intentions to improve the image of the African American women are apparent.

CRITICAL RECEPTION

Shirley Wilson Logan describes how Matthews, "at turn of the nineteenth century, serv[ed] as a prototype of the emerging black woman public intellectual" ("To Embalm Her Memory," 127). Indeed, Matthews asserts what Bill Mullen calls a "recurring theme in African American literature: slavery's traumatic effects on the family," as well as a "suggest[ion] [of] forgiveness as antidote to racism" (13). She explores the role of the

African woman and the significance that religion and spirituality hold for former female slaves who seem to "forgive" the slave master, and it is the recreation of the "True Woman," which reveals her attempts to convince her fellow African female peers to "abandon the self-effacing restrictions associated with middle-class respectability and the cult of true womanhood that prevented them from defending their own name" ("TO Embalm Her Memory," Logan 128). Elizabeth Ammons suggests that oftentimes these typically romantic writers were instead "engaged in focused, mainstream public action to achieve sexual—and even more pressing for women of color, racial—equality . . ." (6). In other words, Matthews's motive was to alter the place that African American women held within society, because for Matthews and Aunt Lindy, the demands of true womanhood could never be fulfilled. She attempts to create an image of a strong woman, one which holds admirable qualities similar, yet different, from those subscribed to through the "Cult of True Womanhood."

BIBLIOGRAPHY

Work by Victoria Earle Matthews

"Aunt Lindy: A Story Founded on Real Life." In *Revolutionary Tales: African American Women's Short Stories, From the First Story to the Present*, edited and introduced by Bill Mullen, 13–19. New York: Dell, 1995.

Studies of Victoria Earle Matthews's Work

Ammons, Elizabeth, ed. "The Limits of Freedom: The Fiction of Alice Dunbar-Nelson, Kate Chopin, and Pauline Hopkins." In *Conflicting Stories: American Women Writers at the Turn into the Twentieth Century*, 7–8, 59–85. Oxford: Oxford University Press, 1992.

Logan, Shirley Wilson, ed. "'To Embalm Her Memory in Song and Story': Victoria Earle Matthews and Situated Sisterhood." In *"We Are Coming": The Persuasive Discourse of Nineteenth-Century Black Women*, 127–51. Carbondale and Edwardsville: Southern Illinois University Press, 1999.

———, ed. "Victoria Earle Matthews (1861–1907)." In *With Pen and Voice a Critical Anthology of Nineteenth Century African-American Women*, 120–25. Carbondale and Edwardsville: Southern Illinois University Press, 1995.

McCaskill, Barbara. "'To Labor . . . and Fight on the Side of God': Spirit, Class, and Nineteenth-Century African American Women's Literature." In *Nineteenth-Century American Women Writers: A Critical Reader*, edited by Karen L. Kilcup, 164–83. Malden and Oxford: Blackwell, 1998.

Mullen, Bill, et al. *Left of the Color Line*. Chapel Hill, NC: University of North Carolina Press, 2003.

Robinson, Fred Miller. "Victoria Earle Matthews: *The Value of Race Literature (1895)*." *Massachusetts Review* 27.2 (1986): 169–91.

Heidi Stauffer

COLLEEN J. McELROY (1935–)

BIOGRAPHICAL NARRATIVE

Colleen J. McElroy is a prolific poet and writer whose words bridge distances and create a unique sense of place. She was born in 1935 in St. Louis, Missouri, to Ruth Celeste and Purcia Purcell Rawls. Her parents divorced in 1938, and she and her mother moved in with her grandmother, where her love of language began. McElroy's mother married an army sergeant named Jesse Dalton Johnson in 1943. It was then that McElroy began the life of a nomad living everywhere from Wyoming to Germany. She earned an associate's degree at Harris-Stowe Teachers College in 1956 and went on to receive her bachelor's degree from Kansas State University in 1958, where she also received her master's degree in 1963. For the next several years, McElroy worked a range of unique jobs from speech clinician to television talk show moderator before taking a position as the director of Speech and Hearing Services at Western Washington University. After receiving her doctoral degree in ethnolinguistic patterns of dialect differences and oral traditions from the University of Washington in 1973, she joined the faculty and went on to become that university's first black female full professor.

McElroy came to writing seriously in her thirties. In 1972, she published a textbook on speech and language development in preschool aged children. She published her first book of poetry in 1973, *The Mules Done Long Since Gone* and followed that with another collection, *Winters Without Snow,* in 1980. During the past thirty years, she has published hundreds of poems, prose, and scholarly work in some of the most prestigious literary journals, such as *Callaloo, Ploughshares, Prairie Schooner,* the *Kenyon Review, Poetry Northwest,* the *African American Review,* the *Massachusetts Review,* the *Manhattan Review* and the *Seattle Review.* In 1975, she received a Pushcart Prize for her poetry. In 2001, her poem "Mae West Chats It Up with Bessie Smith," which originally appeared in the *Crab Orchard Review,* was anthologized in the annual Best American Poetry series.

In 1978, she received a National Endowment for the Arts Creative Writing Fellowship for her poetry, and in 1991 she received a National Endowment for the Arts Creative Writing Fellowship for her fiction. She has also received both a Rockefeller Fellowship and a Dupont Visiting Scholar Fellowship. Her poetry collection *Queen of the Ebony Isles* received the Before Columbus Association's American Book Award in 1985. In 1987, McElroy traveled as a Fulbright Scholar to Yugoslavia and also won a Washington State Governor's Award for her second book, *Bone Flames.* In 1993, McElroy journeyed to Madagascar on a second Fulbright Fellowship, an experience that led to her collection of translations and travel memoirs, *Over the Lip of the World: Among the Storytellers of Madagascar.* McElroy's poetry collection *Travelling Music* was a Bronze finalist in poetry for *ForeWord* magazine's 1998 Book of the Year Awards. Over the years, McElroy's books have been translated into Russian, Italian, German, Malay, and Serbo-Croatian. In addition to teaching and sharing her writing throughout the Pacific Northwest, McElroy serves as the editor-in-chief of the *Seattle Review,* which has published writers such as Sharon Olds, Diane Wakoski, Al Young, Carolyn Kizer, Marilyn Hacker, Yusef Komunyakaa, and Grace Paley.

Never one to forego the pleasures of travel, McElroy visited Aristotle University of Thessaloniki, Greece, in 2005, to commemorate their African American History month. Today, she is highly sought after as a speaker, teacher, and writer. She has traveled throughout the world, from Europe to South America, and Asia to Africa, bridging culture and distance with her words, creating unique literary places that resonate in the human imagination.

MAJOR WORKS

McElroy has widely published across a range of genres, from poetry to fiction to scholarly work to drama.

Jesus and Fat Tuesday and Other Stories (1987) is a collection of McElroy's fiction— fourteen short stories that cover environments from rural America to the inner cities, over the span of nearly 100 years. The stories make the ordinary extraordinary and detail the lives of everyday people with lyrical language and hope.

In McElroy's memoir, *A Long Way from St. Louie* (1997), a collection of essays and poems, she shares her love of movement and travel. This is a book about the world as a place to explore and inhabit, sharing stories of traveling on the famed Route 66, studying in Germany after World War II, adventuring in Fiji, getting to know the country of Malaysia, climbing Machu Picchu, and traveling across Australia on a motorcycle at the age of fifty-eight. In her own words, McElroy describes this book as "impressions of journeys, memories held in fragments like footprints on a sandy beach . . . or the special spice in a dish prepared by a favorite cook." In addition to travel narratives, she also shares stories of her childhood in St. Louis and words of appreciation about role models including Josephine Baker and Ethel Waters.

The poetry collection *Travelling Music* (1998) continues to catalogue McElroy's world travels in the free-verse style she is known for, this time taking readers to the Balkans, Japan, Paris, and throughout the United States. The poems also recall current events, in poems such as "The Verdict: Los Angeles 1992," which speaks to the acquittal of four white police offers who were charged with beating Rodney King. Several of the poems pay homage to prominent African American figures such as Dorothy Dandrige, Josephine Baker, Florence Mills, and Bill Robinson.

McElroy continued to write about her travel abroad in *Over the Lip of the World: Among the Storytellers of Madagascar* (1999), based on her experiences traveling to Madagascar as a Fulbright researcher, where she undertook an ethnographic study of the Malagasy oral traditions and myths. The book opens with an explanation of how McElroy's project in Madagascar began and the oral traditions on which she focused her research. The introduction is followed by an overview of the linguistics of the island, and the ensuing nine chapters deal with the various regions of Madagascar. The narrative includes twenty-eight native folktales and examples of Malagasy poetry interspersed with McElroy's impressions of Madagascar and her adventures interacting with the Malagasy people and immersing herself in the culture.

CRITICAL RECEPTION

McElroy's work has always been well received by audiences and critics alike. She has won numerous awards and grants for her writing, including two prestigious National Endowment for the Arts fellowships. With reference to an early collection of poetry, *What Madness Brought Me Here: New and Selected Poems, 1968–1988,* the *San Francisco Review of Books* wrote, "McElroy is the master of long, finely-crafted poems, each with a particular melodic intensity and tone."

Kirkus Reviews referred to her memoir, *A Long Way from St. Louie,* as a "lovely, lyrical memoir of an African American woman's travels through life," and "a stunning piece of writing, and a fitting summary of a life led to the fullest." *Publishers Weekly* wrote that the book was a "high-spirited, fresh and beautifully written memoir." Kirkus Reviews was equally enamored with *Over the Lip of the World: Among the Storytellers of Madagascar,* which they described as "[a] piquant glimpse into Malagasy storytelling, set to advantage by the kind of poised writing that makes one slow down, read carefully, savor."

Over the Lip of the World was also well reviewed in Seattle's independent weekly newspaper, the *Stranger.* Kent Miller writes, "Whether chatting with renowned poets or sweating out encounters with hissing cockroaches, McElroy is a most amiable companion. Linguists will find much fascinating material in her introductory chapter on the island's 18 dialects, but the rest of us will be impatient to climb aboard an overcrowded jitney, bound for yet another balladeer softly murmuring of ancient doings."

In a review of *Travelling Music, Publishers Weekly* writes, "The pleasure in accompanying McElroy on her excursions and jazz age reconstructions, such as the impressive 'A Charleston for Florence Mills,' allows us to overlook some of the more overstated lines, and find how 'each landscape has its own remark for our lives.' "

BIBLIOGRAPHY

Works by Colleen J. McElroy

Bone Flames. Middletown: CT: Wesleyan University Press, 1987.
Driving under the Cardboard Pines. Berkeley, CA: Creative Arts Book Company, 1989.
Jesus and Fat Tuesday and Other Stories. Berkeley, CA: Creative Arts Book Company, 1987.
Lie and Say You Love Me. Tacoma, WA: Circinatum Press, 1981.
A Long Way from St. Louie. Minneapolis: Coffee House Press, 1997.
Looking for a Country under Its Original Name. Yakima, WA: Blue Begonia Press, 1984.
The Mules Done Long Since Gone. Seattle: Harrison-Madrona Press, 1973.
Music from Home. Carbondale: Southern Illinois University Press, 1976.
Over the Lip of the World: Among the Storytellers of Madagascar. Seattle: University of Washington Press, 1999.
Queen of the Ebony Isles. Middletown, CT: Wesleyan University Press, 1984.
Travelling Music: Poems. Ashland, OR: Story Line Press, 1998.
What Madness Brought Me Here: New and Selected Poems, 1968–1988. Middletown, CT: Wesleyan University Press, 1991.
Winters Without Snow. San Francisco: Ishmael Reed Publishing Company, 1980.

Studies of Colleen J. McElroy's Works

Koolish, Linda. *African American Writers: Portraits and Visions*. Jackson: University Press of Mississippi, 2001.
Strickland, Daryl. "Seattle's Black Voices—For Authors of Color, the Local Literary Scene is Filled with Promise." *Seattle Times*, February 16, 1997, M1.
Watson Sherman, Charlotte. "Walking across the Floor: A Conversation with Colleen J. McElroy—Black Writer and Teacher." *American Visions* (April–May 1995).

Roxane Gay

PATRICIA McKISSACK (1944–)

BIOGRAPHICAL NARRATIVE

Patricia L'Ann Carwell McKissack, a writer of children's fiction, was born in Nashville, Tennessee, on August 9, 1944. She and her husband, Fredrick L. McKissack, are both graduates of Tennessee State University. Married since 1964, their writing careers are deeply entwined. The McKissacks are the co-owners of All-Writing Services. Patricia McKissack also holds a master's degree from Webster University and taught English for several years at the junior high and college level. Long-time residents of St. Louis, they have retired to Chesterfield, Missouri.

MAJOR WORKS

Patricia McKissack has written and published several books by herself, but has also had great success in collaborating with illustrators such as Jerry Pinkney and Rachel Isadore. Her husband Fredrick McKissack is her most frequent and closest writing collaborator. Together, the two have published dozens of titles for children in the areas of African American biography and history. The McKissacks's books have won several notable awards, including the prestigious Coretta Scott King award in 1995 for *Christmas in the Big House, Christmas in the Quarters* and again for *Black Hands, White Sails.*

Patricia McKissack's breakout book for children was *Flossie and the Fox*, published in 1986. Her personable note to her readers introduces the story as part of an oral tradition. The character of Flossie is a satisfying counterpoint to the Eurocentric Red Riding Hood archetype of a young girl journeying in the forest. When Flossie encounters danger in the form of a talking fox, she defeats the trickster at his own game. When Mr. Fox informs her he is a fox, she tells him, "I just purely don't believe it," and through the book continues to verbally vex him through denial until she safely arrives at her destination.

Goin' Someplace Special also features a strong young African American character. Unlike Flossie, who has just one villain to deny, Tricia Ann must run a gauntlet of dangers to reach her Someplace Special, the Public Library. In an interview with Heather Vogel Frederick, McKissack explains how the events in story were prompted by personal experience. Besides illuminating a particular time in history, she wrote the story to convey an encouraging message, "I wanted it to be a book of personal triumph, so that a young person reading it would not just see me as a black child in the South dealing with segregation, but as any child dealing with a challenge—a learning disability or physical challenge or anything that sets them apart" (90).

Narrating African American history is a goal that Patricia and Fred McKissack have achieved through historical fiction and biographies of major figures. Biographies they have created for the "Great African Americans Series" published by Enslow include books on Frederick Douglass, Ida B. Wells-Barnett, Louis Armstrong, Marian Anderson, and Jesse Owens.

CRITICAL RECEPTION

McKissack's individual and collaborative works have been favorably reviewed by major publications like *Publishers Weekly, Kirkus Reviews*, and the *Horn Book*. Sharon McElmeel cites McKissack's work as being "noted for candor and thoroughness" (36). *Sojourner Truth: Ain't I a Woman?* (Scholastic 1994), cowritten with Fredrick, won the 1993 Boston Globe-Horn Book Award for children's literature in the nonfiction category. Besides being critically acclaimed as a children's author, articles in scholarly journals like *African American Review* and *Language Arts* provide substantial literary analysis of McKissack's writings.

BIBLIOGRAPHY

Works by Patricia McKissack

Black Hands, White Sails: The Story of African-American Whalers. With Fredrick L. McKissack. New York: Scholastic, 1999.
Christmas in the Big House, Christmas in the Quarters. With Fredrick L. McKissack. New York: Scholastic, 1994.
Flossie and the Fox. New York: Dial, 1986.
Goin' Someplace Special. New York: Atheneum, 2001.
Mirandy and Brother Wind. New York: Knopf, 1988.
Sojourner Truth: Ain't I a Woman? New York: Scholastic, 1994.

Studies of Patricia McKissack's Works

Brodie, Carolyn S. "Patricia and Fredrick McKissack: Changing Lives." *School Library Media Activities Monthly* 17.5 (2001): 45–48.
Davis, Olga Idriss. "The Rhetoric of Quilts: Creating Identity in African-American Children's Literature." *African American Review* 32 (1998): 67–76.
Frederick, Heather Vogel. "PW Talks with Patricia McKissack." *Publishers Weekly* (August 6, 2001): 90.
McElmeel, Sharon. "Patricia McKissack: Wordsmith and Avid Reader." *Book Report* 18.3 (1999): 36–37.
Yenika-Agbaw, Vivian. "Taking Children's Literature Seriously: Reading for Pleasure and Social Change." *Language Arts* 74 (1997): 446–53.

Rebecca Feind

TERRY McMILLAN (1951–)

BIOGRAPHICAL NARRATIVE

Popular novelist Terry McMillan was born on October 18, 1951 in Port Huron, MI. Her parents, Madeline Washington Tilman and Edward McMillan, divorced when she was thirteen years old, and her father died three years later. McMillan became interested in literature as a teenager when she worked in the local library. McMillan received a bachelor of arts degree in journalism from the University of California at Berkeley in 1986 and a master of fine arts degree in film from Columbia University.

McMillan has an adult son, Solomon. She currently resides in California.

MAJOR WORKS

To date, McMillan has written six novels. The first of those novels, *Mama* (1987) was self-published. *Mama* is the story of Mildred Peacock, a hardworking mother of five children. A single mother by choice-she throws her drunken husband out of the house after a fight—Mildred daily struggles to take care of her children. Initially finding solace in liquor and cigarettes, she eventually finds solace in the bond she develops with her eldest daughter, Freda.

McMillan's second novel, *Disappearing Acts* (1989), is the urban love story of Franklin Swift and Zora Banks. Franklin is a construction worker and Zora is a teacher and aspiring singer and songwriter. The novel follows the ups and downs of their relationship as they learn that sometimes socio-economic differences trump mutual attraction.

Waiting to Exhale (1992) is McMillan's third novel. Four friends—Robin Stokes, Bernadine Harris, Gloria Matthews, and Savannah Jackson—are at the center of this novel. An examination of the bond of friendship among women, the novel follows the four Phoenix friends who support each other through trials such as depression and divorce.

McMillan published her fourth novel in 1996. *How Stella Got Her Groove Back* is semiautobiographical. It is loosely based on McMillan's own experience. In the novel Stella Payne, a 42-year-old investment analyst meets and falls in love with a Jamaican half her age.

A Day Late and a Dollar Short (2001) followed *How Stella got Her Groove Back*. It is similar to *Mama* in that it has a matriarch, Viola Price, at its center. The novel focuses on the Price family's struggles with themselves and one another.

The Interruption of Everything (2005) is McMillan's most recent work. Marilyn Grimes, a middle aged wife and mother, is the novel's heroine. The novel follows Marilyn through her mid-life crisis.

In addition to the six novels, McMillan also edited *Breaking Ice: An Anthology of Contemporary African American Fiction* (1990), a collection of fiction by African American writers.

CRITICAL RECEPTION

McMillan's work has been positively received by both the popular and critical communities. *Waiting to Exhale* was a *New York Times* bestseller. *Waiting to Exhale* and *How Stella Got Her Groove Back* were both developed into movies which grossed millions of dollars. *Disappearing Acts* was produced into a direct to cable film, and McMillan received a National Book Award for *Mama*.

Critics praise McMillan's ability to depict the African American female experience. For example, Tina M. Harris and Patricia S. Hill argue that the screen version of *Waiting to Exhale* was so wildly popular because of its ability to address the tension between African American women's personal and professional lives (9). Similarly, Janet Mason Ellerby argues that McMillan has found success because she "resists following the script written by main stream American discourse that imposes the cultural ideals of white patriarchal domesticity . . ." (106).

Like her predecessors Toni Morrison and Alice Walker, McMillan has been criticized for her negative depiction of African American men (Jackson 20); however, her work promises to continue to have "sister" popularity.

BIBLIOGRAPHY

Works by Terry McMillan

Breaking Ice: An Anthology of Contemporary African American Fiction. New York: Penguin Group, 1990.
A Day Late and a Dollar Short. New York: Penguin Group, 2001.
Disappearing Acts. New York: Penguin Group, 1989.
How Stella Got Her Groove Back. New York: Penguin Group, 1996.
The Interruption of Everything. New York: Penguin Group, 2005.
Mama. New York: Houghton Mifflin, 1998.
Waiting to Exhale. New York: Penguin Group, 1992.

Studies of Terry McMillan's Works

Champion, Laurie. "Terry McMillan." In *Twenty-First Century American Novelists*. Ed Lisa Abney and Suzanne Disheroon-Green, Suzanne. Detroit, MI: Thomson Gale, 2004. 245–51.
Dandridge, Rita B. "Debunking the Beauty Myth in Terry McMillan's Waiting to Exhale." *In Language, Rhythm, and Sound: Black Popular Cultures into the Twenty-First Century.* Ed. Joseph K. Adjaye and Adrianne R. Andrews. Pittsburgh, PA: University of Pittsburgh Press, 1997. 121–33.
———. "Debunking the Motherhood Myth in Terry McMillan's Mama." *CLA Journal* 41.4 (June 1998): 405–16.
———. "Terry McMillan." *Contemporary African American Novelists: A Bio-Bibliographical Critical Sourcebook.* Ed. Emmanuel S. Nelson. Westport, CT: Greenwood, 1999. 319–326.
Ellerby, Janet Mason. "Deposing the Man of the House: Terry McMillan Rewrites the Family." *MELUS* 22.2 (Summer 1997): 105–17.
Harris, Tina M. 'Waiting to Exhale' or 'Breath(ing) Again': A Search for Identity, Empowerment, and Love in the 1990's. *Women and Language* 21.2 (Fall 1998): 9–20.
Jackson, Edward M. "Images of Black Males in Terry McMillan's Waiting to Exhale." *MAWA Review* 8.1 (June 1993): 20–26.
Völz, Sabrina. "Teaching Terry McMillan's Short Fiction." *ELT Journal* 55.2 (Apr 2001): 164–71.

Waltonen, Karma. "Terry McMillan 1951" In *American Writers: A Collection of Literary Biographies, Supplement XIII: Edward Abbey to William Jay Smith*. Ed Jay Parini. New York, NY: Scribner, 2003. 179–211.

Yolanda Williams Page

LOUISE MERIWETHER (1923–)

BIOGRAPHICAL NARRATIVE

Most known, perhaps, for her juvenile biographies of notable African Americans and her novel *Daddy Was a Number Runner*, Louise Meriwether has been and continues to be an advocate for African Americans and women. Her candid writing style and activist voice has impacted American social thinking. She was born the third of five children and the only daughter to Marion Lloyd Jenkins and Julia Jenkins in Haverstraw, New York. Her father, a bricklayer, moved the family to Brooklyn, where he became a numbers runner during the Great Depression, and, from there, the family moved to Harlem, where Meriwether spent her adolescent years.

After high school, Meriwether earned a B.A. in English from New York University, and soon after married a Columbia University graduate student, Angelo Meriwether. She taught in the Midwest before moving with her husband to Los Angeles, where her marriage ended, as did a second marriage to Earl Howe. She earned her master's degree in journalism from the University of California at Los Angeles and published numerous articles and reviews in the 1960s in periodicals such as the *Los Angeles Times*, *Los Angeles Sentinel*, and the *Antioch Review*, catching the eye of Prentice-Hall with her short story "A Happening in Barbados," published in the spring 1968 issue of the *Antioch Review.*

After the publication of *Daddy Was a Number Runner* (1970), Meriwether returned to New York to write three children's biographies of notable African American men and women over the next three years. She did so to remedy what she perceived as a void of influential African American figures in American history education. The biographies— *The Freedom Ship of Robert Smalls*; *The Heart Man: Dr. Daniel Hale Williams*; and *Don't Ride the Bus on Monday: The Rosa Parks Story*—were meant to right that wrong. Most recently, Meriwether has published the adult novels *Fragments of the Ark* (1994) and *Shadow Dancing* (2000).

MAJOR WORKS

Louise Meriwether's first and best-known novel is *Daddy Was a Number Runner*. Inspired by her own adolescence in Harlem, this novel is representative of Depression-era Harlem and the lack of opportunity and hope found in desolate conditions, though not the autobiography it is sometimes alleged to be. The despair of Harlem is portrayed through the eyes of the adolescent protagonist Francie Coffin and focuses on the struggle of young women who are sexually victimized so much that sexuality becomes a commodity traded on a daily basis. The first response is to cover one's eyes, but her scenes assault so quickly and are written so soberly that the reader has no time to look away. Forgoing the rhetoric of what it means to grow up as a young girl in Harlem, Meriwether involves and invades the reader, who wants the best for Francie, but is left in the end feeling that the patterns of Harlem life are all but unalterable and inescapable.

Meriwether followed the success of *Daddy Was a Number Runner* with the children's biographies *The Freedom Ship of Robert Smalls*, *The Heart Man: Dr. Daniel Hale Williams*, and *Don't Ride the Bus on Monday: The Rosa Parks Story*, publishing one a year from 1971 to 1973. Each of these tells the life stories of influential African Americans often left unsung by American education. Although Meriwether simplifies the stories for an audience of children, the poignancy remains. The books leave readers with a sense of the hope inherent in the fortitude of the individuals to whom she gives voice.

In the midst of the publication of these children's biographies, Meriwether also published the short story "That Girl from Creektown" in 1972's *Black Review No. 2*, a collection of works by African American authors edited by Mel Watkins. This short work showcases the best of Meriwether's talents. In this ambiguous story of Lonnie Lyttle, a young southern African American woman, seemingly ensnared by her poverty, race, and gender, Meriwether again paints with candor the friction of desire and circumstance. Lonnie's pride and hunger for success keep her from accepting a menial job that her mother and her poverty push her toward. It is the same pride that strengthens her to reject the advances of Daniel, a past lover now married to another woman. And it is the same hunger that fuels her eventual acquiescence to the affair with Daniel.

Meriwether writes about this desire and pain of the characters masterfully: "Hope fluttered in Lonnie's breast. She waited for him to say he was through with Viola, was moving out of her father's house, but he only looked at Lonnie in silent anguish. For a moment his need for her lay naked between them. Lonnie felt a vague alarm, sensing a hurting in him somewhere where she had presumed only strength" (86).

The reader, though, is uncertain to what Lonnie has finally succumbed —to Daniel, to her own passion, to selling her body? The duplicitous ending leaves the reader questioning whether Lonnie has been empowered or entrapped by her affair with Daniel.

In 1994, Meriwether published *Fragments of the Ark*, an adult historical fiction and extension of one of her earlier children's biographies. This novel narrates the life of Robert Smalls, who saves other slaves from a crumbling south, helps northern forces, and becomes a Union naval officer. Perspicuously representative of slave life during and after the Civil War, in this novel, Meriwether does not romanticize the effects of emancipation, but instead offers a realistic look at the degree to which African American lives are changed and unchanged by the Civil War.

In Meriwether's *Shadow Dancing*, a modern embodiment of her theme of African American female struggle and identity, protagonist Glenda Jackson navigates career, motherhood, friendship, pain, and love. Meriwether's thumbprint is certainly on this novel, and although her other novels can be arguably categorized as young adult fiction, the themes of this work clearly designate it to an adult audience. While this novel details a woman who is perhaps Meriwether's most successful female character, the novel itself carries less impact than her previous works. Her candor seems subdued here.

That telltale candor and the incredible fortitude of the African American spirit in the face of Sisyphean circumstances is what creates a thread of continuity throughout Meriwether's diverse works. Whether writing for children, for adolescents, or for adults, Louise Meriwether writes about real and fictional heroes who face unfathomable odds. Some succeed; others face more indistinct futures. Perhaps that ambiguity, too, is what sets Meriwether's writing apart.

CRITICAL RECEPTION

Given the diversity and amount of Meriwether's writing, surprisingly little critical work focuses on her. Almost all that is published on Meriwether praises her believable characters for their simultaneous innocence and intuitive intelligence and praises her representation of the economic, social, and relational reality of African American lives in whatever historical period she writes. Indicative of the kind of critical reception common to Meriwether, Janelle Collins writes the following in "'Poor and Black and Apt to Stay That Way': Gambling on a Sure Thing in Louise Meriwether's *Daddy Was a Number Runner*": "Meriwether's novel powerfully reminds us of the human tragedy behind the statistics and stereotypes of the black underclass. It is for this reason that the importance of *Daddy Was a Number Runner* extends far beyond both its literary and historical value" (58).

This applause for Meriwether's first novel echoes throughout critical reviews of her adult works, which are repeatedly admired for their poignancy. Perhaps in the best praise possible for any author's writing, James Baldwin expresses in the foreword to *Daddy Was a Number Runner* that the novel is an object he can point to proudly when people ask him why he writes. He continues, "This book should be sent to the White House . . . and to everyone in this country to read" (6–7).

BIBLIOGRAPHY

Works by Louise Meriwether

Daddy Was a Number Runner. New York: The Feminist Press, 1970.
Don't Ride the Bus on Monday: The Rosa Parks Story. Englewood Cliffs, NJ: Prentice-Hall, 1973.
Fragments of the Ark. New York: Pocket Books, 1994.
"James Baldwin: The Fiery Voice of the Negro Revolt." *Negro Digest* (August 1963): 3–7.
"The Negro: Half a Man in a White World." *Negro Digest* (October 1965): 4–13.
"The New Face of Negro History." *Frontier* (October 1965): 5–7.
"No Race Pride." *Bronze America* (June 1964): 6–9.
Shadow Dancing. New York: One World, 2000.
"That Girl from Creektown." In *Black Review No. 2*, edited by Mel Watkins, 79–92. New York: William Morrow and Company, Inc., 1972.
"The Thick End Is for Whipping." *Negro Digest* (November 1968): 55–62.

Studies of Louise Meriwether's Works

Baldwin, James. "Foreword." In *Daddy Was a Number Runner*, edited by Louise Meriwether, 5–7. New York: The Feminist Press, 1970.
Collins, Janelle. "'Poor and Black and Apt to Stay That Way': Gambling on a Sure Thing in Louise Meriwether's *Daddy Was a Number Runner*." *Midwest Quarterly* 45.1 (2003): 49–58.
Dandridge, Rita B. "From Economic Insecurity to Disintegration: A Study of Character in Louise Meriwether's *Daddy Was a Number Runner*." *Negro American Literature Forum* 9 (1975): 82–85.
———. "Louise Meriwether." *Literature Resource Center*. The Gale Group, 2003. University of Texas at Arlington Library. http://www.galegroup.com (accessed January 6, 2005).
Davis, Thadious M., and Trudier Harris, eds. "Louise Meriwether." In *Dictionary of Literary Biography, Volume 33: Afro-American Fiction Writers After 1955*, 182–86. Detroit: Gale Research Co., 1984.

Keymer, David. Rev. of *Daddy Was a Number Runner* by Louise Meriwether. *Library Journal* (January 1, 1994): 163.

McKay, Nellie. "Afterword." In *Daddy Was a Number Runner*, edited by Louise Meriwether, 209–34. New York: The Feminist Press, 1970.

Naylor, Gloria. "Finding Our Voice." *Essence* (May 1995): 193–98.

Schraufnagel, Noel. *From Apology to Protest: The Black American Novel*. Deland, FL: Everett/Edwards, Inc., 1973, 134–35.

Bridgitte Arnold

MAY MILLER (1899–1995)

BIOGRAPHICAL NARRATIVE

Poet and dramatist May Miller was born on January 26, 1899, in Washington, D.C., to Kelly and Annie May Miller. Along with her four siblings, she grew up on the campus of Howard University, where her father worked as a professor and dean. During his last year at Howard, Kelly Miller founded Moorland-Spingarn Research Center, a nationally recognized repository for the documentation of people of African descent. His position at Howard introduced the family to many respected scholars, writers, and activists, including W.E.B. DuBois, Booker T. Washington, and Carter G. Woodson. In addition to being a nationally known educator and sociologist, Miller's father was also a respected orator and published poet. His love for literature inspired Miller at a young age as he encouraged her to read and write.

As a child, Miller was drawn to literature. She read Poe and Whitman, who were among her father's favorites. She attended the well-known M Street School, which was later renamed Paul Laurence Dunbar High School. Her teachers included playwright Mary P. Burrill and poet Angelina Grimké. Burrill encouraged Miller to write, and at fourteen, Miller had her first poem, "Venus," published in the *School Progress* magazine. A year later, *School Progress* also published Miller's first play, *Pandora's Box*.

In 1916, at sixteen, Miller enrolled at Howard University. She joined the Howard University Dramatic Club, which was organized to train students in theater arts. As a member of Howard's theater community, Miller was active in the movement to develop and perform plays written by African American writers at a time when the only plays being staged about African Americans were written by white playwrights. During her four year tenure at Howard, Miller performed in several plays, including Clyde Fitch's *The Truth*. Miller graduated at the top of her class in 1920, and in that same year she received a playwright's award for her one-act play, *Within the Shadows*.

After graduation, Miller moved to Baltimore, where she taught drama, dance, and speech at Frederick Douglass High School. Miller also joined Georgia Douglas Johnson's "S Street Salon." Johnson's Washington, D.C., home became a gathering place for writers to meet and share their works. Miller traveled to S Street on the weekends. There she developed friendships with Langston Hughes, Willis Richardson, Zora Neale Hurston, and Carter G. Woodson, among others. In the summer, Miller studied playwriting at Columbia University under Frederick Koch, a prominent theater scholar of the period.

In 1925, *Opportunity* magazine awarded the third prize to Miller's one-act play *The Bog Guide*. While teaching and living in Baltimore, Miller wrote her most well-known plays, including the 1926 *Cuss'd Thing*, to which *Opportunity* gave an honorable mention. In 1929, the University of North Carolina's *Carolina* magazine published Miller's play *Scratches*. During the summer of 1927, Miller was invited to join the Krigwa Players, which W.E.B. DuBois founded in 1923. Miller performed in the Krigwa Players' production of Georgia Douglas Johnson's *Blue Blood* with Frank Horne. In 1930, Willis Richardson compiled *Plays and Pageants from the Life of the Negro*, an anthology frequently used in schools. Richardson required that none of the contributing playwrights employ dialect, which was used in most African American plays of the period. He included two of Miller's plays, *Graven Images* and *Ridin' the Goat*. Upon the collection's publication, Richardson cited Miller as among the most promising Negro playwrights. Throughout the 1930s, Miller continued to write plays, focusing on history plays for her students at Douglass High School. In 1935, Miller collaborated with Richardson on *Negro History in Thirteen Plays*, an anthology of plays that dramatized the lives of African American men and women. Miller contributed four of her own plays: *Harriet Tubman*, *Samory*, *Christophe's Daughters*, and *Sojourner Truth*. Both Miller and Richardson received national recognition for the anthology.

Miller wrote two plays that remain unpublished. *Stragglers in the Dust* was completed in 1930, and *Nails and Thorns* won the third prize in Southern University's 1933 writing contest. While continuing her work in drama, Miller began writing short stories and poetry. In May 1930, her short story "Doorstops" was published by *Carolina* magazine. She published a second story, "Bidin' Place," in Dillard University's April 1937 edition of *Arts Quarterly*. Like her plays, Miller's short stories are largely concerned with political and social issues and their impact upon African American families.

The year 1943 was a pivotal one for Miller. She wrote her last play, *Freedom's Children on the March*, which was presented at Douglass High School's June commencement exercises. At the encouragement of her husband, John Lewis Sullivan, whom she married in 1940, Miller retired from teaching at the end of that school year to devote herself to writing poetry full time.

Embarking upon her career as a poet with the same determination that she exhibited as a playwright, Miller attended numerous writing workshops in Washington, D.C., to improve her writing, including one headed by Inez Boulton. A devotee of the Imagist School, Boulton drew many budding poets to her workshops, among them Owen Dodson and Paul Lawson, who later published two of Miller's poetry collections. Between 1945 and 1955, several of Miller's poems appeared in the literary magazines *Antioch Review* and *Poetry*. Miller's first major collection of poems, *Into the Clearing*, was printed in 1959 by Lawson's Charioteer Press. *Poems*, her second collection, appeared in 1962. Miller published three books of poetry in the 1970s: *Not That Far* was issued in 1973 and was greatly influenced by her travels in Europe; *The Clearing and Beyond* was printed in 1974; and 1975 saw the publication of *Dust of Uncertain Journey*.

In addition to writing and publishing, Miller continued to teach, serving as poet-in-residence at Monmouth College, West Virginia State College, Exeter Academy, the Bluefield Arts Commission, and the Southern University Poetry Festival. Throughout the 1970s, Miller began reading her poetry at national celebrations, including the Washington, D.C., bicentennials of 1973 and 1974 as well as the inauguration of President Jimmy Carter in 1977. During the 1960s and 1970s, Miller became increasingly active in Washington, D.C.'s community arts programs, serving as the coordinator for performing poets in 1964 and 1965. From 1970 to 1978, Miller served on the District of Columbia Commission of the Arts, chairing the literature panel. In 1979, Miller was elected to the Folger Library's Poetry Advisory Committee. Miller continued to write and publish throughout the 1980s. Her last collection, *Collected Poems*, was printed in 1989. Miller's works, both poetic and dramatic, have been published in numerous anthologies and literary magazines. May Miller died on February 8, 1995, in Washington, D.C.

MAJOR WORKS

Like most African American women writers of the 1920s and 1930s, Miller wrote plays that were primarily concerned with political and social issues, especially those that affected African American women and their families. Miller's work differs from many of her contemporaries, however, because she ventured beyond the domestic sphere, representing life beyond the confines of the home. Miller was also daring in her decision to feature white characters in major roles, something most of her colleagues avoided. Miller seemed to believe that bringing African American and white characters together on stage was an effective means of presenting racial issues and combating racial stereotypes. Most of Miller's early plays center on issues of racism and class.

Written in 1926, *Scratches* highlights class differences and stereotypes between mulattos and darker-skinned African Americans. Set in an urban pool hall, the play tells the story of Dan, a poor young man torn between Abbie, a light-skinned mulatto, and Meldora, who is darker. Meldora is cast as "a cheap imitation, whereas one indefinable feels that Abbie, in spite of dissipation, is to the manner born." Dan ultimately chooses Abbie, whom he believes to be the epitome of class and beauty, and Meldora receives little consideration in the play's conclusion. With *Scratches*, Miller examines the prejudices that exist within the African American community, suggesting that African Americans often accept the same stereotypes about themselves that whites perpetuate.

Miller's *Graven Images* and *Ridin' the Goat*, both published in Willis Richardson's *Plays and Pageants from the Life of the Negro*, focus on an individual's relationship with the community. *Graven Images*, which was inspired by an Old Testament verse, presents an African American hero in a biblical story. Moses's son confronts a hostile environment and triumphs through intelligence rather than force. Several critics have noted that the play could have been read to the children who integrated the public school system in Little Rock, perhaps urging them to rely upon their intellect rather than responding to violence in kind.

Like *Graven Images*, *Ridin' the Goat* draws on themes of the individual at odds with the community. With comical and occasionally satirical look at life in an African American community, the play follows a young doctor through his journey to be accepted into a Baltimore community and to gain the trust of his uneducated clients. In this work, Miller emphasizes the importance of education, casting it as the hope of all African Americans. In some sense, she repeats DuBois's call for educated women and men to share their knowledge with others, thus uplifting their community.

In the 1930s, Miller began writing plays that dramatize the lives of African American men and women who played a crucial role in history. In both *Harriet Tubman* and *Sojourner Truth*, Miller seeks to call attention to the forgotten women of African American history. By presenting strong African American women of the past, Miller seemingly urges all African Americans to remember the strength of their foremothers and urges them to draw upon figures like Truth and Tubman for inspiration.

After retiring from teaching in 1943, Miller began writing and publishing poetry full time, and she quickly gained national recognition as a poet. As with her plays, Miller's poetry confronts social and political concerns, posing moral questions that face a society that lacks humanist values. In her first two collections of poetry, Miller explores her growing concern with morality, sacrifice, and knowledge. Poems like "Green Leaf," "Trails," and "Late Conjecture" consider man's relationship to a higher power, an issue in which Miller became increasingly interested. Miller's poems reveal a simple, straightforward style that encourages readers to reflect on their own lives. As critic Claudia Tate notes, Miller's poetry is contemplative and evocative, placing the reader at the center of each poem. Miller has often been described as a playwright and poet of exceptional vision, incorporating spiritual, social, political, and emotional themes in her works.

CRITICAL RECEPTION

Miller's work has largely been well received. She is frequently described as one of the best African American female playwrights of the early twentieth century, and she is noted for her ability to accurately represent African American urban life. She is also lauded by critics for her insistence upon including white characters in her plays, for her honesty in tackling racial issues, and for portraying African American women as three-dimensional characters who want lives beyond their homes. Similarly, Miller's poetry, which is less concerned with politics and more concerned with virtue than her plays, is said to express a humane vision of quiet strength and moral courage. While both her plays and her poems are widely anthologized and Miller is often cited in works on African American writers, Miller's works have received scant critical attention. Like many African American women who enjoyed successful careers as writers, Miller has been remembered more as a social activist than as a writer who received national recognition at the height of her career. Known as both a member of the Harlem Renaissance and the black Avant-garde movement, Miller is best remembered as an actor, director, collaborator, activist, and artist.

BIBLIOGRAPHY

Works by May Miller

"Bidin' Place." *Arts Quarterly* (April 1937).
The Bog Guide. 1925. Unpublished.
The Clearing and Beyond. Washington, DC: Charioteer Press, 1974.
Collected Poems. Detroit: Lotus Press, 1989.
"Doorstops." *Carolina Magazine* (May 1930).
Dust of Uncertain Journey. Detroit: Lotus Press, 1975.
Freedom's Children on the March. 1943. Unpublished.
Graven Images. In *Plays and Pageants from the Life of the Negro*, edited by Willis Richardson. New York: Associated Publishers, 1930.
Halfway to the Sun. Washington, DC: Washington Writers' Publishing House, 1981.
Into the Clearing. Washington, DC: Charioteer Press, 1959.
Lyrics of Three Women. With Katie Lyle and Maude Rubin. Baltimore: Linden Press, 1964.
Nails and Thorns. 1933. Unpublished.
Negro History in Thirteen Plays. With Willis Richardson. Washington, DC: Associated Publishers, 1935.
Not That Far. San Luis Obispo, CA: Solo Press, 1973.
Poems. Thetford, VT: Cricket Press, 1962.
The Ransomed Wait. Detroit: Lotus Press, 1983.
Ridin' the Goat. In *Plays and Pageants from the Life of the Negro*, edited by Willis Richardson. New York: Associated Publishers, 1930.
Scratches. 1929. Unpublished.
Stragglers in the Dust. 1930. Unpublished.

Studies of May Miller's Works

Christian, Samuel. "Four African-American Female Playwrights, 1910–1950: The Narratives of their Historical, Genteel, and Black Folk Voodoo Plays." Ph.D. Dissertation., City University of New York, 1995.

Hatch, James V., and Leo Hamalian, eds. *The Roots of African-American Theatre.* Detroit: Wayne State University Press, 1991.

Miller, Jeanne Marie A. "Georgia Douglas Johnson and May Miller: Forgotten Playwrights of the New Negro Renaissance." *CLA Journal* 33.4 (1990): 349–66.

Mutima, Niamani. "Hatch-Billops Archives: Interviews with Playwrights." *Negro American Literature Forum* 10.2 (1976): 64–65.

Nouryeh, Andrea J. "Twice Silenced, Twice Oppressed: African American Women Playwrights of the 1930s." *New England Theatre Journal* 13 (2002): 99–122.

Parry, Betty. "Belles Lettres Interview." *Belles Lettres* 2.3 (1987): 9.

Redmond, Eugene. *Drumvoices: The Mission of Afro-American Poetry, A Critical History.* Garden City, NJ: Doubleday, 1976.

Young-Minor, Ethyl A. "Staging Black Women's History: May Miller's Harriet Tubman as Cultural Artifact." *CLA Journal* 46.1 (2002): 30–47.

Miranda A. Green-Barteet

ARTHENIA J. BATES MILLICAN (1920–)

BIOGRAPHICAL NARRATIVE

Born and raised in Sumter, South Carolina, Arthenia J. Bates Millican has had a long career as a writer and an educator. She received formal education at Lincoln High School and Morris College, but was also inspired by her intellectual father, Calvin Shepard Jackson, who encouraged her to write. After completing her studies at Morris, she began her teaching career. After teaching in different schools from 1941 to 1946, she attended Atlanta University, completing a master's degree and studying under Langston Hughes. She married Noah Bates in 1950, a union that concluded in divorce in 1956, and later married Wilbert Millican. Her first book, *Seeds beneath the Snow*, was published in 1969. She completed her dissertation on James Weldon Johnson in 1972 at Louisiana State University. Millican combined her skills as a writer and contributor to African American scholarship with her abilities as a professional educator, attaining the status of full professor at Southern University. Retired from teaching since 1980, she has continued to explore ideas through writing and public speaking.

MAJOR WORKS

Millican is known as a poet and a prose writer. Her writings examine religious themes, seeking answers and explanations about suffering and tragedy. In her essay "The Autobiography of an Idea," she describes her father's influence on her perspective on fate, saying, "I worshipped at his shrine of 'tragedy,' unconsciously bringing a predilection for doom and gloom into my stories and verse" (25). Her tendency toward "doom and gloom" was balanced by advice from her mentors, Langston Hughes and Lance Jeffers. The balance for Millican is in the exploration of painful themes and deep questions with a wry humor that makes her an engaging and believable narrator. For example, in the vignette "Little Jake," she explains the spoiled young man's lack of ambition with a brief statement on his behavior in high school, "Truancy interested him during the first year" (*Seeds* 22). In stories like "Little Jake," Millican combines observation of family dynamics with realistic details that illustrate the lives of her characters.

Parent-child relationships are also a major theme of Millican's writings. She presents several parent-child dyads that hinge on the parent's willingness to raise a child in a strict environment, examining positive and negative aspects of traditional roles. The stories in *Seeds* reflect the multifaceted ironies in raising African American children in the segregated South. Millican's child characters range from the abused Silas, who is faced with the limited definition of manhood that denies emotion, to the fatherless Runetta, the focus of her mother's great devotion.

Besides examining the role of fate through a religious lens, Millican also examines religion in the role of the community, including the division between Christians and black Muslims. As Rita Dandridge explains, "With good intentions and quiet reserve,

Millican broaches a subject few would dare to approach. In doing so, she challenges social mores, questions guarded beliefs, and exposes insecurities, frustrations, and mistrust" (21).

CRITICAL RECEPTION

Millican received critical attention for *Seeds beneath the Snow* when first published in 1969 and positive reviews upon its republication in 1975. However, her second and third novels did not receive wide critical response. Millican's works provide a ripe harvest for scholars interested in deeper understanding of the African American South aesthetic and the literary influences of Jeffers and Hughes on a female writer.

BIBLIOGRAPHY

Works by Arthenia J. Bates Millican

"The Autobiography of an Idea." *African American Review* 27 (1993): 25–28.
The Deity Nodded. Detroit: Harlo, 1973.
Seeds beneath the Snow. New York: Greenwich, 1969.
Such Things from the Valley. Norfolk, VA: Millican, 1977.

Studies of Arthenia J. Bates Millican's Works

Dandridge, Rita. "The Motherhood Myth: Black Women and Christianity in *The Deity Nodded.*" *MELUS* 12.3 (1985): 13–22.
Gill, Glenda. "Arthenia Bates Millican." In *The Oxford Companion to African American Literature*, edited by William L. Andrews, Frances Smith Foster, and Trudier Harris. New York: Oxford University Press, 1997.
Smith, Virginia Whatley. "Arthenia J. Bates Millican." In *Afro-American Writers after 1955: Dramatists and Prose Writers. Dictionary of Literary Biography*, vol. 38. Detroit: Gale, 1985.

Rebecca Feind

MARY MONROE (1949–)

BIOGRAPHICAL NARRATIVE

Fiction writer Mary Monroe, her family's first and only high school graduate (Monroe says she completed "high school by the skin of [her] teeth"), was born in Toxey, Alabama, and is a former Choctaw County cotton picker. She is the third child of sharecroppers Otis and Ocie Mae Nicholson, who she refers to as "Bible-thumping farm workers and domestics." Monroe never attended college or studied writing, but taught herself to write, beginning around age four or five, using her gifts for observation and storytelling. She says, "'I was born to write...'" Monroe spent her first six years in Alabama, moved at seven (her father died, and her mother remarried) to Alliance, Ohio, married at seventeen but later divorced, moved with her two daughters to Richmond, California, in 1973, and moved to Oakland in 1984. Monroe is an avid traveler, and loves "to mingle with other authors." She began sending out her own manuscripts at age twelve, and says, "Over the years I've collected more than two thousand rejection letters." Kensington Books, Monroe's current publisher, says about Monroe, "Mary's ... childhood ... [was] one of passion for reading.... She overcame a range of adversity—mental, physical, and economic—to achieve her ... dream of becoming a writer." Her first book was published on February 27, 1985. Monroe currently has an active agreement with Kensington, calling for three Monroe novels and one Monroe novella to be published by 2009.

MAJOR WORKS

In her teens, to earn spending money, Monroe wrote articles for *Reader's Digest*, *Bronze Thrills*, and for confession magazines, with titles including "I Married a Hairy Beast," "I Married My Rapist," "My Husband and His Mistress Tried to Kill Me with Voodoo," "They Called Me the Lonely Hearts Swindler," and "A Homosexual Preacher Stole My Husband."

Monroe's debut novel is *The Upper Room* (1985). The main character is Ruby Montgomery, an obese woman who steals her best friend's baby daughter and flees to rural Florida. During the course of the story, Ruby develops an unhealthy dependence on her daughter, Maureen, which estranges them as Maureen becomes older.

God Don't Like Ugly (2000) is the coming-of-age story of Annette Goode. Annette is an overweight compulsive overeater. After her father left her domestic mother for a white woman, she began overeating to deal with her feelings of abandonment. In addition to her feelings of abandonment, Annette is constantly molested by the family's male boarder, Mr. Boatwright. Her eventual friendship with Rhoda Nelson, daughter of the town undertaker, helps her put a stop to the molestation.

God Still Don't Like Ugly (2003) is the sequel to *God Don't Like Ugly* (2000). Several years have past and Annette is a young woman with many secrets. The novel focuses on these secrets and their uncovering, which is triggered by her desire to meet her father. When Annette travels to Miami to meet her father, she meets Jerome, a young man who falls in love with her and proposes marriage. It is at their engagement party that her life starts to fall apart, again.

In Sheep's Clothing (2005) introduces a dissatisfied woman from a low-income background, who dreams about her unfulfilled desires and how to satisfy them. She becomes a secretary and later, in an effort to obtain what she considers "the good life," adopts her supervisor's identity, only to become the target of a hit man looking for the supervisor. As the story progresses, the woman learns to value what she has.

CRITICAL RECEPTION

The Upper Room, Monroe's first novel, came out more than a decade before her best seller *God Don't Like Ugly* (one writer says the delay occurred only because Monroe "could not find a publisher"). The *San Francisco Chronicle* describes *The Upper Room* as "magnificent...and terrifying," and the Chicago *Sun-Times* calls the book "visionary," comparing Monroe to William Faulkner and Ralph Ellison. The *Wisconsin State Journal* calls *The Upper Room* "powerful... outlandish... [and] impressive," and "the most impressive debut novel... since [John Kennedy Toole's] *The Confederacy of Dunces*." Widely reviewed throughout the United States and in Great Britain, this Monroe novel is excerpted in Terry McMillan's anthology *Breaking Ice*. Though *The Upper Room* made an obvious impact, it was Monroe's coming-of-age novel *God Don't Like Ugly*, set in 1960s and 1970s Ohio, that made Monroe an *Essence* magazine best-selling author. *God Don't Like Ugly* received the PEN/Oakland Josephine Miles National Literary Award for the year's best fiction, a nomination for Black Writers Alliance's Golden Pen Award, remained on *Essence*, Waldenbooks, and *Blackboard* best seller lists for three months, has more than a quarter million copies in print, and appears, with some other Monroe works, on numerous library-recommended reading lists. Upon receiving her PEN award, Monroe said about publishing in 2001: "'It's a huge market to learn about the black experience. Back in '85 [when *The Upper Room* was published] that wasn't the case." Monroe's other novels include *God Still Don't Like Ugly, Red Light Wives, Gonna Lay Down My Burdens*, and *In Sheep's Clothing*.

God Still Don't Like Ugly was an *Essence* best seller for seven months, and a *Black Issues*'s best seller for four months. *Red Light Wives*, a story about the background, lives, and ultimately redeemable value of six prostitutes (the "wives"), reached number one on *Essence*'s best seller list. Monroe did book signings in her home city of Oakland, California, for this book. *Gonna Lay Down My Burdens*, a 2003 Boston Public Library–recommended fiction book, was a bet.com (an affiliate of Black Entertainment Television) Best Book in 2002. *Booklist* says *Gonna Lay Down My Burdens* "delves both painfully and humorously into the lives of southern African Americans." *Publishers Weekly* calls this Monroe novel "a standout," *Booklist* calls *In Sheep's Clothing* a "pageturner." *In Sheep's Clothing* was selected as the sixth annual book-to-be-discussed-aboard-ship (and Monroe was a "featured guest") for an October 2005 "Afro-centric voyage," a seven-day cruise aboard the ship Carnival's *Pride*, departing from Long Beach, California, and visiting three Mexican ports: Puerto Vallarta, Mazatlan, and Cabo San Lucas. (A "cruise for intellectuals," the African American Book Club Summit at Sea (AABCS) cruise began in 2000 as a book club meeting for African American lovers of books.)

BIBLIOGRAPHY

Works by Mary Monroe

God Don't Like Ugly. New York: Dafina-Kensington Publishing, 2000.
God Still Don't Like Ugly. New York: Dafina-Kensington Publishing, 2003.
Gonna Lay Down My Burdens. New York: Dafina-Kensington Publishing, 2002.
In Sheep's Clothing. New York: Dafina-Kensington Publishing, 2005.
Red Light Wives. New York: Dafina-Kensington Publishing, 2004.
The Upper Room. New York: St. Martin's Press, 1985.

Studies of Mary Monroe's Works

"Bookshelf—Books by, and Concerning, African Americans: *God Don't Like Ugly.*" *Ebony* (February 2001).
"Fiction Round-Up—Review: Reissue of *The Upper Room.*" *Black Issues* (November–December 2001).
McKanic, Arlene, and Kelly Ellis. "*God Don't Like Ugly.* Review—Book Review." *Black Issues* (November 2000).

Freda Fuller Coursey

ANNE MOODY (1940–)

BIOGRAPHICAL NARRATIVE

Anne Moody, a Mississippi writer, chronicled her life and events of the civil rights movement in her autobiography and memoir *Coming of Age in Mississippi* (1968). Born and raised in Centreville, Mississippi, during the Jim Crow era, Moody details her resistance of patriarchal control, racism, and injustice along with documenting her involvement with organizations such as the NAACP, SNCC, CORE, and other grassroots organizations. A graduate of Tougaloo College, Moody reflects upon her participation with other Tougaloo students and local leaders to protest against racial injustices. Having met many leaders and witnessed unforgettable events, her narrative includes history that may otherwise have never been documented and told. She lends her voice and story to narrate events such as Medgar Evers's assassination, Emmett Till's lynching, as well as rallies and sit-ins of which she fully participated. Upon the publication of *Coming of Age in Mississippi*, Moody went on to write and publish a collection of short stories titled *Mr. Death: Four Stories* (1975). Anne Moody has since relinquished her fame and spot in the public eye. She, instead, remains ambiguous about her whereabouts and doings, hoping to fade out of history and memory. Her autobiography will, however, forever remain as one of the most heart-wrenching, truth-telling, unapologetic narratives in southern history.

MAJOR WORKS

Anne Moody's *Coming of Age in Mississippi* details her life growing up in Mississippi during the civil rights era in which she historicizes her involvement with the civil rights movement through Tougaloo College, the NAACP, CORE, SNCC, and other organizations. She captures her fight against racism for equality, voting rights, civil liberties, and personal freedom. As she tells her unique story, Moody creates and re-creates history—a history of African Americans, a history of women, a history of southerners, a history of Mississippians, a history of a people in their fight for freedom and autonomy.

Anne Moody saw race relations at their worst in Mississippi during the Jim Crow era. Quickly realizing that she was both African American and female, Moody learned to adapt to various situations that would have been fatal had she not accepted her imposed "inferior" role as an African American woman. Although she somewhat conformed and came to understand her role in society, Moody never quite became accustomed to or satisfied with the mandated subordination due to whites. She, instead, began to challenge white authority, myths, assumptions, and false heirs of superiority. Moody, like Richard Wright in *Black Boy*, began to question her assumed role and position in opposition with other whites. And similar to Wright, she began to question other African Americans as to why they simply played the role rather than acting or reacting against whites. As Moody continued to mature, she learned of the many lynchings, murders, and threats to African Americans who acted upon the very impudence and rebellion that she longed to demonstrate. While these hate crimes disgusted her, they also prevented her from acting or reacting as she notes, "Negroes are being killed, beaten up, run out of town by these white folks and everything. But Negroes can't even talk about it" (*Coming of Age*, 155).

Coming of age, Moody constantly learned of the differences between behaviors, expectations, and rules governing African Americans and whites. Because she never accepted and believed in the Jim Crow system supporting people because of race, Moody sought to move. In her first attempt to leave Mississippi, where Jim Crow laws and race relations appeared to be the worst in the country, she traveled to Baton Rouge and New Orleans, Louisiana, to live with relatives. Expecting to find more freedom and equality, Moody was disappointed because she was again met with a harsh reality of prejudices and racism which she learned was truly embedded all over the deep south. Upon her return to Mississippi during the academic school terms, race relations became worse as the lynchings, murders, and hate crimes increased making it unbearable for anyone to live without fear of his or her life. It was at this point that Moody became fed up with the indifference shown by her family, friends, and community. She could no longer merely be inactive and afraid; she needed to do something to make a difference as she asserts, "Courage was growing in me too. Little by little it was getting harder and harder for me not to speak out" (*Coming of Age*, 163).

Moody attended community college in Natchez and furthered her education at Tougaloo College—the college serving as her introduction to activity with the civil rights movement. Her involvement with other Tougaloo students and professors, city leaders, and activists gave her a sense of self, identity, purpose, and fulfillment for which she had longed and sought. Because of her fulfillment, a great portion of Moody's narrative details the joys and sorrows she felt as she participated in various riots, marches, rallies, sit-ins, meetings, and other activities to plead and fight for equal rights for all African American citizens. Her inclusion of such events allows her to create and re-create history from an African American woman's point of view, which is short of phenomenal considering that history was and is a field dominated by white men. Moreover, Moody's history is powerful not only because she documents "HERstory" but also because she documents a history of and for America, all African American people, and especially southerners.

Following in the African American literary tradition, Anne Moody's sociopolitical narrative fuses multiple themes and discourses to include: naturalism, existentialism, poverty, classism, perseverance, and education. Naturalism—a type of realism that pays close attention to forces beyond the character's or narrator's control—is a common trope used in African American literature. Moody tropes upon discourses such as poverty and classism explaining the difficulty of growing up in the south due to forces binding people to extreme states of poverty. She also stresses the inability for white and African American people to unite due to class issues. While Moody captures the affects of such forces as they operate in Naturalism, she emphasizes a form of black Naturalism, stressing that she and others in the south were the objects of various forces simply because they were African American.

Another common theme found in Moody's narrative is existentialism—the notion or belief that one must act in order to establish or distinguish oneself. This existentialistic value is inherent in Moody for she is determined to use her education and will for the betterment of society. Moreover, her every action and word is intrinsic to her search for an identity autonomous from race, sex, class, and imposed values or qualities. Yet another common discourse found in the narrative is the importance of literacy and education. Following in the tradition of slave and liberation narrators, Moody appreciates the value of education and, thus, explains her challenges as she strives to be a top scholar. She stresses the importance of education by heavily focusing major parts of her narrative upon her school days at Natchez Community College and, later, at Tougaloo College—the "Mecca" of African American higher education in the south.

In *Coming of Age in Mississippi*, Anne Moody makes use of many strategies of reading and writing common in the African American literary tradition. Strategies include her serving as a griot looking back and recounting stories; her inclusion of childhood memories challenging the reader to place fragmented memories and histories together; her fusion of historical events and personal stories to document the lives and times of a people; her use of spirituals, gospel, and blues to commemorate African American musical contributions; and her focus on the "dogged strength" of which W.E.B. DuBois claims will not let African Americans be torn asunder.

CRITICAL RECEPTION

Although Anne Moody's *Coming of Age in Mississippi* is phenomenal, it has not received the criticism it deserves. The bulk of the criticism on Moody and her narrative can be found in online summaries and entries in various anthologies and compilations. She has, however, been compared to other "major" autobiographers by key critics in the fields of African American and American literature.

In "The Girls Who Became Women: Childhood Memories in the Autobiographies of Harriet Jacobs, Mary Church Terrell, and Anne Moody," Nellie Y. McKay compares the autobiographers' ways of reconstructing their childhoods. McKay is specifically interested in tracing three major steps within the narratives: the Innocent or Edenic stage, the Orphan stage, and the Warrior stage. She compares the three autobiographies analyzing whether they conform to the inclusion of these three stages. According to McKay, Moody did not experience an Edenic stage in her developing childhood because, at an early age, she realized the oppression of her family and all African American people in Mississippi. McKay confirms, "Unlike Jacobs and Terrell, Anne Moody had no consciousness of an Edenic period in her life, only of the physical and psychological fears encumbering her and those around her" (117).

In "Coming of Age in the Segregated South: Autobiographies of Twentieth-Century Childhoods, Black and White," Lynn Z. Bloom also compares autobiographers' ways of reconstructing childhoods. Bloom, however, strictly focuses on autobiographies written by African American and white southerners. In addition to tracing the development of childhood, Bloom also traces a sense of family, community, and place within autobiographies. Her reflections on Moody's narrative echo McKay's sentiments: "Moody's firsthand awareness of the indelible evils of segregation begins at a much earlier age than [other autobiographers]—in the consciousness of early childhood rather than with the dawn of conscience in adolescence. Throughout her growing up the message of segregation is insistent and excoriating" (119).

In *From Girl to Woman: American Women's Coming-of-Age Narratives*, Christy Rishoi examines the autobiographies of a diverse group of women. Rishoi specifically examines Moody's autobiography for its resistance to the objectification of the African American woman's body. Rishoi declares, "In an environment that valued black women primarily as domestic workers and sexual objects, Anne Moody pushed herself to scholastic achievement, economic self-sufficiency, and a sense of self-worth with little support or encouragement" (96). She views Moody's self-characterization as an attempt to set herself apart from other African American women who, like Moody's mother, accepted their fates as oppressed and inferior beings. Rishoi argues that "by highlighting her social and cultural alienation, Moody is adapting the grand narrative of the autonomous individual in an attempt to align herself with 'universal' American values" (98).

In his "In Search of a Common Identity: The Self and the South in Four Mississippi Autobiographies," William Andrews compares the autobiographies of William Alexander Percy's *Lanterns on the Levee*, Richard Wright's *Black Boy*, Willie Morris's *North Toward Home*, and Anne Moody's *Coming of Age in Mississippi*. As he performs an intertextual reading of the four autobiographies, Andrews specifically examines the effects of race in relation to the textual differences. Based upon race, he found that Percy and Morris, two white Mississippians, shared similarities that were uncommon to Wright and Moody, two black Mississippians. However, Andrews also notes that aside from race, the four narrators all share commonalities such as experiences, perspectives, memories, and histories.

BIBLIOGRAPHY

Works by Anne Moody

Coming of Age in Mississippi. New York: Dial Press, 1968.
Mr. Death: Four Stories. New York: Harper & Row, 1975.

Studies of Anne Moody's Works

Anderson, Jace. "Re-Writing Race: Subverting Language in Anne Moody's *Coming of Age in Mississippi* and Alice Walker's *Meridian*." *A/B: Auto/Biography Studies* 8.1 (Spring 1993): 33–50.

Andrews, William. "In Search of a Common Identity: The Self and the South in Four Mississippi Autobiographies." *Southern Review* 24 (1988): 47–64.

Beavers, Gina. "Anne Moody." In *Black Women in America: a Historical Encyclopedia*, edited by Darlene Clark Hines et al., 809–10. Brooklyn: Carlson, 1993.

Bloom, Lynn Z. "Coming of Age in the Segregated South: Autobiographies of Twentieth-Century Childhoods, Black and White." In *Home Ground: Southern Autobiography*, edited by J. Bill Berry, 110–22. Columbia: University of Missouri Press, 1991.

Eckard, Paula Gallant. "Anne Moody." In *The Oxford Companion to African American Literature*, edited by William Andrews, Frances Smith Foster, and Trudier Harris, 506–7. New York: Oxford University Press, 1997.

Hart, James D. "Anne Moody." In *The Oxford Companion to American Literature*, edited by James D. Hart, 441. New York: Oxford University Press, 1995.

McKay, Nellie Y. "The Girls Who Became Women: Childhood Memories in the Autobiographies of Harriet Jacobs, Mary Church Terrell, and Anne Moody." In *Tradition and the Talents of Women*, edited by Florence Howe, 105–24. Urbana: University of Illinois Press, 1991.

Rishoi, Christy. "Hegemonic Inscription of the Body in *Coming of Age in Mississippi*." In *From Girl to Woman: American Women's Coming-of-Age Narratives*. Albany: State University of New York Press, 2003.

White, Elease. "Effects of Poverty on the Social Maturation of Anne Moody: A Commentary on Moody's *Coming of Age in Mississippi*." *Journal of African Children's and Youth Literature* 6 (1994–1995): 43–55.

Meta Michond Cooper

OPAL J. MOORE (1953–)

BIOGRAPHICAL NARRATIVE

Functioning within both the fields of the creative arts and criticism, the specific focus of Opal Moore's work has shifted between children's literature, short stories, and poetry, but her concerns about the black community and women have always remained stable. Growing up in Chicago, Moore began her postsecondary education in her home state at Illinois Wesleyan College, where she received her B.F.A. in 1974. She continued her education at the University of Iowa, Iowa City, where she graduated from the Iowa Writers' Workshop, completing an M.A. in drawing and printmaking and earning an MFA in fiction writing in 1982. In 1994 Moore became a Fulbright Lecturer at Johannes Gutenburg-Universität in Mainz, Germany, and in 1995 she was an associate professor of English at Radford University, as well as a Jessie Ball DuPont Visiting Scholar at Hollins College in Virginia. A Rockefeller Foundation Bellagio Fellow and a Cave Canem alumna, Moore currently serves as the chair of the English Department at Spelman College in Atlanta, Georgia, where she has taught African American literature and fiction and poetry writing.

MAJOR WORKS

Opal Moore's poetry and prose are interested in the emotional and psychological conditions of black people, especially women. Her criticism begins where this condition often originates—childhood. Moore has published numerous articles addressing children's literature. In a 1991 interview with Donnarae MacCann and Olga Richard, Moore speaks about a selection of children's book titles. Moore notes that the problems of colorism, the desire for universality, and the failure to honestly speak about the multicultural experience infuse the structure of many children's texts that are concerned with the lives of children in the African diaspora. But, Moore also suggests that these children's texts can demonstrate positive imaginative escapes from racism in their healthy portrayals of child-parent/grandparent relationships. Communication between the generations seems to be the redeeming quality of some of these stories and for some of these characters. These texts are also a place where art and creative writing meet for Moore, who spends a lot of time critiquing the pictures within the books. She argues that artwork should respond to and enlighten the ideas inherent within the works themselves. Moore's biggest issue in general with the selected children's picture books is that they erase critical issues, such as those listed above, and value shallow portraits over more substantial renderings of children's lives.

Moore's short stories, such as "A Happy Story," also explore the problem of not telling the whole truth in literature. In her attempt to write a "happy story" the protagonist finds that these types of stories tend to erase any sad or troubling parts of the narrative. After much difficulty, the narrator finally concludes that her mother's story was a happy one, not because it would have been considered "perfect" in the traditional sense, but because she "always spoke of her life without excluding any parts."

"The Fence" explores another dominant theme in Moore's works, women within the patriarchy. "The Fence" opens up the ways that the sexual divide influences women's lives. The young girl in "The Fence" struggles to keep up with her brother and his friend when they run off to play but finds that girls are not welcome in the male sphere. The text considers how, at the same time the young boys physically separate themselves from the girl, her life is still often prescribed by the men surrounding her. Her life is dictated by her patriarchal father, her sporting activities are governed by the judging force of the boys at school, and her body is controlled by her Uncle who molests her.

Moore's uncollected published poetry, from 1985 to 1999, serves to speak women's voices into fields where they were not welcome, namely she addresses women's negotiation of their place within the Christian religion. Moore's poetry struggles between the redemptive power of Christianity and its historical repression of women's voices. In "I Fly Away: John's Song" Moore considers the bodily relief from the oppressions of real life that one can find in gospel songs. The voice of the worldly religious singer, John, becomes a transcendent voice shaking its audience from the bodily shackles of life and raising them to an awareness beyond that of the real, an awareness that is instead of the imagination. Much in the same way Moore argues that children's imaginings serve as safe spaces for them to escape the oppressions of racism; this poem praises the ability of the religious song to help its audience escape from the difficulties of daily life. But, in poems such as "The Mother's Board," Moore uncovers the underbelly of Christianity, and the church becomes a space where the pastor's honor is established only through the church women's suppression. This same theme also runs throughout "A Woman's Virtue: Sister I Need to Hear You Sing That Song" and "Eulogy for Sister." In Moore's works, suburbia, church, and sometimes even the home become spaces that are unsafe for a woman's body and a woman's emotional well-being, spaces where women are challenged and subdued.

Moore's first published collection of poetry, *Lot's Daughters*, contains revisions of many of the earlier poems that she published in *Callaloo* and *African American Review*. Therefore, some of those same early themes are transmitted into her new collection, such as the contradictory roles of religion in women's lives and the power of communication between the generations. But, Moore extends those themes and explores new ones in *Lot's Daughters*, themes such as migration, rebirth, agency, and ancestry.

Lot's Daughters is divided into two sections: "Geometry for Leaving" and "Lot's Daughters." Moore explains that, while the first section offers portraits of her mother's and grandmother's generation, the second section considers contemporary challenges and envisions the current world as "another Middle Passage."

CRITICAL RECEPTION

To date, there has been no critical response to Moore's work.

BIBLIOGRAPHY

Works by Opal Moore

"Enter, the Tribe of Woman." *Callaloo, Emerging Women Writers: A Special Issue* 19.2 (1992): 340–47.

"Eulogy for Sister." *Callaloo* 19.3 (1996): 622–23.

"The Fence." *African American Review* 29.1 (1995): 47–54.

"The Fence." In *Honey Hush! An Anthology of African American Women's Humor*, edited by Daryl Dance, 227–37. New York: W. W. Norton, 1998.

"Freeing Ourselves of History: The Slave Closet." *Obsidian II* (1988).

"A Happy Story." *Callaloo* 39 (1989): 274–81.

"I Fly Away: John's Song." *Callaloo* 19.3 (1996): 624–27.

"Landscapes: Shakin'." *Black American Literature Forum* 19.3 (1985): 113.

Lot's Daughters. Chicago: Third World Press, 2004.

"The Mother's Board." *Callaloo* 19.1 (1996): 101–6.

"Othello, Othello, Where Art Thou?" *The Lion and the Unicorn* 25.3 (2001): 375–90.

"Picture Books: The Un-Text." In *The Black American in Books for Children: Readings in Racism*, 2nd ed., edited by Donnarae MacCann and Gloria Woodard, 183–91. Metuchen and London: Scarecrow Press, 1985.

"A Pilgrim Notebook." In *Home Places: Stories of the South by Women Writers*, edited by Mary Ellis Gibson. Columbia: University of South Carolina Press, 1991.

"A Small Insolence." *Callaloo* 24 (1985): 304–9.

"A Woman's Virtue: Sister I Need to Hear You Sing That Song." *Callaloo* 22.4 (1999): 979–80.

Kellie D. Weiss

TONI MORRISON (1931–)

BIOGRAPHICAL NARRATIVE

Toni Morrison, primarily a novelist, has also published works in the fields of literary theory, drama, and short fiction. In addition, she has edited numerous collections of essays and fiction works. She was born Chloe Anthony Wofford on February 18, 1931, in Lorain, Ohio, a working-class Midwestern steel-town which was "neither plantation nor ghetto." Although Lorain was largely populated by European immigrants, Morrison grew up in a small African American community within the town and was raised with a rich sense of racial and cultural history. Her mother, a singer in her church's choir, came from a resourceful family that stressed education. Morrison's father was a dignified man who took pride in his work. As an African American man who left the Jim Crow segregation of Georgia, his race politics were greatly informed by experience; he distrusted "every word and every gesture from every white man on earth." In childhood, Morrison was a good student who loved to read; favorite authors of her youth included Tolstoy, Dostoyevsky, Flaubert, and Austen. Although she sensed a cultural disconnect between European canonical authors and a young African American girl from the Midwest, Morrison responded profoundly to these writers, feeling as though they spoke directly to her out of their own specificity.

Morrison received her B.A. in English from Howard University in 1953. After earning her M.A. from Cornell in 1955, she began teaching at Texas Southern University. She returned to Howard as an English instructor two years later and, within a year, married a Jamaican architect named Harold Morrison. While at her alma mater, Morrison met several important African American political and literary figures, including Amiri Baraka, Andrew Young, Stokely Carmichael, and Claude Brown. In 1961, she gave birth to her first child, Harold Ford. Besides teaching and caring for her infant son, Morrison also began to stage her writing, including a short piece about an African American girl who prayed for blue eyes. The year 1964 held dramatic changes for Morrison; pregnant with her second son, Slade Kevin, she divorced her husband and left her job to become an editor for Random House in Syracuse, New York.

Her twenty-year-long career at Random House demonstrated her commitment to the production of African American literature; she published work from Toni Cade Bambara, Gayl Jones, Angela Davis, Gloria Naylor, Leon Forrest, and Andrew Young, among others. A mother of small children and eventually a senior editor, she also resumed teaching in 1971 at SUNY Purchase. She found time to pursue her desire to write during her few peaceful morning hours "before [her children] said, 'Mama' . . . always around five in the morning." Morrison wrote her first four novels while working at Random House: *The Bluest Eye* (1970), *Sula* (1973), *Song of Solomon* (1977), and *Tar Baby* (1981). Eventually, she left her position as senior editor to continue to write and teach, lecturing at numerous universities including Yale, Bard, Harvard, Rutgers, Trinity College Cambridge, SUNY Albany, the University of California at Berkeley, and Bowdoin College. She became the Robert F. Goheen Professor in Humanities at Princeton University in 1989. To date, Morrison has published eight novels, a work of literary theory, a play, and a short story. More recently, she has written children's literature with her son Slade. Screenplays have been written for *Tar Baby* and *Beloved*.

Toni Morrison's literary career is marked by numerous honors, including the National Book Critics Circle Award, the American Academy and Institute of Arts and Letters Award, the Pulitzer Prize, and the Robert F. Kennedy Award. In 1993, she became the first black woman to receive the Nobel Prize for Literature. Her lyrical and insightful body of work chronicles the intricacies of centuries of the African American experience.

MAJOR WORKS

The Bluest Eye (1970), Toni Morrison's first novel, begins with a primer that structures the entire narrative. Echoing the conventions of children's literature, the narrator describes a middle-class family in grammatically simple sentences. The description is repeated without punctuation, and again without spaces. Here, Morrison disrupts the dominant narrative of bourgeois respectability. She strips it of authority by dismantling standard grammatical constructions, finally representing it almost unintelligibly. This becomes a central concern of the text; Morrison reveals the "American dream" to be exclusionary and unrealizable (for the Breedloves), stifling (for Geraldine), perverting (for Soaphead Church), and ultimately grotesque (for Pecola).

The story's opening invites the reader to participate in community gossip. "Quiet as its kept," the narrator says, "there were no marigolds in the fall of 1941" (*Bluest Eye* 8). This natural image of rupture is immediately aligned with a social one: we learn Pecola is "having her father's baby" (8). This part of the text, italicized and written in the past tense, is set off from the rest of the narrative and frames the story. Claudia comments on the story retrospectively, but narrative position becomes complicated as the novel progresses. Claudia's subjective "I" emerges from an initial "we": the second sentence in the novel begins "We thought..." (8). This is the first instance of Morrison's consistent interest in individual and communal memory. While the central story is Pecola's tale of abjection, violence, and self-hate, it could not be told without the histories of Pauline and Cholly Breedlove, Geraldine, Soaphead Church, and Frieda and Claudia, who become repositories of the community's memory.

Ultimately, Pecola's story is at once personal and collective. Her ridicule, rape, and degeneration are entwined with the same social and economic forces that emasculate Cholly, degrade Pauline, repress Geraldine, privilege Maureen Peal, and produce the "ascetic... misanthrope" Soaphead Church (165). Thus, everyone is involved; everyone is complicit—including the reader, who the narrator implicates through gossip.

While the shifting narrative position assigns guilt, it also complicates the notion of blame. Because we are privy to, for example, Cholly's story, his act of violence against Pecola is contextualized. We are told of his abandonment by his mother; we witness his humiliation at the hands of white men during his first sexual experience; we see his "dangerous freedom" and his despair at married life. Following his personal history, we are given the only description of the rape of Pecola. Morrison embeds this incident in Cholly's story, imbues it with Cholly's subjectivity, encouraging the reader to witness the act as desperate and pathetic rather than merely predatory or lustful.

The Bluest Eye is an assault on accepted notions of beauty, "respectability," race, class, and community. The horrific "transformation" of Pecola (and the ideological roots of desire for "transformation") figures as a sort of inverted fairy tale. The novel becomes, in part, an unrealized coming-of-age story—the image of stunted growth in the marigolds foreshadows this theme.

Morrison's second novel, *Sula* (1973), explores relationships between women and interrogates the functions of an insular African American community. Critics often read this as a feminist text that subordinates heterosexual romance to emotional intimacy among women. The title character, dangerously indifferent to social constraints and gender expectations, certainly seems to invite this reading. However, Morrison problematizes the absoluteness of Sula's freedom, in part by shifting narrative focus among a variety of perspectives.

The novel begins with a sort of folk history of "the Bottom," the neighborhood created, we are told, because of an old "nigger joke." The irony, cruelty, and humor associated with the land come to characterize life in the Bottom as well. Morrison's consistent interest in the interplay between individual, community, and geography figures prominently in *Sula*. Also, the construction of paradox here, through narrative and over time, becomes a trope for the entire novel. To a large extent, *Sula* is a story concerned with deconstructing binaries. It rejects the strict demarcation of male/female by imbuing Sula with traditionally male traits (she is especially reminiscent of Cholly Breedlove). It undermines the notion of "peace" by representing instances of violence, destruction, and trauma during the time between the two world wars.

Morrison's characterization of Nel and Sula also embodies this deconstructive aim. Where Nel lives for her family, community, and church, Sula centers her life on self-discovery and the indiscriminate fulfillment of her desires (or curiosities). Where Nel strives to be a positive figure of African American womanhood, Sula is repeatedly aligned with whiteness (for example, when rumors circulate that she has slept with white men, or when she decides to leave her grandmother in a white nursing home). Nel is a "good woman"—a wife, a mother, a church member; Sula is perceived as an evil conjure woman. Her birthmark, her mysterious unaffectedness, and instances of violence that come to be associated with her wickedness (Teapot's fall and Mr. Finley's death), all contribute to this impression. Yet, Morrison suggests, the evil the community projects onto Sula defines, and makes possible, the existence of good. After Sula's death, Teapot's mama resumes beating him, women "uncoddle their husbands"; and more generally, "affection for others [sinks] into flaccid disrepair" (*Sula* 154). The novel asserts the complicity of good and evil and breaks down the notion of a moral absolute.

Many scholars note Morrison's break with female-centered narrative in *Song of Solomon* (1977). Yet, although she appropriates the traditionally male-quest narrative to structure her third novel, Morrison acknowledges the women who remain behind. When Milkman tells Sweet of his flying African ancestor, she wonders, "Who'd he leave behind?" (*Song of Solomon* 328). Morrison complicates the romance of the quest by emphasizing the importance of rootedness: being rooted in community, in culture, and in history. Macon Dead attempts, and fails, to isolate himself and his family from the surrounding "rank-and-file" African American folks. Part of Hagar's tragedy is her unfulfilled need for the guidance of "a chorus" of African American women. Ultimately, even the quest itself loses its emphasis on the heroic individual—Milkman comes to discard his search for fortune; instead, he seeks to discover his past, his ancestors.

This theme—the reclamation of self and history—figures in the prominent motif of naming. The African American community assigns names to people (Railroad Tommy, Hospital Tommy, Empire State, Guitar Bains, and Milkman are renamed because of their actions or characteristics) and places (such as Not Doctor Street, No Mercy Hospital, and

Blood Bank). Exercising power over one's name becomes a symbolic act of defining one's personal experience. Pilate, by wearing her ominous name on her ear, bravely subverts its power by claiming possession of it.

In Morrison's first novel, the narrator tells us that "love is never any better than the lover" (*Bluest Eye* 206). She returns to this interest in the destructive possibilities of love in *Song of Solomon*. Hagar's unrequited love for Milkman fuels her determination to kill him; Guitar's love for the African American race becomes murderous through his involvement with the Seven Days. If the Dead family offers an example of the absence of love, we witness a potentially ideal love between Milkman and Sweet. The relationship's reciprocity, simplicity, and beauty are even evident in the language: "He made up the bed. She gave him gumbo to eat. He washed the dishes. She washed his clothes and hung them out to dry. He scoured her tub" (*Song of Solomon* 285). As he approaches self-knowledge through a sense of history, Milkman becomes capable of connecting with others.

Morrison's rich sense of literary history is especially evident in *Song of Solomon*. She draws on the Western odyssey and appropriates biblical names, placing them in a matrix of African and American cultural forms. Her interest in the oral tradition is integral to the text—Milkman's discovery of his history would be impossible without Pilate's "Sugarman" blues song, the children's rhyme of Solomon's genealogy, and, of course, the Angolan Gullah folktale of the flying African which underpins the narrative. Song of Solomon holds disparate elements in flux; it blends oral with written, Western with African, and ancient with modern, telling a story that is at once particularly African American and inherently universal.

Morrison's fourth novel, *Tar Baby* (1981), affirms her interest in folklore; the title appropriates a Brer Rabbit tale from the Uncle Remus collection, which itself is rooted in African mythology. Morrison discusses the sacred and binding qualities implicit in the symbolism of tar. Thus the metaphor carries a double meaning: the "tar baby" in the plantation tale is constructed by a white man; the African "tar lady," in contrast, is the embodiment of history and the facilitator of community. This layered understanding of the symbol informs both who Jadine is and who she is not.

Discussions of *Tar Baby* often focus on its various departures from her previous work. Set on a small fictitious Caribbean island rather than the close-knit rural African American communities of her first three novels, *Tar Baby* is also her first text to feature central white characters (Valerian and Margaret). Described by Morrison as "a love story, really," the novel is structured around the relationship between Jadine, a light-skinned African American model aligned with Western culture, and Son, a near-ideal of Afrocentric masculinity. The theme of beauty is taken up in her fourth novel in a significantly distinct way. Where white standards exclude Pecola, repress Nel, and intimidate Hagar, Jadine physically and culturally embodies them. Morrison also presents an alternative to Eurocentric beauty in the dark-skinned "woman in yellow."

As in *Sula* and *Song of Solomon*, naming is a central motif of *Tar Baby*. Rather than asserting agency over the self, however, characters rename one another in acts of dominance, ridicule, and rebellion. Sydney and Ondine Childs refer to the Dominique African Americans as "swamp women" and "horsemen"; they also call Gideon, Thérèse, and Alma Estée "Yardman" and "The Marys." Gideon and Thérèse call Sydney and Ondine "Bowtie" and "Machete hair," respectively. Jadine is derided as "the yalla," "fat ass," and a white girl. The relatively powerful and powerless both participate in this struggle over definition.

As a fictional slave narrative, Morrison's fifth novel, *Beloved* (1987), is also profoundly concerned with definition. A major aim of the neo-slave narrative is the reclamation and revision of history. Thus, though *Beloved* is structured around instances of storytelling, it is also itself an act of narrated "rememory." As a result of this parallel relationship between form and content, the structure of the story becomes especially important.

Scholars often call attention to *Beloved*'s nonlinear temporality. Stories, particularly traumatic ones, are fragmented and retold, sometimes from different perspectives. This emphasizes the communal nature of memory in the text. Characters share possession of a collective account of history. Those who are not incorporated into the oral tradition feel alienated. The narrator reveals Denver's resentment that Sethe and Paul D were "a twosome, saying 'Your daddy' and 'Sweet Home' in a way that made it clear that both belonged to them and not to her. That her own father's absence was not hers" (*Beloved* 13). Shared ownership of memory is the foundation of human connection in the text. Sethe describes her understanding with Paul D: "the mind of him that knew her own. Her story was bearable because it was his as well—to tell, to refine, to tell again" (99). Yet memory also makes relationships impossible: the force of the past, embodied in Beloved, drives Paul D from 124. Storytelling is a moral act in the novel; the decision to retell (and even remember) one's past has profound consequences.

Madness, also a moral choice for Morrison, becomes the inverse of the decision to remember. Sethe laments her willingness to remember: "other people went crazy," she says, "why couldn't she?" (71). Six-O and Halle retreat into madness; even Paul D allows himself to be driven "crazy so he would not lose his mind" (41). Insanity is presented as a sort of escape; it is aligned with maleness as an extreme form of rootless masculinity. Ultimately, it is irresponsible—women are once again left behind to bear the knowledge of cultural history.

Beloved, like *Song of Solomon*, sets the desire for human connection against the weight of the past. Love and history are at once interdependent and antagonistic forces in the text. While *Song of Solomon* shows the impossibility of love when divorced from the past, *Beloved* describes the other extreme: destructive mother-love "too thick" with collective traumatic memory.

Murderous love also figures prominently in Morrison's sixth work, *Jazz* (1992). Incorporating formal and thematic elements of jazz music, the novel tells of Joe Trace's ultimately fatal love of the shallow eighteen-year-old Dorcas. The text is improvisational, open-ended, and participates in call-and-response techniques. Besides love, *Jazz* explores pain, loss, and longing. The absent presence is a central motif of both the novel and the musical form. This is embodied first by the narrator—the "voice" without race, gender, or age. The opening paragraph introduces a number of other absent presences: "the woman" (Violet Trace), who is spoken of but is not there, and Dorcas, whose absence is supposed to sustain the presence of Joe's love. Indeed, the "presence" of Joe's absent mother in Dorcas sparks his desire for her. The orphans who populate the narrative (Joe, Violet, Dorcas, Felice, Golden Gray) also evoke this motif: their missing parents essentially become ever-present by defining their orphan status. The novel's structure emphasizes absences and silences through whitespace between sections, seen by some critics as musical pauses.

Jazz is also intertextual; it engages in a sort of call and response with Morrison's previous work. For example, there are curious similarities between Wild and Beloved: their childish demeanor, language, and their connection with sweet things (Beloved's honey, sugar sandwiches, and cane sticks, Wild's honeycombs and association with the cane field). This connection is left ambiguous, inserting the reader into the construction of the story.

The act of interpretation is also central to both form and content of Morrison's seventh work, *Paradise* (1997). Its nonlinear structure and enigmatic opening line ("They shoot the white girl first") invite and even insist upon reader participation. The story is also fundamentally concerned with contestation over meaning; the Oven exemplifies this theme. Although most explicit in the struggles over the inscription on the oven's "mouth," the mythology of Haven, the Old Fathers, biblical narratives, and the symbolism of the cross all become sites of contested interpretation. (Steward Morgan, expounding on the significance of the cross, notes that "a cross was no better than the bearer" [*Paradise* 154], recalling the view expressed in *The Bluest Eye* that "love is never any better than the lover.") The Convent is a continually appropriated and redefined physical space: from a pornographic structure belonging to an embezzler, to a Catholic school for Arapho girls, and finally a refuge for displaced women, the significance of the Convent is fluid—imbued with history and informed by the needs of its inhabitants.

History is central to the story of *Paradise*. The plot is essentially the convergence of distinct pasts: the stories of the Convent's women (Mavis, Gigi, Seneca, Pallas, and Connie) are juxtaposed against the story of Ruby. It is ultimately the accumulation of history that layers meaning and fuels conflict. In contrast to *Beloved*, where memory of the past is repressed and denied, *Paradise* presents an overpresence of the past. The New Fathers attempt to "repeat exactly" the history of Haven (113). The desire for repetition concretizes in the town's hidden privileging of racial purity ("8-rock blood"). Through a description of the school's Christmas play, Morrison portrays attempts at reenactment as potentially corrupt. The story of Nativity is revised to include a pivotal moment in Ruby's history, the Disallowing. The number of wise men in the Nativity scene is expanded to correlate to the number of Founding Fathers, but this number changes when one family is no longer in the ruling group's good graces. This instance of problematic revisionist history becomes a figure for the novel's larger themes: the idealization of the past, the relationship between the human and the sacred, and the interpretation of narrative as a moral act.

Love (2003), Morrison's latest novel, is essentially the story of the women surrounding Bill Cosey, the owner of the Cosey Hotel and Resort. He marries his granddaughter Christine's eleven-year-old (one-time) friend Heed (short for "Heed the Night"). Contemporaneous to the narration of the text, Christine and Heed find themselves sharing the house of the late Cosey. Other women involved include May, Cosey's daughter-in-law; L, Cosey's cook and one of the novel's narrators; and Junior, a displaced sixteen-year-old who applies to work for Heed and is subsequently haunted by Cosey's ghost. Critics have remarked on the relative underdevelopment of Cosey's character— this is deliberate. Playing on the presence/absence theme consistent in her work, Cosey is rendered a present absence both through his death and his emotional unavailability. The novel presents a patriarchal economy in which relationships between women are defined by their relationships to men (or in this case, a man). May turns Christine against Heed, and only toward the end of the novel do the characters begin to realize that more cooperative relationships between women would have been better than "looking for Big Daddy everywhere." The novel continues to explore several of the dominant themes in Morrison's work, including an interrogation of love, intraracial issues in the African

American community, possibilities of relationships between women, sexual violence, the oral tradition, and mythology. The narrative structure of *Love* is also consistent with Morrison's craft; she uses temporal shifts and flashbacks and makes use of multiple perspectives.

CRITICAL RECEPTION

Scholarship on Toni Morrison spans decades and encompasses a wide variety of approaches. In her introduction to *Toni Morrison's Fiction*, Jan Furman distinguishes between earlier, more thematically focused criticism and more contemporary scholarship concerned with narrative structure. While periodizing critical reception is certainly useful, this overview is thematically organized instead, emphasizing that feminist, Marxist, and Afrocentric readings of her work are not entirely restricted to the past. For the most part, scholarship on Morrison's works can be placed into six categories: those that emphasize her African and African American literary heritage, those that consider the importance of the oral tradition, texts that investigate her role in revising history, those that read her novels as feminist texts, works that attempt to locate Morrison in the Western literary tradition, and, finally, works concerned with narrative structure.

Scholars interested in Morrison's place in the African American literary tradition emphasize her use of African American cultural forms. Trudier Harris describes the "orality" so central to Morrison's fiction as fundamentally African American. Gurleen Grewal reads *The Bluest Eye* (which makes Pecola's invisibility conspicuous) as a response to canonical African American male authors who ignore the African American female experience. Lucinda H. MacKethan contextualizes Morrison within an African American literary tradition that uses naming to emphasize selfhood. Also, Sandra Pouchet Paquet connects *Their Eyes Were Watching God's* Janie Crawford to *Tar Baby's* Jadine Childs to explore the tension between the individual and the community in African American literature. These scholars identify characteristics of Morrison's work that make it distinctively African American.

Comparing her novels to African American musical forms is also a key approach to this perspective. For Barbara Williams Lewis, *Jazz* the novel is structured by formal elements of jazz music—especially open-endedness and ambiguity. Joyce Wegs's "Toni Morrison's *Song of Solomon*: A Blues Song" takes a similar approach: *Song of Solomon* is structurally a blues song in that it is the enunciation of a collective experience. It is also thematically a blues song: characters appropriate gender-specific behavior representative of blues narratives—men respond to life's trials by leaving home, women remain and grieve.

Certain critics argue that Morrison's novels can only be fully understood when contextualized by cultural knowledge and history. Susan Bowers, in "*Beloved* and the New Apocalypse," investigates the particularities of the notion of "apocalypse" within an African American context. She explains that while white hopes for humankind lay in the future, African American expectations of glory involve the reclamation of the past. The latter informs Bowers's reading of *Beloved*: for her, an apocalyptic battle is waged over "rememory." Similarly, Gay Wilentz emphasizes black storytelling and writing traditions as central and necessary to any interpretation of Morrison's works. Wilentz cites characteristics of the oral tradition, the emphasis on reader participation, and "tribal values" (such as community) within Morrison's novels as examples of her African heritage. Philip Page draws on West African concepts of fluidity to analyze Morrison's novels. The coexistence of past, present, and future, as well as "life and death, sacred and secular . . . spiritual and material . . . individual . . . and community" all connect Morrison's work to West African culture (Page 11).

Morrison's participation in oral culture is also often linked to African and American cultural forms. Trudier Harris, in *Fiction and Folklore: The Novels of Toni Morrison*, argues from the position that folklore is the foundation for African American literature, so that literary themes derive from those of the oral tradition. She challenges the traditional dichotomy between folklore and literature, asserting that, in Morrison's texts, lore is not merely "lifted" and represented isolated from the literary content of the novel. It is instead integrated and integral to the thematic aims of her works.

Harris's designation of Morrison's work as "literary folklore" embodies a consistent scholarly concern with her novels: the juxtaposition of the individual literary imagination with a sense of communal history and tradition. Gurleen Grewal's *Circles of Sorrow, Lines of Struggle* also touches on this issue in its examination of temporality. Grewal argues that linear time is disrupted because personal experience must continually be contextualized within history. Morrison's novels, for her, represent the process of shaping narratives from the folk and oral traditions. For example, Grewal reads *The Bluest Eye* as an inversion of the fairy-tale notion of transformation, a complication of long-standing African American belief in the north as a better place for black people, and a challenge to the myth of upward mobility. Catherine Carr Lee, in "The South in Toni Morrison's *Song of Solomon*: Initiation, Healing, and Home," also addresses the ways in which Morrison undermines traditional notions of north and south. Morrison simultaneously represents and revises cultural myths.

Scholars note her similar object/agent position to history. Morrison's novels are historical—they span centuries of African American experience (beginning with *Beloved*'s references to the Middle Passage)—yet they are also fictional. Gurleen Grewal reads Morrison as postcolonial literature that rewrites dominant historical narratives from a marginalized perspective. She draws on Deleuze and Guattari's notion of minor literature in order to examine Morrison's treatment of memory; namely, Grewal views her use of memory as an attempt to make sense of individual experience through the lens of a collective consciousness. Ashraf Rushdy is also concerned with memory; he uses Wordsworth's notion of primal sympathy and Freud's idea of constructed fantasies to emphasize the centrality of primal scenes to Morrison's interrogation of (re)memory. J. Brooks Bouson, similarly, draws on shame and trauma theory to analyze Morrison's treatment of historic racism.

While some critics focus on Morrison's revision of history, others discuss the ways in which her novels deal with existing accounts. In "Dead Teachers: Rituals of Manhood and Rituals of Reading in *Song of Solomon*," Linda Krumholtz analyzes *Song of Solomon* as a narrative of Milkman's quest for African American history. David Lawrence, in "Fleshly Ghosts and Ghostly Flesh: The Word and the Body in *Beloved*," examines how characters deal with knowledge of the past. He argues that acts of remembering and forgetting are both potentially dangerous and enslaving. Ultimately, he concludes, the relationship between control over the body and control over language is central; thus, Sethe and Paul D must struggle with language before reclaiming their lives.

A significant body of scholarship on Morrison focuses on her works as feminist texts. Perhaps this category is a misleading distinction, as most critics acknowledge feminist and womanist influences on her novels even when not making them a central focus. For example, Philip Page mentions Simone de Beauvoir, Virginia Woolf, and

Luce Irigaray, as well as bell hooks, Barbara Christian, Barbara Smith, Patricia Hill Collins, Hazel Carby, and Valerie Smith, among others, in his preface to *Dangerous Freedom: Fusion and Fragmentation in Toni Morrison's Novels.*

Ed Guerrero examines the patriarchal gaze in Morrison's first five novels. He explores the ways in which race, class, and gender intersect in her construction of the gaze. Lauren Lepow's "Paradise Lost and Found: Dualism and Edenic Myth in Toni Morrison's *Tar Baby*" reads the novel as an attempt to overcome dualistic thinking by establishing a mythology which redefines original sin as a form of innocence: a lack of self-knowledge.

Sula is a work particularly emphasized by feminist scholarship. Gurleen Grewal presents *Sula* as a class history of the African American female experience in America: Eva, Hannah, and Sula Peace are working class; Rochelle, Helene, and Nel Wright are upwardly mobile bourgeoisie. Diane Gillespie and Missy Dehn Kubitschek, in "Who Cares? Women-Centered Psychology in Sula," remark on the centrality of female experience and perspective, as well as issues of community, friendship, and empathy among women.

In contrast, Michael Awkward focuses on what some scholars see as the least feminist of Morrison's fiction. In "'Unruly and Let Loose': Myth, Ideology, and Gender in *Song of Solomon*," he departs from most analyses of the novel that emphasize the focus on male consciousness. Instead, he suggests, the novel comments on the marginalization of women within the dominant male narrative.

As Morrison's work becomes increasingly mainstream, many scholars begin to assess her relationship to the American and Western literary traditions. There seem to be three distinct approaches: those who attempt to canonize her within the tradition, those who argue that she participates in the tradition, and those who discuss how she subverts and undermines it. Most notable among the first group is perhaps Harold Bloom, who in *The Western Canon* includes Morrison's *Song of Solomon* for its participation in the quest narrative. David Cowart echoes Bloom's assessment, claiming that *Song of Solomon* is "literature," not "black literature" (Middleton 95). He argues that Morrison is universal and encourages people to read her texts within a "larger tradition" of Western writing.

John Duval, in "Doe Hunting and Masculinity: *Song of Solomon* and *Go Down, Moses*," diverges from critics like Bloom who see Faulkner's work as a "master-narrative" for Morrison. Instead, he emphasizes Morrison's craft and contribution by suggesting a shift in terminology: she "*engages*" Faulkner. Philip Page acknowledges the plurality of Morrison's literary heritage: he locates predecessors for his fusion and fragmentation trope in American culture, deconstruction, and African American culture.

Other critics emphasize Morrison as subversive. Valerie Smith, in "The Quest for and Discovery of Identity in Toni Morrison's Song of Solomon," argues that the novel undermines individualistic notions of identity by insisting that a more authentic identity must be essentially communal. Catherine M. Woidat similarly posits Morrison's work as a challenge to canonical American authors in her article "Talking Back to Schoolteacher: Morrison's Confrontation with Hawthorne in *Beloved*." Gurleen Grewal situates Morrison's work within the tradition of the bourgeois novel while also undermining it with her emphasis on "peasant" oral culture. The narrative perspective within her work is also subversive in that it is "on the side of those who are subordinated to bourgeois power" (Grewal 4).

Finally, a number of critics have remarked on the structure in Morrison's fiction. Scholarship often remarks on several characteristics of Morrison's narrative structure: multiple points of view, conflation of characters, repetition, nonlinear temporality, and ambiguous narration. Philip Page draws on Ralph Ellison's term—the "puzzle of the one-and-the-many"—to characterize Morrison's work as "a unified entity [that] simultaneously exists as a complex configuration of its constituent parts" (Page 3). He applies this idea to themes in the content of her novels as well as their form—particularly her disruption of temporal linearity. Brian Finney also discusses temporality, emphasizing the large gap between the order in which events occur in *Beloved* and the order in which they are told. He sees the intermediary, timeless status of Beloved-as-ghost as parallel to the narrative structure, which he describes as nonlinear and disorienting. Katherine J. Mayberry, in "The Problem of Narrative in Toni Morrison's *Jazz*," diverges from the idea that narrative structure is the result of Morrison's participation in African American cultural forms; instead, she resists closure in her fiction to prevent her texts from being subordinated to hegemonic ideology. Mayberry emphasizes Morrison's agency and craft in constructing her narratives.

New and original scholarship on Toni Morrison's novels continues to be published in major literary journals and volumes of criticism. Her texts offer rich possibilities for critical interpretation of their social and cultural commentary, preservation of history, intertextuality, and intricately crafted aesthetics.

BIBLIOGRAPHY

Works by Toni Morrison

Beloved. New York: Alfred A. Knopf, 1987.
The Bluest Eye. New York: Holt, Rinehart & Winston, 1970.
Jazz. New York: Alfred A. Knopf, 1992.
Love. New York: Alfred A. Knopf, 2003.
Paradise. New York: Alfred A. Knopf, 1997.
Playing in the Dark: Whiteness and the Literary Imagination. Cambridge: Harvard University Press, 1992.
Rac(ing) Justice, (En)gender(ing) Power: Essays on Anita Hill, Clarence Thomas, and the Construction of a Social Reality. New York: Pantheon, 1992.
"Recitatif." In *Confirmation*, edited by Amiri and Amina Baraka. New York: Morrow, 1983.
Song of Solomon. New York: Alfred A. Knopf, 1977.
Sula. New York: Alfred A. Knopf, 1973.
Tar Baby. New York: Alfred A. Knopf, 1981.

Studies of Toni Morrison's Works

Andrews, William L., and Nellie Y. McKay, eds. *Toni Morrison's Beloved: A Casebook*. New York: Oxford University Press, 1999.
Berkman, Anne Elizabeth. *The Quest for Authenticity: The Novels of Toni Morrison*. Ann Arbor: University of Michigan Press, 1987.
Bjork, Patrick B. *The Novels of Toni Morrison: The Search for Self and Place within the Community*. New York: Peter Lang, 1996.
Bloom, Harold. *Toni Morrison*. Bloom's Major Novelist series. Pennsylvania: Chelsea House Publishers, 1999.

————. *The Western Canon: The Books and School of the Ages*. New York: Harcourt, 1994.

Bouson, J. Brooks. *Quiet as It's Kept: Shame, Trauma and Race in the Novels of Toni Morrison*. Albany: State University of New York Press, 2000.

Carmean, Karen. *Toni Morrison's World of Fiction*. Troy, NY: The Whitson Publishing Company, 1993.

Christian, Barbara. "Community and Nature: The Novels of Toni Morrison." *Journal of Ethnic Studies* 7.4 (1980): 65–78.

Conner, Marc C. *The Aesthetics of Toni Morrison:* Speaking the Unspeakable. Jackson: University Press of Mississippi, 2000.

David, Ron. *Toni Morrison Explained*. New York: Random House, 2000.

Furman, Jan. *Toni Morrison's Fiction*. Columbia: University of South Carolina Press, 1996.

Gates, Henry Louis, Jr., and K. A. Appiah. *Toni Morrison: Critical Perspectives Past and Present*. New York: Amistad, 1993.

Grewal, Gurleen. *Circles of Sorrow, Lines of Struggle: The Novels of Toni Morrison*. Baton Rouge: Louisiana State University Press, 2000.

Harris, Trudier. *Fiction and Folklore: The Novels of Toni Morrison*. Knoxville: University of Tennessee, 1991.

Kolmerton, Carol A., Stephen M. Ross, and Judith Bryant Wittenberg, eds. *Unflinching Gaze: Morrison and Faulkner Re-Envisioned*. Jackson: University Press of Mississippi, 1997.

Kubitschek, Missy Dehn. *Toni Morrison: A Critical Companion*. Westport: Greenwood Publishing Group, (1998).

Matus, Jill. *Toni Morrison*. New York: St. Martin's Press, 1998.

McKay, Nellie Y. *Critical Essays on Toni Morrison*. Boston: G. K. Hall, 1988.

McKay, Nellie Y., and William L. Andrews, eds. *Toni Morrison's Beloved: A Casebook*. New York: Oxford University Press, 1998.

McKay, Nellie Y., and Kathryn Earle, eds. *Approaches to Teaching the Novels of Toni Morrison*. New York: The Modern Langauge Association of America, 1997.

Middleton, David L., ed. *Toni Morrison's Fiction: Contemporary Criticism*. New York: Garland Publishing, 1999.

Page, Philip. *Dangerous Freedom: Fusion and Fragmentation in Toni Morrison's Novels*. Jackson: University Press of Mississippi, 1996.

Peach, Linden. *Toni Morrison*. New York: St. Martin's Press, 2000.

————, ed. *Toni Morrison: Contemporary Critical Essays*. New York: St. Martin's Press, 1998.

Reyes-Connor, Marc Cameron. *The Aesthetics of Toni Morrison*. Jackson: University Press of Mississippi, 2000.

Smith, Valerie. *New Essays on Song of Solomon*. Cambridge: Cambridge University Press, 1995.

Spillers, Hortense, and Marjorie Pryse, eds. *Conjuring: Black Women, Fiction, and Literary Tradition*. Bloomington: Indiana University Press, 1985.

Sumana, K. *The Novels of Toni Morrison: A Study in Race, Gender, and Class*. London: Sangam Books, 1998.

Deborah M. Wolf

GERTRUDE BUSTILL MOSSELL (1855–1948)

BIOGRAPHICAL NARRATIVE

Gertrude Bustill Mossell was a journalist and published two books in her literary career. She was born on July 3, 1855, into a pioneering, socially active, and politically aware Philadelphia family. Mossell did not disappoint her family's legacy. She taught school for several years after graduating from Robert Vaux Grammar and published her first text at the age of sixteen when her high school commencement speech "Influence" appeared in the *Christian Recorder*.

As an early feminist, Mossell focused most of her journalistic endeavors on articles concerning women's rights and responsibilities. She published in a variety of periodicals including the *AME Church Review*, *Philadelphia Echo*, *Independent Freeman*, *Our Women and Children*, and *Woman's Era*. In December 1885 Mossell became the first woman to publish an ongoing column in an African American newspaper. "The Woman's Department" ran in the *New York Freeman*, the leading African American newspaper at the time, and was later picked up by *Indianapolis World* and *New York Age*. She also worked for three of Philadelphia's most widely distributed daily periodicals for almost seven years: the *Philadelphia Times*, *Inquirer*, and *Press*.

Mossell had two daughters, Mary Campbell and Florence Alma, with her husband Dr. Nathan Frances Mossell. The two worked together in 1895 to establish the Frederick Douglas Memorial Hospital and Training School. Mrs. Mossell, though rarely noted for her assistance, raised over $30,000 for the hospital's creation, served as president of the Social Service Auxiliary, and spent two years working on the *Alumni Magazine*. Her most notable civic accomplishment, however, may be her support in organizing the Philadelphia branch of the National Afro-American Council, predecessor to the NAACP, in 1899. She died on January 21, 1948, in Philadelphia. Sadly, her obituary headline did not even mention her name; it read, "Widow of Dr. Mossell Succumbs at 92 years."

MAJOR WORKS

While Mossell is most noted for her extraordinary career as a journalist, she published two books during her lifetime. The first, and most widely recognized, is *The Work of the Afro-American Woman*. Published in 1894, this feminist and political text is a collection of original essays and poems by a diverse group of women including businesswomen, journalists, educators, and missionaries. Mossell focuses on the industrious work and writings of contemporary women while highlighting how the legacy of historical figures like Harriet Tubman and Phillis Wheatley enables the current and future race projects. She praises African American women's efforts and accomplishments, emphasizing the extraordinary nature of African American women to prevail and pioneer while maintaining dignity and identity. She encourages young women to make responsible choices concerning their future roles as mothers, wives, and professionals, emphasizing one's need for personal space within the home as a way to retreat and rejuvenate her worldly endeavors. Mossell also focuses on African American history as a point of reference for future hope as well as a critical tool for racial pride. She beautifully crafts her text to inspire, instruct, and offer accolade to African American women without openly antagonizing masculine authority or igniting racial conflict. This was a skill Mossell practiced in all her journalistic efforts for which she was handsomely rewarded with a lengthy list of periodical publications.

Mossell published her second and last book, *Little Dansie's One Day at Sabbath School*, in 1902. It is the story of a little girl who is killed while trying to save her Sunday school teacher from an oncoming train.

CRITICAL RECEPTION

Mossell published *The Work* under her husband's initials, perhaps as a way to highlight her domesticity and mask the progressive nature of the text. Unlike many nineteenth-century race writers, she was able to put into print her ideas regarding race with minimal negative press. Her first book sold 1,000 copies immediately and a second edition was printed in 1908. The *New York Independent*, *Chicago Inter-Ocean*, and *Springfield Republican* all published complimentary reviews. Her work as a journalist was also extremely well received by the public. Like many nineteenth-century African American female writers, Mossell is noticeably absent from contemporary discourse. The few resources in circulation emphasize the irreplaceable and progressive role she played in African American history.

BIBLIOGRAPHY

Works by Gertrude Mossell

Little Dansie's One Day at Sabbath School. Philadelphia: Penn Printing and Pub., 1902.
The Work of the Afro-American Woman. Philadelphia: G. S. Ferguson, 1894.

Studies of Gertrude Mossell's Work

Pero Gaglo, Dagbovie. "Black Women Historians from the Late 19th Century to the Dawning of the Civil Rights Movement." *Journal of African American History* 89.3 (2004): 241–62.
Price-Groff, Claire. *Extraordinary Women Journalists.* New York. Children's Press, 1997.
Streitmatter, Rodger. *Raising Her Voice: African American Women Journalists Who Changed History.* Lexington: University Press of Kentucky, 1994.

Amanda Wray

HARRYETTE MULLEN (1953–)

BIOGRAPHICAL NARRATIVE

Poet Harryette Mullen was born on July 1, 1953, in Florence, Alabama, to James Otis and Avis Ann Mullen. By age four she moved to Fort Worth, Texas, where her life as a writer began. Initially she wrote to entertain family and friends; but before graduating high school, her poetry was published in a local newspaper. Continuing her education and her writing, she attended the University of Texas, Austin, taking an English degree in 1975. Publishing *Tree Tall Woman* in 1981 as her first professional publication, she later entered graduate school at the University of California, Santa Cruz, earning her master's degree in 1987 and doctorate in 1990.

Upon graduating in 1990 Mullen took a position as an assistant professor at Cornell University and by 1991 published *Trimmings*. In 1992 she followed up with the publishing of *S*perm**K*T*. Focusing more in academia and professional scholarship, Mullen published about one critical article per year until 1995. In that year, two significant events occurred; Mullen published *Muse & Drudge* and she left Cornel University to join the University of California, Los Angeles (UCLA) faculty.

MAJOR WORKS

Mullen's work, whether classified as a collection of individual prose-poems or a large unit of poetic-prose, is always experimental poetry in one fashion or another. In *Tree Tall Woman* Mullen seeks to discuss elements of black identity especially as manifested within the context of the Black Arts Movement. She attempted to project a voice telling of the black identity and experience without having that voice scream the identity of the black speaker. To that end Mullen tells Cynthia Hogue in an interview that she created a work that "is really about relationships among black people." As such it allowed her vicariously to reveal her identity in a way that made race central but not overwhelming. In doing this, she makes a niche in and from which she can work to create an authorial identity.

Ten years later when Mullen published the poetic-prose work *Trimmings*, she again experimented with the language to offer a feminist critique of American society through the thematic use of clothing accessories to discuss the image of women in America. This particular work seems to focus less on issues of race and more on issues relating to women, as does *S*perm**K*T* the following year in which the shopping list is explored as a vehicle for offering a feminist critique of American society. While these works are marvelously crafted and are at the zenith of innovation, they indirectly seem to alienate Mullen's minority audience.

Responding directly to this, Mullen published *Muse & Drudge*, a long poetical work discussing the African American woman from the obvious perspective of an African American woman, in 1995. The voice in this work resonates differently than the voice of the earlier works, and the effort is rewarded through a welcoming reception of a more diverse audience. In 2002 she wrote her most critically praised work, *Sleeping with the Dictionary*. In this particular work, Mullen provides the perfect combination of linguistic wordplay and appreciable themes. It is not only pleasing to her target audience, but it extends itself beyond that demographic into the mainstream so that aficionados and casual readers alike take notice.

Sleeping with the Dictionary is a collection of prose-poems treating a variety of themes. Ironically, the language used to express the themes is as important as the themes themselves. In this work, language not only provides a conduit for discussing a subject but also becomes the subject of the discussion. The work riddled with duplicities, and laced with wordplay and word games subtly becomes about language. Just as Mullen directly treats blackness in *Tree Tall Woman* without directly discussing it, she illuminates language in *Sleeping with the Dictionary* without shining a spotlight on it.

CRITICAL RECEPTION

Mullen's reception is broad. Deborah Mix notes Aldon Nielsen's praising Mullen "as . . . critic and poet [who] has helped . . . to identify and sustain a tradition of African American experimentalism that has been marginalized, if not ignored . . ." (Mix 65–66). Mithcum Huehls extols Mullen's experimentation in *Muse and Drudge* as intentional Veil shifting within the DuBoisean paradigm of double consciousness (19). *Sleeping with the Dictionary* was highly praised by many groups simultaneously, winning it a nomination as a finalist for the 2002 National Book Award. Hokes S. Glocver III posits that Mullen's *Sleeping with the Dictionary* challenges how language is obtained by "presenting a wide range of linguistic forces converging in the poems" presented while Carol Muske-Dukes says the work "may be lexicon lust, but it's no one-night stand."

BIBLIOGRAPHY

Works by Harryette Mullen

Blues Baby: Early Poems. Lewisburg: Bucknell University Press, 2002.
Muse & Drudge. Philadelphia: Singing Horse, 1995.
Sleeping with the Dictionary. Berkeley: University of California Press, 2002.
S*perm**K*T. Philadelphia: Singing Horse, 1992.
Tree Tall Woman. Galveston: Energy Earth, 1981.
Trimmings. New York: Tender Buttons, 1991.

Studies of Harryette Mullen's Work

Bedient, Calvin. "Interview with Harryette Mullen." *Callaloo* 19.3 (Summer 1996): 651–69.
Frost, Elisabeth A. "An Interview with Harryette Mullen." *Contemporary Literature* 41.1 (Spring 2000): 397–421.
———. "Signifyin(g) on Stein: The Revisionist Poetics of Harryette Mullen and Leslie Scalapino." *Postmodern Culture* 5.3 (May 1995).
Glover III, Hoke S. Rev. of *Sleeping with the Dictionary*. *Black Issues Book Review* (July–August 2002): 63.

Hogue, Cynthia. "Beyond the Frame of Whiteness: Harryette Mullen's Revisionary Border." In *We Who Love to Be Astonished: Experimental Women's Writing and Performance Poetics*, edited by Laura Hinton and Cynthia Hogue, 81–89. Tuscaloosa: University of Alabama Press, 2002.

———. "Interview with Harryette Mullen." *Postmodern Culture* 9.2 (January 1999).

Hoover, Paul. "Stark Strangled Banjos: Linguistic Doubleness in the Work of David Hammons, Harryette Mullen, and Al Hibbler." *Denver Quarterly* 36.3–4 (Fall–Winter 2002): 68–82.

Huehls, Mitchum. "Spun Puns (and Anagrams): Exchange Economies, Subjectivity, and History in Harryette Mullen's Muse & Drudge." *Contemporary Literature* 44.1 (Spring 2003): 19–46.

Mix, Deborah. "Tender Revisions: Harryette Mullen's Trimmings and S*PERM**K*T." *American Literature* 77.1 (March 2005): 65–92.

Muske-Duke, Carol. Rev. of *Sleeping with the Dictionary. Los Angeles Times Book Review*, March 31, 2002, 6.

Pinto, Samantha. "Feminist Subjectivity and the Everyday Blues: The Casual Erotics of Harryette Mullen." In *Sound as Sense: Contemporary U. S. Poetry &/in Music*, edited by Michael Delville and Christine Pagnoulle, 59–75. Belgium: Peter Lang, 2003.

Williams, Emily Allen. "Harryette Mullen, 'The Queen of Hip Hyperbole': An Interview." *African American Review* 34.4 (Winter 2000): 701–7.

Ordner W. Taylor, III

BEATRICE MURPHY (1908–1992)

BIOGRAPHICAL NARRATIVE

Hailing from Monessen, Pennsylvania, Beatrice Murphy as a young child put down roots in Washington, D.C., where she spent the remainder of her prolific life working as an editor, reviewer, columnist, poet, and bibliographer. Clearly a lesser-known voice among African American women writers, Murphy nonetheless garners recognition for giving voice and support to other African American writers, advocating primarily for young, unknown, and struggling poets.

Throughout her career, Murphy wrote syndicated book and poetry review columns for the Associated Negro Press that ran in African American newspapers. She founded the Negro Bibliographic and Research Center in Washington, D.C., which published the *Bibliographic Survey: The Negro in Print* (1965–1972), a periodical of reviews of black fiction and nonfiction that was subscribed to by public, university, and federal libraries.

MAJOR WORKS

Murphy published three books of original poetry. *Love Is a Terrible Thing* (1945) explores love from its heights of passion to the valley of despair. *The Rocks Cry Out* (1969) takes a definitive nonviolent stance in the midst of the civil rights movement. *Get with It, Lord* (1976) directly calls upon God for strength. Facing impending blindness, Murphy writes of engulfing darkness and contemplates what might happen to the question of race, for she can no longer see visual markers.

Murphy's dedication to young black poets is exemplified in her three edited collections. In *Negro Voices* (1938) she contends that it is her "duty" to bring undiscovered "talent to light" (5–6). A combination of factors—lack of publication venues, "callous indifference" from white publishers, and feeling disloyal to the black race when publishing with white presses —makes the "role of the Negro writer a difficult one" (6).

While still advocating unknown black writers, *Ebony Rhythm* (1948) attempts to erase matters of race. Murphy states that "Negro poets write . . . about love, nature and everyday events in the world they live in—which is an American, not a Negro, world" (i). She was not "swayed by sentimental considerations of race" (ii) yet at least a third of the poems are indeed black-themed.

In stark contrast to her earlier attempt to gloss over race, *Today's Negro Voices* (1970) is "much more race oriented . . . even race saturated." Murphy admits that the sensibilities of black nationalism along with "determination" for change are felt in the "unadorned hate flowing from their pens" (7). Indeed nearly all of the thirty-four poets deal with matters of survival and black pride.

CRITICAL RECEPTION

Despite Murphy's efforts to popularize young black poets, she did not receive the critical recognition that she may have deserved. Keneth Kinnamon's extensive survey of African American anthologies does give a nod to Murphy's first two edited collections, but his assessment is less than stunning. In one throwaway comment he finds her "lack of selectivity" unimpressive (469). It is unfortunate that Kinnamon did not give consideration to her final anthology, which is by far the most race based. Nor does he bother to explain her noble mission to assist black writers as they face publication roadblocks, an impressive undertaking for a Negro woman in 1938.

Indeed the strongest critical blow was delivered by Nikki Giovanni in her 1969 review of *The Rocks Cry Out* in which Murphy points an accusatory finger at the "Negro youth." Entrenched in the Black Pride Movement, Giovanni is saddened at being "so misunderstood by some of our older generation." She charges Murphy with missing the "whole point of being Black in the beginning of Blackness" (97) and resents the "despair and helplessness" in Murphy's poetry (98).

While the works of Beatrice Murphy did not resonate throughout the larger African American literary realm, her nuanced efforts of giving voice to hundreds of unknown writers will always be a noteworthy part of African American literary history.

BIBLIOGRAPHY

Works by Beatrice Murphy

Bibliographic Survey: The Negro in Print. Washington, DC: Minority Research Center, 1965–1972.
Ebony Rhythm: An Anthology of Contemporary Negro Verse. New York: Exposition, 1948.
Get with It, Lord: Poems New and Selected. Washington, DC: Winebury Press, 1976.
Love Is a Terrible Thing. New York: Hobson, 1945.
Negro Voices: An Anthology of Contemporary Verse. New York: Harrison, 1938.
The Rocks Cry Out. Detroit: Broadside, 1969.
Today's Negro Voices: An Anthology by Young Negro Poets. New York: Messner, 1970.

Studies of Beatrice Murphy's Work

Adams, Katherine H. "Beatrice M. Murphy." In *Dictionary of Literary Biography, Afro American Writers, 1940—1955*, ed. Trudier Harris-Lopez. Farmington Hills, MI: Thomson Gale, 1988.
Giovanni, Nikki. Rev. of *The Rocks Cry Out* by Beatrice M. Murphy and Nancy L. Arnez. *Negro Digest* (August 1969): 97–98.
Kinnamon, Keneth. "Anthologies of African-American Literature from 1845 to 1994." *Callaloo* 20.2 (1997): 461–81.

Judy L. Isaksen

PAULI MURRAY (1910–1985)

BIOGRAPHICAL NARRATIVE

Pauli Murray, a novelist, poet, and author of law books and autobiographies, was born in Baltimore in 1910 but lived from the age of three until sixteen in Durham, North Carolina, with her maternal grandparents Robert and Cornelia Fitzgerald and her aunts Pauline Fitzgerald Dame, who eventually adopted Murray, and Sallie Fitzgerald Small. During her time in North Carolina, Murray developed a strongly ambivalent attitude toward the south, abhorring the Jim Crow laws she was forced to live under. She left Durham in 1926 to attend college in New York City. Murray received her undergraduate degree from Hunter College and later went on to attend law school at Howard University, where she engaged in several nonviolent protests in the 1940s, long before their popularity in the 1950s and 1960s. Murray received graduate degrees in law from UC-Berkeley and Yale University; later she would practice law as well as teach at the Ghana School of Law and at Brandeis, where she not only taught law but also was responsible for helping to design their first African American Studies program. Murray was also an ardent advocate for women's rights, coining the phrase "Jane Crow" to refer to women's second-class status in the United States and serving as one of the founding members of the National Organization for Women in 1966. In 1973, at the age of sixty-two, Murray entered divinity school and in 1977 became one of the first women, and *the* first African American woman, ordained a priest in the Episcopal Church in the United States. Murray died on July 1, 1985.

MAJOR WORKS

While Murray is most often recognized as a civil rights' activist, a teacher, and a priest, writing was the vocation she felt most drawn to. Amidst the many pamphlets, newspaper articles, and two law books Murray wrote, three texts should be of particular interest to the scholar of African American women's literature: two autobiographical works and one collection of poetry. *Proud Shoes* (1956) chronicles the story of her maternal grandparents Robert and Cornelia Fitzgerald who raised her, the former a free African American man from Chester County, Pennsylvania, who came to North Carolina during Reconstruction as a teacher devoted to educating the newly freed slaves, and the latter the offspring of a slave woman named Harriet and her owner, Sidney Smith, a member of a prominent Orange County family, who raped her repeatedly. Later Sidney's brother Frank would claim Harriet for himself and produce three more daughters. Mary Ruffin Smith, the Smith brothers' unmarried sister, raised eyebrows when she took the girls into her household, brought them up much differently than other Smith slaves, including instilling in them a sense of their aristocratic blood, and bequeathing each of them substantial parcels of land upon her death. The book is a milestone, not only for its recounting of the success of an African American family during Reconstruction and the early twentieth century but also for the way it tells the national story of America's tangled race relations and racial identities; it makes a worthy companion to Harriet Jacobs's *Incidents in the Life of a Slave Girl*. In 1987, two years after her death, *Song in a Weary Throat: An American Pilgrimage*, her own autobiography she was working on with editors up to the time of her death, was published. The autobiography recounts Murray's awakening to both racial and gender inequities and eloquently explains how she shaped herself into the civil rights' activist and feminist she became. Murray also published one volume of poetry, *Dark Testament and Other Poems* (1970), which has largely been neglected but deserves greater attention. The collection can be characterized as containing a significant number of poems that speak to racial and economic injustices as well as a section of beautiful, striking, and conflicted love poems that are particularly intriguing, especially in light of the struggles Murray underwent in the 1930s and 1940s with her gender identity and sexuality, when most of the love poems were written. Murray found herself emotionally and sexually drawn to women but was unable to accept lesbianism as a respectable identity. Her distress over her attractions to women and her deep belief that she was really biologically a man resulted in several psychiatric hospital stays and finally abdominal surgery to assure her that she did not have "hidden" male sex organs. Following this surgery, Murray seems to have relinquished her struggle over her gender and sexuality and turned her energies toward her work; nonetheless, the love poems are significant for they can be read as helping to establish an African American lesbian tradition in poetry brought to fruition in the work of such writers as Audre Lorde, June Jordan, and Pat Parker.

CRITICAL RECEPTION

Murray's literary texts garnered some critical attention at the times of their publications. *Proud Shoes*, especially, received glowing reviews from major newspapers, including the *New York Times*; a reviewer from the *New York Herald Tribune* deemed *Proud Shoes* more than "a family chronicle . . . [it is] a personal memoir, it is history, it is biography, and it is also a story that, at its best, is dramatic enough to satisfy the demands of fiction. It is written in anger, but without hatred; in affection, but without pathos and tears; and in humor that never becomes extravagant" (quoted in *Song* 311). *Song in a Weary Throat* won the Lillian Smith Award in 1987, was widely and positively reviewed, and was later reprinted by the University of Tennessee Press as *Pauli Murray: The Autobiography of a Black Activist, Feminist, Lawyer, Priest, and Poet*. *Dark Testament and Other Poems* received the least critical attention and, unfortunately, is currently out of print. Lately, Murray has been receiving more scholarly attention. Several dissertations on Murray were completed in the 1990s, and one of those, by Darlene O'Dell has been revised into a book titled *Sites of Southern Memory: The Autobiographies of Katherine Dupre Lumpkin, Lillian Smith, and Pauli Murray*. Most notably, in 2002, the *Journal of Women's History* devoted a section of seven short articles on Murray to encourage, as the editor of the section notes, "readers to take up the story where we left off, and enter into their own personal journeys of discovery and appreciation of Pauli Murray's multifaceted life" (56). Ware also notes that several of the writers who contributed are at work on longer pieces on Murray, including biographies (54), which indicates that there are even more studies on Murray to come. Christina Bucher's recent article on Murray's much-neglected poetry seeks to revive interest in her poems as valuable contributions to the protest tradition of African American poetry.

BIBLIOGRAPHY

Works by Pauli Murray

The Constitution and Government of Ghana. With Leslie Maxwell. London: Sweet & Maxwell, 1961.
Dark Testament and Other Poems. Norwalk, CT: Silvermine, 1970.
Pauli Murray: The Autobiography of a Black Activist, Feminist, Lawyer, Priest, and Poet. 1987. Reprint, Knoxville: University of Tennessee Press, 1989.
Proud Shoes: The Story of An American Family. 1956. Reprint, Boston: Beacon Press, 1999.
Song in a Weary Throat: An American Pilgrimage. New York: Harper & Row, 1987.
States' Laws on Race and Color. 1955. Reprint, Athens: University of Georgia Press, 1997.

Studies of Pauli Murray's Works

Bucher, Christina G. "Pauli Murray: A Case for the Poetry." *North Carolina Literary Review* 13 (2004): 59–73.
"Dialogue: Pauli Murray's Notable Connections." Introduction by Caroline Ware. *Journal of Women's History* 14.2 (2002): 54–86.
Drury, Doreen Marie. "'Experimentation on the Male Side': Race, Class, Gender, and Sexuality in Pauli Murray's Quest for Love and Identity, 1910–1960." Ph.D. diss., Boston University, 2000.
Humez, Jean M. "Pauli Murray's Histories of Loyalty and Revolt." *Black American Literature Forum* 24.2 (1990): 315–35.
McKay, Nellie. "Pauli Murray." In *African American Poets Since 1955 DLB 41*, edited by Trudier Harris and Thadious M. Davis, 248–51. Detroit: Gale Research, 1985.
O'Dell, Darlene. *Sites of Southern Memory: The Autobiographies of Katherine Du Pre Lumpkin, Lillian Smith, and Pauli Murray.* Charlottesville: University of Virginia Press, 2001.
Roses, Lorraine Elena, and Ruth Elizabeth Randolph. *Harlem Renaissance and Beyond: Literary Biographies of 100 Black Women Writers 1900–1945.* Boston: G. K. Hall, 1990.

Christina G. Bucher

GLORIA NAYLOR (1950–)

BIOGRAPHICAL NARRATIVE

Novelist Gloria Naylor was born in 1950 in New York City. Her father was a transit worker; her mother was a telephone operator. Although Naylor grew up in an urban area, she had deep roots in the south since her parents had worked as sharecroppers in Robinsonville, Mississippi. Naylor's parents emigrated from rural Mississippi to north the year before her birth. She inherited her mother's love for books, and from a very young age, she was an avid reader.

In 1963, her family moved to Queens, where Naylor became aware of racism. Gloria was a shy and introverted child. The love of the written word kept her spirits thriving. She wrote her thoughts in a diary while growing up. Her love of reading and writing grew during her high school years when she was exposed to many classics. Naylor graduated high school in 1968. Martin Luther King, Jr., was assassinated that year, and that event had a great impact on her; as a result, she followed in her mother's footsteps and became a Jehovah's Witnesses missionary. For the next seven years, she traveled the country preaching. The Jehovah's Witnesses role made her come out of her shell and offered her an opportunity for community service and travel.

In 1975, Naylor began attending Brooklyn College. From 1975 to 1981, she worked full-time as a switchboard operator, while pursuing writing and her college education. During this time she became familiar with the vast body of African American literature and discovered feminism. She read Toni Morrison's novel *The Bluest Eye* in 1977. It was the very first book she read that was written by an African American woman author. Reading it gave her an inspiration to tell the stories of the world that she knew.

Naylor's early attempts at writing were immediately successful. One of her first short stories was published in *Essence* magazine. She graduated with a Bachelor of Arts degree in English from Brooklyn College in 1981. That same year she completed her first novel *The Women of Brewster Place*. She traveled to Spain and Tangiers during that summer. On her return, she began graduate work in Afro-American Studies at Yale University. In 1983, she graduated with a Master of Arts degree. That same year she received the American Book Award for the Best First Novel for *The Women of Brewster Place*. She served as the writer-in-residence at Cummington Community of the Arts, and as a visiting lecturer at George Washington University. Naylor has continued to receive awards and honors, including fellowships from both the National Endowment for the Arts (NEA) and the Guggenheim Foundation. Naylor next published *Linden Hills* (1985), *Mama Day* (1987), *Bailey's Café* (1992), and *The Men of Brewster Place* (1998). In addition to her novels, Naylor has also written essays and screenplays, as well as the stage adaptation of *Bailey's Café*. In 1989, *The Women of Brewster Place* was made into a television movie starring Oprah Winfrey. Naylor also founded "One Way Productions," an independent film company.

MAJOR WORKS

Naylor's first four novels—*The Women of Brewster Place*, *Linden Hills*, *Mama Day*, and *Bailey's Café*—form a quartet, with the themes and characters from one novel appearing in another novel. In an interview with Diane Osen, Naylor said that she did not want to be a one-book wonder, like so many African American writers before her. She planned to write four interwoven novels. She said in the interview: "... I would write these four novels and think of them as a base, and then go on and build a career."

Naylor's first novel, *The Women of Brewster Place*, is a montage of African American womanhood. It celebrates the complex and diverse lives of African American women. The seven women of the novel manage to survive and support each other in an impoverished and dangerous neighborhood. The novel was critically acclaimed, received several awards, and was made into a television series in 1989. In a March 1989 interview with *Ebony* magazine, Naylor explains her motivation behind writing *The Women of Brewster Place*: "... one character couldn't be the Black woman in America. So I had seven different women, all in different circumstances, encompassing the complexity of our lives, the richness of our diversity, from skin color on down to religious, political, and sexual preference."

In the first few pages of the novel, Naylor offers readers a vivid portrait of the women whose lives she is about to explore in the coming chapters. She writes, "Brewster Place became especially fond of its colored daughters as they milled like determined spirits among its decay, trying to make it a home. . . . Like an ebony phoenix, each in her own time and with her own season had a story" (5).

The women of Brewster Place have all had decent upbringings, but, in almost every case, they ended up in Brewster Place as result of just one mistake that they made. In some cases that mistake was of having too much spirit. In the end each one of them rises above that mistake, conquers injustices to become a positive influence in the lives of other residents. Mattie Michael becomes an unwed mother as result of a youthful indiscretion and this marks the beginning of her downward spiral that brings her to Brewster Place. Independence and free spirit were Etta May Johnson's downfall, because "... Rutheford County wasn't ready for Etta's blooming independence." So she leaves, but she soon finds out that "...America wasn't ready for her yet—not in 1937." Kiswana Browne grows to be an independent woman who quits college to become a community activist. She believes that her place is among her people, fighting for equality and a better community. Her well-to-do parents live on Linden Hills and her brother is a successful lawyer. Kiswana brings the diverse community of Brewster Place together. Lucielia Louise Turner has an unsuccessful and temperamental husband, Eugene, who forces her to have an abortion, and tragically Ciel (Lucielia) loses her only daughter to an illness. Again, it is Mattie who nurses Ciel back to life. Cora Lee, a woman who is emotionally just a child, continues to bear children fathered by a series of useless men, and continues to treat the babies like dolls. She only likes men because they continue to provide her with babies. When Kiswana takes her to see an African American production of Shakespeare in the park, Cora Lee is almost inspired to become active and change her life, and, yet in the end, she accepts the "... the shadow, who has let himself in with his key." Lorraine and Theresa are two lesbian partners who have had to keep moving to find a place that will accept them. Brewster Place is not very accepting of their relationship either. In a stark contrast to the rebirth and hope of the stories of the other ladies, their story ends in death and destruction. Lorraine is gang raped by the neighborhood hoodlums and in the aftermath of that event kills Ben, the resident caretaker of Brewster Place.

Linden Hills portrays a world of economically successful African Americans and the hidden price of that success. The novel is loosely modeled after Dante's *Inferno*. The nine circles of hell from *Inferno* become the crescents of *Linden Hills*. Naylor allegorizes Dante's narrative journey through hell, in a similar journey by Willie and Lester through Linden Hills. In an interview with Angels Carabi, Naylor said she wanted to "look at what happens to black Americans when they move up in America's society. They first lose family ties . . . then there are the community ties. You can create a whole different type of community around you—mostly of a mixture of other professional, middle-class people—but you lose the ties with your spiritual or religious valuesb" (38). This is exactly what happens to many residents of Linden Hills.

Luther Nedeed immigrates to Wayne County from Tupelo, Mississippi. He is sold a useless piece of land by the white landowners of the town. But Luther Nedeed is a resourceful and determined man. He becomes the undertaker for the town, and soon creates a small fortune for himself and his descendents. The five generations of the Nedeed family are the new oppressors of the African American community.

In *Mama Day* Naylor narrates the love story of two people from two different backgrounds. George is an orphan from the urban north and Cocoa is a young woman, coddled by her mother Abigail and her mother's sister Miranda, known as Mama Day. Cocoa is from the rural south. In order to maintain an independent, black cultural identity, Naylor has created a fictional place called Willow Springs, which is not a part of any state. The only external connection to Willow Springs and the rest of the world is a few weakly built bridges, which are frequently washed out by storms.

After their marriage, George and Cocoa spend their vacation in Willow Springs every summer. During one of those vacations, Ruby, a jealous root doctor, poisons Cocoa. Cocoa becomes dangerously ill. George and Cocoa are stranded due to a thunderstorm that washes out the bridge from Willow Springs. George dies in the process of trying to help Cocoa. His death and Mama Day's healing powers lead to Cocoa's healing.

Bailey's Café explores female sexuality and male-female sexual identity. The structure of the novel is similar to the riffing in a blues or jazz song. Each character tells his or her own story which is echoed by another's story. Most of the storytellers are women who have suffered childhood abuse and are scarred for life as a result of that abuse. Each one ends up at Eve's Boarding House. Most of the characters of *Bailey's Café* have led isolated lives. Nadine, Bailey's wife, is a woman of few words; their relationship is missing personal affection. Sadie grew up alone and has lived through a lonely married life. She attempts to earn love by fulfilling everyone's wishes around her. Eve grew up with a doting grandfather, but as she began to show signs of womanhood, he became distant and as result she became emotionally isolated. Esther's brothers used Esther as an economic pawn. They sold her to an older man who performed unspeakable sexual acts on her, and kept her isolated in a dark cellar. Mary (Peaches) is beautiful but hates her mirror image because her beauty is her own prison and men want only one thing from her. Jesse Bell turns to heroin and becomes a lesbian when her marriage to the wealthy Sugar Hill King ends in a bitter divorce. The Ethiopian, Miriam, was subjected to genital mutilation and suffers through a virgin pregnancy. "Miss Maple" is the rich, well-educated son of a wealthy Negro family who becomes the transvestite housekeeper for Eve's Boarding house.

In *The Men of Brewster Place*, Naylor fills in the narrative gaps of *The Women of Brewster Place*, which was originally told from the women's perspective. Naylor returns to the same depressing block of city tenement housing. This time she focuses on the African America men of the struggling community. Each chapter of the novel highlights the life of one man. First, there is Ben, the alcoholic superintendent of Brewster Place. He is stuck with the impossible task of fixing and improving the failing architecture of Brewster Place. There is Autistic Jerome, whose mother wants to use his musical talents for financial gains and refuses to provide him with the institutionalized care that he needs. Also, there is Eugene, Ciel's husband; he is gay, married to Ciel, and a father. In addition there is Basil, Mattie Michael's son, who longs for children of his own and is trying to raise other's children. Also, there is Rev. Moreland T. Woods who wants a new church to glorify himself. Then there is Abshu (Clifford Jackson), a playwright and community activist. He hates greedy, politically ambitious minister, C. C. Baker. Additionally, there are the other men who gather at the barbershop to comment on the general state of the world.

CRITICAL RECEPTION

Critic Henry Louis Gates has noted that Naylor's first novel, *The Women of Brewster Place*, boldly returns to and revives "naturalism as a mode of narration and plot development." Annie Gottlieb of the *New York Times* writes, "Miss Naylor bravely risks sentimentality and melodrama to write her compassion and outrage large, and she pulls it off triumphantly." Sharon Felton and Michelle C. Loris, in *The Critical Response to Gloria Naylor*, summarize the five categories of scholarly perspectives addressed by Naylor critics. The perspectives are (1) Naylor's work as a product of an African American writer, (2) as an example of work positing a feminist or women's studies agenda, (3) as a focus of influence studies or intertextual comparisons, (4) as a study of narrative and/or rhetorical methods, and (5) as an exponent of popular culture. *The Women of Brewster Place* and *Bailey's Café* fall under the first category *Mama Day* and *Linden Hills* squarely fall under the category of intertextual comparisons, as a study of narrative and/or rhetorical methods.

In *Rewriting Shakespeare, Rewriting Ourselves*, Peter Erickson analyzes Naylor's frequent and systematic invocations of Shakespeare. Erickson points out that *The Women of Brewster Place* tries to recreate *A Midsummer Night's Dream*. Erickson further argues that *Mama Day* provides critical analysis of George's attachment to *King Lear*. He shows how the novel recreates *The Tempest*. For example, the title character is an African American female magician named Miranda, who is the matriarch of the island of Willow Springs.

Missy Dehn Kubitschek, in "Shakespeare, Morrison, and Gloria Naylor's 'Mama Day,'" points out that "[*Mama Day*] simultaneously appropriates and signifies on earlier texts to create its own idea of order" (79). She argues that by using voices from Euro-American as well as African American tradition, Naylor strives to create a new social order. Willow Springs is not part of any state, yet it is part of the country, with residents participating in the political process at the national level; thus, giving them freedom from smaller allegiances. Sapphira Wade is of "pure Africa Stock," thus her identity is not American. Kubitschek further argues that Shakespeare is invoked at many points in the narrative. The names of the central characters—Ophelia and Miranda—are from Hamlet. On his first date with Ophelia, George has to interrupt his reading of King Lear.

BIBLIOGRAPHY

Works by Gloria Naylor

Bailey's Café. New York: Harcourt Brace Jovanovich, 1992.
Children of the Night: The Best Short Stories by Black Writers, 1967 to the Present. Boston: Little Brown & Co., 1996.
Linden Hills. New York: Ticknor & Fields, 1985.
Mama Day. New York: Knopf Publishing Group, 1987.
"The Meaning of a Word." In *Language Awareness*, edited by Paul Eschholz, 305–7. New York: St. Martin's Press, 1994.
The Men of Brewster Place. New York: Hyperion Books, 1998.
The Women of Brewster Place. New York: Viking Adult, 1982.

Studies of Gloria Naylor's Works

Carabi, Angels. "An Interview with Gloria Naylor." *Belles Lettres* 7 (1992): 36–42.
Erickson, Peter. *Rewriting Shakespeare, Rewriting Ourselves*. Berkeley: University of California Press, 1991.
Felton, Sharon C., and Michelle C. Loris, eds. *The Critical Response to Gloria Naylor*. Westport, CT: Greenwood Press, 1997.
Fowler, Virginia C. *Gloria Naylor: In Search of Sanctuary*. Boston: Twayne Publishers, 1996.
Gates, Henry Louis, Jr., and K. A. Appiah, eds. *Gloria Naylor: Critical Perspectives Past and Present*. New York: Amistad, 1993.
Kelley, Margot Anne, ed. *Gloria Naylor's Early Novels*. Newark: University of Delaware Press, 2001.
Kubitschek, Missy Dehn. "Toward a New Order: Shakespeare, Morrison, and Gloria Naylor's Mama Day." *MELUS* 19.3 (1994): 75–89.
Whitt, Margaret Earley. *Understanding Gloria Naylor*. Columbia: University of South Carolina Press, 1999.
Wilson, Charles E., Jr. *Gloria Naylor: A Critical Companion*. Westport, CT: Greenwood Press, 2001.

Pratibha Kelapure

BARBARA NEELY (1941–)

BIOGRAPHICAL NARRATIVE

Short fiction writer Barbara Neely was born in 1941 in Lebanon, Pennsylvania, the eldest of three children. She holds a master's degree in Urban and Regional Planning from the University of Pittsburgh. Prior to her career as a novelist and short-fiction writer, Neely applied her graduate work to a position with the Pennsylvania Department of Corrections, overseeing development of the state's first community-based correctional center for women. Her efforts toward social justice are consistently evident in her executive, activist, and literary undertakings.

In addition to her work with Pennsylvania Corrections, Neely has served as director of a YWCA branch, executive director of Women for Economic Justice, producer for Africa News, cofounder of Women of Color for Reproductive Freedom, and host of *Commonwealth Journal* on Boston radio. Her first fiction publication appeared in *Essence* in 1981, and her short fiction continues to appear regularly in anthologies and magazines. Beginning in 1992, with the multiple-award-winning *Blanche on the Lam*, she has published four novels in her Blanche White detective series, for which she is best known. Neely's entertaining murder mysteries take refreshing liberties with generic conventions, not the least of which is Blanche White herself.

MAJOR WORKS

Building on aspects of the diverse personalities of her grandmothers, both of whom worked as domestics, Neely in her Blanche White detective series presents a protagonist who may cook and clean for other people but is never a servant. Blanche is a full-bodied woman who is full of sass, sexual sauciness, and spiritual awareness of her ancestors, and unmarried and childless by choice. Her resistance for societal norms such as marriage and reproduction reflects Neely's own. Blanche is unmarried not because she got no offers—she did—but because of her discomfort with the institution. She also planned not to be a mother, but her sister's death leaves her with a niece and nephew to foster, a situation which puts her in a position to demonstrate a broader notion of social responsibility through the nurture of young people not her own, but of her community.

The novels explore outsiderness, most obviously by having a poor African American woman as the central character, but also by including characters such as the developmentally delayed Mumsfield in *Blanche on the Lam* (1992) and the gay Ray-Ray and lesbian Mick in *Blanche Cleans Up* (1998). Neely creates opportunities to discuss additional social issues such as teen pregnancy, environmental poisoning, political corruption, and scandal, rape, and racism. Blanche does not function outside of these realities, untouched and detached. Rather, she finds herself guilty of assumptions, and the pregnant teen is her own niece, she lives in a neighborhood where children are sickened by lead paint in housing owned by absentee landlords, and she suffers from rape trauma, which she confronts in *Blanche Passes Go*. And as a dark-skinned poverty-class black woman, she encounters intraracial racism and classism in *Blanche among the Talented Tenth* when she visits a light-skinned upper-class enclave.

CRITICAL RECEPTION

Despite the societal issues Neely explores in her fiction, literary critics, for the most part, have overlooked it. One critic who has found merit in Neely's work is Stephen Soitos who admires Neely's meditation on "insidious internal prejudice" and applauds her creation of a setting that mirrors the economic and color conflicts in African American society. He points to her incorporation of "black vernaculars" and "hoodoo awareness" (233) as ways in which she adds dimension to the cultural reality in her books, and recognizes the significance of the resilient African American woman in these novels, defining what Neely calls the "pivotal role that older women play in society" (Cary). For Neely, "the mystery genre [is] perfect to talk about serious subjects" (quoted in Collette). But the talk is never prosaic and preachy. Blanche is a very interesting woman, a dynamic and entertaining character who lives in a believable world.

BIBLIOGRAPHY

Works by Barbara Neely

Blanche among the Talented Tenth. New York: St. Martin's Press, 1994.
Blanche Cleans Up. New York: Viking Penguin, 1998.
Blanche on the Lam. New York: St. Martin's Press, 1992.
Blanche Passes Go. New York: Viking Penguin, 2000.

Studies of Barbara Neely's Works

Bailey, Frankie Y. "*Blanche on the Lam*, or the Invisible Woman Speaks." In *Diversity and Detective Fiction*, edited by Kathleen Gregory Klein, 186–204. Bowling Green: Bowling Green State University Popular Press, 1999.
Cary, Alice. "Grandma Just Liked to Boogie." *Boston Globe* May 9, 2004, 3rd edition, City Weekly: 1ff.
Collette, Ann. "Damn, She Done It: Barbara Neely's Fictional Detective Fights More Than Crime." *Ms. Magazine*, June 2000. *Ms. Magazine* 2005. http://msmagazine.com/jun2k/books.html (accessed February 1, 2005).
Soitos, Stephen F. *The Blues Detective: A Study of African American Detective Fiction*. Amherst: University of Massachusetts Press, 1996.
Tolson, Nancy D. "The Butler Didn't Do It So Now They're Blaming the Maid: Defining a Black Feminist Trickster through the Novels of Barbara Neely." *South Central Review* 18.3–4 (Fall–Winter 2001): 72–85.
Witt, Doris. "Detecting Bodies: Barbara Neely's Domestic Sleuth and the Trope of the (In)visible Woman." In *Recovering the Black Female Body: Self-Representations by African-American Women*, edited by Michael Bennett and Vanessa D., 165–94. Dickerson. New Brunswick: Rutgers University Press, 2000.

A. Mary Murphy

DIANE OLIVER (1943–1966)

BIOGRAPHICAL NARRATIVE

Diane Oliver's literary production comprises six short stories. "Neighbors," her most recognized story, placed third in the 1967 O. Henry Award competition and was later reprinted in several anthologies. She was born in Charlotte, North Carolina, on July 28, 1943, to school administrator William Oliver and piano teacher Blanche Rann Oliver. She grew up within the southern African American middle class, attended segregated public schools, and entered the second integrated freshman class at Women's College (now University of North Carolina at Greensboro). Upon graduation in 1964, she became guest editor of *Mademoiselle* magazine and studied in Switzerland. She then enrolled in the University of Iowa Writers Workshop and was awarded a Master of Fine Arts degree posthumously, days after she was killed in a motorcycle-automobile crash on May 21, 1966, in Iowa City.

MAJOR WORKS

Oliver's first published story, "Key to the City," sketches the character point-of-view identification, which recurs in most of her stories: a relatively young female protagonist, either married with young children or single and the oldest child. "Key to the City" portrays a matriarchal African American family emigrating from the south to join the absent husband in the promised land of Chicago. Upon arrival, they discover that the husband has abandoned his family; the protagonist is so disappointed and bewildered that she tries to reimpose order in her family's life by sorting out their clothing bundles and ironing their Sunday clothes.

Oliver's second story, "Health Service," introduces Libby, a young mother whose husband, Hal, works "upstate," a euphemism for unknown whereabouts. The family reappears in "Traffic Jam," at the end of which Hal unnerves Libby by returning without notice.

"Neighbors," which takes place in Charlotte, North Carolina, quickly became Oliver's most acclaimed story, as suggested by Arthur Mizener: "It is hard to believe this beautifully conceived story was written by a twenty-three-year-old" (*Handbook* 28). Based on a true story of attempted high school integration involving one of Oliver's teenage female friends, Dorothy Counts, Oliver transforms the story to the elementary school and a boy named Tommy. The hatred from elements of the white community and the fears of Tommy's family erupt when their house is bombed the night before school is to start, resulting in Tommy's parents' decision to end the attempt to integrate Jefferson Davis School. Oliver moved the theme to the college level with "The Closet on the Top Floor." The protagonist, Winifred, also suffers defeat by withdrawing into her closet and by being withdrawn from the southern women's college she attempts to integrate.

Oliver's female protagonists must cope with personal problems as well as with the enveloping and often suffocating majority culture. Her last story, "Mint Juleps Not

Served Here," published posthumously, enacts a reversal of the "Goldilocks and the Three Bears" tale with an African American family of three ("bears") comfortably isolated in the woods of Forest Preserve. When a golden-haired woman visits, she, like previous visitors, is killed to preserve the Edenic home of the "three bears."

CRITICAL RECEPTION

Although only little scholarly work has been published, entries in *Cyclopedia of World Authors II* (1989) and *Oxford Companion to African American Literature* (1997) attempt to address the significance of Diane Oliver's work. Arthur Mizener's instructor's manual accompanying *Modern Short Stories* is the longest study of a single work, "Neighbors." In 1984, the South Carolina Educational Television Network produced a trilogy titled *Tales of the Unknown South*, which included a version of "Neighbors."

BIBLIOGRAPHY

Works by Diane Oliver

"The Closet on the Top Floor." In *Southern Writing in the Sixties*, edited by John W. Corrington and Miller Williams, 150–61. Baton Rouge: Louisiana State University Press, 1966.
"Health Service." *Negro Digest* (November 1965): 72–79.
"Key to the City." In *Red Clay Reader II*, edited by Charlene Whisnant, 17–21. Charlotte, NC: Southern Review, 1965. Reprint, *Calling the Wind: Twentieth Century African American Short Stories*, edited by Clarence Major. New York: HarperCollins, 1993.
"Mint Juleps Not Served Here." *Negro Digest* (March 1967): 58–66.
"Neighbors." *The Sewanee Review* 74 (1966): 470–88. Reprints.
"Traffic Jam." *Negro Digest* (July 1966): 69–78.

Studies of Diane Oliver's Works

Alvarez, Joseph A. "Diane Oliver." In *Cyclopedia of World Authors II*, vol. 3., edited by Frank McGill, 1141–42. Pasadena, CA: Salem Press, 1989.
Kratt, Mary N., ed. "Diane Oliver." In *The Imaginative Spirit: Literary Heritage of Charlotte and Mecklenburg County, North Carolina*, 77. Charlotte, NC: Public Library of Charlotte and Mecklenburg County, 1988.
Llorens, David. "Remembering a Young Talent." *Negro Digest* (September 1966): 88–89.
Mizener, Arthur. *A Handbook of Analyses, Questions, and a Discussion of Technique for Use with Modern Short Stories: The Uses of Imagination*. 4th ed. New York: Norton, 1979.
Smith, Virginia Whatley. "Oliver, Diane." In *Oxford Companion to African American Literature*, edited by William Andrews, Frances Smith Foster, and Trudier Harris, 551–52. New York: Oxford University Press, 1997.

Joseph A. Alvarez

BRENDA MARIE OSBEY (1957–)

BIOGRAPHICAL NARRATIVE

Brenda Marie Osbey, poet laureate of Louisiana, was born on December 12, 1957 in New Orleans, which serves as the geographical core of her work—a creative tapestry replete with rich cultural elements of her native place. Inscribed in her poetry and nonfiction are Louisiana Creole and New Orleanian traditions that resonate and capture the essence of this unique dynamic culture. Yet, while Osbey foregrounds New Orleans heritage and customs with a certain particularity, her work and the salient issues she addresses are by no means provincial but, rather, universal and far-reaching. This lends itself to Osbey's own experiences locally, nationally, and internationally. She earned her Bachelor of Arts degree from Dillard University in New Orleans in 1978; a Master of Art from the University of Kentucky, where she studied with Charles Rowell, in 1986; and attended the Université Paul Valéry at Montpélliér, France.

In addition to studying in various geographical locales, Osbey has also taught a range of courses—from African American literature to French language—at a number of institutions in New Orleans and elsewhere. At her alma mater Dillard University, for instance, she taught English, French, and African World literatures. She taught African American literature and creative writing at Loyola University, and was a visiting writer-in-residence at Tulane University. And, among other appointments, she has also taught African American and Third World literatures at the University of California, Los Angeles, and has been a scholar-in-residence at Southern University in Baton Rouge, Louisiana. Likewise, Osbey has been a fellow of the MacDowell Colony, the Fine Arts Work Center in Provincetown, the Kentucky Foundation for Women, the Virginia Center for the Creative Arts, the Millay Colony, and the Bunting Institute at Radcliffe College/ Harvard University.

In several respects, then, Osbey's work is largely experiential: infused with, enriched by, and reflective of not only her firsthand knowledge of Louisiana culture but also her vast experiences residing elsewhere: Kentucky, Virginia, California, Massachusetts, and France, to only name a few. What this has done for Osbey, and her work especially, is enable her to render her artforms—her poetry, characters, and nonfiction—in ways that are adorned with the rich symbolism, language, mythology, and traditions of New Orleans particularly, but along a larger cultural landscape and social backdrop.

MAJOR WORKS

Brenda Marie Osbey has published four volumes of poetry: *Ceremony for Minneconjoux* (1983, 1985), *In These Houses* (1988), *Desperate Circumstance, Dangerous Woman* (1991), and *All Saints: New and Selected Poems* (1997). Her first collection, a compilation of roughly fourteen poems, foregrounds black women—their voices, remembrances, and roots—in New Orleans, which, rich with its African, French, and Spanish heritage, also functions as a character in the text. With poems ranging thematically from love and madness to beauty and murder, Osbey conjures, much like her characters, stories of women—féfé and bahalia women—who, in their unconventional behavior, exhibit haunting power and, other times, a lack thereof. Stories of Lenazette, for instance, told by her daughter Minneconjoux, contain themes of love and death, while others, such as the one involving Ramona Veagis, deal with madness. Then other poems explore these recurring themes with regards to family: "Eileen," for instance, features a character that complicates the family ideal by, rather than showing them love and familial devotion, killing her "people" and waiting five days before going public to announce it. Consistent in this collection of poems, then, is women and their experiences, in all their complexity, on the bayous and streets or "bankettes" of Louisiana.

In These Houses is, as Osbey asserts, her first "planned" volume: that is, in preparation for the collection, she constructed and compiled timelines, photographs, genealogy charts, and landmark maps, which account for the detail and specificity in which she renders these poems. This collection, as did her first, also centers on women of African descent, exploring their various accounts, particularly with love, death, and insanity. In fact, some of the characters in her first collection become the subjects of the poetry of *In These Houses* as well. Divided in three sections—"Houses of the Swift Easy Women," "House of Mercies," and "House of Bones"—Osbey places emphasis on women and their relational aspects, both literally and metaphorically, to houses. Women, such as Thelma V. Picou, run naked into the street calling "freedom"; and, she threatens to kill her Darling Henry if he is in her house—which she misses rather than her children—when she is released. Ophelia, another unconventional woman, surrounds herself with flowers and beautiful things, reminiscing while in the infirmary about the lovers whom she has had and kept long dead. Other poems evoke blues lyricism, as is the case in "How I Became the Blues." While a number of these poems generally end with men dead at the hands or conjuration of women, Augustine in "The House" consumes rat poison, killing herself, and epitomizes a tragic blues genre.

Osbey takes her work into a different trajectory in her third volume *Desperate Circumstance, Dangerous Woman*, which is constituted by a single book-length poem. Comprised of twelve chapters and a glossary, it chronicles the experiences of Marie Crying Eagle and her lover Percy, as well as Ms. Regina, a conjurer and former friend of Marie's deceased mother. Set primarily in Faubourg Marigny, an early suburb or district of New Orleans, this work is infused with spirituality and hoodoo practices, as well as historical links to maroon communities—le màron—to which Marie learns she has familial connections.

In her 1998 American Book Award–winning *All Saints: New and Selected Poems*, comprised of three sections and twenty poems, Osbey continues her exploration of various religious aspects of Louisiana culture. She continues her focus on hoodoo and explores Catholicism, and its deeply rooted practices in Louisiana, which accounts in part for her title, "All Saints," which alludes to the Feast of All Saints. Osbey evokes Louisiana spiritual folklore and legend in "Mother Catherine" and the Seven Sisters of New Orleans, showing the coexistence and influences of hoodoo and Catholicism, as well as the ways traditional African-based religions impact spiritual practices. Likewise, Osbey pays tribute and homage to legendary musical figures and attributes her book title, as well, to the tendency to "deify" musicians and singers, who become almost god-like—hence her poem "The Evening News," which she writes to Nina Simone. She also infuses, in some of the poems of this collection, jazz and blues lyricism and celebrates these musical styles and their influences on New Orleans culture. In addition to exploring religiosity and musical forms and figures, Osbey memorializes the dead, who, as in the African tradition, has "life" and a connection to us long beyond the grave; and, in "Peculiar Fascination with the Dead," she shows the extent to which the dead are honored, celebrated, and ever present.

In addition to these published volumes, Osbey has written creative nonfiction on Buddy Bolden, the father of jazz, and rituals, death, music, and jazz funerals of New Orleans. Her work appears in a multiplicity of journals and anthologies including, but not limited to, the following: *Callaloo*, *Essence*, *Renaissance Noire*, *Southern Review*, *Literature of the American South: A Norton Anthology*, *The American Voice*, *The American Poetry Review*, *Georgia Review*, and *Creative Nonfiction*.

CRITICAL RECEPTION

Osbey has received numerous awards and fellowships for her work: the Carmargo Foundation Fellowship, Cassis France (2004); the American Book Award (1998); the Louisiana Division of the Arts Creative Writing Fellowship (1994); the New Orleans Jazz and Heritage Foundation Maxi-Grant (1993); the National Endowment for the Arts Creative Writing Fellowship (1990); the Associated Writing Program Poetry Award (1984); and the Academy of Poets Loring-Williams Prize (1980), to name a few.

While there is a paucity of scholarship on Osbey's work, some critical attention has been given to her publications in the following: *The Oxford Companion to African American Literature*, edited by William L. Andrews, Frances Smith Foster, and Trudier Harris; and *Forms of Expansion: Recent Long Poems by Women* by Lynn Keller. In "Sequences Testifying for 'Nobodies': Rita Dove's *Thomas and Beulah* and Brenda Marie Marie Osbey's *Desperate Circumstance, Dangerous Woman*—the third chapter of *Forms of Expansion*—Keller examines both Dove's and Osbey's appropriation of the largely Anglo-European epic to present the individual black protagonist's actions as representative of the group's experiences with historical and geographical specificity. Similarly, scholar Violet Harrington Bryan explores geography and culture, particularly Osbey's excavation of New Orleans history and tradition, in "Evocations of Place and Culture in the Works of Four Contemporary Black Louisiana Writers: Brenda Osbey, Sybil Kein, Elizabeth Brown-Guillory, and Pinkie Gordon Lane." Like Keller, Bryan's analysis of Osbey is comparative in nature, as well as historical, cultural, and geographical in scope.

In his coedited volume *The Future of Southern Letters*, John Lowe, in "An Interview with Brenda Marie Osbey," provides an insightful discussion with the author that foregrounds her experiences and illuminates her work. Interviewing Osbey in her New Orleans residence near the French Quarter, Lowe elicits responses that address Osbey's literary influences; the conditions in which she writes; how and why New Orleans and Louisiana have privileged positions in her work; and various other salient aspects that pertain to Osbey's life and literature.

Osbey continues to publish and discuss New Orleans history and culture, which is particularly pertinent and significant during the aftermath of Hurricane Katrina. Her work, like her long narrative poem, is far-reaching and should not be read solely within an individual local culture, but as representative of, as well as along, a larger social, cultural, and historical continuum.

BIBLIOGRAPHY

Works by Brenda Marie Osbey

Books

All Saints: New and Selected Poems. Baton Rouge: Louisiana State University Press, 1997.
Ceremony for Minneconjoux. Lexington: Callaloo Poetry Series, 1983.
Desperate Circumstance, Dangerous Woman. Brownsville: Story Line, 1991.
In These Houses. Middletown: Wesleyan University, 1988.

Essays

"I Thought I Heard Buddy Bolden Say." *Creative Nonfiction* 7 (Winter 1996): 33–48.
"I Want to Die in New Orleans." *American Voice* 38 (Fall 1995): 103–12.
"One More Last Chance: Ritual and the Jazz Funeral" *Georgia Review* 50.1 (Spring 1996): 97–107.

Studies of Brenda Marie Osbey's Works

Bryan, Violet Harrington. "Evocations of Place and Culture in the Works of Four Contemporary Black Louisiana Writers: Brenda Osbey, Sybil Kein, Elizabeth Brown-Guillory, and Pinkie Gordon Lane." *Louisiana Literature Review* 4.2 (1987): 49–80.
Keller, Lynn. "Sequences Testifying for 'Nobodies': Rita Dove's *Thomas and Beulah* and Brenda Marie Osbey's *Desperate Circumstance, Dangerous Woman*." In *Forms of Expansion: Recent Long Poems by Women*. Chicago: University of Chicago Press, 1997.
Lowe, John. "Brenda Marie Osbey." In *The Oxford Companion to African American Literature*, edited by William L. Andrews, Frances Smith Foster, and Trudier Harris, 555–56. New York: Oxford University Press, 1997.
Osbey, Brenda Marie. "An Interview with Brenda Marie Osbey." By John Lowe. In *The Future of Southern Letters*, edited by Jefferson Humphries and John Lowe, 93–118. New York: Oxford University Press, 1996.

Trimiko C. Melancon

PAT PARKER (1944–1989)

BIOGRAPHICAL NARRATIVE

Born to working-class parents in Houston, Texas, poet Pat Parker described herself in her autobiographical poem "Goat Child" as a rebellious tomboy. She declined a college scholarship so she could move to California, where in 1962 she married Ed Bullins, a playwright and Black Panther Party activist. She published her first poem (as P. A. Bullins) in 1963 in *Negro Digest*. By 1969 she had come out as a lesbian, and she soon became an architect of the lesbian-feminist movement on the west coast. Throughout the 1970s she performed her poetry around the country, often with Judy Grahn, with whom she recorded the album "Where Would I Be Without You?" (1976). Parker died of breast cancer at age forty-five and is survived by her partner and their two daughters.

MAJOR WORKS

By most accounts, Parker was the first African American woman to publish poetry openly as a lesbian. Her work addresses the intersections among the African American, feminist, gay, and lesbian communities and movements, challenging exclusions and oppression in all of them. "For the white person who wants to know how to be my friend" confronts racism, while "For the Straight Folks Who Don't Mind Gays But Wish They Weren't So BLATANT" similarly questions the limits of liberal tolerance. Both "Brother" and "Womanslaughter" address violence against women in the African American community, while "have you ever tried to hide" expresses both the racism in the women's movement and the tendency of African American women to avoid each other's gaze in groups of white feminists. "Where Will You Be?" her most frequently anthologized poem, demands that all gays and lesbians come out to fight the homophobia that threatens them.

Like her better-known friend Audre Lorde, Parker insisted on bringing all the parts of herself to her various communities, as articulated in her poem "i have a dream", an obvious riff on King's famous speech, the poem imagines a world in which Parker can safely be a lesbian in many "liberation fronts." The "Love Poems" section of *Movement in Black: The Collected Poetry of Pat Parker, 1961–1978* is similarly political. Parker counts as love poems the expected lyrics ("Let me come to you naked"), but also poems about homophobia ("My lover is a woman") and poems of women's solidarity ("Gente," "Womanslaughter"). Themes of love, oppression, justice, and liberation run throughout her works, from her first chapbook, *Child of Myself* (1972), to her last collection, *Jonestown and Other Madness* (1985).

Showing her roots in the Black Arts Movement, Parker's poems are written to be heard. Her signature poem "Movement in Black" was performed in five voices, usually herself and four African American women in her audience. The poem celebrates the achievements of African American women famous and unknown. Rooted in the African

American oral tradition, Parker uses vernacular language and form rather than what she considered oppressive "academic" diction.

CRITICAL RECEPTION

Perhaps as a result of her refusal to use academic diction, Parker's work was largely ignored by critics. Though the *Lambda Book Report* called Parker one of the "50 Most Influential People in Gay and Lesbian Literature" in the 1980s, most attention came after her death, when tributes were published in feminist and gay publications around the country, as well as in *Black Literature Forum*. Parker's poetry was always more favorably reviewed by African American lesbians than by others, to whom it seemed too strident. Reevaluating Parker's work after her death, Dympna Callaghan read her multiple positioning as a postmodern strategy. Barbara Smith and Pamela Annas both wrote about the importance of naming in Parker's work; Annas placed her in the company of Sylvia Plath, Adrienne Rich, and Audre Lorde. Despite the paucity of critical attention, *Movement in Black* has remained in print on and off since 1978, marking her lasting impact.

BIBLIOGRAPHY

Works by Pat Parker

Jonestown and Other Madness. Ithaca, NY: Firebrand, 1985.
Movement in Black: The Collected Poetry of Pat Parker, 1961–1978. 1978. Ithaca, NY: Firebrand, 1999.

Studies of Pat Parker's Works

Alexander, Ilene. "Pat Parker." *Voices from the Gaps,* August 13, 1998, http://voices.cla.umn.edu/vg/Bios/entries/parker_pat.html (accessed May 30, 2005).
Annas, Pamela. "A Poetry of Survival: Unnaming and Renaming in the Poetry of Audre Lorde, Pat Parker, Sylvia Plath, and Adrienne Rich. *Colby Library Quarterly* 18.1 (March 1982): 9–25.
Callaghan, Dympna. "Pat Parker: Feminism in Postmodernity." In *Contemporary Poetry Meets Modern Theory,* edited by Antony Easthope and John O. Thompson, 128–38. New York: Harvester, 1991.
Garber, Linda. " 'i have a dream too': Pat Parker." In *Identity Poetics: Race, Class, and the Lesbian-Feminist Roots of Queer Theory,* 63–96. New York: Routledge, 2001.
Smith, Barbara. "Naming the Unnameable: The Poetry of Pat Parker." *Conditions: Three* 1.3 (Spring 1978): 99–103.

Linda Garber

SUZAN-LORI PARKS (1964–)

BIOGRAPHICAL NARRATIVE

Dramatist, novelist, and screenwriter Suzan-Lori Parks is one of today's foremost American theater voices and in 2002 she became the first African American woman to win the Pulitzer Prize for drama. Born in Fort Knox, Kentucky, Parks grew up in a military family. Her father was a colonel in the United States Army and her family moved often. Her high school years were spent in Germany where she attended German schools instead of those provided for American military personnel. She began writing short fiction pieces during this period in her second language. Parks attributes this use of a language other than her native tongue as the reason she views language and specifically dialogue as both confrontational and tools of power. She received her bachelor's degree in English and German in 1985 from Mount Holyoke College and soon began writing for the stage after taking a creative-writing course at the school with James Baldwin. It was Baldwin that proposed she should write for the theater. On hearing the young writer read her work aloud, Baldwin predicted her prominence as a playwright. Parks, by her own admittance, knew little of the theater and found those involved in the field as pretentious and foreign to her. However, within Baldwin's class she began to *see* her characters and her stories as created in a dramatic form to be heard. She began to read plays, including those of Ntozake Shange and Adrienne Kennedy, which affected her perception of theatrical structure. She was awakened to the freedom of nontraditional dramatic form and theatrical experiment that would mark her work and also its controversy. Her first play, *The Sinner's Place* (1984), received honors at her college, but was refused a production due to its experimental form.

She went to London after graduating from Holyoke to study acting and within a year moved to New York City. Her second play, *Betting on the Dust Commander* (1987) was produced in a New York bar. However, by 1989 she was working for Off-Broadway and won her first Obie Award for the best new play of 1990 for her drama *Imperceptible Mutabilities in the Third Kingdom*. That same year, *Death of the Last Black Man in the Whole Entire World* was completed, and in 1992 her play *Devotees in the Garden of Love* premiered at the Humana Festival of the Actors Theatre of Louisville. She explored the assassination of Abraham Lincoln in *American Play* (1994) through a black carnival performer who plays the president in white face for customers who pretend to assassinate him. Perceived as her most Brechtian work, *Venus* (1996), directed by Richard Foreman, focused upon racism, sexism, and the deconstruction of African American history through the portrayal of Venus Hottentot's suffering within an early nineteenth-century freak show. The play opened at the Yale Repertory Theatre, then moved to the Public Theatre in New York City and won Parks her second Obie Award for the best Off-Broadway play. Her next plays, *In the Blood* (1999) and *Fucking A* (2000) explore the Hawthorne novel *The Scarlet Letter* and implode the meaning of adultery, class systems, poverty, and race within today's American culture. After opening at Public Theatre, *Topdog/Underdog* (2001), far more linear than her other work, moved uptown. It had been twenty-five years since words written by a black woman had been heard on a Broadway stage. Parks revisited the Abraham Lincoln myth within her Pulitzer Prize–winning play, which reconstructed history through the shadows of the African American journey. Her play, *Fucking A*, after many revisions, opened at Public Theatre in 2003 to critical acclaim.

Although best known for her writings for the stage, Parks wrote her first screenplay in 1996 for Spike Lee's film *Girl 6*. She also adapted the novel *Gal* into a screenplay for Universal and rewrote the screenplay *God's Country* for Jodie Foster and Egg Pictures. She authored an original television pilot for Kennedy/Marshall as well as the teleplay for the 2005 film *Their Eyes Were Watching God* based upon the novel by Zora Neale Hurston and produced by Oprah Winfrey's Harpo Productions. Her most recent screenplay *The Great Debaters* was cowritten with Robert Eisle, directed by Denzel Washington, and is scheduled for release in 2006–2007. In addition, Parks has written three plays for radio: *Locomotive* (1991), *Third Kingdom* (1990), and *Pickling* (1990). Her first novel, *Getting Mother's Body*, published in 2003, takes the narrative form of first-person monologues, which reveal her stage foundation but also her love of Faulkner's *As I Lay Dying*. A prolific writer, who is always challenging herself and experimenting in new fields, Parks is writing a musical called *Hoops* for Disney and a new teleplay, adapting Toni Morrison's *Paradise*. She has taught playwriting at Yale, lectures at leading universities, and currently is the director of A. S. K. Theatre Projects Writing for Performance Program at the California Institute of the Arts.

Parks has been the recipient of major grants from the New York Council on the Arts, New York Foundation of the Arts, the Kennedy Center Fund for New American Plays, TCG-Pew Charitable Trusts, Ford, Rockefeller, W. Alton Jones, Lila Wallace and Whiting Foundations. In 2001 she received the MacArthur Foundation Genus Grant and has twice been a National Endowment of the Arts playwriting fellow. In 1989, the *New York Times* named Suzan-Lori Parks "The year's most promising new playwright." She received a 2000 Guggenheim Fellowship for playwriting and in 2002 the PEN-Laura Pels Award for excellence in playwriting. Her professionally produced plays are all published either singly or in collections. Two of her collections are *The Red Letter Plays* and *The American Play and Other Works*. Parks is also a musician and songwriter. She plays the harmonica, blues guitar, and has studied cello. Her life in music is evident within her plays. After over a decade of residing in Brooklyn, New York, Parks now lives in Venice Beach, California, with her husband, blues musician Paul Oscher.

MAJOR WORKS

Parks is noted for her in-depth road map preceding many of the texts of her plays. She explains her nontraditional format and its musical sense to her readers often using diagrams and clues to unravel the significance of structure within the play. Using poetic language, nontraditional characters, and extraordinary images, Parks creates a work of dense structure that is often impenetrable for an audience. Her dialogue form is based in a repetition and revision style similar to the 1920 writings of Gertrude Stein. Removing herself from conventional dramatic structure, the playwright uses a jazz aesthetic, which necessitates that repetition always creates revision. Repetition also gives her plays a ritual sense. Her plays choreograph sound and silence creating a drama of language with few stage directions allowing the character and the word to be the primary source of theatricality.

Parks combines, what many African American playwrights have focused upon, the double consciousness of the black American, W.E.B. DuBois's sense of always looking at one's self through the eyes of others, with a unique form of ritualistic absurdism. Parks, unlike other African American contemporary writers, dramatizes the process of the self as an object produced by others, but also as an object looking in on itself. She creates a dual reality for her characters who are both subject and object. For example, in *The American Play* (1994), a reflection of the black identity, American history, and theatre, her focus is upon history, but not a history about race but more about historiography. Similar to Brecht, her concern is not our emotional identification with the character, but with a conscious awakening that there are larger societal dynamics operating and acting upon the masses.

Parks's theater is very different from that of her predecessors. In her own words she describes her play *Imperceptible Mutabilities in the Third Kingdom* as "African-American history in the shadow of the photographic image." The play is completely nonnaturalistic and each of its four parts is centered on theatrical metaphors. It possesses the aura of an African American and feminist protest drama, but is delivered through a fusion of Beckett, Ionesco, Fornes, and early Shepard. The program described the play as "an ensemble of actors move through four allegorical phases of African American history." Her work fascinates theoretical scholars who have claimed that in many ways her plays are more experimental than Adrienne Kennedy's, Robbie McCauley's, or even Anna Deavere Smith's. Parks further explains that a play for her is always "a blueprint of an event; a way of creating and rewriting history through the medium of literature." She enacts the process of remembering within her plays, but it is not the traditional history that she recalls, but that which has been forgotten or silenced. Parks feels that the theater "is the perfect place to *make* history, that is, because so much of African American history has been unrecorded, dismembered, washed out." Time is irrelevant upon her stage. The dead and the living simultaneously inhabit the same light. Progress and time are not linear in her dramas, often different eras and localities are play simultaneously, as she illuminates a world where the now is always haunted by the whisperings of a dead past. Parks begins her histories with what she calls a *fabricated absence*. As she explains, "It's the story that you're told that goes, once upon a time you weren't here. You weren't here and you didn't do shit. And it's that, that's fabricated absence." She simply fills in this hole with a created history for the African American, a history of what might have been, the imaginings of a people long absent, but always standing in the middle of the event.

Within *The Death Of the Last Black Man in the Whole Entire World* (1990) Parks combines DuBois's thesis (the sense of self and of race as seen through history) with a Locke form (something similar to ritualistic absurdism). The play is set in a theme park called the Great Hole of History, which reflects the black population in America. It is a history that is in reality an *absence*, because the national mythology or history has been created by whites. The play retains an African American content and theme within an absurdist structure and a ritualistic pattern of performance. The simplistic plot introduces Gamble, a thirty-eight-year-old forerunner of the civil rights movement who during the progress of the play is captured, enslaved, shipped, bred, raped, auctioned, and lynched by Europeans. The playwright replaces realism with absurdism. She uses an authentic African American nineteenth-century rural dialect and names her characters after stereotypical food: Black Man with Watermelon (Gamble) and Black Woman with Fried Drumstick (Gamble's wife). The theme of the play is that Europeans stole not only Africa's people, wealth, and minds, but also its history.

The use of an African American theme is not what sets Parks apart from other contemporary playwrights, but her structure and treatment of her themes. She divides the play into seven sections, beginning with the overture and followed by six *panels*. These divisions, though, do not follow in a cause-and-effect linear form but are episodes. The overture introduces the characters, plot, and subplots while the remainder of the play is divided into three duets and three chorus segments. Parks uses the duets for her dramatic power, which is personalized through the main sporadic plot line and then explodes the history by the object describing and experiencing its own death through a description of contemporary capital punishment. The chorus segments are rituals composed of repetitious sounds, puns, silences, and visions. Gone are the victims of the DuBois era. Parks portrays characters who are recreating a history, who observe that they are history and rejoice in their story and voice. In her essay "Elements of Style," Parks description of her characters states "they are not characters. To call them so could be an injustice. Instead, she says they are figures, figments, ghosts, roles, lovers maybe, speakers, maybe, shadows, slips, players maybe, maybe someone else's pulse. For Parks, form is not a passive thing anymore than language but is a physical and powerful means to communicate message and image.

Topdog/Underdog (2001) winner of the 2002 Pulitzer Prize for Drama is the story of two brothers, Lincoln and Booth, named so by their father as a joke. Lincoln and Booth's parents abandoned them when they were teenagers, and they live together in Booth's apartment.

Lincoln, the older of the two brothers, has a job impersonating Abraham Lincoln at the local arcade. Daily he works as the target for one of the shooting games. Booth, on the other hand, is a petty thief who yearns to master the con game Three-Card Monte. Booth remembers the success Lincoln had at the game before he gave it up for a more "respectable" job. The play's conflict is Booth's attempt to convince Lincoln to give up his arcade job and return to the hustle.

Fucking A, produced in 2003, is stylistically different from her 1999 *In the Blood*. The "A" on this Hester's breast does not identify her as an adulterer, but as an abortionist. Both plays center around an abused woman, but Parks's later play has no historical grounding. It is a parable about revenge composed in an epic, Brechtian style interrupted by dark songs sung by its characters. The playwright creates a world in which good boys are turned into monsters by oppression, and sexuality or fertility must be spoken of through a coded language, which is translated to the audience through over-stage screens. Parks depicts a world of invisible and dangerous power where imprisonment is arbitrary and engulfed with sadistic violence. She places her characters in an environment that breeds its own destruction and depicts her drama through an episodic and ritualistic structure. They are self-aware and simultaneously see themselves through the eyes of the other as they experience themselves as the other. Within this mythic fable, escape is impossible and returns the audience to the ancient tragedies of the Greeks, where bloodletting continues and endless repetition allows us to see a society turning in on itself and eating its own tail. The ghosts of the past haunt the play. Unlike the Hester of *In the Blood*, who admits her own fault and is created and destroyed by her society, this Hester in *Fucking A* is also created and destroyed by her world, but she pulls it down with her. Repetition does necessitate change as Parks once again evokes awareness through structure and ritual for her audience to view itself as butcher, hunter, and victim. In an essay titled "Possession," the playwright states that her task is "to locate the ancestral burial ground, dig for bones, find bones, hear the bones sing, write it down."

CRITICAL RECEPTION

Parks has been acclaimed and ridiculed by her critics. Working in a style poetic, postmodern, and her own, her plays have been described by theater historians as discontinuous postmodern ruminations of the black experience in American society (Brockett 572) or as "the most sophisticated plays in contemporary American theatre" (Hay 133). One critic, Abiola Sinclaire wrote of her second Obie-winning play, *Venus* (1996), *"Venus* is not absurdist, it's insulting and absurd." Many theater producers are uncomfortable because of her racial themes and advant-garde experimental structure that they assume will make their white audiences uncomfortable. A 1993 symposium on her work was abandoned by *Theatre* magazine because not enough African American critics were willing to participate, citing their objections to her politics. She herself admits that her plays are not for an audience that wants something simple. Her plays deal with the controversial issues of race and sexism and as Erika Munk states, "lends itself to connections and expansions, as images and wordplay flow along, inviting little riffs of interpretation" (Barnett 1443).

In 1988, *Imperceptible Mutabilities in the Third Kingdom* opened in a tiny theater in downtown Brooklyn. Usually missed by critics and audiences alike, the play immediately received a buzz as something completely new and visionary. Yale University's *Theatre* magazine stated the play contained "startling stage imagery and a lyrical sense of wordplay that has been scarce in American playwriting for ages . . ." (Barnett 1442).

A little over ten years later, a *New York Times* critic reviewed her play *In The Blood* at Public Theatre and stated, "You will leave *In the Blood* feeling pity and terror. And because it is a work of art, you will leave thrilled, even comforted by its mastery" (Barnett 1472).

Her Pulitzer Prize play, *Topdog/Underdog*, after opening in New York at Papp's Public Theatre fulfilled Baldwin's prophecy for Suzan-Lori Parks as she became one of the preeminent dramatic voices in American theater. August Wilson wrote that she was an original whose fierce intelligence and fearless approach to the craft subverts theatrical convention. *Fucking A* also received praise from her critics. Many stated that it was her best work and darkest to date, and, yet, controversy and critical conflict continue to surround all of her work.

BIBLIOGRAPHY

Works by Suzan-Lori Parks

The American Play (1994). In *The America Play and Other Works.* New York: Theatre Communications Group, 1995.

Betting on the Dust Commander (1987). In *The America Play and Other Works.* New York: Theatre Communications Group, 1995.

The Death of the Last Black Man in the Whole Entire World (1990). In *The America Play and Other Works.* New York: Theatre Communications Group, 1995.

Devotees in the Garden of Love (1992). In *The America Play and Other Works.* New York: Theatre Communications Group, 1995.

Fucking A (2000). In *Red Letter Plays.* New York: Theatre Communications Group, 2001.

Getting Mother's Body: A Novel. New York: Random House, 2003.

Imperceptible Mutabilities in the Third Kingdom (1989). In *The America Play and Other Works.* New York: Theatre Communications Group, 1995.

In the Blood (1999). In *Red Letter Plays*. New York: Theatre Communications Group, 2001.

Pickling (1990). In *The America Play and Other Works*. New York: Theatre Communications Group, 1995.

Topdog/Underdog (2001). New York: Theatre Communications Group, 2002.

Venus (1996). New York: Theatre Communications Group, 1997.

Studies of Suzan-Lori Parks's Works

Bean, Annemarie, ed. *A Sourcebook of African-American Performance*. London: Routledge, 1999.

Brockett, Oscar G., ed. *Plays for the Theatre: A Drama Anthology*. New York: Holt, Rinehart & Winston, 1988.

Drukman, Steven. "Suzan-Lori Parks and Liz Diamond: Doo-A-Diddly-Dit-Dit." In *Redirections: A Theoretical Practical Guide*, edited by Rebecca Schneider and Gabrielle Cody, 352–65. London: Routledge, 2002.

Elam, Harry J., Jr., and Robert Alexander, eds. *The Fire This Time, African American Plays for the 21st Century*. New York: Theatre Communications Group, Inc., 2004.

Elam, Harry J., Jr., and David Krassner, eds. *African American Performance and Theatre History*. New York: Oxford University Press, 2001.

Hay, Samuel A. *African American Theatre*. Cambridge, UK: Cambridge University Press, 1994.

Hill, Errol G., and James V. Hatch. *A History of African American Theatre*. Cambridge, UK: Cambridge University Press, 2003.

Ryan, Laura T. "Interview with Suzan-Lori Parks." *Post Standard*, December 8, 2005, 82.

Savran, David. *The Playwright's Voice*. New York: Theatre Communication Group, Inc., 1999.

Wainscott, Ronald, and Kathy Fletcher, eds. *Plays on Stage*. Boston: Pearson, 2006.

Wilmer, S. E. "Restaging the Nation: The Work of Suzan Lori-Parks." *Modern Drama* 43.3 (Fall 2000), 442–52.

Marla Dean

ANN PETRY (1908–1997)

BIOGRAPHICAL NARRATIVE

Novelist and short story writer Ann Petry was born to Peter Clark Lane, Jr. and Bertha Lane on October 12, 1908 in Old Saybrook, Connecticut. Petry was educated in Old Saybrook public schools and earned a PhG degree from the University of Connecticut School of Pharmacy in 1931. Upon graduation, she worked in family-owned drugstores until 1938.

Petry married George Petry in 1938, and they moved to Harlem soon after their marriage. Upon her move to Harlem, Petry began her writing career. She worked for several journalistic agencies including the *Amsterdam News* and the *People's Voice*. In 1939 her first short story was published. "Marie of the Cabin Club" was published in the *Baltimore Afro-American* under the pseudonym Arnold Petri. That story was followed by "On the Saturday the Siren Sounds at Noon" (1943), "Olaf and His Girl Friend," (1945) and "Like a Winding Sheet" (1945); all of which were published in the *Crisis* magazine. Although "Like a Winding Sheet is the more anthologized of the three stories, it was "On the Saturday the Siren Sounds at Noon" which brought Petry's writing talent to a major publisher's attention. A Houghton Mifflin editor advised her to apply for the company's literary fellowship after reading the short story. She did and won the fellowship in 1945. Her submission was the first three chapters of *The Street*. Houghton Mifflin published the novel in its entirety in 1946. *The Street* was followed by two more novels, *Country Place* (1947) and *The Narrows* (1953). In addition, Petry has published four children's books, *The Drugstore Cat* (1949), *Harriet Tubman: Conductor of the Underground Railroad* (1955), *Tituba of Salem Village* (1964), and *Legends of the Saints* (1970); two essays, "Harlem" (1949) and "The Novel as Social Criticism" (1950); a collection of short stories, *Miss Muriel and Other Short Stories* (1971) and five poems.

Petry and her husband returned to Old Saybrook in 1947, where she resided until her death in 1997. Their daughter, Elizabeth, was born in 1949.

MAJOR WORKS

The Street is Petry's most well-known work. Set in the 1940s, it is the story of Lutie Johnson, a well-meaning woman who seeks a better life for herself and her son, Bub. Lutie believes the best place for this is New York City. She leaves her job and husband behind in Old Saybrook and moves into a three room apartment in Harlem. Despite their less than suitable living conditions, Lutie continues to believe that she can have a good life in Harlem. Like Benjamin Franklin whose story serves as her inspiration, Lutie believes that as long as she works hard, she will be successful. She fails to realize, however, that she is a single mother who lives in a society that is socially and economically oppressive to African Americans. A chain of events, however, cause Lutie's ideal life to spiral out of control: the tenement superintendent attempts to rape her, her son is arrested, and she kills the local bandleader. Realizing that she will never achieve her goal, she leaves New York and her son.

Petry's remaining two novels examine social issues. *Country Place* examines class and gender as it is observed and experienced by a white World War II veteran in smalltown New England. Race is the focus of *The Narrows*; an interracial love affair between a black man and a white woman provide the novel's plot.

Petry's most popular short stories are "Like a Winding Sheet" and "Miss Muriel." "Like a Winding Sheet" is the story of an African American male, Johnson, who succumbs to the racial and societal pressures he experiences daily. Johnson's life has become a meaningless routine over which he has no control. He describes it as "get up, go to work and come home." Finally, fed up with his situation, he violently lashes out at his wife. The story ends with him repeatedly punching her.

Better described as a novella, "Miss Muriel" is told by a 12-year-old narrator, who observes her family and community's reactions to the courting of her aunt Sophronia by three distinct male suitors: an older white gentleman, a working-class blues musician, and a fellow with effeminate mannerisms. During the course of the story, the narrator learns and reveals much about prejudices based on race, gender, sexual preference, and age.

CRITICAL RECEPTION

Petry's work has been well received. In 1946 "Like a Winding Sheet" was included in Martha Fuller's *The Best American Short Stories*. Fuller also dedicated the collection to Petry. *The Street* is the first novel by an African American to sell more than a million copies. Her work, especially *The Street,* has been described as naturalistic. Petry's writing style is often compared to naturalist writers Richard Wright and Ralph Ellison. For example, in her essay "This Strange Communion: Surveillance and Spectatorship in Ann Petry's *The Street*," Heather Hicks articulates that Wright and Ellison's work can be used to illuminate central concerns in *The Street*, that of the dynamics of spectatorship and surveillance. Petry's work has also been hailed by the feminist pact. *The Street*, *Country Place* and *The Narrows* are described as feminist texts. In "Women in the Novels of Ann Petry," Thelma Shinn claims that in both *The Narrows* and *The Street* Petry creates women who might be characterized as feminist.

Petry's work continues to be the subject of criticism. Most recently, William Scott argues that "*The Street* should be read as a story not just about one woman's subjugation and degradation by forces beyond her control but as a story about acts of material resistance as well as the various forms that this resistance may take in an apparently hopeless and predetermined environment" (93).

BIBLIOGRAPHY

Works by Ann Petry

Country Place. Madison, NJ: Chatham Bookseller, 1971.
The Drugstore Cat. Boston: Beacon Press, 1988.
Harriet Tubman: Conductor on the Underground Railroad. New York: Collins, 1996.
Legends of the Saints. New York: Thomas Y. Crowell Company, 1970.
Miss Muriel and Other Stories. Boston: Mariner Books, 1999.
The Narrows. Boston: Mariner Books, 1999.

The Street. Boston: Mariner Books, 1998.
Tituba of Salem Village. New York: Harper Trophy, 1991.

Studies of Ann Petry's Work

Barrett, Lindon. "Further Figures of Violence: *The Street* in the U.S. Landscape." *Blackness and Value: Seeing Double*, 94–128. Cambridge: Cambridge University Press, 1999.

Bernard, Emily. "Raceless Writing and Difference: Ann Petry's Country Place and the African-American Literary Canon." *Studies in American Fiction* 33.1 (Spring 2005): 87–117.

Drake, Kimberly. "Women on the Go: Blues, Conjure and Other Alternatives to Domesticity in Ann Petry's *The Street* and *The Narrows*. *Arizona Quarterly: A Journal of American Literature, Culture, and Theory* 54.1 (Spring 1998): 65–90.

Gross, Theodore L. "An Petry: The Novelist as social Critic." *Black Fiction: New Studies in the Afro-American Novel Since 1945*, 41–53. Edited by. A. Robert Lee. New York: Barnes & Noble, 1980.

Henderson, Carol E. "The Walking Wounded: Rethinking Black Women's Identity in Ann Petry's *The Street*." *MFS: Modern Fiction Studies* 46.4 (Winter 2000): 849–67.

Hicks, Heather. "This Strange Communion: Surveillance and Spectatorship in Ann Petry's *The Street*." *African American Review* 37.1 (2003): 21–37.

Holladay, Hilary. *Ann Petry*. New York: Twayne, 1996.

Lucy, Robin. "Fables of the Reconstruction: Black Women on the Domestic Front in Ann Petry's World War II Fiction." *CLA Journal* 49.1 (Sept 2005): 1–27.

McBride, Kecia Driver. "Fear, Consumption and Desire: Naturalism and Ann Petry's *The Street*." *Twisted from the Ordinary: Essays on American Literary Naturalism*, 304–22. Edited by Mary E. Papke. Knoxville: University of Tennessee Press, 2003.

McKay, Nellie Y. "Ann Petry's *The Street* and *The Narrows*: A Study of the Influence of class, race and Gender on Afro-American Women's Lives." *Women and War: The Changing Status of American Women from the 1930s to the 1950s*, 127–140. Edited by Maria Diedrich and Dorothea Hornung-Fischer. New York: Berg, 1990.

Pryse, Marjorie. "Pattern Against the Sky: Deism and Motherhood in Ann Petry's *The Street*." *Conjuring: Black Women, Fiction and Literary Tradition*, 116–31. Edited by Marjorie Pryse and Hortense J. Spillers. Bloomington: Indiana University Press, 1985.

Scott, William. "Material Resistance and the Agency of the Body in Ann Petry's *The Street*." *American Literature: A Journal of Literary History, Criticism, and Bibliography* 78.1 (Mar 2006): 89–116.

Washington, Gladys. "A World Made Cunningly: A Closer Look at Ann Petry's Short Fiction." *CLA Journal* 30 (Sept 1986): 14–29.

Yolanda Williams Page

ANN PLATO (1820?–1860)

BIOGRAPHICAL NARRATIVE

There are few known details about the life of nineteenth-century poet Ann Plato. It is known that Ann Plato was a free African American who lived in Hartford, Connecticut. Ann Plato was also an essayist and schoolteacher who described herself as a pious woman of modest worth. It is also known that Plato was a member of the Talcott Street Congregational Church.

Ann Plato held education in high regard and stated that "a good education is that which prepares us for our future sphere of action" (*Essays*). Plato taught in the Elm Street School, a school designed by the A.M.E. Zion Church in Hartford, Connecticut. The school, housed in the basement area of the church, allowed African American children the possibility of going to school without harassment from white schoolmates. The church also served as a gathering spot for a vibrant African American writing community in Hartford, Connecticut. Currently, Trinity College offers an Ann Plato Fellowship for underrepresented students working on a dissertation.

There are no records of Plato's life after 1845.

MAJOR WORK

Essays; Including Biographies and Miscellaneous Pieces in Prose and Poetry is Plato's only known publication. The book contains sixteen short essays, four biographical sketches, and twenty poems.

Plato's writing is conceptualized as taking on a motif of romantic escapism. The genre of romantic escapism is especially known for its emphasis on the idea of natural religion—for presenting writings that offer nature as a way of exploring notions of subjectivity via an extended metaphor. Plato's biographical sketches, for example, focus on the piety of four women (Louisa Sebury, Julia Ann Pell, Eliza Loomis Sherman, and Elizabeth Low) who resided in Hartford and died at an early age. These women, according to Plato, were pious because they all died in the bosom of the Christian faith. The notion of natural religion is further conceptualized in a section of the text titled *Lessons from Nature*. In this section, Plato states, "I confessed that I knew naught of knowledge, save that which I learned of the violets that grew, and the lily which appears from the vale, and the vines which clime my father's bowers. I was ashamed, and felt that I had need to be taught of nature; and I yet wished to turn from the wild scenery around, and look into the moral and intellectual views of mankind" (*Essays*). Other concepts explored in this text include: benevolence, obedience, the death of the Christian, and reflections of life upon death.

CRITICAL RECEPTION

Since there is little information regarding Ann Plato's life and writing, there is a lack of critical response to her work. Nonetheless, Ann Plato is an important figure in literature, not only because *Essays* was the first book of essays published by a female writer and the second book published by an African American woman writer, but also because she represents a nineteenth-century female print culture "that gave primacy to everyday life and human connection, building networks of community—centered on women and children" (Gray, xxxii). Rev. James Pennington, in his preface for the text, states: "[M]y authoress has a taste for poetry. And this is much to the advantage of any one who makes an effort in this difficult part of literature. The opinion has too far prevailed, that the talent for poetry is exclusively the legacy of nature. . . . My authoress has followed the example of Phillis Wheatly, and of Terence, and Capitain, and Francis Williams, her compatriots" (quoted in Plato, *Essays*).

Ann Plato is also important to the history of women's rhetoric. Plato's work is thought to "attest to the gulf between rhetoric and reality . . . revealing the limitations of the cultural and social role of rhetorical pedagogy in its failure to address the issue of race (Xavier, 438).

BIBLIOGRAPHY

Work by Ann Plato

Essays; Including Biographies and Miscellaneous Pieces in Prose and Poetry. N.p.: Hartford, 1841. (Reprint). *Essays.* Intro Kenny J. Williams. New York: Oxford University Press, 1988.

Studies of Ann Plato's Work

Bogin, Ruth, and Bert James Loewenberg. *Black Women in Nineteenth-Century American Life. Their Words, Their Thoughts, Their Feelings.* University Park: Pennsylvania State University Press, 1976.

Brown, Hallie Q. *Homespun Heroines and Other Women of Distinction.* New York: Oxford University Press, 1992.

Clay, Katherine. *Spiritual Interrogations: Culture, Gender and Community in Early African American Women's Writing.* Princeton, NJ: Princeton University Press, 1999.

Foster, Frances Smith. *Written by Herself: Literary Production by African American Woman, 1746–1892.* Bloomington: Indiana University Press, 1993.

Gray, Janet, ed. *She Wields a Pen: American Women Writers of the Nineteenth Century.* Iowa City: University of Iowa Press, 1997.

Mossell, N. F. *The Work of the Afro-American Woman.* New York: Oxford University Press, 1988.

Williams, Kenny J. "Introduction." In *Essays; Including Biographies and Miscellaneous Pieces in Prose and Poetry.* The Schomburg Library of Nineteenth-Century Black Women Writers. New York: Oxford University Press, 1988.

Xavier, Silvia. "Engaging George Campbell's Sympathy in the Rhetoric of Charlotte Forten and Ann Plato, African-American Women of the Antebellum North." *Rhetoric Review* 24.4 (2005): 438–56.

Tinola N. Mayfield

CONNIE PORTER (1959–)

BIOGRAPHICAL NARRATIVE

Connie (Rose) Porter was born in New York City and raised in Lackawanna, New York. The eighth of nine children, Porter grew up in a housing project and attended public schools, both of which influence the settings and characterizations of her creative work. Porter earned her undergraduate degree from the State University of New York at Albany in 1981 and holds an M.F.A. in creative writing from Louisiana State University. She has taught English and creative writing at Milton Academy and Emerson College in Massachusetts and at Southern Illinois University at Carbondale.

MAJOR WORKS

Porter's debut novel, *All-Bright Court* (1991), received the *New York Times* Notable Book award and was selected by the American Library Association as one of the Best Books of 1991. Following the tradition of the African American migration narrative, *All-Bright Court* tells the story of Samuel and Mary Kate Taylor who, in 1959, migrate from the segregated south to the industrial north in search of economic opportunity and social equality. Samuel Taylor secures a job in a steel mill and the Taylors settle in All-Bright Court, a housing project in Lackawanna, New York, where they start a family and develop a strong sense of community with their neighbors. Faced with a variety of hardships, from the faltering steel mills and poor working conditions to social unrest and rioting, Samuel Taylor finds that the mythic dream of economic freedom and social equality "up north" is fragile and often elusive. Conscientiously avoiding sentimentality, Porter portrays both the decay of All-Bright Court and the crumbling dreams of its residents. *New York Times* reviewer Michiko Katutani praises Porter for "showing the reader the harsh reality of her characters' daily lives."

Porter is perhaps best known for her series of books for children about the character Addy in the Pleasant Company's "American Girls" historical series. The series features Addy, a young slave girl who escapes to freedom with her mother during the Civil War. The *Addy* series has sold more than 3 million copies and was voted Best Children's Series of 1993 in the annual *Publishers Weekly* Cuffie Awards.

In 1998, Porter returned her attention to the young-adult/adult audience with her novel *Imani All Mine*. The novel chronicles the tragedies and triumphs of 15-year-old Tasha, a rape victim and single mother of daughter Imani. Vividly told from Tasha's perspective in a nonlinear fashion and written in dialect, the novel depicts Buffalo's inner-city violence, frustration, and poverty in what *New York Times* book reviewer Andrea Higby calls a "story of great promise shining through monstrous obstacles." *Booklist* praises *Imani All Mine* as a "sad though ultimately hopeful novel, compelling from its very first page."

CRITICAL RECEPTION

Although Porter has received numerous awards for her creative work, was named a fellow at Bread Loaf Writer's Conference, and was a regional winner in Granta's Best Young American Novelist competition, her work has received no critical attention.

BIBLIOGRAPHY

Works by Connie Porter

Addy Learns a Lesson: A School Story. Illustrated by Melodye Rosales. Middleton: Pleasant Company, 1993.

Addy Saves the Day: A Summer Story. Illustrated by Bradford Brown. Middleton: Pleasant Company, 1994.

Addy Studies Freedom. Illustrated by Dahl Taylor. Middleton: Pleasant Company, 2002.

Addy's Little Brother. Illustrated by Gabriela Dellosso and Dahl Taylor. Middleton: Pleasant Company, 2000.

Addy's Story Collection. Illustrated by Dahl Taylor, Middleton: Pleasant Company, 2001.

Addy's Surprise: A Christmas Story. Illustrated by Melodye Rosales. Middleton: Pleasant Company, 1993.

Addy's Wedding Quilt. Illustrated by Dahl Taylor. Middleton: Pleasant Company, 2001.

All-Bright Court. Boston: Houghton, 1991.

Changes for Addy: A Winter Story. Illustrated by Bradford Brown. Middleton: Pleasant Company, 1994.

Happy Birthday, Addy!: A Springtime Story. Illustrated by Bradford Brown. Middleton: Pleasant Company, 1993.

High Hopes for Addy. Illustrated by John Thompson and Dahl Taylor. Middleton: Pleasant Company, 1999.

Imani All Mine. Boston: Houghton, 1998.

Meet Addy: An American Girl. Illustrated by Melodye Rosales. Middleton: Pleasant Company, 1993.

Studies of Connie Porter's Work

Anderson, Karen. Rev. of *Imani All Mine. Library Journal*, February 1, 1999, 122.

Biography of Connie Porter. *Literature Resource Center site.* Thompson Gale, 2002. http://infotrac.galegroup.com/ (accessed March 4, 2005).

Contemporary Literary Criticism, vol. 70. Detroit: Gale, 1992, 96–101.

Kakutani, Michiko. Rev. of *All-Bright Court. New York Times*, September 10, 1991, C14.

Pearl, Nancy. Rev. of *All-Bright Court. Library Journal*, November 1, 2000, 168.

Rev. of *Addy Learns a Lesson. Publishers Weekly* (July 5, 1993): 73.

Rev. of *Imani All Mine, Booklist*, April 1, 2000, 1449.

Rev. of *Imani All Mine. New York Times Book Review*, June 18, 2000, 28.

Rev. of *Imani All Mine. Publishers Weekly* (November 23, 1998): 58.

Tamra E. DiBenedetto

ELIZA POTTER (1820–?)

BIOGRAPHICAL NARRATIVE

Autobiographer Eliza Johnson Potter was born in Cincinnati in 1820. She was raised in New York, but little else is known of her childhood. While in Buffalo, New York, she married and she and her husband moved to Pennsylvania where her two children were born. This pattern of constant movement continued through Potter's adult life. She traveled to Canada before settling for a time in Cincinnati. A freewoman, Potter was arrested and imprisoned for helping a runaway slave find his way to Canada. After three months she was acquitted as a result of her impassioned speech to the court denying any wrongdoing in "rescuing the soul of an oppressed fellow-being" (Potter 19). Upon her release from prison she found work as a maid and governess and traveled with her employers around Europe. As her employers were "in high position, and possessed much public influence" (Potter 20), she was exposed to high society, once even witnessing the baptism of the Prince of Wales. While in Paris she learned the art of hairdressing, a skill that she used to support herself upon her return to the United States. Although she continued to indulge her "vagabond disposition" by moving from New Orleans to Saratoga to other fashionable resort cities, where her services as a society hairdresser were in high demand, she eventually settled in Cincinnati for at least six years, from 1856 to 1861 (Graber 215). It was during this time that Potter, after years of observing the habits and lifestyles of the wealthy, wrote her book. It caused a great deal of excitement when it was published because most of the people about whom she wrote were recognizable to the members of the society set, despite an attempt at hiding their identities.

MAJOR WORK

The significance of the year of publication of *A Hairdresser's Experience in High Life* cannot be overstated. In 1859 the United States was struggling toward Civil War, divided over the slavery issue. Given this context, it is unusual to read a story written by a free, educated African American woman. She was able to decide her own fate rather than follow the usual path of women in those days. Few people, male or female, African American or white, were able to travel as they wished, but Potter did so by supporting herself. Her book is more a critique of white society rather than of the slavery issue. In fact, at times she seems to use her voice to uphold the "unchanging and steadfast hierarchy among [white] classes" (Huot 354), preserving rather than questioning the idea of white superiority. Because of the intimate nature of the relationship between hairdresser and client, Mrs. Potter garnered a wealth of gossipy information about the people in high society, to whom she catered exclusively; it is this that forms the basis of her book. Nevertheless, the fact that she was able to publish her autobiography at all is remarkable. Because of her status as free, and because she does not allow herself to be fettered long by marriage and motherhood, she is able to decide for herself how to use her voice. She does not fill the traditional role of an African American woman suffering under the oppressions of society.

CRITICAL RECEPTION

Although *A Hairdresser's Experience in High Life* caused a stir when it was first published because of its exposé of white society, it is not generally well known. Despite her avowal that she detested slavery, Potter accords relatively little attention to this matter that was convulsing the United States, and for this her work has been criticized. Despite the book's lack of political influence, Sue Graber points out that it does shed light upon the context of Harriet Wilson's *Our Nig* (1859) and for Toni Morrison's *Beloved* (1987), which incorporates the true story of Cincinnati resident Margaret Garner, an escaped slave who murdered her daughter rather than allow her to go back into slavery.

BIBLIOGRAPHY

Work by Eliza Potter

A Hairdresser's Experience in High Life. New York: Oxford University Press, 1991.

Studies of Eliza Potter's Work

Graber, Susan. "A Hairdresser's Experience in High Life by Mrs. Eliza Potter: Cincinnati Society in the Mid-Nineteenth Century." *Bulletin of the Historical and Philosophical Society of Ohio* 25.3 (1967): 215–24.
Harlow, Alvin Fay. *The Serene Cincinnatians.* New York: Dutton, 1950.
Huot, Nikolas. "Eliza C. Potter." In *African American Authors, 1745–1945: Bio-Bibliographical Critical Sourcebook*, edited by Emmanuel S. Nelson. Westport, CT: Praeger, 2000.

Karen C. Summers

MARY PRINCE (1788–?)

BIOGRAPHICAL NARRATIVE

Mary Prince was born into slavery in 1788 at Brackish Pond, in Devonshire Parish, Bermuda, which was then a British colony. She grew up in the households of white slave owners such as the Darrels, the Williams, and the Prudens (Ferguson 49). Later, she was sold to Captain and Mrs. I——, at Spanish Point, and then to Mr. D——, in Turks Island. In 1810, she returned to Bermuda and lived there for eight years before she was sold to Mr. and Mrs. John Wood in Antigua where she met and married Daniel James, who was a free black carpenter and cooper. In 1827, she accompanied her owners to England and established connections with the Anti-Slavery Society in Aldermanbury in November 1828. Later, Prince refused to return to Antigua with her owners and was backed by abolitionist lawyer Thomas Pringle, the secretary of the Anti-Slavery Society. Shortly before her death, she told her story of the brutality and humanity of slavery in Bermuda, Turks Island, Antigua, and England to Susanna Strickland, a guest of the Pringles. In 1831, her story was published in England as a tract for the Anti-Slavery Society, and Mr. Pringle served as her editor and publisher (Paquet 28–29). Moira Ferguson describes Prince as "The first black British woman to 'walk away' from slavery and claim her freedom" and hails her narrative as "the first known recorded autobiography by a freed West Indian slave" (48).

MAJOR WORK

Prince's narrative, *The History of Mary Prince: A West Indian Slave, Related by Herself* (1831), denounces the exploitation, oppression, exile, deprivations, anxieties, and legal barriers against people of African descent in the diaspora. The story participates in the Pan-Africanist intellectual tradition of early black intellectuals by finding within racist contexts the legal, professional, and spiritual support that could help improve the conditions of enslaved Africans. Though it is a personal account, the narrative was relevant to the lives of millions of people of African descent of the diaspora who were direct victims of slavery, racial prejudice, classism, and sexism. Using the power of eyewitness and first-person's account, Prince describes the painful conditions in which the enslaved Africans in Bermuda and Antigua labored, revealing the immorality and brutality of slavery in the West Indies.

In order to protect herself from the violence of her owners, Prince devises tactics of resistance that draw on the strength of her black community in Antigua and Bermuda. Her first strategy is to build a family based on bloodline, gender identity, and racial solidarity. Her bloodline community is recreated when she seeks refuge from her mother after she is beaten by Mr. I——. The narrator tells us that when Prince was chased by her drunken master Captain Mr. I——, her mother hid her in a hole and brought her food at night certainly because of filial bonds but also because Prince was a young black woman whose life was in danger. Like her mother, Prince's father comes to her rescue.

The latter uses a pacifist strategy consisting of an appeal to the conscience of the slave owner. He says: "Sir, I am sorry that my child should be forced to run away from her owner; but the treatment she has received is enough to break her heart. The sight of the wounds has nearly broke mine" (197). This anecdote reflects Prince's ability to reconstruct her black family that slavery fragmented. Having being separated from her mother, two sisters and two brothers, Prince recreates her lost community on principles based on racial solidarity and gender unity. Her reconnection with her parents is a search for kinship that resonates the primordial importance that slaves in Antiguan society placed on family and community. In his report on the West Indies, Bryan Edwards confides that the African slaves shared a special spirit of solidarity and affection with each other, especially with people from the same countries as theirs (64–76). Through their bonding to protect their daughter from Mr. I——'s tyranny, Prince's parents exhibit this African search for unity.

CRITICAL RECEPTION

In their interpretation of Prince's narrative, many literary critics have represented the story as an individual's struggle against slavery and sexism only, overlooking the importance of African survivals and consciousness in the book. In *The Maroon Narrative: Caribbean Literature in English Across Boundaries, Ethnicities, and Centuries* (2002), Cynthia James writes: "Although she is of African descent, she [Prince] knows neither Africa nor African parentage, and can cite no African comparisons, traditions, and customs. In her case, the famous freedom narrative opening, 'I was born,' records a Caribbean parentage that opens its eyes on slavery as practice and tradition" (44). Later, James contends: "In addition to being cut off at root from her African legacy, Mary Prince knows the dislocated, loveless, and unstable existence of being moved from island to island" (45). James's thesis rejoins that of the Anti-African supporters who claimed that slavery and contact with Europeans were the only forces that shaped the traditions of the West Indian blacks. This Eurocentric perspective minimizes the complex ways in which African cultures survived in the Caribbean in ways that can be analyzed only through reinterpretation of Caribbean cultures themselves. Kamau Brathwaite states that "much of what we have come to accept as 'literature' is work which ignores, or is ignorant of, its African connection and aesthetic." (204). Brathwaite's rationale suggests the necessity for reinterpreting West Indian literature through new eyes. From this perspective, Prince's narrative becomes a work in which the author's individual achievements and resistance are connected with her search for an African Caribbean community that spiritually and ideologically influences her actions. To reflect the multiple sides of Prince's identity, Sandra Pouchet Paquet argues in "The Heartbeat of a West Indian Slave: The History of Mary Prince" (1992) that Prince's struggle in a brutal world must be understood as "an individual and collective state of mind. It is an ideology of survival and resistance. It is the well of being. It engenders a new literary tradition rooted in the values of a transplanted and transformed African community in the Caribbean" (142). While it is transformed to face new situations, the reinvented African community is not devoid of agency and hope because its resistance against oppression is inspired by age-old wisdom preserved in African and Caribbean folktales. This wisdom is apparent in the language, worldview, and search for community that Prince exhibits in her fight against racism in Bermuda, Antigua, and England.

BIBLIOGRAPHY

Work by Mary Prince

The History of Mary Prince: A West Indian Slave. Related by Herself (1831). In *The Classic Slave Narratives*, edited by Henry Louis Gates, Jr., 183–242. New York and Scarborough: New American Library, 1987.

Studies of Mary Prince's Work

Berrian, Brenda F. "Claiming Identity: Caribbean Women Writers in English." *Journal of Black Studies* 25.2 (December 1994): 200–216.

Brathwaite, Kamau. *Roots*. Ann Arbor: University of Michigan Press, 1993.

Edwards, Bryan. "The History, Civil and Commercial, of the British Colonies in the West Indies." In *After Africa: Extracts from British Travel Accounts and Journals of the Seventeenth, Eighteenth, and Nineteenth Centuries Concerning the Slaves, Their Manners, and Customs in the British West Indies*, edited by Roger D. Abrahams and John F. Szwed, 64–76. New Haven, CT: Yale University Press, 1983.

Ferguson, Moira, ed. *Nine Black Women: An Anthology of Nineteenth-Century Writers from the United States, Canada, Bermuda, and the Caribbean*. New York and London: Routledge, 1998.

James, Cynthia. *The Maroon Narrative: Caribbean Literature in English across Boundaries, Ethnicities, and Centuries*. Portsmouth, NH: Heinemann, 2002.

Paquet, Sandra Pouchet. *Caribbean Autobiography: Cultural Identity and Self-Representation*. Madison: University of Wisconsin Press, 2002, 28–29.

———. "The Heartbeat of a West Indian Slave: The History of Mary Prince." *African American Review* 26.2 (Spring 1992): 131–46.

Woodward, Helena. *African-British Writings in the Eighteenth Century: The Politics of Race and Reason*. Westport, CT: Greenwood Press, 1999.

Babacar M'Baye

NANCY PRINCE (1799–?)

BIOGRAPHICAL NARRATIVE

Little is known about the life of Nancy Prince aside from the record of her *Narrative of the Life and Travels of Mrs. Nancy Prince, Written by Herself* (1850). What is known is Prince was born on September 15, 1799, in Newburyport, Massachusetts. Though Prince was born free, her paternal grandparents were brought from Africa as slaves, and Prince identified strongly with their experiences. Prince's paternal grandfather, Tobias Worton, was also kidnapped from Africa as a slave, though later freed for his role in the Battle of Bunker Hill; her Native American paternal grandmother was also enslaved and later freed.

Three months after Prince's birth, her father, Thomas Gardner, died at sea. Prince's mother then married Money Vose, a former slave from Africa who had escaped from his slave ship as it docked in America. Vose made his living as a sailor for twelve years but died when impressed into service by a British privateer. Prince's mother was again a widow, now with eight children to feed. Though Vose was never kind to Prince or her older sister Silvia, his death marked a new era of deprivation for the family. Prince went into service to support her siblings, but soon overworked herself into illness. In 1816, Silvia entered a brothel; Prince and a cane-wielding friend traveled to Boston and removed her by force.

In 1819, Prince was baptized by Rev. Thomas Paul, giving her a new religious consciousness that would shape the rest of her life. Increasingly frustrated with caring for her siblings and her mother's "spells of insanity," Prince resolved to leave the country, marrying Nero Prince, a much older African American sailor journeying to serve as a guard in the court of the Russian Czar. Prince arrived in St. Petersburg in 1824 where she worked with a missionary society to sell Bibles and aided in the creation of an orphanage. She traveled the area around the city, learning several languages and observing local customs, and witnessed the disastrous flood of 1824 and the 1825 Decembrist Revolt.

In 1833, Prince left Russia to return to America, ostensibly on the recommendation of her doctor but possibly as a result of increased government repression. Her husband, who remained at the court, died shortly following her departure. Prince speaks little of the next six years of her life, but there appears to have been a period of personal confusion and financial deprivation. She attempted to found an orphanage in Boston in 1839, but the project failed within three months.

Feeling alienated from the American abolition movement due to a lack of roles for women, Prince set sail for Jamaica in 1840, eager to serve as a missionary and teacher to the island's many newly freed Afro-Jamaican citizens. In this stage of her travels, she encountered many obstacles, including pirates, civil disturbances, greedy locals, and even attempts to sell her into slavery. However, Prince saw these problems not as the fault of the Afro-Jamaican people she lived among, but of the corrupt system of slavery that raised them. Prince returned penniless to New York in 1842 and worked as a seamstress, saving to go into business. In 1848 and 1849 she suffered serious health problems, leading her to write her 1850 *Life and Travels* in hopes of supporting herself. Prince attended the Fifth National Women's Rights Convention in Philadelphia in 1854, and published a third edition of *Life and Travels* in 1856. No record exists of her life beyond this point, including of when or how she died.

MAJOR WORK

Prince published her *The West Indies: Being a Description of the Islands, Progress of Christianity, Education, and Liberty among the Colored Population Generally* while still working in Jamaica in 1841. Targeted to a New England audience, the sixteen-page tract describes the geography, fauna, and political history of the islands. Prince pays particular attention to criticizing imperialism in the West Indies and the institution of slavery, comparing it to England's unjust treatment of the Irish.

However, Prince is primarily remembered for her 1850 *Narrative of the Life and Travels of Mrs. Nancy Prince, Written by Herself*. Half travelogue, half spiritual autobiography, *Life and Travels* is one of the few autobiographical accounts of a free African American woman in the pre-war north. In her brief preface, Prince notes that she writes not from "a vain desire to appear before the public," but in an attempt to ease her poverty. Following the lead of Jarena Lee, Prince published her work at her own expense, becoming one of the first African American self-published authors. The book sold successfully enough to go through three editions in her lifetime (1850, 1853, and 1856).

Prince opens the book with an evocation of her ancestors, including a dramatic recounting of stepfather Money Vose's escape from a slave ship. Following Vose's death, Prince describes her family's destitution and her own efforts to care for her siblings, and later her mother as well. When Prince finally makes up her mind to leave the "anxiety and toil" of the United States behind, she marries Mr. Prince and departs for Russia. Prince gives surprisingly little detail about her husband or her life with him, omitting even his first name, his age, his history, and the year and cause of his death.

Instead, the Russian portion of her narrative focuses on two key events, the terrible St. Petersburg flood of 1824 and the 1825 Decembrist Revolution. In the first, Prince tells of her own dangerous experiences with the flooding and later with a sinkhole, and her efforts to aid survivors. In the second, though Prince implies that she witnessed some of the fighting personally, her narrative takes a broader view of the event, summarizing the action across the city and placing it in a historical context. She also describes Russian holidays and burial rituals with an objectivity rarely found in the travelogues of her day.

The second half of the text deals with Prince's experiences in Jamaica, especially her frustrations in her missionary work. Though she unblinkingly details the moral "corruption" of the Afro-Jamaicans that she meets, Prince observes repeatedly that she feels this corruption to be a result of the slave system, rather than inherent to the race. Prince also includes the text of her 1841 pamphlet on the West Indies, adding a subsection on miscegenation, mulattoes, and the Maroon people. On Prince's return voyage to America, the captain attempts to trick her ashore in both Florida and Texas in order to sell her into slavery, but fails due to Prince's vigilance. The narrative closes with the suggestion that "the world's pilgrimage" is the last of Prince's many voyages, and a reaffirmation of the trust in God that has guided her actions throughout her life.

CRITICAL RECEPTION

Long a neglected text, *Life and Travels* received little critical attention until the mid-1980s. Recent critics have focused on the ways in which Prince's status as a free African American woman shaped her narrative, particularly in her relationship to America as a homeland. Drawing on Paul Gilroy's model of the "black diaspora," Sandra Gunning analyzes Prince's role as "the quintessential black diaspora subject," closely tied to an African genealogy and dissatisfied with her American identity. In discussing how Prince subverts the conventions of travelogue and spiritual autobiography, Cheryl Fish similarly attributes this subversion to Prince's outsider status.

Given Prince's reticence to discuss her personal life, several critics have expressed interest in what she chose to leave out of her text. Ronald Walters examines how Prince evades discussion of racial pride, her marriage, and her childlessness, while Gunning and Darcy Zabel both speculate as to how the prolonged silences in the narrative may reflect abolitionist schisms that Prince could not openly discuss.

BIBLIOGRAPHY

Works by Nancy Prince

A Narrative of the Life and Travels of Mrs. Nancy Prince, Written by Herself. Boston: Author, 1850.

The West Indies: Being a Description of the Islands, Progress of Christianity, Education, and Liberty among the Colored Population Generally. Boston: Dow & Jackson, 1841.

Studies of Nancy Prince's Works

Fish, Cheryl. "Voices of Restless (Dis)continuity: The Significance of Travel for Free Black Women in the Antebellum Americas." *Women's Studies* 26 (1997): 475–95.

Foster, Frances Smith. "Adding Color and Contour to Early American Self-Portraitures: Autobiographical Writings of Afro-American Women." In *Conjuring: Black Women, Fiction, and Literary Tradition*, edited by Marjorie Pryse et al. Bloomington: Indiana University Press, 1985.

Gunning, Sandra. "Nancy Prince and the Politics of Mobility, Home, and Diasporic (Mis)-Indentification." *American Quarterly* 53.1 (2001): 32–69.

Peterson, Carla L. *"Doers of the Word": African-American Women Speakers & Writers in the North (1830–1880)*. New York: Oxford University Press, 1995.

Shockley, Ann Allen. *Afro-American Women Writers 1746–1933*. Boston: G. K. Hall, 1988.

Walters, Ronald G. "Introduction." In *A Black Woman's Odyssey through Russia and Jamaica: the Narrative of Nancy Prince*. New York: M. Weiner, 1989.

Zabel, Darcy A. "Prince, Nancy." In *Dictionary of Literary Biography: American Women Prose Writers 1820–1870*, vol. 239, edited by Amy E. Hudock et al. Detroit: Gale, 2001.

Dave Yost

AISHAH RAHMAN (1939–)

BIOGRAPHICAL NARRATIVE

Dramatist Aishah Rahman was born Virginia Hughes, but changed her name after a religious conversion to Islam. Rahman was raised in Harlem and became a foster child in her early youth. Her coming-of-age experiences and cultural influences during this time became the subject of her 2001 book, *Chewed Water*.

Educated at Howard University, she graduated in 1968 with a degree in Political Science, but began writing as a child. This love for writing eventually led her to Goddard College where she received her M.A. in Playwriting and Dramatic Writing in 1970.

Always interested in nurturing new dramatic voices, Rahman has worked at New Federal Theater as the Director of Playwriting. She is the founder/editor of *NuMuse*, a journal of new dramatic writings and essays published by Brown University where she has been a professor since 1992.

Rahman has also taught at Nassau Community College and Amherst College, and has been a guest artist at several other colleges and universities. Her plays have been performed at the Brooklyn Academy of the Arts, the Chelsea Theater in Brooklyn, Crossroads Theatre in New Jersey, the New York Shakespeare Festival, and several other regional theaters and colleges and universities. Her play *Transcendental Blues* was nominated for an AUDELCO Award. In 1988 she received the Doris Abramson play-writing Award for *The Mojo and the Sayso*. She also received a Rockefeller Fellowship in American Playwriting award and a fellowship from the New York Foundation for the Arts in 1988.

MAJOR WORKS

A prolific writer, Rahman is author of several plays and is widely anthologized and produced. In *Unfinished Women Cry in No Man's Land while a Bird Dies in a Gilded Cage*, Rahman explores the dilemma faced by young teens who find themselves pregnant, unmarried, and living together in a home for unwed mothers. The young women must decide whether or not to give up their babies, whether to accept the hard realities of being a black woman, or to dream of being rescued and redeemed by illusive boyfriends.

The Mojo and the Sayso, first produced by Crossroads Theatre and directed by George Ferencz, addresses the killing of a child and the response of the family and authorities. *If Only We Knew* is a one act that mirrors the Amadou Diallo killing by the New York police department. *Chewed Water* is a book that is autobiographical in nature and chronicles her life as a foster child and her life growing up in Harlem. It is a tale of abuse and triumph. *Plays by Aishah Rahman* is an anthology that features *Only in America*, *The Mojo and the Sayso*, and *Unfinished Women Cry in No Man's Land while a Bird Dies in a Gilded Cage*. Other plays include *The Lady and the Tramp* and *The Tale of Madame Zora*.

Many of her plays incorporate the use of music; rather than simply a background device, the music in her plays often echoes the rhythms of her character's speech. Music is central to the advancement of the story line, and becomes a metaphor for the struggle in which the characters are engaged. In the anthology, *Moon Marked & Touched by Sun*, Rahman states, "The jazz aesthetic in drama expresses multiple ideas and experiences through language, visual art and spirituality simultaneously."

CRITICAL RECEPTION

Although critical commentary of Rahman's work is sparse, what has been written about it is generally positive. About *Chewed Water* Azande Mangeango writes, "The vivid characterization of Harlem and the epic confrontations between foster mother and foster child give this memoir its drive and power. Whenever Harlem is foregrounded, *Chewed Water* explodes into magic. In large part, Harlem is the sweetener in this bittersweet tale. . . . In rich, lyrical language written in the cadence of jazz and blues, the pervasive music of her Harlem Childhood, this uniquely written memoir assumes its own shape. It is a mixed media event, narrative, dramatic and cinematic. . . . Aishah Rahman has written a masterful memoir that fills a void of women's voices in the literature of mid-twentieth century Harlem."

According to Margaret Wilkerson, *Unfinished Women Cry in No Man's Land while a Bird Dies in a Gilded Cage* is an underground classic. It "reaches beyond statistics and sociological theories to find the unarticulated, half-understood longings of teen-age mothers. . . ."

Joyce Meier writes in her critical essay, "The effect of all these voices is of an antiphonal interplay . . . that has its roots on jazz and in the call-and-response form of traditional African and antebellum music. . . . Rahman's five pregnant women (and their nurse) serve as a chorus, a response to the periodical 'call' of Parker's impassioned musical and vocal solos which are interspersed throughout the play."

Sydne Mahone critiques the importance of The *Mojo and the Sayso*, by stating

"Aishah Rahman uses the domestic drama as a launching pad for a highly imaginative flight into new dimensions of style. Her self-defined jazz aesthetic creates a dynamic of several genres including allegory, farce satire and myth, all of which culminate in this reinvention of the miracle play."

BIBLIOGRAPHY

Works by Aishah Rahman

Chewed Water, a memoir. New Hampshire: University Press of New England, 2001.
Plays by Aishah Rahman. New York: Broadway Press, 1997.
Unfinished Women Cry in No Man's Land while a Bird Cries in a Gilded Cage. New York: Drama Jazz House, 1984.

Studies of Aishah Rahman's Works

"Aishah Rahman," *Women of Color, Women of Words*. www.scils.rutgers.edu (accessed June 30, 2006).
Mahone, Sydne, ed. *Moon Marked & Touched by Sun*. New York: Theatre Communications Group, 1994.

Mangeango, Azande. "Broken Ancestry: A Review of *Chewed Water*." *Black Renaissance/ Renaissance Noire* (2002). http://www.highbeam.com (accessed September 2005).

Maynard, Suzanne. "Aishah Rahman. *Interview.*" www.brown.edu.

Meier, Joyce. "The Refusal of Motherhood in African American Women's Theater." *MELUS* 25.3-4 (Fall-Winter 2000): 117–39.

Wilkerson, Margaret, ed. *Nine Plays by Black Women.* New York: Signet Mentor Press, 1986.

Joan McCarty

ALICE RANDALL (1959–)

BIOGRAPHICAL NARRATIVE

Presently the only African American woman ever to write a number-one country song, Alice Randall is also a novelist and screenwriter. She was born in Detroit, Michigan, grew up in Washington, D.C., and graduated from Harvard in 1981. Following an emerging trend for children and grandchildren of the Great Migration, she moved to the south, to Nashville, Tennessee, to become a country songwriter. The more than twenty songs she has had recorded include a song about lynching ("The Ballad of Sally Anne") and a song about honoring both the Confederate dead and the slave dead ("I'll Cry for Yours, Will You Cry for Mine?"). As a screenwriter she has worked on adaptations of *Their Eyes Were Watching God*, *Parting the Waters*, and *Brer Rabbit*.

Randall has published two novels, *The Wind Done Gone* (2001) and *Pushkin and the Queen of Spades* (2004). For *The Wind Done Gone*, she was awarded the Free Spirit Award in 2001 and the Literature Award of Excellence by the Memphis Black Writers Conference in 2002, and she was a finalist for the NAACP Image Award in 2002.

MAJOR WORKS

The Wind Done Gone (2001) was the subject of a failed lawsuit by Margaret Mitchell's estate to prevent publication based on its references to Mitchell's 1939 novel *Gone With the Wind*. After an injunction followed by an appeal with an impressive show of support from most of the leading figures in Southern Letters, *The Wind Done Gone* was released to fairly positive reviews. Whether regarded as a parody of *Gone With the Wind* or as something more, *The Wind Done Gone* includes renamed versions of characters and settings from Mitchell's book. It is presented in the form of a diary written by Cynara, Rhett Butler's ("RB's") mistress and eventual wife, who is the daughter of a long-term liaison between Gerald O'Hara ("Planter") and Mammy, and as such is Scarlett O'Hara's ("Other's") half-sister. Rejected by her mother and sold in her early teens, Cynara still sees the plantation ("Tata") as home. As she becomes increasingly literate, self-aware, and self-assertive, Cynara leaves RB, whom she renames "Debt Chauffeur," to associate with the emerging African American political structure in Washington, where she provides a surrogate child for a congressman and his wife. In an interview, Randall says that she and members of her immediate family circle, who have connections to both the African American elite and to white southern blue blood families, refer to themselves as "not-so-tragic mulattos," and she acknowledges that they are interested in exploring new roles, relationships, and histories in the context of a south that is not divided along racial lines.

CRITICAL RECEPTION

Bettye Williams analyzes the novel as a parody of *Gone With the Wind*, "a revisionist version of American history which inverts and subverts traditional assumptions about issues of African American maleness and womanhood" (323), and points out that Cynara's assertive self possession allows her to avoid censure, recrimination, and punishment, either for her own interracial dalliances or for her mulatto status. In this way, she avoids the "tragic mulatto" stereotype that has haunted American depictions of biracial characters.

Nicole Argall's reading of *The Wind Done Gone* as the product of an "Africana womanist" perspective is somewhat more problematic, first because she wants to present Cyana as an "antihero," and second because she applies only four of the eighteen defining qualities of this perspective, acknowledging that the others do not fit as well. That being said, Argall does provide some interesting insights into the novel, especially in the way that she reads Cynara's self-fashioning through writing in the context of an emerging understanding of the tripartite (raced, classed, gendered) structure of the oppression of African American women in American society.

Randall's second novel is *Pushkin and the Queen of Spades* (2004). It concerns a culture conflict between narrator/protagonist Windsor Armstrong, a professor of Russian literature, and her son Pushkin X, a professional football player who is planning to marry a white Russian stripper. A discursive, rambling novel addressed in part to Pushkin and in part to a larger audience, it allows Armstrong to examine her past (Motown to Harvard) and influences, both literary and family, in order to come to terms with her son's choices. Most reviews have been mixed, pointing to the novel's diffuse structure and the difficulty of liking the abrasive, snotty central character's voice. A rap version of a Pushkin story offered by Armstrong to her son as a peace offering also takes some hits from the reviewers. In her *New York Times* review, Julie Salamon praises Randall's publicity people for bringing the author out to selected book groups rather than relying on reviewers. Like *The Wind Done Gone* but without its controversial court case, the hope is that this book will find its own audience in the public. This makes sense, because this is a novel where postmodern plotting and abundant literary references combine with family melodrama and Randall's sure eye for racial and social contradictions, so that it finds its location somewhere between Windsor Armstrong's world of high culture and Pushkin X's world of popular entertainment.

BIBLIOGRAPHY

Works by Alice Randall

Pushkin and the Queen of Spades. Boston: Houghton Mifflin, 2004.
The Wind Done Gone. Boston: Houghton Mifflin, 2001.

Studies of Alice Randall's Works

Argall, Nicole. "A Rib from My Chest: Cynara's Journey as an Africana Womanist." *CLA Journal* 47.2 (December 2003): 231–43.

Salamon, Julie. "Provocatuer Returns with a New Firebomb." *New York Times*, March 17, 2004, 9.
Williams, Bettye. "Glimpsing Parody, Language and Post-Reconstruction Themes in Alice Randall's *The Wind Done Gone. CLA Journal* 47.3 (March 2004): 310–25.

Louis H. Palmer, III

HENRIETTA CORDELIA RAY (1849–1916)

BIOGRAPHICAL NARRATIVE

Poet H. Cordelia Ray was born in 1849 to a prominent and progressive New York City family. Like her four older siblings, she graduated from college, and, like her beloved sister Florence, became a teacher, eventually earning an M.A. in pedagogy from the University of the City of New York (now known as New York University). She was proficient in French, German, Latin, and Greek, and after three decades of teaching in the New York City public school system, Cordelia moved out to Woodside, Long Island, with Florence, where she taught foreign languages as well as English literature, mathematics, and music in their home. She was very close to her sister, living with her until Florence died, and she generally led a quiet and rather private life.

MAJOR WORKS

H. Cordelia Ray was first publicly recognized for her poem "Lincoln," commissioned for the dedication of the Freedmen's Monument in Washington, D.C., in 1876. The poem, however, did not reach press until 1893, the same year that her *Sonnets* came out. Meanwhile, Cordelia and Florence collaborated on a short biographical work of their father, *Sketch of the Life of the Reverend Charles B. Ray*, published in 1887. Cordelia contributed poems to periodicals, such as the *AME Church Review*, throughout her career. Finally, she published her larger collection, titled *Poems*, in 1910. The themes of her poetry range from morally austere yet optimistic meditations on duty and the human condition, to tributes to specific abolitionists, to passionate treatments of romantic love.

CRITICAL RECEPTION

In her day, Ray was generally praised for her refined, erudite style and diverse subject range. She has since, however, been faulted for this by critics who think that it signals too close an identification with white literary traditions, or that her focus might have been too much on form and not enough on creative expression. Nonetheless, Ray has received increasing positive attention from critics and anthologists in recent years, and thus more acceptance and celebration within the literary community.

BIBLIOGRAPHY

Works by Henrietta Cordelia Ray

"Charles Lamb." *AME Review* 8 (1891): 1–9.
Lincoln. Written for the Occasion of the Unveiling of the Freedmen's Monument in Memory of Abraham Lincoln, April 14, 1876. New York: J. J. Little, 1893.
Poems. New York: Grafton Press, 1910.

Sketch of the Life of the Reverend Charles B. Ray. With Florence T. Ray. New York: J. J. Little, 1887.
Sonnets. New York: J. J. Little, 1893.

Studies of Henrietta Cordelia Ray's Works

Banks, Marva Osborne. "Henrietta Cordelia Ray." In *African American Authors, 1745–1945: A Bio-Bibliographical Critical Sourcebook,* edited by Emmanuel S. Nelson, 366–70. Westport, CT: Greenwood Press, 2000.

Blount, Marcellus. "Caged Birds: Race and Gender in the Sonnet." In *Engendering Men: The Question of Male Feminist Criticism,* edited by Joseph A. Boone and Michael Cadden, 225–38. New York: Routledge, 1990.

Fauset, Jessie Redmon. "What to Read." Rev. of *Poems,* by Henrietta Cordelia Ray. *Crisis* 3–4 (1912): 183.

Flint, Allen. "Black Response to Colonel Shaw." *Phylon* 45.3 (1984): 210–19.

Frazier, S. Elizabeth. "Some Afro-American Women of Mark." *A.M.E. Church Review* 8 (1892): 373 86.

Jackson, Blyden. *A History of Afro-American Literature,* vol. 1. Baton Rouge: Louisiana State University Press, 1989.

Kapai, Leela. "Henrietta Cordelia Ray." In *Dictionary of Literary Biography,* vol. 50, edited by Trudier Harris, 233–37. New York: The Gale Group, 1986.

Kerlin, Robert T. *Negro Poets and Their Poems.* Washington, DC: Associated Publishers, 1947.

Lyons, Maritcha R. "Henrietta Cordelia Ray." In *Homespun Heroines and Other Women of Distinction,* edited by Hallie Quinn Brown. Xenia, Ohio: Aldine, 1926.

Moorehead, Elizabeth A. "Henrietta Cordelia Ray." In *Nineteenth-Century American Women Writers: A Bio Bibliographical Critical Sourcebook,* edited by Denise D. Knight and Emmanuel S. Nelson, 343–46. Westport, CT. Greenwood Press, 1997.

"Ray, H(enrietta) Cordelia." In *Black Writers: A Selection of Sketches from Contemporary Authors,* edited by Linda Metzger et al. Detroit: Gale Research, Inc., 1989.

Robinson, William Henry, Jr. *Early Black American Poets.* Dubuque, Iowa: William C. Brown, 1969, 138 44.

Sampson, Henry T. *Blacks in Black and White.* Metuchen, NJ: Scarecrow Press, 1977.

Sanders, Kimberly Wallace. "Henrietta Cordelia Ray." In *Oxford Companion to African American Literature,* edited by William L. Andrews et al., 261–62. New York: Oxford University Press, 1997.

Sherman, Joan R., ed. *African-American Poetry of the Nineteenth Century: An Anthology.* Urbana: University of Illinois Press, 1992, 265–81.

———, ed. "Introduction." In *Collected Black Women's Poetry,* vol. 3. New York: Oxford University Press, 1988, xxix–xxxiv.

———. *Invisible Poets: Afro-Americans of the Nineteenth Century.* Urbana: University of Illinois Press, 1974, 129–35.

Shockley, Ann Allen. *Afro-American Women Writers (1746–1933).* Boston: G. K. Hall, 1988.

Smith, Jessie Carney, ed. *Notable Black Women.* New York: Gale Research Group, 1992.

Walker, Cheryl, ed. *American Women Poets of the Nineteenth Century: An Anthology.* New Brunswick, NJ: Rutgers University Press, 1992, 352–63.

Walters, Tracey Lorraine. "Reclaiming the Classics: The Emancipatory Strategy of Selected African American Women Poets: Phillis Wheatley, Henrietta Cordelia Ray, and Gwendolyn Brooks." Ph.D. Dissertation, Howard University, 1999.

Ward, Jerry W., Jr., ed. "Henrietta Cordelia Ray." In *Trouble the Water: 250 Years of African-American Poetry.* New York: Penguin, 1997, 55.

Megan K. Ahern

JEWELL PARKER RHODES (?–)

BIOGRAPHICAL NARRATIVE

A writer with both a critical eye and a creative talent, Rhodes's publishing career encompasses several genres, including creative writing, literary criticism, and pedagogical work. As a child, she was an avid reader and writer of stories, yet received little encouragement to develop her artistic talent. Her parents' divorce and her subsequent move to live with her grandmother in Pittsburgh, Pennsylvania, later impacted the substance of her writing as themes of family legacy, rejection, and racial relationships, as well as male and female relationships, often surface in her novels. In college, Rhodes's interest in literature began to blossom. She attended Carnegie-Mellon and received a B.A. in Drama Criticism, an M.A. in English, and a Doctor of Arts in English for Creative Writing.

Rhodes explains that her writing, and particularly her first novel, became the passage for helping her discover the meaning of being African American, female, and particularly, a mother. She worked on her first manuscript, *Voodoo Dreams*, initially titled *Marie Laveau, Voodoo Queen* for years, finally finishing in 1983. No publisher showed interest in printing a book about an African American woman, claiming the story was not universal enough, a situation that led to Rhodes being overlooked for tenure in her university teaching position and her subsequent dismissal. During this time, she also survived a number of other personal challenges, including divorce, remarriage, and her grandmother's death, events that played prominently into her search for self and her subsequent motivation to succeed as an African American female author. Dealing with pain and discouragement, Rhodes ceased writing for a period of over four years. For another three years, after finding the inner strength to return to her writing, she patiently continued to work on her manuscript and to search for a publisher. Rhodes relates this time in her life to the pain her protagonists often must endure in order to self-actualize. *Voodoo Dreams* was finally published in 1993 by St. Martin's Press, and has been followed by six other books, including one soon to be released, *Voodoo Season: A Marie Laveau Mystery*.

A prolific author, Rhodes writes short fictions as well as novels, and these stories have appeared in numerous anthologies and journals. The Institute for the Study of the Arts at Arizona State University also staged a reading of *Voodoo Dreams* as a play in 2001. Additionally, her scholarly and nonfiction articles appear in various academic journals and in many composition texts. She was selected as the Creative Writing Delegate for the Modern Language Association and has served as a professor and the former Director of the MFA Program in Creative Writing at Arizona State University, where she has won numerous teaching awards. She devotes herself to working with her students, assisting them creatively and professionally, presently serving as the Artistic Director at the Virginia G. Piper Center for Creative Writing at Arizona State University. Frequently traveling to speak at literary events and to read on book tours, Rhodes spends her downtime in Scottsdale, Arizona, with her husband Brad and her two children.

MAJOR WORKS

In *Voodoo Dreams*, Rhodes pens the tale of Marie Laveau, a voodooienne of French, Indian, and African ancestry in New Orleans. Reminiscent of Gayl Jones for its attention to family legacy and Toni Cade Bambara's circuitous narrative style, Rhodes details Marie's motherless childhood as she lives with her grandmother, a former voodoo queen herself. In the bayou country of Louisiana, as Marie matures, she begins to receive visions of the past and her mother, as well as visions of the future, seeing her own daughter through her voodoo heritage. Moving to a village in which free African Americans reside outside New Orleans in the early nineteenth century, Marie yearns to experience city life for herself. She struggles with her Christian grandmother's plans for her to marry at sixteen, and laments the power men like Jacques and John, her mother's former lover, hold over her life. Jacques saves her from a white slave owner's son, and then demands that she love him in return. Her grandmother's complicity in this plot hurts Marie, but she aims to prevent Marie from her own mother's mistakes with John, an abusive voodoo businessman who tricks people with his fake version of voodoo in order to make money.

In her quest to discover not only her mother but love and acceptance as well, Marie discovers that her mother has died, and that she never loved her—only her grandmother's love kept her alive. Yet, by subscribing to the power of voodoo and aligning herself with John, Marie chooses a life that limits her future choices. She abandons her marriage to Jacques, her grandmother, and her Christian religion in order to become a voodoo queen. She kills a man attempting to rape her because of her skin color, and ends up in prison, an act that starts a race riot in the city between the Christians and the voodoo practitioners. Marie is freed because she is feared. Pregnant and in an abusive relationship with John, Marie thrives on the power that her popularity gives her. Strangers worship Marie for her powers, cutting her garments for a blessing; yet, she is powerless in her personal life, controlled by John.

Through Marie's tragic relationships with those around her, and the strength she discovers when she has her own child, the fourth Marie, she grows into a strong woman, strong enough to break the legacy of abuse that haunts her. To leave John and to survive, she must murder him, tricking him into holding a snake during one of her conjuring sessions as voodooeinne. Years later, Marie's tale ends on her deathbed as her faithful friend Louis pens her story into his diary. With New Orleans as a slave city, the horrors of slavery are detailed in this novel as new slaves are unloaded, caged, whipped, and beaten, and free African Americans mistreated. The racial differences in the city figure prominently in the novel, as people are tiered according to the mixture of white and African in their blood, where a drop of African blood denigrates whites, African Americans and mulattos to a lower social status. This novel painfully explores the legacy of slavery, the intricacies of voodoo, mother and daughter relationships, and the delicate interconnectivity between Christianity and voodoo, while detailing Marie's own search for self, a quest she finally achieves.

Magic City is based on historical events in Tulsa, Oklahoma, in 1921. Parker Rhodes fictionalizes the story of several days in the life of Joe Samuels and Mary Keane, two people whose lives intersect in downtown Tulsa. Joe, from Deep Greenwood, known as the "Black Wall Street," is a banker's son and a shoe shiner in downtown Tulsa who practices magic religiously, performing escapist routines after his idol, Houdini. With his older brother Henry dead from the war, Joe feels destined for more in life, yet faces his parents' shame and scorn at his lack of career motivation.

The novel then switches narrative to Mary's story, where white, poor, and motherless, raised by an abusive father and a racist brother left handicapped by the war, she already dreams of escaping her fate. When her father promises her hand in marriage to Dell, the farmhand, and he subsequently rapes her, Mary's world begins to shatter. Working as an elevator woman in the same skyscraper as Joe, their worlds collide when Joe mistakenly takes the elevator intended for whites only. Mary's distress at her earlier rape causes her to scream at the sight of Joe's handcuffs that he regularly uses for his escapist routines, and she faints. Joe, immediately scared and worried about his own family problems, runs back to Deep Greenwood. Mary's hysteria and her bruises and other markings from her earlier rape lead the whites in the downtown tower to assume that she was assaulted by Joe, a presumption that sparks a mob in Tulsa, a hot bed for racial hostilities and a city with a large Klan population. Racial tensions figure prominently at a time when all African Americans are presumed guilty and lynched immediately with no defense.

Joe's subsequent arrests, beatings, and escapes eventually lead him back to Deep Greenwood, bent on fighting the mob that he knows will come. Mary's attempts at clearing Joe of the charges fail miserably in light of the Klan's power to murder before Joe's innocence can be proven. Through the help of her new friend Allen, Mary heads to Deep Greenwood, befriending Joe's sister, Hildy, in her attempt to clear Joe's name. Subsequent inflammatory and false newspaper reports, historically documented, as well as the hatred of those involved in the case, flare up racial tensions to the point that national guardsmen drop dynamite on Deep Greenwood, incinerating the entire area and many inhabitants. The novel explores at length Joe's relationship with his father, Douglass, a founding member of Deep Greenwood and one of its prominent citizens. He dies trying to protect his vault at the bank, claiming that white men only respect money and property. Joe and Mary must both decide after everything that has happened whether to leave Tulsa or stay and face the damage from the spark of racial hatred that flared into a fire beyond their control. Rhodes explores family ties, the southern history of racism, abuse, and the power of friendship in this attempt to see beyond the headlines of the newspapers and into the lives of real people.

In *Douglass' Women*, Rhodes writes an historical fictional novel about abolitionist Frederick Douglass and the women who love him—both a wife and a mistress. The novel begins in early nineteenth-century Maryland, with the tale of Anna Murray Douglass, and her recounting of the first time she met Douglass, then a slave. An uneducated southern woman making a living through domestic service, Anna is portrayed, nevertheless, as an extremely sensitive and caring individual who bore Douglass's children while enduring a less than fulfilling relationship with him for many years. The novel details their courtship and marriage as Anna recalls the memories as an old woman on her deathbed. Her voice, filled with hope and often regret for the changes in their relationship over the years, recounts Douglass's journey to freedom. Anna herself gives Douglass the money to escape, and assists him as he creates a new life in New York, transforming into the renowned speaker and abolitionist.

The novel continues with Ottilie Assing's diary, a German woman who immigrates to America and meets Douglass through her involvement in the Anti-Slavery society. An artist and writer, Ottilie served as Douglass's mistress for over twenty years. The reader sees Anna, abandoned by Douglass, alone birthing and raising her children while he travels, speaking out against slavery. In addition, the complications in their relationship because of Anna's uneducated background, and her ignorance at understanding the role

Douglass plays in the abolitionist movement are examined. Anna's strength in raising her children and performing domestic service to keep food on the table speaks to her portrayal as a woman with a larger purpose in life. It is Anna who encourages Douglass to write his story down, the story that will cement his position in the abolitionist movement and in history. Douglass disappears sometimes for as long as three years at a time, leaving Anna and his children to fend for themselves until his freedom is bought. The intricacies of Douglass's humanity are shown through his relationship with both women. Ottilie, his mistress, depends on Douglass for happiness, whereas Anna is portrayed as strong and independent. Both women confront each other at times, knowing the relationships that exist between them and "Freddy," as Anna calls him. For example, Rhodes fictionalizes the moment when Anna discovers their relationship, pregnant with Douglass's third child, and how Ottilie stakes her claim to their oldest child, Rosetta, as she resembles her father in mind and spirit. With no children of her own, Ottilie leads a lonely life, and Anna remains busy with her family of five. The novel continues to track the emotional aspect of their relationships with each other and Douglass's family life in a compelling and fascinating look into the love triangle, up until Anna's death and Ottilie's suicide at learning of Douglass's remarriage eighteen months later.

CRITICAL RECEPTION

Widely published, Rhodes regularly receives kudos from critics who describe her work as "betwitching," with a "deft narrative style." Houston A. Baker, Jr., says that Rhodes writes with a flair for drama. Her most recent novel, *Douglass' Women*, described as "passionate" and "captivating," has achieved greatest acclaim by winning the 2003 American Book Award, the 2003 Black Caucus of the American Library Association Award for Literary Excellence, the 2003 PEN Oakland Josephine Miles Award, and by being recognized as a finalist for the PEN Center USA Award in Fiction and for the Hurston-Wright Legacy Award. She has been twice nominated for the Pushcart Prize. Rhodes has also been the recipient of the Yaddo Creative Writing Fellowship and the National Endowment of the Arts Award in Fiction.

BIBLIOGRAPHY

Works by Jewell Parker Rhodes

The African American Guide to Writing and Publishing Non-Fiction. New York: Broadway, 2001.
Douglass' Women. New York: Atria, 2002.
"Enough Rides." *Callaloo* 14.1 (1991): 12–19.
"Enough Rides." In *Ancestral House: The Black Short Story in the Americas and Europe*, edited by Charles Rowell and John Edgar Wideman. Boulder, CO: Westview Press, 1995.
"Evan." In *Between Mothers and Sons: Women Writers Writing about Their Sons*, edited by Patricia Stevens. New York: Touchstone, 1999.
"Foreword." In *Proverbs for the People*, edited by Tracy Price-Thompson and TaRessa Stovall, ix. New York: Kensington, 2003.
Free within Ourselves: Fiction Lessons for Black Authors. New York: Main Street, 1999.
"The Left Hand of Darkness: Androgyny and the Feminist Utopia." In *Women and Utopia: Critical Interpretations*, edited by Marleen Barr and Nicholas D. Smith, 108–20. Lanham, MD: University Press of America, 1983.

"Long Distances." In *Children of the Night: Best Short Stories by Black Writers*, edited by Gloria Naylor, 172–79. Canada: Little Brown, 1995.

Magic City. New York: HarperCollins, 1997.

"Meeting Frederick." In *Gumbo: An Anthology of African American Writing*, edited by Marita Golden and E. Lynn Harris, 458–63. New York: Broadway Books, 2002.

"Mixed Blood Stew." *Creative Nonfiction* 19 (2002). www.creativenonfiction.org/thejournal/back.htm (accessed September 2006).

Voodoo Dreams: A Novel of Marie Laveau. New York: St. Martin's, 1993.

Studies of Jewell Parker Rhodes's Works

Baker, Houston A., Jr. Rev. of *Voodoo Dreams: A Novel of Marie Laveau*, by Jewell Parker Rhodes. *African American Review* 29 (1995): 157–60.

Quashie, Kevin E. "Interview. Mining Magic, Mining Dreams: A Conversation with Jewell Parker Rhodes." *Callaloo* 20.2 (1997): 431–40.

Rhodes, Barbara C., and Allen Ramsay. "An Interview with Jewell Parker Rhodes." *African American Review* 29 (1995): 593–603.

Tatia Jacobson Jordan

CAROLYN MARIE RODGERS (1943–)

BIOGRAPHICAL NARRATIVE

Carolyn Marie Rodgers is best known as one of the female poets of the Black Arts Movement (BAM), but her work far surpasses that era despite being neglected and overlooked. Born on December 14, 1943, she began writing poetry in her freshman year at University of Illinois as a means of coping with isolation. The next year she transferred to Roosevelt University. Eventually, she received her B.A. in 1981 and M.A. in English in 1984 from the University of Chicago. She has won the Conrad Kent Rivers Award for writing in 1968, an NEA grant in 1969, was named poet laureate of the Society of Midland Authors in 1970, and won the Pen Award in 1987. In addition to her poetry, Rodgers published several short stories; these focus on what may be called ordinary and overlooked people and often show their struggles and spirit of survival.

MAJOR WORKS

As a member of the Organization of Black American Culture (OBAC), Rodgers was mentored by Hoyt Fuller and Gwendolyn Brooks, along with other major writers of BAM, and she developed a militant voice and form. Her first three volumes of poetry were published by Third World Press: *Paper Soul* (1968), *2 Love Raps* (1969), and *Songs of a Black Bird* (1969). Broadside Press published her four subsequent volumes: *Now Ain't That Love* (1970), *For H. W. Fuller* (1970), *For Flip Wilson* (1971), and *Long Rap/ Commonly Known as a Poetic Essay* (1971). The poems in these volumes explore her battle with the militancy of the time and the traditional life in which she was reared. Her use of obscenities and other common language, as well as her nonstandard and inconsistent structure, spelling, capitalization, and punctuation drew much criticism even as her talents were praised.

In struggling with issues of womanhood, battling with racial oppression, and attempting to authentically express the life, pains, and joys of regular people, she examines her own inner conflicts on all these issues as well.

Rodgers broke with OBAC, and the black-owned independent presses, sometime in the mid-1970s. Her next two volumes—*how i got ovah* (1975) and *The Heart as Ever Green* (1978), both published by Anchor/Doubleday—explore identity issues, a desire for creative and personal freedom, and also question the revolution out of which she emerged. Her more recent volumes appear from her own Eden Press: *Translation: Poems* (1980), *Eden and Other Poems* (1983), *A Little Lower Than Angels* (1984), *Finite Forms: Poems* (1985), *Echoes, from a Circle Called Earth* (1988), and *Morning Glory* (1989). Her body of work shows her process from a militant to a religious loyalist. Yet in 1984, after writing for over twenty years, she still saw herself as "... becoming. I am a has-been, would perhaps, going to be. Underneath, I'm a dot. With no i's" (Evans 374).

CRITICAL RECEPTION

Rodgers is, unfortunately, much neglected in current criticism regarding African American poets and especially African American female poets. In analyzing her work, one easily finds much autobiography. Parker-Smith suggests there are three major dilemmas running throughout her texts: "the fear of assimilating the value system of her mother, which interferes with claiming an independent life-style of her own; the attempt to define her 'self' by the standards of the social system responsible for creating her own and her mother's condition; and the search for love (a man) that will simultaneously electrify and save her" (395).

BIBLIOGRAPHY

Works by Carolyn Marie Rodgers

"Blackbird in a Cage." *Negro Digest* 16 (August 1967): 66–71.
"Black Poetry—Where It's At." *Negro Digest* 18.1 (September 1969): 7–16.
Echoes, from a Circle Called Earth. Chicago: Eden Press, 1988.
Eden and Other Poems. Chicago: Eden Press, 1983.
Finite Forms: Poems. Chicago: Eden Press, 1985.
For Flip Wilson. Chicago: Broadside Press, 1971.
For H. W. Fuller. Chicago: Broadside Press, 1970.
The Heart as Ever Green. Garden City: Anchor/Doubleday, 1978.
how i got ovah: New and Selected Poems. Garden City: Anchor/Doubleday, 1975.
A Little Lower Than Angels. Chicago: Eden Press, 1984.
Long Rap/Commonly Known as a Poetic Essay. Chicago: Broadside Press, 1971.
Morning Glory. Chicago: Eden Press, 1989.
Now Ain't That Love. Chicago: Broadside Press, 1970.
Paper Soul. Chicago: Third World Press, 1968.
Songs of a Black Bird. Chicago: Third World Press, 1969.
"A Statistic, Trying to Make It Home." *Negro Digest* 18 (June 1969): 68–71.
Translation: Poems. Chicago: Eden Press, 1980.
2 Love Raps. Chicago: Third World Press, 1969.

Studies of Carolyn Marie Rodgers's Works

Davis, Jean. "Carolyn M. Rodgers." In *Dictionary of Literary Biography: Afro-American Poets Since 1955*, vol. 41, edited by Trudier Harris. Detroit: Gale, 1985, 287–95.
Evans, Mari. "An Amen Arena." In *Black Women Writers (1950–1980): A Critical Evaluation*, edited by Mari Evans, 373–76. Garden City: Doubleday, 1984.
Jamison, Angeline. "Imagery in the Women Poems: The Art of Carolyn Rodgers." In *Black Women Writers (1950–1980): A Critical Evaluation*, edited by Mari Evans, 377–92. Garden City: Doubleday, 1984.
Parker-Smith, Bettye J. "Running Wild in Her Soul: The Poetry of Carolyn Rodgers." In *Black Women Writers (1950–1980): A Critical Evaluation*, edited by Mari Evans, 393–410. Garden City: Doubleday, 1984.

Adenike Marie Davidson

MONA LISA SALOY (1950–)

BIOGRAPHICAL NARRATIVE

Poet Mona Lisa Saloy was born in New Orleans, Louisiana, in 1950. Named by her father after Nat King Cole's popular song "Mona Lisa," his symbolic *Creole* potency beside her mother's rhythmic black beauty bared the beginning of a powerful poet, folklorist, and writer.

Having received her Bachelor of Arts degree from the University of Washington in Seattle, Saloy went on to pursue a Master of Arts degree in Creative Writing and English at San Francisco State University. She received her Master of Fine Arts degree in Creative Writing from Louisiana State University. After relocating to New Orleans, Saloy began teaching at Dillard University as an associate professor of English, where she also developed a successful Creative Writing program.

Saloy continued her educational pursuits at Louisiana State University where she earned the Doctor of Philosophy degree in English and Anthropology. Her research and dissertation focused on Black Beat Poet, Bob Kaufman, who served as an essential link to the Black Arts Movement. This research was funded by fellowships from the National Endowment for the Humanities and from the *United Negro College Fund/Andrew W Mellon Foundation*.

Saloy currently holds her position at Dillard University, however, having been displaced by Hurricane Katrina, she is a visiting associate professor of English and Creative Writing at the University of Washington.

MAJOR WORKS

Several of Saloy's writings perceptively construct Louisiana, allowing readers to engage themselves. Her overall themes employ empathy and evolution for women, African American culture and communities, family (extended family), and notable writers—particularly those often overlooked.

Red Beans and Ricely Yours, Saloy's prize-winning compilation of verse for which she won the 2005 T. S. Eliot Prize, chronicles five sectors of personal geography that prepare, kiss, and coax the human spirit.

"Still Laughing to Keep from Crying: Black Humor," an ethnographic article by Saloy, distinctively displays her talent as a true guru of folklore. She provides in-depth testimony of historic and contemporary black comedians, categorizing the delicate traditions from which they result, featuring their racial anecdotes of *laughing to keep from crying*.

Perhaps one of Saloy's most prominent works is "Word Works," a brilliant poem that emphasizes the beauty of southern culture, recently made into a film by Betsy Weiss.

CRITICAL RECEPTION

Absolute acclaim is a must for Saloy's exceptional verse. She captures the essence of well-rounded literature. In *ChickenBones: A Journal for Literary & Artistic African-American Themes*, literary critic Rudolph Lewis's review of Saloy's *Red Beans and Ricely Yours* enhances these findings: "Mona Lisa's poems are concrete. They are filled with objects (cats, mosquito hawks, word sounds, music and musicians, oaks and mums, colors, houses (shotgun), yards, etc.) and actions (talk, dance, more talk, touching, eating, bereft of abstractions) like good modern poems ought to be" (3).

Fiction novelist Ishmael Reed states: "Mona Lisa Saloy captures the street idioms and culture of New Orleans that challenge tourist misconceptions about that fabulous city. She also succeeds where many performance poets fail. These poems are music to the ear as well as on the page" (Back cover of *Red Beans and Ricely Yours*, 4).

Well-renowned poet Lorenzo Thomas credits Saloy as a voice of creative inspiration for literary critic Fahamisha Patricia Brown's *Performing the Word: African American Poetry as Vernacular Culture:* "By to choosing to explore poetry—beginning with Paul Laurence Dunbar and James Weldon Johnson and covering contemporaries as recent as Mona Lisa Saloy and Saul Williams—Brown attempts to demonstrate that our poetic vernacular 'is not merely colloquial, slang, or vulgar'" (174).

BIBLIOGRAPHY

Works by Mona Lisa Saloy

"African American Oral Traditions in Louisiana." In *Louisiana Folklife Festival Guide*. Baton Rouge: Louisiana Division of Folklife, 1990. www.louisianafolklore.org/LT/Articles_Essays/creole_art_african_am_oral.html (accessed September 2006).
"Black Beats and Black Issues." In *Beat Culture and the New America: 1950–1965*, edited by Lisa Phillips, 153–65. New York: The Whitney Museum of American Art, 1995.
"New Orleans Lagniappe: Terms of Our Endearment." In *Ties That Bind: Making Family New Orleans Style*, 53–59. New Orleans: Ashe Cultural Center and Ebon Images, 2001.
Red Beans and Ricely Yours. Kirksville, MO: Truman State University Press, 2005.
"Still Laughing to Keep from Crying: Black Humor." In *Louisiana Folklife Festival Guide*, 14–15. Baton Rouge: Louisiana Division of Folklife, 2001.
"Word Works." In *Poets in the Dream State: An Anthology of Louisiana Writers*. NOVAC, 2001.

Studies of Mona Lisa Saloy's Works

Lewis, Rudolph. "A Life Won with Blood & Tears." *ChickenBones: A Journal for Literary & Artistic African-American Themes* (2005): 1–7. www.nathanielturner.com/redbeansandricely yours.htm (accessed September 2006).
Thomas, Lorenzo. Rev. of *Performing the Word: African American Poetry as Vernacular Culture*, by Fahamisha Patricia Brown. *African American Review*, 35.3 (Autumn 2001): 174–76.

Delicia Dena Daniels

SONIA SANCHEZ (1934–)

BIOGRAPHICAL NARRATIVE

A combination of artistic engagements and race/gender oppression characterizes the early life of poet and playwright Sonia Sanchez. She was born Wilsonia Sanchez, reportedly because her father, Wilson L., wanted a male child (Melhem, *Heroism* 133). Wilson, a musician by trade, introduced her to such jazz greats as Billie Holiday. She received a Bachelor of Arts from Hunter College in 1955, and later did postgraduate study in poetry, at New York University. Her work with Louise Bogan, the late author of *The Sleeping Fury* (1937), led her to establish a writer's workshop with Don L. Lee, the African American activist and author of *Don't Cry, Scream* (1969). This was her first milestone in a lifetime of contributions to the literary field.

She joined the ranks of the Black Arts Movement, published early poems in a variety of African American circulars, and enlisted in the Nation of Islam all in four-year period (1972–1975). Though she disagreed with the antifemale undertones of the Nation's philosophy, her poetry participates in the assertion of black pride through masculinity, which is a characteristic of the sociocultural efforts of Elijah Muhammad and Malcolm X. Her first anthology of poetry was *Home Coming* (1969), which featured an introduction by her confederate, Don Lee.

Between 1968 and 1974, Sanchez experimented with a variety of literary forms. She produced four plays, *The Bronx Is Next* (1968), *Sister Son/ji* (1969), *Dirty Hearts* (1973), and *Uh Huh, But How Do It Free Us?* (1974), at such stagehouses as Theatre Black and the New York Public. She also composed her first five collections of poetry: *Home Coming* (1969), *We a BaddDDD People* (1970), *It's a New Day* (1971), *A Blues Book for Blue Black Magical Women* (1974), and *Love Poems* (1973). In the same period, she served as editor for a collection of student poems, a product of her own writer's workshop at the Countee Cullen Library titled *Three Hundred and Sixty Degrees of Blackness Comin' at You* (1971), and published her first children's stories, *The Adventures of Fathead, Smallhead, and Squarehead* (1973). She has continued to operate in these diverse segments of the literary arts throughout the last three decades.

Fourteen years passed between *Home Coming* and Sanchez's first formal recognitions from the literary field. She received an American Book Award for *Homegirls & Handgrenades* (1984) and, four years later, was presented the Pennsylvania Governor's Award for Excellence in the Humanities (1988). That same year, the Women's International League for Peace and Freedom recognized her with its highest commendation. In 1989, she received the Paul Robeson Social Justice Award.

Academic foundations seem to have been quicker to acknowledge Sanchez as a figure in American literature. The National Endowment for the Arts presented her with a fellowship in 1978, and Trinity College awarded her an honorary doctorate in 1988. By this year, San Francisco State College, the University of Pittsburgh, Rutgers University, Manhattan Community College, City College of CUNY, Amherst College, the University of Pennsylvania, Temple University, Haverford College, and the University of

Delaware had employed her in a number of educational positions. Temple University selected her for special recognitions, electing her to Laura H. Carnell Professor of English in 1979 (making her the first African American to hold a chair at Temple University), and a Provost Office faculty fellowship in 1986. At the University of Delaware, she was named Distinguished Minority Faculty Fellow (1987). At Spelman College, in Atlanta, Georgia, she was Distinguished Poet-in-Residence (1989). Her academic efforts culminated in a Roots Award from the PAN-African Studies Community Education Program (1993) and a PEN fellowship in the Arts (1993). She has continued to serve the academy in a variety of roles, while maintaining her professorship at Temple, where she teaches African American literature and creative writing.

Sonia Sanchez enjoys an international reputation as poet, having given readings in Asia, Australia, Canada, Central America, and Europe. She traveled on fully funded cultural tours to Bermuda, Guyana, and Jamaica (1972), to China (1973), and Cuba (1979). The latter was sponsored by the Venceremos Brigade, a youth organization dedicated to supporting the revolutionary government and resisting American trade/travel policies directed at Cuba. She published her memories of the pilgrimage to Nicaragua as a semi-poetic essay, "Bullet Holes of Resistance" (1994).

MAJOR WORKS

Though she is generally recognized as a poet first and a playwright second, the spirit of theater pervades her work. Seven of her plays have enjoyed professional production, most recently *Black Cats Back and Uneasy Landings* at the Freedom Theatre in Philadelphia (1995).

And yet, performance is central to her literary endeavors as well. Sanchez has adopted the intense vocal variations of sub-Saharan African speech and music, embedding her remarkable record of national and international readings with a broader sense of the African American spoken tradition. In her publications, she has regularly notated the verbal organization of the text, including a wide variety of accents and slashes. She is adamant that such choices are integral to the poetic themes, having taught her students that "free verse . . . is not free," rather that there are specific reasons for the seemingly random choices in experimental poems (Melhem, *Heroism* 169). In effect, Sanchez provides stage directions for the theatrical annunciation of poetry. This theatricalization of the written word provides the scope for her to examine a variety of topics, including: sexuality, masculinity, feminism, social/political revolution, and spirituality.

In *The Bronx Is Next*, her first drama, she answers Ed Bullins's call for street theater with a story of militant, organized African American resistance. A mere five pages of text enact a mime-show of reversal. A character known only as White Cop chastises African Americans for not "putting forth a little more effort" (49) and for rioting in the streets. Three African American residents of Harlem (Roland, Charles, and Jimmy) offer him a chance to understand their perspectives, by switching roles with him. They become the police; White Cop plays the African American man. They abuse him, accusing him of trying to flee arrest when he does not move, and finally drag him from the stage. As they pull him to his apparent doom, his assailants ignore his protests that he has never hurt nor killed an African American, even if other police he has known have. The building where the play is staged begins to burn, as the last character on the stage predicts, "the Bronx is next" (54). The implicit purpose of such a play, an interest in making performance a factor in community action, may explain her early tendency to stage poetry readings in bars and other community locales.

Many of her poems adopt dramatic techniques. In *Home Coming*, she uses lower-case lettering to undermine the power of cultural monoliths. She lowercases American and that most troublesome of racist signifiers, Nigger, reducing the impact of words that might otherwise be emphasized in oral presentation. In *Homegirls & Handgrenades*, she introduces the reader to a variety of characters, from a child called "Militancy" to a friend called Martin (in a letter written to Dr. Martin Luther King). One of her newest published poems "For Sweet Honey in the Rock," collected in *Shake Loose My Skin* (1999), uses her familiar pattern of repetition to evoke the theatricality of African American cultural performance, colloquially referred to as "running it down" (Baker 332). It is not unreasonable to claim that Sanchez has followed the career path of a poet, but done so with the soul of a dramatist.

On the surface, much of her work has a thematic character that connects her to other feminist poets of the Black Arts Movement. Like Ntozake Shange and others, Sanchez engages African American masculinity and African American spiritual traditions, and challenges the history and heritage of oppression in a divided America. She grieves over the violence she returns to, in the African American communities of *Home Coming*. She celebrates ancestral figures and tribal medicine in *Generations* (1969). She romanticizes feminine healing powers in *Like the Singing Coming off the Drums* (1999). Certainly, her poetry claims a partnership with other poets, in its "revolutionary didacticism meant to inspire mass audiences," and in her "genius for the vernacular" (Baker 332).

However, Sanchez also demonstrates a desire to reconcile with the literary monolith of masculinity, a desire that produces a thematic voice unique to her. The most elaborate examples of this stretch toward empathy with the African American male subject are *Blues Book* and a selection of haikus in *I've Been a Woman* (1978). In these poems, the African American male body becomes a vessel for the same romantic ego displacement that men have traditionally made of the female subject. Man embodies home, history, and the Earth itself, in a series of poems with such hyperbolic connections as seeing Africa in the eyes of a father. Also, she is not afraid to turn an angry eye at other women. In "to all sisters," collected in *Home Coming*, she sends a venomous diatribe at white women who try to seduce African American men. Unlike Shange, whose literary project assaults the perceived sexism in much of the history of African American empowerment, Sanchez works with and through masculinity to achieve mutual goals of self-realization for herself and her African American brothers.

CRITICAL RECEPTION

Many critical responses see a kinship between Sanchez and Malcolm X. For Houston A. Baker, she borrows many of her dramatic techniques from the activist, despite originally seeing him as a dangerous racist (328). For D. H. Melhem, Sanchez's elegy to the fallen leader is both an evocation of his undying anger and a spiritual bonding driven by deep sorrow (*Heroism* 137). Yet, for Melhem, she is no more a student of Malcolm X than she is of any other African American leader or poet. Though she shares the artistic experimentalism and moral asceticism of Lee, for example, she does not reflect his homophobia or segregationism (135–36). Explaining what he sees as her strongest collection of poetry, *Homegirls & Handgrenades*, he celebrates its "influx of

African and Latino influences . . . blues mode, love poems . . . haiku . . . [and] significant development that is the abundance of poetic stories and prose poems that create their own fluid forms" (142).

Lee, himself, in his introduction to *Home Coming*, calls her "dangerous," praising her ability "to do damage to the nigger's control center. His mind" (7). Mimicking the dialect representations in Sanchez and others, he attests that her poetry "helps u face yr/ self. Then, actually u will be able to move thru/out the world and face otherpeople as a true blackperson" (7). More than twenty years later, Kamili Anderson, in a review of *Under a Soprano Sky* (1987), asserts that Sanchez was perhaps "the most undeservedly underspoken of contemporary women poets in America" ("Sonia Sanchez" 1669). Anderson argues that "Sanchez has a penchant for enlisting words to imagery. She can mesmerize with scenarios that require readers to transfuse all of their senses. . . . Few poets write with more succinctness and intensity" (1669). As Sanchez has continued to produce new work into her seventies, she has been, though perhaps underrepresented, consistently celebrated by those who have taken notice.

If Sanchez's poetry has not earned the critical attention it has deserved, virtually no attention has been paid to her dramas. Mike Sell appears to be the only scholar to have given them serious consideration, devoting a portion of his essay in *African American Performance and Theatre History* (2001) to her first three plays. For Sell, Sanchez's drama "demonstrate[s] the power available to a 'whirlwind commonwealth'" (71). Considering mainly *Sister Son/ji* and *Malcolm/Man Don't Live Here No More*, Sell concludes that Sanchez's plays "utilize monologue and movement to highlight personality without celebrating individuality . . . they are . . . among the most acutely self-critical, resolutely revolutionary plays of the Black Arts era" (71–72). It appears that Sanchez has created a poetry that is enriched by the strategies of performance, and a drama that is enriched by the strategies of narrative poetry.

Perhaps Baker best summarizes the theatrical dynamism of Sonia Sanchez's contribution to literature: "There may well be more celebrated Afro-American writers, but Sonia Sanchez helps bring an enduring spirit of black renaissancism to contemporary effectiveness. . . . Nobody performs like Sonia Sanchez; nobody brings quintessential black cultural rituals to the high note she achieves" (345).

BIBLIOGRAPHY

Works by Sonia Sanchez

The Adventures of Fathead, Smallhead, and Squarehead. With Taiwo DuVall. New York: The Third Press, 1973.

Black and in Brooklyn: Creators and Creations. With Linda Cousins. Brooklyn: Universal Black Writer Press, 1983.

A Blues Book for Blue Black Magical Women. Detroit: Broadside Press, 1974.

The Bronx Is Next. In *A Sourcebook of African American Performance: Plays, People, Movements*, edited by Annemarie Bean. New York: Routlege, 1999.

"Bullet Holes of Resistance." In *Life Notes: Personal Writings by Contemporary Black Women*, edited by Particia Bell-Scott. New York: W. W. Norton, 1994.

Crises in Culture-Two Speeches by Sonia Sanchez. New York: Black Liberation Press, 1983.

Dirty Hearts. In *Break Out! In Search of New Theatrical Environments.* Chicago: Swallow Press, 1973.

Does Your House Have Lions? Boston: Beacon Press, 1991.

Generations: Poetry 1969–1985. London: Karnak House, 1969.

Home Coming: Poems by Sonia Sanchez. Detroit: Broadside Press, 1969.

Homegirls & Handgrenades. New York: Thunder's Mouth Press, 1984.

It's a New Day; Poems for Young Brothas and Sistuhs. Detroit: Broadside Press, 1971.

I've Been a Woman: New and Selected Poems. Sausalito, CA: The Black Scholar Press, 1978.

Like the Singing Coming off the Drums: Love Poems. Boston: Beacon Press, 1999.

Love Poems. New York: Third Press, 1973.

Shake Loose My Skin: New and Selected Poems. Boston: Beacon Press, 1999.

Sister Son/ji. In *New Plays from the Black Theatre*, edited by Ed Bullins. New York: Bantam Books, 1969.

A Sound Investment and Other Stories. Chicago: Third World Press, 1979.

Three Hundred and Sixty Degrees of Blackness Comin' at You. New York: FX Publishing, 1971.

Uh Huh, But How Do It Free Us? In *The New Lafayette Theatre Presents: Plays with Aesthetic Comments by Six Black Poets*, edited by Ed Bullins. Garden City, NJ: Anchor Press, 1974.

Under a Soprano Sky. Trenton: Africa World Press, 1987.

We a BaddDDD People. Detroit: Broadside Press, 1970.

We Be Word Sorcerers: 25 Stories by Black Americans. New York: Bantam Books, 1974.

Wounded in the House of a Friend. Boston: Beacon Press, 1995.

Studies of Sonia Sanchez's Works

Anderson, Kamili. "Giving Our Souls Ears." *Belle's Letters* 4.2 (Winter 1989): 14.

Asim, Jabari. "A Revival with Sonia Sanchez." *American Visions* 13 (1998): 27–28.

Baker, Houston A. "Our Lady: Sonia Sanchez and the Writing of a Black Renaissance." In *Reading Black, Reading Feminist: A Critical Anthology*, edited by Henry Louis Gates, Jr. New York: Penguin Books, 1990.

Bell, Bernard W. *The Folk Roots of Contemporary Afro-American Poetry.* Detroit: Broadside Press, 1974.

Cornwell, Anita. "Attuned to the Energy: Sonia Sanchez." *Essence* 10.3 (1979): 10.

Decker, Jeffrey Louis. *The Black Aesthetic Movement.* Detroit: Gale Research, 1991.

Dudley, Randall. *Broadside Memories: Poets I Have Known.* Detroit: Broadside Press, 1975.

Gabbin, Joanne Veal. "The Southern Imagination of Sonia Sanchez." In *Southern Women Writers: The New Generation*, edited by Tonette Bond Inge. Tuscaloosa: University of Alabama, 1990.

Joyce, Joyce Ann. "The Development of Sonia Sanchez: A Continuing Journey." *Indian Journal of American Studies* 13.2 (1983): 37–71.

———. *Ijala: Sonia Sanchez and the African Poetic Tradition.* Chicago: Third World Press, 1996.

Kalasky, Dale, ed. *Poetry Criticism, Volume 9: Excerpts from Criticism of the Works of the Most Significant and Widely Studied Poets of World Literature.* Detroit: Gale Research, 1994.

Leibowitz, Herbert. "Exploding Myths: An Interview with Sonia Sanchez." *Parnassus* 12–13 (1985): 357–68.

Melhem, D. H. *Heroism in the New Black Poetry: Introductions & Interviews.* Lexington: University Press of Kentucky, 1990.

———. "Sonia Sanchez: Will and Spirit." *Melus* 12.3 (1985): 73–98.

Roderick, Palmer R. "The Poetry of Three Revolutionists: Don L. Lee, Sonia Sanchez, and Nikki Giovanni." *CLA Journal* XV (1971): 25–36.

"Sanchez, Sonia." *Contemporary Authors* 74 (1999): 364–68.

Saunders, James Robert. "Sonia Sanchez's *Homegirls and Handgrenades*: Recalling Toomer's *Cane*." *Melus* 15 (1988): 73–82.

Sell, Mike. "The Black Arts Movement: Performance, Neo-Orality, and the Destruction of the 'White Thing.'" In *African American Performance and Theatre History: A Critical Reader*, edited by Harry J. Elam, Jr., and David Krasner. New York: Oxford University Press, 2000.

"Sonia Sanchez." In *Black Literature Criticism: Excerpts from the Criticism of the Most Significant Works of Black Authors over the Past 200 Years*, edited by James P. Draper, Jeffrey W. Hunter, and Jerry Moore. Detroit: Gale Research, 1992.

Walker, Barbara. "Sonia Sanchez Creates Poetry for the Stage." *Black Creation* 5 (1973): 12–14.

Ben Fisler

DORI SANDERS (1934–)

BIOGRAPHICAL NARRATIVE

Novelist Dori Sanders was born on her family's peach farm in Filbert, South Carolina, where she continues to live and work today. This farm, one of the oldest African American owned farms in the state, has played a central role in her writing. She draws on her knowledge of agricultural practices, family history, and life in rural African American communities to create the convincing settings and characters of her fiction. Of the relationship of her experiences to her literary efforts, Sanders has said, "What I'm writing about is so much of what I am really about. I grew up in a place and a time, and I'll never be able to get myself out of where I am. I'll never write about anything else. I shouldn't" (Fein C14).

Although she never deliberately set out to become a writer, preferring farming as her first vocation, Sanders nonetheless began honing her craft at an early age. As a child, she discovered her creativity at the "storytelling rock," where she and her nine siblings would gather to entertain themselves by swapping tales they made up. She began writing while working as a hotel banquet manager during the farm's off-season, jotting stories on discarded menus in her spare moments. After receiving encouragement from Algonquin editor Louis Rubin, who told her to "write what you actually know," Sanders focused her efforts on the manuscript that would become her first novel *Clover* (1990).

Clover, eventually translated into five languages, became an international best seller. In 1992, Sanders won the Lillian Smith Award, which honors authors whose work advocates social justice. Sanders's second novel, *Her Own Place,* followed in 1993. In the wake of the media attention that her writing attracted to her peach farm, Sanders authored *Dori Sanders' Country Cooking: Recipes and Stories from the Family Farm Stand* (1995), a cookbook that blends an homage to traditional southern cooking with family anecdotes. Recently, Sanders has moved beyond fiction in *Promise Land: A Farmer Remembers*, a memoir adapted from an address she delivered at the Southern Foodways Alliance Annual Symposium in 2004. In this slim volume, she relates more stories drawn from Sanders family lore and her own youth, describing the efforts of African Americans to live with dignity and grace despite the oppressions of the Jim Crow South.

MAJOR WORKS

In *Clover*, Sanders traces the developing relationship between the novel's narrator, a ten-year-old African American girl named Clover Hill, and her white stepmother Sara Kate. Clover finds herself forced to live alone with Sara Kate when her father, Gaten, is killed in a car accident shortly after his marriage. Over the objections of Clover's extended family, Sara Kate decides to honor Gaten's dying wish that she be the one to raise Clover. Clover is naturally resistant to this prospect; she sees Sara Kate as a "total stranger" and notes that "anybody who knows the story about Cinderella should know that nobody in the world would want a stepmother unless they were all the way crazy" (34). Moreover, Sara Kate's whiteness makes her seem alien. Clover's preoccupation with her new guardian's race is expressed through images of graphic contrast; at her father's funeral, she remarks that "Sara Kate is wedged between me and Uncle Jim Ed, squeezed in between us on the crowded bench like vanilla cream between dark chocolate cookies" (22). Sanders also presents Clover's sense of racial difference in terms of the unfamiliar cultural preferences that puzzle the young girl. Clover is especially unimpressed by Sara Kate's bland way of preparing food "cooked flat out in water, not a speck of grease" (71). Her ambivalence is reinforced by the members of her family, especially her aunt Everleen, who does not hide her antagonism toward the woman whom she perceives as an intruder. Everleen misreads Sara Kate's behavior, ascribing any action she disapproves of to Sara Kate's race; for instance, she tells Clover that Sara Kate did not cry at Gaten's funeral because "white folks don't cry and carry on like we do when somebody dies. They don't love as hard as we do" (67).

Yet by living with Sara Kate, sharing the intimacy of domestic routines and gradually getting to know her, Clover begins to see through this screen of racial stereotypes and appreciate Sara Kate's sincerity. Sanders's simple plot documents the small moments that lead her characters to a better understanding of one another and the expressions of love and concern that enable them to build a mother-daughter bond. However, as she grows to care for Sara Kate, Clover finds herself feeling conflicted by her loyalty to Everleen. The tensions between Everleen and Sara Kate come to a head in an explosive argument over Clover's well-being, leading the women to realize that they have a shared interest in helping the grieving girl to heal. The novel's conflict is resolved in a final crisis that requires Sara Kate to prove herself, earning the respect of both the Hill family and the townspeople of Clover's rural African American community, Round Hill.

Sanders was inspired to write *Clover* after watching two different funeral processions drive past her peach stand: one comprised of poorer African American mourners in battered cars and the other comprised of wealthy whites in much more expensive vehicles. She has said that observing the equally intense sadness of passengers in both groups "made me think of the things people have in common" (Fein C14). This desire to explore the common humanity of her diverse characters informs Sanders's fiction. Through humor and compassion, Sara Kate and Clover transcend their differences to forge an interracial friendship, one that eventually grows to encompass others in Clover's family and community. Sanders suggests that such personal relationships can be a wellspring for a broader social process of reconciliation, offering a hopeful vision of interracial tolerance in the post–civil rights south.

In her second and most recently published novel, *Her Own Place*, Sanders follows her African American protagonist Mae Lee Barnes throughout her life, spanning more than fifty years. The episodic plot of *Her Own Place* is less focused than that of *Clover*, but most of the novel concerns Mae Lee's struggles to raise a family and establish a profitable farm, all on her own. Her story begins in the present time, as the elderly Mae Lee moves from her rural farm to a modern suburban home. The novel then shifts to a flashback as she travels back in memory to her youth, recollecting her experiences as a naïve war bride, and the plot moves forward from the year 1941. While her husband Jeff Barnes is away fighting World War II, Mae Lee manages to save enough money from her work at a munitions plant to buy farmland to surprise her husband. However, Mae Lee's high expectations are dashed when Barnes returns from the war; he refuses to live the traditional farming life his wife desires and abandons her to raise their five children alone.

Despite the obstacles she faces over the years, Mae Lee succeeds at both farming and childrearing through hard work, faith, and the help of friends and family. Sanders depicts Mae Lee as a nurturing matriarch, cultivating both her land and her young according to the rhythms of nature. As her son and daughters grow into independent adults, Mae Lee feels uncertain about what comes next: "Her children, who had grown up surrounding her like plants in a carefully tended perennial garden, had removed themselves and left visible the now uneven edges of her life" (3). She adapts to this new phase of her life by finding another outlet for her nurturing talents when she volunteers in a hospital. In Mae Lee, Sanders creates a touching, authentic portrait of an older woman trying to build a meaningful life for herself after her work of raising children is done. Yet despite her many accomplishments, Mae Lee struggles against the loneliness produced by her husband's departure. Her yearning for romance is finally realized at an advanced age, when she takes in a boarder named Fletcher Owens. By the novel's end, Mae Lee envisions a blossoming future with her new lover, described in Sanders's characteristic agricultural imagery.

Negotiating a respect for tradition with the necessity of change is one of the central themes of *Her Own Place*. Mae Lee is shaped by the values and circumstances of her past, and her old-fashioned ways lead to generational conflict; she cannot bring herself to approve of her grandson's pierced ear or her daughters' directness in dealing with their husbands. Yet Mae Lee has the self-awareness to realize that she must learn to embrace the present despite realities she occasionally finds frightening. *Her Own Place* continues to explore themes presented in *Clover*, affirming the importance of racial tolerance and the sustaining intimacy to be found in female friendship. Although *Her Own Place* has significant weaknesses (there is not enough conflict to drive the plot and Sanders is unable to create for Mae Lee the same kind of strong, appealing narrative voice that she gives Clover), it is a pleasurable read for its humor, quirky characters, and generous warmth of tone.

CRITICAL RECEPTION

Sanders's literary debut generated a warm critical response. Most of the reviews of *Clover* were positive; critics commend Sanders for her simple, yet engaging, narrative style, the warmth and humor of her tone, and the authenticity of the voice she gives to her wryly observant young narrator. Remarking on the author's artistry, one reviewer wrote: "Sanders sews these family scenes together like a fine quilt maker, delicately fashioning scenes that include distant relatives and old friends with all their peculiarities and local customs" (Camp C1). Critics also note her southern settings, praising her ability to convey a strong sense of place through rich, evocative detail. According to one reviewer, "As a specimen of the new realism in regional fiction, *Clover* is very much the genuine item" (Sullivan 30).

Critics' responses to *Her Own Place* are more muted. Many reviewers appreciate the warmth and optimism of Sanders's style. Mae Lee's characterization also garner praise, especially the traits of strength and endurance that are her defining features; for instance, Monique Guillory admires the fact that Mae Lee "breaks new ground for a woman of her generation" while also maintaining the conventional roles of wife, mother, and daughter

(E9). However, the problems of the novel's plot do not escape comment; as Patricia Smith succinctly puts it, Mae Lee "seems on the verge of everything. Southern-bred racism, the Vietnam War, the Civil Rights Movement, all make cameo appearances, then disappear" (48).

Clover has received some attention from scholars, who tend to situate their readings of Sanders in the broader contexts of African American literature, southern literature, and feminist critique. Linda Tate observes that *Clover* is "innovative" in that it reverses a dominant trope in southern fiction dealing with race by presenting a white character who must enter the domain of African American characters and try to win their acceptance. She contends that "Ultimately, Sanders's vision of black-white relationships in the South may be more optimistic as well as more radical: it posits a deep, significant, ongoing bond between black and white communities in the South and articulates a new vision of integrated southern community" (61). Suzanne Jones also notes Sanders's centering of an African American perspective: "Sanders is primarily concerned with blacks' assumptions about whites, and she uses her novel to show that some black assumptions about white people are based on preconceived and unsubstantiated beliefs" (63). Critics also note Sanders's tendency to present racial differences as a matter of contrasting cultural tastes rather than innate differences. Lara Putnam focuses on the role that food plays in *Clover* to signify both personal and racial differences, suggesting that "Sara Kate, Everleen, and Clover use food to express, explore, and occasionally cross the seemingly impermeable demarcation line that exists between blacks and whites" (63). Taking a different tack, Laura Zaidman reads *Clover* as an example of young adult literature, noting that although the book was marketed to adults, school-age readers appreciate its "realism, humor, and honesty" and respond to the narrator's struggle to grow up, a process reflected by Sanders's pastoral imagery of farm life. Zaidman notes that the novel's "metaphor of growth ties all the literary elements into an aesthetic whole." Finally, Nicholyn Hutchinson's reference article is noteworthy for its cogent analysis of *Her Own Place*, one of the few treatments of Sanders's second novel.

BIBLIOGRAPHY

Works by Dori Sanders

Clover. Chapel Hill, NC: Algonquin, 1990.
Dori Sanders' Country Cooking: Recipes and Stories from the Family Farm Stand. Chapel Hill, NC: Algonquin, 1995.
Her Own Place. Chapel Hill, NC: Algonquin, 1993.
Promise Land: A Farmer Remembers. Charlotte, NC: Novello Festival Press, 2004.

Studies of Dori Sanders's Works

Camp, Margaret. Rev. of *Clover. Washington Post*, April 5, 1990, C1.
Fein, Esther B. "Becoming a Writer, Remaining a Farmer." *New York Times*, May 3, 1993, C11ff.
Guillory, Monique. "Places in the Heart." *New Orleans Times-Picayune*, June 27, 1993, E9.
Hutchinson, Nicholyn. "Dori Sanders." In *Contemporary African American Novelists: A Bio-Bibliographical Sourcebook*, edited by Emmanuel S. Nelson, 407–10. Westport, CT: Greenwood Press, 1999.

Jones, Suzanne. *Race Mixing: Southern Fiction Since the Sixties*. Baltimore: Johns Hopkins University Press, 2004.

Putnam, Lara. " 'This Chicken Is Some Kind of Good': The Power of Food in Dori Sanders's *Clover*." *Xavier Review* 17.2 (1997): 63–76.

Smith, Patricia. "*Her Own Place* Feels Good, Goes Nowhere." *Boston Globe*, May 28, 1993, 48.

Sullivan, Jack. Rev. of *Clover*. *New York Times*, May 20, 1990, 30.

Tate, Linda. *A Southern Weave of Women: Fiction of the Contemporary South*. Athens: University of Georgia Press, 1994.

Zaidman, Laura M. "A Sense of Place in Dori Sanders' *Clover*." *ALAN* 22.3 (1995), http://scholar.lib.vt.edu/ejurnals/ALAN/spring95/Zaidman.html (accessed March 12, 2005).

Chandra Wells

MARY SEACOLE (1805–1881)

BIOGRAPHICAL NARRATIVE

Mary Seacole was born Mary Jane Grant in Kingston, Jamaica, in 1805 to a Scottish army officer and a free black "doctoress" and boardinghouse keeper. Although she spent her early years with an unnamed "patroness" who might had educated her, Seacole's early memories of bandaging dolls and assisting her mother with convalescent military officers and their wives are evidence that she was drawn to her mother's profession at an early age. Seacole also displayed a marked turn for business: after her first visit to England, she made a second trip there to sell preserves. She also made small but successful import/export ventures in Haiti and Cuba.

She became a widow shortly after she married the ailing Edwin Seacole in 1836. Although she had inherited her mother's boardinghouse, Seacole left Jamaica for New Grenada (now Panama) in 1851 to help her brother run a small store/hotel, which he had established to serve travelers on their way to the gold fields of California. Seacole later set up her own establishment. When a cholera epidemic struck, she nursed its victims, performed a postmortem, and tested the efficacy of various remedies. Wearied by her efforts and the ingrained prejudice of American travelers, Seacole returned to Jamaica only to be confronted by a yellow fever epidemic. At the request of British army authorities, she provided nursing services at Up Park.

In 1854, when Seacole heard about the wretched conditions that wounded British soldiers faced in the Crimea, she resolved to offer her services there. Although she possessed letters of introduction and significantly more nursing experience than Florence Nightingale, she was not allowed to join the latter in the field. Undaunted, Seacole financed her own journey and, with Mr. Day, her husband's relative, established a combination store, restaurant, and nursing station near the front line. Drawing on her experience in Panama, the popular "Mother Seacole" treated cholera, dysentery, knife and bullet wounds, and other diseases while selling champagne and other delicacies to officers. In spite of the business' initial success, pilfering, disregarded IOUs, and the sudden end of the Crimean War forced Day and Seacole to declare bankruptcy upon returning to England in 1856. A subsequent benefit concert failed to provide Seacole with an income. In need of funds, she published *Wonderful Adventures of Mrs. Seacole in Many Lands* in 1857. A later subscription fund, established by Lord Rokeby and other influential patrons, allowed her to live comfortably in London until her death in 1881.

MAJOR WORK

Because she wrote few letters, and did not keep a journal, *Wonderful Adventures of Mrs. Seacole in Many Lands*, Seacole's only work, is the primary source of information about her. In it, she strategically depicts herself as a British subject who has done her civic duty, crediting her "Scotch blood" for her energy and decisiveness and occasionally displaying the xenophobia characteristic of her British audience. At the same time, Seacole uses her declared Britishness to castigate the racial prejudice of Americans she encounters in Panama. She resists patronizing attitudes and praises the abilities of black Panamanian officials. Even as she depicts herself as a respectable Briton, Seacole firmly and proudly steps over gender boundaries. Although Victorian convention prevents respectable women from traveling alone, Seacole does so, making her own business decisions alone and without apology. Similarly, Seacole makes no apologies for trespassing into the masculine domain of medicine. Championing the heroism of British soldiers, she also unabashedly and humorously declares "the unselfishness of [her] motives" and her "struggles to become a Crimean *heroine!*" (Seacole 76–79).

CRITICAL RECEPTION

Critical approaches to Seacole's narrative focus on the complexities surrounding her identity as a black colonial subject. Writing that many Caribbean authors exhibit "a negotiation of intercultural identities," Paul Baggett notes that Seacole allies herself with the colonial power, "even demonstrating an enthusiastic loyalty toward England and its imperialist enterprises" (45). Sandra Paquet agrees, criticizing the way Seacole occasionally minimizes her Jamaican origins. At the same time, however, the text is also slyly subversive: Evelyn Hawthorne argues that Seacole's declaration of her "good Scotch blood" and her confusing use of the word "creole"—usually applied to European settlers—allow Seacole to declare her value in the face of a racist discourse which would label her illegitimate and sexually immodest. Seacole also "counters prevailing views of black dependency" by emphasizing her own decisiveness (320). Bernard McKenna notes that while Seacole stereotypes Amerindians and dark-skinned blacks in order to project these stereotypes outside of herself—thus "implicitly casting herself as the insider"—contradictions appear in the narrative, as she represents Central American blacks as equal to the English. He suggests that Seacole uses stereotypes to pacify her audience before presenting the notion that "blacks do not always conform to stereotype, [and] . . . have an existence beyond conventional representation" (227). Still, in *Black and White Women's Travel Narratives*, Cheryl Fish writes that Mary Seacole, as "Mother Seacole," was treated as a mammy figure; "most illustrations of Seacole play up her flamboyant dresses and hat . . . and minimize the threat of her politics of trespass and medical intervention" (80).

Both Cheryl Fish and Lorraine Mercer compare *Wonderful Adventures of Mrs. Seacole in Many Lands* to nineteenth-century travel narratives. Mercer writes that, unlike other female travel writers of the era, Seacole was not a privileged white woman traveling to the fringes of the empire. Seacole traveled from margin to center and her narrative "shores up her claim to ladylike behavior while at the same time it illustrates how she transcends the values and abilities of the prescribed feminine behaviors and achieves near epic hero status" (5). Cheryl Fish writes that Seacole "adapts for her travelogue a female version of the picaro": unlike the slave narrators that were her contemporaries, she "shifts the emphasis [of her narrative] from bodily constraint to the realm of adventure" (*Black and White Women's Travel Narratives* 71).

BIBLIOGRAPHY

Work by Mary Seacole

Wonderful Adventures of Mrs. Seacole in Many Lands. 1857. Shomburg Library of Nineteenth-Century Black Women Writers Series, edited by Henry Louis Gates, Jr. New York: Oxford University Press, 1988.

Studies of Mary Seacole's Work

Alexander, Ziggi, and Audrey Dwejee, eds. "Editor's Introduction." In *Wonderful Adventures of Mrs. Seacole in Many Lands.* 1857, 1–45. Bristol: Falling Wall, 1984.

Andrews, William L. "Introduction." In *Wonderful Adventures of Mrs. Seacole in Many Lands.* 1857. Schomburg Library of Nineteenth-Century Black Women Writers Series, edited by Henry Louis Gates, Jr. New York: Oxford University Press, 1988.

Baggett, Paul. "Caught between Homes: Mary Seacole and the Question of Cultural Identity." *MaComère: Journal of the Association of Caribbean Women Writers and Scholars* 3 (2000): 45–56.

Cooper, Helen M. "England: The Imagined Community of Aurora Leigh and Mrs. Seacole." *Studies in Browning and His Circle* (1993): 123–31.

Fish, Cheryl J. *Black and White Women's Travel Narratives: Antebellum Explorations.* Gainesville: University Press of Florida, 2004, 65–95.

———. "Voices of Restless (Dis)continuity: The Significance of Travel for Free Black Women in the Antebellum Americas." *Women's Studies* 262 (1997): 475–95.

Hawthorne, Evelyn J. "Self-Writing, Literary Traditions and Post-Emancipation Identity: The Case of Mary Seacole." *Biography* 23.2 (Spring 2000): 309–31.

Judd, Catherine. *Bedside Seductions: Nursing and the Victorian Imagination.* New York: St. Martin's, 1998, 101–21.

McKenna, Bernard. " 'Fancies of Exclusive Possession': Validation and Dissociation in Mary Seacole's England and the Caribbean." *Philological Quarterly* 76.2 (Spring 1997): 219–32.

Mercer, Lorraine. "Shall Make No Excuse: The Narrative Odyssey of Mary Seacole." *Journal of Narrative Theory* 35.1 (Winter 2005): 1–24.

Moakler, Laura L. "Mary Seacole." In *African American Authors, 1745–1945: A Bibliographical Critical Sourcebook,* edited by Emmanuel S. Nelson, 371–74. Westport, CT: Greenwood Press, 2000.

Paquet, Sandra Pouchet. "The Enigma of Arrival: *The Wonderful Adventures of Mrs. Seacole in Many Lands.*" *African American Review* 26.4 (Winter 1992): 651–63.

Parry, Mel Melanie, ed. "Mary Seacole." In *Larousse Dictionary of Women,* 590. New York: Larousse, 1996.

Rappaport, Helen. "The Invitation That Never Came: Mary Seacole After the Crimea." *History Today* 55 (February 2005): 9–15.

Robinson, Amy. "Authority and Public Display of Identity: *Wonderful Adventures of Mrs. Seacole in Many Lands.*" *Feminist Studies* 20.3 (Fall 1994): 537–57.

Robinson, Jane. *Mary Seacole: The Most Famous Black Woman of the Victorian Age.* New York: Carroll and Graf Publishers, 2004.

Salih, Sara. "Introduction." In *Wonderful Adventures of Mrs. Seacole in Many Lands.* 1857, edited by Sara Salih, l–lii. New York: Penguin Books Ltd., 2005.

Simpson, LaJuan. "Architecting Humanity through Autobiography: Mary Seacole's *Wonderful Adventures of Mrs. Seacole in Many Lands.*" *Revista/Review Interamericana* 31 (Winter 2001): 1–4.

Woodward, Loretta G. "Mary Seacole." In *African American Autobiographers: A Sourcebook,* edited by Emmanuel S. Nelson, 328–32. Westport, CT: Greenwood Press, 2002.

Nanette Morton

FATIMA SHAIK (1952–)

BIOGRAPHICAL NARRATIVE

Adult children fiction writer Fatima Shaik was born on October 24, 1952, in New Orleans, Louisiana, daughter of Mohamed and Lily Shaik. She attended Xavier University–New Orleans, Louisiana, from 1970 to 1972 and obtained a Bachelor of Science degree from Boston University in 1974. Shaik continued her education, and in 1978, received a master's degree from New York University in New York. Shaik worked as a summer intern reporter for the *New Orleans Times-Picayune* in 1973 and 1975, and the *Miami News*, Miami, Florida, in 1974. Also, in 1974 she worked for Gulf South Publishing as assistant editor of the *Newsleader*. From 1976 until 1988 she attained various editorial positions during her employment with McGraw-Hill in New York City. From 1976 to 1981, she held the position of assistant editor in the World News Division, foreign digests editor in 1981–1986, and copy editor in Standard and Poor's Division in 1987–1988. In 1990–1991 at Southern University in New Orleans, Shaik held assistant professor/instructor position in print journalism.

Shaik currently is a lecturer and gives readings from her works. She is on the English Department faculty of Saint Peter's College in New Jersey where she is the Director of the Communication/Mass Media Program and a member of the Board of Director-Writers Room. Her freelance writing has appeared in such publications as the *New York Times*, *Working Woman*, *Black Enterprise*, and *Essence*.

Shaik has received several honors and awards: a Fellowship from the National Endowment for the Humanities (1981), a grant from the Kittredge Fund (1997), "Pick of the Lists" citation, and from the American Booksellers Association for the children's novel Melitte. Shaik is married to painter James Little and is the mother of two children, Celeste and Sophia. She resides both in New York City and New Orleans, Louisiana.

MAJOR WORKS

Shaik has authored four books including three for children: *Melitte*, *On Mardi Gras Day*, and *The Jazz of Our Street*, and one adult collection of fiction, *The Mayor of New Orleans: Just Talking Jazz*. The most acclaimed of her children's books is *Melitte*. Written in first-person narrative for ages ten to fourteen or grades four to eight, *Melitte* is set in the late eighteenth century in Louisiana and is Shaik's first novel.

"Melitte didn't even know she was a slave. She just assumed that all children were treated like this. When her owner married a cruel woman who seemed to enjoy taunting Melitte, things got worse. Melitte even had thoughts of poisoning Madame just to be rid of her. But then the baby was born. The most precious little girl that anyone ever saw. Madame didn't want to care for her so she gave Melitte the responsibility. As baby Marie grew, the two girls became fast friends. To allow Marie to have a Christian education, both Marie and Melitte were allowed to visit a nearby plantation to attend worship. This is where Melitte learned that there were other brown skinned folks. And they were slaves. She never realizes she was a slave. Now she is determined to leave the family and become a free woman. Can a 13 year old girl ever hope to be free?" (Shaik, *Melitte*)

One review of *On Mardi Gras Day* states, "In this disjointed picture book, two young narrators describe their activities on New Orleans' 'day of street parties', a time when Mardis Gras Indians don feathers, beads, and gemstones to dance through neighborhoods. Unless readers are already familiar with Mardi Gras, they will be at sea here" (*Publishers Weekly*, February 8, 1999) *Booklist* describes *The Jazz of Our Street*, "like Medearis and Ransome's Rum-a-Tum-Tum (1997), this is a celebration of the marching bands of New Orleans. Poetic words and stunning, light-filled watercolors express the rhythm and feeling of individual people who play in the band and of those who listen hard and dance and follow the musicians as they wind through the streets of the Treme neighborhood" (May 1, 1998).

The *Black Collegian* reviews *The Mayor of New Orleans: Just Talking Jazz* "a collection of three beautifully written heart-warming stories set in and around New Orleans. Each of the stories gives the readers a glimpse and feel of New Orleans as seen through the eyes of the characters in the book who are all Black but whose backgrounds differ" (March–April 1988).

In each of Ms. Shaik's works she shares and exposes the reader to the culture of New Orleans.

CRITICAL RECEPTION

Although critical analysis of Shaik's works is scant, there have been numerous reviews of *Melitte*. The reviews have ranged from comments such as: "Shaik points out the dehumanizing effect of slavery on the slaveholder as well as on the enslaved as readers watch Melitte's owner (who in actuality is her father) become increasingly callous toward the girl, stealing the money she earned to purchase her freedom" (*School Library Journal*, 138) to "Melitte's intelligence allows her to question the institution of slavery, and her capacity to love eventually helps her to escape. The incidents described are not monumental historical events, but rather a relentless documentary of day-to-day cruelty ultimately—and triumphantly—transformed into a struggle for survival" (*Horn Book Magazine*, 685).

BIBLIOGRAPHY

Works by Fatima Shaik

The Jazz of Our Street. Illustrated by E. B. Lewis. New York: Dial Books for Young Readers, 1998.
The Mayor of New Orleans: Just Talking Jazz. Berkeley, CA: Creative Arts Book Co., 1987.
Melitte. Illustrated by Bill Dodge. New York: Dial Books for Young Readers, 1997.
On Mardi Gras Day. Illustrated by Floyd Cooper. New York: Dial Books for Young Readers, 1999.

Studies of Fatima Shaik's Works

Rev. of *The Jazz of Our Street*. *Booklist* 94.17 (May 1, 1998): 1523.
Rev. of *The Jazz of Our Street*. *Publisher's Weekly* 245.20 (May 18, 1998): 78.
Rev. of *The Jazz of Our Street*. *Horn Book Magazine* 73.6 (November-December 1997): 685.

Rev. of *The Mayor of New Orleans: Just Talking Jazz*. *Publisher's Weekly* 232.18 (October 30, 1987): 52.

Rev. of *The Mayor of New Orleans: Just Talking Jazz*. *Booklist* 84 (December 15, 1987): 676.

Rev. of *The Mayor of New Orleans: Just Talking Jazz*. *Black Collegian* 18.4 (March-April 1988): 150.

Rev. of *Melitte*. *Booklist* 98.12 (February 15, 2002): 1028.

Rev. of *Melitte*. *School Library Journal* 43.10 (October 1997): 138.

Rev. of *Melitte*. *Booklist* 94.4 (October 15, 1997): 398.

Rev. of *Melitte*. *Publisher's Weekly* 244.44 (October 27, 1997): 76.

Rev. of *Melitte*. *Horn Book Magazine* 73.6 (November-December 1997): 685.

Rev. of *On Mardi Gras Day*. *Publisher's Weekly* 246.6 (February 8, 1999): 214.

Rev. of *On Mardi Gras Day*. *Booklist* 95.13 (March 1, 1999): 1223.

Rev. of *On Mardi Gras Day*. *School Library Journal* 45.4 (April, 1999): 109.

Sharon T. Silverman

NTOZAKE SHANGE (1948–)

BIOGRAPHICAL NARRATIVE

The various elements of autobiographer, poet, and fiction writer Shange's biography have not been collected into a full-length work, but much information can be gleaned in fragments from various interviews and from the splashes of autobiography found in Shange's texts. Born in 1948 in Trenton, New Jersey, Paulette Williams moved with her family to St. Louis, met many famous musicians, black activists, and athletes, and attempted suicide four times before changing her name to Ntozake Shange, a Zulu name meaning "she who comes with her own things" and "who walks like a lion" (Lester, *Ntozake Shange*, 10). As the child of two working professionals—a doctor and a psychiatric social worker—Shange never suffered financial deprivations. However, Shange's childhood was not without strife. Perhaps the most traumatic element of her childhood was her forced participation in the St. Louis school integrations, a topic that surfaces in several of her works, most prominently in *Betsey Brown*.

Married and then quickly divorced, Shange's early adulthood was marred by loss, depression, and alienation. Once she found her artistic voice, though, Shange began channeling her pain as well as her optimism for the future into her many female heroines who took the stage, initially, and later championed her novels.

Shange holds a B.A. in American Studies from Barnard College and an M.A. in American Studies from the University of Southern California. She has taught in a variety of disciplines—from the humanities to women's studies—at the University of Houston, the University of Florida (Gainesville), Yale, Douglass, Howard, NYU, the City College of New York, Brown, and Sonoma State.

MAJOR WORKS

Only one of a few works authored by an African American woman to be staged on Broadway, *for colored girls who have considered suicide / when the rainbow is enuf* (1974) is Shange's most influential work. Because of its fusion of dance, poetry, drama, and music, the work's classification is complex, though the preferred term "choreopoem" was first provided by Shange herself. In the work, seven women explore their lives through extended poetic monologues and dance, and each woman represents one of the colors of the rainbow or the color brown. The implication, given the second half of the choreopoem's title and the strong bonds expressed between women throughout the piece, is that women's primary sources of strength and unity lie in other women.

This is not to suggest that the poem is always about all women; for women of color are the focus of the poem, as the title suggests. Although Shange's vision may resonate with women of all colors, especially when dealing with topics such as abortion and date rape, the unique oppression experienced by minority women is highlighted in poems such as Sechita's story of sexual exploitation or the Lady in Orange's struggle to transcend stereotypes of black women.

One of the most remarkable facets of *for colored girls* has been its fluidity, its organic ability to change and grow as it transitioned from its original status as a collection of a few poems, to a collection of a few poems set to dance by Shange and Paula Moss, to a collection of poems set to dance and accompanied by the music of a horn trio and reggae blues band, to a full-scale Broadway production. Although its current productions are fairly standardized, in the early days, Shange and Moss would rearrange the poems selected for performance, varying the choreopoem as they saw fit.

Shange writes of the genesis of *for colored girls*, "In the summer of 1974 I had begun a series of seven poems, modeled on Judy Grahn's *The Common Woman*, which were to explore the realities of seven different kinds of women" ("A History" xii). This early influence of Grahn's work is suggestive, for the women in both works are "common" (although certainly not dull) and united in their common or average lives, their lived lives. Shange's unnamed women experience beatings and other tragedies such as the deaths of children, as well as triumphs of first loves and the sisterhood of other black women in what may initially appear as unrelated snapshots of black womanhood. Shange's poem-as-photo technique is also reminiscent of Grahn's work, and both poets make their snapshots combine into—as Michael Davidson notes is the case of Grahn's *The Common Woman*—the photo album. Shange has also stated her fondness for Grahn's attempt to "murder . . . the King's English" (Lester, "At the Heart," 726). For her part, Shange commits linguistic regicide by violating the rules of capitalization, spelling, and punctuation, and she also peppers her English with both African American Vernacular English and Spanish. Finally, like Grahn, Shange infuses her work's pathos with occasional militant calls to action.

Like *for colored girls*, *A Daughter's Geography* (1983) blends genres, though not all of the poems in the text are performance pieces. Also like *for colored girls*, a number of the poems indict men's abuse of women. For example, in the poems appearing under the heading "Some Men," Shange explores men's exploitation and abuse of women in the forms of rape, sodomy, pornography, stalking, and verbal criticisms. Though the poems uniformly criticize men, they do not criticize all men, just "some men." They are the worst of the worst, the men who belittle women in order to feel big, who rape, mutilate, and silence the women they encounter. But these are not all men, and not even all of the men in the text are abusive. Perhaps the biggest contrast to "Some Men," as Neal A. Lester notes, is that of Greens, the masculine hero in "From Okra to Greens / A Different Kinda Love Story" ("Shange's Men" 325). Greens and Okra (the feminine hero) are both depicted, in the opening poem, as "crooked," which Lester interprets as beaten, mistreated, and abused (325). Though both are undervalued in their mutual society, in each other they find their own worth and means of expressing themselves. Basking in the influence of Greens, Okra begins to relish her black heritage and shun the white faces, voices, and even scents emerging from her television set (59). Though the relationship has its turmoil—one poem is titled "Revelations (The Night Greens Went Off with That Hussy, Rutabaga)"—Okra and Greens work through their disputes and betrayals, and the final poem in the collection celebrates their marriage and incredibly romantic honeymoon.

Innovative in its blending of genres and polyphonic perspectivism, *Sassafrass, Cypress & Indigo* (1982) is Shange's most successful novel to date. The style can be initially daunting for the reader unfamiliar with Shange's work, but as the multiple voices come together via poems, journal entries, letters, traditional narrative fragments, incantations, and recipes, the novel pulls the reader into a culturally rich black female history.

Sassafrass, Cypress, and Indigo—siblings and title characters—each come of age and come into their own black aesthetic as the novel progresses. Indigo, the character most closely aligned with the black south and gifted with a natural musical brilliance, expresses herself through her fiddle. Although her gift is supernatural and ultimately becomes a healing art, Indigo still retains poetic reign over her musicality, refusing to take lessons, as her mother repeatedly requests. Even after she has practiced enough to master the fiddle, Indigo still finds her music stunted whenever she tries to imitate the songs of others. Cypress finds her self-expression in dance, though the particulars of her dance aesthetic shift drastically once she encounters African dance and puts classical ballet mostly aside. Sassafrass and the matriarch of the novel, Hilda Effania, both find their artistic voices in the weaving of cloth, though Sassafrass later supplements her early artistry with poetry.

Though in the novel the main characters are women and perspectives provided are theirs, the novel is sprinkled with male characters, many of whom are artists as well. Mitch, Sassafrass's temperamental lover, and Leroy, Cypress's down-to-earth lover, are both professional musicians. In fact, much of the seduction in the novel occurs through music or dance rather than words or traditional gestures of courtship. The other significant male characters are Hilda's deceased husband, whom she romanticizes although her daughters remember a darker side to their father, and Uncle John, an elderly junk man revered by all area hoodlums, young and old. Both Leroy and Uncle John play significant roles in helping two of the female characters find their voices—Leroy provides Cypress with unconditional love and financial backing and Uncle John introduces Indigo to the gift of musical expression—and therefore illustrate that while *Sassafrass* may be first and foremost a novel about female expression, it also pays homage to black men's roles in paving the way for women's voices.

Reminiscent of Mark Twain's masterpiece for reasons beyond its setting on the Mississippi River, Shange's second novel, *Betsey Brown* (1985) is a Bildungsroman that features the title character's attempts to reconcile white hostility or indifference to blacks with her own family's contradictory impulses to uplift the black race and simultaneously avoid interacting with poor blacks. The daughter of a doctor and a social worker, just as Shange herself was, Betsey Brown finds that her parents have different philosophies about their children's destinies. Dr. Greer Brown is a race man, a man who awakens his children with conga drums each morning, insists that his children be among the first to integrate white schools in St. Louis, introduces his children to Ike and Tina Turner, and risks his marriage in order to take his children to a protest demonstration aimed at defeating hotel segregation. Jane Brown, though not born into great wealth, clings to her middle-class existence and fifteen-room home with passionate determination. She and her mother, Vida, both have a touch of southern gentility in their light-skinned and delicate compositions. Although both women prove themselves loving at various points in the novel, neither is able to see how her own elitism (and colorism, in the case of Vida) robs the family of much happiness.

Perhaps the most egregious error made by Jane Brown occurs at the end of the novel as she dismisses Carrie, the black female servant and nanny to the children. Carrie first appears after she rescues the family from grief and chaos in the wake of Jane Brown's temporary desertion. Giving the children confidence, genuine attention, and abundant domestic chores, Carrie nurtures the Browns into a version of themselves they have never known—their best, most cooperative, most loving selves. Throughout Jane's absence, Carrie helps the children cherish their memories and love for their mother, constantly reassuring them that she will soon return. When she does return, however, Carrie's days are numbered. At the first sign of trouble, Jane asks Carrie to remove her things from their home and be on her way. This signals the end of childhood for Betsey, the eldest daughter and now surrogate mother to her siblings. Still an adolescent herself, Betsey, like Huck Finn in Twain's celebrated novel, must make the adult decisions that reflect a better morality than her social environment has provided. She will love and nurture where her mother was unable or unwilling, and, having loved Carrie, she will judge those around her on more than the color of their skin or their dialect or income.

Despite the interesting plot and historical insights provided by the novel, it fails to achieve the literary quality of Shange's *Sassafrass, Cypress & Indigo*. Limited by a traditional narrative structure and nearly dialect-free vocabulary, the novel is incredibly bland when compared to the magic of *Sassafrass*. Though Betsey is a thoroughly lovable little girl, her voice remains largely submerged by the voices of her oppressors, and even the influence of Carrie, a rural black Arkansan who wears double-layered housecoats cinched with a rope belt and drinks homemade blackberry wine, will not save Betsey from her mother's black middle-class respectability.

Then, too, where so much of the richness of *Sassafrass* comes from the artistry of black women as they weave, write, cook, play music, and conjure, Betsey and her sisters, mother, and grandmother barely scratch the surface of any of these arts, though there is mention of Jane Brown's love of literature and Betsey's mastery of the clarinet. Never, though, do we actually encounter the women in the process of creating, excepting the moments when the children improvise rhymes as they march off to the white schools or perform their chores under Carrie's direction. Gone are the extended descriptions of meal preparation and wool dying; instead, we merely get the chaotic tangle of children's nervous voices as they rush off to slay the racist dragons of ignorance.

A compilation of essays, *See No Evil: Prefaces, Essays & Accounts, 1976–1983* (1984) collectively represents Shange's artistic philosophies told in the highly poetic voice akin to those found in *for colored girls*. The first essay provides fascinating historical commentary on *for colored girls*, ending with a statement on Shange's long wait for recognition and need to move on to other projects: "i am on the other side of the rainbow / picking up the pieces of days spent waitin for the poem to be heard / while you listen / I have other work to do/" (17).

Shange's second essay is a polemic against imitative drama, urging black playwrights to take chances and tap into their rich cultural history. Sounding much like Langston Hughes in his "The Negro Artist and the Racial Mountain," Shange writes, "we are selling ourselves & our legacy quite cheaply / since we are trying to make our primary statements with somebody else's life / and somebody else's idea of what theater is" (19). Further, Shange argues that black playwrights are spilling far too much ink on the lives of black musicians and other famous entertainers, presumably because they offer the audience interesting stories of achievement. Instead, says Shange, playwrights need to focus more on the common black men and women who help to shape the black aesthetic through lived experience (18–19).

The third essay, or, "Program Note," introduces Shange's use of Franz Fanon's "combat breath." The intense exercise of will required to live in an occupied or colonized area, Fanon asserted, made breathing itself an expression of combat. So, too, does Shange feel the oppression of living as a black woman in a society privileging whiteness and maleness. Shange suggests that those who criticize her on the grounds that she is "too self-conscious of being a writer" and doing great harm to the English language have missed the point of her struggle: writing, especially in the oppressor's language, is suffocating. Therefore, Shange writes, "i cant count the number of times i have viscerally wanted to attack deform n main the language that i was taught to hate myself in" (21).

In her most famous essay, "takin a solo / a poetic possibility / a poetic imperative," Shange argues that black writers need to better distinguish themselves from others and readers need to become more discerning interpreters of poetic self-expression. She lightly chides, "you never doubt bessie smith's voice. i cd not say to you / that's chaka khan singin 'empty bed blues'" (26). Although the essay begins by criticizing those authors who are content with imitation, the essay quickly progresses into a keen critique of the audience's poor ear for poetry. There is clearly a difference between the poets you fail to recognize, writes Shange, "a difference / in syntax, imagery & rhythm & theme" (27).

CRITICAL RECEPTION

Shange may well be the least studied most important African American author alive. Though the early success of *for colored girls* earned her a solid reputation, many of her works remain unexplored in the academic presses, with only one full-length study of her works published to date. This, despite two Obies, a two-year run on Broadway, multiple Guggenheim and NEA fellowships, Grammy, Tony, and Emmy nominations, and an Outer Circle Critics Award.

While Shange's work has not received enough attention, much of the attention received has been related to the single topic of negative masculine representations in her works. What began as a controversy started with Curtis E. Rogers's comment on her "'unrelenting stereotyping of Black men'" (quoted in Watson 381) became a full-blown battle when Robert Staples attacked Shange and Michele Wallace in "The Myth of Black Macho: A Response to Angry Black Feminists." Seventeen authors involved in the controversy were asked to respond to the debate in a 1979 issue of the *Black Scholar* (Hernton 141). Ntozake Shange was represented in the two-part series on black sexism, as were Audre Lorde, Robert Staples, and Alvin Poussaint (141). Although the women were diplomatic though insistent that they had a right to express both their feminist and black loyalties, as Calvin Hernton notes, "the men claimed that the women had fallen prey to white feminist propaganda" (141). The controversy reached epic proportions when Alice Walker and *The Color Purple* were pulled into the fray, and several of the parties involved were called together in a watered-down "discussion" promising to stir the pot even further—a debate hosted by Phil Donahue. The superstar panelists appearing on this historic episode of *Phil Donahue* were Ntozake Shange, Maya Angelou, Michele Wallace, Angela Davis, and Alice Walker. The audience was composed mostly of black men, many of whom seemed fairly sympathetic with what the black women panelists were trying to accomplish, and many of whom echoed the sentiments of Alice Walker that the media had overstated the disagreement between black men and women writers and intellectuals.

Whether the media is to be blamed or not, much of the academic criticism of Shange's work continues to focus on the issue of male bashing. In addition to Hernton's overview of the black sexism debate published in 1984 and Neal A. Lester's refutation of the charge respecting Shange, "Shange's Men: For Colored Girls Revisited, and Movement Beyond," Ann duCille, Elizabeth Brown-Guillory, and Mary Helen Washington have all written on various aspects of black feminism in Shange's works. Each of these works is crucial to understanding Shange, but Shange's works are much more comprehensive and complicated than these studies suggest. A few notable additions to the critical study of Shange are Maria V. Johnson and Arlene Elder's studies of blues music in *Sassafrass, Cypress & Indigo*, P. Jane Splawn's study of black folklore in Shange's drama, and Karen Cronacher and Sandra L. Richards's studies of minstrelsy in Shange's *spell #7*. The one full-length study of Shange's dramatic works, Lester's *Ntozake Shange: A Critical Study of the Plays* provides numerous insights and careful research of unpublished as well as published texts, but Lester's work is by no means exhaustive, particularly since Shange continues to write. Then, too, Lester's focus is mostly on Shange's plays. As a novelist, poet, and critic, Shange remains largely unexplored.

BIBLIOGRAPHY

Works by Ntozake Shange

Drama

Daddy Says. In *New Plays for the Black Theatre*, edited by Woodie King, Jr. Chicago: Third World, 1989.

For colored girls who have considered suicide / when the rainbow is enuf. 1974. Reprint, New York: Scribner, 1997.

"A History." Forward for *colored girls who have considered suicide when the rainbow is enuf.* New York: Scribner, 1997: ix–xvi.

A Photograph: Lovers-in-Motion. New York: French, 1981.

See No Evil: Prefaces, Essays, and Accounts, 1976–1983. San Francisco: Momo's Press, 1984.

Spell #7. London: Methuen, 1985.

Three Pieces. Spell #7, A Photograph: Lovers-in-Motion, Boogie Woogie Landscapes. New York: St. Martin's Press, 1981.

Poetry

Black & White Two-Dimensional Planes. Callaloo 5 (1979): 56–62.

A Daughter's Geography. New York: St. Martin's Press, 1983.

The Love Space Demands: A Continuing Saga. New York: St. Martin's Press, 1991.

Nappy Edges. New York: St. Martin's Press, 1978.

Natural Disasters and Other Festive Occasions. San Francisco: Heirs, 1977.

Ridin' the Moon in Texas: Word Paintings. New York: St. Martin's Press, 1987.

Novellas

Melissa & Smith: A Story. St. Paul: Bookslinger, 1976.

Sassafrass. Santa Cruz: Shameless Hussy Press, 1976.

Novels

Betsey Brown. New York: St. Martin's Press, 1985.

Liliane: Resurrection of the Daughter. New York: St. Martin's Press, 1994.

Sassafrass, Cypress & Indigo. New York: Picador, 1982.

Studies of Ntozake Shange's Works

Anderlini, Serena W. "Drama or Performance Art? An Interview with Ntozake Shange." *Journal of Dramatic Theory and Criticism* 6 (1991): 85–97.

Betsko, Kathleen, and Rachael Koenig, eds. "Ntozake Shange." In *Interviews with Contemporary Women Playwrights*, 365–78. New York: Beech Tree Books, 1987.

Blackford, Holly. "The Spirit of a People: The Politicization of Spirituality in Julia Alvarez's *In the Time of Butterflies*, Ntozake Shange's *Sassafrass, Cypress & Indigo*, and Ana Castillo's *So Far from God*." In *Things of the Spirit: Women Writers Constructing Spirituality*, edited by Kristina K. Groover, 224–55. Notre Dame: University of Notre Dame Press, 2004.

Blackwell, Henry. "An Interview with Ntozake Shange." *Black American Literature Forum* 13.4 (1979): 134–38.

Brown-Guillory, Elizabeth. "Black Women Playwrights: Exorcising Myths." *Phylon* 48.3 (1987): 229–39.

Cronacher, Karen. "Unmasking the Mistrel Mask's Black Magic in Ntozake Shange's 'spell #7.'" *Theatre Journal* 44.2 (1992): 177–93.

Damon, Maria. "Kozmic Reappraisals: Revising California Insularity." In *Women Poets of the Americas: Toward a Pan-American Gathering*, edited by Jacqueline Vaught Brogan, 254–71. Notre Dame: University of Notre Dame Press, 1999.

Dong, Stella. "Ntozake Shange." *Publishers Weekly* (May 5, 1985): 74–75.

duCille, Ann. "Phallus(ies) of Interpretation: Toward Engendering the Black Critical 'I.'" *Callaloo* 16.3 (1993): 559–73.

Early, James. "Interview with Ntozake Shange." In *In Memory and Spirit of Frances, Zora, and Lorraine: Essays and Interviews on Black Women and Writing*, edited by Juliette Bowles, 23–26. Washington: Institute for the Arts and the Humanities, Howard University, 1979.

Ecker, Gisela. "Eating Identities—From Migration to Lifestyle: Mary Antin, Ntozake Shange, Ruth Ozekl[i]." In *Wandering Selves: Essays on Migration and Multiculturalism*, edited by Michael Porsche and Christian Berkemeier, 171–83. Essen, Germany: Blaue Eule, 2000.

Effiong, Philip U. "The Subliminal to the Real: Musical Regeneration in Ntozake Shange's *Boogie Woogie Landscapes*." *Theatre Studies* 39 (1994): 33–43.

Elder, Arlene. "*Sassafrass, Cypress & Indigo*: Ntozake Shange's Neo-Slave/Blues Narrative." *African American Review* 26.1 (1992): 99–107.

El-Shayal, Dalia. "Nonverbal Theatrical Elements in Ntozake Shange's *for colored girls . . .* and Intissar Abdel-Fatah's *Makhadet El-Kohl* (*The Kohl Pillow*)." *Comparative Drama* 37.3–4 (2003–2004): 361–78.

Erickson, John. "The Face and the Possibility of Performance." *Journal of Dramatic Theory and Criticism* 13.2 (1999): 5–21.

Flowers, Sandra Hollin. "*Colored Girls*: Textbook for the Eighties." *Black American Literature Forum* 15.2 (1981): 51–54.

Hayes, Ned Dykstra. "Whole 'Altarity': Toward a Feminist A/Theology." In *Divine Aporia: Postmodern Conversations about the Other*, edited by John C. Hawley, 172–89. Lewisburg: Bucknell University Press, 2000.

Hernton, Calvin. "The Sexual Mountain and Black Women Writers." *Black American Literature Forum* 18.4 (Winter 1984): 139–45.

Holloway, Karla F. C. "Revision and (Re)membrance: A Theory of Literary Structures in Literature by African-American Women Writers." *Black American Literature Forum* 24.4 (1990): 617–31.

Hubert, Susan J. "Singing a Black Girl's Song in a Strange Land: *for colored girls* and the Perils of Canonicity." *Literary Griot* 14.1–2 (2002): 92–102.

Huse, Nancy. "Because the Rainbow Is Not Enuf." *Paradoxa* 2 (1996): 490–93.

Johnson, Maria V. "Shange and Her Three Sisters 'Sing a Liberation Song.'" In *Black Orpheus: Music in African American Fiction from the Harlem Renaissance to Toni Morrison*, edited by Saadi A. Simawe, 181–203. New York: Garland Publishing, 2000.

Kent, Assunta. "The Rich Multiplicity of *Betsey Brown*." *Journal of Dramatic Theory and Criticism* 7.1 (1992): 151–61.

Kim, Jeongho. "Aesthetic of Liberation and Subversion: Discursive Strategy in Shange's Choreopoem." *Journal of English Language and Literature* 50.2 (2004): 543–62.

Lester, Neal A. "At the Heart of Shange's Feminism: An Interview." *Black American Literature Forum* 24.4 (1990): 717–30.

———. *Ntozake Shange: A Critical Study of the Plays*. New York: Garland, 1995.

———. "Shange's Men: *For Colored Girls* Revisited, and Movement Beyond." *African American Review* 26.2 (1992): 319–28.

McDowell, Deborah E. " 'The Changing Same': Generational Connections and Black Women Novelists." *New Literary History* 18.2 (1987): 281–302.

Mullen, Harryette. " 'Artistic Expression Was Flowing Everywhere': Alison Mills and Ntozake Shange, Black Bohemian Feminists in the 1970s." *Meridians* 4.2 (2004): 205–35.

Murray, Timothy. "Facing the Camera's Eye: Black and White Terrain in Women's Drama." In *Reading Black, Reading Feminist: A Critical Anthology*, edited by Henry Louis Gates, Jr., 155–75. New York: Meridian, 1990.

"Ntozake Shange." *New Yorker* (August 2, 1976): 17–19.

Richards, Sandra L. "Conflicting Impulses in the Plays of Ntozake Shange." *Black American Literature Forum* 17.2 (1983): 73–78.

Rushing, Andrea Benton. "*For Colored Girls*: Suicide or Struggle." *Massachusetts Review* 22.3 (1981): 539–50.

Splawn, P. Jane. " 'Change the Joke(r) and Slip the Yoke': Boal's 'Jokcr' System in Ntozake Shange's *For Colored Girls* and *Spell #7*." *Modern Drama* 41.3 (1998): 386–98.

Tate, Claudia, ed. "N.S." In *Black Women Writers at Work*, 149–74. New York: Continuum, 1983.

Taylor-Thompson, Betty. "Female Support and Bonding in *for colored girls...*" *Griot* 12.1 (1993): 46–51.

———. "Ntozake Shange." In *The Concise Oxford Companion to African American Literature*, edited by William L. Andrews, Frances Smith Foster, and Trudier Harris, 363–65. New York: Oxford University Press, 2001.

Washington, Mary Helen. "New Lives and New Letters: Black Women Writers at the End of the Seventies." *College English* 43.1 (1981): 1–11.

Watson, Kenneth. "Ntozake Shange." In *American Playwrights since 1945: A Guide to Scholarship, Criticism, and Performance*, edited by Philip C. Kolin, 379–81. New York: Greenwood Press, 1989.

Waxman, Barbara Frey. "Dancing out of Form, Dancing into Self: Genre and Metaphor in Marshall, Shange, and Walker." *MELUS* 19.3 (1994): 91–106.

Whitney, Elizabeth. "When White Girls Act Black: Reconsidering Performances of Otherness." In *Casting and Gender: Women in Intercultural Contexts*, edited by Laura Lengel and John T. Warren, 109–28. New York: Peter Lang, 2005.

"Women and the Creative Process: A Discussion (with Susan Griffin, Norma Leistiko, Ntozake Shange, and Miriam Schapiro)." *Mosaic* 8 (1974–1975): 91–117.

Young, Jean. "Ritual Poetics and Rites of Passage in Ntozake Shange's *for colored girls who have considered suicide / when the rainbow is enuf*." In *Black Theatre: Ritual Performance in the African Diaspora*, edited by Paul Carter Harrison, Victor Leo Walker III, and Gus Edwards, 296–310. Philadelphia: Temple University Press, 2002.

Young-Minor, Ethel. "Performance Pedagogies for African American Lit: Teaching Shange at Ole Miss." *Radical Teacher* 65 (2003–2004): 27–32.

Cammie M. Sublette

ANN ALLEN SHOCKLEY (1927–)

BIOGRAPHICAL NARRATIVE

Ann Allen Shockley has written reference books, nonfiction and fiction for newspapers and journals, as well as book reviews, essays, novels, and a collection of short stories. She was born on June 21, 1927, in Louisville, Kentucky. She began publishing short stories in the *Louisville Defender* at age eighteen. After receiving a B.A. at Fisk University, Shockley went on to pursue an M.A. in Library Science at Case Western Reserve University. She has worked at Delaware State College, University of Maryland (Eastern Shore Branch), and at Fisk University where she still works as the curator for African American collections. Although a majority of Shockley's fictional characters are lesbian, she identifies as a feminist with lesbian sympathies.

MAJOR WORKS

Loving Her, Shockley's first published novel, is a lesbian romance. Terry, a wealthy white writer, and Renay, a lounge pianist and mother, fall in love. Renay's relationship with Terry saves Renay from her abusive husband, Jerome, who raped her and impregnated her—forcing their marriage. Terry replaces everything that Renay has lost or never had during her heterosexual marriage to Jerome. Terry buys Renay another piano, encourages her musically, gives her plenty of money to buy groceries, and loves her and her daughter Denise. Terry is also the first sexual relationship Renay chooses. During the course of the text Renay and Terry's relationship investigates racism, patriarchy, and heterosexism.

Terry and Renay's love for one another is not fully understood—even in the lesbian community. Terry's former lover Jean is overtly racist. Jean calls Renay a "nigger bitch" (56) and refuses to drink with her because she is African American. Other lesbian characters such as Lorraine and Vance fail to understand Renay and Terry as an interracial lesbian couple. Although the other white lesbian characters make attempts to understand Renay, she remains a manifestation of African American stereotypes.

Renay is also oppressed by patriarchal society. She remains passive in her relations with Jerome and also, to a lesser degree, with Terry. Renay allows Jerome to sell the most important thing to her—the piano. Jerome does not work, drinks too much, kills Denise, and rapes and beats Renay. Renay allows her will to be thwarted by her husband in many ways until she meets Terry. However, Renay is still in a subservient position with Terry. Renay is younger and depends on Terry for money, education, and support. Terry is also the sexual aggressor with only one exception. But even when Renay is the aggressor she is still subservient because she is "trying to please her lover" (48). Renay cannot escape the dichotomy of aggressive and subservient—nor can Terry.

Terry, although she gives Renay a satisfying relationship both mentally and physically, uses language that is dominating. Terry speaks of Renay as an object to be owned. Instead of Renay belonging with, she "belongs to" Terry (88). Terry also drinks in almost every scene throughout the novel—paralleling her to Jerome. However loving and supportive their relationship, it is flawed as a result of sexist indoctrination. At the close of the novel, after Denise's death resulting from Jerome's drunk driving, Terry and Renay's relationship has grown. Both women reunite after a short absence while Renay grieves Denise and waits "for the morning, which promised to be even better than the night" (187). Although Terry and Renay have grown in their relationship the society does not mirror the girl's progress.

As a lesbian Renay encounters homophobia from the African American community and remains closeted. Renay's best friend Fran takes care of Denise while Renay works and helps her cope while she is married to Jerome. However, when Renay meets and falls in love with Terry, Fran is both jealous of their relationship and angry that Renay is friends with a white woman. Renay wants to tell her best friend that Terry is not simply a friend but rather a lover. But Renay knows that Fran will not accept this relationship due to her sexual fixation on men. Fran's homophobia is exposed when she yells out at a nightclub "Fag!" and Renay begins to pass as a straight—becoming a "stranger among her own" (153). Sadly, Fran and Renay's mother are both astounded that Renay can live with a white woman and Renay knows that they will not accept their relationship as interracial lesbian lovers.

Renay faces homophobia from the African American community while Terry and Renay receive acceptance from their much older white neighbor. Terry gives Mrs. Stilling a copy of a book that she has written about her relationship with Renay. Mrs. Stilling likes Terry's book and asks Terry whether she has considered their relationship racially. Terry says that she does not think about it. Mrs. Stilling replies knowingly and acceptingly. Although, the novel does not equate oppression of African Americans and homosexuals, there is however a paradox exposed: white lesbians accept African Americans because lesbians experience discrimination while African American heterosexuals blame Lesbianism "on white women" (31).

Renay is poor, female, African American, and lesbian. Terry can understand her position only partially because she is not African American or poor. However, their love is more powerful than the problems each face in society. Shockley exposes the paradox between lesbians accepting African Americans while African Americans blame white women for lesbianism. In doing so, the text illustrates that the only space Renay can be both African American and lesbian is in the white lesbian community—but Renay still yearns for an African American lesbian community.

The Black and White of It is the first published short story collection containing African American lesbian experience. However, there are only ten stories in the collection and three do not refer to racial identity directly. Probably the most successful of the essays is "The Meeting of the Sapphic Daughters." This story is similar to Shockely's longer fiction in that it exposes the ostracization of African American lesbians by white lesbians. In this collection there are relationships unlike in *Loving Her* and *Say Jesus and Come to Me* because not all the relationships end happily. There is also a divergence in the collection as a whole regarding its relative lack of focus on politics and sex. Overall the collection illustrates a greater thematic range of Shockley's writing.

Say Jesus and Come to Me is Shockley's second novel and is much more complex and less trite than *Loving Her*. Myrtle Black, the female protagonist, is an evangelical lesbian minister. Myrtle is an extremely flawed character—she preaches for money, uses the media to gain attention for her church, and has sex with her congregation members.

However, for all of Myrtle's negative traits she also strives, however selfishly, for political change.

Myrtle's focus, therefore, is both selfish and altruistic. When Myrtle arrives in Nashville she reads about two prostitutes who have been shot and are in the hospital. Happily, Myrtle realizes that Nashville is in need of God and proceeds to make plans to use the situation to her advantage. While at the Reverend Cross's house, the minister of New Hope Unity Church, Myrtle makes connections with George Clemons—a journalist. Myrtle convinces Clemons to run a story about her visiting the prostitutes to advertise her sermons. Although Myrtle is using the prostitutes to greedily fill her church pews, she tries her best to get the prostitutes, Earthly Treasures and Heavenly Delight, to change their ways. Ultimately she is successful with only Heavenly Delight.

Myrtle's plan of action to fill her pews sets off a chain of profound consequences. First a blues singer Travis Lee, who Myrtle is already fascinated with, is born again when she hears Myrtle on the radio. Travis Lee's popularity also brings in people to the church. Myrtle is then able to disseminate her beliefs about the Bible, God, and social injustice more effectively. She is also making a large sum of money from the large numbers in attendance. However Cross knew that "there wasn't a man in the church, including himself, who hadn't paid for [sex] one time or another" (79). Consequently Myrtle is asked to leave the church even though her sermons have been successful.

Directly after Myrtle's dismissal from Cross's church, Myrtle sets out to have a Women's March. The march allows Myrtle to stay in Nashville and make real change for herself and the community. During this time Myrtle is given a place to stay and preach from a wealthy white landowner—Wilma Freelander. During this time Myrtle has the freedom to preach what she likes, but also has to compromise with the women's march. The freedom within the church allows Myrtle to court Travis Lee and consummate a loving relationship. The work of the women's march pulls Myrtle and Travis apart. There are opposing views between men and women, African Americans and whites, and lesbians and heterosexuals for the march. Ultimately the committee decides that the march will be for issues affecting straight women of any color.

During the march Travis is symbolically ran over by a car. Myrtle decides that it is time to come out as a lesbian to her church. Previously Myrtle felt that the church was not ready, but believes that she must now give the most important sermon of her life. Her sermon is titled "Freedom and Acceptance" (279) and calls for the church to change its teachings on homosexuality. She announces to her congregation that she is a lesbian and asks anyone who is uncomfortable to leave. No one does. At the opening of the novel Myrtle is concerned with money, clothes, and finding women but she progresses to find loving relationships through political and social change.

The novel calls for intersections of sexual and spiritual, gay and straight, African American and white in order to find love and acceptance. The progress of the novel is a process of social change. Indeed, when no one in Myrtle's congregation leaves as a result of her homosexuality—this is a radically different society compared to the one that forces Myrtle to leave due to her teachings on prostitution. In making Myrtle flawed, the text suggests that political and social change can be accomplished by those who are less than perfect.

CRITICAL RECEPTION

Loving Her reached the *Christopher Street* bestseller list when it was first published in 1974 (Dandridge 26). However, critics had varying views—some extremely harsh. Frank Phillips in *Black World* writes "this bullshit should not be encouraged" (90) while Karla Jay in *WIN* suggests that *Loving Her* commits "all the deadly sins lesbians preach against" (20). Others, however, note that *Loving Her* is the first to address race issues in lesbian relationships and therefore give Shockley credit for her attempts to represent what has never been done before and sympathy for her failures in character development and realism.

Reception of *The Black and White of It* was also mixed. Alexis De Veaux reviewed the work in *13th Moon* and believes that the characters throughout the collection lack depth. De Veaux goes on to mention that in the short story "A Birthday Remembered," the girls are simply "victims of their sexuality" (144). While in *Motherroot Journal*, Gayle White gives the collection of short stories praise despite their predictability. Because *The Black and White of It* is the first collection of short stories about African American lesbian experience, most reviewers tend to suggest that the visibility of African lesbian experience outweigh the lack of aesthetic and character development.

When *Say Jesus and Come to Me* was published in 1982, it received more positive reviews than *Loving Her* and *The Black and White of It*. However, John Tremaine calls Shockley's work "pathetic" and the male characters "fools or morons" (66). The other reviews of the novel were mostly if not entirely positive. Helen Eisenbach in the *New York Native* reviews the novel, calling it "peculiar, dreadfully written, yet somehow fascinating[ly] trashy . . . vaguely evil lesbian" novel (39). However, Eisenbach mistakes central characters' racial identities. Two different reviewers state that the novel would make an excellent movie.

Shockley's fiction often received poor reviews. Responding to this, Karla Jay suggests that Shockley's negative reception is a function of male criticism. Even the essay that Jay wrote on *Loving Her* in *WIN* the editors cut "the positive comments and left the bad ones" (17). Jay considers *The Black and White of It* to be a better work of fiction and is grateful that Shockley continues writing in the face of criticism.

BIBLIOGRAPHY

Works by Ann Allen Shockley

The Black and White of It. Tallahassee: Naiad Press, 1980. Reprint, 1987.
"The Black Lesbian in American Literature: An Overview." In *Home Girls: A Black Feminist Anthology*, edited by Barbara Smith. New York: Kitchen Table Women of Color Press, 1983.
Living Black American Authors: A Bibliographical Directly. Edited with Sue P. Chandler. New York: Bowker, 1973.
Loving Her. New York: Bobbs-Merrill, 1974. Reprints, New York: Avon, 1978; Boston: Northeastern University Press, 1997.
Say Jesus and Come to Me. New York: Avon, 1982.

Studies of Ann Allen Shockley's Works

Dandridge, Rita B. *Ann Allen Shockley: An Annotated Primary and Secondary Bibliography*. New York: Greenwood Press, 1987.
Eisenbach, Helen. *New York Native* 2 (November 22–December 5, 1982): 39.

Jay, Karla. "Deny, Deny, Deny." *New Women's Times Feminist Review* 15 (April–May 1981): 17–18.

———. *WIN* 12 (December 1974): 20.

Josey, E. J., and Ann Allen Shockely, comps. and eds. *Handbook of Black Librarianship*. Littleton: Libraries Unlimited, 1977.

Phillips, Frank Lamont. *Black World* 24 (September 1975): 89–90.

Smith, Barbara. "Toward a Black Feminist Criticism." *Conditions: Two* 1 (October 1977): 25–44.

Tremaine, John S. *West Coast Review of Books* 8 (September–October 1982): 66.

White, Gayle. *Motherroot Journal* 2 (Summer 1980): 4.

Adriane Bezusko

AMANDA BERRY SMITH (1837–1915)

BIOGRAPHICAL NARRATIVE

Amanda Berry Smith was born on January 23, 1837, in Long Green, Maryland, to Samuel Berry and Miriam Matthews, slaves on neighboring farms. By 1840 Samuel had earned enough money to purchase his own freedom and that of Miriam and their children. The Berrys then moved to York County, Pennsylvania, a station on the Underground Railroad. As a result of her family's free status, Amanda received minimal formal education at a school for white children, and her parents helped her learn to read. In 1854 she married Calvin M. Devine and moved to Columbia, Pennsylvania. She found Devine "profane and unreasonable" when he indulged in alcohol (*Autobiography* 42). She underwent conversion in 1856. Devine enlisted in the Union Army and never returned from the Civil War. Moving to Philadelphia, she joined the African Methodist Episcopal (AME) Church and married James H. Smith. The couple relocated to New York City. Because James was not a steady provider, Amanda worked as a servant and took in laundry. In 1868 she experienced sanctification, the "second blessing" that, according to Wesleyan tradition, purifies converts from intentional sin. She began testifying at AME churches and became prominent in Holiness: a predominantly white interdenominational movement that promoted the controversial doctrine of immediate sanctification by faith and encouraged all believers to testify publicly about their spiritual lives. After James died in 1869, she devoted herself to full-time evangelism, but because the AME Church refused to ordain women, she depended on donations from well-wishers.

An enthusiastic speaker with a beautiful singing voice, Smith received many invitations to preach, though some AME pastors adamantly opposed women preachers. She also campaigned for the Woman's Christian Temperance Union. In 1878 her tour of England on behalf of temperance and Holiness led to an invitation to serve as a missionary in India. In 1882 she proceeded to Africa, again with "no official backing or financial support" (Israel 74). Like many westerners, Smith considered Africans deeply ignorant and superstitious. Still, she maintained that blacks given equal opportunities could equal whites, and she spoke out against the whites' alcohol trade in Africa.

A celebrity upon returning to the United States in 1890, Smith spoke widely even while working on her autobiography. In 1893 she settled in Harvey, Illinois, determined to found a home and school for black orphans. After years of national fund-raising tours, she opened her orphanage in Harvey in 1899. Not tax supported, the institution was insolvent by the time Smith retired to Sebring, Florida, in 1912 to a home provided by an admirer. She died in Sebring on February 25, 1915. The school closed after a fire in 1918.

MAJOR WORK

Smith's *An Autobiography: The Story of the Lord's Dealings with Mrs. Amanda Smith the Colored Evangelist* incorporates elements of the spiritual autobiography, travel narrative, and slave narrative. The author focuses on her spiritual experiences and evangelistic and reformist activities. She omits certain personal details—saying little, for example, about her siblings and bypasses exciting incidents such as her flight to Philadelphia as the Confederate Army marched toward central Pennsylvania in 1863. Unlike evangelist-autobiographers Jarena Lee and Julia Foote, she does not argue for the ordination of women, declaring instead that God validates her. The *Autobiography* as a whole affirms the universal need for, and accessibility of, sanctification; it presents the love of God along with "common sense" (41) as remedies for social problems.

Prominent themes include the need for self-control and courage; joy in enthusiastic worship; the evils of alcohol and tobacco; the importance of education; and racism and sexism in India, Africa, and the United States. Smith's prose, though sometimes weighted down with details, is clear and graced with touches of humor. Dialogues with God and with Satan vividly capture her sense of the drama of the devout life. A master of the memorable anecdote, Smith conveys the difficulties of being marginalized—as a woman, an African American, a preacher, an advocate of Holiness, and a person whose determination to get along with others leads some of her own people to criticize her as a "white folks' nigger" (232, 453).

A selective account of the life of an individual for whom faith and racial identity were vital issues, the *Autobiography* provides insights into styles of religious expression, reforms grounded in the African American and evangelical communities, and race and gender relations on four continents.

CRITICAL RECEPTION

Praised and promoted by friends and offered for sale by Smith herself, the *Autobiography* sold well enough to help support her orphans' home. An abridged version appeared in 1977, and the entire work was reprinted several times during the twentieth century. Long a popular author, Smith has recently been examined in scholarly books by historians and literary critics, including Betty Collier-Thomas, Richard J. Douglass-Chin, and Susie C. Stanley.

BIBLIOGRAPHY

Work by Amanda Berry Smith

An Autobiography: The Story of the Lord's Dealings with Mrs. Amanda Smith the Colored Evangelist. Chicago: Meyer & Brother, 1893.

Studies of Amanda Berry Smith's Work

Dodson, Jualynne E. "Introduction." In Smith, *Autobiography*, xxvii–xlii. Reprint, New York: Oxford University Press, 1988.
Israel, Adrienne M. *Amanda Berry Smith: From Washerwoman to Evangelist.* Lanham, MD: Scarecrow Press, Inc., 1998.

Mary G. De Jong

ANNA DEAVERE SMITH (1950–)

BIOGRAPHICAL NARRATIVE

Anna Deavere Smith was born on September 18, 1950 in Baltimore, Maryland. Her mother, Anna, was an elementary school teacher and her father, Deavere, was a coffee merchant. Smith grew up the eldest of her parents' five children. Although she was an extremely shy child, Smith was able to develop a circle of friends because of her talent for mimicry. Smith studied acting at Beaver College in Pennsylvania. She earned the B.A. in 1971 and the MFA in 1977 from San Francisco's American Conservatory Theater.

Upon her relocation to New York from San Francisco, Smith became very active on the stage; she appeared in several off-Broadway productions. Those parts served as precursors to small and big screen acting roles. Smith has appeared in the soap opera *All My Children*; the television dramas *Presidio Med* and *The West Wing;* and the films *The American President, Dave, The Human Stain* and *Philadelphia*. In addition to her acting and screen credits, Smith has also taught at Carnegie-Mellon, Stanford, University of Southern California and Yale. She is currently a tenured professor at New York University.

MAJOR WORKS

Over the course of her career, Smith has developed a oeuvre of documentary shows she refers to as *On the Road: A Search for American Character. On the Road* includes *Fires in the Mirror: Crown Heights, Brooklyn and Other Identities* (1993), *Twilight: Los Angeles, 1992* (1994) and *House Arrest: A Search for American Character in and Around the White House* (2003). The shows are Smith's attempt to explore national identity and American character. They have been described as combining the journalistic technique of interviewing with the art of interpretation. For each theatrical show, Smith interviews hundreds of people and interprets their words through her performance.

For *Fires in the Mirror* Smith interviewed more than 600 people. The show presents the viewpoints of those people affected by the 1991 Crown Heights riots. First performed at the Joseph Papp Public Theatre in New York, *Fires in the Mirror* examines the motivations behind the rioting. Not only does Smith reveal the mitigating circumstances that led to the riots—a young African American child is killed when a Jewish driver runs a red light; in retaliation a group of black men kill a Jewish student—but she delves into the problem that underlies the people's actions, the years of racial tension between the two groups. The play's dialogue contains the voices of the Jewish and African American communities as they provide their account of the situation and problem.

Twilight: Los Angeles, 1992 is an examination of the rioting that erupted in Los Angeles after white police officers were acquitted of beating African American motorist Rodney King. Smith interviewed 175 people for the play and assumes the voice of 26 of them, including Reginald Denny, the driver who was pulled from his truck and beaten by African American males after the verdict was read; former Los Angeles police chief Daryl Gates; and a pregnant young woman who was shot in the cross fire.

In *House Arrest* Smith explores American national identity as it has been embodied by the American presidency. The play is a result of interviews with over 400 people from all walks of life. The play opened at Washington, D.C.'s Arena Stage; unlike its predecessors, Smith did not play all the roles in *House Arrest*. It had a cast of actors.

Smith's other works include *Piano* (1989), a dramatic depiction of gender and racial tension in an affluent Cuban household prior to the Spanish-American War; *Talk to Me: Travels in Media and Politics* (2001), which documents the creative process behind *House Arrest*; and *Letters to a Young Artist: Straight-up Advice on Making a Life in the Arts—For Actors, Performers, Writers and Artists of Every Kind* (2006), a practical manual for aspiring artists.

CRITICAL RECEPTION

Smith has received many accolades for her work. She was named the Ford Foundation's first artist in residence. In 1996 she received a MacArthur Genius Award. She has won many major awards including two Obie Awards and two Drama Desk Awards. *Fires in the Mirror* received a Pulitzer Prize nomination in 1992.

Critics praise Smith's work and performances. In the introduction to "The Circle of Confusion: A Conversation with Anna Deavere Smith" Barbara Lewis refers to Smith's work "as having something [to say] about race and urban America in the '90s that's real and riveting" (54). Elizabeth Brown-Guillory describes *Twilight* as a "razor-sharp play script . . . a major contribution to American theater." (373). In "Teaching the Politics of Identity in a Post-Identity Age: Anna Deavere Smith's Twilight" Sandra Kumamoto Stanley concludes that Smith succeeds in breaking the barrier to "blackness and whiteness by exposing and questioning the apparatus of representation that governs both groups." (202). Finally, Debby Thompson in "Is Race a Trope?:" Anna Deavere Smith and the Question of Racial Performativity" argues that Smith performance style is worthy of emulation.

BIBLIOGRAPHY

Works by Anna Deavere Smith

Fires in the Mirror: Crown Heights, Brooklyn, and Other Identities. New York: Anchor, 1993.
House Arrest and Piano: Two Plays. New York: Anchor, 2004.
Letters to a Young Artist: Straight-up Advice on Making a Life in the Arts-For Actors, Performers, Writers, and Artists of Every Kind. New York: Anchor, 2006.
Talk to Me: Travels in Media and Politics. New York: Random House, 2001.
Twilight: Los Angeles, 1992. New York: Anchor, 1994.

Studies of Anna Deavere Smith's Work

Blanchard, Bob. "'Twilight: Los Angeles 1992'." *The Progressive* 57.12 (1993): 35(2).
Brown-Guillory, Elizabeth. "'Twilight: Los Angeles 1992'." *African American Review* 31 (1997): 372–373.

Brustein, Robert. "'Twilight: Los Angeles 1992'." *The New Republic* 210.18 (May 1994): 29(2).

Connor, Kimberly Rae. "Negotiating the Differences: Anna Deavere Smith." *Imagining Grace: Liberating Theologies in the Slave Narrative Tradition*, 194–238. Urbana: University of Illinois Press, 2000.

Fitzgerald, Sharon. "Anna of a Thousand Faces." *American Visions* 9.5 (Oct–Nov 1994): 14(5).

Lahr, John. "Under the Skin." *New Yorker* (June 28, 1993): 90–93.

Leonard, John. "Humane Voices: Anna Deavere Smith's Astonishing Gift for Mimicry is Enhanced by Her Openhearted Ability to Listen to People." *New York Metro: Best of the Year 2001*. http://www.newyorkmetro.com/nymetro/arts/tv/reviews/4617/.

Lewis, Barbara. "The Circle of Confusion: A Conversation with Anna Deavere Smith." *Kenyon Review* 15.4 (1993): 54–64.

Lloyd, Carol. "Voice of America: Anna Deavere Smith." *Salon Brilliant Careers Series* No. 5. 1998. http://www.salon.com/bc/1998/12/cov_08bc.html.

Martin, Carol. "Anna Deavere Smith: The Word Becomes You." *Drama Review* 37.4 (1993): 45–62.

Marvel, Mark. "Ms. Smith Goes to Washington." *Interview* 26.9 (September 1996): 46(2).

Mermelstein, David. "Legit Reviews: 'House Arrest: An Introgression'." *Variety* 374.10 (April 1999): 57–58.

O'Quinn, Jim. "Getting Closer to America." *American Theatre* 13.8 (October 1996): 18(3).

Reinelt, Janelle. "Performing Race: Anna Deaver Smith's 'Fires in the Mirror'." *Modern Drama* 39.4 (1996): 609–617.

Schechner, Richard. "Anna Deavere Smith: Acting As Incorporation." TDR: The *Drama Review* 37.4 (1993): 63–64.

Stanley, Sandra Kumamoto. "Teaching the Politics of Identity in a Post-Identity Age: Anna Deavere Smith's Twilight." *MELUS: The Journal of the Society for the Study of the Multi-Ethnic Literature of the United States*, 30.2 (Summer 2005): 191–208.

Stayton, Richard. "A Fire in a Crowded Theatre: Anna Deavere Smith Relives the Los Angeles Riots." *American Theatre* 10.7–8 (July–August 1993): 20(7).

Thompson, Debby. 'Is Race a Trope?': Anna Deavere Smith and the Question of Racial Performativity" *African American Review* 37.1 (Spring 2003): 127–38.

Yolanda Williams Page

ELLEASE SOUTHERLAND (1943–)

BIOGRAPHICAL NARRATIVE

Ellease Southerland (now known as Ebele Oseye or Ellease Ebele Oseye) is the third of fifteen children, the eldest daughter of Ellease Dozier and Monroe Penrose Southerland. Though she is sometimes associated with the southerness of her mother's North Carolina girlhood, which she recreated in her lyrically resonant, critically appreciated 1979 novel, *Let the Lion Eat Straw*, she was born in Brooklyn June 18, 1943, and raised in Queens, New York, where she still makes her home. She visited the south for the first time as a young woman, though she is southern enough through collective family memory to have been included in Alex Harris's 1987 anthology of snapshots and stories, *A World Unsuspected: Portraits of Southern Childhood*, alongside such southern mainstays as Barry Hannah and Bobbie Ann Mason.

Monroe Southerland insisted that his children work to become both physically and mentally fit. Regular exercise and organized sports were routine. To this day, Southerland is deeply concerned with the integration of physical and mental health and is an advocate of sound nutrition and exercise. Reading was encouraged. At ten, after hearing an elegiac poem written by her uncle, Southerland began writing her own poetry. With characteristic enthusiasm and purposeful determination, she organized ongoing poetry days at her father's church, edited her elementary school newspaper, and went on to serve as an editor of both her high school and college magazines.

Southerland completed her B.A. in 1965 and received an M.F.A. from Columbia University in 1974. Her deep interest in African history and culture is reflected in her scholarly study of Zora Neale Hurston's use of folklore; her travels to Ghana, Egypt, and Nigeria; her conference papers delivered yearly at the Africa Conference convened at the University of Texas at Austin; her membership in the Association of Nigerian Authors; and her appointment as professor of Creative Writing and the Literature of African Peoples at Pace University in New York. She has taught at Pace since 1975. She has also taught in the Columbia University Community Educational Exchange Program and at the Borough of Manhattan Community College. In 1989, she was made a Fellow of the Institute of African Studies at the University of Nigeria, Nsukka. She has been traveling to Nigeria since the early 1970s and has for years supported Nigerian literacy projects through philanthropic contributions of books. A life-long resident of Queens, Southerland received a Citation of Honor for Literary Achievement from Borough President Claire Schulman in 1990.

Southerland's abiding belief in the interconnectedness of mind and body, the individual and the cosmic, the physical and the spiritual manifests itself in her serious study of Egyptology and astronomy. In 1996, according to Diane McKinney-Whetstone (181), Southerland changed her name to Ebele (Igbo for "mercy") Oseye (a Beninese name for "the happy one"—though some sources list the origin of the name as Nigerian or Egyptian).

MAJOR WORKS

Let the Lion Eat Straw (1979) is the lovingly told story of Abeba Williams Lavoisier Torch's curtailed, constricted but ultimately expansive life. Forty years is compressed into less than 200 pages, yet the unfolding of this intergenerational tale never seems hurried. The relative brevity of the work underscores the twin themes of evanescence and renewal. At the same time, Southerland takes the full measure of these brief, complicated, workaday lives and offers them with knowing reverence, dignifying the individual dramas while evoking the aching vitality of our collective lot.

The intermingled histories of the gifted, life-affirming Abeba and her stern, bitter mother, Angela, are presented with unsentimental spareness. Southerland's prose, at once concretely descriptive and eerily fragmented, both earthbound and dreamily imagistic, is closely akin to poetry. She counts Yeats and Gwendolyn Brooks (as well as Amiri Baraka and Hurston) as early influences, and Yeats's symbol-laden, myth-infused work helped spark her own cross-cultural mythological explorations. The almost mythological significance of ordinary lives seen in their historical fullness and inter connected, familial dimensionality is emphasized in *Lion* through the telling amplitude of biblical symbols as well as through undisguised biographical references. The title comes from Isaiah 11: 6–7, the evocative passage prophesying harmony and deliverance from threat: "The wolf also shall dwell with the lamb . . . and a little child shall lead them."

The suffering of children is a key theme in Southerland's book. Abeba is torn away from her nurturing guardian; her beloved and protective stepfather dies; and she is repeatedly raped by an uncle. Yet her life force is, almost miraculously, undiminished. Her grievous losses are offset by a startling fecundity. Her musical gift is transmuted into finely tuned mothering. Her brilliance is transferred to her children and community. Because Abeba is the fictional incarnation of Ellease Dozier Southerland, she becomes a kind of sacred space, embodying the fierce delicacy of a remarkable life as well as symbolizing hope and creative fire. Abeba is contrasted with her mother, Angela, who is unable to transcend the harshness of her life and is unable to find, as did her daughter, lasting love or a lasting peace.

Southerland's novella *White Shadows* won the 1964 John Golden Award for Fiction. Her poetry appeared in such publications as *Black World*, *Poet Lore*, and *Presence Africaine*. "Beck-Junior and the Good Shepherd"—a Torch family story that heralded the 1979 achievement of *Let the Lion Eat Straw*—was published in the *Massachusetts Review* in 1974. In 1972, her poem "Warlock" won *Black World's* Gwendolyn Brooks Poetry Award and the poetry collection *The Magic Sun Spins* came out in 1975. *Let the Lion Eat Straw* was named a Book of the Month Club alternate selection and a "Best Book for Young Adults" by the Young Adult Services Division of the American Library Association. In 1987 it was included in the Black Heritage Series by the New York Public Libraries. Later work includes *A Feast of Fools* (1998), which continues the saga of the Torch family into the next generation. Southerland's own press, Eneke Publications, brought out her travel memoir, *This Year in Nigeria* (2001), and the first of a projected series of books on writing and communication, *Opening Line: The Creative Writer: From Blank Page to Finished Story* (2000). She is currently at work on a third novel, a second collection of poetry, and a book on communication techniques developed through her many years of teaching.

CRITICAL RECEPTION

Let the Lion Eat Straw was immediately lauded as a debut novel of rare worth and delicacy. Critics noted its potent lyricism, stylistic grace, and affecting narrative. Writing in the *Library Journal*, Janet Boyarin Blundell sums up the work's impact: "It's hard to convey the special beauty of this accomplished first novel; Southerland, with her sparse prose and sharp imagery, has captured the essence of one black woman's life" (850). *New York Times* critic Mel Watkins considered the prototypical significance of this "one life" as Abeba confronts the "formidable barriers" of the urban north and, like innumerable numbers of southern blacks "in search of a better life in the north," is "forced to transfer [her] hopes to [her] children" (BR 2). John Leonard, also writing in the *New York Times*, testifies to the novel's scope and poignancy: "In these few pages, an entire history of desire and talent and frustration and triumph—from boiled peanuts to Nebuchadnezzar—is whittled to an arrow in the heart" (C21). *Los Angeles Times* reviewer, Anne Wittels, noted the haunting effect of the "condensed, distilled . . . style." The story, she writes, has "the effect . . . of a play seen through Venetian blinds. It is all there. We can see it, really, quite clearly. And yet half is not there; half is hidden by thin shadows; half is between the lines" (N4). *Washington Post* critic Jabari Asim describes Southerland's style as "urban minimalism" and likens her "sparse, evocative phrasing" to the poetry of June Jordan and Audre Lorde (T15).

Despite nearly rhapsodic critical accolades, *Let the Lion Eat Straw* went quietly out of print. Reissued by Amistad in a fittingly "commemorative" 25th anniversary edition, the work is once again being affirmed as, in the words of Jabari Asim, "a bittersweet gem of a novel." Asim speculates that though the work belongs in the same company as its contemporaries, Alice Walker's *The Color Purple* (1982) and Toni Morrison's *Song of Solomon* (1977), it may have been eclipsed by the critical and popular reception of these now-classics. Hailed as a classic itself, *Let the Lion Eat Straw* is finding new life and inspiring a new generation of readers.

BIBLIOGRAPHY

Works by Ellease Southerland

"Beck-Junior and the Good Shepherd." *Massachusetts Review* 15 (Autumn 1974): 719–32.
"A Feast of Fools." In *Breaking Ice: An Anthology of Contemporary African-American Fiction*, edited by Terry McMillan. New York: Penguin, 1990.
A Feast of Fools. New York: Africana Legacy Press, 1998.
"I Got a Horn, You Got a Horn." In *A World Unsuspected*, edited by Alex Harris. Chapel Hill: University of North Carolina Press, 1987.
"The Influence of Voodoo on the Fiction of Zora Neale Hurston." In *Sturdy Black Bridges: Visions of Black Women in Literature*, edited by Roseann P. Bell, Bettye J. Parker, and Beverly Guy-Sheftall, 172–83. Garden City, NY: Doubleday, 1979.
Let the Lion Eat Straw. New York: Charles Scribner's Sons, 1979.
Let the Lion Eat Straw. 25th Anniversary Edition. New York: Reissued by Harper/Collins (Amistad), 2004.
The Magic Sun Spins. London: Paul Bremen, 1975.
Opening Line: The Creative Writer: From Blank Page to Finished Story. New York: Eneke Publications, 2000.

"Seventeen Days in Nigeria." *Black World* 21 (January 1972): 29–41.
This Year in Nigeria: *A Memoir*. New York: Eneke Publications, 2001.

Studies of Ellease Southerland's Works

Asim, Jabari. Rev. of *Let the Lion Eat Straw. Washington Post*, July 20, 2005, T15.
Blundell, Janet Boyarin. Rev. of *Let the Lion Eat Straw. Library Journal* 104.7 (April 1, 1979): 850.
Brookhart, Mary Hughes. "Ellease Southerland." In *Dictionary of Literary Biography, v 33: Afro-American Fiction Writers After 1955*, edited by Thadious M. Davis and Trudier Harris, 239–44. Farmington Hills, MI: Gale Research, 1984.
Leonard, John. "Homage Is Paid." *New York Times*, May 10, 1979, C21.
McKinney-Whetstone, Diane. "First Person Singular." *Essence* 36 (May 2005): 181.
Swan, Annalyn. "Love Story." *Time* 113.25 (June 18, 1979): 85–86.
Towers, Robert. "In the Trap." *New York Review of Books* 26.15 (October 11, 1979): 43–44.
Trescott, Jacqueline. "*Let the Lion Eat Straw*. Let the Author Win Glory." *Washington Post* August 6, 1979, B1, B11.
Watkins, Mel. "One Woman Surviving." *New York Times Book Review* June 3, 1979, BR4, 2.
Wittels, Anne. "Abeba's Journey into Maturity." *Los Angeles Times* July 15, 1979, N4.

Kate Falvey

MARIA W. STEWART (1803–1879)

BIOGRAPHICAL NARRATIVE

Essay writer Maria W. Stewart was born Maria Miller to free parents in Hartford, Connecticut, in 1803. When she was five years old, her parents died, and she was "bound out" as a servant for a clergyman's household for the next ten years. She subsequently worked as a domestic servant while educating herself by attending Sabbath School classes and studying the Bible. In the 1820s, she moved to Boston. There she met James W. Stewart, a veteran of the War of 1812 and successful shipping agent who outfitted whaling and fishing vessels, whom she married on August 10, 1826, and settled into the activist-minded free African American community.

After only three years of marriage, Maria Stewart's husband became ill and died, plunging her into grief and destitution. James Stewart had amply provided for his wife in his will, but his white business associates defrauded her of her inheritance. Maria Stewart's sorrow deepened when her close friend David Walker, author of the radical *Appeal*, died in 1830, and then Thomas Paul, founder of the First African Baptist Church that she attended and the minister who officiated at her wedding, died in 1831. The young widow sought solace in Christianity and experienced religious conversion. She believed God called her to address the spiritual and political issues facing the African American community. In 1832, Stewart became the first American woman to deliver a speech to a "promiscuous" audience composed of African American and white males and females. During her three-year public career, she published a political pamphlet, spiritual meditations, and antislavery writings, and she delivered four lectures. William Lloyd Garrison advertised and published her work in the *Liberator*, a weekly abolitionist newspaper.

In 1833 Maria Stewart ended her controversial public-speaking career and began moving south in search of a place where she could continue her community activism and support herself. She first settled in New York and worked in the abolitionist movement and women's literary societies and began a teaching career. In 1835, she published a collection of meditations and lectures she had presented in Boston. Stewart moved on to Baltimore and continued teaching before relocating to Washington, D.C., in 1861 where she founded a school before accepting a position as the Matron of the Freedmen's Hospital. Near the end of her life, Stewart petitioned the U.S. government and received a pension as a veteran's widow. She secured her legacy by investing the money in a new edition of her work. Stewart died in December 1879.

MAJOR WORKS

Stewart's writings and speeches reflect her belief that God called her to embark on a public career to rouse African Americans to fight for freedom and equality. She revealed the spiritual nature of her calling in her *Lecture Delivered at the Franklin Hall* (1832): "Methinks I heard a spiritual interrogation—'Who shall go forward, and take off the reproach that is cast upon the people of color? Shall it be a woman? And my heart made this reply—'If it is thy will, be it even so, Lord Jesus!'" Stewart realized the danger she faced by stepping into the public arena but expressed a willingness to die for God's cause and her people. She relied on the Bible as the chief source for her work. Her speeches and essays also reflected David Walker's revolutionary ideas regarding racial uplift and her knowledge of history and current events.

In her work, Stewart focused her attention on the free African American community, whom she considered only slightly better off than slaves did because they refused to challenge restrictions on their liberty. She expressed concern for African Americans' temporal affairs and eternal salvation and urged them to develop their talents and intellect, live moral lives, and devote themselves to racial activism. Stewart challenged her audience to emulate the valor of the pilgrims and American revolutionaries in demanding freedom, and advised them to establish institutions such as grocery stores and churches to support their community. She was particularly concerned with the plight of African American women whom she encouraged to be virtuous mothers and use their influence in the home to affect change in their communities. Stewart directed most of her ire at African American men, however, whom she chided for not fulfilling their role as community leaders.

Stewart also included admonitions to white members of her audience. She scolded white women for failing to acknowledge their privileged position and ignoring the needs of African American children. Stewart demanded white Americans' support for African American freedom as they had backed other nations, such as Poland, in their fight for liberty. She particularly decried colonization. In *An Address Delivered at the African Masonic Hall*, Stewart declared, "They would drive us to a strange land. But before I go, the bayonet shall pierce me through." Stewart reminded white Americans that African blood had enriched America's soil and warned them that God would repay them for wrongs done to African Americans.

CRITICAL RECEPTION

Scholars have described Stewart in a variety of ways, including abolitionist, evangelist, feminist, journalist, and prophet, and have examined her writings through African and Western literary traditions. In *Maria W. Stewart, America's First Black Woman Political Writer: Essays and Speeches*, Marilyn Richardson characterizes Stewart's work as "political thought," situates her as a feminist, and examines how abolitionist rhetoric, the Black Jeremiad, and call-and-response cadence inform her work. In *Written by Herself*, Frances Smith Foster analyzes how Stewart helped to create a literary tradition for African American women and "wrote herself into history" by giving speeches and publishing her writings that advocated militant Christianity as the means by which African Americans could transform their lives during a time when women were unwelcome in the public sphere. Carla Peterson builds on Foster and Richardson's work in *Doers of the Word* by describing Stewart's writings and speeches as "political sermonizing," and arguing that her *Meditations* reflect the inner struggles that led her to engage in social activism, while her other work exemplifies the depth of her commitment to racial uplift.

Some scholars focus on Stewart's role in her community. In her entry on Stewart published in *Women Public Speakers in the United States*, Laura R. Sells posits Stewart as a forerunner for key abolitionists and activists and examines the rhetorical strategies

Stewart used to surmount the challenge the African American female faced in being a "true woman" in nineteenth-century America. In *Raising Her Voice*, Roger Streiltmatter portrays Stewart as the first African American female journalist and critiques her writings and speeches published in the *Liberator* as journalistic efforts to bring about racial reform from within the African American community. In "The Productions of Maria W. Stewart: Rebellious Domesticity and Black Women's Liberation," Opal Moore examines the contradictions in Stewart's work as she created a new voice for African American women who sought to redefine their role in their families, community, and country. Other scholars focus on Stewart's rhetorical strategies. In *Traces of a Stream*, Jacqueline Jones Royster analyzes how Stewart creates an ethos within her essays to justify her entry into the public sphere and provide the authority she needed to encourage her audience to participate in racial uplift. In *We Are Coming*, Shirley Logan employs classifications from *The New Rhetoric* to examine how Stewart created communion with her audience by highlighting their African heritage and the liberation it offered through biblical references to Ethiopia stretching forth her hand unto God.

BIBLIOGRAPHY

Works by Maria W. Stewart

"Lecture Delivered at The Franklin Hall." In *Maria W. Stewart: America's First Black Woman Political Writer: Essays and Speeches*, edited by Marilyn Richardson. Bloomington: Indiana University Press, 1987.
Meditations from the Pen of Mrs. Maria W. Stewart. Washington, DC: n.p., 1879.
Productions of Mrs. Maria W. Stewart Presented to the First Africa Baptist Church & Society, of the City of Boston. Boston: Friends of Freedom and Virtue, 1835.

Studies of Maria W. Stewart's Works

Foster, Frances Smith. *Written by Herself: Literary Production by African American Women, 1746–1892*. Bloomingdale: Indiana University Press, 1993.
Logan, Shirley Wilson, ed. "African Origins/American Appropriations: Maria Stewart and 'Ethiopia Rising.'" In *We Are Coming: The Persuasive Discourse of Nineteenth Century Black Women*, 23–43. Carbondale: Southern Illinois University Press, 1999.
Moody, Jocelyn. *Sentimental Confessions: Spiritual Narratives of Nineteenth-Century African American Women*. Athens: University of Georgia Press, 2001.
Moore, Opal. "The Productions of Maria W. Stewart: Rebellious Domesticity and Black Women's Liberation." In *Early America Re-Explored: New Readings in Colonial, Early National, and Antebellum Culture*, edited by Klaus H. Schmidt and Fritz Fleischman, 441–65. New York: Peter Lang, 2000.
Peterson, Carla L. *Doers of the Word: African-American Women Speakers and Writers in the North, 1830–1880*. New Brunswick, NJ: Rutgers University Press, 1998.
Richardson, Marilyn, ed. *Maria W. Stewart, America's First Black Woman Political Writer: Essays and Speeches*. Bloomington: Indiana University Press, 1987.
Royster, Jacqueline. *Traces of a Stream: Literacy and Social Change Among African American Women*. Pittsburgh: University of Pittsburgh Press, 2000.
Rycenga, Jennifer. "Maria Stewart, Black Abolitionist, and the Idea of Freedom." In *Frontline Feminisms: Women, War and Resistance*, edited by Marguerite R. Waller and Jennifer Rycenga. New York: Garland, 2000.

Sells, Laura R. "Maria W. Miller Stewart (1803–1879), first African-American woman to lecture in public." In *Women Public Speakers in the United States, 1800–1925, A Bio-Critical Sourcebook*, edited by Karlyn Kohrs Campbell, 339–48. Westport, CT: Greenwood Press, 1993.

Streitmatter, Roger. *Raising Her Voice: African-American Women Journalists Who Changed History.* Lexington: University of Kentucky Press, 1994.

Rhondda Robinson Thomas

BARBARA SUMMERS (1944–)

BIOGRAPHICAL NARRATIVE

Barbara Summers has written and edited a number of books, including *I Dream a World: Portraits of Black Women Who Changed America*. She was born in Springfield, Massachusetts, and grew up in Hartford, Connecticut. She graduated from the University of Pennsylvania with a major in French literature. Summers completed doctoral degree in French at Yale, and spent time studying at the Sorbonne in France. Summers has taught French, English, and journalism and currently teaches English Composition at a CUNY institution. She lives in New York City and is at work on a novel about the Harlem Renaissance.

MAJOR WORKS

I Dream a World: Portraits of Black Women Who Changed America is a pictorial of African American women who in Summers's opinion have been instrumental in shaping America. In this book Summers captures the life of seventy-five magnificent women through their heart and mind outside of race, gender, age, and class.

Nouvelle Soul is a collection of twenty-four short stories, which introduced Barbara Summers as a new literary voice. The book represents diverse men and women confronted with every day life. Different in subject and style from typical stories, the stories in *Nouvelle Soul* provide new perspectives on scenes people often overlook. In one of the stories "Me and Superman," the writer obliges the reader to ponder a homeless street person that he would otherwise prefer not to see.

The Price You Pay has been labeled both a mystery and love story. It explores the mixed blessings bestowed on women who live off their looks and dreams. Through a pleasant trip Summers identify the richness of African American life and culture.

Black and Beautiful: How Women of Color Changed the Fashion Industry is a collection of 250 photos that Summers acquired while interviewing her modeling friends. The book emphasizes more than sixty years of the African American fashion model's conquest and struggles. *Black and Beautiful* depicts and celebrates the beauty of the African American woman who has been historically viewed as unattractive. This book tries to eliminate the blinders to correct our cultural vision, and unfold the definition of the beauty.

Open the Unusual Door, Summers's most recent book, includes sixteen autobiographical essays from a diverse group of African Americans. These stories are examples of challenges and choices of what happened to these people and what they did to make things happen. The anthology teaches us how to recognize the right door, open it, and walk through it.

Skin Deep: Inside the World of Black Fashion Models is a book of more than 250 pictures about the history of black models in America and abroad for the past fifty years. Summers, a Ford model for seventeen years, spent a decade interviewing models on three continents to record their experiences.

CRITICAL RECEPTION

Reception of Summers's work is generally favorable. In a *Los Angeles Times* article, Lynell George writes that Summers has provided a record—oral remembrances, antique advertisements, fantasy high-fashion spreads, working girl composite shots—that stitches together the flourish and fanfare with the contortions and compromise that black women endured to fit ideals of imagination—without losing their sense of self (back cover). Likewise, in a review of *Nouvelle Soul* that appeared in *Publishers Weekly*, the author wrote, "the author of the story collection *Nouvelle Soul* makes her novelistic debut with a glitzy tale of racism and intrigue in the world of modeling. Summers a former Ford model, writes with firsthand knowledge about the dilemmas faced by women of color in this line of work; glimpses of their rarefied world distinguish this otherwise unexciting example of glamour fiction from the pack of Danielle Steel wannabes" (408). Finally about *I Dream a World*, Yvonne Easton writes, "*I Dream a World* established a cultural meeting point of racial and sexual polarities in America and it created a new page in America history books where succeeding generations can write their names. If that's not changing America, I don't know what it is" (17).

BIBLIOGRAPHY

Works by Barbara Summers

Black and Beautiful: How Women of Color Changed the Fashion Industry. New York: HarperCollins, 1998.
I Dream a World: Portraits of Black Women Who Changed America. New York: Stewart, Tabori & Chang, 1989.
Nouvelle Soul: Short Stories. New York: Amistad Press, 1992.
Open the Unusual Door. Boston: Graphia, 2005.
The Price You Pay: A Novel. New York: Amistad Press, 1993.
Skin Deep: Inside the World of Black Fashion Models. New York: Amistad Press, 1998.

Studies of Barbara Summers's Works

Easton, Yvonne. Intro. *I Dream a World: Portraits of Black Women Who Changed America,* edited by Barbara Summers. New York: Stewart, Tabor & Chang, 1999. 17.
George, Lynell. Back Cover. *Black and Beautiful: How Women of Color Changed the Fashion Industry.* New York: HarperCollins, 2001.
Rev. of *Nouvelle Soul. Publishers Weekly* 241.3 (January 17, 1994): 408.

Firouzeh Dianat

ELLEN TARRY (1906–)

BIOGRAPHICAL NARRATIVE

Writer of children literature, Ellen Tarry has also written biographies of many African Americans. Born to mulatto parents, she was set apart from other African American children by her light skin, reddish-blonde hair, and blue eyes. Growing up in Birmingham, Alabama, she attended public school before leaving for a Catholic school in Virginia. She later studied at Alabama State College, Bank Street College, and Fordham University School of Communications.

In Virginia, she converted to Catholicism against the wishes of her father and spoke out against problems and policies that she felt prevented other African Americans from embracing the Catholic Church. For several years, Tarry was a journalist and contributor to *Commonweal* and *Catholic World* magazines where she wrote about these issues in such articles as "Native Daughter" and "Why Is Not the Negro Catholic?"

Tarry was a cofounder of Friendship House in New York, an interracial Christian center, and a director of the Chicago branch. She served in many organizations dedicated to social justice as well as fighting poverty, racism, and Communism, including several positions with the Department of Housing and Urban Development. Tarry is best known for her involvement in the Harlem Renaissance along with James Weldon Johnson, Claude McKay, Langston Hughes, and others. With this group, she worked to bring about reform through her writing. Tarry's stories advocate social change through compassion and understanding between races.

MAJOR WORKS

Tarry taught elementary school and realized that there were no books that gave children a realistic view of city life, which inspired her to create stories of her own. Her first book, *Janie Belle*, presents the story of an abandoned child and her adoption by a white nurse. It was a significant breakthrough in African American children's stories, depicting a positive relationship between different races. *Hezekiah Horton* and *The Runaway Elephant* both feature an African American boy growing up in an urban setting in sharp contrast to the stereotypical southern countryside. Although Hezckiah's relationship with Mr. Ed in *Hezekiah Horton* can be seen as subservient and undesirable, it is important to remember that the friendship would have been shocking to some readers at the time.

My Dog Rinty, written with Marie Hall Els, tells the story of an African American boy who loses his dog and finds it with the help of kind white strangers. The photographs in this book are also noteworthy, as they provide a realistic view of a Harlem neighborhood. Tarry also wrote biographies of several African Americans whose stories had been largely neglected, including her friend James Weldon Johnson.

CRITICAL RECEPTION

Unfortunately, very little has been written on Tarry's life and works. She is often cited as a member of the Harlem Renaissance and as a pioneer in African American children's writing. However, her portrayal of African Americans in a positive and active role was groundbreaking for its time. She constantly stresses that it is possible to overcome poverty and racial prejudice. Her stories focus on people from her own life, helping her achieve a sense of realism that had been lacking in many other writers. Although children's literature met with some resistance in the Harlem Renaissance, Tarry felt it was important to teach children about life outside their hometowns. As Tarry claims in an interview with Katharine Capshaw Smith, she can think of no better way to be remembered as a writer than "as a person who tried to depict life as she saw it" (Smith 283).

BIBLIOGRAPHY

Works by Ellen Tarry

Hezekiah Horton. New York: Viking Press, 1942.
Janie Belle. New York: Garden City, 1940.
Katharine Drexel: Friend of the Neglected. New York: Farrar, Strauss & Giroux, 1958. (Reprinted after Drexel's canonization as *St. Katharine Drexel: Friend of the Oppressed*. Boston: Pauline Books & Media, 2000.)
Martin De Porres Saint of the New World. Fairfield, CA: Vision, 1963.
My Dog Rinty. New York: Viking Press, 1946.
The Other Toussaint: A Modern Biography of Pierre Toussaint, a Post-Revolutionary Black. Boston: St. Paul Editions, 1981.
The Runaway Elephant. New York: Viking Press, 1950.
The Third Door: The Autobiography of an American Negro Woman. Detroit: McKay, 1955.
Young Jim: The Early Years of James Weldon Johnson. New York: Dodd, 1967.

Studies of Ellen Tarry's Works

Scally, Sr. Mary Anthony. *Negro Catholic Writers, 1900–1943: A Bio-Bibliography*. Sr. Mary Anthony Scally. Detroit: Walter Romig, 1945.
Smith, Jessie Carney, ed. *Notable Black American Women*. Detroit: Gale, 1992.
Smith, Katharine Capshaw. "From Bank Street to Harlem: A Conversation with Ellen Tarry." *The Lion and the Unicorn* 23.2 (April 1999): 271–85.
Sternsher, Bernard, and Judith Sealander. *Women of Valor: The Struggle Against the Great Depression as Told in Their Own Life Stories*. Chicago: I. R. Dee, 1990.

Kevin Hogg

CLAUDIA TATE (1946–2002)

BIOGRAPHICAL NARRATIVE

Claudia Tate, literary critic, was born in Long Branch, New Jersey, on December 14, 1946. Tate's parents, Harold Tate and Mary Austin Tate, were college-educated professionals who were able to provide a comfortable, middle-class upbringing for their daughter. The material success of the Tates, their emphasis on the importance of education, and their close connections to both the south and north offered Claudia Tate a perspective on African American identity and culture that diverged sharply from the common perception that African American identity is defined solely by racial oppression and economic deprivation. After graduating from Rumson-Fair Haven Regional High School with honors, Tate enrolled in the University of Michigan at Ann Arbor program in English and American Literature. She received her B.A. in 1968 and continued her studies in English at Harvard University, where she encountered Cheryl Wall, Arnold Rampersad, and Nellie McKay, scholars who, along with Tate, later helped establish African American literature as a modern field of literary study. Tate was awarded her Ph.D. in 1977. She taught at Howard University (1977–1989), George Washington University (1989–1996), and Princeton University (1997–2002). Tate died of small cell lung cancer July 29, 2002.

MAJOR WORKS

Tate's major books, *Black Women Writers at Work* (1983), *Domestic Allegories of Political Desire: The Black Heroine's Text at the Turn of the Century* (1992), and *Psychoanalysis and Black Novels: Desire and the Protocols of Race* (1998), were groundbreaking explorations of previously ignored issues and approaches to reading African American literature.

Black Women Writers at Work is a collection of fourteen interviews of then-established and -emerging African American women writers. Tate, according to the introduction to the volume, envisioned her work as an exploration of the impact of African American women's dual status as racial minority and women in a male-dominated society on their literature. Tate also describes her interviews as:

carefully controlled dialogue fashioned to engage the writer in an analytical discussion of her work with regard to theme and technique, as well as the intellectual and social climates from which the work arose. Each writer presents an understanding of her own sensibility, and explains aspects of her craft that are rendered in particular rhetorical, dramatic, and lyrical details. As a result, the interviews provide firsthand accounts for appreciating a specific body of literature and the creative process in general. (xviii–xix)

Tate's interviews emphasize the craft of these women's texts, a point that needed to be made given the tendency of literary critics—when they read African American literature as a part of the American canon—to focus on the sociological and historical aspects, to the exclusion of literary aspects, in works by African American women. Tate's discussion of the characteristics of writing by African American women, based on her reading and the interviews included in the volume, help to outline the connections between the works of women. The articulation of those connections was an important step in the establishment of African American women's writing as a sub-field. Her discussion of the characteristics of "the black heroine," the central figures in the works of the interviewees, anticipates her work in *Domestic Allegories of Political Desire. Black Women Writers* was well received by critics.

Domestic Allegories of Political Desire offers an examination of African American women's post-Reconstruction domestic novels, a genre that was often ignored or dismissed because of its focus on heroines intent on marriage, the acceptance of a femininity rooted in Victorian ideals, and the achievement of middle-class economic status. Tate's methodology in her study of these novels involves close reading and careful contextualization of the works through a discussion of the historical period and the expectations of the contemporaneous audience for the works. Tate's overarching argument is that critics' dismissal of these novels from the African American canon is a result of a failure to appreciate the importance of these works in consolidating African American citizenship and participation in public life. For the audiences reading these works, the lives of these African American heroines—adventures, followed by marriage, an idealized family life, and economic success—offer a vision of an affirmative African American culture in a time when the promise of Reconstruction was rapidly receding. More contemporary critics read these texts out of the African American literary canon because they fail to adhere to a model of African American literature that emphasize the impact of racial oppression and discrimination on African American families and communities, and that offered overt social protest within the novel. Ignoring this significant body of work suppressed the contribution of African American women writers and the diversity of perspectives encompassed by African American literature.

Psychoanalysis and Black Novels: Desire and the Protocols of Race (1998) is another study motivated by Tate's desire to broaden the canon of African American literature. As with *Domestic Allegories of Political Desire*, Tate uses psychoanalysis to examine texts that have been neglected because of their authors' refusal of the "racial protocol" of overt social protest against racial oppression in the lives of African Americans. Instead, the authors of these novels focus on the issue of personal desire or longing by using white protagonists or by de-emphasizing the issue of racial oppression in the lives of African Americans protagonists. While some critics took Tate to task for applying psychoanalysis to African American literature, Tate's ability to bring a fresh (and rigorous) perspective to these works was praised by many.

CRITICAL RECEPTION

Black Women Writers at Work was lauded as a collection of rich primary texts. In her review of Tate's life and works, critic Nell Irwin Painter argues that the text "set a new standard for the interview as a genre and mapped new directions for critical and theoretical discourse on African American women writers." *Domestic Allegories of Political Desire* was well received by critics, with some reservations expressed by those critics. Tate's work emphasizes the need to pay attention to the original contexts in which these texts were written and received. By bringing these texts to the attention of contemporary readers of African American literature, Tate helped to expose the impact that preconceptions about what African American literature is "supposed to do"—register protest—had on the critical reception of texts. Criticism of the work focus on whether or not some of the texts analyzed by Tate (Hurston's *Seraph on the Suwanee*, for example) receive less critical attention because of the poor quality of the texts, as opposed to the ideological biases of the critics. *Psychoanalysis and Black Novels* (and in other works) helps to legitimize the use of psychoanalytical criticism in African American literature. Many critics laud Tate's work as a pioneering first step in such readings, even as they acknowledge that her eclectic approach to psychoanalysis (Tate uses several schools of psychoanalysis in her readings, including work based on Sigmund Freud and Jacques Lacan) at times generated readings that would have functioned well enough or better without the application of psychoanalytic theory. Tate was a prolific writer whose rigorous theoretical work and innovative approaches to African American literature earned her the respect of her peers. Her involvement with African American literature as an editor of scholarly editions, a reviewer of works within the field of African American literature, and as a writer of her own scholarly texts helped to change the shape of African American literary studies.

BIBLIOGRAPHY

Works by Claudia Tate

Black Women Writers at Work (edited by Tate). New York: Continuum, 1983.
Domestic Allegories of Political Desire: The Black Heroine's Text at the Turn of the Century. New York: Oxford University Press, 1992.
"The Occult of True Black Womanhood." With Ann duCille. In *American Literary Studies: A Methodical Reader*, edited by Michael A. Elliot and Claudia Stokes. New York: New York University Press, 2003.
Psychoanalysis and Black Novels: Desire and the Protocols of Race. New York: Oxford University Press, 1998.
"Reshuffling the Deck; Or, (Re)Reading Race and Gender in Black Women's Writing." *Tulsa Studies in Women's Literature* 7.1 (1988): 119–23.
The Selected Works of Georgia Douglas Johnson. New York: G. K. Hall; London: Prentice Hall, 1997.
The Works of Katherine Davis Chapman Tillman. New York: Oxford University Press, 1991.

Studies of Claudia Tate's Works

Carby, Hazel. "African American Intellectuals Symposium: Claudia Tate." *Journal of African American History* 88.1 (2003): 78–81.
"Claudia Tate: In Memoriam." *African American Review* 36.4 (2002): 705.
Ervin, Hazel Arnett. "In Memoriam-Claudia Tate (December 14, 1946–July 29, 2002)." *CLA Journal* 46.2 (2002): 270–73.
Hoeveler, Diane Long. Rev. of *Psychoanalysis and Black Novels: Desire and the Protocols of Race*, by Tate. *African American Review* 33.4 (1999): 691.
Jones, Clara B., and Matthew V. Johnson. Rev. of *Psychoanalysis and Black Novels: Desire and the Protocols of Race*, by Tate. *The Western Journal of Black Studies* 22.3 (1998): 205.
Painter, Nell Irvin. "Introduction: Claudia Tate and the Protocols of Black Literature and Scholarship." *Journal of African American History* 88.1 (2003): 60–65.

Angela Shaw-Thornburg

MILDRED D. TAYLOR (1943–)

BIOGRAPHICAL NARRATIVE

Mildred Taylor, juvenile writer, was born September 13, 1943, in Jackson, Mississippi, to Wilbert Lee and Deletha Marie (Davis) Taylor. At three months old, her family moved to Toledo, Ohio, because her father refused to raise Taylor and her sister Wilma in the racist, segregated south. Despite moving north, the family never forgot their southern roots and frequently vacationed in the south, returning to visit family members.

As an adolescent Taylor loved reading, and read books from home and the library. She dreamed of writing novels with African American main characters, portraying the culture accurately. Taylor decided to become a writer around the age of nine or ten (Crowe 17). She was exposed to the art of storytelling during her childhood and adolescence. On her trips down south, she was mesmerized by all the adventurous stories she heard her family tell.

After finishing high school, she attended the University of Toledo majoring in education. In 1965, after graduating with a baccalaureate degree, she served in the Peace Corps. Taylor spent two years in Ethiopia, from 1965 to 1967, teaching English and history to Ethiopian students. When she returned to the United States, she moved to Boulder, Colorado, and enrolled in the journalism graduate program at the University of Colorado. She redefined their Black Studies Program and developed a study skills and tutorial program for the Bachelor of Science curriculum. After receiving her master's degree in journalism, she moved to Los Angeles and became a proofreader and editor for a tax firm. In the back of her mind was the desire to write and, during her spare time, she wrote down familial stories. The stories she remembered hearing down south transpired into the Logan sagas.

MAJOR WORKS

Taylor's first published book stemmed from an old manuscript. She heard about a contest sponsored by the Council of Interracial Books for Children. She had entered the manuscript in contests but each time it was rejected. Eight months after entering the contest, she received confirmation that she won the contest in the African American category. That manuscript is Taylor's first novella, *Song of the Trees* (1975). It debuted the Logan family: Stacey, Christopher-John, Little Man, Cassie, Mama, Big Ma, Papa, and Uncle Hammer. Taylor's story depicts an actual incident and is narrated through the voice of eight-year-old Cassie Logan. There are three generations of Logans living on land Grandpa Logan bought in 1887. David Logan leaves for Louisiana to take a job laying railroad track. Meanwhile, a white man threatens to cut down all the trees on their land. David returns to confront the white man before the trees are cut.

Taylor's second book *Roll of Thunder, Hear My Cry* (1976) is set in Great Faith, Mississippi, in 1933. It earned the prestigious Newbery medal in 1977 and continues the saga of the Logan family. Now considered a classic in children's books, Taylor wrote her author's note as a tribute to the familial influence in her writing. She credits her father for instilling strong moral values and a sense of self-respect and dignity despite living in a racist society. The book chronicles the Logan family's life and shows how they cope with racial discrimination everyday. Cassie must wait for help until the white customers are served in Mr. Barnett's store; the Logan children are splashed with mud by a school bus transporting white children to school. Mama defies the school administration by discussing slavery in a history lesson, therefore, losing her job. A childhood friend of Cassie and her brothers, T. J. Avery, is involved in a robbery of a store owned by Mr. Barnett. T. J. is then accused of murder after T. J.'s accomplices, the Simms brothers, who are white, murder Mr. Barnett.

Let the Circle Be Unbroken (1981) continues the story of the Logans. It won the Coretta Scott King Award in 1982 and was nominated for the American Book Award. It begins with T. J. Avery's trial, which results in an all-white jury convicting him. Other incidents include a sixty-five-year-old African American woman being denied the right to vote, local white boys harassing a biracial girl, and Cassie's brother, Stacey, almost dying because of his boss.

The next book, *The Friendship*, written in 1987, also won a Coretta Scott King Award and a 1988 Boston Globe–Horn Book Award. It is a short novel, in which Cassie and her siblings witness the murder of a family friend, Mr. Tom Bee. Taylor's other books include *The Gold Cadillac* (1987), a story set in the 1950s about an African American family's car trip down south in an expensive car. Jeremy Simms, the Logan children's white friend, narrates *Mississippi Bridge* (1990). It tells the story of a bridge collapsing because of an overcrowded bus. *The Road to Memphis* (1990) deals with Moe, a friend of the Logan children, who beats up three white boys and faces a lynching because of it. *The Well* (1995) features a young David Logan, Cassie's father, who narrates the story. It is set in the early 1900s during a sweltering summer, when most of the wells have dried. The Logans share their well water with neighbors. Jealousy fueled by the Simms family results in the poisoning of Logan's well. *The Land* (2001) is the first book in the Logan family saga.

Two themes evident in Taylor's work are family unity and land ownership. Coming from a strong familial background spanning several generations, she infuses a theme of family into her stories. As a child, she always felt African Americans were mis-represented and incorrectly portrayed in history books.

"I envisioned presenting an aspect of American history which during my own childhood was not presented in the history books. I envisioned presenting a family united in love and self-respect, and parents, strong and sensitive, attempting to guide their children successfully without harming their spirits, through the hazardous maze of living in a discriminatory society." (Acceptance Speech)

CRITICAL RECEPTION

Roll of Thunder, Hear My Cry is praised for its honesty in portraying racial dis-crimination. Mildred Taylor pioneered children's literature at a time when few children's books about African Americans existed. She is considered a pioneer in writing books depicting African Americans realistically and truthfully. Dianne Johnson from *World Literature Today* says, ". . . Mildred Taylor's writing is timeless; in a most profound way, it is bound neither to date nor place because she writes not only about American civil rights but about human rights and the human spirit" (4).

Taylor has, however, received criticism from some parents regarding her use of the "n" word. Some people feel children should not be introduced to the harsh side of

American history. Sometimes, schools have responded to the backlash. *Roll of Thunder* in schools has been a constant censored book throughout the country. " ... I understand not wanting a child to hear painful words. . . . I do not understand trying to prevent a child from learning about history that is a part of America ... " (Scales).

BIBLIOGRAPHY

Works by Mildred D. Taylor

The Friendship. Illustrated by Max Ginsburg. New York: Dial Books for Young Readers, 1987.
The Gold Cadillac. Illustrated by Michael Hays. New York: Dial Books for Young Readers, 1987.
The Land. New York: Phyllis Fogelman Books/Penguin Putnam, 2001.
Let the Circle Be Unbroken. New York: Dial Books for Young Readers, 1981.
Mississippi Bridge. Illustrated by Max Ginsburg. New York: Dial Books for Young Readers, 1990.
"My Life as a Writer." *World Literature Today, 78.2* (May–August 2004).
The Road to Memphis. New York: Dial Books for Young Readers, 1990.
Roll of Thunder, Hear My Cry. New York: Dial Books for Young Readers, 1976.
Song of the Trees. Illustrated by Jerry Pinkney. New York: Dial Books for Young Readers, 1975.
The Well: David's Story. New York: Dial Books for Young Readers, 1995.

Studies of Mildred D. Taylor's Works

Bader, Barbara. "How the Little House Gave Ground: The Beginnings of Multiculturism in a New Black Children's Literature." *Horn Book Magazine* (November/December 2002): 657–74.
Bontempo, B., and R. Jerome. "Exploring Diversity in Adolescent Literature." Workshop Presentation, National Council of Teachers of English Annual Convention, Baltimore, Maryland. November 19, 1989.
Crowe, Chris. *Presenting Mildred D. Taylor*, edited by Patricia J. Campbell. New York: Twayne Publishers, 1999.
Hayn, Judith, and Deborah Sherril. "Female Protagonists in Multicultural Young Adult Literature: Sources & Strategies." *ALAN Review* 24.1 (1996): 43–46.
Huber, Angela. "Beyond the Image: Adolescent Girls Reading and Social Reality." *NWSA Journal* 12.1 (Spring 2000): 84–99.
Johnson, Dianne. "A Tribute to Mildred D. Taylor." *World Literature Today* 78.2 (May–August 2004): 4.
Mikkelsen, Nina. "Insiders, Outsiders, and the Question of Authenticity: Who Shall Write for African-American Children?" *African American Review* 32.1 (Spring 1998): 33–49.
Rochel, Hazel. "The Booklist Interview: Mildred Taylor." *Booklist* 98.2 (September 15, 2001): 221.
Scales, Pat. "Profile: Mildred D. Taylor: Keeper of Stories." *Language Arts, Urbana* 80.3 (Jan 2003): 240–45.
Schafer, Elizabeth. "I'm Gonna Glory in Learnin': Academic Aspirations of African American Characters in Children's Literature." *African American Review* 32.1, Children's and Young-Adult Literature Issue (Spring 1998): 57–66.
Simon, Daniel. "Introducing the NSK Neustadt Prize for Children's Literature." *World Literature Today* 78.2 (May–August 2004): 5–7.
Smith, Karen Patricia,ed. "African-American Voices in Young Adult Literature." *Tradition, Transition and Transformation* (1994).

Shawntaye M. Scott

SUSIE KING TAYLOR (1848–1912)

BIOGRAPHICAL NARRATIVE

Laundress, nurse, teacher, and autobiographer, Susie King Taylor was born Susie Baker in 1848 on a slave plantation in Georgia. She was sent to live with her grandmother in Savannah, where she learned to read and write clandestinely: "We went every day about nine o'clock, with our books wrapped in paper to prevent the police or white persons from seeing them." After the announcement that all slaves in the vicinity of Fort Pulaski would be free, Taylor and her family went to Saint Simons Island to obtain their liberty. Teenage Susie found herself living with and working for the 33rd United States Colored Troop commanded by Colonel T. Higginson. While she remained with the troop, Taylor worked as a laundress, healed the injured, and taught reading and writing to soldiers. She witnessed some crucial events of the American Civil War and eventually married a black soldier, Edward King.

After the war, Taylor continued to be engaged with education and opened several schools (including a public institution for black children and a night one for adults). When her last school closed in 1868, Taylor started working in domestic service. In 1879 she remarried. Her second husband was Russell L. Taylor.

Susie King Taylor continued to be extremely engaged in both social and political causes ("my interest in the boys in blue had not abated") and in 1886 she helped organize the Corps 67, Women's Relief Corps, where she collaborated as guard, secretary, treasurer, and president. She was encouraged to write her autobiography which she published in 1902 under the title: *Reminiscences of My Life in Camp with the 33rd U.S. Colored Troops, Late 1st South Carolina Volunteers: A Black Woman's Civil War Memoirs*. She died in 1912.

MAJOR WORKS

Susie King Taylor only published one book in which she told her experiences in the American Civil War. Although the autobiography *Reminiscences* starts by giving a brief account of her past as a slave and also deals with her life after the Civil War, the main theme of the book is her experience with the 33rd Colored Troops. Told in a very direct and objective style, Taylor wants to emphasize the deep commitment and bravery of African Americans in the Civil War as opposed to the postwar lack of involvement of the American nation toward blacks. The book is filled with her anecdotes and experiences in camp, although the most powerful and outspoken chapter is number XIII where she overtly deals with racial problems in the United States: "I wonder if our white fellow men realize the true sense or meaning of brotherhood? . . . when I read almost every day of what is being done to my race by some whites in the South, I sometimes ask, was the war in vain?" The tone used by Taylor throughout *Reminiscences* is a combination between patriotism and disillusionment at the treatment of African Americans before and after the Civil War.

CRITICAL RECEPTION

Susie King Taylor's work has not been widely reviewed, so she still remains a pretty much-unknown autobiographer. The scholars who have studied her work agree that her *Reminiscences* is an exceptional book that describes the Civil War from an unusual perspective. As W. L. Rose states it: "there is nothing vaguely resembling Susie King Taylor's small volume of random recollections in the entire literature of the Civil War" (7).

In J. Stover's "African-American 'Mother Tongue' Resistance in Nineteenth-Century Postbellum Black Women's Autobiography: Elizabeth Keckley and Susie King Taylor" (2003), Taylor and Elizabeth Keckley are analyzed as examples of postbellum narrators who sought new ways of expressing the African American reality after the Emancipation. Taylor's style is described in the article as "documentary" (120), "clever," and "creative" (123).

Joanne Braxton's chapter "Fugitive Slaves and Sanctified Ladies: Narratives of Power and Vision" (1989) focuses on several African American women who wrote their autobiographies and who offered other textual possibilities besides the widely known slave narrative. Taylor is praised here for her concern with "the bond between freedom and literacy" (44) and for the "nurturing and self-sacrificing qualities of the heroine" she portrays in her book.

BIBLIOGRAPHY

Work by Susie King Taylor

Reminiscences of My Life in Camp with the 33rd U.S. Colored Troops, Late 1st South Carolina Volunteers: A Black Woman's Civil War Memoirs. Princeton and New York: Markus Wiener Publishing, Inc., 1988. Reprint, 1992.

Studies of Susie King Taylor's Work

Baum, Rosalie Murphy. "Susie King Taylor." In *African American Women—A Biographical Dictionary*, edited by D.C. Salem. New York: Garland Publishing, 1993.

Braxton, Joanne. "Fugitive Slaves and Sanctified Ladies: Narratives of Power and Vision." In *Black Women Writing Autobiography: A Tradition within a Tradition*. Philadelphia: Temple University Press, 1989.

Moody, J. K. "Twice Other, Once Shy: Nineteenth-Century Black Women Autobiographers and the American Literary Tradition of Self-Effacement." *A/B: Auto/Biography Studies* 7.1 (Spring 1992): 46–61.

Nulton, K. "The War of Susie King Taylor." In *Separate Spheres No More: Gender Convergence in American Literature, 1830–1930*, edited by Monika M. Elbert. Tuscaloosa: University of Alabama Press, 2000.

Ostrom, Hans, and J. David Macey, eds. *The Greenwood Encyclopedia of African American Literature*. Westport, CT: Greenwood Press, 2005.

Rose, W.L.. "Introduction." *A Black Woman's Civil War Memoirs*, edited by Patricia W. Romero. New York: Markus Wiener Publishing, 1988.

Stover, Johnnie. "African-American 'Mother Tongue' Resistance in Nineteenth-Century Postbellum Black Women's Autobiography: Elizabeth Keckley and Susie King Taylor." *A/B: Auto/Biography Studies* 18.1 (2003) 115–144.

Laura Gimeno Pahissa

LISA TEASLEY (1962–)

BIOGRAPHICAL NARRATIVE

Fiction writer Lisa Teasley was born the oldest of three daughters to Larkin and Violet Teasley in Los Angeles. She recalls a very sheltered childhood, but one filled with encouragement of her artistic endeavors at a very early age. Her mother taught her to draw, and around the age of five or six, Teasley began to write and illustrate her own stories, sure even at that young age that she would one day be a writer.

Teasley stayed close to home during her college years, earning a bachelor's in English with an emphasis in creative writing from UCLA. While at UCLA, Teasley nurtured the seeds of short stories that would later mature into *Glow in the Dark*, her debut work. She published an essay in a 1997 anthology, *An Ear to the Ground: Presenting Writers from 2 Coasts*, and has to date released two works—a collection of short stories, *Glow in the Dark* (2002), and a novel, *Dive* (2004).

MAJOR WORKS

While Teasley may describe her life as rather ordinary, the lives of her characters are extraordinary in a way only an imaginative girl from a sheltered upbringing might envision. The characters of both *Glow in the Dark* and *Dive* abound with folks who would be, for the most part, out of sorts with Teasley's parents and friends in the Baldwin Hills area of Los Angeles. From a forlorn ten-year-old to a drug-addicted female surfer, the characters all reflect Teasley's purpose as a fiction writer: to transport her readers into the thick of her characters' psyches at that moment just before "breakdown or breakthrough."

Teasley told the *Los Angeles Times*, "I just happen to be attracted to those kind of situations, just in wondering what is the human spirit in those kind of dire circumstance[s], or just at the point of epiphany." Thus, in *Dive*, Teasley presents Ruby, an indifferent spirit who spins out of control after a murder occurs outside her Laurel Canyon guest home, and Ray, a construction worker whose past includes three ex-wives and someone else's blood on his hands. Love, or the possibility of it, seems to be the impetus moving these characters from the brink of breakdown to the brink of a breakthrough.

CRITICAL RECEPTION

Readers and critics have been most impressed with Teasley's characterizations, particularly her willingness as an African American woman to write in voices clearly alien to her own. Ray, in *Dive*, is a white Floridian construction worker, for example, far divorced from Teasley's own experience as a black Los Angelino artist, but as *Los Angeles Times* writer Reed Johnson notes, her prose is so "blunt and elliptical" that readers never get a chance to question the authenticity of her characters. Some critics have taken exception to the violence that her characters perpetrate or suffer through, calling the situations "over the top," yet the same critics applaud the unflinching eroticism in Teasley's works, particularly *Dive*. Miriam Wolf's review of *Dive* indicates that "Teasley seems to be at her best when she's illuminating the interplay between a man and a woman. Her writing is ribald and romantic at the same time." The critical praise has resulted in several awards for her work, most recently the 2002 Gold Pen Award for Best Short Story Collection and the 2002 Pacificus Literary Foundation Best Short Story Writer award for fiction, both for *Glow in the Dark*.

BIBLIOGRAPHY

Works by Lisa Teasley

Dive. New York: Bloomsbury, 2004.
Glow in the Dark. Seattle: Cune Press, 2002.

Studies of Lisa Teasley's Works

Galipeaux, Jeff. Rev. of *Glow in the Dark*, by Lisa Teasley. *San Francisco Chronicle on the Web*, April 28, 2002, http://www.sfgate.com (accessed April 22, 2005).

Johnson, Reed. "Words from a Street-Smart Tale Teller." *Los Angeles Times on the Web*, February 24, 2002, http://www.lisateasley.com/latimes.html (accessed April 22, 2005).

Nicholson, Joy. "Chewing Tobacco and Big Feet." *LA Weekly on the Web*, May 28–June 3, 2004, http://www.laweekly.com/ink/04/27/wls-nicholson.php (accessed April 22, 2005).

Palmer, Nichole. Rev. of *Glow in the Dark*, by Lisa Teasley. *Black Issues Book Review* (May/June 2002): 44.

Rev. of *Dive*, by Lisa Teasley. *Kirkus Reviews* 72.1 (2004): 15.

Rev. of *Dive*, by Lisa Teasley. *Publishers Weekly* 251.6 (2004): 55.

Tate, Greg. "Adventures in the Skin Trade." *Village Voice on the Web*, March 27–April 2, 2002, http://www.villagevoice.com/books/0213,tate,33310,10.html (accessed April 22, 2005).

Turrentine, Jeff. Rev. of *Dive*, by Lisa Teasley. *New York Times Book Review*, March 21, 2004, 16.

Wolf, Miriam. Rev. of *Dive*, by Lisa Teasley. *San Francisco Chronicle on the Web*, March 28, 2004, http://www.sfgate.com (accessed April 22, 2005).

Jeremy Griggs

LUCY TERRY (1730–1821)

BIOGRAPHICAL NARRATIVE

The first African American writer, Lucy Terry was born in Africa where she was kidnapped and sold into slavery as an infant. At the age of five, Terry was purchased by Ebenezer Wells of Deerfield, Massachusetts, where she lived until 1756 when she married a wealthy free landowner, Abijah Prince. Terry converted to Christianity as a child during the Great Awakening, and at the age of fourteen was admitted into the "fellowship" of the local church, an unusual occurrence for an African American during slavery. When she was twenty-five, the Prince family moved to Guildford, Vermont, where Terry spent the remainder of her life. Terry and her husband had six children and their home was a central gathering place in the community where Terry read her poems and told stories about Africa. Terry was very much a skilled orator, an abolitionist, and worked to promote and defend African American civil rights. When Williams College denied her son entry based on his race, Terry gave a compelling, though futile, three-hour address to the Board of Trustees in his defense. Lucy Terry was the first African American to present, and win, an argument in front of the Supreme Court in a land ownership dispute. Lucy Terry died at the age of ninety-one.

MAJOR WORKS

Lucy Terry is the author of the first known literary work by an African American. Terry wrote the poem "Bars Fight" when she was sixteen years old and though she was known to have written many more, it is Terry's only surviving work. The poem recounts the Indian ambush of two white families in the Bars, a common colonial term for meadow, on August 25, 1746, near Deerfield, Massachusetts. Though "Bars Fight" is not of significant literary style, the poem consists of simple rhymed couplets, that the poem exists at all challenges commonly held beliefs about African Americans in colonial America and particularly African American women. The colonial age was not conducive to poetic creativity and most colonials did not read or write; very few were inclined to write poetry. Terry's authorship demonstrates the extent to which African Americans rejected the repressive atmosphere of slavery and, instead, empowered themselves through language. Though the poem itself is simple in structure, its characterizations are richly textured for the time and demonstrate a social awareness that belies standard beliefs about African American exclusion from social discourse. Terry gives the most attention in her poem to Eunice Allen, devoting six lines to Allen's desire to "save herself by running." But Allen was tripped up by her petticoats and suffered a "tommy hawk" on her head and left to die. Terry's focus on Eunice Allen's fate may be read as a criticism of the restrictive vestments woman of all races were required to wear in colonial America. Though African American and white women lived vastly different lives in terms of social standing and acceptance, Terry's focus on the petticoats as the cause of Allen's fate elicits a particular acknowledgement of the universality of women's oppression by men. Though some of the known facts of the ambush differ slightly from the information in Terry's poem, those disparities merely signal an independent minded poet who valued and demonstrated creative license, despite social attitudes about African American women.

CRITICAL RECEPTION

Critical reception of "Bars Fight" has been mixed. Some critics lament the poem's lack of social commentary about the state of African American slaves at the time. Other scholars read the lack of social commentary as an attempt by Terry to be accepted by her community, a position that assumes Terry's objective is motivated by social concerns. Other scholars read the poem's subject as Terry's recalcitrance against the belief that African Americans cannot command or understand white language, a reading more closely aligned with what is known about Terry's authoritative involvement in community affairs. That a close textual reading of this poem unfortunately reveals nothing of the author or her life is a common critique of "Bars Fight." Indeed, some scholars have questioned the authorship of the poem, a criticism which assumes a uniform" type" or "style" for any early African American literary work to be considered authentic. The very fact that the authorship of "Bars Fight" is questioned presumes a skepticism of authorship rooted in the pervasive history of American racism.

BIBLIOGRAPHY

Work by Lucy Terry

"The Bars Fight," 1746. Springfield, MA: Samuel Bowles and Company, 1855.

Studies of Lucy Terry's Work

Foster, Frances Smith. *Written by Herself: Literary Production by African American Women, 1746–1892.* Bloomington: Indiana University Press, 1993.
Harris, Sharon M. *Executing Race: Early American Women's Narratives of Race, Society, and the Law.* Columbus: Ohio State University Press, 2005.

Debbie Clare Olson

JOYCE CAROL THOMAS (1938–)

BIOGRAPHICAL NARRATIVE

Joyce Carol Thomas has contributed to the literary field through poetry, plays, and novels. She was born in a poor, rural family in Oklahoma that supplemented their livelihood by picking cotton during the Great Depression. She was fortunate to be surrounded by a long oral-storytelling tradition in the African American subculture, as well as a very strong influence from her church and close-knit family. Thomas feels she was compelled to write by this background and her very close relationships and church ties. She focuses upon family and values, recasting the tales she has heard within her family and community, and shows how people are all interconnected, interdependent, and important parts of a whole. Notably, Thomas does not focus on racial issues or take political stands in her writing.

Ponca City, Oklahoma, was Thomas's first home, and she was born to Floyd David and Leona Thompson Haynes in 1938. The fifth of nine children and the first of two girls, Thomas was surrounded by family. She still maintains a strong personal and literary connection with her hometown and state, using them frequently as the settings for her novels, stories, and poems. Thomas's father worked as a barber. Thomas and her eight siblings augmented the family income by picking cotton in the summers with their parents. The family existed within a large and protected African American community. This community was homogenous unto itself, so Thomas experienced little of the turbulence of racial discrimination. A very strong grounding in a fundamentalist Christian faith was part of the overall community structure and contributed to Thomas's love of words, music, stories, and rhythm. Her focus on patterns of speech and words derives from this.

The Haynes family moved to Tracy, California, when Thomas was ten. There, as in Oklahoma, the family picked seasonal fruits to supplement their living. In California, many of the people Thomas worked alongside were hardworking Mexican Americans, and she formed strong attachments to their culture, as well as became fluent in Spanish. Thomas put herself through college at night while working full time as a phone operator. Thomas has four children from two marriages. After receiving a bachelor's degree in Spanish from San Jose State College, Thomas began teaching, and eventually earned a master's degree in education from Stanford in 1967. Her interest in Spanish is directly tied to her days as a fruit and vegetable picker.

Thomas taught at various schools for over twenty-five years as she raised her own family. Eventually, she began a shift into academia and creative-writing instruction in colleges. Assignments at California State University, Purdue, and the University of Tennessee, Knoxville, among others, fostered her writing career. She began publishing in the early 1970s, with several small volumes of poetry and four plays to her credit. Her first novel, *Marked by Fire*, was published in 1982, to great acclaim. Several of her novels and poetry anthologies would later be adapted for the stage. Thomas retired from teaching to pursue her writing career full time in 1995.

Joyce Carol Thomas now lives in Berkeley, California, close to her family, and friends. She spends much of her time writing. She also enjoys making school visits. Over the years she has participated in many national and international conferences and festivals. She loves to see the light of comprehension and a love of language in students' eyes. She also remains dedicated to sharing the experience of community and the strength of family and faith. For Thomas, life is not idyllic, but it is roughly balanced between good and evil.

MAJOR WORKS

Thomas writes for all ages, but has been most recognized for her work for children and young adults. She has consciously chosen to write for these age groups because she feels they are more open to the beauty of the world and the wonder of human life. Her choice of audience, however, does not limit her grasp of characterization and community, of beauty and personal strength. And while her works are often lyrical and idealistic, they are not without recognition of evil and terrible incidents. Thomas's point is to show that life is both good and bad and that people need to support each other and approach life in a positive manner.

The most important work by Joyce Carol Thomas is her first novel, *Marked by Fire*. This is the story of a young African American girl born in the cotton fields of Ponca City, Oklahoma. Abyssinia Jackson, as she is named, is born into a homogenous community of African American rural agricultural workers who work side by side, worship together, and have a very strong bond. Love, family, wonder, music, faith, and magic surround Abby. Nonetheless, she is raped in her early teens, and becomes mute. The annual floods cause great hardship, and her father abandons the family. Through it all Abby takes in the music of language, the magic of healing, and the discovery of her own value. She overcomes her reaction to the assault, learns about herbs and plants for healing, and brings her family back together within the safety of the community and love.

Written in a particularly lyrical manner, *Marked by Fire* (1982) was awarded the National Book Award in 1983. The Coretta Scott King Foundation and the American Library Association also recognized it for its complex yet accessible layers of story and character. Thomas has been recognized as being a master of beautiful prose, intuitive characterizations, and a very positive influence upon readers without resorting to sentimentality or stereotype.

This novel spawned three sequels, a play, and then a musical. *Bright Shadow* is the story of Abby's first love, more hardship through murder, and her own maturity into a real doctor against very large odds. *Water Girl* is about Abby's granddaughter, and *The Golden Pasture* is about the childhood of her future husband, Carl Lee Jefferson. The central theme of all of these novels is that although tragedy and evil do exist and can be terribly painful or even crippling, people have untapped strength within themselves and as a community that can carry them through hard times. Adversity can be overcome through grit, honesty, faith, an appreciation of beauty, and a belief in dreams. Threaded throughout these novels in service to this theme are the motifs of family love, music as a strengthening and fulfilling entity, wonderful food, and the importance of hope.

I Have Heard of a Land is a poem that celebrates and illustrates the history of African Americans in the development of the frontier. Oklahoma encouraged settlers in the late nineteenth century by staging land rushes, or free land given to those who would stake a claim and work it. These poems tell the story of a young African American woman and her family as they pursued the dream of owning their own land and building a community against great difficulties and all expectations. This book also won the Coretta Scott King award and tells a little-known story of African American history.

Joyce Carol Thomas is not limited to one format of writing, let alone one audience. She has written many poetry works addressed to young children, the most important of which are *Brown Honey in Broomwheat Tea*, and its companion piece, *Gingerbread Days*. Broomwheat tea is an herbal concoction that Thomas herself grew up on in Oklahoma. It is used for healing, for comfort, and for all manner of ills. A very inadequate comparison would be to compare this to current comfort foods such as meatloaf or macaroni and cheese. Thomas celebrates its simplicity and profundity as a healing nostrum, as well as its value as a community tie and wonderful memory of a rural childhood. Other poetry books address the beauty of one's first born infant, *You Are My Perfect Baby*, and the bond between a mother and a daughter, *A Mother's Heart, a Daughter's Love* and *Cherish Me*. It is very obvious from interviews with the author and from the poetry itself that Thomas intends for many of her poems to be read aloud to small children. They are characterized by a verbal rhythm and Thomas's usual themes of family and goodness.

Many picture books for early readers have been produced by Thomas in collaboration with a wide variety of illustrators. The most important of these is *The Gospel Cinderella*. There is no handsome prince looking for a bride here, but a young orphan girl taken in to be a servant to an evil woman and her two terrible daughters. Cinderella knows that there must be something more in life for her and someone to love her, but she is unable to seek it out directly. Her one solace is singing in church. Queen Mother Rhythm, the lead singer of the gospel choir, is looking for a protégé to take over the choir as she retires. She accidentally hears Cinderella singing in the woods. It develops that Queen Mother Rhythm lost a young girl child and has been mourning her loss for many years, just as Cinderella has hoped for a real family. Lo and behold, they realize that they are mother and daughter. A beautiful and meaningful new life built around gospel music is before them.

This story is all about rhythm and melody. Thomas's point is that life has a rhythm, and if you let it, it has a melody, as well. You just have to learn how to sing, metaphorically. Her use of words and rhythm to create a melody is inspired, and well served by the vibrantly brilliant illustrations by David Diaz. Family again is celebrated, as well as the strength of an individual and her dreams.

Zora Neale Hurston has been an icon of Joyce Carol Thomas's since she discovered the stories from the south that Hurston collected and published. When Thomas was in graduate school, she found an old, rather neglected copy of one of Hurston's "pourquoi" books and wondered why she had never heard of this author. At the time, Hurston's works were virtually out of print. Recently, Thomas has taken some of these stories of poor, rural, African American life in the south in the early part of the twentieth century and adapted them for a children's audience, along with copious illustrations. *What's the Hurry, Fox?* and *The Skull Talks Back* contain nearly twenty-five of Hurston's stories. Thomas chose to adapt them in order to give children better access to their own oral heritage, and to ensure that the stories and the voices in them are well preserved for a long time. They have been received very well.

Thomas has also compiled and edited two collections of stories from other authors. The first, *A Gathering of Flowers*, features stories and poetry from several authors to illustrate and promote multiracial and ethnic diversity. *Linda Brown, You Are Not Alone*

(2003) gives the reader memories and anecdotes concerning the *Brown v. Board of Education* supreme court decision that brought an end to legal discrimination and segregation in the United States. Certain of the authors write about their own experiences at the time, while others detail instances of discrimination. This book was published on the eve fiftieth anniversary of this controversial and far-reaching court decision.

Joyce's success and hard work has garnered many awards, such as the Coretta Scott King award from the American Library Association for *Brown Honey in Broomwheat Tea*. Her first novel won the 1983 National Book Award, the 1982 Best Book for Young Adults from the American Library Association, and was named the 1983 "Outstanding Book of the Year" by the *New York Times*. Further recognition has come from the state of Oklahoma, where she served as poet laureate from 1996 to 2000. All in all, Thomas has achieved a great deal, continues to toil in the literary vineyard, and has brought joy and entertainment to many people.

CRITICAL RECEPTION

Joyce Carol Thomas has written for so many age groups and in so many formats that the critical reception of her work is somewhat diffused. Repeatedly, however, the words "lyrical," "joyous," "celebration," and "uplifting" are used to describe her writing. Musical terms are frequently applied as well, and this is how Thomas intended her material to be received by readers. Her children's materials tend to be reviewed by the library review journals and children's magazines and Web sites, rather than more traditional, literary sources. Even her first novel, *Marked by Fire*, which won major awards, did so in the children's categories. Finally, however, this novel and its sequels have given Thomas international recognition. Thomas has also written plays whose reviews were sometimes rather negative. Her novels have generally fared better, although at least once her writing style was referred to as saccharine and self-consciously moralizing. Younger reviewers have occasionally taken Thomas to task for not writing more about the evils of racism and segregation, but her subtle style is designed to show that all people are alike and to explore the character of people.

BIBLIOGRAPHY

Works by Joyce Carol Thomas

Ambrosia. Produced in San Francisco at Little Fox Theatre, 1978.
Angel's Lullaby. Illustrated by Pamela Johnson. New York: Hyperion, 2001.
Bittersweet. San Jose: Firesign, 1973.
Black Child. Illustrated by Tom Feelings. New York: Zamani Productions, 1981.
The Blacker the Berry: Poems. Illustrated by Brenda Joysmith. New York: HarperCollins, 1997.
Blessing. Berkeley: Jocato, 1975.
The Bowlegged Rooster and Other Tales That Signify. New York: HarperCollins, 2000.
Bright Shadow. New York: Avon, 1983.
Brown Honey in Broomwheat Tea. Illustrated by Floyd Cooper. New York: HarperCollins, 1993.
Cherish Me. Illustrated by Nneka Bennett. New York: HarperCollins, 1998.
Crowning Glory: Poems. Illustrated by Brenda Joysmith. New York: HarperCollins 2002.
Crystal Breezes. San Jose: Firesign, 1974.
Gingerbread Days. Illustrated by Floyd Cooper. New York: HarperCollins, 1995.

The Golden Pasture. New York: Scholastic, 1986.

The Gospel Cinderella. Illustrated by David Diaz. Hew York: HarperCollins, 2004.

Gospel Roads. Produced in Carson, CA, at California State University, 1981.Unpublished.

House of Light. New York: Hyperion, 2001.

Hush Songs: African American Lullabies. Illustrated by Brenda Joysmith. New York: Hyperion, 2001.

I Have Heard of a Land. Illustrated by Floyd Cooper. New York: HarperCollins, 1998.

Inside the Rainbow. Palo Alto: Zikawana Press, 1982.

Journey. New York: Scholastic, 1988.

Joy! Illustrated by Pamela Johnson. New York: Hyperion, 2001.

Linda Brown, You Are Not Alone: The Brown v. Board of Education Decision: a Collection, edited by Joyce Carol Thomas. Illustrated by Curtis James. New York: Jump at the Sun/Hyperion Books for Children, 2003.

Look! What a Wonder! Produced in Berkeley at Berkeley Community Theatre, 1976. Unpublished.

Magnolia. Produced in San Francisco at Old San Francisco Opera House, 1977. Unpublished.

Marked by Fire. New York: Avon, 1982.

A Mother's Heart, a Daughter's Love. New York: HarperCollins, 2001.

A Song in the Sky. Produced in San Francisco at Montgomery Theatre, 1976. Unpublished.

Water Girl. New York: Avon, 1986.

When the Nightingale Sings. New York: HarperCollins, 1992.

You Are My Perfect Baby. Illustrated by Nneka Bennett. New York: HarperCollins, 1999.

Studies of Joyce Carol Thomas's Works

Bader, Philip. *African-American Writers: A to Z of African Americans.* New York: Facts On File, 2004.

Cart, Michael. *Linda Brown, You Are Not Alone, A Study Guide.* New York: Hyperion, 2003.

Henderson, Darwin L., and Anthony J. Manna. "Evoking the 'Holy and the Horrible': Conversations with Joyce Carol Thomas." *African American Review* 32.1 (Spring 1998): 139–46.

Hudson, Theodore R. "Affirming Rainbows and Flames: A Conversation with Joyce Carol Thomas." *SAGE: A Scholarly Journal on Black Women* 5.1 (Summer 1988): 68–70.

Kovacs, Deborah. *Meet the Authors: 25 Writers of Upper Elementary and Middle School Books Talk about Their Work.* New York: Scholastic, 1995.

Marowski, Daniel G., ed. *Contemporary Literary Criticism*, vol. 35. Detroit: Gale, 1985, 405–7.

Nakamura, Joyce, ed. *Something about the Author: Autobiography Series*, vol. 7. Detroit: Thomas Gale, 1993, 299–312.

Nelson, Emmanuel S., ed. *Contemporary African American Novelists: A Bio-Bibliographical Critical Sourcebook.* Westport, CT: Greenwood Press, 1999.

Rockman, Connie C., ed. *Eighth Book of Junior Authors and Illustrators.* New York: Wilson, 2000, 518–21.

Senick, Gerard, ed. *Children's Literature Review*, vol. 19. Detroit: Gale, 1990, 219–23.

Scot Peacock, ed. Something about the Author, vol. 137. Detroit: Thomson Gale, 2003, 194–207.

Toombs, Charles P., ed. "Joyce Carol Thomas." In *Dictionary of Literary Biography: Afro American Writers after 1955*, vol. 33. Detroit: Gale, 1984, 245–51.

Yalom, Marilyn, ed. *Women Writers of the West Coast: Speaking of Their Lives and Careers.* Santa Barbara: Capra, 1983.

Elizabeth Malia

ERA BELL THOMPSON (1905–1986)

BIOGRAPHICAL NARRATIVE

Era Bell Thompson is a significant but overlooked figure in twentieth-century American letters. Originally from Virginia, Thompson's family migrated west: first to Des Moines, Iowa, then to a homestead in North Dakota. Thompson was born in Des Moines in 1905 where, according to her autobiography *American Daughter*, she experienced a short but idyllic childhood. In Des Moines, her father, Tony, who worked as a waiter, and her mother, Mary, were able to provide their family (two sons and a daughter) a middle-class existence. But in 1914, Tony followed his half brother to North Dakota, settling the family on a homestead near Mandan. As seen in *American Daughter*, this experience— growing up African American on the Northern Plains in the early twentieth century— speaks in large part to Thompson's unique American experience. (The 1920 census indicates that of the 646,872 citizens of the state only 467 were African American.)

Thompson's mother died in 1918. By 1920 her father had moved the family to Bismarck, where Thompson attended high school and excelled in athletics and wrote articles for and published poetry in the school newspaper. Thompson eventually saved enough money to attend the University of North Dakota, where, among other things, she ran track (she broke five UND records) and wrote for the *Dakotah Daily Student*. Persistent financial and health problems prevented her from graduating, however.

Thompson moved to Chicago in 1928 and found a position as a writer with a small black magazine. But shortly thereafter she returned to North Dakota to care for her dying father.

Through the generosity of a Methodist minister for whom she had begun to work, Thompson was able to graduate in 1933 from Morningside College in Sioux City, Iowa. After graduation, she immediately returned to Chicago where she spent the rest of her life as a writer.

MAJOR WORKS

American Daughter (1946) is Thompson's most important work. First, it is unique, one of only a handful of autobiographies and memoirs by African Americans—such as Oscar Micheaux—who grew up or spent time in the Northern Plains. Second, it is unique in terms of its tone. Unlike other autobiographies by African Americans of the same period, Thompson's tone is not one of protest, rage, bitterness, or disappointment. Instead, Thompson portrays herself as an idealist and optimist, whether she is writing about race or about overcoming personal travail and tragedy. Third, in style and content, *American Daughter* is ambitious in scope. Thompson writes poetically of the geography and ethos of the Great Plains; she writes poignantly of the various types of tragedy and hardships her family encounters; she writes lovingly and admiringly of her parents; and she writes optimistically about the future. Moreover, she seamlessly integrates self-deprecating humor. For these reasons and others, *American Daughter* remains a noteworthy literary and historical document.

Thompson published two more books. *Africa: Land of My Fathers* (1954), a memoir of her travels there, written in her signature style. And in 1963 she and Herbert Nipson, another editor at *Ebony*, edited and published a collection of essays: *White on Black: The Views of Twenty-Two White Americans on the Negro*. This collection features figures ranging from William Faulkner to Jack Dempsey.

CRITICAL RECEPTION

American Daughter was well received when University of Chicago Press published it in 1946. Ralph Ellison wrote a complimentary review of it. In *Black Women Writing Autobiography: A Tradition within a Tradition*, critic Joanne Braxton examines Thompson's use of tone and espouses that unlike many similar texts of the time Thompson's tone is quite optimistic.

Perhaps the major indication of her critical reception is the state of North Dakota recognition of Thompson's life and work in two significant ways: it awarded her the Roughrider Award—the state's highest honor—and in 1979 the University of North Dakota renamed its Black Cultural Center the Era Bell Thompson Cultural Center in her honor.

BIBLIOGRAPHY

Works by Era Bell Thompson

Africa: Land of My Fathers. Garden City: Doubleday, 1954.
American Daughter. 1946. Reprint, St. Paul: Minnesota Historical Press, 1986.
White on Black: The Views of Twenty-Two White Americans on the Negro, edited by Era Bell Thompson and Herbert Nipson Thompson. Chicago: Johnson Publishers, 1963.

Studies of Era Bell Thompson's Works

Anderson, Kathie R. "Era Bell Thompson: A North Dakota Daughter." In *The Centennial Anthology of North Dakota History: Journal of the Northern Plains*, edited by Janet Daley Lysengen and Ann M. Rathke, 307–19. Bismarck: State Historical Society of North Dakota, 1996.
Braxton, Joanne M. *Black Women Writing Autobiography: A Tradition within a Tradition*. Philadelphia: Temple University Press, 1989, 144–80.
Cole, Kevin L., and Leah Weins. "Religion, Idealism, and African American Autobiography in the Northern Plains: Era Bell Thompson's *American Daughter*." *Great Plains Quarterly* 23.4 (Fall 2003): 219–29.
Johnson, Michael K. " 'This Strange White World': Race and Place in Era Bell Thompson's American Daughter." *Great Plains Quarterly* 20.2 (Spring 2000): 101–11.
Long, Judith. Rev. of *American Daughter*, by Era Bell Thompson. *Nation* 244.25 (1987): 899–900.

Kevin L. Cole

KATHERINE DAVIS CHAPMAN TILLMAN (1870–?)

BIOGRAPHICAL NARRATIVE

Katherine Tillman, essayist, poet, dramatist, and fiction-writer of the post-Reconstruction era, was born in Mound City, Illinois, February 19, 1870. Although Tillman's work focuses primarily on the standard themes of the nineteenth-century sentimental narrative, it emphasizes that black women can fight racism in their roles as wives and mothers. As Claudia Tate has expressed, Tillman, along with other contemporary black women writers, transformed this genre into "liberational discourses" ("Allegories" 126).

Katherine Tillman began to write in childhood. The short stories she published as a high school student in Yanktown, South Dakota, in *Our Women and Children* are among works that are no longer extant. She published her first poem, "Memory," in the *Christian Recorder*, an A.M.E. publication, at the age of eighteen, and occasional articles and poems appeared in the *Indianapolis Freeman*.

She attended the State University of Louisville in Kentucky and Wilberforce University in Ohio. After her marriage to the Rev. George M. Tillman, minister of Allen Chapel African Methodist Episcopal Church, she proceeded to publish widely in A.M.E. Church publications, most notably the *A.M.E. Church Review*. That review serialized her novellas, *Beryl Weston's Ambition: The Story of an African American Girl's Life* and *Clancy Street*, and published a short play, *Heirs of Slavery: A Little Drama of To-day*.

In 1902, the A.M.E. Book Concern published Tillman's volume of poetry, *Recitations*, and later several plays as well. All of Katherine Tillman's available texts have been published in one volume, *The Works of Katherine Davis Chapman Tillman*, edited and introduced by Claudia Tate.

MAJOR WORKS

Tillman's works argue for education, uplift of the race, social reform, hard work, and ambition tempered by Christian piety and womanly purity.

The protagonist of the novella *Beryl Weston's Ambition* successfully combines domesticity, intellectual achievement, and social responsibility through hard work, devotion to family, and Christian faith. The heavy family responsibilities Beryl inherits when her mother dies forces her to leave college; however, domesticity and marriage do not defeat Beryl, but provide the context in which she can realize her goals. She marries happily and becomes a college teacher. The novella also introduces the subjects of expatriation and repatriation at a time when many African Americans were torn between leaving the United States as missionaries or seekers of a less racist society and committing to the fight for racial equality in this country.

Clancy Street is set in the gritty urban realism of an interracial and multiethnic poor neighborhood in Louisville, Kentucky. More caustic in tone than the first novella, it fiercely critiques a racist society that has abandoned the poor of all races. The text also admonishes the recently emancipated race that "too often acted like so many children in the face of the grave responsibilities that confronted them" (251). Through the characters of Caroline and Hettie, Tillman lays out the harsh choices and fates available to sexually vulnerable poor "colored girls." Obedient Caroline heeds her mother's advice to "stay in her place and keep white men folks in theirs" (273). Her dedication to Christ and devotion to education contrast with Hettie's fall into a "disgrace . . . worse than death" (271). This work confronts, as well, the gruesome social problems of alcoholism, domestic abuse, "the habit of wastefulness" (252), prostitution, and anti-Christian "cunjerin', fixin', trickin', poisonin', and hoodooin'" (261) that plague the Clancy Street neighborhood.

Tillman's two short stories feature idealized African American male characters, both of whom embody commitment to education, Christian values, and social change. In "Miles the Conquerer," Miles Brown's "Christ-like patience" (248) over six years enables him to "conquer" the racism at college and eventually become the president of an Afro-American college. In "The Preacher at Hill Station," Elder Clark uses his authority to reform and empower the community, fight for a library and an extended school term, and heroically confront a crowd of violent whites who deny blacks access to the polls.

The subject matter of Tillman's essays ranges from practical advice to literary criticism. "Some Girls That I Know," "Afro-American Women and Their Work," and "Paying Professions for Colored Girls" instruct and inspire women to cultivate self-reliance and economic independence. Her essays on Afro-American poets reaffirm their contributions to the literary tradition. Essays on Alexander Dumas Père and Alexander Pushkin incorporate into the American literary tradition great writers with Negro blood, who, had they lived in the United States, would be classified as African American.

In Tillman's single volume of poetry, *Recitations*, the themes of racial affirmation and uplift dominate; however, as Tate points out, Tillman's poetry also challenges her own and her readers' intraracial prejudices primarily through nonconfrontational methods—methods that "may have been a most potent subversion of racist allegations" ("Introduction" 21). Some of the most memorable are the persona poems that are written in dialect and address specific racist issues.

The speaker in the heart-rending "She Who Never Had a Chance" is a victim of family violence, poverty, ignorance, and early death, despite her sincere desire for love, home, and respectability. The poem clearly condemns not "She" the sinner but the societal indifference and hypocrisy that predestine many girls to utter misery. Also a searing indictment of racism is the poem "Bashy," which pointedly mentions the intraracial hatred practiced by Negroes who "hate a black face" and "prize" the white.

"A Southern Incident" invites today's readers to draw a startling contrast between the kindness of the "rale" southern lady who offers her seat to an elderly "old colored woman" on a bus or streetcar, and the racism that confronted Rosa Parks on a Montgomery, Alabama, bus. "Sen' Me Back to De Souf" explores the paradoxical nostalgia for the south experienced by blacks who have moved to the north.

Given African American women writers' lack of access to the professional theater, it is doubtful that Tillman's dramatic works were ever formally produced. The themes of both *Aunt Betsy's Thanksgiving* and *Thirty Years* are the reuniting of the family and the economic prosperity brought by hard work. *Fifty Years of Freedom, or From Cabin to Congress* chronicles orphan Benjamin Banneker Houston's determined struggle for an education that eventually takes him to Congress. The emotional center of the drama, however, is Aunt Rhoda, who personifies the older generation's ambivalence about emancipation, complicated by old loyalties and memories. Tillman's last drama, *The Spirit of Allen: A Pageant of African Methodism*, is a tribute to the AME Church, and is assumed to have been self-published.

CRITICAL RECEPTION

Claudia Tate is the only critic to have published extensively on Tillman. She places Tillman's work in the context of nineteenth-century black writers, who "inscribe racial oppression and black people's desire to participate in . . . an emergent bourgeois-capitalistic society." Significantly, Tate differentiates between the "racial protestation in male texts" and the "ideal familial formation" of female texts, including Tillman's ("Allegories" 104).

Tate argues that fiction by Tillman and other postbellum African American women writers has been misread—mostly in opposition to both the Victorian ideals sanctioned in white women's fiction and the African American male heroic standards in the more prominent narratives of writers such as Frederick Douglass. Quite simply, reading these nineteenth-century romance and marriage narratives with twentieth-century eyes has blinded critics to the black female authority inscribed in the texts. In fact, the narratives do not portray marriage as "a negation of personal autonomy" ("Allegories" 101), but as a liberating base from which to challenge racism and promote social progress.

Tate argues masterfully that Tillman and other writers such as Frances Ellen Watkins Harper, Amelia E. Johnson, and Emma Dunham Kelley critiqued and revised the concepts of race, class, and gender. She corrects the dismissive assumption that Tillman's work merely conforms to narrow sentimental-narrative conventions.

BIBLIOGRAPHY

Works by Katherine Davis Chapman Tillman

Published in *The Works of Katherine Davis Chapman Tillman*

"Afro-American Poets and Their Verse" (1898).
"Afro-American Women and Their Work" (1895).
"Alexander Dumas, Père" (1907).
"Alexander Sergeivich Pushkin" (1909).
Aunt Betsy's Thanksgiving (n.d.).
Beryl Weston's Ambition: The Story of an African American Girl's Life (1893).
Clancy Street (1898–1899).
Fifty Years of Freedom, or From Cabin to Congress: A Drama in Five Acts (1910).
Heirs of Slavery: A Little Drama of To-day (1901).
How To Live Well on a Small Salary (lost; mentioned in the *Christian Recorder*, 1895).
"Miles the Conqueror" (1894).
"The Negro among Anglo-Saxon Poets" (1898).
"Paying Professions for Colored Girls" (1907).
"The Preacher at Hill Station" (1903).
Quotations from Negro Authors (anthology) (1921).
Recitations (1902).
"Some Girls That I Know" (1893).

The Spirit of Allen: A Pageant of African Methodism (1922).
Thirty Years of Freedom: A Drama in Four Acts (1902).

Studies of Katherine Davis Chapman Tillman's Works

Tate, Claudia. "Allegories of Black Female Desire; or Rereading Nineteenth-Century Sentimental Narratives of Black Female Authority." In *Essays on Criticism, Theory, and Writing by Black Women*, edited by Cheryl A. Wall. New Brunswick, NJ: Rutgers, 1989.
———. *Domestic Allegories of Political Desire: The Black Heroine's Text at the Turn of the Century.* New York: Oxford University Press, 1992.
———. "Introduction." In *The Works of Katherine Davis Chapman Tillman*, edited by Claudia Tate. New York: Oxford University Press, 1991.

Gerri Reaves

RUTH D. TODD (1878?–?)

BIOGRAPHICAL NARRATIVE

Between March 1902 and March 1904, Ruth D. Todd contributed three short stories and one serial novella to the *Colored American Magazine*. Then she disappeared. Since her biographical information was never featured in the magazine, what is known of Todd's life must be pieced together from federal census records, operating under the assumption that she was publishing under her own name.

The 1900 census lists Ruth D. Todd, an African American woman, living and working as a servant in the Philadelphia home of a physician named George M. Cooper. This census record also indicates that Todd was born in September 1878 in Virginia. Following this lead backward to the 1880 census, there is a one-year-old Ruth A. Todd living in Fairfield, Virginia with her mother, Mattie Todd, and her father, Edward P. Todd. Despite the different middle initials, the coincidences of birth date and geography suggest that the Ruth D. Todd of 1900 and the Ruth A. Todd of 1880 are the same person.

By 1910, the thirty-one-year-old Todd was a self-employed seamstress, living as a boarder in a more modest section of Philadelphia with a fellow native Virginian, twenty-seven-year-old Alice Byers, a chambermaid. After this date, Todd vanishes from the census rolls. Work to uncover more information about her life is ongoing.

MAJOR WORKS

Ruth Todd's stories were never featured in the *Colored American Magazine*'s previews for upcoming issues, and they were consistently overshadowed by fiction from the magazine's most eminent contributor, Pauline Hopkins. And yet, her abbreviated oeuvre offers an interesting counterpoint to what Claudia Tate has termed the "domestic fictions" written by her more well-known contemporaries. Todd is the author of four known works, all of which appeared in the *Colored American Magazine*, and all of which fly in the face of stock "tragic mulatta" storylines. "The Octoroon's Revenge" tells the story of a southern belle who falls in love with, and finally elopes with, her father's African American coachman; at the end, the reader discovers that her octoroon nurse was her birth mother, who switched her own daughter with the master's legitimate baby girl after the latter's death in infancy. On learning of her heritage, the belle embraces the nurse as her "poor abused mother," and the happy threesome move to France to live openly as a mixed-race family. The eponymous heroine of "Florence Grey: A Three-Part Story" is a belle of African American society of Washington, D.C., who is pursued and finally abducted by an obsessed wealthy white man. Florence refuses to give in to her would-be seducer, and is finally saved by Susie Hill, a schoolteacher-in-training and temporary servant in the white man's household who recognizes Florence from the society pages and alerts her family. "The Folly of Mildred: A Race Story with a Moral" indicts its snobbish title character for discriminating against darker-skinned African Americans; she marries a light-skinned man with loose morals, shunning her darker-skinned mother and friends, and ends up a "veritable slave" working to support her infant and her profligate husband. "The Taming of a Modern Shrew" is a comedic piece that mocks flirtation and, ultimately, the romantic frivolity of many male writers; its lightness, Elizabeth Ammons argues, constitutes a "political act" in itself.

CRITICAL RECEPTION

Todd's work is just beginning to receive critical attention. In her introduction to *Short Fiction by Black Women, 1900–1920*, Elizabeth Ammons makes important initial forays into Todd's biography and briefly discusses the political chutzpah of the deceptively lighthearted "The Taming of a Modern Shrew." Amy Blair's "Rewriting Heroines: Ruth Todd's 'Florence Grey,' Society Pages, and the Rhetorics of Success" reads "Florence Grey" in the context of contemporaneous African American society pages, and, seeing the novella as a direct response to Pauline Hopkins's serial novel *Hagar's Daughter*, argues that Susie Hill is to be seen as the true heroine of the piece. Carrie Tirado Bramen reads "The Octoroon's Revenge" alongside Frances Harper's *Iola Leroy* as a text exemplifying what she calls the "Mendelist allegory" of race, in which a biracial subject's blackness triumphs over her whiteness, thereby "unsettl[ing] dominant assumptions about the desirability of whiteness."

BIBLIOGRAPHY

Works by Ruth D. Todd

"Florence Grey: A Three-Part Story." *Colored American Magazine* 5.1 (August 1902): 307–13; 5.2 (September 1902): 391–97; 5.3 (October 1902): 469–77.
"The Folly of Mildred: A Race Story with a Moral." *Colored American Magazine* 6 (March 1903): 364–70.
"The Octoroon's Revenge." *Colored American Magazine* 4 (March 1902): 291–95.
"The Taming of a Modern Shrew." *Colored American Magazine* 7 (March 1904): 191–95.

Studies of Ruth D. Todd's Works

Ammons, Elizabeth, ed. "Introduction." In *Short Fiction by Black Women, 1900–1920*, 3–20. New York: Oxford University Press, 1991.
Blair, Amy L. "Rewriting Heroines: Ruth Todd's 'Florence Grey,' Society Pages, and the Rhetorics of Success." *Studies in American Fiction* 30 (Spring 2002): 103–28.
Bramen, Carrie Tirado. *The Uses of Variety: Modern Americanism and the Quest for National Distinctiveness*. Cambridge, MA: Harvard University Press, 2000, 201–49.

Amy L. Blair

MARY ELIZABETH VROMAN (1925–1967)

BIOGRAPHICAL NARRATIVE

Mary Elizabeth Vroman was a short story writer, novelist, and screen writer. Born in Buffalo, New York, in 1925 and reared in the West Indies, she earned her B.A. at Alabama State University, and went on to teach in the public schools of Alabama, Chicago, and New York. A member of Delta Sigma Theta Sorority—founded on January 13, 1913, by twenty-two students at Howard University—Vroman later published *Shaped to Its Purpose: Delta Sigma Theta, the First Fifty Years* in 1961, providing a history of the sorority which highlighted among other things, the Delta Founders' participation in the Women's Suffrage march in Washington, D.C., in March 1913. She died in 1967.

MAJOR WORKS

Vroman is best known for "See How They Run," her short story about a rural teacher in the south reaching out to a troubled child, which ran in the June 1951 issue of *The Ladies' Home Journal*, and subsequently won that year's Christopher Award. It was made into the 1953 film *Bright Road*; a major studio production with an almost all-black cast, the film deviated markedly from the glamorous MGM productions during that time. Starring newcomers Dorothy Dandridge and Harry Belafonte, the film impressed Dandridge in that according to her it "showed that beneath any color skin, people are simply people" With her writing credit on the film, Vroman became the first black woman of the Screenwriter's Guild.

Vroman also wrote two compelling novels—*Esther*, published in 1963, and *Harlem Summer*, published in 1967—notable for their frank exploration of controversial racial issues. *Esther* focuses on the protagonist Esther Kennedy's maturity, developing its plot initially around young Esther's formative relationship with her grandmother, Grandear, and her older sister Lucy. As a young girl, Esther takes a job as a domestic for a wealthy white family to earn money for nursing school, a move that results in the life-altering event of Esther giving birth to a daughter, Hope, as a result of her rape by the family's decadent eldest son. While the novel relates the shame heaped upon Esther, it more emphatically highlights Esther's subsequent achievement as a supervisor of nurses. Still, rather than suggesting her heroism, the novel routinely connects Esther to her community: When she visits Hope's father Paul to parlay his guilt over raping her into building a decent wing for black people at the hospital that employs her, Paul remarks that he finds her "extraordinary," a characterization Esther rejects. The novel further engages issues of class distinctions within African American communities by suggesting the backlash heaped upon the man Esther dated as a young woman, Joe, when, as a doctor, he shuns the poor man who raised him, and by illustrating the tensions between Esther and her sister when Esther marries Joe while Lucy remains married to a carpenter. Finally, in its depiction of Esther as a professional success and as a wife and mother frustrated by staying home to take care of her second child, the novel also explores tensions between traditional and modern roles for women.

Written for a young adult audience, *Harlem Summer* engages frankly with how race informs issues such as bullying, being away from home, and young love. At times educational in a literal sense, the novel reproduces conversations that detail moments in African American history such as Marcus Garvey's ideas about addressing racial inequities, and Rosa Parks and the bus boycott. Yet the novel also offers a compelling storyline as it traces the friendship between the southern John and the northern Mark, and carves out an important female role in Mark's girlfriend Deena, who helps John navigate his new surroundings. When John bewilderingly looks around as crowds gather in front of speakers in Harlem, Deena explains that these discussions help diffuse potential violence between blacks and whites. The novel portrays both young men positively and as having a lot in common, positioning the honest and considerate Mark as an obvious friend for the equally likeable John, as they explore their common love of reading and share the impact on their young lives of losing their fathers at an early age. John's bringing to justice, at the novel's end, the men who bullied Mark when Mark was younger solidifies the male friendship that focuses the novel.

CRITICAL RECEPTION

"See How They Run" has been included in the recently published short story anthologies, *Modern Fiction about School Teaching: An Anthology*, edited by Jay S. Blanchard and Ursula Casanova; Edith Bliksilver's *Ethnic American Woman, Problems, Protests, Lifestyle*; and John Henrik Clarke's *American Negro Short Stories*, a reprint of the original published in 1966. These reprintings highlight the story's merit, and can help revive critical interest in Vroman's other work as well. Vroman's work is also included in *The Best Short Stories by Black Writers, 1899–1967* by Langston Hughes, an anthology which reproduces more canonical African American writers such as Zora Neale Hurston, Alice Walker, James Baldwin, and Ralph Ellison as well.

Much remains to be written about Vroman. *Bright Road,* the film adaptation of "See How They Run," has received some critical attention. Writing for Turner Classic Movies, Frank Miller writes that the film, an anomaly in a period when Hollywood was producing glamorous musicals, had a "quiet daring [that] has earned it a faithful fan following, particularly in light of the starring performances of Dorothy Dandridge and Harry Belafonte before they became major stars." Miller relates that "[t]hough the studio only gave [the film] a 19-day shooting schedule, they still put a good deal of talent behind the cameras, with Alfred Gilks, a recent Oscar-winner for *An American in Paris* (1951), shooting the film and composer David Rose, currently scoring a major hit as on-camera musical director for television's *The Red Skelton Show*, composing the score." Both Dandridge and Belafonte successfully downplayed their sexuality to evoke the dignity of Vroman's characters: a hardworking, caring low-income schoolteacher and the principal who falls in love with her. As Miller writes, "[a] year later, the two would team in the much more torrid *Carmen Jones*, which made Dandridge the first African-American performer nominated for a Best Actress Oscar. Belafonte's career would take off in 1957 when he recorded 'Day O' and created the '50s rage for calypso music."

BIBLIOGRAPHY

Works by Mary Elizabeth Vroman

Esther. New York: Bantam, 1963.
Harlem Summer. New York: Putnam, 1967.
Shaped to Its Purpose: Delta Sigma Theta, the First Fifty Years. New York: Random, 1961.

Studies of Mary Elizabeth Vroman's Works

Conrad, Earl. *Everything and Nothing: The Dorothy Dandridge Traagedy*. New Yorkk: Harper Collins, 2000.
Miller, Frank. "Bright Road." http://tcmdb.com/title/title.jsp?stid=639&atid=5350&category =Articles&titleName=Bright%20Road&menuName=MAIN (accessed June 10, 2006).

Jean Forst

GLORIA WADE-GAYLES (1938–)

BIOGRAPHICAL NARRATIVE

Gloria Jean Wade was born in Memphis, Tennessee, during a period when racial segregation was still prevalent and enforceable by Jim Crow laws. She was raised by her
mother, Bertha, and grandmother, Nola Ginger Reese. She grew up in a low-income
housing project along with her sister, Faye, her aunt Mae and three uncles. Although her
father lived in Chicago, Wade-Gayles was still close to him, taking annual visits, writing
letters, and speaking to him on the phone. As she writes in her memoir, *Pushed Back to
Strength*, her childhood, while tinged with the harsh realities of racism, was not without
the love and care of an entire black community.

Wade-Gayles attended LeMoyne College in 1955. At the time LeMoyne was the
only college in the area that would admit African American students. She earned her
bachelor's degree in English in 1959, and moved north to pursue her master's degree in
American literature at Boston University as a Woodrow Wilson Fellow. Boston held
none of the warmth and kind sentiments of the south. She realized her time there would
be short. During her studies, Wade-Gayles became more aware of civil inequalities and
became heavily involved in the civil rights struggle. She was an active member of the
Boston Committee on Racial Equality (CORE), as she reports, "In 1959 Boston was a
venomously racist city."

After obtaining her graduate degree she moved to Atlanta, Georgia, and taught at the
all-female, historically black college, Spelman College. Still committed to the fight for
equal rights, she was dismissed from the school because of her activism. She left Atlanta
and obtained a teaching position at another historically black college, Howard University
in Washington, D.C. In 1967 she married Joseph Nathan Gayles and had her first child a
year later. Within six months of the birth she was pregnant again, and she and Joseph
decided they would leave San Jose, California, and raise their family in the south.
Returning to Atlanta, she entered the doctoral program at Emory University and received
her degree in American Studies in 1981. Two years later Wade-Gayles returned to
Spelman College, where she is currently a tenured faculty member. While many African
American professors have left historically black colleges and universities (HBCUs) to
teach at historically white universities for monetary gain, career progression, and
scholarly validation, Wade-Gayles has remained faithful to teaching within the Atlanta
University Center (AUC) for a number of reasons. She writes in *Rooted Against the
Wind*, "Everything at Spelman, as at other historically black colleges, speaks to students.
The buildings say, 'Enter. We have a seat for you in the classroom, a carrel for you in the
library, a terminal for you in the computer center, and a station for you in the science lab.'
The trees say, 'You have deep roots here, You will grow tall and sturdy. No winds will
attempt to uproot you.' Faculty, staff and administrators say, 'You have talent and genius
and that means you have an obligation to our people to develop both. You must soar.'
And the sky promises never to fall." Wade-Gayles holds the Eminent Scholar Endowed
Chair at Spelman and is the mother of two, Jonathan and Monica.

MAJOR WORKS

She gained popularity in the early 1980s along with other writers who strove to increase the criticism of black female literature, which was largely nonexistent. Wade-Gayles has received acclaim as editor of several collections devoted to testimony as a means of remembering and honoring the personal history of those writers who contribute to her anthologies. Her collections focus on a connectedness with family and community, spirituality and strength.

Gloria Wade-Gayles's writing exemplifies a dedication to uncovering truth by highlighting stories of the past. By focusing on memory and rememberings, Wade-Gayles creates texts that help shape the future of her readers. As Johnetta Cole writes, "Indeed, she does teach us about the power that is lodged within a caring family; about the enduring strength of black people; about the centrality of education not only for mobility of an individual but also for the progress of a people; and about the complexity of issues like divorce, abortion, and interracial friendships—issues we too often simplify." Centering on the themes of self-reflection, recovery, ancestry, and community, she uncovers a rich tradition of storytelling. She balks a traditional approach to literary studies and criticism by exploring the significance of personal testimonies.

In 1984 she published *No Crystal Stair: Visions of Race and Sex in Black Women's Novels, 1946–1976*. The text examines selected novels that Wade-Gayles considers "representative of black women's reality." In scrutinizing the work of authors such as Toni Morrison, Ann Petry, and Gayl Jones, she received criticism for her larger claims of black womanhood in America, rather than a solid analysis of the effects of racism and sexism on the characters. As with much of the literary criticism of the decade, many theorists assumed a logical connection between the written word and an understanding of the black experience, positing that the literature conveyed an accurate portrait of black life.

Pushed Back to Strength: A Black Woman's Journey Home (1993) is a testament to her belief in self-reflection and generational continuity. Not necessarily an autobiography, Wade-Gayles prefers to call the work a "book of rememberings." Throughout the text she remembers the cultural atmosphere living in Memphis during a period of great racial inequality. She remembers going to Main Street, a visible site of racial oppression and violence:

"The law gave one white woman, man, or child in a bus filled with blacks the right, the power, to determine where we sat. Even when we outnumbered them, we obeyed. Because of the law. Because of their faces. They had a way of lynching us with their eyes which said they were capable of lynching us with their hands. Especially on Main Street."

She recounts the three years she and her sister worked after school at the Georgia Theatre, her Uncle Prince's influence on her love of teaching and poetry, and her mother's determination to see her daughters succeed.

In *My Soul Is a Witness: African American Women's Spirituality* (1995), Wade-Gayles edits the anthology of poetry, prayers, essays, and songs. The text aims to celebrate the connectedness of African American women to the power of the Spirit interweaving writings by a host of literary notables such as Rita Dove, Alice Walker, bell hooks, and Sonia Sanchez. Spirituality has been the hallmark of black female survival in America. In *My Soul Is a Witness*, Wade-Gayles celebrates the significance of a religious tradition and spirituality on the lives of black women. Wade-Gayles introduces the text writing, "I must 'do what the Spirit says do' and serve as a conduit for the testimonies included herein." The testimonies included are as rich and varied as the contributors. Speaking of the indefinable power of the Spirit, Wade-Gayles contends, "We cannot hear it, but we hear ourselves speaking and singing and testifying because it moves, inspires, and directs us to do so." She makes two contributions to the diverse anthology in "The 'Finny-Finny' Rain: Three Women's Spiritual Bonding on Sapelo Island," an essay written with Ellen Finch and the "Epilogue: Remembering Roseann Pope Bell."

In *Rooted Against the Wind*, Wade-Gayles scribes a collection of personal essays, expressing her responses to provocative issues such as rape, homophobia, interracial relationships, and ageism. Not one to ascribe to the belief that the personal is private, she candidly writes in her introductory address to her readers, "Perhaps, like me, you have come to accept that we can never dress ourselves in any clothes until/unless we become naked. I did that in this ritual in order to put on the right clothes for these un-right times, knowing, as the drums told me, that right clothes are made only when the past and the present work together with threads of love for the people. In this ritual, I am trying to earn the right to wear those clothes."

The first essay, "Who Says an Older Woman Can't/Shouldn't Dance?" Wade-Gayles arms herself against a culture which values being white, male, and young. She writes, "Becoming older is a gift, not a curse, for it is that season when we have long and passionate conversations with the self we spoke to only briefly in our younger years." While the essay confronts a serious issue facing aging women, Wade-Gayles is not above injecting humor in the piece comparing asking a woman her age to the invasiveness of a gynecological exam.

Father Songs: Testimonies by African-American Sons and Daughters is an anthology of stirring accounts of black fatherhood. Again, Wade-Gayles compiles a collection of stories written from the heart. Preferring not to recount sociological studies and statistics, which are rarely without flaw, as with other collections she has edited, *Father Songs* is about memories. Unapologetically, writers share stories of their relationship with cruel fathers, missing fathers, heroic fathers, and fathers who have passed away.

In Praise of Our Teachers: A Multicultural Tribute to Those Who Inspired Us, edited by Wade-Gayles, is an impressive collection of stories about teachers and the art of teaching. The work highlights a moment in the educational foundation of various successful actors, writers, and educators in which a teacher impacted their lives in remarkable ways. From public grade schools to college classrooms, contributors reflect on the methods and varying styles educators implored to transform generations of students. Maya Angelou, James Earl Jones, Angela Davis, and Nikki Giovanni are just a few of the contributors who honor teachers with their personal accounts. Noting, "Really great teachers have this kind of x-ray vision that allows them to look at a young person and see right into that important intersection of emotion and intellect and see how to harness that."

In *Conversations with Gwendolyn Brooks*, Wade-Gayles edits the only collection of interviews devoted solely to Brooks (1917–2000). The interviews span three decades in the life of the first African American woman to win the Pulitzer Prize for poetry. Interviews by Haki Madhubuti and Roy Newquist, among others, highlight the humility of one of America's most beloved poets.

Wade-Gayles has contributed poems, chapters in edited collections, and numerous scholarly articles for periodicals such as *Callaloo*, *Black Scholar*, *Black World*, and *Atlantic Monthly*. An accomplished poet, Wade-Gayles published her own book of poetry in 1991. The poetry in *Anointed to Fly* touches on the sensations of love and grief, of longing and the pursuit of freedom. She has also received many awards in her professional career including: Boston University Woodrow Wilson Fellow (1962); Merrill Travel Grant, Charles Merrill Foundation (1973); Danforth Fellow (1974); National Endowment for the Humanities Fellow (1975); Faculty of the Year Award, Morehouse College (1975); Outstanding Young Woman of America (1975); United Negro College Fund Mellon Research Grant (1987–1988); Rosa Mary Eminent Scholar's Chair in Humanities/Fine Arts, Dillard University; DuBois Research Fellow, Harvard University (1990); Emory Medal; CASE Professor for Excellence in Teaching for the State of Georgia (1991); Honorary Doctor of Humane Letters, Meadville-Lombard Theological School of the University of Chicago; Spelman College President's Award for Outstanding Scholarship; and Malcolm X Award for Community Service. She is also director of RESONANCE, a choral group at Spelman College, which celebrates the literature and history of African Americans.

She has been praised as being a "master teacher," educating her readers with each new text on the necessity of education, the power of spirituality, and the unwavering strength of black families and black communities. In her 1996 interview with Benilde Little for *Essence* magazine, Wade-Gayles states, "We stopped passing on the short stories, and this generation is growing up without them. In those stories were the metaphors, the symbols, the images, the expressions that were passed down. Now our children grow up empty." With her work, Wade-Gayles attempts to fill in those empty spaces using personal testimonies as her medium. She has devoted much of her career to telling the stories that the next generation needs to hear. Wade-Gayles is currently at work on another project researching community as savior in African American fiction.

CRITICAL RECEPTION

Although Gloria Wade-Gayles has been acclaimed as a pioneer in African American feminist scholarship, much of her writing has not received the critical attention it merits. While her texts have been widely reviewed, there has yet to be a comprehensive study done of her works. With the publication of *No Crystal Stair: Visions of Race and Sex in Black Women's Novels, 1946 1976*, much of the criticism associated Wade-Gayles with many African American female authors emerging during the 1980s and early 1990s who strove to expand the scholarship of African American women in terms of literary study. While the text established her as an African American feminist scholar, it was not without critique. Frances Smith Foster writes, "I admire the work that Wade-Gayles has done; however, I have two major concerns, both of which stem from the question of methodology and application" (93). Foster questioned the selection of authors Wade-Gayles had included in the text as "representative" of African American female life.

Wade-Gayles went on to distinguish her tone as a writer when she ventured beyond literary criticism and into memoir writing that focused on self-reflection. She received praise for both *Pushed Back to Strength* and *Rooted Against the Wind* as Allison O. Adams explains, "Gloria Wade-Gayles' scholarly writings reject traditional approaches to literary criticism by presenting a deeply personal perspective" (para. 11). The tone of the works is both strong and engaging. Sandra Gunning contends, "It would be unfair to expect all black feminist intellectuals to write with the controversial edge you often find in essays by bell hooks, Patricia Williams, Alice Walker, or Michele Wallace; for me, part of the experience of reading this book [*Rooted Against the Wind*] was learning to recognize the different tonality of Wade-Gayles' voice" (18).

Her writer's voice struck a cord with African American female scholars on a personal as well as academic level. In many of her essays Wade-Gayles battles the ascribed definitions of what it means to be African American and female in American society. As Trudier Harris contends in the Afterword to *Body Politics and the Fictional Double*, "I felt Gloria Wade-Gayles' frustration and at times her anger at being categorized as a woman whom others judge to be too old to look as good as she does, too old to participate in certain activities, or too old to wear certain clothes or even to say certain things, and I celebrated the ways in which she has resolved those socially imposed issues of growing older" (180). In essence, Wade-Gayles's provocative narratives reaffirm and ultimately redefine African American womanhood.

BIBLIOGRAPHY

Works by Gloria Wade-Gayles

Anointed to Fly. New York: Writers and Readers Publishing, 1991.

Conversations with Gwendolyn Brooks. Jackson: University Press of Mississippi, 2003.

Father Songs: Testimonies by African-American Sons and Daughters. Boston: Beacon Press, 1997.

"Hemorrhaging, and a Call to Arms for the Poor: A Response to the Clarence Thomas Confirmation Hearings." *Sage: A Scholarly Journal on Black Women* 7.2 (1990).

In Praise of Our Teachers: A Multicultural Tribute to Those Who Inspired Us. Boston: Beacon Press, 2003.

My Soul Is a Witness: African American Women's Spirituality. Boston: Beacon Press, 1995.

No Crystal Stair: Visions of Race and Sex in Black Women's Novels, 1946–1976. Cleveland: Pilgrim Press, 1984.

Pushed Back to Strength: A Black Woman's Journey Home. New York: HarperPerennial, 1993.

Rooted Against the Wind: Personal Essays. Boston: Beacon Press, 1996.

"She Who Is Black and Mother: In Sociology and Fiction, 1940–1970." In *The Black Woman*, edited by La Frances Rodgers-Rose. Thousand Oaks, CA: SAGE Publications, 1980.

Sturdy Black Bridges: Visions of Black Women in Literature. With Roseann Bell, Bettye Parker, and Beverly Guy-Sheftall. Lancaster: Anchor Books, 1979.

"The Truths of Our Mothers' Lives: Mother Daughter Relationships in Black Women's Fiction." *Sage* 1.2 (1984): 8–12.

Studies of Gloria Wade-Gayles's Works

Adams, Allison O. "Coloring Outside the Circles." *Emory Magazine* (Spring 1995) http:www.emory.edu/EMORY_MAGAZINE/spring95/Wade-Gayles.html (accessed March 19, 2005).

Foster, Frances Smith. Rev. of *No Crystal Stair: Visions of Race and Sex in Black Women's Fiction. Black American Literature Forum.* (1985): 93–94.

Govan, Sandra Y. "The Narrow Space, the Dark Enclosure." *Callaloo* 25 (1985): 661–664.

Gunning, Sandra. "The Roads Not Taken," *Women's Review of Books* 14.4 (1997): 18

Harris, Trudier. "Afterword." In *Body Politics and the Fictional Double*, by Debra Walker King. Bloomington: Indiana University Press, 2000.

Peterson, Carla L. Rev. of *My Soul is a Witness: African-American Women's Spirituality. African American Review* 31.2 (Summer 1997): 355–56.

Cameron Christine Clark

ALICE WALKER (1944–)

BIOGRAPHICAL NARRATIVE

A prolific and diverse writer, adept at poetry, novels, short stories, and essays, Alice Walker was born on February 9, 1944, in Eatonton, Georgia. She was the eighth child of Willie Lee and Minnie Lou Grant Walker, who were both sharecroppers. From early childhood, she witnessed violent racism, poverty, and the injustice of the sharecropping system. The young Walker was certainly affected by the impact it had on African American families. When she was eight years old, Walker lost the sight of one eye from an accidental gunshot wound. Isolated and partially blinded by such an injury to her eye, she nevertheless read widely. This disfigurement eventually enabled her to develop a writer's voice, because she withdrew from others and became an acute observer of her surroundings, human relationships, and interactions. In high school, Walker became valedictorian of her class, and that achievement, combined with a "rehabilitation scholarship," made it possible in 1961 for her to go to Spelman College in Atlanta, Georgia.

During her years at Spelman (1961–1963), Walker was drawn into a Civil Rights Movement that contrasted with the college's conservative mission—to refine students according to traditional standards of southern womanhood. Disappointed at Spelman's limitations, Walker transferred to Sarah Lawrence College in Bronxville, New York, and received her Bachelor of Arts degree in 1965. While in college, she not only became involved in political activism, but also began to produce her first literary works. The summer before her senior year, she visited Kenya and Uganda on an educational grant. She returned to college pregnant and suicidal. After an arranged abortion, she wrote poems to keep her from despair. Just after graduation, with help from the poet Muriel Rukeyser, then writer-in-residence at Sarah Lawrence, Walker had her first poetry collection, *Once*, accepted by the company Harcourt Brace Jovanovich, which was to become her longtime publisher.

After college, Walker worked for the New York City welfare department for a short time, an experience that formed the basis for certain sections of *Meridian* and her controversial story about *interracial rape*, "Advancing Luna—and Ida B. Wells." In 1966 she moved to Mississippi to teach and continue her social activism. From the late 1960s to the mid-1970s, she worked in Mississippi in voter registration and welfare rights. While working there, Walker discovered the writings of the nearly forgotten Zora Neale Hurston, who would have a great influence on her later work.

In March 1967, Walker married Melvyn Leventhal, a Jewish lawyer active in the civil rights movement. At the time, they were the only legally married interracial couple living in Jackson, Mississippi. A year after that, she gave birth to Rebecca. She left Mississippi for good in 1974 to become an editor at *Ms.* magazine. In 1976, she divorced Leventhal, and in 1978 moved from Brooklyn to San Francisco with Robert Allen, a writer and former member of the board of directors of *Black Scholar* and since 1984 one of her partners at Wild Trees Press.

Since the civil rights movement of the 1960s, Walker has been an involved activist. She has spoken for the women's movement, the antiapartheid movement, for the anti-nuclear movement, and against female genital mutilation. Amidst her political activism, Walker has taught writing and African American studies at several colleges and universities, including Jackson State (1968–1969), Tougaloo (1970–1971), Wellesley (1972–1973), Yale (1977–1978), Berkeley, and Brandeis (both 1982).

During the last three decades, Walker has been recognized as one of the most prolific, controversial, and respected African American writers. She received the Pulitzer Prize in 1983 for *The Color Purple*. Among her numerous awards and honors are the Lillian Smith Award from the National Endowment for the Arts, the Rosenthal Award from the National Institute of Arts & Letters, a nomination for the National Book Award, a Radcliffe Institute Fellowship, a Merrill Fellowship, a Guggenheim Fellowship, and the Front Page Award for Best Magazine Criticism from the Newswoman's Club of New York. She also has received the Townsend Prize and a Lyndhurst Prize.

MAJOR WORKS

In her works Walker consistently reflects her concern with racial, sexual, and political issues—particularly with the African American women's struggle for spiritual survival. She has said that her one overriding preoccupation was "the spiritual survival, the survival whole of my people. But beyond that, I am committed to exploring the oppressions, the insanities, the loyalties, and the triumphs of black women" (O'Brien 192). Throughout her work, she records the courage, resourcefulness, and creativity of African American women of various ages, circumstances, and conditions. Indeed, Walker has become a focal spokesperson and symbol for black feminism; however, she describes herself as a "womanist"—her term for a black feminist—which she defines in the introduction to her book of essays, *In Search of Our Mothers' Gardens: Womanist Prose*, as one who "appreciates and prefers women's culture, women's emotional flexibility . . . women's strength" and is "committed to [the] survival and wholeness of entire people, male and female." Her work often reflects this stance. Walker's central characters are almost always African American women, because she admires the struggle of African American women throughout history to maintain an essential spirituality and creativity in their lives, and their achievements serve as an inspiration to others.

In addition, she has expressed a special concern about the cruelty and inhumane abuse that African American women have endured. While exposing issues such as domestic violence, child abuse, and women's sexuality in her works, Walker sees writing as a way to correct wrongs that she observes in the world and has dedicated herself to delineating the unique dual oppression from which African American women suffer: racism and sexism. Her writings portray the struggle of African American people throughout history, and are praised for their insightful and riveting portraits of African American life, in particular the experiences of African American women who have struggled within themselves to discover who they are in a sexist and racist society. Her works often explore the individual identity of the African American woman and how embracing her identity and bonding with other women affects the health of her community at large.

Walker is best known for her novels. Her first novel, *The Third Life of Grange Copeland* (1970), introduces many of the themes that would become prevalent in her works, particularly the domination of powerless women by equally powerless men. It displays Walker's interest in social conditions that affect family relationships, in addition to her recurring theme of the suffering of African American women at the hands of African American men. The novel describes the racism-ravaged life of an impoverished southern African American sharecropping family in which cycles of male violence affect three generations. Grange, the father, cannot withstand racist pressures and sadistically takes out his frustrations on his wife and children. He then abandons his abused wife and young son for a more prosperous life in the north, and returns years later to find his son similarly abusing his own family. Grange tries in vain to keep his son from making the mistakes that he himself has made. Only his granddaughter, Ruth, receives his love, as he tries to make up for past sins.

Walker explored similar terrain in her second novel, *Meridian* (1976), one of the first books based on the lives of women in the civil rights struggle. She recounts the personal evolution of a young African American woman against the backdrop of the politics of the civil rights movement, extending her attacks on racial injustice to castigate the sexism she observed in some African American relationships. Like Walker, Meridian was born in the rural south, and uses education as a means of escape. Pregnant and married to a high school dropout, Meridian struggles with thoughts of suicide or killing her child, but eventually decides to give the child up and attend college. After graduating she enters an organization of African American militants in Mississippi, but realizes that she is not willing to kill for the cause. With this knowledge she resolves to return to rural Mississippi to help its residents struggle against oppression.

In *The Color Purple* (1982), Walker brings together in one book many of the characters and themes of her previous works. She continues to expose the oppression of African American women in sexual as well as political situations. She draws a searing picture of sexual abuse within a context of white racism, depicting the search for selfhood of the central figure, Celie, and her emergence as a strong creative individual through friendship with other women. Walker uses the form of letters in creating a woman-centered focus for her novel. The letters span thirty years in the life of Celie, a poor southern African American woman victimized physically and emotionally by men. First, it is her stepfather, who repeatedly rapes her and then takes her children away from her. Later, she is abused by a husband, an older widower, who sees her more as a beast of burden than as a wife. The letters are written to God and Celie's sister, Nettie, who has escaped a similar life by becoming a missionary in Africa. Celie eventually overcomes her oppression with the intervention of an unlikely ally, her husband's mistress, Shug Avery. Shug helps Celie find self-esteem and the courage to leave her marriage. The end of the novel reunites Celie with her children and her sister.

The Temple of My Familiar (1989), Walker's fourth novel, is a complex spiritual novel in which Miss Lissie is presented as an ancient African goddess. As such, she has been incarnated hundreds of times, in periods ranging from a prehistoric world during which humans and animals lived harmoniously within a matriarchal society to the reign of slavery in the United States. She thus represents an African cultural heritage. She befriends Suwelo, a narcissistic university professor whose marriage is threatened by his need to dominate and sexually exploit his wife. Through a series of conversations with Miss Lissie and her friend Hal, Suwelo learns of Miss Lissie's innumerable lives and experiences and regains his capability to love, nurture, and respect himself and others.

Walker's fifth novel, *Possessing the Secret of Joy* (1992), exposes the horrors of female genital mutilation. Practiced mainly on the continents of Asia and Africa, particularly in the Middle East, genital mutilation is performed to ensure a girl's virginity or purity before marriage. In this novel, Walker brings back a character, Tashi, who has previously appeared in *The Color Purple* and *The Temple of My Familiar*. After undergoing therapy, the young African woman comes to terms with the genital mutilation she endured while with her tribe in Africa and eventually questions such unchallenged but incredibly harmful traditions.

In *By the Light of My Father's Smile* (1998), Walker extends her exploration of female sexuality. The text is a life-affirming, sensuous, and unusually sexually explicit account of an African American family who travel to a remote part of Mexico to study the Mundo people. Their encounter with the Mundo belief system, with its gentleness and spirituality, changes their lives and challenges the sexual hypocrisy of their own culture. *By the Light* is, in Walker's own words, "a celebration of sexuality, its absolute usefulness in the accessing of one's mature spirituality, and the father's role in assuring joy or sorrow in this arena for his female children." The main characters are the Robinsons, a husband-and-wife team of anthropologists. Unable to secure funding for research in Mexico in the 1950s, the husband poses as a minister to study the Mundo, a mixed black and Indian tribe. The couple brings along their daughters to this new life in the Sierra Madre. The father reacts violently upon discovering that one of his daughters has become involved with a Mundo boy. The daughter, however, ultimately overcomes the sexual repression forced on her by her anthropologist father.

Walker's next book, *The Way Forward Is with a Broken Heart* (2000), employs a narrative strategy different from those in her more conventional novels and stories. In a "quasi-autobiographical reflection," she tells stories of her own past, including ones about her marriage to Melvyn Leventhal, the birth of her daughter, and her life after her divorce. Looking back at their happy years together in "the racially volatile and violent Deep South State of Mississippi," she evokes a place and time in which her union with Leventhal was not only unconventional but also illegal. In this collection of stories, Walker reflects on the nature of passion and friendship, pondering the emotional trajectories of lives and loves. Some of the pieces are directly autobiographical. As Walker explains in her preface, "To My Young Husband" is about her marriage as a young woman to a white civil rights lawyer and their difficult but mostly happy decade in Mississippi and Brooklyn. Many years later, Walker wonders how she and her ex-husband, once so close, could have become such strangers. Other stories are "mostly fiction, but with a definite thread of having come out of a singular life." Infusing her intimate tales with grace and humor, Walker probes hidden corners of the human experience, at once questioning and acknowledging sexual, racial, and cultural rifts.

Her next work of fiction, *Now Is the Time to Open Your Heart* (2004), is clearly a novel, as Walker returns to a more conventional form. It is the story of a successful African American female novelist, Kate Talkingtree. As she is fearful of aging and uncertain about continuing her relationship with her boyfriend, Yolo, Kate decides to set off on a journey of spiritual discovery. After dreaming of a dry river, Kate makes voyages down the Colorado River and later down the Amazon. After the first voyage, an all-female white-water rafting trip down the Colorado, Kate decides that it is time to give up her sexual life and "enter another: the life of the virgin." Soon off on another quest, this time into the Amazon rain forest, she hopes to heal herself through trances induced by yage, a South American medicinal herb, also known as Grandmother to the native peoples. Indeed, it turns out that Kate's Grandmother archetype—representing the Earth, the ancestors, and those violated by patriarchy and racism—has been calling out to her.

Under the influence of yage, Kate is able to keep in touch with the elders and finally unburden her self of her past.

Besides the novels, Walker has published collections of short stories and books of poetry. Walker's short story collections, *In Love and Trouble* (1974) and *You Can't Keep a Good Woman Down* (1981), expand upon the problems of sexism and racism facing African American women. *In Love and Trouble* features thirteen African American women protagonists—many of them from the south—who, as Barbara Christian notes, "against their own conscious wills in the face of pain, abuse, even death, challenge the conventions of sex, race, and age that attempt to restrict them." In *Our Mothers' Gardens*, Walker states that she intends to present a variety of women—"mad, raging, loving, resentful, hateful, strong, ugly, weak, pitiful, and magnificent"—as they "try to live with the loyalty to black men that characterizes all of their lives." Barbara Smith in *Ms.* praises the collection, stating it "would be an extraordinary literary work if its only virtue were the fact that the author sets out consciously to explore with honesty the textures and terror of black women's lives." Smith adds: "The fact that Walker's perceptions, style, and artistry are also consistently high makes her work a treasure."

While the protagonists of *In Love and Trouble* wage their struggle in spite of themselves, the heroines of *You Can't Keep a Good Woman Down* consciously challenge conventions. Published eight years apart, these two collections are rooted in the same perspective yet demonstrate a clear progression of theme. Like her first collection of short stories, *You Can't Keep a Good Woman Down* proves the extent to which African American women are free to pursue their own selfhood in a society permeated by sexism and racism. And though the stories in the book are contemporary in subject matter, they are contextualized in the history of African American women. Moreover, the stories represent an evolution in subject matter, as Walker delves into issues raised by feminists in the 1970s—such as rape, abortion, and pornography. Indeed, in her analyses of these themes, she suggests that intimate relationships are not only personal but also political. Many of the stories in this volume, showing the connection between racist and sexist stereotypes, particularly reveal how sexuality affects the quality of the lives of African American women.

Although she is much better known as a prose writer, Walker began her professional career as a poet, and has continued, though less prolifically than early on, to produce volumes of verse that reflect a deep passion for language along with her commitment to activism and social change. Though not widely reviewed, *Once*, the first collection of poems, marked Walker's debut as a distinctive and talented writer. Walker wrote many of the poems in the span of a week in the winter of 1965, when she wrestled with suicide after deciding to have an abortion. The poems recount the despair and isolation of her situation, in addition to her experiences in the civil rights movement and of her trip to Africa. In 1973 Walker published her second volume of poetry, *Revolutionary Petunias & Other Poems*, a National Book Award nominee. The volume contains poems; she writes in the preface, "about Revolutionaries and Lovers; and about the loss of compassion, trust, and the ability to expand in love that marks the end of hopeful strategy." The title poem of this volume concerns Sammy Lou, a woman who has killed her husband's white murderer and, on her way to the electric chair, reminds her children to water her petunias. The title of Walker's third volume of poetry, *Good Night, Willie Lee, I'll See You in the Morning* (1979), is her mother's farewell to her father at his funeral. Among other topics, the poems in the volume deal with love and the history of slavery. These poems are, according to Walker, "a by-product of the struggle to be, finally, an adult—grown up, responsible in the world—to put large areas of the past to rest."

Walker's fourth volume of poetry, *Horses Make a Landscape Look More Beautiful* (1984), is made up of poems written between 1979 and 1984. The subjects of the poems range from the very personal (her daughter's return, daily exercise) to the political (the assassination of Martin Luther King's mother, Golda Meir's trip to Africa). The political content of these poems reflects Walker's continuing concern with the preservation of people, animals, indeed, of the whole planet. *Her Blue Body Everything We Know: Earthling Poems, 1965–1990 Complete* (1991) collects all the poems from Walker's four previous volumes, adding a new introduction to each, along with a section of sixteen previously uncollected works. In *Sent by the Earth: A Message from the Grandmother Spirit after the Bombing of the Trade Center and Pentagon* (2001), Walker uses a combination of political commentary and poetry to draw attention to the detrimental environmental effects of war. The 2003 collection *Absolute Trust in the Goodness of the Earth* explores a range of topics including further reflections on post–September 11 discrimination and long-term spiritual and ecological interests.

Walker declares most of her political concerns and social consciousness in her influential essay collections. *In Search of Our Mother's Gardens: Womanist Prose* (1983) celebrates African women who kept the spark of creativity alive in spite of the racism and sexism that often denied them the means of expressing their art. *Living by the Word: Selected Writings 1973–87* (1988) records her journey out of isolation in search of the planet she had known and loved as a child. *Warrior Marks: Female Genital Mutilation and the Sexual Blinding of Women* (the script for a documentary film directed by Pratibha Parmar, 1993) is a nonfiction account of this ceremony still practiced throughout the world.

Walker has also drawn scholarly attention to other important African American women writers. She was mainly responsible for the rediscovery of Zora Neale Hurston, for example, and edited the collection *I Love Myself when I'm Laughing . . . and Then Again when I Am Looking Mean and Impressive: A Zora Neale Hurston Reader* for the Feminist Press in 1979. She also edited *The Audre Lorde Compendium* (1996). Whether rescuing from oblivion the writing and reputation of other women writers who are frequently devalued or producing her own portraits of black women whose rich and complex lives have been little known, Walker continues to be a central figure in reshaping and expanding the canon of African American literature.

CRITICAL RECEPTION

Within the last two decades, Walker has emerged, both nationally and internationally, as one of the most versatile and controversial woman writers of African American literature. While Walker achieved early recognition as a poet, it is through her novels that she has found her larger audience and has more fully established the subject matter and premises of her work. Her fictional works have elicited praise for their authentic treatment of women and portrayal of the vital struggle of ordinary people to preserve their humanity. Many critics have commented on Walker's apparently natural authority as a writer, and her assurance with words. Those qualities have made her, according to Renee Tawa in the *Los Angeles Times*, "one of the country's bestselling writers of literary fiction. . . . More than ten million copies of her books are in print."

Walker's first novel, *The Third Life of Grange Copeland*, has received little critical attention. When first published it was reviewed sparsely but called a powerful, compassionate view of African American family life. Her second novel *Meridian* has received more widespread attention than Walker's first novel. Critics such as Marge Piercy and Margo Jefferson have praised the work for its ambitious and sharp exploration of the civil rights movement. Some have remarked Walker's gift for storytelling and her talent in creating subtle, yet compelling, characters. Feminist critics have commented on Walker's strong portrait of an emergent woman. Indeed, on the basis of this novel, they began to regard Walker as a mature and important writer.

Walker's literary reputation was secured with her Pulitzer Prize–winning third novel, *The Color Purple*. Adapted for a popular film by Steven Spielberg in 1985, *The Color Purple* won the high praise of reviewers and the hearts of millions of readers, especially for her accurate rendering of African American folk idioms and her characterization of Celie. Peter S. Prescott echoed the opinion of most reviewers when he called Walker's work "an American novel of permanent importance." Although the novel won public and critical acclaim, the book seemed heretical to some African American male critics who resented its depiction of African American men in the novel and in the Steven Spielberg film made from it. As a result, *The Color Purple* subjected her to extensive, heated criticism in the 1980s. Many reviewers condemn her portrayals of African American men as unnecessarily negative. They disagree with her so much that they accuse her of having "a feminist agenda at the expense of black men" (Winchell 132). Walker's response to these and other attacks upon her work is contained in *The Same River Twice: Honoring the Difficult* (1996), a volume that gathers a number of her own essays, her original screen treatment of the novel (which is not the version that was ultimately filmed), reprints of several articles by others about *The Color Purple*, and a selection of letters sent to her by readers. Addressing detractors who fault her "unabashedly feminist viewpoint," Walker explained that she simply strives to create a meaningful story that allows for all of her characters to "come to recognize and acknowledge the divine both within themselves and in everything in the universe."

Of her next novel, *The Temple of My Familiar*, critical opinions are mixed. The novel was criticized upon its publication for its lack of plot and its "new age" spirituality, but academic critics have seen it as an important statement of an affirmative African American feminism. Luci Tapahonso noted in the *Los Angeles Times Book Review* that the novel focuses on familiar Walker themes, such as "compassion for the oppressed, the grief of the oppressors, acceptance of the unchangeable and hope for everyone and every thing." Although *The Temple of My Familiar* has proved too much a novel of ideas for many readers, it stayed on the *New York Times* best-seller list for more than four months. Walker's next novel, *Possessing the Secret of Joy* (1992), is seen by many critics as more controlled and artistically satisfying than its predecessor. In commenting on *Possessing the Secret of Joy*, Alyson R. Buckman states that Walker's "text acts as a revolutionary manifesto for dismantling systems of domination," echoing the sentiments of many reviewers. *By the Light of My Father's Smile* (1998) has drawn praise from many for its innovative narrative technique but critics have also complained that the novel is too didactic. The novels following fared better. Linda Barrett Osborne, writing in the *New York Times Book Review*, called *The Way Forward* a "touching and provocative collection." And *Booklist*'s Vanessa Bush praised *Now Is the Time to Open Your Heart* as a "dreamlike novel [that] incorporates the political and spiritual consciousness and emotional style for which [Walker] is known and appreciated."

Walker has also become a central figure in the academic study of African American literature and culture; her work is much acknowledged in gender studies and African American literature. Books on her works include *Alice Walker: Critical Perspectives Past and Present* (1993), *Critical Essays on Alice Walker* (1999), and Maria Lauret's *Alice Walker* (2000). Most critical assessments of Walker's novels address her presentation of black women. Barbara Christian sees Walker working through themes of contrariness and waywardness in such characters generally and artist characters in particular. Bettye J. Parker-Smith observes a transformation of African American women from victims to heroines in *The Color Purple*. Karen C. Gaston argues that in "Grange Copeland," female characters serve as the moral centers of the work, even though the males are the central characters. Mary Helen Washington describes Walker's ambition to be an "apologist and chronicler" of African American women's lives. Her works reveal the complexity of moral decision making and the tattered fabric of life in the daily existence of African American women. Elliot Butler-Evans examines the gendered production of history in the first two novels. He describes a dual process, in which a generalized narrative of racial history is doubled (and displaced) by a feminine counternarrative, a historical struggle that mirrors the personal struggles of the protagonists. The passage from *The Third Life of Grange Copeland* to *Meridian* is shown to consist in the eruption of this second, female narrative or historical voice.

Scholars also note "Womanism" as an ideological stance and as the basis for Walker's works. W. Lawrence Hogue read *The Third Life of Grange Copeland* as an example of feminist discourse arguing that the social order dehumanizes African American men who then abuse their families. Chikwenge Okonjo Ogunyemi defines womanism as the focus on women's issues in the context of African American culture. While he considers several writers, he presents Walker as one who is optimistic on such issues, especially in *The Color Purple*. Barbara Smith shows how the emphasis on women enables Walker to see through the myths surrounding the lives of African American women and to reveal the problems of their married life.

There is also unanimous consent that Walker is a writer of great gifts and important themes. Wendy Wall examines the relationship between writing and the body in *The Color Purple*. In her interpretation, the violence Celie initially sustains is transformed into a textual inscription in her letters to God; writing serves as a strategy for psychic survival by creating a second body, unmarred by physical force. Wall further elaborates on the consequences of the epistolary structure of much of the novel. Linda Abbandonato, in a provocative reading of *The Color Purple*, maintains that its form (Hurstonean vernacular) and its content (black lesbian triumph) undermine white patriarchal political and linguistic structures. Houston A. Baker, Jr., and Charlotte Pierce-Baker situate Walker's writing in the context of quilt making in Afro-America. Both represent, they argue, a specifically female craft that confronts chaos and orders it through the skillful arrangement of patches, recreating the literary art of bricolage. In Mae G. Henderson's perspective, *The Color Purple* strongly "subverts the traditional Eurocentric male code which dominates the literary conventions of the epistolary novel." Deorah E. McDowell credits Walker with having helped to create a purely female aesthetic and even an African American female aesthetic.

Covering a broad spectrum of emotions, Walker's poems have long been her warmest, least artful utterances, invoking the solidarity and the compassion she invites her readers to feel. Walker's poetry has always been admired for its ostensible simplicity of statement and construction and its easy accessibility. Although she often addresses the reader directly, speaking eloquently of the most intense sorts of pain and struggle, there is nothing rhetorical or artificial in her work. In an affirmative essay, Hanna Nowak recounts the engaging simplicity of Walker's poetry, noting themes of love, death, and tradition. Thadious Davis reads Walker's poetry in the context of her other fiction and nonfiction work. Davis detects the resonance of her poetic concerns in all of Walker's artistic works. Both Gail Gilliland and Sonia Gernes express the view that the best poems are those based on personal experience.

As a major voice for contemporary African American women, Walker has helped to expand contemporary understanding of African American women and promote an African American women's literary tradition. Walker is dedicated to the continuation and preservation of African American cultural traditions. Her works can be read as an ongoing narrative of an African American woman's emergence from the voiceless obscurity of poverty and racial and sexual victimization. And she has articulated a black feminist criticism that has had a major impact on the increase in critical writings by African American women scholars. As she continues to write from her unique intellectual and spiritual perspective, her contribution to literature and social change is expected to grow ever more solid and abiding. Undoubtedly, Walker's versatility as a writer along with her role as public intellectual has enabled her to occupy an extraordinary position in contemporary American letters.

BIBLIOGRAPHY

Works by Alice Walker

Absolute Trust in the Goodness of the Earth: New Poems. New York: Random House, 2003.

Alice Walker Banned. With Introduction by Patricia Holt. San Francisco, CA: Aunt Lute Books, 1996.

Anything We Love Can Be Saved: A Writer's Activism. New York: Random House, 1997.

By the Light of My Father's Smile: A Novel. New York: Random House, 1998.

The Color Purple. New York: Harcourt Brace Jovanovich, 1982.

Dreads: Sacred Rites of the Natural Hair Revolution. With Francesco Mastalia and Alfonse Pagano. New York: Artisan, 1999.

Finding the Green Stone. Illustrations by Catherine Deeter. San Diego: Harcourt Brace Jovanovich, 1991.

Good Night, Willie Lee, I'll See You in the Morning: Poems. New York: Dial, 1979.

Her Blue Body Everything We Know: Earthling Poems, 1965–1990 Complete. San Diego: Harcourt, 1991.

Horses Make a Landscape Look More Beautiful. San Diego: Harcourt Brace Jovanovich, 1984.

I Love Myself when I'm Laughing . . . and Then Again when I Am Looking Mean and Impressive: A Zora Neale Hurston Reader. Introduction by Mary Helen Washington. New York: Feminist Press, 1979.

In Love & Trouble: Stories of Black Women. New York: Harcourt Brace Jovanovich, 1974.

In Search of Our Mothers' Gardens: Womanist Prose. San Diego: Harcourt Brace Jovanovich, 1983.

Langston Hughes: American Poet. New York: Harper & Row, 1974.

Living by the Word: Selected Writings, 1973–87. San Diego: Harcourt Brace Jovanovich, 1988.

Meridian. New York: Harcourt Brace Jovanovich, 1976.

Now Is the Time to Open Your Heart: A Novel. New York: Random House, 2004.

Once: Poems. New York: Harcourt Brace and World, 1968.

A Poem Traveled down My Arm: Poem and Drawings. New York: Random House, 2002.

Possessing the Secret of Joy. New York: Harcourt Brace Jovanovich, 1992.

Revolutionary Petunias & Other Poems. New York: Harcourt Brace Jovanovich, 1973.

The Same River Twice: Honoring the Difficult; A Meditation of Life, Spirit, Art, and the Making of the Film "The Color Purple," Ten Years Later. New York: Scribners, 1996.

Sent by the Earth: A Message from the Grandmother Spirit after the Bombing of the Trade Center and Pentagon. New York: Open Media, 2001.

The Temple of My Familiar. San Diego: Harcourt Brace Jovanovich, 1989.

The Third Life of Grange Copeland. New York: Harcourt Brace Jovanovich, 1970.

To Hell with Dying. Illustrations by Catherine Deeter. San Diego: Harcourt Brace Jovanovich, 1987.

Warrior Marks: Female Genital Mutilation and the Sexual Blinding of Women. With Pratibha Parmar. San Diego: Harcourt Brace Jovanovich, 1993.

The Way Forward Is with a Broken Heart. New York: Random House, 2000.

You Can't Keep a Good Woman Down: Stories. New York: Harcourt Brace Jovanovich, 1981.

Studies of Alice Walker's Works

Abbandonato, Linda. "Rewriting the Heroine's Story in *The Color Purple.*" In *Alice Walker: Critical Perspectives Past and Present,* edited by Henry Louis Gates, Jr., and K. A. Appiah, 296–308. New York: Amistad, 1993.

Baker, Houston A., Jr., and Charlotte Pierce-Baker. "Patches: Quilts and Community in Alice Walker's 'Everyday Use.'" *Southern Review* 21 (1985): 706–20.

Bloom, Harold, ed. *Alice Walker: Modern Critical Views.* New York: Chelsea House Publishers, 1989.

Butler-Evans, Elliott. *Race, Gender, and Desire: Narrative Strategies in the Fiction of Toni Cade Bambara, Toni Morrison, and Alice Walker.* Philadelphia: Temple University Press, 1989.

Christian, Barbara, ed. "Alice Walker: The Black Woman Artist as Wayward." In *Black Women Writers (1950–80): A Critical Evaluation,* edited by Mari Evans, 457–77. Garden City, NY: Anchor/Doubleday, 1984.

———. "The Contrary Women of Alice Walker: A Study of Female Protagonists in *In Love and Trouble.*" In *Black Feminist Criticism: Perspectives on Black Women Writers,* 31–46. New York: Pergamon Press, 1985.

Davis, Thadious. "Poetry as Preface to Fiction: Alice Walker's Recurrent Apprenticeship." *Mississippi Quarterly* 44.2 (1991): 133–42.

Dieke, Ikenna, ed. *Critical Essays on Alice Walker.* Westport, CT: Greenwood Press, 1999.

Gaston, Karen C. "Women in the Lives of Grange Copeland." *CLA Journal* 24 (1981): 276–86.

Gates, Henry Louis, Jr., and K. A. Appiah, eds. *Alice Walker: Critical Perspectives Past and Present.* New York: Amistad, 1993.

Henderson, Mae G. "*The Color Purple*: Revisions and Redefinitions." *Sage* 2 (1985): 14–18.

Hogue, W. Lawrence. "History, the Feminist Discourse, and Alice Walker's *The Third Life of Grange Copeland.*" *MELUS* 12 (1985): 45–62.

Lauret, Maria. *Alice Walker.* New York: Pallgrave Macmillan, 2000.

McDowell, Deborah E. "'The Changing Same': Generational Connections and Black Women Novelists." *New Literary History* 18 (1987): 281–302.

Nowak, Hanna. "Poetry Celebrating Life." In *Alice Walker: Critical Perspectives Past and Present,* edited by Henry Louis Gates, Jr., and K. A. Appiah, 179–92. New York: Amistad, 1993.

O'Brien, John, ed. *Interviews with Black Writers.* New York: Liveright, 1973.

Parker-Smith, Bettye J. "Alice Walker's Women: In Search of Some Peace of Mind." In *Black Women Writers (1950–80): A Critical Evaluation,* edited by Mari Evans, 478–93. New York: Pergamon, 1985.

Piercy, Marge. "Rev. of *Meridian*." In *Alice Walker: Critical Perspectives: Past and Present*, edited by Henry Louis Gates, Jr., and K. A. Appiah, 9–11. New York: Amistad, 1993.

Prescott, Peter S. "A Long Road to Liberation." *Newsweek* (June 21, 1982): 67–68.

Smith, Barbara. "The Souls of Black Women." *Ms.* (February 1974): 42–43.

Wall, Wendy. "Lettered Bodies and Corporeal Tests in *The Color Purple*." *Studies in American Fiction* 16 (1988): 83–97.

Washington, Mary Helen. "An Essay on Alice Walker." In *Sturdy Black Bridges: Visions of Black Women in Literature*, edited by Roseann P. Bell, 133–49. New York: Anchor/Doubleday, 1979.

White, Evelyn C. *Alice Walker: A Life*. New York: W. W. Norton, 2004.

Winchell, Donna Haisty. *Alice Walker*. New York: Twayne, 1992.

Su-lin Yu

MARGARET WALKER (1915–1998)

BIOGRAPHICAL NARRATIVE

Prolific poet and fiction writer, Margaret Abigail Walker was born in Birmingham, Alabama, on July 7, 1915, to Methodist Minister Sigismund Walker and music teacher Marion Dozier Walker. Her middle-class environment exposed her to Christian values, music, and books and to the importance of education. This family standing, however, could not shield her from the cruel realities of southern racism. She later conveyed her awareness of race matters in her first collection of poetry, *For My People* (1942). In 1925 the Walkers moved to New Orleans, Louisiana, where the young Margaret Walker attended Gilbert Academy and graduated at the age of fourteen. She then spent two years at New Orleans University (now Dillard University). In her teenage years she met famed literary figures such as James Weldon Johnson, Roland Hayes, W.E.B. DuBois, and Langston Hughes. Encouraged by the latter, she left the south to seek education in the north. In 1932, she enrolled at Northwestern University in Chicago, Illinois, graduating with a B.A. in English in 1935. In 1934 she had her first poems published in *Crisis* (edited by W.E.B DuBois) and began working on *Jubilee*.

Walker worked for the Works Project Administration (WPA) as a social worker and for the Federal Writers' Project as a writer assigned to the *Illinois Guidebook*. These two experiences helped sharpen her craftsmanship and her appreciation of urban life. Living in Chicago in the 1930s made her aware of the realities of the Great Depression and put her in contact with other writers in the city such as Richard Wright. She admired Wright's writing and shared his view of literature as an instrument for political change. It is in this context that she drafted *Goose Island*, a novel that has remained unpublished. In 1939, the year Walker and Wright's friendship and her work with the Federal Writers' Project ended, she enrolled at the University of Iowa for a master's in creative writing. Her first major publication, *For My People* (1942), was developed as her M.A. thesis. The following year she married Firnist James Alexander. For the next few years she held teaching positions at Livingston College in North Carolina and West Virginia State College. In 1949, her husband, three children (she later had a fourth), and herself moved to Jackson, Mississippi, where she started a new teaching job at Jackson State University; she stayed there until her retirement in 1979. In 1962 she returned to the University of Iowa for a Ph.D. in English, which she received in 1965 after presenting her dissertation, a novel titled *Jubilee*, published the following year by Houghton Mifflin.

Between 1966 and her death in 1998 Walker wrote several other books. During her tenure at Jackson State University she established the Institute for the Study of the History, Life and Culture of Black People (1968), later renamed the Margaret Walker Alexander National Research Center to honor her. It focuses on the preservation of, and research on, black experience in America.

Walker's achievements are reflected in the many recognitions she received, including six honorary degrees, the Yale Series for Young Poets Award for *For My People* (1942), a Rosenwald Fellowship (1944), a Ford Fellowship (1953), the Houghton Mifflin Literary

Award (1968) for her novel *Jubilee*, a Fulbright Fellowship to Norway (1971), a senior Fellowship from the National Endowment for the Humanities (1972), the College Language Association Lifetime Achievement Award (1992), the State of Mississippi Lifetime Achievement Award for Excellence in the Arts (1992), the White House Award for Distinguished Senior Citizen given by President Jimmy Carter, and induction into the African American Literary Hall of Fame on October 17, 1998.

MAJOR WORKS

Margaret Walker's work can be read as the fulfillment of her wish to write "songs for my people," as she sings in the poem "I want to write." Indeed, in her poetry and fiction, she has written and recorded the history, culture, fear, and hope of her people. Taken together, her work is an assembly of forms such as the blues, spirituals, jazz, tales, songs, animal tales, sermons, prayers, and the black vernacular serving as oral depositories of African American life. At the same time she also constructs myths for the future, imagining a prophetic and humanistic vision in spite of the difficulties of the moment. The main setting of her opus is the south, with its historical burden of moral decay, shame, and marginality, resulting from the practices of slavery and a long history of racism. Margaret Walker conceives a cave myth of her own, offering the south possibilities of redemption and regeneration from the darkness and wilderness of oppression to the brilliant dawn and light that come from forgiveness, reconciliation, belief, and hope, ideas embodied in poems such as "For My People," "We Have Been Believers," and "I Want to Write" and in *Jubilee*.

Margaret Walker's poetry pays tribute to the resilience of African Americans throughout their historical experience in America, celebrating the joys of simple things in life and vividly chronicling the anguish and pleasures of a people often disheartened by hardships. Walker counters this bleak background with her belief in the power of humanism as a creative force that transforms despair into hope. Using the south as the locale of many of her poems, in the manner of Martin Luther King, Jr.'s "I Have a Dream," Walker projects a "new earth" and a new "race of men" characterized by peace, courage, and freedom. Walker's poetry articulates black historical consciousness through the blending of African American oral traditions, biblical typology (the appropriation of the holy history of salvation or Heilsgeschichte), free verse, conventional poetic forms, and multiple literary traditions—a palimpsest that helps to create what Maryemma Graham calls "acts of cultural recovery" in the process of "reconstructing [Walker's] own family as a communal history of African Americans" (*Fields Watered with Blood* 14–15). In this respect, Margaret Walker paves the way for, and participates in, the work of memory with other contemporary African American writers, such as Alice Walker, Sherley Anne Williams, Toni Morrison, and John Edgar Wideman.

As she later disclosed in *How I Wrote Jubilee* (1972), Margaret Walker wrote *Jubilee* as a fulfillment of a promise she had made to her maternal grandmother to write down the story of her maternal great-grandmother, Margaret Duggans Ware Brown— Vyry in the novel—who lived in the south before, during, and after the Civil War. After hearing harrowing stories about slavery from her grandmother, Walker promised her that "when I grew up I would write her mother's story" (*How I Wrote Jubilee* 12). *Jubilee* extensively depicts the life of a female slave and the folk tradition that African American women have preserved through time to sustain their survival within the trying institution of slavery. The folk tradition fosters a strong sense of community, nurturing, and sisterhood among slave women. Deprived of her mother, who is a victim of intensive childbearing resulting from repeated rape by her master, Vyry leads a life of tremendous suffering at the hands of her father's wife. Instead of bitterness, she returns love, forgiveness, and caring for others regardless of race. At a time of racial tension during the civil rights movement of the 1950s and 1960s, Margaret Walker promotes the power of humanism in the face of intolerance. Vyry has been said to bring sanity to the chaos of slavery, the Civil War, and the Reconstruction, but the novel's publication in the 1960s brings the same sanity to one of the most turbulent periods in the history of the United States.

Margaret Walker dedicates her novel to her family and to the memory of her grandmothers: her "maternal great-grand mother, Margaret Duggans War Brown, whose story this is, my maternal grandmother, Elvira Ware Dozier, who told me this story; and my paternal grandmother, Margaret Walker" (v). Margaret Walker's namesake, Alice Walker, cogently asserts in *In Search of Our Mothers' Gardens* that "so many of the stories that I write, that we all write, are my mother's stories" (232). Margaret Walker's and other African American women's writings are acts of recording their (grand)mothers' stories. In the novel, young Vyry is told stories and hears songs, and later on she tells stories and sings for her own children. In her book, Alice Walker also portrays mothers and grandmothers as "artists" and "Creators...so rich in spirituality"(233). In this tradition even the domestic activities African American women perform in *Jubilee* convey the creativity that they use to convey humanism and participate in the spiritual rebirth of the south.

Against the horrors of slavery and racism, Vyry opposes the resilience of the African American woman, love for others, forgiveness, and reconciliation as well as the expression of a rich cultural life evolving around a community of African American women. From this perspective, the novel links the African American woman's history and culture to Vyry, to her family's own history and to future generations of women. This is seen notably in the use of oral traditions, folk medicine, feminine art, the art of cooking and food preparation, and the sustaining power of sisterhood and motherhood. Vyry learns about the use of herbs and roots in African American folk medicine and later gathers them by herself. Vyry's knowledge about herbs and roots, taught to her by a community of women, contributes to the recording of the folk tradition that could otherwise be lost.

The same community of African American women teaches Vyry about the herbs and roots used for medicinal purposes but also for cooking. *Jubilee* also describes the transmission of the art of cooking, passed from generation to generation within the slave family. Since her biological mother dies when she is still an infant, Vyry learns the different aspects of the folk tradition from Aunt Sally and other slave women. Aunt Sally, the chief cook at the Big House, becomes a surrogate mother to her. She initiates Vyry to the art of cooking and taking care of the kitchen (35). Later on, Vyry herself teaches the same cooking skills to her daughter Minna (342). With the skills slave women learn, they feed both their masters' families and their own families. The visible presence of the culinary art is metonymic of the nurturing and caring aspect of the African American woman in *Jubilee* and in African American literature in general, even though it is sometimes corrupted by slavery.

Feminine art (sewing and quilt making) plays a special role in the novel. The art of sewing is also passed from mother to daughter: as she learned from her "mothers," Vyry also teaches her daughter Minna. In a remarkable display of humanism, quilt making becomes an occasion for racial harmony in chapter 54. As men are helping to build a new house for Innis Brown and Vyry for her to stay in the community as a midwife, Vyry is working with her white female neighbors on a piece of quilt. This activity creates, around a female activity, a new community that respects difference, as each housewife uses her own design pattern, but it also invokes the possibility of racial forgiveness and reconciliation generated by shared interest. This proposition may sound too idealistic for the Reconstruction south, but it potently conveys Margaret Walker's humanistic vision.

The novel turns the south, the place of the cruel and inhumane regime of slavery, into a location of humane possibilities through the character of Vyry. When she has all the reasons to be bitter after surviving white cruelty and oppression, she chooses love and forgiveness. Vyry's continuous availability to help white women in the face of war and poverty is a redemptive moral choice that is conveyed through motherhood, an idea that frames the novel. At the beginning, Sis Hetta dies of intensive childbearing. At the end, Vyry is expecting her fourth child and is a midwife. This is particularly significant, given the fact that she does not really know her mother. She also loses her surrogate mothers, Mammy Suckey and Aunt Sally. Mammy Suckey's death early in the novel leaves Vyry devastated. She shakes "like a leaf in a whirlwind" when Aunt Sally is sold. As Vyry wants to go with Aunt Sally, Big Missy slaps her "so hard she saw stars and when she saw straight again Aunt Sally was gone" (71), a scene that vividly portrays the terror of southern slavery. In spite of this ordeal, Vyry stays the course of love and compassion.

The Civil War section shows Vyry taking care of white women after their world of power and privilege has been shattered by war. Amid the physical and psychological ravages of the war, Vyry does not abandon her half sister Lillian and her children. She diligently takes care of them. As the old south disintegrates, the African American female's redemptive will is affirmed in Vyry's humanism. Even when she marries Inns Brown, she does not leave Lillian until another relative of Lillian's, Lucy Porter, arrives to take care of her. Years later, Vyry goes back to visit the debilitated Lillian; she has forgiven Lillian's thoughtlessness. Even after the Ku Klux Klan burns Vyry's and Innis Brown's house and despite the generalized bias against African Americans, she keeps her humanistic sense of duty to fellow human beings intact, guided by the principle that "I feels like it's my duty to help anybody I can wheresomever I can" (360). In spite of the persistence of the codes and practices of slavery after the Civil War, they do not deter Vyry from seeking friendship with white women. When Vyry improvises as a granny to Betty-Alice Fletcher and takes care of both mother and child, it also becomes an occasion to dispel racist myths, leading Henry Fletcher, his wife Betty-Alice and her parents to acknowledge her humanity. This episode projects Walker's vision of the transformative possibilities of love and compassion, values that bring the human race together.

In a moment of epiphany, Vyry chastises Randall Ware, who views the relationship between whites and African Americans as one between exploiters and exploited. Vyry insists that African Americans and whites need each other. She revisits her childhood and the abuse she received from Big Missy. Taking her clothes off, she exposes the scars that resulted from a severe whipping after her failed attempt to meet and flee with Randall Ware. In spite of this indelible mark of her suffering, unlike Ware, she does not hold any grudge, but instead she reaffirms the force that has always defined and sustained her life: humanism.

CRITICAL RECEPTION

Margaret Walker is most known for her poetry collection *For My People* (1942) and her novel *Jubilee* (1966), both of which received literary prizes, respectively the Yale Series of Younger Poets Award and the Houghton Mifflin Literary Fellowship. In spite of these immediate accolades and the popular reception of her work, Margaret Walker did not attract the same kind of critical attention that greeted such writers as Alice Walker and Toni Morrison. In fact, Nikki Giovanni has dubbed her "the most famous person nobody knows," an assessment echoed by Maryemma Graham and Deborah Whaley (*Fields Watered with Blood* 1).

Of all Walker scholars, Maryemma Graham is probably the most devoted student, having edited two of her works—*How I Wrote Jubilee and Other Essays on Life and Literature* (1990) and *On Being Female, Black, and Free: Essays by Margaret Walker, 1932–1992* (1997)—and two critical volumes—*Conversations with Margaret Walker* (2002) and *Fields Watered with Blood: Critical Essays on Margaret Walker* (2001), undoubtedly the best critical book yet on Walker's oeuvre. In the words of the editor, this volume contains "the best essays" (*Field Watered with Blood,* xiii) written between 1977 and 1999 and conveys an "increasingly diverse, intergenerational, intercultural, and international" scholarly interest in the work of Margaret Walker (*Field Watered with Blood,* xv). The different contributions capture the power of Walker's humanistic vision, informed by her family history; the south as setting; African American folklore, language, and culture; an African American woman's perspective; and multiple literary traditions. Discussing Walker's themes in *Jubilee*, Graham argues that they "are moral ones: love conquers violence and hatred; suffering makes us strong; the search for home and community prevails over all else" (Graham, *Conversations*, ix). This humanistic vision proves particularly salutary against racism, against the violence and anger of the tumultuous 1960s, and against the easy drift to racial intolerance at times of tension. Walker counters this wilderness with poems and stories that offer a non-self-destructive way of dealing with the past, forges a common past with its hardships and joys, and expresses the necessity to record history and to remember and redeem African American heritage without succumbing to the detrimental forces of the past.

BIBLIOGRAPHY

Works by Margaret Walker

The Ballad of the Free. Detroit: Broadside Press, 1966.
For Farish Street Green. Jackson: University of Mississippi, 1986.
For My People. New Haven: Yale University Press, 1942.
How I Wrote Jubilee. Chicago: Third World Press, 1972.
How I Wrote Jubilee and Other Essays on Life and Literature, edited by Maryemma Graham. New York: Feminist Press at the City University of New York, 1990.
Jubilee. Boston: Houghton Mifflin, 1966.
October Journey. Detroit: Broadside Press, 1973.
On Being Female, Black, and Free: Essays by Margaret Walker, 1932–1992, edited by Maryemma Graham. Knoxville: University of Tennessee Press, 1997.
A Poetic Equation: Conversations between Nikki Giovanni and Margaret Walker. Washington, DC: Howard University Press, 1974.

Prophets for a New Day. Detroit: Broadside Press, 1970.

Richard Wright, Daemonic Genius: A Portrait of the Man, a Critical Look at His Work. New York: Warner Books, 1988.

This Is My Century: New and Collected Poems. Athens: University of Georgia Press, 1989.

Studies of Margaret Walker's Works

Carmichael, Jacqueline M. *Trumpeting a Fiery Sound: History and Folklore in Margaret Walker's Jubilee.* Athens: University of Georgia Press, 1998.

Goodman, Charlotte. *Tradition and the Talents of Women.* Urbana: University of Illinois Press, 1991.

Graham, Maryemma, ed. *Conversations with Margaret Walker.* Jackson: University Press of Mississippi, 2002.

———, ed. *Fields Watered with Blood: Critical Essays on Margaret Walker.* Athens: University of Georgia Press, 2001.

Gwin, Minrose. *Black and White Women of the Old South: The Peculiar Sisterhood in American Literature.* Knoxville: University of Tennessee Press, 1985.

Aimable Twagilimana

MILDRED PITTS WALTER (1922–)

BIOGRAPHICAL NARRATIVE

African American children's writer Mildred Pitts Walter was born on September 8, 1922, in DeRidder, Louisiana. Walter received her Bachelor of Arts degree in English from Southern University, and later earned a master's degree in Education from Antioch (Colorado). Earl Lloyd Walter, the late husband of Mildred Pitts Walter, was a social worker and civil rights activist. Together they raised two sons, Earl Lloyd, Jr., and Craig Allen Walter. Throughout her adult life, Walter has occupied various roles including kindergarten teacher, consultant at the Western Interstate Commission of Higher Education in Boulder, Colorado, and lecturer at Metro State College. Since 1969, Mildred Pitts Walter has devoted her time exclusively to authoring books intended for children and young adults.

MAJOR WORKS

Mildred Pitts Walter's thirty-six-year career has produced over twenty-five published texts. A major theme of Walter's fiction is that African Americans who achieve high academic standing are typically excluded from their community. Emma Walsh, the main character of *Because We Are* (1983), has ambitions to study medicine, and is a perfect 4.0 student, but she fears that her strive toward perfection will ultimately lead her to lose the companionship of her friends. The anxiety Emma feels is based on a guilt that is normally associated with African American pedagogical success that inherently places those students who cannot reach the same level of accomplishment on the lower end of the educational hierarchy. Academically inclined pupils usually receive rewards and are praised for overcoming the oppression of being African American in a white-dominated school system.

Perhaps Walter's most widely read book is *My Mama Needs Me* (1984). Walter's protagonist, Jason, learns the responsibilities of domestic life when his mother brings home a newborn baby. The introduction of a younger sibling into Jason's home life instructs him that he must now sacrifice his personal desires to satisfy the needs of a newborn infant. Jason continually reminds his friends and neighbors that he is now obliged to divide his time between his personal and home life by repeating the phrase, "I can't. I've got to go. My Mama needs me" (11). The most prevalent motif that Walter incorporates into her work is that parental figures always attempt to include every member of their family in domestic responsibilities.

CRITICAL RECEPTION

Walter has enjoyed great critical acclaim for her fiction. *Mississippi Challenge* won the Coretta Scott King Honor Book Award in 1993, as did *Trouble's Child* in 1986.

Literary critics and educationalists have defined Walter's writing as a positive, realistic portrait of Afro-American family life that studies African American history and culture. Parents have praised Walter for producing work that gives an interpretation of the African American experience with a comprehension that race implies more than simply skin color. Walter's books have been taught during Black History Month across the United States. Although few scholarly studies deal exclusively with Walter, many critics use her writings as a reflection of the concerns surrounding the intellectual ambitions and family scenarios of African American adolescents. These concerns and scenarios are then juxtaposed to the public constraints under which African Americans are forced to live. Walter has collaborated with illustrators Carole Byard, Pat Cummings, and Leo Dillion to provide pictorial depictions of her written texts. She was inducted into the Colorado Women's Hall of Fame in 1993.

BIBLIOGRAPHY

Works by Mildred Pitts Walter

Alec's Primer. Vermont: Vermont Folklife Center, 2004.
Because We Are. New York: Lothrop, Lee and Shepard Books, 1983.
Brother to the Wind. New York: HarperCollins, 1985.
Darkness. New York: Simon and Schuster Books for Young Readers, 1995.
The Girl on the Outside. New York: Lothrop, Lee and Shepard Books, 1982.
Have a Happy Birthday. New York: Lothrop, Lee and Shepard Books, 1989.
Justin and the Best Biscuits in the World. Caledonia, MN: Turtleback Books, 1986.
Kwanzaa: A Family Affair. New York: Avon Books, 1996.
Lillie of the Watts Takes a Giant Step. Garden City: Doubleday, 1971.
Mariah Keeps Cool. New York: Bradbury Press, 1990.
Mariah Loves Rock. New York: Bradbury Press, 1988.
Mississippi Challenge. New York: Aladdin Paperbacks, 1996.
My Mama Needs Me. New York: Lothrop, Lee and Shepard Books, 1984.
Ray and the Best Family Reunion Ever. New York: HarperCollins, 2002.
The Second Daughter: The Story of a Slave Girl. New York: Scholastic, 1996.
Suitcase. New York: Lothrop, Lee and Shepard Books, 1999.
Tiger Ride. New York: Scholastic, 1995.
Trouble's Child. New York: Lothrop, Lee and Shepard Books, 1985.
Two Much and Too Much. New York: Bradbury Press, 1990.
Ty's One-Band. New York: Scholastic, 1984.

Studies of Mildred Pitts Walter's Works

Englebaugh, Debi. *Integrating Art and Language Arts through Children's Literature.* Westport, CT: Teacher Ideas Press, 2003.
Kutenplon, Deborah, and Ellen Olmstead. *Young Adult Fiction by African American Writers, 1968–1993: A Critical and Annotated Guide.* New York: Garland, 1996.
Murphy, Barbara Trash, ed. "Mildred Pitts Walter." In *Black Authors and Illustrators for Books for Children and Young Adults: A Biographical Dictionary,* 3rd ed., 386–87. New York: Garland, 1999.
Rudman, Marsha Kabakow, ed. *Children's Literature: Resource for the Classroom.* Norwood: Christopher-Gordon Publishers, 1989.

Schafer, Elizabeth. "I'm Gonna Glory in Learnin': Academic Aspirations of African American Characters in Children's Literature." *African American Review* 32.1 (1998): 57–66.

Smith, Katherine Capshaw. *Children's Literature of the Harlem Renaissance*. Bloomington: Indiana University Press, 2004.

Gerardo Del Guercio

MARILYN NELSON WANIEK (1946–)

BIOGRAPHICAL NARRATIVE

Born in Cleveland, Ohio, on April 26, 1946, poet Marilyn Nelson grew up on military bases around the United States where her father Melvin, a Tuskegee Airman, was stationed. Her mother, Johnnie, was a teacher. The family eventually settled in Sacramento, California, where the poet attended high school. She was educated at the University of California at Davis (B.A., 1968), the University of Pennsylvania (M.A., 1970), and the University of Minnesota (Ph.D., 1978). In 1970, Nelson married a German scholar; they divorced in 1978, but until 1997 she published under the name Marilyn Nelson Waniek. She has taught at colleges and universities around the United States and in Europe, most of her career at the University of Connecticut.

Nelson was named Poet Laureate of Connecticut in 2001. Nelson has been awarded two fellowships from the National Endowment for the Arts and one from the J. S. Guggenheim Foundation. Nelson has two children, Jacob and Dora, from her second marriage, to English professor Roger Wilkenfeld. In 2004, she founded Soul Mountain Retreat, a poets' colony in East Haddam, Connecticut.

MAJOR WORKS

Nelson's first book, *For the Body*, was published in 1978 and her second, *Mama's Promises*, in 1985. With the publication of her third book, *The Homeplace*, in 1990, Nelson began to be recognized as a major poetic voice. That book, and later, *The Fields of Praise: New and Selected Poems* (1997) and *Carver: A Life in Poems* (2001) were finalists for the National Book Award. Her other volumes are *Magnificat* (1994), *Fortune's Bones: The Manumission Requiem* (2004), *A Wreath for Emmett Till* (2005), and *The Cachoeira Tales and Other Poems* (2005). Nelson has also published verse for children, translations, and essays.

As the title *The Fields of Praise: New and Selected Poems* suggests, Nelson celebrates the self's relation to a contradictory, hostile, but ultimately compassionate universe. Nelson's first book foregrounds the major themes of her later work: the interplay between history and identity, and the earthly wisdom borne of spiritual love. In her second book, *Mama's Promises*, celebratory images of an African American mother figured as "the feminine face of God" are balanced with the quotidian tensions of a modern professional, wife, and mother. The theme of family is amplified and nuanced in Nelson's third book, *The Homeplace*, a watershed publication in her career. In this book narrative elements come to the fore, as the poet tells stories of both her maternal ancestors and of the Tuskegee Airmen her father knew as a U.S. Air Force officer. A new, more formal prosody complements the innovative structure. The poet weaves a rich vernacular seamlessly into traditional verse forms, while continuing to use freer verse as well. *The Homeplace* was followed by *Magnificat*, which similarly combines formal and free verse in a narrative of desire and spiritual growth inspired by Nelson's friendship with a Benedictine monk. *The Fields of Praise: New and Selected Poems* received critical acclaim, as did her next book, *Carver: A Life in Poems*, a lavishly illustrated poetic biography of George Washington Carver. The year 2005 saw the publication of three books written entirely in received forms: *Fortune's Bones: The Manumission Requiem* commemorates the life of an eighteenth-century Connecticut slave; *A Wreath for Emmett Till* (an heroic crown of Petrarchan sonnets) tries to find healing in the wake of the infamous 1955 lynching; *The Cachoeira Tales and Other Poems* includes a rollicking Chaucerian narrative which chronicles a trip to Brazil.

CRITICAL RECEPTION

Response to Nelson's work has been for the most part restricted to reviews and reference-book articles. Major critical work remains to be done. Judging by the poet's growing recognition, such attention is imminent. Paul A. Griffith notes how Nelson's "dual awareness of African and American ancestry—impacts her search for poetic forms" (Griffith 234). In an as yet unpublished conference paper, David Anderson, writing of the poet's use of allusion in *The Homeplace*, writes that "Nelson's conception of tradition remains open, rather than dictatorial or restrictive. By writing in a multitude of forms, and referring to several vernacular and literary traditions, the poet acknowledges and celebrates her connections to a complex cultural past" (Anderson 1). Like Ralph Ellison, Nelson has upheld African American writers' prerogative to utilize both the prevailing canon and the rich African American literary and oral traditions. One point of interest concerns Nelson's decision to publish for the young adult audience three books dealing with African American historical figures—*Carver: A Life in Poems*, *Fortune's Bones: The Manumission Requiem*, and *A Wreath for Emmett Till*. These three volumes are in no sense "children's" poems. Betty Adcock comments about *Carver*: "Though clearly written for an adult audience . . . this book was marketed for young readers" (658). One result of the young adult designation has been beautifully illustrated books of a kind rare in the world of poetry publication. The reviews that the poet has garnered for these books have been overwhelmingly laudatory. It remains to be seen what the status of these books will be in Nelson's oeuvre.

BIBLIOGRAPHY

Works by Marilyn Nelson Waniek

The Cachoeira Tales and Other Poems. Baton Rouge: Louisiana State University Press, 2005.
Carver: A Life in Poems. Asheville, NC: Front Street, 2001.
The Fields of Praise: New and Selected Poems. Baton Rouge: Louisiana State University Press, 1997.
For the Body, as Marilyn Nelson Waniek. Baton Rouge: Louisiana State University Press, 1978.
Fortune's Bones: The Manumission Requiem. Asheville, NC: Front Street, 2004.
The Homeplace, as Waniek. Baton Rouge: Louisiana State University Press, 1990.
Magnificat, as Waniek. Baton Rouge: Louisiana State University Press, 1994.
Mama's Promises, as Waniek. Baton Rouge: Louisiana State University Press, 1985.
"Marilyn Nelson" (autobiographical essay). In *Contemporary Authors Autobiography Series*, vol. 23, edited by Shelly Andrews, 247–67. Detroit: Gale Group, 1996.
"Owning the Masters." *Gettysburg Review* 8.2 (Spring 1995): 201–9.
A Wreath for Emmett Till. Boston: Houghton Mifflin, 2005.

Studies of Marilyn Nelson Waniek's Works

Adcock, Betty. Rev. of *Carver: A Life in Poems*. *Southern Review* 39.3 (Summer 2003): 650–70.

Anderson, David. "Building the Homeplace: Rewriting Family and Cultural History in Marilyn Nelson's *The Homeplace*." Unpublished paper. English Department, University of Louisville.

Boelcskevy, Mary Anne Stewart. "Waniek, Marilyn Nelson." In *The Oxford Companion to African American Literature*, edited by William L. Andrews, Frances Smith Foster, and Trudier Harris, 756. New York: Oxford University Press, 1997.

Dick, Rodney Franklin. "Creative and Constructive Tensions: A Discussion of the Poetry of Marilyn Nelson (Waniek)." M.A. thesis, University of Louisville, 2000.

Gardiner, Susan. "Bootleg, Jackleg Medicine: Curing as Only Generations Can." Rev. of *The Homeplace*. *Parnassus* 17.1 (1992): 65–78.

Griffith, Paul A. "Marilyn Nelson." In *Dictionary of Literary Biography*, vol. 282, edited by Jonathan N. Barron and Bruce Meyer, 233–40. Detroit: Gale Group, 2003.

Hacker, Marilyn. "Double Vision." Rev. of *The Fields of Praise: New and Selected Poems*. *Women's Review of Books* 15.8 (May 1998): 17–18.

Kitchen, Judith. "I Gotta Use Words." Rev. of *The Fields of Praise: New and Selected Poems*. *Georgia Review* 51.4 (Winter 1997): 756–76.

Pettis, Joyce. "Marilyn Nelson." In *African American Poets: Lives, Works, and Sources*, 262–69. Westport, CT: Greenwood Press, 2002.

Rosengarten, Theodore. "America in Black and White." Rev. of *A Wreath for Emmett Till*. *New York Times Book Review*, November 11, 2004, 43.

Williams, Miller. Rev. of *The Fields of Praise: New and Selected Poems*. *African American Review* 33.1 (Spring 1999): 179–81.

Jacob Nelson Wilkenfeld

IDA B. WELLS-BARNETT (1862–1931)

BIOGRAPHICAL NARRATIVE

Journalist and activist, Ida Bell Wells was born on July 16, 1862, in Holly Springs, Mississippi, during the Civil War. She was the oldest of eight children. Her father, James Wells, the son of a white slave owner, was a carpenter, and her mother, Elizabeth Warrenton, was a cook. After the war, Wells's parents were highly regarded in Holly Springs for their character and principles; these characteristics they also instilled in their children while also emphasizing the importance of education and religion. Wells-Barnett and her siblings attended Rust University, a school established for former slaves by the Freedmen's Bureau. She left Rust, however, after her parents died in the yellow fever epidemic of 1878 to take care of her five younger siblings. She eventually became a school teacher.

In 1880, Wells-Barnett moved to Memphis, Tennessee, to live with her aunt and two of her sisters. In Memphis she continued to teach and began writing a weekly column, "Iola" (her pen name) for the *Living Way*, an African American Christian weekly paper. She also became the editor of the *Evening Star*.

In 1884, Wells-Barnett was involved in a lawsuit against the Chesapeake, Ohio, and Southwestern Railroad Company. While traveling from Memphis, the conductor told Wells that she could not sit in the ladies' car; when she refused to move to the smoking car, she was forcibly removed by three men. Although Wells-Barnett won the lawsuit, the Tennessee State Supreme Court overturned the lower court's ruling in 1887. Wells wrote about the incident and lawsuit in the *Living Way*.

In 1889, Wells-Barnett became the co-owner of the *Free Speech and Headlight* newspaper with Rev. Taylor Nightingale and J. L. Fleming. In 1891, because of an editorial that criticized the Memphis Board of Education and the poor and unequal condition of schools for African Americans, Wells failed to gain reelection as a teacher. At this point she began traveling throughout the south obtaining subscriptions for the *Free Speech*, trying to make a living from the paper; she was quite successful and wrote in her autobiography, "I had found my vocation" (39).

The year 1892 marked a turning point in Wells-Barnett's life. Already an outspoken journalist with a sharp mind and pen, Wells learned that three of her friends had been lynched. To this point Wells-Barnett had not questioned the culture of lynching. The American public, including Frederick Douglass, accepted the white mobs' argument that those lynched were guilty of raping white women. However, Wells knew that this was not the case with her friends, so she began to investigate incidents of lynching, which eventually lead to the publication of three pamphlets over the next eight years: *Southern Horrors: Lynch Law in All Its Phases* (1892), *A Red Record* (1895), and *Mob Rule in New Orleans* (1900). On May 21, several months after the lynching of her friends, Wells published her own editorial of the incident in the *Free Speech*, questioning the reasons for the lynching and accusing those who committed the act of lying. When her editorial was published she was in Philadelphia on business. In response to her editorial, Wells's newspaper office was burned and her life was threatened if she returned to Tennessee. She remained in exile from the south for thirty years.

Wells-Barnett became a reporter for the *New York Age*, signing her columns "Exiled," and began her campaign against lynching as a public speaker. In 1893 and 1894, Wells made a strategic move by taking the national issue abroad. She traveled to England, Scotland, and Wales, gaining support for her antilynching campaign among antilynching groups in England. When questioned as to why white northerners and/or Christian groups were not supporting her cause, she replied that they sometimes condone the lynchings either through their silence, or like Frances Willard, president of the Women's Christian Temperance Union and famous in the United States and England, desire the support of southerners and, therefore, publicly condone such behavior. Her reports of her speaking tour are printed in the Chicago *Inter Ocean*.

Between trips to England, Wells produced, with Frederick Douglass, Ferdinand L. Barnett, and I. Garland Penn, *The Reason Why the Colored American Is Not in the World's Columbian Exposition* (1893). Her contribution to the pamphlet, chapter 4, "Lynch Law," details the numerous lynchings of African Americans. In 1895, Wells-Barnett married Ferdinand Barnett, an attorney in Chicago. Together they had four children: Charles Aked, Herman Kohlsaat, Ida B. Wells, Jr., and Alfreda M. During this time, Wells-Barnett began to devote more of her time to her family. She concentrated much of her political activism to the local politics of Chicago and even ran for state senator of Illinois in 1930 as an Independent. Wells-Barnett founded the Negro Fellowship League in 1910 and was a founding member of the NAACP in 1909. Wells died on March 25, 1931.

MAJOR WORKS

Wells-Barnett is most remembered for her antilynching campaign. In *Southern Horrors*, Wells-Barnett's first pamphlet, she makes several devastating claims about the racial and sexual politics of America in the post-Reconstruction era. In the decades following the end of Reconstruction, lynching became a means of white supremacist control over the African American population, not only in the south but throughout the United States. Historically, lynching was justified on the grounds that African American men were raping white women ("violating their purity") and that white southern men were defending the honor of their women. In *Southern Horrors*, Wells makes several arguments to prove that this cannot be true for all the victims of lynching:

1. Why were white women in danger at that time, if they were not in danger before or during the Civil War, when many plantations and homes were left with only the slaves to protect the master's family while the master was away?
2. Why were white northern Christian women not in danger during Reconstruction, when they came to the south to help establish schools for blacks?
3. The victims of lynchings were not only black men but also black women and children. How can they be guilty of rape?

Those who advocated lynching made several arguments, which Wells also challenges:

1. Lynch Law was supposedly used by communities beyond the reach of the law and civilization; yet, Wells's points out that many lynchings took place in civilized areas with laws, and, therefore, there is no need for mob violence.
2. Rape was not the only reason being used to lynch people. In *A Red Record*, which provides extensive background of the circumstances leading up to many reported lynchings as well as the graphic details of the murder, Wells-Barnett reveals that some African Americans were lynched for "stealing hogs," "because they were saucy," and even for "no offense" at all (Royster 106–7).
3. The crimes of African people were, in reality, often achievements, such as the financial success of the People's Grocery Store.
4. There were white women who had consensual relationships with African American men. Moreover, white women sometimes seduced African American men and lied about their attraction for them since this attraction was not socially acceptable.

Wells-Barnett also points out that with regard to the lynchers' claims of African American men raping white women, the reverse is true: white men were and had been guilty of raping African American women since slavery. Mulattos were the evidence of this common occurrence. In general, Wells-Barnett insists that lynching is a form of control and terrorism to limit African Americans economically, politically, and socially. Wells-Barnett ends *Southern Horrors* by urging the African American community to take action in three ways: (1) boycott white-owned businesses; (2) emigrate; and (3) use the press to disseminate the truth and expose the lies. She even advocated protecting oneself with a "Winchester," if need be.

In all three of her pamphlets, Wells-Barnett closely examines the incidents reported in white-owned newspapers, such as the *Chicago Tribune* and the *Cleveland Gazette*, to question the supposed crime and to challenge unsubstantiated beliefs surrounding the culture of lynching. Also included are sketches and detailed facts surrounding the deaths of the victims. For instance, in *Mob Rule in New Orleans*, she inserts a table listing the number of lynchings of African Americans for each year from 1882 to 1899.

Wells-Barnett also wrote three diaries and an autobiography in addition to several other pamphlets and countless articles. Wells-Barnett began writing her autobiography in 1928 but was unable to finish it before she died; its voice is that of a mature woman reflecting back on her life and includes many interesting stories of the inner politics of her world. Her diaries, however, are different in tone from her autobiography. In her diary entries during her twenties, the voice is that of an anxious young woman working hard to support herself and help her siblings, find a male companion whom she can respect and who is her intellectual equal, and develop a writing career.

CRITICAL RECEPTION

Many critics consider Wells-Barnett an early civil rights activist. In recent decades, the issue of lynching has been brought to the public's attention through the recovery of forgotten Americans, such as Wells-Barnett, who made important contributions to U.S. political history but who have not been given adequate attention or credit.

Jacqueline Jones Royster's *Southern Horrors and Other Writings* reproduces Wells-Barnett's three antilynching pamphlets in a small textbook format. Her introduction is helpful in contextualizing the historical period and Wells-Barnett's political work.

Trudier Harris's compilation of Wells-Barnett's works includes *The Reason Why the Colored American Is Not in the World's Columbian Exposition* in addition to her three antilynching pamphlets.

Alfreda M. Duster, Wells-Barnett's youngest child, is the editor of Wells-Barnett's autobiography, *Crusade for Justice*. Linda McMurry's *To Keep the Waters Troubled* is a biography of Wells-Barnett. Patricia Schechter's informative *Ida B. Wells-Barnett and American Reform* focuses less on her biography and more on her social activism and the political climate of the period. *The Memphis Diary of Ida B. Wells* reproduces Wells's diaries written at different periods in her life: her midtwenties as a teacher and journalist, at age thirty-one when she is traveling abroad, and at age sixty-eight. Almost every entry is preceded with a paragraph contextualizing Wells-Barnett's situation and the numerous people about whom Wells-Barnett wrote in her entries. This text also includes a few of the articles Wells-Barnett wrote for the *Living Way*, the *New York Freeman*, and the *Fisk Herald*.

BIBLIOGRAPHY

Works By Ida B. Wells-Barnett

"Afro-Americans and Africa." *AME Church Review* (July 1892): 40–44.
The Arkansas Race Riot. Chicago: Author, 1920.
"Booker T. Washington and His Critics." *World Today* 6 (1904): 518–21.
Crusade for Justice: The Autobiography of Ida B. Wells, edited by Alfreda M. Duster. Chicago: University of Chicago Press, 1970.
"Functions of Leadership." In *The Memphis Diary of Ida B. Wells*, edited by Miriam DeCosta-Willis, 178–79. Boston: Beacon Press, 1995.
"How Enfranchisement Stops Lynching." *Original Rights Magazine* (June 1910): 42–53.
"Iola on Discrimination." *The Memphis Diary of Ida B. Wells*, edited by Miriam DeCosta-Willis, 186–87. Boston: Beacon Press, 1995.
"Liverpool Slave Traditions and Present Practices." *Independent* 46 (May 19, 1894): 617.
"Lynching and the Excuse for It." *Independent* 53 (May 1901): 1133–36.
"Lynching: Our National Crime." In *National Negro Conference: Proceedings*, 174–79. New York: Schomburg Center for Research in Black Culture, 1909.
"Lynch Law in America." *Arena* 24 (January 1900): 16–24.
Lynch Law in Georgia. Chicago: Author, 1899.
Mob Rule in New Orleans: Robert Charles and His Fight to the Death. In *Selected Works of Ida B. Wells-Barnett*, compiled by Trudier Harris. New York: Oxford University Press, 1991.
"The Model Woman: A Pen Picture of the Typical Southern Girl." In *The Memphis Diary of Ida B. Wells*, edited by Miriam DeCosta-Willis, 187–89. Boston: Beacon Press, 1995.
"The National Afro-American Council." *Howard's American Magazine* 6.10 (1901): 413–16.
"The Negro's Case in Equity." In *Ida B. Wells-Barnett: An Exploratory Study of an American Black Woman*, edited by Mildred I. Thompson, 245–46. Brooklyn, NY: Carlson, 1990.
"The Northern Negro Woman's Social and Moral Condition." *Original Rights Magazine* (April 1910): 33–37.
"Our Country's Lynching Record." *Survey*, February 1, 1913, 573–74.
"Our Women." 1887. In *The Memphis Diary of Ida B. Wells*, edited by Miriam DeCosta-Willis, 184–86. Boston: Beacon Press, 1995.
The Reason Why the Colored American Is Not in the World's Columbian Exposition. In *Selected Works of Ida B. Wells-Barnett*, compiled by Trudier Harris. New York: Oxford University Press, 1991.

A Red Record: Tabulated Statistics and Alleged Causes of Lynchings in the United States, 1892–1893–1894. In *Selected Works of Ida B. Wells-Barnett*, compiled by Trudier Harris. New York: Oxford University Press, 1991.

"The Requirements of Southern Journalism." *AME Zion Church Quarterly* (April 1892): 189–96.

Southern Horrors: Lynch Law in All Its Phases. In *Selected Works of Ida B. Wells-Barnett*, compiled by Trudier Harris. New York: Oxford University Press, 1991.

"A Story of 1900." In *The Memphis Diary of Ida B. Wells*, edited by Miriam DeCosta-Willis, 182–84. Boston: Beacon Press, 1995.

"Two Christmas Days. A Holiday Story." *AME Zion Church Quarterly* 4 (January 1894): 129–40.

United States Atrocities: Lynch Law. London: Lux Press, 1894.

"Woman's Mission." In *The Memphis Diary of Ida B. Wells*, edited by Miriam DeCosta-Willis, 179–82. Boston: Beacon Press, 1995.

Studies of Ida B. Wells-Barnett's Works

Adams, Samuel L. "Ida B. Wells: A Founder Who Knew Her Place." *Crisis* 101 (January 1994): 43–44.

Aptheker, Bettina. "The Suppression of the *Free Speech*: Ida B. Wells and the Memphis Lynching, 1892." *San Jose Studies* 3 (1977): 34–40.

Davis, Simone W. "The 'Weak Race' and the Winchester: Political Voices in the Pamphlets of Ida B. Wells-Barnett." *Legacy* 12 (1995): 77–89.

DeCosta-Willis, Miriam, ed. *The Memphis Diary of Ida B. Wells*. Boston: Beacon Press, 1995.

Humrich, Shauna L. "Ida B. Wells-Barnett: The Making of a Public Reputation." *Purview Southeast* (1989): 1–20.

Logan, Shirley W. "Rhetorical Strategies in Ida B. Wells's *Southern Horrors: Lynch Law in All Its Phases*." *Sage* 8 (Summer 1991): 3–9.

McMurry, Linda O. *To Keep the Waters Troubled: The Life of Ida B. Wells*. New York: Oxford University Press, 2000.

Ochiai, Akiko. "Ida B. Wells and Her Crusade for Justice. An African American Woman's Testimonial Autobiography." *Soundings* 75 (Summer/Fall 1992): 365–82.

Royster, Jacqueline Jones, ed. *Southern Horrors and Other Writings: The Anti-Lynching Campaign of Ida B. Wells, 1892–1900*. The Bedford Series in History and Culture. Boston: Bedford Books, 1997.

Schechter, Patricia A. *Ida B. Wells-Barnett and American Reform, 1880–1930*. Chapel Hill: University of North Carolina Press, 2001.

Thompson, Mildred I. *Ida B. Wells-Barnett: An Exploratory Study of an American Black Woman, 1893–1930*. Brooklyn: Carson Publishing, 1990.

Tucker, David M. "Miss Ida B. Wells and Memphis Lynching." *Phylon* 32 (Summer 1971): 112–22.

Joy M. Leighton

DOROTHY WEST (1907–1988)

BIOGRAPHICAL NARRATIVE

Dorothy West was a literary and journalistic maverick who wore many artistic hats in her illustrious ninety-one years of life that began with her birth to Isaac Christopher and Rachel Pease Benson West on June 2, 1907, in Boston, Massachusetts, and ended with her death on August 16, 1998, in Boston. West's literary career lasted sixty years and, as a result, she may be described in a number of ways: short story writer, novelist, actress, welfare investigator researcher and writer (for the New York branch of the WPA Federal Writers' Project), editor of two short-lived black literary magazines of the 1930s and post–Harlem Renaissance years (*Challenge* and *New Challenge*), and cashier.

Langston Hughes and other Harlem Renaissance notables referred to Dorothy West as "the Kid" because of her youthful age of seventeen when she (and first cousin, Helene Johnson) first arrived in Harlem and brushed competitive, literary shoulders with the older, more mature members of the Harlem Literati. In the 1990s, when she experienced a second and prolific literary awakening—when she was well into her eighties—with the publication of two books, *The Wedding* (1995) and *The Richer, the Poorer* (1995), in editorial collaboration with Jackie Kennedy Onassius and Henry Louis Gates, Dorothy West earned the distinction of being called, as Sally Ferguson describes her, "a national gift, the last surviving member of the Harlem Renaissance," and as other critics envisioned her as being "the last leaf on the artistic tree of the Harlem Renaissance Literary Movement."

Dorothy West's upbringing in Boston, at 478 Brooklin Avenue in an economically prosperous and socially affluent black middle-class family, nurtured and influenced her literary path as writer and journalist. Only child of Rachel and Isaac West, who was known as the Black Banana King of Boston, West was encouraged to excel in all areas of her Victorian-styled, Bostonian existence where identities and distinctions of race, class, and gender were heavily ingrained in her young psyche. The ideals of education, class, social manners, racial pride, family love, loyalty, and solidarity were often stressed to West by her fair-skinned mother, Rachel, and by other members of West's large, extended family of aunts and cousins. The family's Boston and Martha's Vineyard homes further illuminated upper-middle-class values and traditions in the precocious West. By contrast to her mother and other female members of the family, Mr. West, an ex-slave from Virginia, emphasized to West the value of self-help, self-employment, thrift, and the entrepreneurial opportunities available with sacrifice and hard work.

An imaginative child, who was fascinated by the family stories she heard told in their home, West set her fancy on storytelling rather than on a serious engagement with business and the great prospects of money-making ventures Mr. West described to her each evening upon his return from the fruit store he owned and operated in the Boston market. Mr. West's business philosophy and habits would later impact economic and class themes in West's fictional writings, but not in her real, everyday life or in her eventual career. Her mother's influence in shaping West's individualism and in dominating her own three sisters and other members of the extended family would have a supreme impact on her freedom to be individual with an unrestrained artistic and social vision. West often interjected her own imaginative, hyperbolic ideas and fancied stories in the adult conversation that the women elders of the home engaged. On one occasion, West's creative outpouring of stories became so profound and mature in nature that one of her aunts, according to Sally Ferguson, remarked, "That's no child. That's a little sawed-off woman."

MAJOR WORKS

West's intellectual brilliance and breath for dynamic storytelling were realized and she exerted it at will so much so that she began actually writing stories at age seven and formally publishing them at fourteen, beginning with her first story, "Promise and Fulfillment," which was published in the *Boston Post* as the best story of the week. West continued on the short story writing path with the publication of "The Typewriter" (1926) in *Opportunity* magazine. For this story she earned a second prize award. To West's credit, the story would later be published in Edward J. O'Brien's *The Best Short Stories of 1926*. Later, in the 1940s when she became a contributing writer to the *New York Daily News*, her most anthologized story, "Jack in the Pot," which she termed her manifesto on poverty, would receive the Blue Fiction Prize Award from the *New York Daily News*.

As West's writing career flourished, she published a prolific assortment of stories in literary venues such as *Opportunity*, *Messenger*, the *Saturday Evening Quill*, the *New York Daily News*, and the *Vineyard Gazette*. Although her stories focus on middle-class American dream themes, many are not stories about the black race; they are simply people-oriented stories about life, racism, classism, and sexism. According to Sally Ferguson and Margaret Perry, Dorothy's stories are characteristically influenced by her preoccupation with the Russian writer, Dostoyevski and her "tendency to emphasize moral, psychological, and social confinement," to focus on childhood and innocence and to show the irony of black urban existence and the superficiality and contradictions of urban middle-class life.

To promote writing excellence in writers displaced by the poverty of the Depression, West edited two short-lived literary journals with her own finances she earned from theatrical work in Russia: *Challenge* (1934) and *New Challenge* (1937) which she coedited with Richard Wright and Marion Minus. West stressed high quality work over the representation in the journals of poorly written essays propagandizing political ideologies under the Communism umbrella. She introduced writings by Chester Himes, Langston Hughes, Arna Bontemps, Margaret Walker, and Richard Wright—most notably his essay, "Blueprint for Negro Writing." She also wrote stories in disguised names. To West's dismay, both *Challenge* and *New Challenge* folded because of hard, financial times.

With the demise of *New Challenge*, West began writing a novel while contributing over thirty short stories from 1940 to 1960 to the *New York Daily News*. She would later write columns about life in Oak Bluffs for the *Martha's Vineyard Gazette* until she was infirmed by illness in 1998.

West also expanded her short story themes in two novels. *The Living Is Easy* (1948) is an autobiographical novel based on the character of her mother, Rachel, as represented in the aggressive and manipulative Cleo Judson who dominates her husband, Bart, a successful businessman whom she calls "Mr. Nigger." The novel reached brief critical acclaim, even though it did not sell as well as expected, especially when *Ladies' Home Journal*, yielding to southern prejudice, decided not to serialize in its monthly journal a novel about a powerful black woman protagonist. Feminist Press reissued the novel in 1982 when renewed critical interest in West escalated. Some forty years later, on the persuasion of Doubleday editor and Martha's Vineyard neighbor, Jackie Kennedy Onassis, West published her second much-anticipated novel, *The Wedding*. Set during the weeks prior to the wedding of a white jazz musician and a black, upper-class woman, *The Wedding* examines intraracial class and color prejudice among Martha's Vineyard residents. It received rave critical reviews and Oprah Winfrey produced a two-part television miniseries of the novel several months before West's death in July 1988.

CRITICAL RECEPTION

Prior to Margaret Perry's critical study of a few of West's selected short stories in the book, *Silence to the Drums: A Survey of the Literature of the Harlem Renaissance* (1976), West's works received limited critical assessment. However, in the 1990s with the publication of *The Wedding* (1995) and *The Richer, the Poorer: Stories, Sketches, and Reminiscences* (1995), a slight surge in critiques of West's works emerged. Critics have been enthusiastically receptive to West, beginning in 1998 with Pearlie Peters's critical study, "The Resurgence of Dorothy West as Short Story Writer," which assesses West's career and lifelong talent as a skilled short story craftswoman before, during and after the Harlem Renaissance. In 1999, Lionel Bascom wrote an assessment of West's contributions to the Federal Writers' Project of New York in the 1940s. In *A Renaissance in Harlem: Lost Voices of an American Community*, Bascom locates unpublished writings by West held at The Library of Congress Federal Writers' Project Archives and calls attention to West's little-known literary contributions to African American literature of the Depression era.

Bascom has also edited several of West's short narratives written about Harlemites struggling through the Depression. As critical interest in West gains momentum, three other pivotal critical studies of West's life, novels, and short stories have served as catalysts in the Dorothy West revival.

Trudier Harris Lopez's "Strength as Disease Bordering on Evil: Dorothy West's Cleo Judson," provides a provocative study of *The Living Is Easy* protagonist, Cleo Judson, as "a strong black female character who lives up to the stereotype of being destructive and domineering" (101). By way of this acerbic analysis of Cleo, Lopez draws attention to West's social views about the black upper-class society and its snobbery and pretentiousness.

In the book *Rereading the Harlem Renaissance: Race, Class and Gender in the Fiction of Jessie Fauset, Zora Neale Hurston, and Dorothy West* (2002), Sharon L. Jones devotes a chapter to a study of West and "the multiplicity of voices and aesthetics" (119) that she represents to readers and publishers. Such multiplicity presented misperceptions of West to readers and publishers, for as Jones argues, "West truly functions as a closet revolutionary, for while on the surface her work and her life seem to reflect the black bourgeoisie, her novels, short stories, and essays reflect a proletarian stance" (Jones 119).

Verner D. Mitchell and Cynthia Davis, in 2004, published an anthology of West's selected writings from 1930 to 1950 with the inclusion of short stories by West and an unpublished novel about aging and lesbianism called *Where the Wild Grape Grows*.

Mitchell and Davis present a startling revelation about West's personal life that had never surfaced before in critical studies of her life. Despite the talk in critical circles that West may have had an affair with Langston Hughes at some time in their literary friendship, Mitchell and Davis argue that West had a lesbian relationship with Marian Minus, who at one time assisted West with the editing of the *New Challenge* literary journal during the 1930s. Certainly Mitchell and Davis's findings will warrant further critical investigations into the life and times of Dorothy West.

BIBLIOGRAPHY

Works by Dorothy West

The Living Is Easy (reprint). New York: The Feminist Press, 1982.
The Richer, the Poorer: Stories, Sketches, and Reminiscences. New York: Anchor, 1995.
The Wedding. New York: Anchor, 1995.

Studies of Dorothy West's Works

Bascom, Lionel. *A Renaissance in Harlem: Lost Voices of an American Community.* New York: Avon Book, 1999.
Dalsgard, Katrine. "Alive and Well and Living on the Island of Martha's Vineyard: An Interview with Dorothy West, Oct. 29, 1988." *Langston Hughes Review* 12.2 (Fall 1983): 28–44.
Ferguson, Sally Ann. "Dorothy West." In *Dictionary of Literary Biography, Vol. 76. African American Writers, 1940–1955*, edited by Trudier Harris and Thadious M. Davis, 187–95. Detroit: Gale Research, 1988.
———. "Dorothy West and Helene Johnson in *Infants of the Spring*." *Langston Hughes Review* 2.2 (Fall 1983): 22–24.
Jones, Sharon L. *Rereading the Harlem Renaissance: Race, Class and Gender in the Fiction of Jessie Fauset, Zora Neale Hurston, and Dorothy West.* Westport, CT: Greenwood Press, 2002.
Lopez, Trudier Harris, ed. "Strength as Disease Bordering on Evil: Dorothy West's Cleo Judson." In *Saints, Sinners and Saviors: Strong Black Women in African American Literature*, 57–79. New York: Palgrave, 2001.
Mitchell, Verner D., and Cynthia Davis. *Dorothy West: Where the Wild Grape Grows, Selected Writings, 1930–1950.* Amherst: University of Massachusetts Press, 2005.
Perry, Margaret. *Silence to the Drums: A Survey of the Literature of the Harlem Renaissance.* Westport, CT: Greenwood Press, 1976.
Peters, Pearlie. "The Resurgence of Dorothy West as Short Story Writer." *Abafazi* 8.2 (Spring/Summer 1998): 16–21.
Roses, Lorraine. "Interviews with Black Women Writers: Dorothy West at Oak Bluffs, Massachusetts, July, 1984." *SAGE* 2.1 (Spring 1985): 47–49.

Pearlie Mae Peters

PHILLIS WHEATLEY (1753–1784)

BIOGRAPHICAL NARRATIVE

Phillis Wheatley was one of America's first African American female poets. She was born in Senegal, Africa. At the age of seven, she was sold in a slave market. John and Susannah Wheatley of Boston bought her as a household servant and as an attendant for Susannah. They treated her as a member of the family, and she was raised with the Wheatleys' other two children. Mary, the Wheatleys' daughter, took it upon herself to teach Phillis how to read and write English. Phillis surprised everyone by her quick and sharp intellect. By the time she was twelve, Phillis was reading Greek and Latin classics, and passages from the Bible. By fourteen, she had become a poet. She had some minor household duties, but was free to write whenever inspiration struck. The Wheatleys introduced her to the Boston Literary Circle and she soon became a literary sensation. Through this literary and theological circle, Wheatley was exposed to a wide variety of books and religious texts. Her poetry is clearly influenced by the Scriptures. Major English poets, Milton, Pope, and Gray also exerted a strong influence on her verse. Although she was free to write anything that she wanted, Wheatley was frequently called upon to write poems for special occasions. Many of her elegiac poems were borne out of such requests. Her first poem was published in the *Newport Mercury* newspaper in 1767. In 1770, she wrote a poetic elegy for the popular Rev. George Whitefield. Although this elegy made her an overnight sensation in Boston, Phillis and the Wheatleys were unable to get her poems published in Boston. About the same time, Countess Selina of Huntington invited Wheatley to London to assist her in the publication of her poems. In 1773, thirty-nine of Wheatley's poems were published as *Poems on Various Subjects, Religious and Moral*. The governor of Massachusetts, her master John Wheatley, and dozens of other clergymen and dignitaries from Boston wrote a signed letter to the public vouching the text as Wheatley's original work. In addition to the Wheatleys and Countess Selina, Obour Tanner, a former slave who made it through the middle passage journey with Wheatley, was also one of the strong supporters of her poetry. Eventually, Wheatley returned to America to take care of ailing Mrs. Wheatley. Back in America, she was rewarded—perhaps her greatest gift, with freedom from slavery. Mrs. Wheatley died in 1774. The Revolutionary War changed Wheatley's life quite dramatically. Mr. Wheatley and his daughter Mary died in 1778. Soon afterward Wheatley married John Peters, a free man from Boston. Due to either a lack of personal qualities or racial prejudices and the lack of opportunities, John Peters was unsuccessful as businessman and was unable to support his wife and their children. They moved briefly to Wilmington, Massachusetts. Two of their children died during this period. Wheatley was able to publish a few poems during this period; a few were published as pamphlets.

In 1776, while her owner was still alive, Wheatley wrote a poem to George Washington, praising his appointment as commander of the Continental Army, and it was well received. After her marriage, she addressed several other poems to George Washington. She sent them to him, but he never responded again. Wheatley was a strong supporter of independence during the Revolutionary War. She felt that the issue of slavery separated whites from true heroism. Eventually John Peters deserted Wheatley, and, to support herself and her surviving child, she took a job as a maid in a boardinghouse. She died on December 5, 1784; hours after, her surviving child also died.

MAJOR WORKS

Phillis Wheatley displays a classical quality and restrained emotion in her poetry. Two plausible explanations of this restraint can be offered. First, she was influenced by classical poets such as Milton and Pope, and second, she was very aware of her status as a slave and was unable to speak freely. Examination of her works and her essays indicates that she was not a meek person. Phillis Wheatley's strongest antislavery statement is contained in the letter to the Rev. Samson Occom dated February 11, 1774. She writes, "...*for in every human breast God has implanted a principle, which we call ~ it is impatient of oppression, and pants for deliverance.*"

This shows that the reason for her poetic restraint was the influence of her classical literary training, and not any lack of courage. Christianity was a very important theme in Wheatley's poetry. Her first published poem, about two soldiers who barely escaped drowning, demonstrates Wheatley's Christian spirituality. The poem states that the soldiers were saved by the grace of God alone. Most of her poems are occasional pieces, written on the death of some notable person or on some special occasion. Wheatley uses classical mythology and ancient history as allusive devices. She maintains that people of all races need salvation.

One example of this is Wheatley's most anthologized poem: "On Being Brought from Africa." On the surface, this poem seems like an enthusiastic response of a sincere convert. But later in the poem Wheatley expresses that, according to the Christian message, God makes no distinctions between blacks and whites, and that all believers are promised redemption. This was a subtle but powerful message against prevailing racism. She comments on her being brought from her *pagan* land to the *Saviour* and to *redemption* by *mercy*. She thus turns her kidnapping and enslavement into a positive experience, an act of mercy, an act willed by God. She thus denies any power to the people who kidnapped and sold her. The choice of the word *benighted* is also an interesting one. it means, "overtaken by night or darkness." Metaphorically, it means "being in a state of moral or intellectual darkness." Thus, she equates her skin color with her original state of ignorance of Christian redemption. She describes her race as *sable*. Sable is very valuable and desirable. This word is directly in contradiction with the phrase *diabolic die* used in the next line. Here she is able to make the readers question their belief that slaves are an inferior race. She uses the verb *remember* in the form of a direct command, thus, assuming the role of a teacher or a preacher.

The first poem in her published collection is "To Mæcenas." She invokes the male muse to grant her permission to speak. Wheatley addresses her muse as *sire*. Mæcenas lived in 70 BC and was a friend of the emperor Augustus. The fact that Wheatley chooses to invoke the wealthy, white male Roman as her muse is important. She sees herself as helpless without the white male master and muse. Only after obtaining permission, can she speak her mind. She thus gains power by subjugating herself to the forces stronger than hers.

In later poems such as "An Hymn to the Morning," Wheatley claims that Bright Aurora demands her song, thus claiming that the forces more powerful than her master exist, and that she is governed by those. In some ways she is claiming freedom from her master's will.

In "On Imagination," Wheatley announces the power of imagination; she calls the imagination the *leader of the mental train*. Yet another power that is higher than the powers any humans can ever exert. Alas, the flights of fancy are short and the poet must *cease* her song.

Death is a major theme in Wheatley's numerous elegies. She treats death and the rewards of an afterlife as a continuum of the life itself. In "On the Death of the Rev. Dr. SEWELL," she calls on the mourning crowd to come and watch the saint ascend to his *native skies*, implying that he had been there before. She thus invokes the theme of a "circular pattern" of life and afterlife.

CRITICAL RECEPTION

The historical significance of Phillis Wheatley as one of the first African American woman poets sometimes overshadows her poetical achievements. From the beginning, Wheatley had a bifurcated audience. The signatories of her first volume of poetry assured the readers that *Poems on Various Subjects* was indeed "written by Phillis, a young Negro Girl, who was but a few years since, brought an uncultivated Barbarian from Africa." When Wheatley arrived in Boston after the publication of her book, the *Boston Gazette*, the newspaper of revolutionary, lauded the young slave woman as "the extraordinary Poetical Genius."

Several critics have noted the significance of the book's frontispiece as a skillful marketing tool. Betsy Erkkila refers to this portrait as the emblem of "Wheatley's complex position as a black woman slave in revolutionary America." Mukhtar Ali Isani notes that in the four months following the publication of *Poems on Various Subjects*, "nine British periodicals reviewed the work, usually contributing space in generous amounts. . . . All [the] reviews were favorable."

Regarding the quality of her poetry, two respected people of the time had two entirely opposite opinions. Voltaire announced that her poetry is the proof of the facts that: the genius exists in all parts of the world, and the *perfectibility of the Negroes*.

Thomas Jefferson on the other hand declared that her poetry proved that the Negroes lacked imagination and her poetry was "dull, tasteless, and anomalous." There is similar disagreement about the politics of her poetry. Critics like John Shields maintain that Wheatley uses her poetry to comment on white oppression through expert use of classical and biblical references. Philip Richards and others contend that Wheatley used her poetry to embrace the dominant white culture and tried to assimilate into it. Shields maintains that the poems "To Mæcenas," "On Imagination," and "On Recollection" carry a subversive message. Richards claims that her public poems such as her elegies are the evidence of her wish to assimilate into Colonial America. One thing most critics agree on is that her use of language, meter, and the rhyme scheme is flawless.

BIBLIOGRAPHY

Works by Phillis Wheatley

"An Elegiac Poem on the Death of the Celebrated Divine, and Eminent Servant of Jesus Christ, the Late Reverend, and Pious George Whitefield, Chaplain to Right Honourable the Countess of

Huntingdon," 1770. The Project Gutenberg Etext of Poems by Philllis Wheatley. http://www.gutenberg.org/dirs/etext96/whtly10.txt (accessed January 3, 2005).

Poems on Various Subjects, Religious and Moral, London: A. Bell, 1773.

"To His Excellency General Washington." 1775. The Project Gutenberg Etext of Poems by Philllis Wheatley. http://www.gutenberg.org/dirs/etext96/whtly10.txt (accessed January 3, 2005).

Studies of Phillis Wheatley's Works

Bly, Antonio T. "Wheatley's 'To the University of Cambridge, in New-England.'" *Explicator* 55.4 (1997): 205–8.

Choucair, Mona M. "Phillis Wheatley (1754–1784)." In *African American Authors, 1745–1945: A Bio-Bibliographical Critical Sourcebook*, edited by Emmanuel S. Nelson, 463–68. Westport, CT: Greenwood Press, 2000.

Erkkila, Betsy. *Mixed Bloods and Other Crosses: Rethinking American Literature from the Revolution to the Culture Wars*. Philadelphia: University of Pennsylvania Press, 2004.

Finch, Annie. "Phillis Wheatley and the Sentimental Tradition." *Romanticism on the Net* 29–30 (February–May 2003).

Flanzbaum, Hilene. "Unprecedented Liberties: Re-reading Phillis Wheatley." *Melus* 18.3 (Fall 1993): 71.

Gates, Henry Louis, Jr. "Phillis Wheatley and the Nature of the Negro." In *Critical Essays on Phillis Wheatley*, edited by William H. Robinson, 215–33. Critical Essays on American Literature. Boston: Hall, 1982.

———. *The Trials of Phillis Wheatley: America's First Black Poet and Encounters with the Founding Fathers*. New York: Basic Civitas Books, 2003.

Hayden, Lucy K. "Classical Tidings from the Afric Muse: Phillis Wheatley's Use of Greek and Roman Mythology." *College Language Association Journal* 35.4 (1992): 432–47.

Isani, Mukhtar Ali. "The Contemporaneous Reception of Phillis Wheatley: Newspaper and Magazine Notices During the Years of Fame, 1765–1774." *Journal of Negro History* 24.3 (September 2000): 565–66.

Kendrick, Robert. "Re-membering America: Phillis Wheatley's Intertextual Epic." *African American Review* 30.1 (Spring 1996): 71–89.

Mason, Julian. *Poems of Phillis Wheatley*. Chapel Hill: University of North Carolina Press, 1966.

Nott, Walt. "From 'Uncultivated Barbarian' to 'Poetical Genius': The Public Presence of Phillis Wheatley." *Melus* 18.3 (Fall 1993): 21.

Richards, Phillip M. "Phillis Wheatley and Literary Americanization." *American Quarterly* 44.2 (June 1992): 163–91.

Rizzo, Betty M. "The Poems of Phillis Wheatley." *Eighteenth-Century Studies* 28.3 (1995): 345.

Robinson, William H. *Critical Essays on Phillis Wheatley*. Boston: G. K. Hall, 1982.

———. *Phillis Wheatley: A Bio-Bibliography*. Boston: G. K. Hall, 1981.

———. *Phillis Wheatley and Her Writings*. Boston: G. K. Hall, 1984.

Shields, John C., ed. "Phillis Wheatley's Struggle for Freedom in Her Poetry and Prose." In *The Collected Works of Phillis Wheatley*. New York: Oxford University Press, 1988.

———. "Wheatley's 'On the Affray in King Street.'" *Explicator* 56.4 (1998): 177–80.

———. "Wheatley's 'On the Death of a Young Lady of Five Years of Age.'" *Explicator* 58.1 (1999): 10–13.

Pratibha Kelapure

PAULETTE CHILDRESS WHITE (1948–)

BIOGRAPHICAL NARRATIVE

Paulette Childress White, a poet and short-story writer, was born on December 1, 1948, in Hamtramck, Michigan, to Norris Childress, a welder, and Effie (Storey) Childress. White grew up in Ecorse, Michigan, a small segregated suburb of Detroit, and attended public high school in the same town. She married Bennie White, Jr., a postal worker and artist, and has five sons—Pierre, Oronde, Kojo, Kala, and Paul. After her divorce from Bennie White in 1989 and wanting to feel closer to her origins and identity, White changed her name back to Paulette Childress.

White began her writing career at the age of twenty-four. In 1998, she received her Ph.D. in English from Wayne State University. White currently serves as English instructor at Henry Ford Community College. Most recently and for the third time, she has been honored in *Who's Who Among American Teachers, 2004*. White writes about female cohesion and everyday urban living. She stated in *Contemporary Authors Online, 2002*: "I write from a sense of irony, because I want to make sense of my experience of life. I am also a painter. I write and paint because I have a need to give substance to my ideas, feelings, and experiences, and because I believe it is good and important work."

MAJOR WORKS

Lotus Press, a nonprofit literary organization, still publishes both of White's major works of poetry—*Love Poem to a Black Junkie* (1975) and *The Watermelon Dress: Portrait of a Woman* (1983). White's short story "Getting the Facts of Life" (1989) was anthologized in three different publications from 1991 to 1993.

Love Poem to a Black Junkie, a collection of twenty-six poems, describes White's personal and political experiences as an African American woman—from following leaders as they marched against injustice to talking to her son about slavery. The collection also bestows respect upon several African Americans, including Nina Simone and Malcolm X.

The Watermelon Dress, a poem spanning from the 1950s through the 1980s, narrates the journey of a woman and her dresses. Sometimes wearing a calico dress, sometimes a cotton dress, and eventually wearing stretch pants, the speaker discovers that her clothes do not fit; that is, her position as a political activist, homemaker, and lover does not always satisfy. In the end, she proudly discovers her life as an artist.

Twelve-year-old Minerva Blue, the protagonist and narrator of the autobiographical "Getting the Facts of Life," encounters the urbanized bureaucracy of the welfare system in 1960s America, as well as the impending responsibility of a female life defined by domesticity and sexuality.

CRITICAL RECEPTION

White's work has received minimal critical attention. Gerald Barrax, in "Six Poets: From Poetry to Verse," describes her writing in *The Watermelon Dress* as "pleasant, easy, accessible verse that might be understood and enjoyed even by people who ordinarily 'don't like poetry'" (265). While noting that some of her poetry does not include functional metaphors, he credits White's work with "an intensity and control (a masterful combination of forces)" (268).

Despite the lack of critical attention, White's writing garners recognition for its cultural relevance, subtle humor, and questioning of the African American female condition. Connecting art with her own spiritual development, White stated in January 2006: "The work of other artists and the creation of my own art have been among my most profound spiritual experiences. Creating a thing of value and beauty satisfies my soul."

BIBLIOGRAPHY

Works by Paulette Childress White

"Alice." In *Midnight Birds: Stories of Contemporary Black Women Writers*, edited by Mary Helen Washington, 8–11. New York: Anchor/Doubleday, 1980.
"Bessie." *Callaloo* 16 (1982): 18.
"The Bird Cage." In *Midnight Birds: Stories of Contemporary Black Women Writers*, 33–41. New York: Anchor/Doubleday, 1980.
"The Boulevard House." *Callaloo* 16 (1982): 19.
"Claudie Mae." *Callaloo* 16 (1982): 130.
"Getting the Facts of Life." In *Memory of Kin: Stories about Family by Black Writers*, edited by Mary Helen Washington. New York: Anchor/Doubleday, 1991.
Love Poem to a Black Junkie. Detroit: Lotus Press, 1975.
Rev. of *Mufaro's Beautiful Daughters: An African Tale*, by John Steptoe. *New York Times*, June 28, 1987, A27.
"This Chain." *Callaloo* 16 (1982): 129.
"Three Seconds before Sleep." *Callaloo* 16 (1982): 131.
The Watermelon Dress: Portrait of a Woman. Detroit: Lotus Press, 1983.

Studies of Paulette Childress White's Works

Barrax, Gerald. "Six Poets: From Poetry to Verse." *Callaloo* 26 (1986): 248–69.
Davis, Ella Jean. "African-American Women Writers of Detroit." Ph.D. Dissertation, University of Michigan, 1990.
Washington, Mary Helen. "Commentary on Paulette Childress White." In *Memory of Kin: Stories about Family by Black Writers*, edited by Mary Helen Washington, 140–42. New York: Anchor/Doubleday, 1991.

Jessica Margaret Brophy

BRENDA WILKINSON (1946–)

BIOGRAPHICAL NARRATIVE

Children and young adult fiction writer Brenda Scott Wilkinson was born on January 1, 1946, in Moultrie, Georgia, to Malcolm Wilkinson and Ethel Scott. After graduating from Hunter College of the City University of New York, Wilkinson became a published author of children's books. Between 1976 and 2003, she served as staff writer for the United Methodist Church's Board of Global Ministries in New York. Recently, she participated in the Medgar Evers College Center for Black Literature 7th Annual National Black Writers Conference: A Tribute to and Symposium on John Oliver Killens (2004). Wilkinson is a National Book Award nominee, a Georgia Writers Hall of Fame nominee, and a recipient of School Library Journal Best Children's Book, *New York Times Book Review* Outstanding Children's Book of the Year Award, and American Library Association Best Books for Young Adults Award. She is divorced and has two daughters: Kim and Lori.

MAJOR WORKS

Wilkinson is best known for her 1975 debut novel, *Ludell*, and its sequels, *Ludell and Willie* (1976) and *Ludell's New York Time* (1980). In the first book of this coming-of-age trilogy, Ludell Wilson navigates the pros and cons of African American life in Waycross, Georgia, during the 1950s. The book begins with Ludell daydreaming in her fifth grade class. She dreams about her mother, Dessa, sending a television from New York and wonders "what clouds taste like." One of Ludell's dreams is realized, and Dessa sends to the Wilson household a television. Ludell subsequently suffers a disappointment that serves as an initiation into the reality of southern African American life outside of school. However, her imagination and flair for sensory details carry her through hard times and, often through her own creative works, enable her to balance reality with idealism.

In *Ludell and Willie*, the trilogy explores the more complex issues that affect teenagers. Ludell no longer moves in a world where clouds have a taste, and the maturity she developed at the end of the first book is tested and refined. Ludell is now a high school senior in the late 1950s and her dream is to graduate; marry Willie, the high school football hero who has been Ludell's neighbor and friend since childhood; and leave Waycross. However, the couple confronts many obstacles. Mama, Ludell's grandmother, imposes strict, old-fashioned rules that circumscribe the relationship. Mama does not want Ludell to end up like Dessa or like Willie's oldest sister, both of whom ran away and left their children with their mothers to rear. Ludell and Willie also have to deal with poverty. Their financial situation partly determines whether Willie will stay in high school instead of going to work, and his only chance to get to college is based on winning a football scholarship. In parallel, Ludell enters an essay writing contest that will award a scholarship to the winner. However, none of the plans work out. Mama becomes sick and dies. Dessa returns and takes Ludell to a school in New York. Ludell's optimism and determination reign strong despite hardship, and her dream changes only slightly: Willie will join the army after his high school graduation, come to New York to marry Ludell, and then take her away.

In *Ludell's New York Time*, Ludell has the opportunity to reconcile her relationship with Dessa and also her rural southern background with the urban north. Now that Dessa is a full-time mother, she determines to give Ludell the opportunities she never had. Like Mama, though, Dessa imposes upon Ludell rules and regulations she believes are in Ludell's best interest. In response, Ludell remains detached from her environment. The only thing of importance to her is marking time until Willie comes to take her back home. Again, Ludell's dream comes true. However, it is at a cost. While growing up in Georgia, Ludell was part of history. In *Ludell*, she experiences segregation and her life partly was constructed in accordance with Jim Crow laws. In *Ludell and Willie*, she experiences and is a proponent of school desegregation. In *Ludell's New York Time*, Ludell meets people who represent the issues of the civil rights era in the north: a young family struggling to make financial ends meet, a young man unable to obtain gainful employment due to racial ideology and who speaks about civil rights and African heritage, and a sexually uninhibited girl who revolts against rules. Ludell's focus, though, remains on Willie, and she fails to be fully present in her New York life. The balance between reality and idealism shifts as Ludell closes her eyes to the significance of the present in favor of a dream. However, it is because of this shift that *Ludell's New York Time* remains a testimony to the power of dreams and determination in the face of obstacles.

Other books by Wilkinson focus on themes raised in the trilogy. *Definitely Cool* mirrors *Ludell* in its depiction of the rocky world of childhood and the accompanying family matters, peer pressure, friendships, and romantic relationships. *Jesse Jackson: Still Fighting for the Dream* and *African American Women Writers* profile individuals who significantly impacted African American history. In *Not Separate, Not Equal*, seventeen-year-old Malene Freeman experiences integration in Georgia during 1965 while *The Civil Rights Movement: An Illustrated History* pictorially examines the civil rights movement.

CRITICAL RECEPTION

Wilkinson's books are successful because she recreates the world of children without interference from the adult persona. She skillfully develops her characters, right down to their very nuances and idiom. Critics note that Wilkinson portrays "the day to day give and take between kids and the jumble of sassy perceptions and vague misunderstandings" that children often have (*Kirkus Reviews*). Critics also note that the characters in *Ludell and Willie* "are developed believably; their dialect . . . and interplay with one another and with the rigors of Black life in a small Georgia town before desegregation are portrayed with honesty, immediacy, warmth, and humor" (Silver 128).

Lending to this social realism is the incorporation of thematically multilayered plots. In the trilogy, Wilkinson develops the themes of love and romance; female relationships and friendship; and "race" and poverty within the domestic, rural, and urban spheres. Rather than being didactic or rhetorical regarding controversial personal and social issues, Wilkinson records the issues and weaves them into the characters' daily lives. Primarily because of Wilkinson's focus on African American life, Addison Gayle compares *Ludell* with Richard Wright's *Native Son*. Gayle draws comparisons between the two writers. Among other things, he notes that "[t]he members of the Wright school . . . were moral warriors who believed that the novel should function as an instrument for improving the human condition" (470). *Ludell*, with its focus on love and caring as the foundation of the black family, functions to improve the human condition by suggesting "that the black novel will return to an explication of the ethics and values which have assured black survival in this society" (471).

Although *Ludell* makes a significant contribution to African American society and African American literature, the issue of balance that partly characterizes *Ludell's New York Time* recurs in Wilkinson's work. This time, the issue appears when the marriage between character and plot falters as one or the other becomes too dominant. Pamela Pollack notes that *Ludell's New York Time* is "all talk and no action," and Roger Sutton states that *Definitely Cool* is "basically plotless." Conversely, Gerry Larson states, "Readers will find [*Not Separate, Not Equal*] an action-packed account and a palatable history lesson (115). Reflecting this conflicting split between character and plot are the types of books Wilkinson wrote: fiction featuring characters living through historical events, and plot-heavy nonfiction about historical events or historical figures and their contributions to society. This split was resolved when Wilkinson eventually stopped writing fiction in favor of plot-heavy work, and she became known as a chronicler of African American history.

In *African American Women Writers*, Wilkinson remarks that she wished as a child for books that contained characters and experiences to which she could relate. Her own books seem to be responses to her pre–civil rights southern childhood and the lack of African American characters in literature during that time. Her characters' believable perspectives personalize history, making it accessible to young readers even as they fill that literary lack. Like Ludell, Wilkinson fulfills her dream. Ultimately, her works, which are "rich in events, feelings, and customs of the time, . . . provide a record, positive and negative, or an era of black frustration" (ElLaissi 3).

BIBLIOGRAPHY

Works by Brenda Wilkinson

African American Women Writers. New York: Jossey-Bass, 1999.
Civil Rights Movement: An Illustrated History. New York: Gramercy, 1996.
Definitely Cool. New York: Scholastic, 1995.
Jesse Jackson: Still Fighting for the Dream. Englewood, New Jersey: Silver Burdett Press, 1990.
Ludell. New York: Harper, 1975.
Ludell and Willie. New York: Harper, 1976.
Ludell's New York Time. New York: Harper, 1980.
Not Separate, Not Equal. New York: Harper, 1987.

Collaborative Works

Haskins, Jim, Clinton Cox, and Brenda Wilkinson. *Black Stars of Colonial Times and the Revolutionary War: African Americans Who Liver Their Dreams*. New York: Jossey-Bass, 2002.
Haskins, Jim, Eleanor E. Tate, Clinton Cox, and Brenda Wilkinson. *Black Stars of the Harlem Renaissance*. New York: Jossey-Bass, 2002.
Wilkinson, Brenda, and Tom Feelings. *Teacher's Guide to Under the Boab Tree: Children of Africa*. New York: The United Methodist Church General Board of Global Ministries, 2000.

Wilkinson, Brenda, and Tom Feelings. *Under the Boab Tree: Children of Africa*. New York: The United Methodist Church General Board of Global Ministries, 2000.

Studies of Brenda Wilkinson's Works

"Books." *American Visions* 8.6 (December 93/January 94): 35.

Boyd, Herb. "Wilkinson Captures Civil Rights Movement in Pictures." *New York Amsterdam News* 87.49 (December 7, 1996): 24.

ElLaissi, Bobbie. "Ludell and Willie." *Masterplots II: Juvenile and Young Adult Fiction Series* (1991): 1–3. MagillOnLiterature Plus.

Gayle, Addison. "Ludell: Beyond Native Son." *Nation* 222.15 (April 17, 1976): 469–71.

King, Cynthia. "Children's Books." *New York Times Book Review* (August 3, 1980): BR5.

Kirkus Reviews. *Ludell*. Brenda Wilkinson. New York: Harper, 1975.

Kornfield, Matilda R. "Ludell." *School Library Journal* 22.4 (December 1975): 62.

Kutenplon, Deborah. *Young Adult Fiction by African American Writers, 1968–1993: A Critical and Annotated Guide*. New York: Garland Publishing, 1995. 304–13.

Larson, Gerry. "Not Separate, Not Equal." *School Library Journal* 34.8 (April 1988): 114–15.

Lindsay, Leon W. "Growing Up and Going to School in the South." *Christian Science Monitor* (November 5, 1975): 38.

McHargue, Georgess. "Children's Books." *New York Times Book Review* (May 22, 1977): 263.

Meisner, Sylvia V. "Book Review: Grades 3–6." *School Library Journal* 39.3 (March 1993): 202.

Norris, Jerrie. "Love Story Set in Harlem." *Christian Science Monitor* (April 14, 1980): B7.

Pollack, Pamela D. "Ludell's New York Time." *School Library Journal* 26.6 (February 1980): 73.

Silver, Linda. "Ludell and Willie." *School Library Journal* 24.2 (October 1977): 128.

Sutton, Roger. "Definitely Cool." *Bulletin of the Center for Children's Books* 46.7 (March 1993).

Thompson, Betty. "Books." *Christian Century* 114.5 (February 5, 1997): 171–74.

Washington, Idella. "Reviews: Fiction." *Book Report* 12.2 (September/October 1993): 50.

Tamara Zaneta Hollins

FANNIE BARRIER WILLIAMS (1855–1944)

BIOGRAPHICAL NARRATIVE

Journalist, orator, sociologist, schoolteacher—these are just a few of the influential roles that Fannie (Frances) Barrier Williams assumed during her eighty-nine years. She was born in Brockport, New York, and died there, but lived much of her adult life in Chicago (1887–1926). There she and her husband S. Laing Williams, an attorney, were leaders in the Prudence Crandall Club, a literary society that aggressively promoted social activism on behalf of African Americans and whites alike. Williams was born on February 12, 1855, to Harriet Prince and Anthony J. Barrier. Of her formative years in western New York, Williams writes that "[w]e suffered from no discriminations on account of color . . . and lived in blissful ignorance of the fact that we were practicing the unpardonable sin of 'social equality'" (*New Woman* 6). At the State Normal School in Brockport she pursued both academic and classical coursework, and graduated in 1870 with a certificate to teach school. Her education was profoundly impacted by the transcendentalists, especially the writings of Emerson and Thoreau (*New Woman* xvi).

Seeking adventure and wanting to contribute to sweeping historical change, Williams moved south during Reconstruction to be a schoolteacher. Her insulated northern childhood proved poor preparation for the level of racism she encountered while traveling and teaching in the southern states. Nevertheless, she stayed true to her mission for a number of years, eventually ending up in Washington, D.C., where she became acquainted with many black intellectuals and activists. In 1887, at the age of thirty-two, she married, and the newlyweds moved to Chicago. During their Chicago years, the Williamses worked and socialized with a plethora of distinguished African Americans, including Booker T. Washington, Frederick Douglass, Ida B. Wells, and W.E.B. DuBois.

Williams's speech, "The intellectual progress of the Colored Women of the United States since the Emancipation Proclamation," at the World's Columbian Exposition of 1893 put her in the national spotlight for the first time. That same year Williams and Mary Church Terrell were instrumental in the establishment of the National League of Colored Women, and three years later they worked to found the National Association of Colored Women. Williams began writing newspaper articles in 1895 when she became a correspondent for *Woman's Era*, the first publication for and by African American women. In the summer of 1904, Williams's "A Northern Negro's Autobiography" appeared in the widely read journal the *Independent*. Williams was reacting to a series of articles the journal ran in the spring that she thought gave the impression black women lived only in the south. In 1905 and 1906, the *New York Age*, an important African American national newspaper, published several articles by Williams. Also about this time Williams wrote columns for the white *Chicago Record Herald*.

Williams was a pioneering sociologist, focusing on issues related to the home and education, and she associated with other "feminist pragmatists" in Chicago, including Jane Addams, Mary McDowell, and Celia Parker Woolley. As such, Williams was actively involved with each one's social project: Addams's Hull-House, McDowell's University of Chicago Social Settlement, and Woolley's Frederick Douglass Center. Williams's work in sociology, which focused not only on black women but on other disenfranchised groups as well, was marginalized or dismissed entirely by the white male-dominated field as it developed after 1920 (*New Woman* xxxvi).

Williams's last major accomplishment was in 1924 when she became the first female and the first African American to be named to the Chicago Public Library Board. She held the position for two years before resigning to return to Brockport, New York, where she lived out her remaining years with her sister. Her husband died in 1921, after having survived a serious automobile accident the previous year.

MAJOR WORKS

Williams's articles and reprinted addresses are difficult to come by as virtually all were published in newspapers and journals long defunct; however, in 2002, Northern Illinois University Press published *The New Woman of Color: The Collected Writings of Fannie Barrier Williams, 1893–1918*. Skillfully edited and introduced by Mary Jo Deegan, the collection includes many of Williams's more significant pieces, including her 1904 "Autobiography" and her speech at the World's Columbian Exposition of 1893. There are twenty-four of Williams' pieces all together, and among them are eulogies for Philip D. Armour and Susan B. Anthony.

The prose of "Autobiography" is lively and much more akin to the economical style that would continue to evolve in the new century, showing little of the floridness often associated with writers of the 1800s. Though brief, Williams recounts her racism-free childhood and tells of her family's history. Then, via a series of personal anecdotes she discusses the overt bigotry of the south versus the more Machiavellian practices of northern racists: ". . . I can but believe that the prejudice that blights and hinders is quite as decided in the North as it is in the South, but does not manifest itself so openly and brutally" (10). In particular, Williams talks about trying to find employment for young black women in companies owned by white men. She baldly criticizes churchgoing whites, both men and women, who claim to have Christian values but are bigots in their daily lives. She closes her autobiography, however, with restrained optimism: "I dare not cease to hope and aspire and believe in human love and justice, but progress is painful and my faith is often strained to the breaking point" (13).

Williams had expressed many of these same ideas a decade earlier when she spoke at the World's Columbian Exposition. In the speech, originally published in *The World's Congress of Representative Women* (1894), she identifies Christianity and education as the keys for women of color to achieve equality in American society. "[O]ur women," she writes, "find congeniality in all the creeds, from the Catholic creed to the no-creed of Emerson" (19). And she says that for "thirty years education has been the magic word among the colored people" (19). Her interests in sociology are clear from the beginning of the address when she notes that "[l]ess is known of our women than of any other class of Americans" (17). She further claims that "[t]he power of organized womanhood is one of the most interesting studies of modern sociology" (20).

CRITICAL RECEPTION

Scholarship on Williams has been meager, owed in large part to the scarcity of her published work prior to the 2002 collection. Deegan asserts that Williams was controversial in her lifetime and is to this day. Various historians have characterized Williams as an "accommodationist," an "elitist," and as a "dilettante" (xiv). In her autobiography, Williams tells of having to pass as a Frenchwoman while in the south to avoid being subjected to Jim Crow laws, especially while traveling by train. According to Deegan, some biographers have blown Williams's admission out of proportion to make it seem as though she habitually misrepresented her ethnicity. Deegan writes, "Such a harsh interpretation of Williams, who did *not* pass as white in her everyday life and who fought for African American rights, ideas, and history throughout her life, blames the victim of discrimination instead of the oppressor" (xvi–xvii). As far as the charge of elitism, Williams does differentiate between black women who are educated and moral, like herself—primarily northerners—and those who are ignorant and lacking a sense of Christian morality. She does not criticize the women of the south themselves, but places blame on the institution of slavery and its tenacious aftermath (21). She also charges that African Americans of her day have difficulty living and working in harmony: "For peculiar and painful reasons the great lessons of fraternity and altruism are hard for colored women to learn. Emancipation found the colored Americans of the South with no sentiments of association" (20). Williams does say, though, that black women have taken a leading role in trying to bring communities together for the common good (21).

Moreover, her 1893 address shows anticipation of great contributions to American literature, art, and music by African American women of the coming generation (20). As far as being a dilettante, there is no question that Williams's father was a well-to-do man of business who made sure his children were well educated and well cared for, and Williams's husband was a successful attorney—so she did not suffer the same ignorance, poverty, and indignities that plagued most African American women of her day. Williams, therefore, could have lived a quiet, comfortable life in New England or Chicago, but instead she worked on behalf of the downtrodden, regardless of race and gender, and risked her personal safety to do so. She moved south as a schoolteacher while still a teenager, and after making a name for herself nationally with her pen and voice, Williams went on lecture tours throughout the south. Deegan writes, "It is not her flaws that fascinate me: it is her frequent transcendence of her own limits that is exciting" (lvi).

BIBLIOGRAPHY

Works by Fannie Barrier Williams

The New Woman of Color: The Collected Writings of Fannie Barrier Williams, 1893–1918. Edited by Mary Jo Deegan. Dekalb, IL: Northern Illinois University Press, 2002.

Note: All works listed below are collected in *The New Woman of Color.*

"Club Movement among Colored Women." In *Progress of a Race: The Remarkable Advancement of the American Negro*, edited by J. W. Gibson and W. H. Grogman, 197–281. Naperville, IL: J.L. Nichols, 1912.
"The Club Movement among the Colored Women." *Voice of the Negro* 1.3 (1904): 99–102.
"The Colored Girl." *Voice of the Negro* 2.6 (1905): 400–403.
"Colored Women of Chicago." *Southern Workman* 43 (October 1914): 564–66.

"Do We Need Another Name?" *Southern Workman* 33 (January 1904): 33–36.

"An Extension of the Conference Spirit." *Voice of the Negro* 1.7 (1904): 300–303.

"The Frederick Douglass Centre." *Southern Workman* 35 (June 1906): 334–36.

"The Frederick Douglass Centre: A Question of Social Betterment and Not of Social Equality." *Voice of the Negro* 1.12 (1904): 601–4.

The History of Woman Suffrage. Eulogy of Susan B. Anthony, vol. 5 (1900–1920). 1922. Edited by Ida Husted Harper. New York: Arno Press, 1969.

"Industrial Education—Will It Solve the Negro Problem?" *Colored American* (July 1904): 491–505.

"The Need of Social Settlement Work for the City Negro." *Southern Workman* 33 (September 1904): 501–6.

"The Negro and Public Opinion." *Voice of the Negro* 1.1 (1904): 31–32.

"A New Method of Dealing with the Race Problem." *Voice of the Negro* 3.7 (1906): 502–5.

"A Northern Negro's Autobiography." *Independent* 57 (July 14, 1904): 91–96.

"Philip D. Armour." Eulogy. *Southern Workman* 30 (May 1901): 24–25.

"The Problem of Employment for Negro Women." Address delivered at the Hampton Conference, July 1903. *Southern Workman* 32 (September 1903): 432–37.

"Refining Influence of Art." *Voice of the Negro* 3.3 (1906): 211–14.

"Religious Duty to the Negro." In *The World's Congress of Religion*, edited by J. W. Hanson, 893–977. Chicago: W.B. Conkey, 1894.

"Report of Memorial Service for Rev. Celia Parker Woolley, April 7, 1918, at the Abraham Lincoln Centre, Chicago." *Unity* 81 (April 18, 1918): 116–17.

"The Smaller Economies." *Voice of the Negro* 1.5 (1904): 184–85.

"Social Bonds in the 'Black Belt' of Chicago: Negro Organizations and the New Spirit Pervading Them." *Charities* 15 (October 7, 1905): 40–44.

"Vacation Values." *Voice of the Negro* 2.12 (1905): 863–66.

"The Woman's Part in a Man's Business." *Voice of the Negro* 1.11 (1904): 543–47.

The World's Congress of Representative Women. Edited by Mary Wright Sewell. Chicago: Rand, McNally, 1894, 2: 696–711.

Studies of Fannie Barrier Williams's Works

Fishel, Leslie H., Jr. "Fannie Barrier Williams." In *Notable American Women*, edited by Edward T. James, 3: 620–22. Cambridge, MA: Belknap Press, Harvard University, 1971.

Lamping, Marilyn. "Fannie Barrier Williams." In *American Women Writers*, edited by Lina Mainiero, 432–33. New York: Frederick Ungar Publishing, 1982.

Logan, Rayford W. "Fannie Barrier Williams." In *Dictionary of American Negro Biography*, edited by Rayford W. Logan and Michael R. Winston, 656–57. New York: W.W. Norton, 1982.

Riggs, Marcia Y. "Fannie [Barrier] Williams." In *African American Women: A Biographical Dictionary*, edited by Dorothy C. Salem, 556–58. New York: Garland, 1993.

Smith, Jessie Cary. "Fannie B. Williams (1855–1944)." In *Notable Black American Women*, edited by Jessie Cary Smith, 1251–54. Detroit: Gale Research, 1992.

Spear, Allan H. "Fannie Barrier Williams." In *Dictionary of American Biography*, edited by Edward T. James et al., 827–28. New York: Charles Scribner's Sons, 1973.

Ted Morrissey

SHERLEY ANNE WILLIAMS (1944–1999)

BIOGRAPHICAL NARRATIVE

Most widely acclaimed for her 1986 novel *Dessa Rose*, Sherley Anne Williams played an important role in twentieth-century African American literature as writer, teacher, and scholar. Williams, groundbreaking in her first-person representations of rural and poor African American women, wrote one of the first neo-slave narratives that followed Margaret Walker's *Jubilee*, with *Dessa Rose* appearing just prior to Morrison's 1987 *Beloved*. One of the pioneers who established a place for African American literature in academia, Williams's literary criticism highlights matters including the changing ideology of the African American heroic figure and the impact of the blues on the literary tradition. Her poetry and fiction often reflect the life she and her three sisters experienced as the daughters of agricultural workers who followed the crops in California's San Joaquin valley. As a writer, she filled a void that had frustrated her younger self by depicting in books the girls and young women who grew up and lived in such a world. Williams combined her work as a poet and fiction writer with her ongoing scholarship as well as with the teaching of African American literature as a professor at the University of California, San Diego, from 1973 to 1999.

Williams was born on August 25, 1944, in Bakersfield, California, and spent her early years in the projects in Fresno. Her father, Jesse, died of tuberculosis when she was eight and her mother, Lelia-Lena, died when she was sixteen. Williams's older sister Ruby, who at eighteen had returned home with her daughter following the breakup of her marriage, cared for Williams following their mother's death. In the introduction to her story "Meditations on History" in Mary Helen Washington's *Midnight Birds*, Williams attributes much of her early success to Ruby's support. Her early short stories, "Tell Martha Not to Moan" (1968) and "The Lawd Don't Like Ugly" (1974), drew characters and language from the poor, rural California environments where she grew up, where the "heroic young women" she knew "who despite all they had to do and endure laughed and loved, hoped and encouraged, [and] supported each other with gifts of food and money" ("Meditations" 197). Though she found few representations of women like her sisters and herself in the books at her school library, she did find autobiographies by Eartha Kitt, Katherine Dunham, Ethel Waters, and Richard Wright that inspired her to endure. Her early literary influences also included Louisa May Alcott, Frank Yerby, and Sterling Brown. In Langston Hughes's *Montage of a Dream Deferred*, she found a representation of the language she knew and which she ultimately incorporated into her own fiction and poetry.

A woman of letters in every respect, Williams braided writing into her life as a mother, scholar, and teacher. She earned her B.A. in history from Fresno State College (now California State University, Fresno) in 1966 and attended graduate school at the Fisk University (1966) and Howard University (1966–1967). She taught adult education at Miles College in Birmingham, Alabama, in the midsixties and worked as a community educator in Washington, D.C., from 1970 to 1972. In 1972 she received her M.A. in

American literature from Brown University. The same year, *Give Birth to Brightness: A Thematic Study in Neo-Black Literature* was published and she returned to Fresno with her young son, Malcolm, to take a position as an associate professor of English. In 1973 she became assistant professor at the University of California, San Diego, where she served as department chair from 1976 to 1982. Her first book of poetry, *The Peacock Poems*, was published in 1975, and her second, *Some One Sweet Angel Chile*, in 1982. In 1984, she was senior Fulbright lecturer at the University of Ghana. Her two children's books, *Working Cotton* and *Girls Together*, appeared in 1992 and 1999, respectively. She continued to teach at the University of California, San Diego, until her death from cancer on July 6, 1999.

MAJOR WORKS

Williams first gained recognition as a poet. *The Peacock Poems* (1975), her earliest collection, speaks of giving birth and motherhood, of relations between African American women and men, of driving the roads of the San Joaquin Valley, and of the power of words and poetry. Frances Smith Foster, who refers to these poems as "so technically perfect that technique seems non-existent," describes them as "first of all about a woman, all women, and black women especially." This is especially evident in the opening poem, "Any Woman's Blues," and in "I Sing This Song for Our Mothers." The theme of the blues emerges more explicitly in Williams's second book of poetry, *Some One Sweet Angel Chile* (1982), in homage to Bessie Smith. The first of its three sections is Williams's "Letters from a New England Negro." Written in the voice of a Negro woman who went south following the Civil War to teach those freed from slavery, the "Letters" reemerged as a full-length, one-woman drama performed at the 1991 National Black Theatre Festival and the 1992 Chicago International Theatre Festival. The central section evokes Bessie Smith's life, her influence, and her music through the poems "Regular Reefer," "The Hard Time Blues," and the widely anthologized "I Want Aretha to Set This to Music," a blues lyric that echoes the "one-sided bed Blues" of the *Peacock Poems*. The final section returns to an autobiographical voice; the most poignant, "the wishon line," tells of a journey to visit her father before he died of tuberculosis.

Give Birth to Brightness (1972), Williams's first published text of literary criticism, established her engagement with the nature of the African American hero. This rich text, written at a time when the neo-black literary movement was taking shape, traces the types of African American heroic figures in America, from the slave rebel and the trickster figure through the street man and the modern revolutionary hero, noting the ways that the historical and social situations of African American life in America produce different kinds of heroes. Williams reads Amiri Baraka's early works, *The Dutchman* and *The Slave* as examples of where African American literature has been, and James Baldwin's *Blues for Mister Charlie* and Ernest Gaines's *The Autobiography of Miss June Pittman* as evidence of a newly emerging neo-black hero that represents African American life for African American audiences, rather than as a subtext to white America. She explained later in an interview with Shirley Jordan that "[w]hen I wrote *Give Birth to Brightness*, Toni Morrison said that the book was very masculine. . . . If I had found women [in literature] who fit my subject—a certain kind of heroic black character—I would have dealt with that too" (210). Indeed, her short story "Meditations on History" and her novel *Dessa Rose* were inspired by an abbreviated historical account of just such a heroine.

Williams first encountered the story that became *Dessa Rose* in Angela Davis's 1971 "Reflections on the Black Woman's Role in the Community of Slaves," which includes an account of a slave woman who led a rebellion from a slave coffle. In tracing Davis's account of Herbert Aptheker's *American Negro Slave Revolts*, Williams came across the story of a white woman accused of harboring runaway slaves on her plantation. She framed her novel with an opening in which Dessa's viewpoint counters and reveals the inaccuracy of an invented white male "researcher" and writer of guides for slaveholders. In part, the historically fictional *Dessa Rose* is a response to William Styron's controversial reimagination of Nat Turner's revolt as he renders it in *The Confessions of Nat Turner*. However, Williams's primary objective was to represent a historical voice that she had been unable to find in the books she read growing up in California: the voice of the African American woman. At the same time, the latter sections of *Dessa Rose* contain subtle allusions to canonical white male authors, with the ghosts of William Faulkner and Mark Twain haunting the novel—Sutton Glen, Williams's setting for the middle section, parodies Faulkner's *Sutpen's Hundred* and the third and final section invokes Twain's picaresque style and recalls the tragicomic selling and rescuing of Jim in *Huckleberry Finn*. Williams was working on a sequel to *Dessa Rose* when she died. In the spring of 2005, a version of *Dessa Rose* by Lynn Ahrens and Stephen Flaherty appeared as an Off-Broadway production at the Lincoln Center in New York City.

During the 1990s, Williams composed two children's books. *Working Cotton*, illustrated by Carole Byard, is a selection from *The Peacock Poems*' "The Trimming of the Feathers," which represents a girl's-eye view of a family working in a field from sun-up to sun-down. Williams's second children's book, *Girls Together* (1999), with illustrations by Synthia Saint James, is a simple but compelling story of a group of girls playing together in the projects—climbing a tree, sharing a bicycle, and taking a flower home for a friend.

Recognized most often for her poetry and fiction, Williams was also a brilliant literary scholar. Just as *Give Birth to Brightness* was an important critical work at a time when African American literature was beginning to receive attention, Williams's more recent work in literary criticism has been timely and important. Between them, her introductions to the 1978 reprint of Zora Neale Hurston's *Their Eyes Were Watching God* and to a 1996 edition of Twain's *The Tragedy of Pudd'nhead Wilson* mark the dramatic changes that the field of literature saw during her career. The first introduced readers to Hurston's rural African American heroine, Janie, whose language and experience resonated with that of the rural African American culture Williams knew from her own life. The second, less a critical celebration and more a case of hard-nosed praise for an already canonical writer, calls Twain's text "a clever, ironic, and caustic rebuke of the notion of the Negro's 'inherent'—that is *natural*—inferiority" (xxxii).

"Some Implications of Womanist Theory" (1986) is Williams's entry into the conversation about the role of African American women as literary scholars in relation to the whole of a black aesthetic and in relation to feminist projects that largely failed to address the position of African American women in society. This essay, which builds on her work in *Give Birth to Brightness*, traces the changing nature of the heroic quest of the African American male character. It is notable especially for its attention to the nature of the African American male literary hero prior to 1940, a hero whom she identifies as notably nonviolent, with his heroism dependent on moral superiority or "intellectual parity" and his care for family and others. "The Blues Roots of Contemporary Afro-

American Poetry" (1997) and "Returning to the Blues: Esther Phillips and Contemporary Blues Culture" (1991) define the importance of the blues to contemporary African American literature and culture, while "The Lion's History: The Ghetto Writes B(l)ack" (1993) stakes a place for African American writers to write their own stories. "The Lion's History" is, in part, a response to criticism of *Dessa Rose*, and there Williams outlines in greater detail her impetus in writing the novel, claiming her need to write those like herself into history, "even though [she] seemed to have no place there except as slave and savage" (247). She observes that "'History' is often no more than who holds the pen at a given point in time" (258). Williams wielded her own pen compellingly, claiming through her writing a place in history for herself, for African American women, and for all women.

CRITICAL RECEPTION

In 1976, *The Peacock Poems* garnered nominations for both the National Book Award and the Pulitzer Prize. *Some One Sweet Angel Chile* was likewise nominated for the National Book Award, and a televised reading from the collection won an Emmy Award in 1982. *Dessa Rose* was named a notable book of the year by the *New York Times* in 1986. The children's book *Working Cotton* was selected as both a Caldecott Honor Book and a Coretta Scott King Honor Book in 1993.

David Bradley, reviewing *Dessa Rose* for the *New York Times*, notes Williams's skill as a novelist. He describes *Dessa Rose* as "an absorbing fusion that is both elegant poetry and powerful fiction" and draws a parallel between Alice Walker's storyline in *The Color Purple* and Williams's story of "a liberating relationship between two women."

BIBLIOGRAPHY

Works by Sherley Anne Williams

"The Blues Roots of Contemporary Afro-American Poetry." *Massachusetts Review* 18.3 (1977): 542–54.

Dessa Rose. New York: Morrow, 1986.

Dessa Rose. Musical. Adapted by Lynn Ahrens and Stephen Flaherty. Dir. Graciela Daniele. Perf. La Chanze and Rachel York. Mitzi E. Newhouse Theater, Lincoln Center. New York, 2005.

Foreword to *Their Eyes Were Watching God*, by Zora Neale Hurston, v–xv. Urbana: University of Illinois Press, 1978.

Girls Together. With Illustrations by Synthia Saint James. San Diego: Harcourt, 1999.

Give Birth to Brightness: A Thematic Study in Neo-Black Literature. New York: Dial, 1972.

"In Time: *The Tragedy of Pudd'nhead Wilson*." Introduction to *The Tragedy of Pudd'nhead Wilson*, by Mark Twain, xxxi–xliii. New York: Oxford University Press, 1996.

"The Lawd Don't Like Ugly." *New Letters* 41.2 (1974): 15–37.

"The Lion's History: The Ghetto Writes B(l)ack." *Soundings* 76.2–3 (1993): 245–60.

"Meditations on History." In *Midnight Birds: Stories by Contemporary Black Women Writers*, edited by Mary Helen Washington, 200–248. Garden City, NY: Anchor-Doubleday, 1980.

The Peacock Poems. Middletown, CT: Wesleyan University Press, 1975.

"Returning to the Blues: Esther Phillips and Contemporary Blues Culture." *Callaloo* 14.4 (1991): 816–28.

"Some Implications of Womanist Theory." *Callaloo* 27 (1986): 303–8.

"Someone Sweet Angel Child." *Massachusetts Review* 18.3 (1977): 567–72.
Some One Sweet Angel Chile. New York: Morrow, 1982.
"Tell Martha Not to Moan." *Massachusetts Review* 9 (Summer 1968): 443–58.
Working Cotton. With Illustrations by Carole Byard. San Diego: Harcourt, 1992.

Studies of Sherley Anne Williams's Works

Bradley, David. "On the Lam from Race and Gender." Rev. of *Dessa Rose*. *New York Times*, August 3, 1986, late city final edition, sec. 7:7.
Foster, Frances Smith. "The Line Converges Here." Rev. of *The Peacock Poems*. *Callaloo* 5 (February 1979): 151–52.
Griffin, Farah Jasmine. "Textual Healing: Claiming Black Women's Bodies, the Erotic and Resistance in Contemporary Novels of Slavery." *Callaloo* 19.2 (1996): 519–36.
McDowell, Deborah E. "Negotiating between Tenses: Witnessing Slavery after Freedom—*Dessa Rose*." In *Slavery and the Literary Imagination*, edited by Deborah E. McDowell and Arnold Rampersad. Baltimore: Johns Hopkins University Press, 1989.
Mitchell, Angelyn. *The Freedom to Remember: Narrative, Slavery, and Gender in Contemporary Black Women's Fiction*. New Brunswick, NJ: Rutgers University Press, 2002.
Rushdy, Ashraf H. A. "Reading Mammy: The Subject of Relation in Sherley Anne Williams' *Dessa Rose*." *African American Review* 27.3 (1993): 365–89.

Gretchen Michlitsch

HARRIET E. WILSON (1828?–1863?)

BIOGRAPHICAL NARRATIVE

Very little is known about the life of Harriet E. Wilson, the first African American female novelist and author of *Our Nig; or, Sketches from the Life of a Free Black*. After its first printing in 1859, the novel and its author disappeared from American literary consciousness. In 1983, Henry Louis Gates, Jr., reintroduced Wilson and her text to American readers. Three letters included in the original appendix of *Our Nig* provide some biographical details about Wilson. The text of *Our Nig* can also be mined for information on Wilson. However, scholars emphasize that the novel cannot be read as purely autobiographical.

Gates determined that the author of *Our Nig* was a black woman named Harriet E. Wilson. She was born Harriet Adams near the town of Milford, New Hampshire, around 1828. She was subsequently abandoned by her mother and indentured in the home of a white family until her eighteenth birthday. David A. Curtis provides two sources that confirm Wilson's birth date and location: the 1850 federal census for the state of New Hampshire, and the marriage record of Harriet Adams and Thomas Wilson, dated 1851. Barbara A. White discovered the identity of the family to which the child Harriet Adams was indentured: the family of Nehemiah Hayward. Wilson worked as a slave for the Hayward family, and she was often physically and mentally abused. According to the novel, from the age of six, the narrator worked for Mrs. "Bellmont" as a field hand and house servant. She was often whipped at her mistress's whim. White asserts, "Documentary evidence regarding the Haywards shows that many of Wilson's stories in *Our Nig* are literally true" (ix). Ironically, the Hayward family had strong connections to the abolitionist movement. According to the novel, the letters of the appendix, and historical information uncovered by White, Wilson's descriptions of the abuse she endured in the Hayward home can be believed. Wilson managed to survive until her eighteenth year, but her health had been severely damaged by the hard life she had lived.

After she escaped the Haywards, Wilson found work in the home of a local family in Milford, whose identity is not yet ascertained. The 1850 Milford town records list Wilson among the poor supported by the town during the previous year. The 1850 federal census states that Wilson was a resident of the Boyles family and that she was twenty-two years old. Wilson soon moved to a town in Massachusetts to find work. "Allida" writes in her letter in the appendix that the town's name begins with a "W" and that it had a straw hat industry. According to "Allida," Wilson lived in the home of a Mrs. Walker and earned her room and board as a straw-sewer. Shortly after her arrival in Massachusetts, Wilson met a black man named Thomas Wilson, who claimed to be a former slave and lectured to abolitionist groups. They married in 1851 in Milford, according to the town's marriage records. A few months later, shortly before the birth of their son, Thomas abandoned his wife. Wilson's son George was born in May or June of 1852 in the county poorhouse. After George's birth, Thomas returned for a short while, but then abandoned his family again for good. Unable to support her son in Milford,

Wilson left George first in the poorhouse, then in a foster home with a white famly. According to the letters of "Allida" and "Margaretta Thorn," this new foster family treated George well. The 1855 and 1856 Milford town records indicate that Wilson again was supported by the town the years prior.

Wilson moved to Boston in 1855 or 1856. The Boston city directory lists a Harriet Wilson, widow, living in the city from 1856 to 1863. Wilson published *Our Nig* in 1859 in Boston. She states in her preface that she undertook the project to raise money to support her child. According to his death certificate, George died on February 15, 1860, within six months of the publication of *Our Nig*. He was seven years, eight months old. Harriet Wilson disappears from official records in 1863.

MAJOR WORKS

Harriet E. Wilson self-published *Our Nig* anonymously in 1859, through the Boston publishing company George C. Rand and Avery. Scholars believe this initial printing was the only edition of the novel before its first modern printing. The 1983 edition is accompanied by a long introduction by Henry Louis Gates, Jr. His 1983 research has been supplemented over the years, and has yielded another edition in 2002. These modern printings contain facsimiles of the original 1859 edition. The facsimile includes the preface, written by Wilson, and the appendix containing three letters in support of Wilson's project. The novel's title page reads: "*Our Nig; or, Sketches from the Life of a free Black, in a two-story white house, North. Showing that Slavery's Shadows Fall Even There. By 'Our Nig.'*" The page prior to the title page indicates that a Mrs. H. E. Wilson entered the copyright for the novel at the District Court of Massachusetts.

Our Nig is the narrative of the life of Alfrado, a free black woman living in New Hampshire. It begins with the marriage of the heroine's parents and ends with the birth of her own child and subsequent abandonment by her husband. The narrative is told primarily in the third person, removing it from the traditional autobiography genre. Yet its *semiautobiographical* nature is attested by the author in the preface and by the three letter writers in the appendix.

From the very start, *Our Nig* is highly complex. The novel opens with the marriage of Alfrado's mother Mag, a white woman, to Jim, a black man. Theirs is not a marriage of love, but rather a business transaction. Jim wants a white wife, as whiteness is valuable property in the economy of the novel. In return, he provides Mag a home and food, saving her from poverty. In its portrayal of an ordinary marriage that happens to be interracial, Wilson's novel is radical. After the birth of a few children, Jim dies. Mag forms a relationship with another man, Seth, although they do not marry. Unable to support the children, they leave six-year-old Alfrado at the home of a neighbor family, the Bellmonts.

From the age of six to the age of eighteen, Alfrado, or Frado, works as an indentured servant in the Bellmont home. She is abused physically and mentally by Mrs. Bellmont and her youngest child, Mary. Mrs. Bellmont works Frado like a slave. Frado does all of the household labor and helps with the farm labor as well. Mrs. Bellmont brutally punishes Frado, and the author describes these punishments in awful detail. Mrs. Bellmont whips Frado with a rawhide, gags her with rags and pieces of wood, starves her, and locks her in closets. Other members of the Bellmont family try to protect Frado: Mr. Bellmont, his maiden sister Abby, and other Bellmont children. They are unsuccessful, though, and Frado lives in misery until she turns eighteen.

After Frado leaves the Bellmonts, she takes a position in the home of Mrs. Moore as a seamstress. Mrs. Moore is kind to Frado, but soon Frado's health begins to fail her. She becomes an invalid as a result of the difficult labor she performed since early childhood. She works some, then returns to the Bellmont home when she is struck by illness. She recovers, finds work, but again becomes ill. She is taken in by a woman who is paid by the town to care for invalids. Frado then travels to Massachusetts to a town where "girls make straw bonnets" (124). She finds a job and starts a pleasant life. In the final chapter of the book, Frado meets Samuel, the man she marries. He claims to be a fugitive slave and makes a living giving speeches about slavery on the abolitionist circuit, but it turns out he never was a slave at all. Frado and Samuel return to her home town to marry, and then Samuel abandons his pregnant wife. She puts herself on the charity of the town and bears her child. Her husband then returns for a short while, but soon leaves her again. He meets his death by yellow fever in New Orleans. The book ends with the narrator reiterating that Frado seeks the reader's support: "Reposing in God, she has thus far journeyed securely. Still an invalid, she asks your sympathy, gentle reader" (130).

A major theme of this text is the power of speech: who has it, and who controls it in others. In one scene, Mrs. Bellmont believes that Frado has told others about her cruelty, and punishes Frado for speaking out. She forces a piece of wood into Frado's mouth, symbolically and literally silencing her, and then whips her. Mrs. Bellmont tells Frado that she intends to "cure her of tale-bearing" (93). Mrs. Bellmont recognizes that Frado's only power lies in her ability to tell others of Mrs. Bellmont's horrid behavior and therefore seeks to control Frado's speech. In another scene, Mrs. Bellmont tells Frado not to pray, because "prayer was for whites, not for blacks" (94). Frado is not even allowed to ask her God for assistance. Frado's moment of rebellion against Mrs. Bellmont finally comes in chapter ten. Mrs. Bellmont lifts a stick to strike Frado, and Frado yells, "Stop!" (105). She warns Mrs. Bellmont, "Strike me and I'll never work a mite more for you" (105). Frado realizes that "she had a power to ward of assaults." This power consists solely of her voice: she never makes a move to strike Mrs. Bellmont in return. She performs a vocal, not physical, rebellion.

CRITICAL RECEPTION

Our Nig was not well received at the time of its publication. White abolitionists comprised the primary audience of the work of African American authors. Indeed, slave narratives were tools of the abolitionist movement to persuade other northern whites to support the cause. Wilson's narrative resembles a slave narrative in form, but differs in one significant respect: the "slaveowner" in *Our Nig* is a northern white woman. Furthermore, it is now known that her real-life counterpart had ties to the abolitionist movement. Thus, Wilson seems to have deliberately alienated her readership. Eric Gardner has done excellent research on the publication history of *Our Nig*. He writes: "My research . . . suggests not only that abolitionists knew about the book but that they may have consciously chosen *not* to publicize it" (227). Wilson seems to have been aware of the consequences of her actions. In the preface to the novel, she writes that her northern mistress was "imbued with *southern* principles," an apparent attempt to win northern readers. And, in the last paragraph of the preface, Wilson appeals to her "colored brethren" to support her, perhaps anticipating rejection of her text by white people. However, Gardner has discovered that although "Wilson clearly addresses a black readership in her preface, this readership may never have been reached by the original edition of *Our Nig*" (227). Gardner continues, "[I]t appears that it instead attracted primarily white, middle-class readers who lived close to Wilson's home in Milford, New Hampshire" (227–28). According to Gardner, it is probable that Wilson distributed the book herself to her friends and neighbors in Milford.

In her novel, Wilson radically combines the two prevailing genres available to her in the 1850s: the woman's sentimental novel and the slave narrative. Gates writes, "By this act of formal revision [of the white woman's novel], she *created* the black woman's novel" (xlvi, emphasis in original). In her essay, "Excavating Genre in *Our Nig*," Julia Stern observes that "*Our Nig* marks a transitional moment in the history of American women's narrative" (439). She continues: "[W]hile the novel's sentimental frame attempts to function as a structure of containment, it cannot quite suppress, and indeed underscores, the gothic protest seething beneath the narrative's surface" (439). Furthermore, Wilson's novel "raises important questions about what Gates has called 'the innocence of the mother-daughter relationship'" (440). Thus, *Our Nig* should be considered radical, in both a literary and political sense.

BIBLIOGRAPHY

Work by Harriet E. Wilson

Wilson, Harriet E. *Our Nig; or, Sketches from the Life of a Free Black.* 3rd ed. Edited by and Introduction by Henry Louis Gates, Jr. New York: Vintage, 2002.

Studies of Harriet E. Wilson's Work

Ellis, R. J. *Harriet Wilson's* Our Nig: *A Cultural Biography of a "Two-Story" African Novel.* Kenilworth, NJ: Rodopi, 2003.
Ernest, John. "Economics of Identity: Harriet E. Wilson's *Our Nig*." *PMLA* 109 (1994): 424–38.
Gardner, Eric. "'This Attempt of Their Sister': Harriet Wilson's *Our Nig* from Printer to Readers." *New England Quarterly* 66 (1993): 226–46.
Gates, Henry Louis, Jr., and David Ames Curtis. "Establishing the Identity of the Author of *Our Nig*." In *Wild Women in the Whirlwind: Afra-American Culture and the Contemporary Literary Renaissance*, edited by Joanne M. Braxton and Andree Nicola McLaughlin. New Brunswick, NJ: Rutgers University Press, 1990.
Leveen, Lois. "Dwelling in the House of Oppression: The Spatial, Racial, and Textual Dynamics of Harriet Wilson's *Our Nig*." *African American Review* 35.4 (2001): 561–80.
Stern, Julia. "Excavating Genre in *Our Nig*." *American Literature* 67.3 (1995): 439–66.
White, Barbara A. "*Our Nig* and the She-Devil: New Information about Harriet Wilson and the 'Bellmont' Family." *American Literature* 65.1 (1993): 19–52.

Katie Rose Guest

SARAH ELIZABETH WRIGHT (1928–?)

BIOGRAPHICAL NARRATIVE

Born on December 9, 1928, to Mary Amelia Moore and Willis Charles Wright, poet and novelist Sarah Elizabeth Wright grew up one of nine children in Wetipquin, Maryland. Wright's parents raised their nine children with love, care, and dignity, although their lives were often a struggle. In addition to overseeing her children's education, Wright's mother worked on the family's farm and in a local factory; her father was an oysterman, a farmer, and a barber. Their example of hard work and care, laborers outside and inside the home, stayed with Wright and appear as major themes in her writing.

Encouraged by teachers and the school librarian, Wright began writing poetry during her early elementary school years. At age sixteen, she left home to enter Howard University to study under the tutelage of poet Sterling Brown. While there she added to her writing experience by working as a contributing editor/reporter at the *49er*, the *Hilltop*, and the *Stylus*, developing her understanding of the symbiotic relationship between writing and society, particularly as writing affects the lives of African Americans and their search for a positive self-identity. It was at this point that she began a lifelong involvement in social activism. At Howard, Wright also had the opportunity to meet Langston Hughes, who once wrote a poem in her honor and remained a mentor until his death.

Wright moved to Philadelphia in 1949, leaving Howard without graduating. She found a job at a small publishing/printing firm owned by the Kraft family. Her interest in social issues and injustice is reflected in her poetry of this time, as seen in the volume titled *Give Me a Child*, which she published with Lucy Smith in 1955. In 1957, she moved to New York, where she worked with Maya Angelou, Abbey Lincoln, and Rosa Guy to found the Cultural Association for Women of African Heritage. The association's purpose was to promote and affirm black women's natural beauty—Wright herself had abandoned the practice of straightening her hair and conforming to white standards of beauty while attending Howard. The movement for social justice for African Americans frequently meant black men sought to increase their power by making attacks on black women. Wright sought to balance gender inequities and create positive role models for black women as she believed black women's self-respect was a prerequisite for race reform. During this time, Wright also joined the Harlem Writer's Guild and turned her attention to fiction. The result is her novel *This Child's Gonna Live*, published in 1969, in which she shows how racism and sexism are interconnected and come from the same source.

In the final years of the twentieth century, Wright continued to write poetry and articles, to argue for a black power movement grounded in gender equity. Wright is currently working on a sequel to her novel with the working title *Twelve Gates to the City, Hallelujah! Hallelujah!*

Wright married Joseph Kay in 1959. They have two children, Michael Wright and Shelly Wright Chotai. The couple lives in Manhattan.

MAJOR WORKS

Wright's goal in her writing is to define and reclaim the "black experience" from the myths and misconceptions perpetuated by the media. Social injustice toward black Americans and the gender inequities suffered by black women are the major themes in her work. Because of the positive influence of her parents, her work also shows an optimistic bias that equity is a possibility if people work together. Wright utilizes poetry, fiction, and nonfiction to get her message across.

Wright's first love is poetry, and her interest in social activism informs *Give Me a Child* (1955), which was cowritten with Lucy Smith. The poems encompass the daily lives of African Americans, the struggles in their lives dealing with injustice and violence in a society fighting for democracy abroad yet ignoring racial inequity at home. Yet, her poems have a sense of optimism and pride in race and their abilities and accomplishments.

This Child's Gonna Live (1969) is set in a small harbor town called Tangierneck, where the African American residents struggle to raise their children and improve their futures for their families while fighting a culture of poverty, racism, and sexism. One of the remarkable aspects of the novel is the blending of African and American spiritual beliefs in Mariah's (the main character) religion. The novel is told in third person, primarily from Mariah's perspective, although several chapters are from the main male character, Jacob's, perspective. The double perspective allows for an inclusiveness that is missing in most novels. Wright's aim is to reveal the gendered and economic history of her characters while she exposes the economic, racial, and sexual oppression of the surrounding white society.

A. Philip Randolph: Integration in the Workplace is a nonfiction account of the life of Asa Philip Randolph. The article is a continuation of her dialogue on African American culture.

CRITICAL RECEPTION

Although Wright does not have a large body of work, her literary endeavors have been well received and she is a respected member of the literary community. She is considered a voice of the Harlem Renaissance as well as a contemporary voice portraying the black experience.

Much of Wright's recognition is for her novel. *This Child's Gonna Live* has been in print continuously from the time of its publication. Some reviewers writing when the novel was first published found it to be a "local color" story and the heroine to be poor and desperate, but reviewers such as John Killens and Henry Du Bois praised Wright for the depth and complexity of her narrative and her portrayal of the black experience in a white, racist and sexist society. In a critical analysis of the novel written in 1997, Jennifer Campbell writes that the novel endures for current audiences because Wright "shows how subtly entwined are racism and sexism, and how both are deployed in the service of capitalism by monied white men who stand to benefit." The strengths that made the novel "the most important book of 1969" (*New York Times*, June 29, 1970) are the strengths that critics see in the novel today, issues that society still faces today.

Wright has received several literary honors for her work, including an award from the American Women Writers of Color in 1997; a plaque from the Harlem Writer's

Guild, honoring the thirty years of continuous sales of her novel, in 1998; and the Zora Neale Hurston Award for Literary Excellence in 1999.

BIBLIOGRAPHY

Works by Sarah Elizabeth Wright

A. Phillip Randolph: Integration in the Workplace. Englewood Cliffs, NJ: Silver Burdett Press, 1990.
"Black Writers' Views of America." *Freedomways* 19.3 (1979): 161–62.
Give Me a Child. With Lucy Smith. Philadelphia: Kraft, 1955.
"I Have Known Death." *Tomorrow* 10 (November 3, 1950): 46.
"Lament of a Harlem Mother." American Pen 4 (Spring 1972): 23–27.
"*Lorraine Hansberry* on Film." *Freedomways* 19.4 (1979): 283–84.
"Lower East Side: A Rebirth of World Vision." *African American Review* 27 (1993): 593–96.
"The Negro Woman in American Literature." *Freedomways* 6 (1966): 8–10.
"The Responsibility of the Writer as Participant in the World Community." *Zora Neale Hurston Forum* 3.1 (1988): 35–39.
"Roadblocks to the Development of the Negro Writer." In *The American Negro Writer and His Roots.* New York: American Society of African Culture, 1960.
This Child's Gonna Live. New York: Delacorte, 1969.
"Until They Have Stopped." *Freedomways* 5.3 (1965): 378.
"Urgency." In *Beyond the Blue,* edited by Rosey E. Pool. Detroit, MI: Broadside Press, 1971.
"Window Pictures." In *Beyond the Blue,* edited by Rosey E. Pool. Detroit, MI: Broadside Press, 1971.

Studies of Sarah Elizabeth Wright's Works

Campbell, Jennifer. "'It's a Time in the Land': Gendering Black Power and Sarah E. Wright's Place in the Tradition of Black Women's Writing." *African American Review* 31.2 (1997): 211–26.
Guilford, Virginia B. "Sarah Elizabeth Wright." In *Dictionary of Literary Biography,* 33: 293–300. Ann Arbor, MI: Gale, 1984.
Killens, John O. "An Appreciation." In *This Child's Gonna Live,* edited by Sarah Elizabeth Wright, 277–78, 282. New York: Delacorte, 1969.
White, Linda M. "Sarah Elizabeth Wright." In *Contemporary African American Novelists,* edited by Emmanuel S. Nelson, 500–504. Westport, CT: Greenwood Press, 1999.

Althea Rhodes

SHAY YOUNGBLOOD (1959–)

BIOGRAPHICAL NARRATIVE

Born in Columbus, Georgia, in 1959, Shay Youngblood was educated at Clark College (now Clark-Atlanta University) in Georgia, where she received her B.A. in mass communications in 1981. Youngblood was raised communally after her mother died in the early sixties. At the time she did not appreciate the experience, but now feels that she actually grew up in a very rich world. She gleaned stories from women and men with advice as various as "You catch more flies with honey," and "You punch them before they punch you!" Youngblood says these different voices, from her family and other "big mamas" in her community, helped her figure out how to shape herself as a young woman in the world. Youngblood says she learned

to be very, very quiet . . . if I wanted to get the good stories. But as they got older and I got older . . . I would ask them to tell me their stories. And they would say, "Aww, nobody wanna hear about all that!" But I'd say, "Well I think it's important." So in a way I wrote out of sense of wanting to give them a voice. Because I thought they had done an incredible job raising me, this whole community of people raising me, both men and women, and I wanted to tell their stories. (Jake-ann Jones)

According to Youngblood, she always loved words and after college wrote her first published story in the *Dominican Republic*, where she served as an agriculture information officer for the Peace Corps. The story, titled "In a House of Wooden Monkeys," was published in an anthology of African American fiction edited by Gloria Naylor. After several years of taking odd jobs to support herself while she wrote, Youngblood landed a contract to publish her first book, *The Big Mama Stories*. It came together fortuitously. She met Nancy Bereano, the publisher of Firebrand Books at a conference, and Bereano expressed interest in Youngblood's writing and asked her to send a manuscript when she felt she was ready. Youngblood worked on the stories for three months and sent off the manuscript. Two weeks later, she had a contract. Firebrand Books published *Big Mama Stories* in 1989. While she was working on the book manuscript, she adapted the material into a play, *Shakin' the Mess Outta Misery*. Horizon Studios in Atlanta had told her she had a gift for dialogue and they would be interested in producing a play if she ever wrote one. *Shakin' the Mess* opened at Horizon in 1988, directed by Glenda Dickerson. Writing the play also provided Youngblood with the last story in *Big Mama Stories*: "They Tell Me, Now I Know," in which the narrator is named as a rite of passage.

After this very successful period, Youngblood was in and out of artists' retreats and still working odd jobs. Then a friend recommended that she apply to Brown University's M.F.A. program to study playwriting with Paula Vogel. Youngblood says Vogel kept her fed with inspiration and confidence that allowed her to see her possibilities. She received her M.F.A. in creative writing in 1993, and by then she had already seen two of her plays produced.

Youngblood has won a number of awards. She won a Pushcart Prize for "Born with Religion" in *Big Mama Stories*; an NAACP Theatre Award in 1991 for *Shakin' the Mess Outta Misery*; a Lorraine Hansberry Playwriting Award in 1993 for *Talking Bones*; and a Paul Green Foundation National Theatre Award for *Square Blues* in 1993.

Youngblood believes part of her responsibility is to pass on the love she received from her "big mamas," so she encourages young writers to commit to their work and take themselves seriously as writers, to read and then go write the books they want to read. Part of Youngblood's giving back is in her teaching, which she has done in places ranging from the Rhode Island Adult Correctional Institution for Women to Brown University. She has also taught at the Syracuse Community Writers Project and at the New School for Social Research in New York.

MAJOR WORKS

By her own account, Shay Youngblood grew up obsessed with words, a passion that is reflected in her novels. Mariah Santos, the protagonist of *Soul Kiss*, eats words—not only because they bring her closer to her mother, but also because they taste delicious to her. She reads the dictionary and caresses the words on her tongue. She plants scraps of paper with words written on them and hopes they will grow. Mariah comes from an uncertain childhood, in which she was raised with the absolute (and sometimes boundary-crossing) love of her mother, who taught her how to see beauty in the world, who tucked words into her lunch bag, and who shared soul kisses with her every day. Then Mariah's mother begins to mysteriously degenerate, losing interest in the world and even in her daughter. Only later will Mariah recognize these as effects of heartbreak and drug addiction. Mariah and her mother take a trip on a Greyhound bus from their home in Manhattan, Kansas, to visit her mother's aunts Faith and Merleen in Columbus, Georgia. Mariah's mother leaves and Mariah ends up staying with Faith and Merleen for seven years. Much of *Soul Kiss* is Mariah's attempt to come to terms with her mother's absence, her father's absence, and her own growth into womanhood against the backdrop of the civil-rights-strained sixties. Mariah's burgeoning creativity leads her into experiments with her own erotic feelings, and her loneliness keeps her constantly looking for love.

Mariah thinks she has found the solution to the missing love in her life when her father agrees to let her live with him in Los Angeles. Mariah and her father try to make their family work, but they both miss her mother, and Mariah's resemblance to her mother and her own incipient longing for erotic fulfillment make the union tricky to navigate. In *Soul Kiss*, Shay Youngblood deals with issues that she will continue to evocatively limn in *Black Girl in Paris* and that she began sorting out in *Big Mama Stories*—What kinds of love are there? How much love is enough? How are creativity and imagination helpful and harmful to a young woman? Creativity seems at times to betray Mariah, making her invest in things that those with less giving imaginations would steer clear of. Finally, the novel deals with the value and weight of innocence.

Youngblood writes about the world in a knowing and clever way that has sometimes struck critics as slightly too knowing for her often young protagonists. From *Big Mama Stories*: "One Sunday Maggie got saved. During the call to sinners she walked that slow, sexy, smelling-the-roses walk of hers right up to the preacher, looked him dead in the eye, and shouted, 'Save me!' Then she leaned into Reverend Waters arms like a fallen angel" (86). Youngblood's language delights and the observations of the small town's wide cast of characters draw the reader into the world that Rita (more often referred to as Chile or Daughter in the book) inhabits.

Rita, like Mariah, Eden in *Black Girl in Paris*, and Youngblood herself, is an effective orphan, but is raised by a cast of women who teach her the intricacies of the world. Their stories contain love as well as a warning of boundaries. In the story "Snuff Dippers," Big Mama tells Rita about the maids' bus that drove the route from the poor side of town, where it picked up the African American maids—of which Big Mama and her friend Miss Emma Lou were two—and took them to work in the wealthy suburbs. Youngblood handles this story in a masterful and poignant manner. Big Mama and Miss Emma Lou ride the bus and Emma Lou chews tobacco. She has forgotten her snuff cup and so she spits tobacco juice out the window. It lands on a white couple in a convertible. Up to this point, Youngblood through Big Mama has made the story a light comedy, mildly embittered by its contact with the reality of racially based division and economic disadvantage. But then Youngblood moves the tale into nightmarish humiliation as the driver of the convertible makes the bus pull over and has each of the grown women line up by the side of the road so the man can spit in their faces one by one. Youngblood relieves the horror of this injustice and humiliation by having the man's convertible battered by a truck as he pulls back onto the highway, but the reader feels changed along with Rita by this revelation of cruelty. This is Youngblood's art, to bend a deceptively simple story into a multilayered commentary on injustice and power.

In *Black Girl in Paris*, Youngblood deals with similar issues but with an older narrator. Eden is a young woman who wants to be a writer and dreams of going to Paris to join the ranks of the great African American writers who flourished there. But the Paris that she finds is troubled by terrorism, poverty, and racism. Eden is the protagonist with the most advanced years in Youngblood's work to date, and her differences from Mariah are telling. She, too, is looking for family, but she takes Mariah's search one step further by looking for a made family, a family of words—those who produce them, like her idol and patron saint, James Baldwin, and the words that she hopes to illuminate her own world with. She goes to Paris with little money and many romantic hopes for what her stay there will bring. Eden must work her way through the reality of Paris, which for her means fear that she or one of her new friends will be dismembered or killed by the bombs planted on buses and in squares in protest of France's racist practices. Paris for Eden also means low-paying and sometimes humiliating jobs as an artist's model, poet's helper, and nanny, and when these jobs are depleted, hunger. Eden must also work out her own trades in love. She barters sex for street education in her alliance with Indego, an older African American poet who lives by his wits and understanding of Paris's back ways. She explores sympathy and fascination with Ving, a white saxophone player with whom she must try to answer the question of how much their skins matter, and she finds a surprising sense of home at her lowest moment in the company of Luce, a girl like herself, on the edge of giving in to poverty. It seems that if Eden can overcome these things she can overcome anything, and earn the right to write the words that will shape her life.

Youngblood's writing is sexually frank and intimately rendered. She explores various kinds of longing, including that between parents and children. But this probing is in the service of a deep kind of honesty that her characters hope will help them to shake off the chains of the world they have been delivered into in exchange for the keys to a world they can make for themselves. Youngblood's novels and plays are essential contributions to the literature of African American female awakening and are sensitive to the challenges of consciousness and creativity. For Youngblood, imagination is always a hard road well-traveled, one that leads through its pitfalls to a better understanding of the self and the forces of the world.

CRITICAL RECEPTION

Critics largely praise *Soul Kiss* as a searing and poetic novel; it was named as an alternate selection for the Book of the Month Club, as a finalist for the Lambda Literary Award, and was included in Barnes & Noble's Discover New Writers series. Some critics, however, find its subject matter unpleasant and claim that the novel borders on the pornographic. Critics call *Black Girl in Paris* "stirring and engaging"; it, too, has received largely positive reviews, though some complain that the plot is episodic and that the language at times is almost too insular. Several critics have made the mistake of reading Youngblood's sometimes difficult characters as entirely autobiographical. Youngblood denies this claim, saying that though the emotions are real, the situations are entirely created. It is a tribute to her talent that her intimacy with the characters' inner lives can seem so effortless. Critics often point out Youngblood's ear for poetry and her fresh and interesting dialogue. Her talent for dialogue led her into playwriting, and though her plays receive mixed reviews—some rejoice in their ability to speak their own language, others feel that they do not break new enough ground—critics and audiences alike seem eager to hear more from Shay Youngblood.

BIBLIOGRAPHY

Works by Shay Youngblood

Amazing Grace. Woodstock, IL: Dramatic Publishing Company, 1993.
Big Mama Stories. Ithaca, NY: Firebrand Books, 1989.
Black Girl in Paris. New York: Riverhead Books, 2000.
Black Power Barbie in Hotel de Dream. 1992. Unpublished.
Communism Killed My Dog. 1991. Unpublished.
"In a House of Wooden Monkeys." In *Snapshots: 20th Century Mother-Daughter Fiction*, edited by Joyce Carol Oates, et al. Boston: David R. Godine Publisher, 2000.
Shakin' the Mess Outta Misery. Woodstock, IL: Dramatic Publishing Company, 1993.
Soul Kiss. New York: Riverhead Books, 1997.
Square Blues. 1992. Unpublished.
Talking Bones. Woodstock, IL: Dramatic Publishing Company, 1993.

Studies of Shay Youngblood's Works

Coyne, John. "Talking with Shay Youngblood." April 2005. http://www.peacecorpswriters.org/pages/2000/0007/prntvers007/pv007talkyngbld.html (accessed April 2005).
Jones, Daniel Alexander. "Shay Youngblood Flying Solo (Interview)." *Lambda Book Report* 8.7 (February 2000): 15.
Jones, Jake-ann. "Interview with Shay Youngblood." April 2005. http://www.brown.edu/Departments/Literary_Arts/youngblood.html (accessed April 2005).

Jones, Joni L. "Conjuring as Radical Re/Membering in the Works of *Shay Youngblood*." In *Black Theatre: Ritual Performance in the African* Diaspora, edited by Paul Carter Harrison, Victor Leo walker, and Gus Edwards, 227–35. Philadelphia: Temple University Press, 2002.
Waugh, Debra Wiggin. "Delicious, Forbidden: An interview with Shay Youngblood. (Interview)." *Lambda Book Report* 6.2 (September 1997): 1(3).

Samira C. Franklin

APPENDIX: LIST OF AWARDS AND AUTHORS

Academy of Arts and Letters Award
Shirley Graham DuBois

Agatha Award
Barbara Neely

**Alain Locke-Gwendolyn Brooks
Award for Excellence in Literature**
Mari Evans

**American Academy of Arts and
Letters Award**
Adrienne Kennedy
Toni Morrison

American Book Award
J. California Cooper
Edwidge Danticat
Adrienne Kennedy
Audre Geraldine Lorde
Paule Marshall
Colleen J. McElroy
Gloria Naylor
Brenda Marie Osbey
Jewell Parker Rhodes
Sonia Sanchez

American Library Association Award
Doris Jean Austin

**American Library Notable Book
Citation**
Eloise Greenfield

American Writers of Color Award
Sarah Elizabeth Wright

Anisfeld-Wolf Award
Toi Derricotte
Shirley Graham DuBois
Jamaica Kincaid

Art Book for Children Award
Alexis De Veaux

Art Seidenbaum Award
Carolyn Ferrell

**Associated Writing Program
Poetry Award**
Brenda Marie Osbey

Audelco Award
Pearl T. Cleage
Kathleen Conwell Collins
Patricia Joann Gibson

Barbara Deming Award
Jewelle Gomez

Barnes and Noble Writers Award
Marita Golden
Terry McMillan

Beard's Fund Award
Jewelle Gomez

**Best Books for Young Adults Award
(American Library Association)**
Brenda Wilkinson

**Black Caucus of the American Library
Association Award**
Grace Edwards-Yearwood
Helene Elaine Lee
Jewell Parker Rhodes

Black Playwright of the Year Award
J. California Cooper

Boston Globe-Horn Book Award
Patricia McKissack
Mildred D. Taylor

**Boston Globe-Horn Book Honor
Book**
Sharon Bell Mathis

Bronze Jubilee Award
Pearl T. Cleage

Caldecott Honor Book
Sherley Anne Williams

CAPS Award for Fiction
Sarah Elizabeth Wright

Carl Sandburg Award
Barbara Chase-Riboud
Rita Dove

Carter G. Woodson Book Award
Eloise Greenfield

Children's Book Award (African Studies Association)
Joyce Hansen

Conrad Kent Rivers Memorial Award
Julia Fields
Mae Jackson
Carolyn Marie Rodgers

Coretta Scott King Award
Candy Boyd (Marguerite Dawson)
Alexis De Veaux
Eloise Greenfield
Rosa Guy
Joyce Hansen
Sharon Bell Mathis
Patricia McKissack
Mildred D. Taylor
Joyce Carol Thomas
Mildred Pitts Walter

Coretta Scott King Honor Book
Sherley Anne Williams

DeWitt Wallace/Reader's Digest Fellowship Award
Doris Jean Austin

Distinguished Pioneering of the Arts Award
Toi Derricotte

Doris Abramson Playwrighting Award
Aishah Rahman

Dudley Randall Award for National Contributions to Literature
Toi Derricotte

Edgar Allen Poe Award
Virginia Hamilton

Emmy Award
Lucille Clifton
Wanda Coleman
Sherley Anne Williams

Fannie Lou Hamer Award
Alexis De Veaux
Safiya Holmes-Henderson

Fisk Fiction Award (Boston Book Review)
Jamaica Kincaid

Folger Shakespeare Library Poetry Award
Toi Derricotte

Ford Fellowship
Jewelle Gomez
Margaret Walker

Frances Steloff Award for Fiction
Gayl Jones

Free Spirit Award
Alice Randall

Fulbright Fellowship
Colleen J. McElroy
Margaret Walker

Gay Caucus Book of the Year Award (American Library Association)
Audre Geraldine Lorde

Golden Pen Award for Best Short Story Collection
Lisa Teasley

Golden Plate Award
Rita Dove

Guggenheim Fellowship
Wanda Coleman
Toi Derricotte
Adrienne Kennedy
Nella Larsen
Paule Marshall
Gloria Naylor
Ntozake Shange
Alice Walker
Paulette Childress White

Gwendolyn Brooks Award for Fiction
Eugenia W. Collier

Gwendolyn Brooks Center Award
Barbara T. Christian

Gwendolyn Brooks Poetry Award
Ellease Southerland

Hans Christian Anderson Award
Virginia Hamilton

Harmon Award
Nella Larsen

Harriet Tubman Award
Doris Davenport

Horatio Alger Award
Maya Angelou

Hugo Award
Octavia Butler

James Baldwin Writing Award
J. California Cooper

Janet Heidinger Kafka Prize
Barbara Chase-Riboud

Jean Stein Award
Andrea Lee

John Dos Passos Award for Literature
Paule Marshall

John Golden Award for Fiction
Ellease Southerland

Julian Messner Award
Shirley Graham DuBois

Lambda Literary Award for Lesbian Fiction
Jewelle Gomez

Langston Hughes Award
Elaine Jackson

Lavan Younger Poets Award
Rita Dove

Leila-Wallace Reader's Digest Award
Suzan-Lori Parks

Lenore Marshall Poetry Prize
Wanda Coleman

Lifetime Achievement Award (National Black Writers Conference)
June Jordan

Lifetime Achievement Award for Excellence in the Arts
Margaret Walker

Lillian Smith Award
Pauli Murray
Gloria Naylor
Dori Sanders
Alice Walker

Literary Lion Award
J. California Cooper

Loring-Williams Prize (Academy of American Poets)
Brenda Marie Osbey

Lorraine Hansberry Playwrighting Award
Alexis De Veaux
Shay Youngblood

Louise Patterson African American Studies Award
Barbara T. Christian

Lucille Medwick Memorial Award
Toi Derricotte

Lucretia Mott Award
Sonia Sanchez

MacArthur "Genius" Award
Virginia Hamilton
Paule Marshall
Suzan-Lori Parks

McCavity Award
Barbara Neely

MLA Melus Award
Barbara T. Christian

Moonstone Black Writing Celebration Lifetime Achievement Award
Kristin Hunter Lattany

Morton Dauwen Zabel Award
Jamaica Kincaid

NAACP Image Award
Pinkie Gordon Lane

NAACP Theatre Award
Shay Youngblood

National Association of Black Journalists Award
June Jordan

National Award for Achievement (College Language Association)
Pinkie Gordon Lane

National Book Award
Lucille Clifton
Virginia Hamilton
Joyce Carol Thomas
Alice Walker

National Book Critics Circle Award
Toni Morrison

National Endowment for the Arts Award in Fiction
Jewell Parker Rhodes

National Endowment for the Arts Creative Writing Award
Mari Evans

National Endowment for the Arts Fellowship
Wanda Coleman
Toi Derricotte
Elaine Jackson
Colleen J. McElroy
Terry McMillan
Gloria Naylor
Brenda Marie Osbey
Ntozake Shange
Paulette Childress White

National Institute of Arts Award
Paule Marshall

Nebula Award
Octavia Butler

Newbery Honor
Virginia Hamilton

Newbery Medal
Virginia Hamilton
Mildred D. Taylor

New York Daily News Blue Fiction Prize
Dorothy West

New York Drama Critics Award
Lorraine Hansberry

New York Times Book Review Outstanding Children's Book of the Year Award
Brenda Wilkinson

New York Times Most Promising New Playwright Award
Suzan-Lori Parks

New York Times Notable Book of the Year
Tina McElroy Ansa
Connie Porter
Sherley Anne Williams

New York Times Outstanding Book of the Year Citation
Rosa Guy

Nobel Prize
Toni Morrison

Notable Book Award (American Library Association)
Rosa Guy
Sharon Bell Mathis

Obie Award
Maya Angelou
Alice Childress
Adrienne Kennedy
Ntozake Shange

Outer Circle Critics Award
Ntozake Shange

Pacificus Literary Foundation Best Short Story Writer Award
Lisa Teasley

Parent's Choice Award
Joyce Hansen

Paul Green Foundation National Theatre Award
Shay Youngblood

PEN/Faulkner Award
Paule Marshall

PEN-Laura Pels Award for Excellence in Playwrighting
Suzan-Lori Parks

PEN/Oakland Josephine Miles National Literary Award
Mary Monroe
Jewell Parker Rhodes
Mona Lisa Saloy

Pierre LeComite duNouy Foundation Award
Adrienne Kennedy

Ploughshares Zacharias Award
Carolyn Ferrell

Pulitzer Prize
Gwendolyn Brooks
Rita Dove
Toni Morrison
Alice Walker

Pushcart Prize
Toi Derricotte
Colleen J. McElroy
Shay Youngblood

Robert F. Kennedy Award
Toni Morrison

Rockefeller Fellowship
Elaine Jackson

June Jordan
Adrienne Kennedy
Opal J. Moore
Aishah Rahman

Rosenthal Award
Alice Walker

Rosenwald Fellowship
Margaret Walker

School Library Journal Best Children's Book Award
Brenda Wilkinson

Stanley W. Lindberg Award
Tina McElroy Ansa

The Story Prize
Edwidge Danticat

T.S. Eliot Prize
Mona Lisa Saloy

Walt Whitman Citation of Merit
Audre Geraldine Lorde

Whiting Writers' Award
Suzan-Lori Parks

William Carlos Williams Award
Safiya Holmes-Henderson

Yale Series for Young Poets Award
Margaret Walker

Zora Neale Hurston Award for Literary Excellence
Sarah Elizabeth Wright

BIBLIOGRAPHY OF WORKS

Andrews, William L., ed. *Classic African American Women's Narratives.* Oxford, England: Oxford University Press, 2003.

Bailey, Frankie Y. "Telling Our Stories: African-American Women Writers and the Mystery Genre." *Mystery Scene* 73 (2001): 14–17.

Baker, Houston A., Jr. "There Is No More Beautiful Way: Theory and the Poetics of Afro-American Women's Writing." In *Afro-American Literary Study in the 1990s*, edited by Houston A. Baker, Jr., and Patricia Redmond, 135–63. Chicago: University of Chicago Press, 1989.

———. *The Workings of the Spirit: The Poetics of Afro-American Women's Writing.* Chicago: University of Chicago Press, 1991.

Bassard, Katherine Clay. "Gender and Genre: Black Women's Autobiography and the Ideology of Literacy." *African American Review* 26, no. 1 (Spring1992): 119–29.

Bell, Roseann P., Beverly Guy-Sheftall, and Bettye J. Parker. *Sturdy Black Bridges: Visions of Black Women in Literature.* New York: Anchor Books, 1979.

Berlant, Lauren. "Cultural Struggle and Literary History: African-American Women's Writing." *Modern Philology: A Journal Devoted to Research in Medieval and Modern Literature* 88.1 (August 1990): 57–64.

Bollinger, Laurel. "'A Mother in the Deity': Maternity and Authority in the Nineteenth-Century African-American Spiritual Narrative." *Women's Studies: An Interdisciplinary Journal* 29.3 (June 2000): 357–82.

Braxton, Joanne M. *Black Women Writing Autobiography: A Tradition within a Tradition.* Philadelphia: Temple University Press, 1989.

Brown, Martha H. "African-American Women's Autobiography." In *Fissions and Fusions*, edited by Lesley Marx, Loes Nas, and Lara Dunwell, 32–40. Bellville, South Africa: University of the Western Cape, 1997.

Carby, Hazel V. "On the Threshold of Woman's Era: Lynching, Empire, and Sexuality in Black Feminist Theory." *Critical Inquiry* 12.1 (Autumn 1985): 262–77.

Christian, Barbara. *Black Feminist Criticism: Perspectives on Black Women Writers.* New York: Pergamon, 1985.

———. *Black Women Novelists: The Development of a Tradition, 1892–1976.* New York: Greenwood Press, 1980.

———. "Trajectories of Self-Definition: Placing Contemporary Afro-American Women's Fiction." In *Conjuring: Black Women, Fiction, and Literary Tradition*, edited by Marjorie Pryse and Hortense J. Spillers, 233–48. Bloomington: Indiana University Press, 1985.

Connor, Kimberly Rae. *Conversions and Visions in the Writings of African-American Women.* Knoxville: University of Tennessee Press, 1994.

Dalke, Anne. "Spirit Matters: Re-Possessing the African-American Women's Literary Tradition." *Legacy: A Journal of American Women Writers* 12.1 (1995): 1–16.

Davies, Carole Boyce, ed. "Black Women's Writing: Crossing the Boundaries." *Matatu: Journal for African Culture and Society* 3.6 (1989).

Decure, Nicole. "In Search of Our Sisters' Mean Streets: The Politics of Sex, Race, and Class in Black Women's Crime Fiction." In *Diversity and Detective Fiction*, edited by Kathleen Gregory, 158–85. Bowling Green, OH: Popular, 1999.

duCille, Ann. *The Coupling Convention: Sex, Text, and Tradition in Black Women's Fiction*. New York: Oxford University Press, 1993.

Ellmann, Maud. "The Power to Tell: Rape, Race and Writing in Afro-American Women's Fiction." In *An Introduction to Contemporary Fiction: International Writing in English since 1970*, edited by Rod Mengham, 32–52. Cambridge, England: Polity, 1999.

Evans, Mari. *Black Women Writers, 1950–1980, a Critical Evaluation*. New York: Anchor Books, 1983.

Fabre, Geneviève. "Genealogical Archeology: Black Women Writers in the 1980s and the Search for Legacy." *Revue Francaise d'Etudes Americaines* 11.30 (November 1986): 461–67.

———."Selected Bibliography of Essays on Black Women and Black Feminist Criticism." *Revue Francaise d'Etudes Americaines* 11.30 (November 1986): 501–2.

Fleischner, Jennifer. *Mastering Slavery: Memory, Family, and Identity in Women's Slave Narratives*. New York: New York University Press, 1996.

Foster, Frances Smith. "Adding Color and Contour to Early American Self-Portraitures: Autobiographical Writings of Afro-American Women." In *Conjuring: Black Women, Fiction, and Literary Tradition,* edited by Marjorie Pryse and Hortense J. Spillers, 25–38. Bloomington: Indiana University Press, 1985.

———. "Between the Sides: Afro-American Women Writers as Mediators." *Nineteenth-Century Studies*, 3 (1989): 53–64.

———. *Written By Herself: Literary Production by African American Women, 1746–1892*. Bloomington: Indiana University Press, 1993.

Fox-Genovese, Elizabeth. "My Statue, My Self: Autobiographical Writings of Afro-American Women." In *The Private Self: Theory and Practice of Women's Autobiographical Writings*, edited by Shari Benstock, 63–89. Chapel Hill: University of North Carolina Press, 1988.

———. "Slavery, Race, and the Figure of the Tragic Mulatta; or, the Ghost of Southern History in the Writing of African-American Women." In *Haunted Bodies: Gender and Southern Texts*, edited by Anne Goodwyn Jones and Susan V. Donaldson, 464–91. Charlottesville: University Press of Virginia, 1997.

———. "Southern History in the Imagination of African American Women Writers." In *The History of Southern Women's Literature*, edited by Carolyn Perry and Mary Louise Weaks, 156–63. Baton Rouge: Louisiana State University Press, 2002.

———. "To Write My Self: The Autobiographies of Afro-American Women." In *Feminist Issues in Literary Scholarship*, edited by Shari Benstock, 161–80. Bloomington: Indiana University Press, 1987.

Guy-Sheftall, Beverly. *Words of Fire: An Anthology of African American Feminist Thought*. New York: New Press, 1995.

Harris, Trudier. "From Exile to Asylum: Religion and Community in the Writings of Contemporary Black Women." In *Women's Writing in Exile*, edited by Mary Lynn Broe and Angela Ingram, 151–69. Chapel Hill: University of North Carolina Press, 1989.

———. "What Women? What Canon? African American Women and the Canon." In *Speaking the Other Self: American Women Writers*, edited by Jeanne Campbell Reesman, 90–95. Athens: University of Georgia Press, 1997.

Henderson, Mae Gwendolyn. "Speaking in Tongues: Dialogics, Dialectics, and the Black Woman Writer's Literary Tradition." In *Women, Autobiography, Theory: A Reader*, edited by Sidonie Smith and Julia Watson, 343–51. Madison: University of Wisconsin Press, 1998.

Hernton, Calvin. "The Sexual Mountain and Black Women Writers." *Black American Literature Forum* 18.4 (Winter 1984): 139–45.

Hobson, Janell. "Early African American Women Writers." In *The History of Southern Women's Literature*, edited by Carolyn Perry and Mary Louise Weaks, 87–96. Baton Rouge: Louisiana State University Press, 2002.

Holloway, Karla F. C. *Moorings & Metaphors: Figures of Culture and Gender in Black Women's Literature*. New Brunswick, NJ: Rutgers University Press, 1992.

————. "Revision and (Re)membrance: A Theory of Literary Structures in Literature by African-American Women Writers." In *African American Literary Theory: A Reader*, edited by Winston Napier, 387–98. New York: New York University Press, 2000.

Hull, Gloria T. "Rewriting Afro-American Literature: A Case for Black Women Writers." In *Politics of Education: Essays from Radical Teacher,* edited by Robert C. Rosent and Leonard Vogt, 99–109. Albany: State University of New York Press, 1990.

Hull, Gloria T., Patricia Bell Scott, and Barbara Smith, eds. *All the Women Are White, All the Blacks Are Men, But Some of Us Are Brave: Black Women's Studies*. New York: Feminist Press, 1981.

Kafka, Phillipa. *The Great White Way: African American Women Writers and American Success Mythologies*. New York: Garland, 1993.

Kiah, Rosalie Black. "African-American Women Writers of Adolescent Literature." *Journal of African Children's and Youth Literature* 3 (1991–1992): 80–92.

Levin, Amy K. *Africanism and Authenticity in African-American Women's Novels*. Gainesville: University Press of Florida, 2003.

Liddell, Janice Lee, and Yakini Belinda Kemp, eds. *Arms Akimbo: Africana Women in Contemporary Literature*. Gainesville: University Press of Florida; 1999.

Lindberg-Seyersted, Brita. "The Color Black: Skin Color as Social, Ethical, and Esthetic Sign in Writings by Black American Women." *English Studies: A Journal of English Language and Literature* 73.1 (February 1992): 51–67.

Logan, Shirley Wilson, ed. *With Pen and Voice: A Critical Anthology of Nineteenth-Century African-American Women*. Carbondale: Southern Illinois University Press, 1995.

Lynch, Acklyn. "Notes on Black Women Writers of the Past Two Decades." In *In the Memory and Spirit of Frances, Zora, and Lorraine: Essays and Interviews on Black Women and Writing,* edited by Juliette Bowles, 45–52. Washington, DC: Institute for the Arts & the Humanities, Howard University, 1979.

Mason, Mary G. "Travel as Metaphor and Reality in Afro-American Women's Autobiography, 1850–1972." *Black American Literature Forum* 24.2 (Summer 1990): 337–56.

McCaskill, Barbara. "'To Labor . . . and Fight on the Side of God': Spirit, Class, and Nineteenth-Century African American Women's Literature." In *Nineteenth-Century American Women Writers: A Critical Reader,* edited by Karen L. Kilcup, 164–83. Malden, MA: Blackwell; 1998

McDowell, Deborah E. *"The Changing Same": Black Women's Literature, Criticism and Theory.* Bloomington: Indiana University Press, 1995.

McKay, Nellie Y. "The Narrative Self: Race, Politics, and Culture in Black American Women's Autobiography." In *Women, Autobiography, Theory: A Reader,* edited by Sidonie Smith and Julia Watson, 96–107. Madison: University of Wisconsin Press, 1998.

————. "Reflections on Black Women Writers: Revising the Literary Canon." In *The Impact of Feminist Research in the Academy,* edited by Christie Farnham, 174–89. Bloomington: Indiana University Press, 1987.

Mehaffy, Marilyn Maness. "Shifting Canons: African-American Women Writers, 1746–1910." *College Literature* 22.3 (October 1995): 132–36.

Mittlefehldt, Pamela Klass. "A Weaponry of Choice: Black American Women Writers and the Essay." In *The Politics of the Essay: Feminist Perspectives,* edited by Ruth-Ellen Boetcher and Elizabeth Mittman, 196–208. Bloomington: Indiana University Press, 1993.

Moody, Joycelyn K. "On the Road with God: Travel and Quest in Early Nineteenth-Century African American Holy Women's Narratives." *Religion and Literature* 27.1 (Spring 1995): 35–51.

Mullen, Bill. "A Revolutionary Tale: In Search of African American Women's Short Story Writing." In *American Women Short Story Writers: A Collection of Critical Essays*, edited by Julie Brown, 191–207. New York: Garland; 1995.

Nankoe, Lucia. "To Keep the Memory of the Past Alive: A Theoretical Approach to Novels of Black Women Writers." In *Crisis and Creativity in the New Literatures in English: Cross/*

Cultures, edited by Geoffrey V. Davis and Hena Maes-Jelinek, 481–97. Amsterdam: Rodopi, 1990.

Nash, Margaret. "Patient Persistence: The Political and Educational Values of Anna Julia Cooper and Mary Church Terrell." *Educational Studies: A Journal of the American Educational Studies Association* 35.2 (April 2004): 122–36.

―――. "Reflections on Black Women Writers: Revising the Literary Canon." In *Feminisms: An Anthology of Literary Theory and Criticism*, edited by Robyn R. Warhol and Diane Price Herndl, 151–63. New Brunswick, NJ: Rutgers University Press, 1997.

O'Connor, Mary. "Subject, Voice, and Women in Some Contemporary Black American Women's Writing." In *Feminism, Bakhtin, and the Dialogic*, edited by Dale M. Bauer and Susan Jaret McKinstry, 199–217. Albany: State University of New York Press, 1991.

Pierce, Yolanda. "African-American Women's Spiritual Narratives." In *The Cambridge Companion to Nineteenth-Century American Women's Writing*, edited by Philip Gould and Dale Bauer, 244–61. Cambridge, England: Cambridge University Press, 2001.

Pryse, Marjorie, and Hortense J. Spillers, ed. *Conjuring: Black Women, Fiction, and Literary Tradition*. Bloomington: Indiana University Press, 1985.

Roses, Lorraine Elena, ed. *Harlem's Glory: Black Women Writing, 1900–1950*. Cambridge, MA: Harvard University Press, 1996.

Shockley, Ann Allen. "Afro-American Women Writers: The New Negro Movement, 1924–1933." In *Rereading Modernism: New Directions in Feminist Criticism*, edited by Lisa Rado, 123–35. New York: Garland, 1994.

Smith, Barbara, ed. *Home Girls: A Black Feminist Anthology*. New Brunswick, NJ: Rutgers University Press, 2000.

Stover, Johnnie M. *Rhetoric and Resistance in Black Women's Autobiography*. Gainesville: University Press of Florida, 2003.

Tally, Justine. "History, Fiction, and Community in the Work of Black American Women Writers from the Ends of Two Centuries." In *The Black Columbiad: Defining Moments in African American Literature and Culture*, edited by Werner Sollors and Maria Diedrich, 357–68. Cambridge, MA: Harvard University Press, 1994.

Tate, Claudia. *Black Women Writers at Work*. New York: Continuum Intl Pub Group, 1984.

―――. "On Black Literary Women and the Evolution of Critical Discourse." *Tulsa Studies in Women's Literature* 5.1 (Spring 1986): 111–23.

―――. "Reshuffling the Deck; or, (Re)Reading Race and Gender in Black Women's Writing." *Tulsa Studies in Women's Literature* 7.1 (Spring 1988): 119–32.

Wade-Gayles, Gloria. *No Crystal Stair: Visions of Race and Gender in Black Women's Fiction*. New York: Pilgrim Press, 1984.

Walker, Alice. In *Search of Our Mothers' Gardens*. Caledonia, MN: 1984.

Walker, Melissa. "The Verbal Arsenal of Black Women Writers in America." In *Confronting the Crisis: War, Politics, and Culture in the Eighties,* edited by Francis Barker, et al., 118–30. Colchester: University of Essex, 1984.

Wall, Cheryl A., ed. *Changing Our Own Words: Essays on Criticism, Theory, and Writing by Black Women*. New Brunswick, NJ: Rutgers University Press, 1989.

―――. *Worrying the Line: Black Women Writers, Lineage and Literary Tradition*. Chapel Hill: University of North Carolina Press, 2005.

Ward, Kathleen L. "Creating a Legacy: Black Women Writing for Children." In *Images of the Child*, edited by Harry Eiss, 229–44. Bowling Green, OH: Popular, 1994.

Washington, Mary Helen. "The Darkened Eye Restored: Notes for a Literary History of Black Women." In *Within the Circle: An Anthology of African American Literary Criticism from the Harlem Renaissance to the Present*, edited by Angelyn Mitchell, 442–53. Durham, NC: Duke University Press, 1994.

―――. "New Lives and New Letters: Black Women Writers at the End of the Seventies." *College English* 43.1 (January 1981): 1–11.

————. "Teaching Black-Eyed Susans: An Approach to the Study of Black Women Writers." *Black American Literature Forum* 11.1 (Spring 1977): 20–24.

Wilentz, Gay. "Toward a Diaspora Literature: Black Women Writers from Africa, the Caribbean, and the United States." *College English* 54.4 (April 1992): 385–405.

Willis, Susan. "Black Women Writers: Taking a Critical Perspective." In *Making a Difference: Feminist Literary Criticism*, edited by Gayle Greene and Coppelia Kahn, 211–37. London: Methuen, 1985.

INDEX

Bold-faced page numbers indicate main entries.

Abby (Caines), 71
Abramson, Doris, 82
Adams, Elizabeth Laura, **1–5**
"Adventures of the Dread Sisters, The"
  (De Veaux), 156–57
Affrilachia, 141
Africa Dream (Greenfield), 227
African American Women Writers (Wilkinson),
  618
African Methodist Episcopal (AME) Church,
  366, 367, 527, 565
After the Garden (Austin), 23–24
Albert, Octavia Victoria Rogers, **7–8**
All-Bright Court (Porter), 470
Allen, Clarissa Minnie Thompson, **9–10**
Allen, Eunice, 554
Allen, Samuel, 130
All God's Children Need Traveling Shoes
  (Angelou), 16
All Saints (Osbey), 454–55
American Daughter (Thompson), 561–62
American Negro Theatre (ANT), 79
American Play (Parks), 459, 461
American Smooth (Dove), 166
Anaporte-Easton, Jean, 97
And Do Remember Me (Golden), 220, 222
Anderson, Kamili, 500
Anderson, Mignon Holland, **11–12**
Anderson, T. J., III, 122
Andrews, William, 297, 419
Angelou, Maya, **13–17**, 23
Anna Lucasta (Childress), 80, 81
Annas, Pamela, 458
Annie Allen (Brooks), 50
Annie John (Kincaid), 343, 345
Ansa, Tina McElroy, **19–21**
Anthologies on black women's literature, 237,
  238
"Apocalypse," 429
Argall, Nicole, 484
Art, 187. *See also* Black Arts Movement
Asim, Jabari, 534

Austin, Doris Jean, **23–25**
Austin, Gayle, 81–82
Autobiographical writings, 95, 219, 264–65,
  301, 335–38, 342, 344, 345, 369, 370, 374,
  399, 402, 457, 480, 508–9, 514–18, 540, 581,
  629–32. *See also* Memoirs; Slave narratives
Autobiographies, 13–16, 46–47, 51–52, 145,
  207, 289, 303, 416–19, 442, 472, 473,
  477–79, 508–9, 527–28, 550–51, 561–62,
  604; fictional, 50, 51; spiritual, 182–84,
  204–5, 366–67
Autobiography of My Mother, The (Kincaid),
  344, 345
"Autobiography" (Williams), 621
Awkward, Michael, 431

Babylon Sisters (Cleage), 89
Baby of the Family (Ansa), 19
Baggett, Paul, 509
Bailey, Cathryn, 114
Bailey's Café (Naylor), 446, 447
Baker, Houston A., 500
Baker, Nikki, **26–27**
Baldwin, James, 404, 459
Balshaw, Maria, 40
Bambara, Toni Cade, **28–33**
Barras, Jonetta, 239
Barrax, Gerald, 615
"Bars Fight, The" (Terry), 554–55
Barton, Rebecca Chalmers, 4–5
Bascom, Lionel, 608
*Behind the Scenes or Thirty Years a Slave, and
  Four Years in the White House* (Keckley),
  331–33
Belafonte, Harry, 570
Bell, Bernard W., 323
"Belle Isle" (Hodges), 271–72
Beloved (Morrison), 246, 427–31
Benjamin, Shanna Greene, 32
Bennett, Gwendolyn, **35–37**
Berg, Allison, 243
Beryl Weston's Ambition (Tillman), 563

Betsey Brown (Shange), 514, 516–17

Big Mama Stories (Youngblood), 636–38

Biographers, 227. *See also specific authors*

Black and Beautiful (Summers), 540

Black and White of It, The (Shockley), 523, 525

Black Arts Movement (BAM), 122, 187, 188, 223, 379, 436, 457, 493, 497, 499

"Black English" (Bambara), 29–30

Black experience, 186–88

Black Feminist Criticism (Christian), 85

Black Girl in Paris (Youngblood), 637–39

"Black Man, My Man, Listen!" (Stokes), 29

"Black," meanings of, 188, 189

Black Notebooks, The (Derricotte), 151–53

Black Southern Voices (Killens and Ward), 24

Black Unicorn, The (Lorde), 372

Black Woman: An Anthology, The (Bambara), 29, 33

Black Women Novelists (Christian), 85

Black Women Writers at Work (Tate), 544–45

Black Women Writing Autobiography (Braxton), 46, 47

Blair, Amy, 568

Blessing the Boats (Clifton), 96

Bloom, Lynn Z., 418

Blue Blood (Johnson), 312, 314

Blues for Alabama Sky (Cleage), 89

Bluest Eye, The (Morrison), 423–26, 428–30, 444

Blundell, Janet Boyarin, 534

Bond, Jean, 256–57

Bonner, Marita, **39–41**

Book of Light (Clifton), 96

"Bottled" (Johnson), 317–18

Bowers, Susan, 429

Boyd, Candy Dawson, **43–44**

Bradley, David, 627

Bramen, Carrie Tirado, 324

Brand Plucked from the Fire, A (Foote), 204–5

Brathwaite, Kamau, 475

Braxton, Joanne "Jodie" Margaret, **46–47**, 304, 551, 562

Breaking Away (Lattany), 357

Breast cancer, 370, 373

Breath, Eyes, Memory (Danticat), 132–34

Bright Road (film), 570

Bronx Is Next, The (Sanchez), 498–99

Bronze (Johnson), 313–14

Brooks, Gwendolyn, **49–54**, 574

Brothers, The (Collins), 108, 110

Brown, Elizabeth Barnsley, 297

Brown, Kimberly, 124

Brown, Linda Beatrice, **56–58**

Brown, Patricia, 496

Browngirl, Brownstones (Marshall), 382, 383, 385

Bryan, C.D.B., 33

Bryan, Violet Harrington, 177, 455

Bryant, Cynthia, 120

Bryant, Janice K., 239

Buckman, Alyson R., 584

Burton, Annie Louise, **59–60**

Bush, Vanessa, 584

Bush-Banks, Olivia Ward, **61–62**

Bush-Banks School of Expression, 61

Butler, Octavia, **64–68**

Butler-Evans, Elliot, 585

Byerman, Keith, 323

By the Light of My Father's Smile (Walker), 581, 584

Cade, Miltona Mirkin. *See* Bambara, Toni Cade

Caines, Jeanette Franklin, **71–72**

Campbell, Bebe Moore, **74–75**

Campbell, Jennifer, 634

Cancer Journals, The (Lorde), 370, 373

Caribbean cultures, 475

Carroll, Mary, 221

Carter, Steven, 257

Carver, George Washington, 599

Carver (Waniek), 598, 599

Catholicism, 1–3

Chapman, Abraham, 358

Chase-Riboud, Barbara, **76–77**

Chewed Water (Rahman), 480, 481

Childress, Alice, **79–82**

Chilly Stomach (Caines), 71–72

Chinaberry Tree, The (Fauset), 196

Chopin, Kate, 176, 177

Chosen Place, The Timeless People, The (Marshall), 382, 383

Christian, Barbara T., **85–86**

Christianity, 59–60, 118, 182–84, 205, 303, 304, 309, 366–67, 391, 523–24, 536–37, 542, 564, 565. *See also* African Methodist Episcopal (AME) Church; Spiritual autobiographies

Christmas in the Big House, Christmas in the Quarters (McKissack), 397

Civil rights activism, 174–76, 238, 239, 252, 439, 441, 442, 579, 582, 633

Clancy Street (Tillman), 563–64

Clarence and Corinne, or God's Way (Johnson), 309, 310

Classism, 417. *See also* Social class

Cleage, Pearl T., **88–90**

Cliff, Michelle, **92–93**

Clifton, (Thelma) Lucille Sayles, **94–98**

Clover (Sanders), 503–6

Clurman, Harold, 82

Cole, Johnetta, 573

Coleman, Wanda, **101–2**

Collier, Eugenia W., **103–4**

Collins, Janelle, 404

Collins, Kathleen Conwell, **106–10**

Color, Sex and Poetry (Hull), 40

Color complex, 221

Colored Girl Beautiful, The (Hackley), 242–43

Color Purple, The (Walker), 579, 584, 585

Comedy (Fauset), 196

Coming of Age in Mississippi (Moody), 416–19

Common Woman, The (Grahn), 515

Contending Forces (Hopkins), 279–80

Conwell, Kathleen. *See* Collins, Kathleen Conwell

Cook, Martha, 215

Cooper, Anna Julia Hayward, **112–14**

Cooper, J. California, **116–20**

Corregidora (Jones), 322, 323

Cortez, Jayne, **121–24**

Coward, David, 431

Creole culture, 175–77

Crossing Over Jordan (Brown), 57–58

Crouch, Stanley, 122

Daddy Was a Number Runner (Meriwether), 402, 404

Dandridge, Dorothy, 570

Dandridge, Rita, 411–12

Danner, Margaret Esse, **127–30**

Danticat, Edwidge, **132–37**

Dark Symphony (Adams), 2–4

Daughters (Marshall), 384–85

Davenport, Doris, **141–43**

Davies, Carole Boyce, 386

Davis, Angela Yvonne, **145–47**, 626

Davis, Arthur P., 197

Davis, Cynthia, 608–9

Davis, Thadious M., 194, 195, 586

Death, 612

Deegan, Mary Jo, 621, 622

Delaney, Lucy, **149–50**

Derricotte, Toi(nette) Marie, **151–53**

Desperate Circumstance, Dangerous Woman (Osbey), 454

Dessa Rose (Williams), 625–27

Detective fiction, 26–27

De Veaux, Alexis, **155–58**, 376, 525

Dew Breaker, The (Danticat), 135

Diaries, 176, 200

Dias, Risasi-Zachariah, 266

Didacticism, 117–18, 188

Dillard, J. L., 29

Dillou, Amadou, 299

Disappearing Acts (McMillan), 399, 400

Dive (Teasley), 552, 553

Dixon, Edwina Streeter, **161**

Domestic Allegories of Political Desire (Tate), 545

Domestic violence, 579–81. *See also specific writings*

Don't Erase Me (Ferrell), 200

Don't Play in the Sun (Golden), 221, 222

Dorscy, David, 188

Double-voiced strategy, 1

Douglass, Frederick, 490–91, 601, 602

Douglass' Women (Rhodes), 490–91

Dove, Rita, **163–66**

Dowdell, Jennifer. *See* Baker, Nikki

Driftwood (Bush-Banks), 61–62

Drinking Gourd, A (Hansberry), 254–56

Drumgoold, Kate, **169–70**

Dubey, Madhu, 68

DuBois, Shirley Graham, **171–72**

DuBois, W.E.B., 113, 171, 246, 461

Dugan, Olga, 82

Dunbar, Paul Lawrence, 50–51, 62, 174, 175

Dunbar-Nelson, Alice, **174–78**

Duster, Alfreda M., 604

Dust Tracks on a Road (Hurston), 289

Duval, John, 431

Dystopian fiction, 67

Easton, Yvonne, 541

Ebonics. *See* "Black English"

Eder, Richard, 82

Edge of Heaven, The (Golden), 221, 222

Education, 417, 595

Edwards, Solomon, 188

Edwards-Yearwood, Grace, **180–81**

Eisenbach, Helen, 525

Elaw, Zilpha, **182–84**

Ellerby, Janet Mason, 400

Ellison, Ralph, 466

Embree, Edwin R., 5

Empowerment, 40

Enchanted Hair Tale, An (De Veaux), 157

End of Dying, The (Anderson), 11

Enomoto, Don, 362
Erickson, Peter, 328, 447
Erotic, the, 373. *See also* Sexuality and sexual politics
Essays (Plato), 468, 469
Essex, Mark, 336
Esther (Vroman), 569–70
Evans, Mari, 96–97, **186–89**
Eva's Man (Jones), 322, 323
Everett Anderson's Goodbye (Clifton), 95
Existentialism, 417

Fabio, Sarah Webster, **191–92**
Fabricated absence, 461
Family (Cooper), 119, 120
Farming of Bones, The (Danticat), 134–35
Fashion industry, 540
Father Songs (Wade-Gayles), 574
Faulkner, William, 626
Fauset, Jessie Redmon, **193–98**
Female genital mutilation, 579–80
Feminist issues and writings, 113–14, 146, 175, 177, 232, 233, 237–39, 274, 430–31, 434, 499, 518, 537–38. *See also* Lorde, Audre Geraldine; Womanism
"Feminist pragmatists," 620–21
"Fence" (Moore), 421
Ferrell, Carolyn, **200–201**
Fields, Julia, **202–3**
Finney, Brian, 432
Fires in the Mirror (Smith), 529, 530
First Cities, The (Lorde), 370, 371
Fish, Cheryl, 509
Fisher King, The (Marshall), 385, 386
Fledgling (Butler), 67–68
Florence (Childress), 80, 81
Flyin' West (Cleage), 88, 90
Foote, Julia A. J., **204–5**
for colored girls who have considered suicide / when the rainbow is enuf (Shange), 514, 515, 517, 518
Forgiveness, 391–92
For My People (Walker), 589, 593
Foster, Frances Smith, 8, 367, 537, 625
Friendship, The (Taylor), 548
From the Darkness Cometh the Light, or, Struggles for Freedom, 149–50
"*Fucking A*" (Parks), 459, 460, 462

Gaines, Patrice, **207–8**
Gardner, Eric, 631–32
Gates, Henry Louis, Jr., 324, 447, 632

Gather Together in My Name (Angelou), 15
Gay and lesbian issues, 457, 458. *See also* Lesbian literature and lesbian politics
Gender issues, 40, 101, 195, 196, 373. *See also* Feminist issues and writings; Sexuality and sexual politics
Gender Talk (Guy-Sheftall), 238, 239
Genital mutilation, female, 579–80
George, Lynell, 541
Gibson, Patricia Joann, **209–10**
Gifts of Power (Jackson), 303
Gilbert, Mercedes, **211–12**
Gilda Stories, The (Gomez), 224–25
"Gilded Six-Bits, The" (Hurston), 286
Giles, Freda Scott, 90
Giovanni, Nikki, 124, **213–16**, 440, 593
"Girl" (Kincaid), 342–43
Glow in the Dark (Teasley), 552
God Bless the Child (Lattany), 355–56, 358
God Don't Like Ugly (Monroe), 413, 414
God Still Don't Like Ugly (Monroe), 413–14
Goin' Someplace Special (McKissack), 397
Golden, Marita, **218–22**
Gomez, Jewelle, **223–25**
Gone with the Wind (O'Hara), 483, 484
Good Times (Clifton), 95
Good Woman (Clifton), 96
"Gorilla, My Love" (Bambara), 30
Gorilla, My Love (Bambara), 29–31
Gospel of Cinderella, The (Thomas), 558
Gottlieb, Annie, 447
Grace Notes (Dove), 164, 165
Graham, Maryemma, 590, 593
Graham, Shirley. *See* DuBois, Shirley Graham
Grahn, Judy, 515
Graven Images (Meriwether), 408
Greenfield, Eloise, **227–28**
Grewal, Gurleen, 430, 431
Griffith, Ada Gay, 376
Griffith, Paul A., 599
Grimké, Angelina Weld, **229–33**
Grimké, Charlotte Forten, 113
Guerrero, Ed, 431
Gunning, Sandra, 576
Guy, Rosa, **235–36**
Guy-Sheftall, Beverly, **237–39**

Hackley, Madame Emma Azalia Smith, **241–42**
Hagar's Daughter (Hopkins), 280
Hairdresser's Experience in High Life, A (Potter), 472–73

Haiti and Haitian Americans, 132–36, 155–56
Haley, Alex, 77
Hamilton, Denise, 27
Hamilton, Virginia, **244–47**
Hand I Fan With, The (Ansa), 20
Hanley, Karen, 389
Hansberry, Lorraine, **251–57**
Hansen, Joyce, **259–60**
"Happy Story, A" (Moore), 420–21
Harlem, 402, 606, 608
Harlem Renaissance writing, 318
Harlem Summer (Vroman), 569, 570
Harper, Frances Ellen Watkins, **261–62**
Harris, Janet, 389
Harris, Trudier, 120, 430, 576
Harris, Will, 232
Harrison, Juanita, **264–65**
Hatch, James, 232
Healing, The (Jones), 322, 324
Heart of a Woman, The (Johnson), 312–14
Heart of a Woman (Angelou), 15–16
Helford, Elyce Rae, 68
Henderson, Mae G., 585
Henderson-Holmes, Safiya E., **266–67**
Hernton, Calvin, 518
Heroes, 625, 626
Her Own Place (Sanders), 503–6
Herron, Carolivia, **268–69**
Hershman, Marcie, 324
Hirsch, David, 233
History of Mary Prince, The (Prince), 474–75
Hodges, Frenchy Jolene, **271–72**
Holiday, Billie, 157, 358
Home Coming (Sanchez), 497, 499, 500
Homegirls & Handgrenades (Sanchez), 497, 499–500
Homeplace (Waniek), 598, 599
Homophobia, 523. *See also* Lesbian literature and lesbian politics
Honey, Maureen, 231
hooks, bell, **273–75**
Hopkins, Pauline Elizabeth, **278–81**
House Arrest (Smith), 530
House of Bondage, The (Albert), 7, 8
How Stella Got Her Groove Back (McMillan), 399, 400
Hughes, Langston, 129–30, 186–88
Hughes, Sheila Hassell, 53–54
Hughes, Virginia. *See* Rahman, Aishah
Hull, Gloria, 40, 231
Humanism, 592
"Human Spirit, The" (Guy), 235

Hurston, Zora Neale, 118, **283–90**, 558, 583, 626

I Am a Black Woman (Evans), 186–87
Identity, 156, 157, 186–89, 321–22, 328–29, 351, 375; national, 529
I Dream a World (Summers), 540, 541
If I Should Die (Edwards-Yearwood), 180
I Know Why the Caged Bird Sings (Angelou), 13–16
Imani All Mine (Porter), 470
Imperceptible Mutabilities in the Third Kingdom (Parks), 459, 463
Incest, 424, 580
Incidents in the Life of a Slave Girl (Jacobs), 306–7
I Need a Lunch Box (Caines), 72
In Love and Trouble (Walker), 582
In Praise of Our Teachers (Wade-Gayles), 574
In Search of Satisfaction (Cooper), 118
In the Blood (Parks), 459, 463
"In the Face of Fire I Will Not Turn Back" (Anderson), 11
In the Midnight Hour (Collins), 108–9
In These Houses (Osbey), 454
Isani, Mukhtar Ali, 612

Jackson, Angela, **292–94**
Jackson, David Earl, 267
Jackson, Elaine, **296–97**
Jackson, Mae, **299–300**
Jackson, Mattie Jane, **301–2**
Jackson, Rebecca Cox, **303–4**
Jacobs, Harriet Ann, **305–8**
James, Cynthia, 475
Jay, Karla, 525
Jazz (Morrison), 427–28, 432
Jazz aesthetic in drama, 481
Jazz poetry, 123, 124
Jefferson, Thomas, 612
Jesus and Fat Tuesday and Other Stories (McElroy), 394
Johnson, Amelia E., **309–10**
Johnson, Dianne, 548
Johnson, Georgia Douglas, **312–15**
Johnson, Helen, **317–19**
Johnson, James Weldon, 37
Johnson, Joyce, 97
Jonah's Gourd Vine (Hurston), 284, 286–87, 289, 290
Jones, Gayl, **321–24**
Jones, Sharon L., 608

Jones, Suzanne, 506
Jordan, June, **326–29**
Jordan, Michael, 227
Joyce, Joyce Ann, 53
Jubilee (Walker), 589–93
Juhasz, Suzanne, 215
Just Us Women (Caines), 71

Kali, 95
Kaplan, Carla, 1, 3, 4
Karrer, Wolfgang, 119
Katutani, Michiko, 470
Kaufman, Ellen, 152
Keating, AnnaLouise, 375
Keckley, Elizabeth Hobbs, **331–33**
Keller, Frances Richardson, 114
Keller, Lynn, 455
Kelly, Katherine, 41
Kennedy, Adrienne, **334–39**
Kent, George, 12
"Key to the City" (Oliver), 451
Kincaid, Jamaica, **341–45**
Kindred (Butler), 65–66
King, Martin Luther, Jr., 499
King, Rodney, 394, 529–30
Kinnamon, Keneth, 440
Kinnell, Galway, 151
Knopf, Marcy Jane, 197
Krasner, David, 232–33
Krik? Krak! (Danticat), 133, 134
Kubitschek, Missy Dehn, 447
Ku Klux Klan (KKK), 490

Landlord, The (Lattany), 356, 357
Lane, Pinkie Gordon, **347–49**
Larsen, Nella, **350–54**
"Last Supper, The" (Adams), 4
Lattany, Kristin Hunter, **355–58**
Laughing in the Dark (Gaines), 207
Lee, Andrea, **360–62**
Lee, Helen Elaine, **364–65**
Lee, Jarena, **366–68**
Leibovich, Lori, 386
Leonard, John, 534
Lesbian literature and lesbian politics, 26, 27,
    156–58, 223, 225, 229, 446, 449, 522–25.
    See also Gay and lesbian issues; Lorde,
    Audre Geraldine
Les Blancs (Hansberry), 254, 256
"Lesson, The" (Bambara), 31
Lester, Neal A., 518, 519
Let the Circle Be Unbroken (Taylor), 548

Let the Lion Eat Straw (Southerland), 532–34
Lewis, Derrick C., 297
Lewis, Rudolph, 496
*Liberating Voices: Oral Tradition in African
    American Literature* (Jones), 322, 323
"Liberation literature," 245–47
"Life of Lincoln West, The" (Brooks), 52
Lincoln, Abraham, 459, 460, 462
"Lincoln" (Ray), 486
Lindberg, Kathryne V., 53
Linden Hills (Naylor), 446
"Literary folklore," 430
Loeffelholz, Mary, 177
Logan, Shirley Wilson, 391–92, 538
Long, Octavia, 379–80
Long Distance Life (Golden), 220, 222
Long Time since Yesterday (Gibson), 209
Long Walk, The (Brown), 56–57
Long Way Home from St. Louie, A (McElroy),
    394, 395
Looking for Harlem (Balshaw), 40
Lopez, Trudier Harris, 608
Lorde, Audre Geraldine, 157–58, 223,
    369–76, 457, 583
Losing Ground (Collins), 107, 110
Lot's Daughters (Moore), 421
Lotus Press, 379
Love (Morrison), 428–29
"Love Poems" (Parker), 457
Loving Her (Shockley), 522–23, 525
Lowe, John, 455
Lucy (Kincaid), 343–44
Ludell (Wilkinson), 616–18
Lynching, 230–31, 314, 601–3

Madagascar, 394, 395
Madgett, Naomi Long, **378–80**
Mahone, Sydne, 481
Major, Clarence, 41
Malcolm X, 16, 299, 336, 499, 614
"Malcolm X" (Brooks), 52
Mali Anderson Mysteries, 180
Mama Day (Naylor), 446, 447
Mama's Promises (Waniek), 598
Mandela, Nelson, 49, 51
Mandela, Winnie, 49, 51
Mangeango, Azande, 481
Marked by Fire (Thomas), 556, 557, 559
Marshall, Barbara, 119
Marshall, Paule, **382–86**
Marsh-Lockett, Carol P., 21
Masculinity, 238

Mathis, Sharon Bell, **388–89**
Matthews, Victoria Earle, **391–92**
Maud Martha (Brooks), 50, 51
Mayberry, Katherine J., 432
McCluskey, Audrey, 97, 239
McDowell, Deborah, 196, 197
McDowell, Margaret B., 215
McElroy, Colleen J., **393–95**
McKenna, Bernard, 509
McKissack, Patricia L'Ann Carwell, **397–98**
McLendon, Jacqueline Y., 195, 197–98
McMillan, Terry, **399–400**
McWhorter, Deane, 221
Meier, Joyce, 232, 481
Melhem, D. H., 122, 499–500
Melitte (Shaik), 511–12
Memoirs, 94, 96, 97, 152, 182 84, 274, 394, 395, 480, 481, 503, 561–62. *See also* Autobiographical writings; Autobiographies
Memoirs (Elaw), 182–84
Memories of Childhood's Slavery Days (Burton), 59
Men of Brewster Place, The (Naylor), 444, 447
Menstruation, 336
Mental illness, 74, 75
Mercer, Lorraine, 509
Meriweather, Louise, **402–4**
Middle Massage Project, 47
Migrations of the Heart (Golden), 219–21
Miller, Ericka M., 233
Miller, Frank, 570
Miller, James, 141, 142
Miller, James A., 324
Miller, Jeanne-Maria, 231–33
Miller, Kent, 395
Miller, May, **406–9**
Millican, Arthenia J. Bates, **411–12**
Mills, David, 124
Miracle Every Day, A (Golden), 221, 222
Misunderstandings, 255
Mitchell, Verner D., 608–9
Mojo and the Sayso, The (Rahman), 480, 481
Moments of Grace, Meeting the Challenge to Change (Gaines), 208
Monroe, Mary, **413–14**
Montgomery, Helena Louise, 142
Moody, Anne, **416–19**, 419
Moore, Alice Ruth. *See* Dunbar-Nelson, Alice
Moore, Opal J., **420–21**, 538
Morris, Willie, 419
Morrison, Emily, 50
Morrison, Toni, 247, **423–32**, 460, 625

Mosquito (Jones), 323, 324
Mossell, Gertrude Bustill, **434–35**
Mostly Womenfolk and a Man or Two (Anderson), 11, 12
Motherhood, 230. *See also Rachel*
Mother Love (Dove), 165
Mothers, single, 221
Mourning and allegory, Benjamin's theory of, 232–33
"Movement in Black" (Parker), 457–58
Mulattos, 194, 198. *see also specific writings*
Mules and Men (Hurston), 287–88
Mullen, Bill, 41
Mullen, Harryette, **436–37**
Munk, Erika, 463
Murphy, Beatrice, **439–40**
Murray, Pauli, **441–42**
Music, 242, 480–81
Musser, Judith, 41
My Great, Wide, Beautiful World (Harrison), 264–65
My Mama Needs Me (Walter), 595
My Soul Is a Witness (Wade-Gayles), 573–74
Mystery novels, 26, 180, 449, 450, 488
Mystic Female, The (Kincaid), 348, 349

Na-Ni (De Veaux), 157
Narrative of the Life and Travels of Mrs. Nancy Prince, Written by Herself (Prince), 477–79
National Association for the Advancement of Colored People (NAACP), 80
Naturalism, 417, 447
Naylor, Gloria, 210, **444–47**
Neely, Barbara, **449–50**
"Negro Novel," stereotype of, 358
"Neighbors" (Oliver), 451, 452
New Negro, 5
New Orleans, 174, 175, 177, 453–55
Newton, Huey, 146
Nielsen, Aldon, 437
"Nigger," 351–52, 548
No (De Veaux), 157, 158
Nouvelle Soul (Summers), 540, 541
Now Is the Time to Open Your Heart (Walker), 581–82, 584

Of One Blood, or The Hidden Self (Hopkins), 280–81
Ohio State Murders, The (Kennedy), 337
Oliver, Diane, **451–52**
"On Being Brought from Africa" (Wheatley), 611

"On Being Young–a Woman–and Colored" (Bonner), 39–40
O'Neale, Sondra, 16
On the Bus with Rosa Parks (Dove), 165–66
Oppression, 255–56
Ordinary Woman, An (Clifton), 95
Organization of Black American Culture (OBAC), 292, 493
Organization of Women Writers of Africa (OWWA), 121
Original Poems (Bush-Banks), 61
Osbey, Brenda Marie, **453–55**
Oseye, Ellease Ebele. See Southerland, Ellease Dozier
Othering, 65
Our Nig; or, Sketches from the Life of a Free Black (Wilson), 629–32
Over the Lip of the World (McElroy), 394, 395

Page, Philip, 429–32
Page, Thomas Nelson, 8
Painter, Nell Irwin, 545
Paper Dolls (Jackson), 296–97
Paquet, Sandra Pouchet, 475
Parable of the Sower (Butler), 67
Parable of the Talents (Butler), 67, 68
Paradise (Morrison), 428
Parent-child relationships, 411
Parker, Pat, **457–58**
Parker-Smith, Bettye J., 494, 585
Parks, Rosa, 165, 166
Parks, Suzan-Lori, **459–63**
"Pa Sees Again" (Dixon), 161
Passing (Larsen), 351–53
"Passing," racial, 40
Patternmaster (Butler), 64, 65, 68
Peacock Poems, The (Williams), 625–27
Pennington, James, 469
Peterson, Carla, 537
Petry, Ann, **465–66**
Plato, Ann, **468–69**
Plum Bun (Fauset), 195–96
"Poem" (Johnson), 317–18
Poems on Miscellaneous Subjects (Harper), 261–62
Poems on Various Subjects (Wheatley), 612
"Poems to My Father" (Lane), 348
Poetry for the People program, 327
"Poetry Is Not a Luxury" (Lorde), 372–73
Poetry magazine, 128, 129
Porter, Connie (Rose), **470–71**

Possessing the Secret of Joy (Walker), 580–81, 584
Postmodern discourse, 68, 362
Potter, Eliza Johnson, **472–73**
Power, 352
Praisesong for the Widow (Marshall), 382, 384, 386
Prettyman, Kathleen Collins. See Collins, Kathleen Conwell
Prince, Mary, **474–75**
Prince, Nancy, **477–79**
Printz, Jessica Kimball, 181
Prisons, 207, 208
Prostitution, 224–25
Proud Shoes (Murray), 441, 442
Psychic phenomena. See Supernatural phenomena
Psychoanalysis and Black Novels (Tate), 545, 546
Pushed Back to Strength (Wade-Gayles), 573
Pushkin and the Queen of Spades (Randall), 483, 484

Quicksand (Larsen), 352–53
Quilting (Clifton), 96

Rachel (Grimké), 230–33
Racial "passing." See "Passing"
Rahman, Aishah, **480–81**
Rainbow Roun' Mah Shoulder (Brown), 57
Rainbow Signs (Fabio), 191
Raisin in the Sun, A (Hansberry), 252–56
Randall, Alice, **483–84**
Randolph, Asa Philip, 634
Rape, 14, 15, 331, 335, 336, 424, 470, 578, 580; lynchings and, 601–3
"Rape" (Cortez), 124
Rat's Mass (Kennedy), 336
Ray, Henrietta Cordelia, **486**
Raymond, Harry, 81
"Raymond's Run" (Bambara), 30–31
Red Beans and Ricely Yours (Saloy), 495, 496
Redmond, Eugene, 124
Reed, Ishmael, 496
Reid, Mark A., 110
Religion. See Christianity; Spirituality
"Remember Him a Outlaw" (De Veaux), 156
"Rememory," 245, 246, 429
Reminiscences (Taylor), 550–51
"Requiem for Willie Lee" (Hodges), 271
Resilience, 590–92
Revius, Alesia, 227

Rhodes, Jewell Parker, **488–91**
Rich, Adrienne, 375
Rich, Frank, 110
Richardson, Judy, 389
Richardson, Mattie, 177
Richardson, Thomas, 176–77
Richardson, Willis, 406–7
"Riddle of Egypt Brownstone, The"
   (De Veaux), 156
Ridin' the Goat (Meriwether), 408
Rishoi, Christy, 418–19
Rocks Cry Out, The (Murphy), 439, 440
Rodgers, Carolyn Marie, **493–94**
Rogers, Curtis E., 518
Roll of Thunder, Hear My Cry (Taylor), 547–49
Romantic escapism, 468
"Room 1023" (Austin), 24
"Rootbound" (Johnson), 318–19
Rose, W. L., 551
Rosemont, Penelope, 123
Royster, Jacqueline Jones, 538, 603
Russia, 607
Russian Journal (Lee), 360

Sadomasochism, 374
Sally Hemings (Chase-Riboud), 76, 77
Saloy, Mona Lisa, **495–96**
Salt Eaters, The (Bambara), 31–32
Salvaggio, Ruth, 68
Sanchez, Sonia, **497–500**
Sanders, Dori, **503–6**
Sanford & Son (TV sitcom), 104
Sarah Phillips (Lee), 360–62
Sassafrass, Cypress & Indigo (Grahn), 515–17
Saving Our Sons (Golden), 221
Say Jesus and Come to Me (Shockley), 523–25
Schroeder, Patricia, 232
Science fiction, 64
Scratches (Meriwether), 408
Seacole, Mary, **508–9**
Searle, Elizabeth, 201
Seeds beneath the Snow (Millican), 411, 412
"See How They Run" (Vroman), 569, 570
Segregation, 74
Self: reclamation of, 425–26. *See also* Identity
Sell, Mike, 500
Serpent's Gift, The (Lee), 364, 365
Sexual abuse, 14, 15, 322. *See also* Incest; Rape
Sexuality and sexual politics, 101, 196, 238,
   353, 373, 442, 446, 579–81. *See also*
   Lesbian literature and lesbian politics
Shadow Dancing (Meriwether), 403

Shaik, Fatima, **511–12**
Shakespeare, William, 447
Shakhovtseva, Elena, 21
Shakin' the Mess Outta Misery (Youngblood),
   636, 637
Shange, Ntozake, **514–19**
Shine, Ted, 232
Shinn, Thelma, 466
Shockley, Ann Allen, 9–10, 281, **522–25**
Short stories, 32–33. *See also specific authors*
Sign in Sidney Brustein's Window, The
   (Hansberry), 253–54
Simone, Nina, 614
Sinclaire, Abiola, 463
Singin' and Swingin' and Gettin' Merry Like
   Christmas (Angelou), 15
Sisterhood, 156
Skaggs, Merrill, 177
Slave Girl's Story: Being an Autobiography
   of Kate Drumgoold, A (Drumgoold), 169, 170
Slave narratives, 7, 59–60, 67, 149–50, 169,
   170, 259–60, 301–2, 306, 307, 331–33,
   473–75. *See also Beloved*; *Gilda Stories*;
   Jubilee; *Our Nig*
Slavery, 66, 145–46, 195, 254–55, 391–92,
   611. *See also* Underground Railroad
Slavery and the French Revolutionists
   (Cooper), 113
Sleeping with the Dictionary (Mullen), 437
Small Place, A (Kincaid), 343, 345
Smith, Amanda Berry, **527–28**
Smith, Anna Deavere, **529–30**
Smith, Patricia, 506
Smith, Valerie, 239, 361, 362, 431
Social activism. *See* Civil rights activism
Social class, 194–97. *See also* Classism
Social system, 103–4
Sojourner Truth (McKissack), 398
Sollers, Werner, 338
Some People, Some Other Place (Cooper), 119
Sommers, Sally R., 82
Song in a Weary Throat (Murray), 442
Song of Solomon (Morrison), 423, 425–26,
   429–31
"Sonnet to a Negro in Harlem" (Johnson),
   317–18
Soul Brothers and Sister Lou, The (Lattany),
   356, 358
Soul Kiss (Youngblood), 637, 639
Southerland, Ellease Dozier, **532–34**
Southern Christian Leadership Conference
   (SCLC), 16

Southern Horrors: Lynch Law in All Its Phases (Wells-Barnett), 601–3
Southern Horrors and Other Writings (Royster), 603–4
Southern writers, 21. *See also specific writers*
South Side Community Art Center (SSAC), 127–28
Speech, power of, 631
Spiritual autobiographies, 182–84, 204–5, 366–67
Spiritual individualism, radical, 184
Spirituality, 573–74. *See also* Christianity; Supernatural phenomena
"Spunk" (Hurston), 283, 285
St. John, Janet, 142–43
Stephens, Judith, 233
Stewart, Maria W., **536–38**
Stokes, Gail, 29
Storm, William, 232
Stover, J., 551
Street, The (Petry), 465–66
Street Lights: Illuminating the Tales of the Urban Black Experience (Austin), 24, 25
Sula (Morrison), 423, 425, 431
Sullivan, James D., 54
Summers, Barbara, **540–41**
Supernatural phenomena, 19–21, 532
Surrealism, 122
"Sweat" (Hurston), 283, 285–86
Sylvander, Carolyn Wedin, 197

Tapahonso, Luci, 584
Tapestry, The (De Veaux), 157
Taranto, James, 143
Tar Baby (Morrison), 423, 426, 429, 431
Tarry, Ellen, **542–43**
Tate, Claudia, 310, 313, **544–46**, 565
Tate, Linda, 506
Tawa, Renee, 583
Taylor, Mildred D., **547–49**
Taylor, Susie King, **550–51**
Teachers, 574
Teacup Full of Roses (Mathis), 388–89
Teasley, Lisa, **552–53**
Temple of My Familiar, The (Walker), 580, 584
Terry, Lucy, **554–55**
Their Eyes Were Watching God (Hurston), 288–90
There Is Confusion (Fauset), 194–95, 197
Third Life of Grange Copeland, The (Walker), 579–80, 584, 585

This Bridge Called My Back: Writings by Radical Women of Color (Moraga and Anzaldua), 29
This Child's Gonna Live (Wright), 633, 634
Thomas, Joyce Carol, **556–59**
Thomas, Lorenzo, 496
Thomas and Beulah (Dove), 163–65
Thompson, Era Bell, **561–62**
Those Bones Are Not My Child (Bambara), 32
Tillman, Katherine Davis Chapman, **563–65**
Todd, Ruth D., **567–68**
Toe Jam (Jackson), 296, 297
Topdog/Underdog (Parks), 459–60, 463
"To Usward" (Bennett), 36
Travelling Music (McElroy), 393–95
Treading the Winepress (Allen), 9
Trouble in Mind (Childress), 80–82
Truth, Sojourner, 408
Tubman, Harriet, 408
Turner, Nat, 626
Twain, Mark, 626
Twilight: Los Angeles, 1992 (Smith), 529–30
Two-Headed Woman (Clifton), 95–96

Ugly Ways (Ansa), 20
Ullman, Leslie, 96
Underground Railroad, 245, 278
Unfinished Women Cry in No Man's Land while a Bird Dies in a Gilded Cage (Rahman), 480, 481
"Urban minimalism," 534

Valentine, Victoria, 118
Vampire stories, 224
Venus (Parks), 459, 463
Violets and Other Tales (Dunbar-Nelson), 174, 176, 177
Voice from the South by a Black Woman of the South, A (Cooper), 112–13
Voodoo Dreams (Rhodes), 488, 489
Voodoo/Love Magic (Jackson), 293
Vroman, Mary Elizabeth, **569–70**

Wade-Gayles, Gloria, **572–76**
Waiting to Exhale (McMillan), 399, 400
Walk, Lori L., 375
Walker, Alice, 373, **578–86**
Walker, David, 537
Walker, Margaret Abigail, **589–93**
Walker, Pierre, 17
Wall, Wendy, 585

Wallinger, Hanna, 113–14
Walter, Mildred Pitts, **595–96**
Waniek, Marilyn Nelson, **598–99**
Warrior Poet: A Biography of Audre Lorde
  (De Veaux), 157–58
Washington, George, 610
Washington, Harold, 52
Washington, Helen, 113
Washington, Mary Helen, 40
Water Marked (Lee), 364
Watermelon Dress, The (White), 614, 615
Watkins, Gloria. *See* hooks, bell
Watkins, Mel, 534
Way Forward Is with a Broken Heart, The
  (Walker), 581, 584
Wedding Band (Childress), 81, 82
Wells-Barnett, Ida Bell, **601–4**
West, Dorothy, **606–9**
What Looks Like Crazy on an Ordinary Day
  (Cleage), 89, 90
What Use Are Flowers? (Hansberry), 255
Wheatley, Phillis, **610–12**
White, Mark, 97
White, Paulette Childress, **614–15**
Whitley, Edward, 97
Wilderson, Margaret B., 297
Wilentz, Gay, 429
Wilkerson, Margaret, 481
Wilkinson, Brenda Scott, **616–18**
Williams, Bettye, 484
Williams, Dana A., 297
Williams, Fannie (Frances) Barrier, **620–22**
Williams, John, 110
Williams, Sherley Anne, **624–27**
Wilson, Harriet E., **629–32**

Wind Done Gone, The (Randall), 483–84
Winfrey, Oprah, 90, 460, 608
Winona (Hopkins), 280
*Witness to Freedom: Negro Americans in
  Autobiography* (Chalmers), 4–5
Wolf, Miriam, 553
Womanism, 110, 118, 119, 219, 484, 579, 583,
  585, 626
"Womanist model," 119
Woman's Place, A (Golden), 220
Women of Brewster Place, The (Naylor), 444,
  445, 447
Women's club movement, 176, 177
*Wonderful Adventures of Mrs. Seacole in Many
  Lands* (Seacole), 508–9
Wood, Susan, 222
Work of the Afro-American Woman, The
  (Mossell), 434–35
Wright, Richard, 466
Wright, Sarah Elizabeth, **633–34**

Yellin, Jean Fagan, 307
Yellow Bird and Me (Hansen), 259, 260
Yellow House on the Corner, The (Dove),
  163, 165
You Can't Keep a Good Woman Down
  (Walker), 582
You Know Better (Ansa), 20–21
Young, Patricia, 233
Youngblood, Shay, **636–39**

Zaidman, Laura, 506
Zami (Lorde), 369, 374
Zandy, Janet, 267
"Zimbabwe: Women Fire" (De Veaux), 155

ABOUT THE EDITOR
AND THE CONTRIBUTORS

Yolanda Williams Page is coordinator of collegiate success at the University of Arkansas at Little Rock. Prior to that position she worked at Dillard University, where she served as assistant dean of Humanities and was an associate professor of English. Yolanda has published bio-bibliographical essays in *African American Playwrights: A Sourcebook* and *African American Autobiographers: A Sourcebook*; and a historical essay in *Encyclopedia of Ethnic American Literature*. She has also published an interview in *August Wilson and the New Black Arts Movement*.

Megan K. Ahern is currently a graduate student of comparative literary and cultural studies at the University of Connecticut. She received her B.A. in women's and gender studies from Dartmouth College and is interested in questions of gender, ethnicity, and language within literature.

Jessica Allen received a master's degree in English from the University of Washington, where she specialized in twentieth-century literature. She currently works as an editor in educational publishing and writes freelance articles and book reviews in New York City.

Joseph A. Alvarez resides in Charlotte, NC.

Lena Marie Ampadu is an associate professor of English and vice-chair of the English Department at Towson University, where she teaches African American literature, African women writers, and composition and rhetoric. She has scholarly work published in *Callaloo, Composition Studies, African American Rhetoric(s): Interdisciplinary Perspectives*, and *Journal of the Association for Research on Mothering*. Her current research interests include the rhetoric of nineteenth century African American women, the rhetoric of masculinity, and oral traditions in the literature of women of African descent.

Christopher J. Anderson is a Ph.D. candidate in American religious studies at Drew University in Madison, New Jersey. His dissertation explores early-twentieth-century U.S. Protestant missionary expositions. He is an instructor of history and religion at Fairleigh Dickinson University and Asbury Theological Seminary.

Bridgitte Arnold is an English Ph.D. candidate and graduate teaching assistant at the University of Texas at Arlington, where her studies are concentrated on American women's literature. She completed her M.A. in English at Southern Connecticut State University, focusing on twentieth-century African American literature and twentieth-century southern women's literature. Prior to her Ph.D. work, she was a member of the English faculty at Nyack College, teaching American literature and composition.

Marlo David Azikwe is a McKnight doctoral fellow in English at the University of Florida in Gainesville. She received her master's degree in liberal studies from Rollins College in Winter Park, Florida, where she completed her thesis, "Folklore and Oral Culture in Black Women's Fiction, 1925–1975." Her research interests include African diaspora literatures, speculative fiction/Afrofuturism, African American vernacular expression, and gender and sexuality.

Iva Balic is a Ph.D. candidate in English at the University of North Texas, where she is writing her dissertation on utopian fiction. She has presented at various conferences and published an article on spatial politics of Charlotte Perkins Gilman's *Herland*.

Sue E. Barker holds an M.A. in English language and literature from the University of Chicago. She has contributed articles on American literature to several reference works.

Sharon L. Barnes is assistant professor of Interdisciplinary and Special Programs at the University of Toledo, where she teaches academic writing as well as women's studies. Her areas of research include African American women poets and teaching writing to underprepared students. She is currently at work on a book-length manuscript about the work of Audre Lorde.

Jane M. Barstow is professor of English at the University of Hartford, where she teaches courses on nineteenth-century and contemporary women writers and on African American literature. She is the author of *One Hundred Years of American Women Writing, 1848–1948* (Scarecrow Press, 1997). Her most recent articles include "Reading in Groups: Women's Clubs and College Literature Classes," in *Publishing Research Quarterly* (Fall 2003) and "Edwidge Danticat" in *Cyclopedia of World Authors* (Gale Press, 2003).

Lopamudra Basu is assistant professor of English at the University of Wisconsin-Stout. She received her Ph.D. in English from the Graduate Center of the City University of New York. She completed her undergraduate education and received an M.A. from the University of Delhi, India. Her scholarly interests include postcolonial literatures of South Asia, Africa, and the Caribbean; Asian American studies; transnational feminist theory; and the contemporary world novel.

Ann Beebe, Ph.D., is assistant professor of English at the University of Texas at Tyler. She is currently working on a short article on Langston Hughes as well as an essay on counterfeiting in the works of Charles Brockden Brown and James Fenimore Cooper.

Adriane Bezusko is currently pursuing her master's degree in English literature at the University of North Texas and plans on pursing a Ph.D. in English literature concentrating on feminist theory.

Amy L. Blair is assistant professor of English at Marquette University. Her work on late-nineteenth- and early-twentieth-century American literature focuses on the ways readers concerned about social and financial upward mobility read and productively misread texts critical of American success culture.

Sophie Blanch recently completed her Ph.D. in English at the University of Warwick, UK, where she also works as a part-time teacher. Having a masters degree in gender, literature, and modernity, she explores in her doctoral thesis the dialogue between female modernisms and feminist revisions to psychoanalysis in the 1920s and 1930s that effectively rewrote the narrative of the modern woman. She has published articles on a range of Anglo-American women writers of the modernist period, including Antonia White, Nella Larsen, Vita Sackville-West, and the little-known poet and novelist Emily Holmes Coleman. Blanch's postdoctoral research interests are aimed at exploring the strategic uses of comedy in early-twentieth-century women's writing.

Ruth Blandón has written extensively on feminist issues, which include the articles "On Drag, Gender and Fashionable Stupidity: An Interview with Judith 'Jack' Halberstam," and "Cinderella Dreams—Silence, Ignorance and AIDS in America." She is currently working on her dissertation, "Trans-American Modernisms—Latin America, the United States and the Politics of Being" at the University of Southern California.

Sarah Boslaugh received her M.A. in English from the University of Massachusetts and her Ph.D. in measurement and evaluation from the City University of New York. Dr. Boslaugh is a senior statistical data analyst at the Washington University School of Medicine in St. Louis, where she frequently publishes on public health and information technology topics.

Patricia Kennedy Bostian teaches at Central Piedmont Community College, where she is editor of the *Wild Goose Poetry Review*. She has published articles on many poets such as Lorna Dee Cervantes, Garrett Hongo, and Joy Harjo.

Barbara Boswell is a doctoral student and Fulbright Fellow at the University of Maryland's Department of Women's Studies. She has an M.Phil. degree in women's and gender studies from the University of the Western Cape, South Africa. Her research interests are black South African women's literature, South African feminisms, and diasporic women's writing.

Kimberly Downing Braddock received her B.A. and M.A.I.S. from the University of Houston-Victoria and her D.A. from Idaho State University. She currently teaches rhetoric and composition at the University of Arkansas at Fort Smith.

Jana Evans Braziel is an assistant professor of English and Comparative Literature at the University of Cincinnati.

Lisa Pertillar Brevard is an internationally-recognized scholar and creative artist, specializing in the study of African-American traditions. Active in music and poetry, her most recent project to-date is a novel set in New Orleans, called, *Sugar Free*. She is currently Visiting Associate Professor of English at Roanoke College.

Gabriel A. Briggs is currently an instructor and English Ph.D. candidate at the University of Kentucky. Briggs's research/teaching interests include African American literature of the nineteenth and twentieth centuries, African American literary criticism and theory, and early American literature. Briggs is particularly interested in nineteenth-century women writers of protest literature (abolitionist and suffragist).

Jessica Margaret Brophy, a New Jersey native, is currently working toward her Ph.D. in English literature at Morgan State University. Her interests include nineteenth- and twentieth-century aesthetic philosophy and twentieth-century African American literature.

Tenille Brown is a southern writer whose short fiction has been featured online and in several print anthologies including *Chocolate Flava*, *Amazons: Sexy Tales of Strong Women*, and *Glamour Girls*. The short-film adaptation of her story "Her Mama's House" will be released in the summer of 2006. She keeps a blog on writing on her Web site, www.tenillebrown.com.

Josie A. Brown-Rose is assistant professor of English and director of the Minor in African American Studies at Western New England College. She received her Ph.D. from Stony Brook University, focusing on African American, Caribbean, and black British literatures.

Jacqueline Imani Bryant is associate professor of English and an affiliate faculty member of African American studies at Chicago State University. Her presentations center mainly on the life and works of Gwendolyn Brooks and selected literary works of early black women writers. Publications include articles and reviews in *Journal of Black Studies*, *Warpland: A Journal of Black Literature and Ideas*, and *College Language Association Journal*. Her book *The Foremother Figure in Early Black Women's Literature: "Clothed in My Right Mind"* is a part of the Studies in African American History and Culture Series (1999). She is the editor of the book titled *Gwendolyn Brooks' Maud Martha: A Critical Collection* (2002). Additionally, her chapter appears in the book titled *African American Rhetoric(s)* (2004). Finally, she is editor of the forthcoming work *Gwendolyn Brooks and Working Writers*.

Christina G. Bucher is associate professor of English, rhetoric and writing at Berry College in Rome, Georgia, where she teaches nineteenth-century American literature, African American literature, and women's literature. She has published articles and book reviews in *Mississippi Quarterly*, the *North Carolina Literary Review*, and the *CATESOL Journal*, and has entries in *The Encyclopedia of the Harlem Renaissance* and *The Feminist Encyclopedia of African American Literature*.

Joi Carr is assistant professor of English in the Humanities and Teacher Education division at Pepperdine University.

Warren J. Carson is assistant dean of Arts and Sciences and professor of English at the University of South Carolina Upstate. He holds a B.A. in English from the University of North Carolina at Chapel Hill, M.A. in African American studies from Atlanta University, and Ph.D. in English from the University of South Carolina, where he wrote his dissertation on the early career of Zora Neale Hurston. He has published many essays and reviews on works by African American writers including Hurston, James Baldwin, and Richard Wright.

Adrienne Carthon is a doctoral student at Howard University. She is a graduate of Howard University (B.A., Journalism) and North Carolina State University (M.A., English). She is also a teacher, and her research interests include women's literature by African American, Caribbean, and Hispanic writers, as well as cultural studies.

Teresa Clark Caruso is editor of *"On the subject of the feminist business": Re-Reading Flannery O'Connor*, a collection of essays that focuses on a feminist reevaluation of O'Connor's fiction. She received her Ph.D. in literature and criticism from Indiana University of Pennsylvania. She serves as secretary for the Pennsylvania College English Association and currently teaches literature, women's studies, and composition at Penn State's Behrend College in Erie, Pennsylvania.

Adrienne Cassel is assistant professor of English at Sinclair Community College. She received her M.F.A. in poetry from Bennington College. Her poetry has appeared in the *Northwest Review*, *5 A.M.*, *Nexus*, *Amulet*, and the *Bennington Review*. She lives in the historic Wright-Dunbar neighborhood in Dayton, Ohio, with her husband and two dogs.

Heejung Cha is a doctoral candidate in the English department at Indiana University of Pennsylvania. Her scholarly interests broadly range from postcolonial and multicultural literature, to cultural studies, to women's studies and pedagogy. She wrote a book review of Greg Garrard's *Ecocricism* and many entries on Ngugi wa Thiong'o, Bessie Head, Carol Lee Sanchez, Linda Hogan, and others.

Denisa E. Chatman-Riley is a writer and lecturer in southern California. She received a B.A. in English from the University of California at Riverside and a master's degree in English from Claremont Graduate University, where she is presently a Ph.D. candidate. She is currently doing research for her dissertation on racial, gender, and social passing as an American construct. She has written biographies and book reviews for various publications and the media. Her research interests include African American women writers, science fiction, and mythology.

Cameron Christine Clark received her B.A. in English-creative writing from Western Michigan University and her M.A. in English from the University of Florida, where she specialized in cultural studies. She wrote her master's thesis on the depictions of trauma and testimony in Toni Morrison's *Song of Solomon*. She is currently working on a collection of poetry.

Tanya N. Clark is assistant professor of English and Africana studies at Rowan University. She teaches a variety of courses on African American literature and culture, American literature, and women's studies. A graduate of Temple University having received her doctorate in English in 2004, Clark is currently revising her manuscript titled "Quilting the Race: Pauline Elizabeth Hopkins, *The Colored American* magazine, and the African American Family, 1900–1905."

Kevin L. Cole is associate professor of English and chair of Humanities at the University of Sioux Falls.

Meta Michond Cooper is currently doing her M.A. in English and African American literature at Howard University. As a Mississippi resident and Tougaloo College undergraduate, Meta's interest was piqued by Anne Moody's *Coming of Age in Mississippi*. She is pursuing her interest in Moody's autobiography for her thesis project as she explores Moody's reinscriptions of canonical authors such as Harriet Jacobs and Richard Wright. Moreover, Meta explores ways in which Moody rewrites history and paves the way for black women writers such as Toni Cade Bambara, Toni Morrison, and Alice Walker.

Freda Fuller Coursey teaches World Literature, Cinema and Violence, Technical Communication, and other courses at Binghamton University in New York. Coursey publications include: reviews of books on Edna St. Vincent Millay in *Phoebe: Journal of Feminist Scholarship, Theory and Aesthetics*; an article on Henry Adams in the *European Journal of American Culture*; and an article on incorporating technology into the English/Writing classroom in the *Louisiana English Journal*, plus numerous additional book reviews, short stories, essays, and poems. Coursey has Masters degrees in English and History, and has completed the coursework for a Ph.D. in Comparative Literature at Binghamton-SUNY. She also has completed an as-yet unpublished biography of Russian poet Yevgeny Yevtushenko.

Ginette Curry obtained her Ph.D. in English at the Sorbonne University, Paris III, specializing on African American and postcolonial literatures. She is the author of *Awakening African Women: The Dynamics of Change* (2004), which is a comparative study of African novels and films about women's issues in contemporary West Africa and their role in the development of Africa. She is a professor in the Department of English at Florida International University.

Delicia Dena Daniels, a native of Houston, Texas, is a poet, writer, and educator. She is currently an instructor in the English Department at Wiley College in Marshall, Texas. She received her M.F.A. in creative writing at Chicago State University and her B.A. in English at Dillard University in New Orleans.

Adenike Marie Davidson is associate professor at Fisk University. Her research interests include black nationalism, feminist theory, African American literature, and turn-of-the-century American literature. She is currently working on a book manuscript on black nationalism and the African American novel.

Amanda J. Davis is a Ph.D. candidate in the Department of English at the University of Florida, where she teaches courses through the Center for Women's Studies and Gender Research. Her dissertation focuses on autobiographical texts written by incarcerated women.

Carol Bunch Davis is a doctoral candidate in English at the University of Southern California and a lecturer in English at Texas A&M University–Galveston. Her dissertation, *Troubling the Boundaries: "Blacknesses," Performativity and the African-American Freedom Struggle*, considers how the performance of visual and textual "blackness" in the drama produced during the 1960s mediate, rehearse, and constitute multiple black identities or "blacknesses" in dialogue with the social and political upheaval of the African American freedom struggle.

T. Jasmine Dawson is a staff writer for *Black Reign News* and is a contributor at *Upscale* magazine. She completed her B.A. at San Francisco State University and M.F.A. in creative writing at Mills College. She has taught at Mills College, guest lectured at Louisiana State University and McClymond's High School. She is currently working on a novel.

Marla Dean completed her masters degree in theater history and criticism at the University of Texas at Austin and her Ph.D. in theater at Louisiana State University in Baton Rouge. She is an award-winning playwright and director of some forty plays and musicals. Marla is currently a professor of theater at the University of Montevallo in Alabama and is a consultant with *Remembrance through the Performing Arts* in Austin, Texas (a theater group that specifically develops new plays.) Her articles have appeared in *Being Native/Native Being* and Modern Drama. She has presented at numerous conferences and is a scholar of ancient indigenous ritual and performance. Marla is currently writing a book on the development of the new play in academia.

Mary G. De Jong, associate professor of English and women's studies at Penn State Altoona, has published several articles on American hymnody. She is particularly interested in styles of performance and autobiographers' uses of hymn texts to tell their stories and affirm their values.

Gerardo Del Guercio is a Montreal born freelance writer whose research interests lie greatly in American literature, and race and gender studies. He received his B.A. in English from Concordia University (Montreal, Quebec, Canada) and M.A. in English from the université de Montréal. Currently, he is publishing book reviews for *Cercles* and is working on his first book manuscript.

Firouzeh Dianat is a Ph.D. candidate at Morgan State University. She received her M.A. at the Tehran Azad University and B.A. in English from Kurdistan University. Having spent most of her life in Kurdistan, Iran, she is in the process of publishing a book of folktales of her people. She taught English as a second language at the Kurdistan Medical University, Teacher Training Center, and high schools. Her research interests are children's literature, race, American literature of the eighteenth and nineteenth centuries, and religion.

Tamra E. DiBenedetto is associate professor of English at Riverside Community College, Riverside, California.

Helen Doss is a tenure-track faculty member in the Department of Communications and Fine Arts at Malcolm X College, one of the City Colleges of Chicago. She teaches intermediate composition and literature courses, particularly research writing, Shakespeare, Beowulf to Johnson, contemporary American and English literature, and women's literature. She received her undergraduate degree in anthropology from University of Minnesota, Twin Cities. Dr. Doss completed her doctorate in literature at the University of California, Santa Cruz. Her dissertation considers the connections among Milton's

"Paradise Regained", messianic prophecy, and early-Restoration experimental science. Dr. Doss's scholarly interests include pre- and early-modern studies, the history and philosophy of science, Victorian literature, and the writings from the African and American diasporas.

Judy Massey Dozier is associate professor of English and chairperson of the English Department at Lake Forest College. She is currently at work on a novel as she markets her dissertation, *Conjure Women: Culture Performances of African American Women Writers*, for publication. She is also a member of OBAC Writers Workshop.

Kalenda C. Eaton received her Ph.D. from the Ohio State University in twentieth-century African American literature. Her research interests include African American literature and culture, social protest writing, the black power movement, and women's studies. She has taught at universities in Ohio and Florida, and is currently assistant professor of English and ethnic studies at the University of Nebraska-Lincoln.

Julie Ellam teaches in the English Department at the University of Hull, United Kingdom. She is currently writing a book, which is provisionally titled *Love in Jeanette Winterson's Novels*. Her other research areas include literary theory, writing by women, and contemporary fiction.

Kate Falvey holds a Ph.D. in English and American literature from New York University, where she taught for many years. She currently teaches at New York City College of Technology at the City University of New York. Her specialty areas are race and gender in literature, women's narratives, and the literary gothic, and she has published work on nineteenth- and early-twentieth-century American women writers.

Alex Feerst holds an A.B. from Columbia University and a Ph.D. in English from Duke University.

Rebecca Feind, M.L.S., is reference librarian and the outreach coordinator for San Jose State University at the Dr. Martin Luther King, Jr., Library in San Jose, California. She served on the steering committee of the 2004 Furious Flower Poetry Conference held at James Madison University in Harrisonburg, Virginia.

Ben Fisler holds a Ph.D. in theatre and performance studies from the University of Maryland and is currently director of the theater program at Otero Junior College in La Junta, Colorado. He has published articles with *The Puppetry Yearbook*, *Theatron*, and *Research in Drama Education*. Other biographical entries of his appear in sources related to African American literature, Native American literature, modern drama, and Enlightenment culture and arts.

Jean Forst is a Ph.D. candidate in later American literature at the University of Illinois at Urbana-Champaign. She has taught courses in literature, film, rhetoric, and business writing.

Samira C. Franklin is working toward her Ph.D. in English at UC Berkeley. She holds an M.F.A. in fiction writing from New York University and is currently at work on her second novel. She lives in Oakland with her husband, Christopher Perrius.

Imani Lillie B. Fryar teaches at Lemoyne-Owen College in Memphis, TN.

Linda Garber is associate professor of English and women's and gender studies at Santa Clara University. She is the author of *Identity Poetics: Race, Class, and the Lesbian-Feminist Roots of Queer Theory* (2001).

Roxane Gay is a graduate student in the Rhetoric and Technical Communication program at Michigan Technological University. Her writing can be found in many anthologies as well as in the *Greenwood Encyclopedia of African American Literature* and *Writing African American Women*.

Elissa Gershowitz is an editor in the Boston area. She holds a master's degree in children's literature, and is a freelance writer of children's book reviews.

Sarah Estes Graham teaches poetry and composition at the University of Virginia. She is currently at work on her first book of poems *Fall Gently to the River*.

Miranda A. Green-Barteet is a doctoral student at Texas A&M University. She recently completed her coursework and is in the initial stages of researching her dissertation, which will explore nineteenth-century constructions of domesticity and sentimentality as they were employed by ethnic American women. Her interests include nineteenth-century American literature, African American literature, American women writers, as well as issues of race, gender, and ethnicity.

Jeremy Griggs is an instructor of English at Lewis & Clark Community College in Godfrey, Illinois. He is a graduate of Southern Illinois University Carbondale and Edwardsville, where he studied under poet Eugene B. Redmond and was editorial assistant for *Drumvoices Revue*.

Katie Rose Guest is a doctoral student in English, her areas of interest being rhetoric and cultural studies at the University of North Carolina at Greensboro. She earned her J.D. in 2003 from the University of North Carolina School of Law.

Shayla Hawkins is a freelance writer and editor. Her poems, essays, and book reviews have been published in magazines and journals throughout North America and Europe, including *Poets and Writers*, *Carolina Quarterly*, *Windsor Review*, *Calabash*, and *Paris/Atlantic*. Hawkins served as an events coordinator for the 2001 United Nations/Rattapallax Press worldwide poetry readings and was featured in the "Poets Among Us Series" at the 2002 Geraldine R. Dodge Poetry Festival. She is a graduate of the Cave Canem Workshop/Retreat for African American Poets and lives in Detroit, Michigan.

DaMaris Hill is a professor at Towson University and Sojourner-Douglass College and a member of the National Writing Project. She is a graduate of Morgan State University with an M.A. degree in English. Her story "On the Other Side of Heaven—1957" won the Zora Neale Hurston/Richard Wright Award for Short Fiction. The majority of her poetry is spiritually based on and addresses issues of gender, race, and identity in a capitalistic society. She is also working on a novel about slavery and social identity in Bermuda. Some of her writing has been published with *African American National*

Biography Project, *Warpland*, *Women in Judaism*, and *The Sable Quill*. In addition to her creative pursuits, she is currently aiming to document the lives and careers of African American women.

Kevin Hogg is originally from British Columbia and holds a B.A. degree from the University of Lethbridge. He is currently working on his master's degree in English at Carleton University in Ottawa, Ontario. His main research interest is twentieth-century dystopian literature; he also has a strong interest in African American history, which stems from living in Mississippi when he was younger.

Tamara Zaneta Hollins is a professor and healer living in Pennsylvania. She holds degrees in art, writing and literature, cultural studies, and English. Her creative writing, scholarly writing, and art have appeared in various publications, and she has presented scholarly papers at several conferences. Her research interests include the production and construction of identity as well as spirituality and self-authenticity.

Peggy J. Huey received her Ph.D. in English from the University of South Florida. She currently teaches in the Department of Speech, Theater and Dance at the University of Tampa in Florida. She has previously published work on the Breton Lay, Geoffrey Chaucer's "The Squire's Tale," Jane Austen's *Sanditon*, as well as numerous book reviews. Forthcoming are articles on Thomas Heywood, John Steinbeck, E. A. Robinson, Persia Wooley, Harry Potter, and John Hersey's *A Bell for Adano*.

Richard A. Iadonisi is visiting assistant professor at Grand Valley State University. He has published articles on the poetry of Richard Wright, Sonia Sanchez, and Robert Frost.

Judy L. Isaksen, an associate professor of English and Communications at High Point University in North Carolina, teaches rhetorical theory and writing, visual rhetoric, media theory and production, communication and cultural studies, and literature. Her scholarly interests primarily focus on the intersection of rhetoric and race, with print publications on critical race theory and whiteness studies as well as an audio documentary on black voices on public radio and a video documentary on D. W. Griffith's *The Birth of a Nation*.

Katarzyna Iwona Jakubiak is a Ph.D. candidate at Illinois State University. Her dissertation explores the benefits of using translation theory in the study of African diaspora literature. She has translated a collection of Yusef Komunyakaa's poetry into Polish and recently contributed to the *Callaloo* special issue on Komunyakaa.

Raymond Janifer is an associate professor of English and Director of the Ethnic Studies Interdisciplinary Minor at Shippensburg University in PA. He has recently published articles in the *Encyclopedia of Multiethnic Literature Vols. 1 & 5* on Ed Bullins and John Edgar Wideman and an article on Howard Dotson, Curator of the New York Public Library's Schomburg Center for Research in Black Culture in the *Encyclopedia of African American Literature*.

David M. Jones is assistant professor of English and women's studies at the University of Wisconsin, Eau Claire. His writing examines social movements and popular culture using tools from critical race studies. His essay on Lorraine Hansberry and sexuality in the civil rights movement is collected in *Growing Up Postmodern* (2002), and he is working on a full-length manuscript on the Black Arts Movement as well as essays on blues and social change in American culture.

Regina V. Jones, Ph.D., is visiting assistant professor of Afro-American studies and an adjunct assistant professor in women's studies at Indiana University Northwest. She is interested in the writings, narrative voices, and culture of African American women from the eighteenth to the twentieth centuries. Dr. Jones has written on African American women for *Black Women in America*, *Encyclopedia of African American Literature*, and the forthcoming *African American National Biography*. Dr. Jones is currently working on a book about the resistant voices of nineteenth-century narrative women.

Heather Hoffman Jordan is a Ph.D. student in rhetoric and technical communication at Michigan Technological University. Jordan recently completed a review of Shirley Brice Heath's *ArtShow2Grow* DVD and became an editorial and production assistant for *Community Literacy Journal*.

Tatia Jacobson Jordan, a Ph.D. student in Florida State University's English Department, specializes in nineteenth- and twentieth-century American literature. Exploring issues of race and gender within texts, Jacobson Jordan earned her M.A. in 2004 from Georgia State University. She teaches composition and literature in Tallahassee, and is an active member of the South Atlantic Modern Language Association, The Modern Language Association, and the American Studies Association.

Nancy Kang is completing her doctorate study at the University of Toronto Department of English. A Social Sciences and Humanities Research Council of Canada Fellow, Chancellor Jackman Graduate Research Fellow, and Sir James Lougheed Scholar of Distinction, she focuses on ethnic American literature and culture in the twentieth century.

Pratibha Kelapure lives in the San Francisco Bay area California where she has spent most of her adult life.

Nita N. Kumar, reader of English at Shyama Prasad Mukherji College, University of Delhi, has a Ph.D. in African American drama. Her recent publications include "The Logic of Retribution: Amiri Baraka's Dutchman" in *African American Review* (2003), "Black Arts Movement and Ntozake Shange's Choreopoem" in *Black Arts Quarterly* (2001), and several other essays and reviews on African American and postcolonial literatures. She has been granted a Mellon Fellowship at the Harry Ransom Humanities Research Centre, University of Texas at Austin, to work on Adrienne Kennedy papers. Her forthcoming works include an essay on Kennedy in *Journal of American Theater and Drama* and an essay titled "The Colour of the Critic: An Intervention in the Critical Debate in African American Theory on Interpretive Authority" in *White Scholars/ African American Texts*, edited by Lisa Long.

Joy M. Leighton received her Ph.D. in English from SUNY Buffalo. She is an assistant professor at Auburn University. She teaches and researches on nineteenth-century U.S. literature, Asian-American literature, and multiethnic literature.

Jeehyun Lim is a Ph.D. student in English at the University of Pennsylvania. Her primary interest is ethnic literature of the United States. She is a contributing editor to *The North Carolina Roots of African American Literature*.

Katherine Madison is an undergraduate English major at the University of Sioux Falls. She will pursue graduate studies in literature.

Elizabeth Malia earned a B.A. (Whitworth College, 1976) and an M.A. (Eastern Washington University, 2004) in English literature. She also holds an M.A. in librarianship and information management. Over twenty-four years, she has worked in a wide variety of public and academic libraries in Colorado, Kansas, and Washington State. She is currently employed at EWU in the Kennedy Library as manager of the Curriculum and Media Center and the Tech-Eze student support desk.

Elizabeth Marsden, a native New Orleanian, is a former assistant professor of English at Dillard University. She has lived in Texas since Hurricane Katrina. Besides loving her profession, she rescues animals and works with several humane no-kill shelters. A published poet, she is one of the 100 poets featured in *From the Bend in the River: An Anthology of 100 New Orleans Poets*.

Tinola N. Mayfield is a photographer, poet, and activist. She currently teaches sociology at Owens Community College and will be starting art school in the fall at Bowling Green State University. Tinola received her undergraduate degree in women and gender studies and her master's degree in sociology, both from the University of Toledo.

Babacar M'Baye teaches black studies at the Evergreen State College. His publications include "The Image of Africa in the Travel Narratives of W.E.B. DuBois, Richard Wright, James Baldwin, and Henry Louis Gates, Jr." (*BMA: The Sonia Sanchez Literary Review*, Fall 2003, 153–177) and "Dualistic Imagination of Africa in the Black Atlantic Narratives of Phillis Wheatley, Olaudah Equiano, and Martin R. Delany" (*The New England Journal of History*, Spring 2002, 15–32).

Joan McCarty is the author of the plays *A Time to Dance* and *Last Bus to Stateville*. She has also written a collection of short stories titled *Through My Windows*. She is a contributor to the *Greenwood Encyclopedia of African American Literature*, *This Day in the Life—Diaries from Women Across America*, and *Life Spices from Seasoned Sisters*, an anthology of life stories. She received the first place short story award from the Georgia Writer's Association in 2003. Formerly a faculty member at Spelman College, she is currently assistant professor at Savannah State University.

Trimiko C. Melancon is visiting assistant professor of English at St. Lawrence University, where her teaching and scholarly interests lie primarily in African American, American, and Africana literature and culture, critical race and feminist theory, and gender and sexuality studies. She has received numerous grants and fellowships from the Woodrow Wilson National Fellowship Foundation, Social Science Research Council, Andrew Mellon Foundation, and Nellie Mae Foundation. Currently, she is working on her book manuscript, which examines post–civil rights representations of unconventional black women in the literary imagination.

Gretchen Michlitsch is assistant professor of English at Winona State University in Minnesota, where she teaches multicultural American literature. She recently completed her dissertation, *Expressing Milk: Breastfeeding in Contemporary American Literature*, at the University of Wisconsin-Madison and has published articles on the works of Sherley Anne Williams and Nalo Hopkinson.

Maria Mikolchak is currently associate professor in the Department of Foreign Languages and Literatures and in the English Department at St. Cloud State University in Minnesota. She received her Ph.D. in comparative literature and a Graduate Certificate in women's studies from University of South Carolina. Her research interests include women's studies, critical theory, and comparative studies of the novel as a genre.

Shamika Ann Mitchell is a doctoral student in the Department of English at Temple University. Her area of study is contemporary black and Latino American fiction, with a focus on constructions of identity.

Tabitha Adams Morgan is currently an American Studies doctoral student in the Department of English at the University of Massachusetts. She is an instructor at the University of Massachusetts and at Holyoke Community College. Her primary research interest and dissertation centers in exploring working class and immigrant women's artistic and cultural productions as social protest discourse, 1880s–1930s.

Ted Morrissey teaches in the Division of Languages and Literature at Springfield College in Illinois, including an introductory course on women authors. He is also a Ph.D. candidate in English studies at Illinois State University, where he is concentrating on postmodern American literature, especially Thomas Pynchon and William Gaddis. His articles on literature pedagogy have appeared in *Eureka Studies in Teaching Short Fiction*, and his own fiction has been in *Glimmer Train Stories*, *Paris Transcontinental*, and *Eureka Literary* magazine.

Nanette Morton is a lecturer at the Brantford, Ontario, campus of Wilfrid Laurier University, Canada. She is in the process of completing a book on the African Canadian west.

Chandra Tyler Mountain is chairperson and associate professor of English at Dillard University in New Orleans. Her research centers on Africana women's literature.

A. Mary Murphy works primarily in life writing, particularly literary biography, and twentieth-century poetry. She also publishes as a poet. She has a Ph.D. from Memorial University of Newfoundland and teaches film and literature in Calgary, Alberta, Canada.

Joy R. Myree-Mainor is assistant professor of English at Morgan State University in Baltimore, Maryland. She teaches undergraduate and graduate courses in literary theory and criticism, African American literature, world literature, and composition. She earned her Ph.D. in English at the University of Kentucky, completing a dissertation titled "Rereading the Social Protest Tradition: Progressive Race, Class, and Gender Politics in the Fiction of Ann Petry and Dorothy West." She specializes in black women's literature from the late nineteenth to the midtwentieth century with an emphasis on social protest fiction and race, gender, and class issues. Her forthcoming essay is on nineteenth-century black women writers and activists in the forthcoming *Sparks of Resistance, Flames of Change: Black Communities and Activism.* Currently she is completing a manuscript on Dorothy West.

Debbie Clare Olson is a lecturer in English and films at Central Washington University.

Keren Omry lectures, has published, and continues to explore science fiction and the popular narrative, with particular focus on the work of Octavia Butler, investigating how the dialogue between aesthetics and technology is articulated in terms of gender and genre. Omry was awarded her PhD in English Literature at the University of London, where she explored the relationship between jazz and African American literature of the twentieth century. She is currently developing her investigation of racialised discourses in contemporary Jewish American and African American texts, writing on the intersections of popular imagination and culture with constructions of ethnic identity.

Born in Australia, **Deirdre Osborne** is a lecturer in drama and theater arts at Goldsmiths College, University of London. She has published essays on black British writers including Roy Williams, Lemn Sissay, Kwame Kwei-Armah, and Winsome Pinnock. Her research focuses on late Victorian motherhood and colonial ideology, and she also writes about women spies in World War II.

Laura Gimeno Pahissa holds a B.A. and an M.A. in English philology from the Universitat Autonoma de Barcelona (Spain) and teaches American history and literature there. Her research interests are African American literature and autobiography. Gimeno Pahissa was awarded a research grant in 2005 at the Freie Universität-John F. Kennedy Institut für Nordamerikasstudien in Berlin, Germany.

Louis H. Palmer, III, is assistant professor of American literature at Castleton State College in Castleton, Vermont. He teaches genre and survey courses in American literature as well as general education courses and courses in African American literature and women's writing. He received a Ph.D. from Syracuse University. He serves as a member of the editorial board for the *Journal of Popular Culture* and serves as the Gothic chair for the Popular Culture Association. His research interests include Southern literature, popular cultural studies, and environmental literature.

Valerie Palmer-Mehta is assistant professor of communication in the Department of Rhetoric, Communication and Journalism at Oakland University in Rochester, Michigan. Her research focuses on the intersection of hegemony, ideology, and the social construction of gender, race, and sexuality in public discourse and the media.

Roy Pérez is a doctoral candidate in English and American literature at New York University, where he is studying society and aesthetics in nineteenth- and twentieth-century minority writing. He has published entries on Gloria Anzaldúa, Lorna Dee Cervantes, and June Jordan.

Pearlie Mae Peters is professor of English at Rider University in Lawrenceville, New Jersey, and is author of the book *The Assertive Woman in Zora Neale Hurston's Fiction, Folklore and Drama.*

Hermine Pinson is an associate professor of literature at the College of William and Mary. She is the author of two poetry collections, Ashe and Mama Yetta and Selected Poems and a cd, Changing the Changes in Poetry & Song in special collaboration with Yusef Komunyakaa. Her fiction and essays have appeared in a variety of journals, including *Callaloo, Paintbrush, Mississippi Quarterly*, and *African American Review*.

Julia Marek Ponce is a graduate student at Purdue University Calumet, where she also teaches composition. Her research interests include women's literature and using technology in the classroom.

Myisha Priest is a University of California President's Postdoctoral Fellow at UCLA. She is completing a manuscript examining the relationship between adult and children's works in African American literature.

Gerri Reaves is a freelance writer and editor living in South Florida. Her publications include *Mapping the Private Geography: Autobiography, Identity, and America* (2001), and her critical essays, creative nonfiction, and environmental pieces that have appeared in *Southern Ocean Review, Passages North, Literature/Film Quarterly, ZCPortal*, and others. She also contributed an essay to *Footnotes: On Shoes* (2001), titled "The Slip in the Dance Slipper: Illusion and the Naked Foot."

Althea Rhodes teaches at the University of Arkansas-Fort Smith.

Maria J. Rice is a Ph.D. candidate in English at Rutgers, the State University of New Jersey. Her dissertation studies the experience of postmemory and migration in contemporary African American and ethnic American literature. A former high school teacher, she has taught literature and composition at all secondary and undergraduate levels. She is currently an American Association of University Women Dissertation Fellow and is a former Mellon Fellow in humanistic study.

Bennie P. Robinson received her B.A. from Tougaloo College and M.L.S. from Atlanta University. She is a reference librarian and collection developer for black studies and women studies at the University of Akron, where she also serves on the Black Studies Advisory Council and the Women's Studies Advisory Council.

Frank A. Salamone, Ph.D., is chair of the Sociology and Anthropology Department of Iona College and an instructor at the University of Phoenix. He has authored and edited more than twenty books and 100 articles. He is the editor of the *Encyclopedia of Religious Rituals and Performances* (2004), and *Gods and Goods in Africa, Popular Culture in the Fifties*, among others.

Joshunda Sanders is a writer and journalist who has written for the *Houston Chronicle,* the *Seattle Post-Intelligencer* and most recently, the *San Francisco Chronicle*. The Bronx native is at work on her first book and resides in Oakland, California.

Shawntaye M. Scott is a graduate of Pennsylvania State University with a Bachelor of Science degree in information science and technology. She is currently a research associate for the University of Pittsburgh Medical Center. Scott's poems have been published on the e-zines *Holler, Subjective Substance, The Writers Crib, Now and Forever, Nubian Mindz, MagNetique, Timbooktu, The Soul of Pittsburgh, Confused in a Deeper Way*, and the Canadian e-magazines *Poetry Stop* and *3 Cup Morning*.

Kelly O. Secovnie is completing her Ph.D. in writing, teaching, and criticism in the English Department at the University at Albany, SUNY. Her research and teaching interests include West African Anglophone literature, African American drama, transatlantic diasporic studies, and postcolonial and feminist theory.

Denise R. Shaw earned a Ph.D. from the University of South Carolina. Her dissertation is titled "Lowly Violence: Rape, Loss, and Melancholia in the Modern Southern Novel." Her areas of interest are twentieth-century American literature, specifically the modern and postmodern novel, Southern literature, and African American literature. She has published articles in *African American History Reference Series* (volume 2); *The World of Frederick Douglass, 1818–1895*; *Voices of Infanticide: Toward a Global Understanding*; *Cleave: A Journal of Literary Criticism*; *Journal for the Association of Research on Mothering*; and *Stepping through the Looking Glass: Reflections on, Revisions of, and Premonitions about English Studies in the 21st Century*.

Angela Shaw-Thornburg is an assistant professor of English at Newberry College.

Gloria A. Shearin is an associate professor in the Liberal arts Department at Savannah State University

Sharon T. Silverman is a native of Chicago. She earned her B.A. at Stillman College in Tuscaloosa, Alabama, and her M.A. from the University of Illinois-Urbana/Champaign in library and information science. She is currently employed with the University of Illinois at Chicago as a visiting professor and professional library associate. During her leisure time, Silverman enjoys fiction novels written by African Americans, and comedies and drama/suspense movies.

Karen S. Sloan is assistant professor of English at the University of Texas at Tyler, where she teaches undergraduate and graduate courses in American literature and bibliography. She has published articles in the *Explicator* and *ANQ*, and has authored entries in the *Greenwood Encyclopedia of African American Literature*.

Dorsia Smith is a Ph.D. student in Caribbean literature at the University of Puerto Rico, Río Piedras. She has several forthcoming articles in *La Torre* and has presented at conferences in Tobago, Tortola, and Puerto Rico. Her primary interests are the Caribbean writers V. S. Naipaul and Jamaica Kincaid.

Rochelle Spencer earned her M.F.A. from New York University. She is the recipient of a Burke-Marshall fellowship (sponsored by Paule Marshall), a Hurston-Hughes fellowship (sponsored by Alice Walker), and a Starr fellowship (sponsored by Teachers and Writers Inc.). Spencer was a finalist for the Chesterfield Writers Program fellowship, and her writings have appeared in the *African American Review*; *Cake Train*; *Stickman Review*; *Upscale*; Sweet Fancy Moses; and the anthology *Sometimes Rhythm, Sometimes*

Blues: Young African Americans on Love, Relationships, and the Search for Mr. Right (*Seal Press* 2004). She currently teaches English at Spelman College.

Tarshia L. Stanley is an associate professor of English at Spelman College in Atlanta, GA. She teaches courses in Film Studies and visual imagery particularly as it pertains to images of women. She has authored several articles critiquing black women in African American, African, and Caribbean cinema as well as black female iconography in popular culture.

Heidi Stauffer received her Bachelor of Arts degree in English from Michigan State University and her Master of Arts degree in English from the University of Central Florida. Her areas of interest are nineteenth-century literature, regionalist literature, and African American literature. She is currently teaching English at Bethune-Cookman College in Daytona Beach, Florida.

Eric Sterling earned his Ph.D. in English at Indiana University. He is Distinguished Research Professor of English at Auburn University Montgomery. He has published two books and dozens of articles. He is currently writing a book on the drama of August Wilson.

Susan M. Stone is assistant professor of American literature at Loras College in Dubuque, Iowa, where she teaches courses on nineteenth-century literature by and about African Americans, Native Americans, and women. Her recent scholarly work includes publications on the Transcendentalists William Dean Howells, Susan Warner, and Lucretia Hale. She is currently working on two projects, one about rhetoric and writing in nineteenth-century HBCUs, and a second about the plays and poetry of Josephine Preston Peabody.

Cammie M. Sublette is assistant professor of English at the University of Arkansas-Fort Smith. She teaches African American literature, popular culture, genre studies, composition, and literary theory.

Karen C. Summers is in the Ph.D. program at the University of North Carolina, Greensboro, specializing in medieval literature. Additional scholarly interests include gender issues in literature and intersections of literature and history.

Claire Taft, presently an English lecturer at Texas A&M University-Kingsville, has also taught at the University of Tennessee, Knoxville, Ave Maria College of the Americas in Nicaragua, and Centro Colombo Americano in Bogota, Colombia.

Ordner W. Taylor, III, is a doctoral student at Morgan State University. He is particularly interested in comparative criticism that encompasses British romanticism and literature from the black diaspora.

Lynnell Thomas earned a Ph.D. from Emory University's Graduate Program of the Liberal Arts and is currently assistant professor of American studies at Umass Boston. Her teaching and research fields include African American studies, American literature and culture, and the history and culture of New Orleans. She is a native New Orleanian whose research focuses on race and tourism in New Orleans.

Rhondda Robinson Thomas is a Ph.D. candidate at the University of Maryland, College Park. Her dissertation, "Exodus: Literary Migration of Afro-Atlantic Authors, 1760—1903," explores how African Americans appropriated fragments from the biblical story of Exodus, Moses leading the children of Israel to freedom in the Promised Land, into a literary tradition that challenged white Americans' embrace of the narrative and enabled them to forge persuasive arguments for freedom and equality. She has also contributed an essay on Lucy Bagby Johnson to *African American Lives*.

Bridget Harris Tsemo is assistant professor of rhetoric at the University of Iowa. She is presently working on a book that focuses on American democracy as an essentially racist project that began at the turn of the nineteenth and twentieth centuries and still continues today.

Aimable Twagilimana is professor of English at the State University of New York College at Buffalo (Buffalo State College). He teaches African American literature, world literature, postcolonial theory, literature of continental Europe, and comparative literature. Some of his publications are *Race and Gender in the Making of an African American Literary Tradition* (1997), *The Debris of Ham: Ethnicity, Regionalish and the 1994 Rwandan Genocide* (2003), *Heritage Library of African Peoples: Hutu and Tutsi* (1998), *In Their Own Voices: Teenage Refugees from Rwanda Speak Out* (1997), and *Manifold Annihilation: A Novel* (1996). Aimable is currently working on two book manuscripts, *A Historical Dictionary of Rwanda* and *Romancing the Past: Toni Morrison's Historiography*.

Jasmin J. Vann is currently working toward an M.A. in English and American literature at the University of Houston, where she also teaches English composition I.

Sathyaraj Venkatesan is a doctoral student in the Department of Humanities and Social Sciences, Indian Institute of Technology (IIT) Kanpur, India. His current research interests are literary theories and African American women literature. He has published articles in both international and national journals.

Wendy Wagner is an assistant professor of English at Johnson & Wales University. She wrote her dissertation on nineteenth and twentieth century African American woman writers and has published an essay on Amelia E. H. Johnson in *The Black Press: New Literary and Historical Essays* (Rutgers University Press). She has recently been working on papers on Harriet Jacobs and on feminism and popular culture.

A doctoral candidate in twentieth-century literary studies, **Terri Jackson Wallace** holds a B.A. in English from Dillard University and an M.A. from the University of Vermont. She is currently completing the final stages of her dissertation prospectus in which she discusses the depiction(s) and definition(s) of blackness in the works of William Faulkner and various Harlem Renaissance authors.

Rebecca Walsh is currently visiting assistant professor of English at Duke University, where she teaches critical theory and nineteenth- and twentieth-century literature. She has guest-edited a special issue on global diasporas in the international postcolonial journal *Interventions*, and has also published on feminist locational theory. Her current book project, *Modernism's Geopoetics*, explores representations of space and place in a range of African American and Euro-American long poems, while other projects explore space and Native American identity in contemporary film.

Rachelle D. Washington is a doctoral student at the University of Georgia, Department of Language Education and Literacy. Her areas of interests include oral narratives, black women's schooling narratives, children's literature, black feminism/women's studies, critical pedagogy,ss and reflexive practice. Rachelle is an instructor of preservice teachers at UGA.

Mary McCartin Wearn is an assistant professor of English at Macon State College. Her research interests include American literature, gender studies, and abolitionist writing. Dr. Wearn has articles published or forthcoming on Adrienne Rich, Harriet Jacobs, and Sarah Piatt, and she has a book forthcoming on literary representations of motherhood in nineteenth-century America.

Kellie D. Weiss is a student at Howard University, where she is pursing a Ph.D. in multicultural literatures in America and teaches composition. She is currently working on the study of Asian American literature and has a publication in progress on the scholarship of teaching and learning at minority serving institutions.

Chandra Wells is a doctoral candidate in English at the University of Connecticut. Her dissertation is titled "Befriending the Other(ed) Woman: Fictions of Interracial Female Friendship." Her article "'Unable to Imagine Getting on without Each Other': Katherine Anne Porter's Fictions of Interracial Female Friendship" is forthcoming in *Mississippi Quarterly*.

Jacob Nelson Wilkenfeld is a graduate student in comparative literature at the University of North Carolina at Chapel Hill, concentrating in nineteenth-century American and Brazilian poetry.

Laura Madeline Wiseman is an award-winning writer currently teaching in the southwest. Over 100 pieces and two chapbooks of her work have been published. Her works have appeared in *13th Moon*, *Poetry Motel*, *Vs*, *Fiction International*, *Driftwood*, *Familiar*, *Spire* magazine, *Colere*, *Clare*, *42opus*, *Dicey Brown*, *Flyway Literature Review*, *Nebula*, *Altar* magazine, and other publications. In addition, she is a columnist for *Empowerment4Women* and the literary editor for *In the Fray*.

Deborah M. Wolf is an English literature major in the CUNY Honors College at the City College of New York. Her current research focuses on temporality in the neo-slave narratives of contemporary African American women writers. In addition, she is the contributing editor of a forthcoming collection of feminist folk tales, fairy tales, and fables titled *The Heroic Young Woman*. She is particularly interested in the relationship of formal and thematic elements of folklore to the American (and, more specifically, the African American) literary tradition(s). A single mother of a small child, Ms. Wolf is also currently working to organize a network of resources and support for City College students with children.

Loretta G. Woodard is an associate professor of English at Marygrove College, where she teaches African American literature, writing, speech, and interdisciplinary studies. She is also president of the African American Literature and Culture Society. Her essays and reviews have appeared in a number of scholarly works, including *African American Review*, *Obsidian II & III*, *The Journal of African American History*, *The Dictionary of Literary Biography*, *Contemporary African American Novelists*, *African American Autobiographers*, *Women in Literature*, *African American Dramatists*, *Writing African American Women*, *The Greenwood Encyclopedia of Multiethnic American Literature*, and *The Facts on File Companion to the American Novel.*

Amanda Wray completed her M.A. in English at the University of Kentucky and currently teaches in the Department of English and Theatre at Eastern Kentucky University. She is newly acquainting herself with motherhood, taking advantage of late night feeding sessions to tackle the stack of feminist theory texts on her nightstand and to peruse Maya Angelou's cookbook.

Dave Yost is currently pursuing an M.A. in fiction writing at the University of Louisiana at Lafayette. He has served in the U.S. Peace Corps in Mali, and the Burmese Volunteer Program in Thailand.

Su-lin Yu is an associate professor in the Department of Foreign Languages & Literature at National Cheng Kung University, Taiwan. She has contributed chapters and entries to numerous scholarly reference works and published scholarly articles on ethnic American Literature in a variety of journals, including *Jouvert*, *The Journal of Southwest*, and *Critique.*